THE LAW OF NATIONS TREATED ACCORDING
TO THE SCIENTIFIC METHOD

NATURAL LAW AND
ENLIGHTENMENT CLASSICS

Knud Haakonssen
General Editor

Christian Wolff

NATURAL LAW AND
ENLIGHTENMENT CLASSICS

The Law of Nations Treated According to the Scientific Method

Christian Wolff

Translated by Joseph H. Drake

Translation revised by Thomas Ahnert

Edited and with an Introduction by
Thomas Ahnert

LIBERTY FUND

This book is published by Liberty Fund, Inc., a foundation established
to encourage study of the ideal of a society of free and responsible individuals.

The cuneiform inscription that serves as our logo and as the design motif for
our endpapers is the earliest-known written appearance of the word
"freedom" (*amagi*), or "liberty." It is taken from a clay document written
about 2300 B.C. in the Sumerian city-state of Lagash.

The text of this edition is a reprint with revisions of the translation of
Jus Gentium Methodo Scientifica Pertractatum by Joseph H. Drake, first
published in 1934 in the Classics of International Law series by the Carnegie
Endowment for International Peace.

Portrait of Christian Wolff is reproduced by permission
of Herzog August Bibliothek Wolfenbüttel: B 118.

16   17   18   19   20   C   5   4   3   2   1
16   17   18   19   20   P   5   4   3   2   1

Library of Congress Cataloging-in-Publication Data
Names: Wolff, Christian, Freiherr von, 1679–1754, author. | Ahnert, Thomas,
writer of introduction, translator. | Drake, Joseph H. (Joseph Horace),
1860–1947, translator.
Title: The law of nations treated according to the scientific method / Christian
Wolff ; edited and with an Introduction by Thomas Ahnert ; translated by
Joseph H. Drake ; translation revised by Thomas Ahnert.
Other titles: Jus naturae methodo scientifica pertractatum. English.
Description: Indianapolis : Liberty Fund, 2017. | Series: Natural law and
enlightenment classics | Includes bibliographical references and index.
Identifiers: LCCN 2016057737 | ISBN 9780865977655 (hardcover : alk. paper) |
ISBN 9780865977662 (pbk. : alk. paper) | ISBN 9781614879244 (pdf)
Subjects: LCSH: International law—Early works to 1800. | Natural law—Early
works to 1800.
Classification: LCC KZ2347.A3 J8713 2017 | DDC 341—dc23
LC record available at https://lccn.loc.gov/2016057737

LIBERTY FUND, INC.
11301 North Meridian Street
Carmel, Indiana 46032-4564

CONTENTS

INTRODUCTION

Christian Wolff (1679–1754) was one of the most famous and influential German thinkers in the first half of the eighteenth century. He began his academic career as a mathematician, but over the course of almost five decades he taught and wrote on nearly every aspect of eighteenth-century philosophy, including the human mind, economics, political science, and physics, as well as logic, metaphysics, ontology, natural theology, natural law, and moral philosophy. Uniting Wolff's many different intellectual pursuits was his commitment to the "scientific method." This method, as Wolff understood it, was a form of reasoning that began from principles that were certain, and in which all steps of the argument were so closely linked to each other that the conclusions to which they led were necessarily true.[1] Although the "scientific method" was exemplified particularly well by mathematics, Wolff believed that it was also applicable to philosophical argument. Wolff's *Law of Nations* is one example of the "scientific method." He published this work in 1749, toward the end of his life, after his triumphant return to the territories of the Prussian king, from which he had been banished in 1723 after his philosophy had been judged offensive and dangerous by the then ruler, Frederick William I. In this introduction a brief biography of Wolff will be followed by a discussion of the main principles of his "scientific method" and a short note on the text and translation of his *Law of Nations*.

---

1. "[A]sserta demonstrandi, hoc est, ex principiis certis & immotis per legitimam consequentiam inferendi." "Discursus praeliminaris de philosophia in genere," chap. 2, §30, in Wolff, *Philosophia rationalis sive logica* (1740; ed. J. École, Hildesheim: Georg Olms, 1983), vol. 1, p. 14.

Christian Wolff (1679–1754)

Christian Wolff was born in 1679 in Breslau, a flourishing and wealthy Silesian city of around 40,000 inhabitants.[2] The dominant religious confession in Breslau was Lutheranism, but the city also had a significant Catholic population because the province of Silesia was under Austrian Habsburg rule. Wolff, who was a Lutheran, thus grew up in an environment in which he was constantly reminded of the existence of confessional differences. Even schoolboys appear to have debated theological questions, and Wolff said he often attended mass in order to study Catholic beliefs and practices.[3] Looking back on his childhood, Wolff later claimed that his interest in mathematics had been inspired by a desire to establish an intellectual foundation for resolving the kinds of religious disagreements he had witnessed in his early life.[4]

Christian Wolff's father, Christoph Wolff, was a tanner. Unusually for an artisan, he had attended a *Gymnasium*, a school that prepared boys for entry to a university. Although Christoph Wolff had not continued his education beyond school, he had vowed that his son Christian would do so and train for the Lutheran clergy.[5] After completing the Lutheran *Magdalenen-Gymnasium* in Breslau with great success, Christian Wolff enrolled at the University of Jena as a student of divinity in 1699. It soon became clear that Wolff was more interested in mathematics and physics than theology. In his first few months at Jena he went to lectures on the theories of Johann Christoph Sturm (1635–1703), a famous mathematician and natural scientist who was teaching at the University of Altdorf near Nuremberg.[6] Eventually, Wolff would abandon a clerical career, though he later claimed that he had hesitated for a long time, because he had wanted to obey his father's wishes.[7] He even preached in the Leipzig

---

2. Marcel Thomann, introduction to *Jus gentium* by Christian Wolff (1749, Halle; ed. Marcel Thomann, Hildesheim: Georg Olms, 1972), p. vii.

3. Christian Wolff, *Christian Wolffs eigene Lebensbeschreibung*, ed. Heinrich Wuttke (Leipzig: Weidmann, 1841), p. 117.

4. Wolff, *Lebensbeschreibung*, pp. 120–21.

5. Wolff, *Lebensbeschreibung*, pp. 111–12.

6. Wolff, *Lebensbeschreibung*, p. 120.

7. Wolff, *Lebensheschreibung*, p. 121.

Nicolai Church as late as 1706.[8] It may be that his protestations about his plans to become a clergyman were mainly a reflection of filial piety, but whatever the reasons for his final decision, it does not seem to have been motivated by doubts about religion. Wolff remained a conventionally pious Lutheran in many respects until the very end of his life.

In 1702 Wolff traveled to Leipzig to take his examination for a master's degree in philosophy. He returned to Jena to work on a dissertation that would qualify him for a university teaching post in the faculty of philosophy. This dissertation was *Universal Practical Philosophy, Written according to the Mathematical Method,* which Wolff defended successfully at Leipzig in January 1703.[9] It was read by the Leipzig professor of moral philosophy, Otto Mencke, who was also editor of the most important academic review journal in the Holy Roman Empire, the Leipzig *Acta Eruditorum.* Mencke was eager to recruit Wolff as a contributor to the journal and asked Gottfried Wilhelm Leibniz to provide an opinion on Wolff's dissertation. Leibniz responded by generously praising Wolff's work and sent him a congratulatory letter, thereby inaugurating their correspondence, which continued until Leibniz's death in 1716.[10]

By the time Wolff was awarded the title of lecturer (*magister legens*) in 1703 he was regarded as a promising young scholar. He was soon offered and accepted a position teaching mathematics at the University of Leipzig, remaining there until 1706. He then agreed to take up a position at the University of Giessen. While traveling to his new post, however, he was persuaded by the more prestigious University of Halle to join its faculty as a professor of mathematics and moved there instead.

At first Wolff was disappointed by the state of teaching at Halle. Mathematics, he said, had been neglected, and philosophy was dominated by the doctrines of Christian Thomasius (1655–1728), whose outlook was very different from Wolff's.[11] Thomasius had little interest in mathematics. He

---

8. Wolff, *Lebensbeschreibung,* p. 128.

9. Wolff, *Philosophia practica universalis, mathematica methodo conscripta* (Leipzig, 1703).

10. Wolff, *Lebensbeschreibung,* p. 133.

11. For Thomasius's main writings on moral and political subjects, see his *Institutes of Divine Jurisprudence, with Selections from the Foundations of the Law of Nature and Nations,* ed. and trans. Thomas Ahnert (Indianapolis: Liberty Fund, 2011), and

was also far more skeptical than Wolff about the powers of the human intellect, arguing that wisdom was founded in the proper management of the passions, which he opposed to the subtle but vain and fruitless reasoning of "scholastic" philosophers, among whom Thomasius included his orthodox Lutheran opponents.[12] Initially, Wolff confined himself to lecturing and writing on mathematics, staying clear of philosophical subjects. But when the professor of medicine and physics, Friedrich Hoffmann, was appointed personal physician to the Prussian king and left Halle for the court at Berlin, Wolff replaced him as lecturer in natural philosophy. Wolff now had the opportunity of expanding the range of his teaching. In 1709 he published a work on the physics of air, the *Aërometriae elementa*.[13] In the following years Wolff extended his teaching to other parts of philosophy, including metaphysics, ethics, and politics. In 1720 his German treatise on metaphysics appeared, *Rational Thoughts concerning God, the World, and the Soul of Man, and All Things in General*,[14] followed by his treatise on ethics, *Rational Thoughts concerning the Actions of Humans*,[15] and in 1721 his treatise on politics, *Rational Thoughts concerning the Social Life of Humans, in Particular the Commonwealth, Communicated for the Purpose of Furthering the Happiness of Humankind*.[16]

The broadening of Wolff's interests, however, brought him into conflict with his academic colleagues. Some members of the Halle theological faculty were becoming especially hostile to him. Wolff's most prominent critic among them was the Pietist professor of theology, Joachim Lange, who would be the main person responsible for persuading Frederick

---

Essays on Church, State, and Politics, ed. and trans. Ian Hunter, Thomas Ahnert, and Frank Grunert (Indianapolis: Liberty Fund, 2007).

12. Thomas Ahnert, *Religion and the Origins of the German Enlightenment: Faith and the Reform of Learning in the Thought of Christian Thomasius* (Rochester, N.Y.: Rochester University Press, 2006). See also Carl Hinrichs, *Preußentum und Pietismus* (Göttingen: Vandenhoeck and Ruprecht, 1971), p. 389.

13. Christian Wolff, *Aërometriae elementa* (Leipzig, 1709).

14. *Vernünftige Gedanken von Gott, der Welt und der Seele des Menschen, auch allen Dingen überhaupt* (Halle, 1720). The book was printed in December 1719 but was released in the following year.

15. *Vernünftige Gedanken von der Menschen Thun und Lassen* (Halle, 1720).

16. *Vernünftige Gedanken von dem gesellschaftlichen Leben der Menschen und insonderheit dem gemeinen Wesen zur Beförderung der Glückseligkeit des menschlichen Geschlechtes mitgeteilt* (Halle, 1721).

William I to remove Wolff from his post in 1723. Wolff later suggested (probably not without some justification) that Lange had been envious of Wolff's popularity as a lecturer, but Lange and others, such as Johann Franz Budde at the University of Jena, also put forward genuine and well-founded philosophical criticisms of some of Wolff's key doctrines. Their concerns centered on Wolff's views on the foundations of moral obligation and on his notion of human free will. Wolff argued that moral conduct required no belief in a deity, a view he set out in a speech he gave on the occasion of demitting office as prorector of the university in July 1721, "On the Practical Philosophy of the Chinese."[17] According to Wolff, the ancient Chinese had had no clear idea of a deity, which, though they lacked Christian revelation, they might have derived from natural religion. The Chinese were not full-blown atheists. They believed in some kind of creator of the universe. But their knowledge of the divine attributes was so limited and confused that it was of no use for their moral theory. Even without a clear idea of a deity, however, Chinese philosophers had understood the principles of morality and been capable of acting according to them, because morality was founded on the obligation to strive toward the perfection of human nature.[18] Moral action depended on a clear and distinct idea of human nature, not belief in a deity. Acting immorally was always contrary to the idea of the perfection of human nature. It was also to the disadvantage of the agent, since

> [t]he property of good is to keep us in repose and tranquillity, and that of evil is to confuse everything, turning upside down and bringing

17. Christian Wolff, "Christiani Wolfii . . . Oratio de *Sinarum philosophia practica,*" in Christian Wolff, *Meletemata mathematico-philosophica quibus accedunt dissertationes,* "Sectio III. Scripturas Wolfianas varii argumenti continens velut programmata, orationes, epistolas, praefationes" (1755; Hildesheim: Georg Olms, 1974), pp. 22–126. For a modern edition and translation, see Christian Wolff, "Discourse on the Practical Philosophy of the Chinese (1721–26)," in *Moral Enlightenment: Leibniz and Wolff on China,* Monumenta Serica 26, ed. Julia Ching and Willard G. Oxtoby (Nettetal: Steyler Verlag, 1992), pp. 145–86.

18. On Wolff's theory of moral obligation, see Dieter Hüning, "Christian Wolffs Begriff der natürlichen Verbindlichkeit als Bindeglied zwischen Psychologie und Moralphilosophie," in *Die Psychologie Christian Wolffs: Systematische und historische Untersuchungen,* ed. Oliver-Pierre Rudolph and Jean-François Goubet (Tübingen: Max Niemeyer, 2004), pp. 143–67.

about lasting chaos; the mind, which sees these possibilities in advance, turns to the attractions of good and hates evil, to the extent that it adheres to the judgement of reason. Consequently, we have a spur to seek the good that we know and to flee the evil that we recognize.[19]

Lange, by contrast, subscribed to a voluntarist view of moral obligation, according to which morality was binding because it was founded on the will of God, who was the lawgiver and judge of all mankind. Certain kinds of action might be advantageous, but they were not morally good unless they were commanded by a legitimate superior, such as God, who had the right to punish all transgressions of his law. Without a clear belief in God, morality lacked any solid foundation.

Another reason Wolff's philosophy occasioned controversy was that he appeared to deny the existence of free will. Lange, among others, accused him of "fatalism" and of reducing human beings to automata who had no power to choose their actions but were determined to act in certain ways by factors beyond their control. Without free will it was futile to teach morality, since nobody had the power to choose one kind of action over another. Lange was referring in particular to Wolff's work on metaphysics, *Rational Thoughts concerning God, the World, and the Soul of Man, and All Things in General* where Wolff had cautiously endorsed Leibniz's theory of a preestablished harmony as the best available explanation for the relationship between mind and body. The system of a preestablished harmony was a response to the classical problem in seventeenth- and eighteenth-century philosophy of how the human mind could influence and direct actions of the physical body, even though mind and body were two different kinds of substance: the mind was generally thought to be an immaterial being without spatial dimensions; the body was material and extended. It was difficult to imagine how the former could be the cause of movement in the latter. Leibniz had concluded that mind and body did not interact with each other causally at all. Each of the two followed its own internal and necessary laws of development. They only appeared to influence each other because God had taken care that the

---

19. Wolff, "Practical Philosophy of the Chinese," pp. 166–67.

changes in both were closely coordinated, like the movements of two synchronized clocks. This idea of a preestablished harmony, however, contradicted a conventional belief in the freedom of the human will. For if mind and body each followed its own necessary laws of change, humans appeared to have no power of acting differently from the way they did. Lange, for example, believed that the human will, in order to be free, had to be "indifferent" to several possible courses of action and capable of choosing between them. Wolff replied that the acts of human volition could never be free in the sense of being indifferent to various courses of action. Every act of the human will required a sufficient reason. Unless the will was determined by such a sufficient reason, the will would never arrive at a decision. The will, Wolff added, was nevertheless free, because its choices were not determined by external, physical causes, but by its own, internal reasons. It was therefore "free" in the sense of acting according to its own impulses.[20]

Wolff's critics replied that such a state of affairs would represent no genuine freedom at all. Humans had to have a capacity for choice between different actions, and the decisions of the will had to influence the actions of the body directly. Lange argued that this influence occurred by means of a "physical influx" (*influxus physicus*), which was probably the most common theory used to describe the relationship between mind and body. Wolff's theory, Lange claimed, was just a variation on the philosophical "fatalism" associated with the thought of the Dutch Jewish philosopher Baruch Spinoza, which made it impossible to hold humans morally accountable for their actions. It was on the

---

20. For an account of the controversy between Lange and Wolff, see Carl Hinrichs, *Preußentum und Pietismus* (Göttingen: Vandenhoeck and Ruprecht, 1971), pp. 388–441. For a discussion of the philosophical issue of "fatalism," see Bruno Bianco, "Freiheit gegen Fatalismus: Zu Joachim Langes Kritik an Wolff," in *Aufklärung und Pietismus,* ed. Norbert Hinske (Heidelberg: Lambert Schneider, 1989), pp. 111–55. See also Tim Hochstrasser, *Natural Law Theories in the Early Enlightenment* (Cambridge: Cambridge University Press, 2000), chap. 5; Thomas P. Saine, "Who's afraid of Christian Wolff?," in *Anticipations of the Enlightenment in England, France and Germany,* ed. Alan Charles Kors and Paul J. Korshin (Philadelphia: University of Pennsylvania Press, 1987), pp. 102–33; and Ian Hunter, *Rival Enlightenments: Civil and Metaphysical Philosophy in Early Modern Germany* (Cambridge: Cambridge University Press, 2001), pp. 265–73.

grounds of Wolff's "fatalistic" philosophical teachings that Lange finally persuaded King Frederick William I of Prussia to force Wolff into exile and forbid him on pain of death from returning. According to Wolff, the "soldier-king," as he was often known, was finally convinced by Lange's argument that it would no longer be possible to punish army deserters if Wolff's theory were true.[21] In November 1723, as soon as he had received the king's order to leave, Wolff departed for the University of Marburg, which had already offered him a professorial chair some months before. Toward the end of his reign, Frederick William acknowledged that Wolff's doctrines were probably not as harmful as he had been led to believe, and in 1739 gave Wolff permission to return and take up a chair at the University of Frankfurt an der Oder. Wolff declined the offer, but when Frederick William's son and successor Frederick II, later known as "the Great," invited him to return to Halle, he accepted. Wolff arrived in December 1740, eventually rose to the office of chancellor at the university, was made a baron of the Holy Roman Empire, and remained in Halle until his death in 1754.

The "Scientific Method" in Philosophy

Throughout his career Wolff followed what he called the "scientific method." His commitment to it is reflected in the titles of many of his main works. In 1728, for example, Wolff's *Rational Philosophy or Logic, according to the Scientific Method* appeared.[22] In 1730 he published his *Ontology*, which was, again, "according to the scientific method."[23] There followed several more works that were all "according to the scientific method": *Empirical Psychology,* 1732;[24] *Rational Psychology,* 1734;[25] *Natural Theology,* 1736;[26] *Universal Practical Philosophy*, published between

21. On Lange's accusation of "fatalism," see especially Bianco, "Freiheit gegen Fatalismus."

22. *Philosophia rationalis sive logica, methodo scientifica pertractata* (Frankfurt and Leipzig, 1728).

23. *Philosophia prima sive ontologia methodo scientifica pertractata* (Frankfurt and Leipzig, 1730).

24. *Psychologia empirica, methodo scientifica pertractata* (Frankfurt, 1732).

25. *Psychologia rationalis, methodo scientifica pertractata* (Frankfurt, 1734).

26. *Theologia naturalis, methodo scientifica pertractata* (Frankfurt, 1736–37).

1738 and 1739;[27] *The Law of Nature*, which appeared between 1740 and 1748;[28] and *Moral Philosophy or Ethics* (1750–53), to name just a few.[29] The model for this "scientific method" was mathematical reasoning, which, according to Wolff, was founded on clear and distinct notions, and in which each step of the argument followed necessarily from what went before. But the usefulness of the "scientific method" was not limited to mathematics; it extended to improving philosophical argument.

Many other thinkers similarly believed that philosophy might benefit from mathematical forms of reasoning. An important part in encouraging this belief was played by Descartes's mathematical discoveries in the first half of the seventeenth century, in particular his successful application of algebraic notation to the solution of geometrical problems. One main advantage of the use of algebraic notation, as Descartes and others argued, was that progression from one step in the solution of a geometrical problem to the next was always clear and perspicuous. Descartes distinguished this "modern" method from the approach of the ancient mathematicians such as Euclid or Pappus, who had relied on geometrical constructions rather than algebraic formulae to solve problems in geometry. The approach of these ancients meant that each step in the solution of a problem was always capable of being represented visually. This made it immediately evident how the solution was applicable to the relevant geometrical problem. It was less clear, however, how the principles on which this answer was based were discovered in the first place. The approach of the ancients seemed to depend on intuition and a process of trial and error, not a method that could be learned and then applied to other cases. Descartes argued that the system of algebraic notation, which he used and which had first been applied by the French mathematician François Viète (1540–1603) to equations with more than one unknown variable, was superior to ancient geometry because each step in the argument leading to the answer to the problem

27. *Philosophia practica universalis, methodo scientifica pertractata* (Frankfurt and Leipzig, 1738–39).

28. *Jus naturae methodo scientifica pertractatum.* 8 vols. (Frankfurt and Leipzig/ Halle and Magdeburg, 1740–48).

29. *Philosophia moralis sive ethica, methodo scientifica pertractata,* 5 vols. (Halle, 1750–53).

was transparent, even if none of these steps could be expressed in pictorial terms as the geometric constructions of the ancient mathematicians could.[30] The method proposed by Descartes was to substitute variables for unknown lengths of lines and angles and express the relationship between these in algebraic formulae, which were then manipulated until a general solution for the geometrical problem had been found. This method of "analysis" (or *resolutio*), as Descartes called it, made it possible to ascend from the particular facts that required explanation to the general principles on which they depended. The particular facts that had been the starting point of the "analysis" could then be derived from these general principles by a reverse process of deductive reasoning, termed "synthesis" (or *compositio*), which moved from definitions to axioms to propositions about these particular facts. A powerful demonstration of the value of this method was Descartes's solution to Pappus's four-line problem, which had defeated ancient geometers, but which Descartes solved by using his analytical method.[31]

Not every prominent mathematician of the seventeenth century was won over by this "modern" method. Isaac Newton believed that one had to be able to picture each step of the solution to a geometrical problem. It was not possible to work blindly through a series of permutations of algebraic formulae that did not relate in any evident way to the geometrical figure in question and yet trust the correct result to emerge at the end. Contrary to Descartes, Newton believed that the ancient mathematicians had in fact possessed a proper method for solving geometrical problems, which had been lost and needed to be recovered.[32]

Many other thinkers, however, were persuaded by the apparent success of Descartes's method, which he had always intended to be applied

30. Stephen Gaukroger, "Picturability and Mathematical Ideals of Knowledge," in *The Oxford Handbook of Philosophy in Early Modern Europe*, ed. Desmond Clarke and Catherine Wilson (Oxford: Oxford University Press, 2011), pp. 338–60. See also Hans-Werner Arndt, *Methodo Scientifica Pertractatum: Mos geometricus und Kalkülbegriff in der philosophischen Theoriebildung des 17. und 18. Jahrhunderts* (Berlin: Walter de Gruyter, 1971).

31. See Gaukroger, "Picturability and Mathematical Ideals."

32. Niccolo Guicciardini, *Reading the Principia: The Debate on Newton's Mathematical Methods for Natural Philosophy from 1687 to 1736* (Cambridge: Cambridge University Press, 1999), p. 101.

to other areas of learning.[33] From the mid-seventeenth century it became popular to present a philosophical argument *more geometrico*, in quasi-mathematical terms, as a sequence of definitions, axioms, and propositions. Like Descartes, other thinkers hoped that the method of "analysis," which had appeared to yield such remarkable results in mathematics, could be transferred to philosophy. At the University of Jena the philosopher Erhard Weigel (1625–99) was one of the most influential German proponents of the new "geometric method."[34] His students included two of the most famous thinkers of the early German Enlightenment, Wolff's later patron Gottfried Wilhelm Leibniz, and the jurist, historian, and philosopher Samuel von Pufendorf (1632–94). Weigel's influence prompted Pufendorf to write his 1660 treatise on natural jurisprudence, *Two Books of the Elements of Universal Jurisprudence,*[35] in the geometric style, though he later more or less abandoned this in his better known work, *On the Law of Nature and Nations* of 1672.[36] An important figure in Christian Wolff's intellectual development, even before he became acquainted with Leibniz, was Ehrenfried Walther von Tschirnhaus (1657–1708). Tschirnhaus was a nobleman from Upper Lusatia who studied law and medicine at the University of Leiden from 1668, at a time when Cartesian philosophy was the subject of considerable controversy there.[37] In 1674 he was introduced to the circle around Spinoza, who gave Tschirnhaus a manuscript copy of his *Ethics, Demonstrated according to the Geometric Method*. Following travels to London, Paris, and Italy, Tschirnhaus returned to the Netherlands in 1679 and completed the manuscript of

33. See René Descartes, *A Discourse on the Method*, ed. and trans. Ian Maclean (Oxford: Oxford University Press, 2006).

34. See, for example, Weigel's *Philosophia mathematica, theologia naturalis solida*, ed. Thomas Behme (Stuttgart–Bad Cannstatt: Frommann–Holzboog, 2013).

35. Samuel Pufendorf, *Two Books of the Elements of Universal Jurisprudence*, ed. Thomas Behme (Indianapolis: Liberty Fund, 2009).

36. For a summary of Pufendorf's natural law theory, see Knud Haakonssen, "Samuel Pufendorf (1632–1694)," in *The Oxford Handbook of the History of International Law*, ed. Bardo Fassbender, Anne Peters, Simone Peter, and Daniel Högger (Oxford: Oxford University Press, 2012), pp. 1102–5.

37. Gerhard Wiesenfeldt, *Leerer Raum in Minervas Haus: Experimentelle Naturlehre an der Universität Leiden, 1675–1715* (Amsterdam: Koninklijke Nederlandse Akademie der Wetenschappen; Berlin: Verlag für Geschichte der Naturwissenschaften und Technik, 2002).

his treatise *Medicine of the Mind, or an Attempt at a Genuine Logic, in Which the Method of Finding Unknown Truths Is Discussed*,[38] in which he expressed his great admiration for the "incomparable" Descartes.[39] Wolff had heard of *Medicine of the Mind* when he was still at school, but failed to obtain a copy. He certainly read it at university, however, and in 1705 met Tschirnhaus himself to discuss *Medicine of the Mind*, an event he thought sufficiently memorable to record in his autobiography.[40]

The importance of mathematics for Wolff's philosophy is already evident from the title of his 1703 dissertation, *Universal Practical Philosophy, Written according to the Mathematical Method*. In the preface, Wolff summed up the significance of recent progress in mathematics for philosophy. Over the past century, he said, mathematics had flourished, and

> the other disciplines derived the great splendour, with which they now shine, from the fact, that their scholars now philosophize according to mathematical principles, that is, they are now used to distinguish accurately the concepts of the understanding from the perceptions of the imagination; examining first the nature of things, and deducing everything else from that; and finally progressing from universal and simple principles to more specific and complex conclusions, according to the laws of the genuine method for finding the truth.[41]

38. Ehrenfried Walther von Tschirnhaus, *Medicina mentis, sive tentamen genuinae logicae, in qua disseritur de methodo detegendi incognitas veritates* (Amsterdam, 1687). A second edition appeared in Leipzig in 1695.

39. Siegfried Wollgast, *Ehrenfried Walther von Tschirnhaus und die deutsche Frühaufklärung* (Berlin: Akademie-Verlag, 1988). Jonathan Israel, *Radical Enlightenment: Philosophy and the Making of Modernity* (Oxford: Oxford University Press, 2001), pp. 637–38. See also Jean-Paul Wurtz, "Über einige offene oder strittige die Medicina Mentis von Tschirnhaus betreffende Fragen," *Studia Leibnitiana* 20, no. 2 (1988): 190–211.

40. Wolff, *Lebensbeschreibung*, p. 125.

41. "[R]eliquae autem disciplinae splendorem, quo nunc effulgent, insignem ideo consecutae, quod earum cultores Mathematice philosophari, h.e. conceptus intellectus a perceptionibus imaginationis accurate distinguere, rerum naturas primo omnium loco investigare & ex iis reliqua deducere, tandemque ab universalibus & simplicioribus ad specialiora & magis involuta progredi juxta leges genuinae cujusdam methodi inveniendi verum sueverint." (Christian Wolff, "Philosophia practica universalis, mathematica methodo conscripta," in Wolff, *Meletemata*

Although mathematics and philosophy were different types of knowledge—philosophy was concerned with causal explanation, mathematics with measurement and quantification—the standards of mathematical and philosophical demonstration were essentially the same. For in mathematical argument

> terms are explained by accurate definitions . . . ; propositions, that are accurately defined as regards the subject and predicate, are rigorously proved on the basis of definitions and propositions that have been demonstrated previously. . . . At all times careful attention is paid to the rule that those things are stated first which are used to understand and to prove subsequent statements.[42]

In philosophical argument, too,

> one must not use terms unless they have been defined precisely. . . . [N]othing may be accepted as true, unless it has been sufficiently demonstrated. . . . [I]n propositions the subject as well as the predicate are accurately determined . . . and everything is arranged in such a way, that all that is necessary to understanding the subsequent argument and for providing its foundation is stated first.[43]

"Who does not see," Wolff concluded, "that the rules of the mathematical method are the same as those of the philosophical method?"[44]

---

mathematico-philosophica quibus accedunt dissertationes (1755; Hildesheim: Georg Olms, 1974), p. 190.

42. "[I]n tradenda quoque Mathesi terminos accurata definitione explicari . . . ; ex definitionibus ac propositionibus in antecedentibus jam evictis propositiones, quoad subjectum & praedicatum accurate determinatas, rigorose demonstrari. . . . Ubique ea lex sancte custodiatur, ut praemittantur ea, unde cetera intelliguntur & demonstrantur." "Discursus praeliminaris de philosophia in genere," chap. 4, §139, p. 69.

43. "Nam in methodo philosophica non utendum est terminis nisi accurata definitione explicatis . . . , nec admittitur tanquam verum, nisi quod sufficienter demonstratum . . . , in propositionibus subjectum pariter & praedicatum accurate determinantur . . . & omnia ita ordinantur, ut praemittantur ea, per quae sequentia intelliguntur & adstruuntur. . . ." "Discursus praeliminaris de philosophia in genere," chap. 4, §139, p. 69.

44. "Quis ergo non videt, methodi mathematicae easdem esse regulas, quae sunt methodi philosophicae?" "Discursus praeliminaris de philosophia in genere," chap. 4, §139, p. 69.

The aim of both mathematical and philosophical reasoning was to develop a chain of rigorous, syllogistic argument. The principles that were the starting point of this argument varied. They could be definitions, empirical matters of fact that were absolutely certain, axioms, or propositions that had already been demonstrated.[45] It was also possible to construct an argument from uncertain principles, but in that case the conclusions lacked certainty too. Only when the principles were unquestionably true, and each step in the argument followed necessarily from the previous ones, was the conclusion also reliable. Like Wolff's other works, *The Law of Nations according to the Scientific Method* was intended as an application of this kind of argument. A paragraph typically begins with a hypothesis, followed by a definition, which is used to develop a demonstration. This leads to a proof of the initial hypothesis, which is restated at the end of the paragraph to conclude the argument.

Wolff's influence on the teaching of philosophy at German, Dutch, and Scandinavian universities was profound. In the second half of the eighteenth century Wolffians occupied academic positions all over the Protestant territories of the Holy Roman Empire.[46] Faithful disciples, such as Daniel Nettelbladt (1719–91) in Halle and Joachim Georg Darjes (1714–91) in Frankfurt an der Oder, lectured to generations of students, many of whom later pursued successful careers in the Prussian state bureaucracy.[47] Wolff's system was also popular at Catholic universities in Germany, Austria, and Italy, where his philosophy was often welcomed as a modernized, updated version of the scholastic philosophy that had been taught there before.[48] His views on international law were also of great significance for the ideas of the Swiss jurist Emer de Vattel (1714–67), author of the classic *The Law of Nations* of 1758. There Vattel

45. Wolff, *Philosophia rationalis sive logica. Pars II*, §562.

46. Haakonssen, "German Natural Law," in *The Cambridge History of Eighteenth-Century Political Thought*, ed. Mark Goldie and Robert Wokler (Cambridge: Cambridge University Press, 2006), p. 276; Lewis White Beck, *Early German Philosophy: Kant and His Predecessors* (Bristol: Thoemmes Press, 1996), pp. 276–78.

47. On the importance of the teaching of Wolffian natural law for the outlook of the Prussian bureaucracy, see Eckhart Hellmuth, *Naturrechtsphilosophie und bürokratischer Wertehorizont: Studien zur preußischen Geistes- und Sozialgeschichte des 18. Jahrhunderts* (Göttingen: Vandenhoeck and Ruprecht, 1985).

48. Haakonssen, "German Natural Law," p. 277.

remarked that had he "every-where pointed out what I have borrowed [from Wolff], my pages would be crowded with quotations equally useless and disagreeable to the reader."[49] Yet Vattel also emphasized his disagreements with "[t]hat great philosopher."[50]

One of the most important of these concerned Wolff's idea of a *civitas maxima*. Like other philosophers, Wolff regarded the law of nations as a direct extension of the law of nature.[51] Nations, he wrote in *The Law of Nations*, were considered as "individual free persons living in a state of nature" (§16). But he also believed that all states together formed a "supreme state" (*civitas maxima*), which was analogous to a political community of ordinary citizens. That "supreme state" had "a kind of democratic form of government," mainly because no particular state or group of states exercised sovereignty over all other members of that "supreme state" (§19). It was not feasible, however, for nations to assemble in one place and reach collective decisions, as the citizens of an ordinary democratic state did. Therefore the law of that supreme state had to be "the will of all nations which they are bound to agree upon, if following the leadership of nature they use right reason" (§20); it was not the actual common will of the assembled nations of the world, but the will they all ought to have concerning their mutual relations if they followed the guidance of reason.[52]

Vattel regarded the idea of a *civitas maxima* as irrelevant to the conduct of relations between states. Although the different states of Europe, for example, were more than a "confused heap of detached pieces, each of which thought herself very little concerned in the fate of the others,"[53] they did not form a state comparable to a political community

49. Emer de Vattel, *The Law of Nations*, ed. Béla Kapossy and Richard Whatmore (Indianapolis: Liberty Fund, 2008), p. 13.

50. Vattel, *The Law of Nations*, p. 10.

51. See Knud Haakonssen, "Christian Wolff (1679–1754)," in *The Oxford Handbook of the History of International Law,* ed. Bardo Fassbender, Anne Peters, Simone Peter, and Daniel Högger (Oxford: Oxford University Press, 2012), pp. 1106–9.

52. On Wolff's idea of a *civitas maxima*, see Knud Haakonssen, "German Natural Law," p. 278; Richard Tuck, *The Rights of War and Peace: Political Thought and the International Order from Grotius to Kant* (Oxford: Oxford University Press, 1999), pp. 187–91.

53. Vattel, *The Law of Nations*, III, iii, §47, p. 496.

of ordinary citizens. Modern Europe, Vattel wrote, was "a kind of republic," but its members, unlike those of Wolff's *civitas maxima*, were ruled by "that famous scheme of the political balance, or the equilibrium of power; by which is understood such a disposition of things, as that no one potentate be able absolutely to predominate, and prescribe laws to the others."[54] Although Wolff in §§642–51 of *The Law of Nations* discussed the question of equilibrium between states and considered the measures that were justified to preserve this equilibrium, he did not present the balance of power as the defining principle of the system of modern European states. In that regard Vattel seems to have captured the nature of eighteenth-century great power politics more accurately than Wolff ever did.

ACKNOWLEDGMENTS

I am very grateful to Knud Haakonssen for inviting me to contribute this edition of Christian Wolff's *The Law of Nations* to Liberty Fund's Natural Law and Enlightenment Classics series.

54. Vattel, *The Law of Nations*, III, iii, §47, p. 496.

A NOTE ON THE TEXT

The first edition of *The Law of Nations* appeared in Halle in 1749. The second edition, which is the basis of the translation in this volume, was published in Frankfurt and Leipzig in 1764. The English text used here is essentially that of the translation by Joseph H. Drake, which was published in 1934 in the Classics of International Law series by the Carnegie Endowment for International Peace, though it has been revised (substantially in a few places) to make it more readable. Minor errors in the original translation have also been silently corrected. One significant terminological change concerns the English equivalent of the Latin term *status*, which Drake often translated as "form of government." In most cases, however, the more general term "condition" seemed more appropriate and has been silently used instead. Another change concerns the title: "a scientific method" in the 1934 translation has been replaced by "the scientific method." The definite article seemed more appropriate since Wolff had in mind a very specific method.

The reader should note that the abbreviation "h" (*hic*) is used to indicate when a reference is to a different passage in the book just cited.

Footnotes in this edition have been kept to a minimum. Notes in square brackets are those of the original translator. There are very few references to other authors in the original text, presumably because Wolff believed that the truth ought to be evident from the argument itself, though there are numerous references to passages in his other works. The abbreviations used to refer to these works are explained below.

ABBREVIATIONS

Cosmol.

Christian Wolff, *Cosmologia generalis, methodo scientifica pertractata, qua ad solidam, inprimis Dei atque naturae cognitionem via sternitur* (Frankfurt, 1731).

Disc. Praelim.

"Discursus praeliminaris de philosophia in genere," in Christian Wolff, *Philosophia rationalis sive logica, methodo scientifica pertractata* (Frankfurt and Leipzig, 1728).

Jus Nat.

Christian Wolff, *Jus naturae methodo scientifica pertractatum*, 8 vols. (Frankfurt and Leipzig/Halle and Magdeburg, 1740–48).

Log.

Christian Wolff, *Philosophia rationalis sive logica, methodo scientifica pertractata* (Frankfurt and Leipzig, 1728).

Ontol.

Christian Wolff, *Philosophia prima sive ontologia methodo scientifica pertractata* (Frankfurt and Leipzig, 1730).

Phil. Pract. Univ.

Christian Wolff, *Philosophia practica universalis, methodo scientifica pertractata* (Frankfurt and Leipzig, 1738–39).

Psych. Emp.

Christian Wolff, *Psychologia empirica, methodo scientifica pertractata* (Frankfurt, 1732).

Psych. Rat.

Christian Wolff, *Psychologia rationalis, methodo scientifica pertractata* (Frankfurt, 1734).

Theol. Nat.

Christian Wolff, *Theologia naturalis, methodo scientifica pertractata* (Frankfurt, 1736–37).

THE LAW OF NATIONS TREATED ACCORDING
TO THE SCIENTIFIC METHOD

THE LAW OF NATIONS
TREATED ACCORDING TO THE
SCIENTIFIC METHOD

In which the Natural Law of Nations
is carefully distinguished from that which is voluntary,
stipulative and customary

by

CHRISTIAN WOLFF

State Counselor of the Most Powerful King of the Swedes and
of the Landgrave of Hesse, Principal Professor of Mathematics
and Philosophy in the University of Marburg, Honorary
Professor of St. Petersburg, Member of the Royal
Academy of Sciences of Paris and of the
Royal Societies of England and of Russia

A more accurate and polished edition than the preceding ones

FRANKFURT and LEIPZIG

1764

At the Expense of the Venetian Society
By the authority and with the privileges granted by the Government

Who Is Most Benign:

That eternal and unchangeable law, which nature herself has established, governs all the acts of individuals as well as those of nations also, by prescribing duties both toward themselves and toward each other. And just as it has united individuals to each other by the closest bond and has established among them a certain society, so that one human being is necessary to another, and nothing is more useful to man than man; so by no less close a bond has it united nations, and moulded them into one enormous state, so that nation is necessary to nation, and nothing is more useful to nation than nation. Indeed, just as it provides for the happiness of individual humans, so also does it provide for that of individual nations, which is promoted and preserved by mutual assistance. Therefore the entire human race is likened to a living body whose individual members are individual nations, and it retains unimpaired health so long as the individual members perform their functions properly. The rulers of nations give life to the members of this body, since the members are as it were endowed with the bare capacity to act, and their power to act rightly is derived from the rulers, as long as they are controlled by the wisdom and foresight of the rulers, so that they are kept healthful, and contribute what they ought to the healthfulness of the body as a whole. For that reason the rulers of states tower above their

3

nations, just as the soul is superior to the body, and as the law of their nations abides in them, so also do that intellect and will, without which it is not possible to use that law. It has seemed fitting to communicate a knowledge of this law by that method which I have used in all of the law of nature and in other departments of philosophy, so that the truth can be clearly seen. But since, indeed, the force of examples is very great, both in knowledge and action, an example ought to be cited. But why should I seek an ancient example, when I may use one present and living? For Your Highness offers an example of such a nature that, if all rulers of states would follow it, there would be no complaints of the misfortunes of the times. Your skill in action, your wisdom and foresight, your love of humanity implanted in you by nature, your desire to give consideration to the welfare of those who repose all confidence as to their well-being in you, your zeal in promoting the fortunes of others without advantage to yourself, and finally, to mention nothing else, that exalted and perfect reputation, in which you excel, has induced the citizens of the whole Confederacy of the Netherlands, by unanimous consent in these most troublous times, as though filled by a certain divine inspiration, to desire to have you, Most Serene Prince, as governor, supreme commander in war on land and sea, and perpetual ruler of the East Indies. Such is your kindness that you have readily consented to their pleas and have willingly assumed this very heavy burden. Now you shine like the sun among the planets throughout the allied provinces, but you are never idle. For just as the sun by its power keeps the planets in their orbits and preserves the whole system by mutual actions and reactions, so that the individual planets complete their circuits around it according to fixed law; so also Your Highness holds the allied provinces united together by a very strong bond of union, and while the performance of duties demanded by mutual affection is secured, their entire system exists in such a form that each province enjoys those blessings which produce a happy state. The artist has portrayed this elegantly on the gold medal, by which the memory of the hereditary rule over the whole of the Confederacy of the Netherlands conferred upon Your Highness, is handed down to posterity. Since, Most Gracious Master, contrary to all my hope and expectation I have been honoured by you with that decoration; wherever learned men have recognized therefrom and publicly honoured your patronage of letters, I too have been fully convinced that my effort to make philosophy definite and useful to the human race, is not displeasing to Your Highness, and I experience daily the influence of so splendid a gift upon the mind, an influence which usually attends gifts conferred by princes upon learned men, when I turn my attention to the continuation of the work which was begun so many years ago. Therefore, relying upon this perfectly assured hope, Most Wise Prince, that you will not disapprove of my coupling the splendour and authority of your name with my learning, I appear with most humble mind to offer this volume to Your Highness. May God preserve you, Most Exalted and Serene Prince, that by your example you may show how nations may be happy and useful to other nations; which is the desire of Your Highness's.

Most humble and devoted admirer
Christian Freiherr von Wolff

Since nations in their relations with each other use no other law than that which has been established by nature, a separate treatment of the law of nations and the law of nature might seem superfluous. But those, indeed, who feel thus do not weigh the laws of nations in scales that are perfectly balanced. Nations certainly can be regarded as nothing else than individual free persons living in a state of nature, and therefore the same duties are to be imposed upon them, both as regards themselves and as regards others, and the rights arising therefrom, which are prescribed by the law of nature and are bestowed on individual humans, to the extent that they are by nature born free, and are united by no other bond than that of nature. And so whatever right arises and whatever obligations result therefrom, come from that unchangeable law which has its source in human nature, and thus the law of nations is undoubtedly a part of the law of nature, and therefore it is called the natural law of nations, if you should look at its source, but the necessary, if you should look at its power to bind. And this is a law common to all nations, so that any nation which does anything contrary to it, violates the common law of all nations, and does a wrong. But since, indeed, nations are moral persons and therefore are subject only to certain rights and duties, which by virtue of the law of nature arise from the society entered into, their nature and essence undoubtedly differ very much from the nature and essence of individual humans as physical persons. When therefore the duties, which the law of nature prescribes to individuals, and when the rights, which are given to individuals to demand the performance of these duties, are applied to nations, since they can be such only as are allowed by their subjects, they must be suitably changed by them, that they may take on a certain new form. And thus the law of nations does not remain the same in all respects as the law of nature, in so far as it governs the acts

7

of individuals. What therefore stands in the way of treating it separately as a law peculiar to nations? Indeed, he who speaks of the law of nature and nations, shows by that very fact, unless he should wish to utter sound without sense, that there is some difference between the law of nature and the law of nations. But if, indeed, any one shall be too obstinate to admit that the law of nations is different from the law of nature, he may call our present volume, which we have written on the former subject, the ninth part of "The Law of Nature." For we consider it unseemly to quarrel over such a trifle. But as indeed the condition of men is such that in a state one cannot completely satisfy in all details the rigour of the law of nature, and for that reason there is need of positive laws, which do not differ altogether from the law of nature, nor observe it in all details; so likewise the condition of nations is such that one cannot completely satisfy in all details the natural rigour of the law of nations, and therefore that law, immutable in itself, should be adapted only so much that it neither departs entirely from natural law, nor observes it in all details. But since the common welfare itself of nations demands this very adaptation; therefore nations are none the less bound to admit as between themselves the law arising therefrom, than they are bound by nature to an observance of natural law; and the former no less than the latter, if consistency in the law is preserved, is to be considered a law common to all nations. But this law itself we, in company with Grotius, have been pleased to call the voluntary law of nations, although with not exactly the same signification, but with a slightly narrower meaning. But far be it from you to imagine that this voluntary law of nations is developed from the will of nations in such a way that their will is free in establishing it and that free will alone takes the place of reason, without any regard to natural law. For as we have proved in the eighth part of "The Law of Nature," civil laws are not matters of mere will, but the law of nature itself prescribes the method by which the civil law is to be fashioned out of natural law, so that there can be nothing which can be criticized in it; so also the voluntary law of nations does not depend upon the free will of nations, but natural law itself defines the means by which voluntary law may replace natural law, which is only admissible when necessity demands it. Since nature herself has united nations into one supreme state in the same manner as individuals have united into particular states, the manner also in which the voluntary law of nations ought to be fashioned out of natural law, is exactly the same as that by which civil laws in a state ought to be fashioned out of natural laws. For that reason the law of nations, which we call voluntary, is not, as Grotius thought, to be determined from the acts of nations, as though from their acts their general consent is to be assumed, but from the purpose of that supreme state which nature herself established, just as she established society among all men, so that nations are bound to agree to that law, and it is not left to their whim as to whether they should prefer to agree or not. Those are not lacking who, when they condemn the voluntary law of nations, speak of it as natural law, so that they seem to disagree only in words, but agree in fact; nevertheless if you wish to examine the matter more carefully, you could not deny that the obligation which comes from natural law is not in the least diminished by the voluntary law, although this gives immunity of action among men and permits those things to be tolerated which could not be avoided without greater evil, consequently it is undoubtedly necessary that natural law must be distinguished from voluntary law, by whatever names indeed you may have preferred to call these different laws. We prefer the custom of not changing terms once introduced into science except for urgent necessity, but the concepts corresponding to them, as there may have been need, are to be so limited and corrected, that they may correspond to the truth. For it seems too childish, with the arrogance of a weak mind, to change terms or their signification, and on this account to claim the reputation of a discoverer with those among whom even the one-eyed is king. That most perfect law of nature constantly retains its force, so that we should do right, and should not wish to do the things which can be done with impunity, unless they are also right, and thus there may arise a consciousness of duty done as a reward, inasmuch as that is a great part of happiness, and as good deeds produce a true and great reputation, delight in which is also to be attributed to this genuine happiness. But just as individuals can acquire rights by stipulations and contract obligations through them; so also nations can acquire rights from nations, by stipulations and contract obligations through them. This is appropriately called the stipulative law of nations, and it gets its validity from natural law, which commands that agreements should be observed. Moreover, natural law enjoins that agreements should be made with a sense of obligation, although the voluntary law does not base their validity upon the same considerations, and there may be a violation of natural law without a penalty and that is to be endured. It is self-evident that stipulative law is only a particular law of nations, which is not valid except between those nations which have contracted. It has been decided before that there can be a tacit no less than an express agreement, and by nature there are certain tacit provisions in every express agreement, since the law of nature makes no distinction between contracts *bona fide* and *stricti juris.*[1] On these tacit agreements are based those provisions which have been introduced by custom among nations, and which, as we have said, constitute the customary law of nations. This is similar to the stipulative law, therefore it holds good only between nations which have made those customs their own by long observance. But although the characteristics which belong to this law are carelessly referred to the common law of nations, nevertheless the great number of erring nations does not provide a defence for this error, so that it could be referred either to the natural or the voluntary law. We do not follow the mass of jurists, who decide concerning a fact before the reasons have been considered as to why it must be so decided, and then that they may protect their preconceived opinion, they finally seek out reasons as to why they should so decide. We admit as true only what is inferred as a necessary consequence from previous conclusions, but we do not invent doubtful principles, so as to deceive those endowed with a weak intellect, to whom it is not permitted to see very far ahead. The method by which we have determined to present the law of nature and nations and which we use in our philosophy, does not admit of these devices; it requires truth without colouring and childish deceit. Therefore in the present work also we have so presented the law of nations, that what is natural may be separated from that which is voluntary but common to all nations, what is customary from either, what finally is stipulative from all the rest, and that by a careful reader those things may be easily distinguished which come from different

---

1. In Roman Law a contract *bonae fidei* ("of good faith") allowed the judge some discretion in determining the obligations derived from it, whereas a contract *stricti juris* ("of strict right") demanded a precise adherence to the terms of the agreement.

sources. But as it is human to err, so it will not seem wonderful that nations, even the most learned and civilized, have erroneously considered those things the law of nature which are diametrically opposed to it, and that perverse customs have arisen therefrom, by which right has been transformed to reckless licence, which we do not in the least confuse with the voluntary law of nations, but refer to an unjust customary law of nations, by which the most sacred name of law is defiled. And in that we part company with Grotius. In his age, "system" was an unknown term, which is subject to abuse even in our own times, and he can be easily excused for uniting the voluntary and customary law of nations into one, and failing to distinguish good customs from bad in the latter. But it is to the advantage of the human race that things so different should not be confused with one another, since nations and their rulers would become the authors of disaster and troubles, if a sense of duty should be divorced from the exercise of a right, and right transformed into reckless licence. In fact it is rather to be desired than hoped for, that nations should be brought back to the straight road from the by-paths into which they have strayed too far; nevertheless on this account a knowledge of the truth is not to be considered absolutely useless. For in order that we may not be unjust to the Supreme Being, it is fitting that we understand the source of evils, and that we should not be so hopeless of the human race, as to believe that there may never be any one who would be unwilling to put his hands into the keeping of truth. May God bring it about that the times may come in which, if not all, at least very many rulers of nations may recognize what they owe to their own nation and to other nations.

Halle, April 9, 1749.

§ 1. *Definition of the Law of Nations*

By the Law of Nations we understand the science of that law which nations or peoples use in their relations with each other and of the obligations corresponding thereto.

§ 23, part 1, Jus Nat.[1]

§ 25, part 1, Jus Nat.

We propose to show, of course, how nations as such ought to determine their actions, and consequently to what each nation is bound, both to itself and to other nations, and what laws of nations arise therefrom, both as to itself and as to other nations. For laws arise from passive obligation, so that, if there were no obligation, neither would there be any law.

§ 2. *How nations are to be regarded*

§ 5, part 8, Jus Nat.

§ 54, part 8, Jus Nat.

Nations are regarded as individual free persons living in a state of nature. For they consist of a multitude of people united into a state. Therefore since states are regarded as individual free persons living in a state of nature, nations also must be regarded in relation to each other as individual free persons living in a state of nature.

Here, of course, we are looking at nations as they are at their beginning, before one has bound itself to another by definite promises restricting the civil liberty which belongs to a people, or has been subjected, either by its own act or that of another, to some other nation. For that the liberty of nations, which originally belongs to them, can be taken away or diminished, will be evident from proof later.

1. [Unless otherwise designated, all marginal notes either refer to other works of Wolff or are cross references to other sections of this book. The complete title of the other works of Wolff to which he makes reference may be found on p. xxvi.—Tr.]

§ 3. *Of what sort the law of nations is originally*

Since nations are regarded as individual persons living in a state of nature, moreover, as men in a state of nature use nothing except natural law, nations also originally use none other than natural law; therefore the law of nations is originally nothing except the law of nature applied to nations.

§ 2.

§ 125, part 1, Jus Nat.

The only law given to men by nature is natural law. This then can be changed by the act of men voluntarily, by agreement between individuals, so far as concerns those things which belong to permissive law, and so far as concerns the performance of those actions that are required by the principles of humanity; it can be changed in the state by force of the legislative power, as we have shown in our natural theory of the civil laws. In like manner the only law given to nations by nature is natural law, or the law of nature itself applied to nations. This then can be changed by the act of nations voluntarily, so far as concerns those things which belong to permissive law, and so far as concerns the performance of those actions that are required by the principles of humanity, as we shall see in the following discussion. But far be it from you to think that therefore there is no need of our discussing in detail the law of nations. For the principles of the law of nature are one thing, but the application of them to nations another, and this application produces a certain diversity in the law of nations, which is inferred from the fact that the nature of a nation is not the same as human nature. For example, man is bound to preserve himself by nature, every nation by the agreement through which it is made a definite moral person. But there is one method of preservation required for man, another for a nation. Likewise the right of defending one's self against the injuries of others belongs to man by nature, and the law of nature itself assigns it to a nation. But the method of one human being's defence against another is not, of course, the same as the proper method of defence for nations. There will be no difficulty in this for those who have understood the force of the fundamental principle of reduction, which is of especial importance in the art of logic. And if any mists still obscure the minds of some, the following discussion will dispel them. Therefore we are not embarrassed by the objections of those who argue that the law of nations ought not to

Chapter 4, part 8, Jus Nat.

be distinguished from the law of nature, and that the law of nations ought to be presented as nothing other than the law of nature. So far as we are concerned, each may indulge his own belief. With none shall we start a dispute. For us it is sufficient to have explained those things which seem to us to be in harmony with the truth.

§ 4. *Definition of the necessary law of nations*

We call that the necessary law of nations which consists in the law of nature applied to nations. It is even called by Grotius and his successors, the internal law of nations, since it evidently binds nations in conscience. It is likewise called by some the natural law of nations.

Of course, the necessary law of nations contains those things which the law of nature prescribes to nations, which, just as it regulates all acts of men, so likewise governs the acts of nations as such.

§ 5. *Of the immutability of this law*

§ 4.

§142, part 1, Phil. Pract. Univ.

Since the necessary law of nations consists in the law of nature applied to nations, furthermore as the law of nature is immutable, the necessary law of nations also is absolutely immutable.

§§ 136, 142, part 1, Phil. Pract. Univ.

§ 5, part 8, Jus Nat.

§ 136, part 1, Phil. Pract. Univ.

§ 4, part 8, Jus Nat.

The immutability of the necessary law of nations arises from the very immutability of natural law, and is finally derived from the essence and nature of man as a source whence flows the very immutability of natural law. The law of nature therefore rules the acts of nations, because men coming together into a state and thereby becoming a nation, do not lay aside their human nature, consequently they remain subject to the law of nature, in as much as they have desired to combine their powers for the promotion of the common good.

§ 6. *The nature of the obligation which comes from the necessary law of nations*

§ 4.

In like manner since the necessary law of nations consists in the law of nature applied to nations, and consequently the obligation which arises from the necessary law of nations comes from the law of nature, furthermore, since this obligation itself, which comes from the law of nature, is necessary and immutable, the obligation also which comes from the law of nations is necessary and immutable; consequently neither can any nation free itself nor can one nation free another from it.

§ 142, part 3, Phil. Pract. Univ.

These things are to be well considered, lest some one may think, when he sees that a certain licence of action must be tolerated among nations, that the necessary law of nations is of no use. For this would be just as if one should argue that the law of nature is of no use, because the abuse of their liberty must be allowed to men in a state of nature and the same is turned to licence of action, nor can this be prohibited except by positive law in a civil state, where they can be compelled by a superior by force to do what they are unwilling to do of their own accord. The abuse of power remains illicit even among nations, even though it cannot be checked. Nor do good nations do all they can, but they have respect for conscience no less than every good man has, who does not gauge his right by might, but by the obligation that comes from the law of nature. A good nation differs from a bad in the same way that a good man differs from a bad, or, if you prefer, the virtuous from the vicious.

§§ 150, 156, part 1, Jus Nat.

§ 7. *Of the society established by nature among nations*

Nature herself has established society among all nations and binds them to preserve society. For nature herself has established society among men and binds them to preserve it. Therefore, since this obligation, as coming from the law of nature, is necessary and immutable, it cannot be changed for the reason that nations have formed a state. Therefore society, which nature has established among individuals, still exists among nations and consequently, after states have been established in accordance with the law of nature and nations have arisen thereby, nature herself also must be said to have established society among all nations and bound them to preserve society.

§ 138, part 1, Jus Nat.
§ 135, part 1, Phil. Pract. Univ.
§ 142, part 1, Phil. Pract. Univ.
§ 5, part 8, Jus Nat.
§ 26, part 8, Jus Nat.
§ 5, part 8, Jus Nat.

If we should consider that great society, which nature herself has established among men, to be done away with by the particular societies, which humans enter, when they unite into a state, states would be established contrary to the law of nature, in as much as the universal obligation of all toward all would be terminated; which assuredly is

§ 5, part 8,
Jus Nat.
absurd. Just as in the human body individual organs do not cease to be organs of the whole human body, because certain ones taken together constitute one organ; so likewise individual men do not cease to be members of that great society which is made up of the whole human race, because several have formed together a certain particular society. And in so far as these act together as associates, just as if they were all of one mind and one will; even so are the members of that society united, which nature has established among men. After the human race was divided into nations, that society which before was between individuals continues between nations.

§ 8. *Of the purpose of that state*

§ 7.

§ 142, part 7,
Jus Nat.

§ 144, part 7,
Jus Nat.

§ 141, part 8,
Jus Nat.

Since nature herself has established society among all nations, in so far as she has established it among all men, as is evident from the demonstration of the preceding proposition, since, moreover, the purpose of natural society, and consequently of that society which nature herself has established among men, is to give mutual assistance in perfecting itself and its condition; the purpose of the society therefore, which nature has established among all nations, is to give mutual assistance in perfecting itself and its condition. Consequently the common good must be promoted by its combined powers.

Just as one human being alone is not sufficient unto himself, but needs the aid of another, in order that thereby the common good may be promoted by their combined powers; so also one nation alone is not sufficient for itself, but one needs the aid of the other, that thereby the common good may be promoted by their combined powers. Therefore since nature herself unites men together and compels them to preserve society, because the common good of all cannot be promoted except by their combined powers, so that nothing is more beneficial for man than man; the same nature likewise unites nations together and compels them to preserve society, because the common good of all cannot be promoted except by their combined powers, so that nothing can be said to be more beneficial for a nation than a nation. For although a nation can be thought of which is spread over a vast expanse, and does not seem to need the aid of other nations; nevertheless it cannot yet be said that it could not improve its condition still more by the aid of other nations, much less that other nations could not be aided by it, however much it could itself dispense with the aid of others. Just as man ought to aid man, so too ought nation to aid nation.

§ 9. *Of the state which is made up of all nations*

All nations are understood to have come together into a state, whose separate members are separate nations, or individual states. For nature herself has established society among all nations and compels them to preserve it, for the purpose of promoting the common good by their combined powers. Therefore since a society of men united for the purpose of promoting the common good by their combined powers, is a state, nature herself has combined nations into a state. Therefore since nations, which know the advantages arising therefrom, by a natural impulse are carried into this association, which binds the human race or all nations one to the other, since moreover it is assumed that the others will join it, if they know their own interests; what can be said except that nations also have combined into society as if by agreement? So all nations are understood to have come together into a state, whose separate nations are separate members or individual states.

§§ 7, 8.

§§ 4, 9, part 8, Jus Nat.

§ 504, part 5, Jus Nat.
§ 5, part 8, Jus Nat.

Reasoning throws a certain light upon the present proposition, by which we have proved that nature has established society among men and compels them to protect society. Nay, rather the state, into which nature herself orders nations to combine, in truth depends on that great society which she has established among all men, as is perfectly evident from the above reasoning. But that those things may not be doubtful which we have said concerning the quasi-agreement, by which that supreme state is understood to have been formed between nations; those things must be reconsidered which we have mentioned elsewhere. Furthermore, in establishing this quasi-agreement we have assumed nothing which is at variance with reason, or which may not be allowed in other quasi-agreements. For that nations are carried into that association by a certain natural impulse is apparent from their acts, as when they enter into treaties for the purpose of commerce or war, or even of friendship, concerning which we shall speak below in their proper place. There is no need to persuade yourself that there

§ 138, part 7, Jus Nat.

§ 7.

Note, § 142, part 7, Jus Nat.

is no nation that is not known to unite to form the state, into which nature herself commands all to combine. Just as in tutelage it is rightly presumed that the pupil agrees, in so far as he ought to agree, nay, more, as he would be likely to agree, if he knew his own interest; so in the same way nations which through lack of insight fail to see how great an advantage it is to be a member of that supreme state, are presumed to agree to this association. And since it is understood in a civil state that the tutor is compelled to act, if he should be unwilling to consent of his own accord, but that even when the agreement is extorted by a superior by force that does not prevent the tutelage from resting upon a quasi-agreement; why, then, is it not allowable to attribute the same force to the natural obligation by which nations are compelled to enter into an alliance as is attributed to the civil obligation, that it is understood to force consent even as from one unwilling? But if these arguments seem more ingenious than true, and altogether too complicated; putting them aside, it is enough to recognize that nature herself has combined nations into a state, therefore whatever flows from the concept of a state, must be assumed as established by nature herself. We have aimed at nothing else.

§ 10. *What indeed may be called the supreme state*

The state, into which nations are understood to have combined, and of which they are members or citizens, is called the supreme state.

The size of a state is determined by the number of its citizens. Therefore a greater state cannot be conceived of than one whose members are all nations in general, inasmuch as they together include the whole human race. This concept of a supreme state was not unknown to Grotius, nor was he ignorant of the fact that the law of nations was based on it, but nevertheless he did not derive from it the law of nations which is called voluntary, as he could and ought to have done.

§§ 17, 23, Proleg.

§ 11. *Of the laws of the supreme state*

§ 10.
§ 4, part 8, Jus Nat.

Since the supreme state is a certain sort of state, and consequently a society, moreover since every society ought to have its own laws and the right exists in it of promulgating laws with respect to those things which concern it, the supreme state also ought to have its own laws and the right exists in it of promulgating laws with respect to those things which concern it; and because civil laws, that is, those declared in a state, prescribe the means by which the good of a state is maintained, the laws of the supreme state likewise ought to prescribe the means by which its good is maintained.

§ 46, part 7, Jus Nat.

§ 965, part 8, Jus Nat.
§ 969, part 8, Jus Nat.

It occasions very little difficulty that laws may be promulgated in the state by a superior such as nations do not have, and certainly do not recognize. For since the law of nature governs the will of the ruler in making laws, and since laws ought to prescribe the means by which the good of the state is maintained, by virtue of the present proposition, then, it is evident enough of what sort those laws ought to be that nations ought to agree to, consequently may be presumed to have agreed to. No difficulty will appear in establishing a law of nations which does not depart altogether from the necessary law of nations, nor in all respects observe it, as will appear in what follows.

§ 965, part 8, Jus Nat.
Note, § 965, part 8, Jus Nat.

§ 12. *How individual nations are bound to the whole and the whole to the individuals*

Inasmuch as nations are understood to have combined in a supreme state, the individual nations are understood to have bound themselves to the whole, because they wish to promote the common good, but the whole to the individuals, because it wishes to provide for the especial good of the individuals. For if a state is established, individuals bind themselves to the whole, because they wish to promote the common good, and the whole binds itself to the individuals, because it wishes to provide for adequate life, for peace and security, consequently for the especial good of the individuals. Inasmuch then as nations are understood to have combined in a supreme state, individual nations also are understood to have bound themselves to the whole, because they wish to promote the common good, and the whole to the individuals, because it wishes to provide for the especial good of the individuals.

§ 28, part 8, Jus Nat.

§§ 9 and fol., part 8, Jus Nat.

Nature herself has brought nations together in the supreme state, and therefore has imposed upon them the obligation which the present

§ 7, 9.

proposition urges, that because they ought to agree, they may be presumed to have agreed, or it may rightly be assumed that they have agreed,
just as something similar exists in patriarchal society, which we have said
is valid as a natural quasi-agreement. But if all nations had been equipped
with such power of discernment as to know how effort might be made
for the advantage of themselves, and what losses might be avoided by
them, if the individual nations performed the duty of a good citizen, and
their leaders did not allow themselves to be led astray by some impulse
of passion, certainly there would be no doubt that in general all would
expressly agree to that to which nature leads them, which produces and
maintains harmony even among the ignorant and unwilling. But this
must be shown by us, how nature provides for the happiness of the
human race in accordance with the human lot. For humans ought not
to be imagined to be what they are not, however much they ought to be
so. And for this reason it will be plain from what follows, that laws which
spring from the concept of the supreme state, depart from the necessary
law of nations, since on account of the human factor in the supreme state
things which are illicit in themselves have to be, not indeed allowed, but
endured, because they cannot be changed by human power.

Note, § 635,
part 7, Jus Nat.

§ 13. Of the law of nations as a whole in regard to individual nations

In the supreme state the nations as a whole have a right to coerce the individual nations, if they should be unwilling to perform their obligation, or
should show themselves negligent in it. For in a state the right belongs to
the whole of coercing the individuals to perform their obligation, if they
should either be unwilling to perform it or should show themselves negligent in it. Therefore since all nations are understood to have combined
into a state, of which the individual nations are members, and inasmuch
as they are understood to have combined in the supreme state, the individual members of this are understood to have bound themselves to the
whole, because they wish to promote the common good, since moreover
from the passive obligation of one party the right of the other arises;
therefore the right belongs to the nations as a whole in the supreme state
also of coercing the individual nations, if they are unwilling to perform
their obligation or show themselves negligent in it.

§ 29, part 8,
Jus Nat.

§ 9.

§ 12.

§ 23, part 1,
Jus Nat.

This will seem paradoxical to those who do not discern the connexion of truths and who judge laws from facts. But it will be evident in what follows that we need the present proposition as a basis of demonstration of others which must be admitted without hesitation. And in general it must be observed that our question is one of law, for which men are fitted in their present state, and not at all of facts, by which the law is either defied or broken. For there would be no purpose in the supreme state, into which nature has united nations, unless from it some law should arise for the whole in regard to the individuals. Of what sort this is will be shown in what follows.

§ 14. *How this is to be measured*

The law of nations as a whole with reference to individual nations in the supreme state must be measured by the purpose of the supreme state. For the law of the whole with reference to individuals in a state must be measured by the purpose of the state. Therefore, since in the supreme state too a certain right belongs to nations as a whole with reference to the individual nations, this right also must be measured by the purpose of the supreme state.

§ 30, part 8, Jus Nat.

§ 13.

Since in any state the right of the whole over the individuals must not be extended beyond the purpose of the state, so also the right of nations as a whole over individual nations cannot be extended beyond the purpose of the supreme state into which nature herself has combined them, so that forthwith individual nations may be known to have assigned a right of this sort to the whole.

Note, § 30, part 8, Jus Nat.

§ 15. *Of what sort this is*

Some sovereignty over individual nations belongs to nations as a whole. For a certain sovereignty over individuals belongs to the whole in a state. Therefore, as is previously shown, some sovereignty over individual nations belongs also to nations as a whole.

§ 31, part 8, Jus Nat.

§ 14.

That sovereignty will seem paradoxical to some. But these will be such as do not have a clear notion of the supreme state, nor recognize the benefit which nature provides, when she establishes a certain civil society among nations. Moreover, it will be evident in its own place that nothing at all results from this, except those things which all willingly recognize as in accordance with the law of nations, or what it is readily understood they ought to recognize. Nor is it less plain that this sovereignty has a certain resemblance to civil sovereignty.

§ 32, part 8, Jus Nat.

§ 16. *Of the moral equality of nations*

§ 2.

§ 81, part 1, Jus Nat.

By nature all nations are equal the one to the other. For nations are considered as individual free persons living in a state of nature. Therefore, since by nature all humans are equal, all nations too are by nature equal the one to the other.

It is not the number of humans coming together into a state that makes a nation, but the bond by which the individuals are united, and this is nothing else than the obligation by which they are bound to one another. The society which exists in the greater number of humans united together, is the same as that which exists in the smaller number. Therefore just as the tallest person is no more a human being than the dwarf, so also a nation, however small, is no less a nation than the greatest nation. Therefore, since the moral equality of humans has no relation to the size of their bodies, the moral equality of nations also has no relation to the number of people of which they are composed.

§ 17. *In what it consists*

§ 16.

§ 78, part 1, Jus Nat.

Since by nature all nations are equal, since moreover all humans are equal in a moral sense whose rights and obligations are the same; the rights and obligations of all nations also are by nature the same.

Therefore a great and powerful nation can assume no right to itself against a small and weak nation such as does not belong to the weaker against the stronger, nor is a small and weak nation bound to a great and powerful one in any way in which the latter is not equally bound to it.

§ 18. *Whether by nature anything is lawful for one nation which is not lawful for another*

§ 17.

Since by nature the rights and obligations of all nations are the same, and since that is lawful which we have a right to do, and unlawful which

we are obliged not to do or to omit; what is lawful by nature for one
nation, that likewise is lawful for another, and what is not lawful for one,
is not lawful for another.

§ 170, part 1,
Jus Nat.

Might gives to no nation a special privilege over another, just as
force gives none to one man over another. Just as might is not the
source of the law of nature, so that any one may do what he can to
another, so neither is the might of nations the source of the law of
nations, so that right is to be measured by might.

§ 19. What form of government is adapted to the supreme state

The supreme state is a kind of democratic form of government. For
the supreme state is made up of the nations as a whole, which as individual nations are free and equal to each other. Therefore, since no nation
by nature is subject to another nation, and since it is evident of itself that
nations by common consent have not bestowed the sovereignty which
belongs to the whole as against the individual nations, upon one or more
particular nations, nay, that it cannot even be conceived under human
conditions how this may happen, that sovereignty is understood to have
been reserved for nations as a whole. Therefore, since the government is
democratic, if the sovereignty rests with the whole, which in the present
instance is the entire human race divided up into peoples or nations, the
supreme state is a kind of democratic form of government.

§ 10.

§ 50, part 8,
Jus Nat.

§ 16.

§ 136, part 1,
Jus Nat.

§ 131, part 8,
Jus Nat.

The democratic form of government is the most natural form of
a state, since it begins at the very beginning of the state itself and is
only *de facto* changed into any other form, a thing which cannot even
be conceived of in the supreme state. Therefore for the supreme state
no form of government is suitable other than the democratic form.

§ 20. What must be conceived of in the supreme state as the will of all the nations

Since in a democratic state that must be considered the will of the whole
people which shall have seemed best to the majority, since moreover the
supreme state is a kind of democratic form of government, and is made
up of all the nations, in the supreme state also that must be considered

§ 157, part 8,
Jus Nat.

§ 19.

§ 10.

the will of all the nations which shall have seemed best to the majority. Nevertheless, since in a democratic state it is necessary that individuals assemble in a definite place and declare their will as to what ought to be done, since moreover all the nations scattered throughout the whole world cannot assemble together, as is self-evident, that must be taken to be the will of all nations which they are bound to agree upon, if following the leadership of nature they use right reason. Hence it is plain, because it has to be admitted, that what has been approved by the more civilized nations is the law of nations.

§ 173, part 8, Jus Nat.

Grotius recognized that some law of nations must be admitted which departs from the law of nature, the inflexibility of which cannot possibly be observed among nations. Moreover, he does not think that this law is such that it can be proved otherwise than by precedents and decisions, and especially the agreements of the more civilized nations. We indeed shall enter upon a safer course if we point out that nations following reason ought to agree as to either this or that which has prevailed, or now prevails, among them as law—a thing which can be proved from the concept of the supreme state no less plainly than the necessary or natural law of nations can.

Prolegomena, De Jure Belli ac Pacis, § 46.

§ 21. *Of the ruler of the supreme state*

Since in the supreme state that is to be considered as the will of all nations, to which they ought to agree, if following the leadership of nature they use right reason, and since the superior in the state is he to whom belongs the right over the actions of the individuals, consequently he who exercises the sovereignty, therefore he can be considered the ruler of the supreme state who, following the leadership of nature, defines by the right use of reason what nations ought to consider as law among themselves, although it does not conform in all respects to the natural law of nations, nor altogether differ from it.

§ 20.
§ 141, part 8, Jus Nat.
§§ 30, 31.

Fictions are advantageously allowed in every kind of science, for the purpose of eliciting truths as well as for proving them. For example, the astronomers, in order to calculate the movements of the planets, assume that a planet is carried by a regular motion in a circular orbit concentric with the sun and about it, and, in the reckoning of time, the sun is assumed to be carried by a regular motion around the equator. Nay, all moral persons and, too, the supreme state itself in the law of nature and nations have something fictitious in them. Those who disapprove of such things, abundantly show that they are only superficially acquainted with the sciences. That fictitious ruler of the supreme state is believed to adapt the natural or necessary law of nations to the purpose of the supreme state, as far as human conditions allow, using the right of making laws, which we have shown above belongs to the supreme state.

§ 11.

§ 22. *Definition of the voluntary law of nations and what it is*

With Grotius we speak of the voluntary law of nations, which is derived from the concept of the supreme state. Therefore it is considered to have been laid down so to speak by its fictitious ruler and so to have proceeded from the will of nations. The voluntary law of nations is therefore equivalent to the civil law, consequently it is derived in the same manner from the necessary law of nations, as we have shown that the civil law must be derived from the natural law in the fifth chapter of the eighth part of "The Law of Nature."

§ 21.

§ 965, part 8, Jus Nat.

And so we have a fixed and immovable foundation for the voluntary law of nations, and there are definite principles, by force of which that law can be derived from the concept of the supreme state, so that it is not necessary to rely blindly on the deeds and customs and decisions of the more civilized nations, and from this there must be assumed as it were a certain universal consensus of all, just as Grotius seems to have perceived.

§ 23. *The stipulative law of nations*

There is a stipulative law of nations, which arises from stipulations entered into between different nations. Since stipulations are entered into between two or more nations, as is plain from the meaning of "pact," since moreover no one can bind another to himself beyond his consent, therefore much less contrary to his consent, nor acquire from him a right which he does not wish to transfer to him; stipulations therefore bind only the nations between whom they are made. Therefore the law of nations, which arises from stipulations, or the stipulative, is not universal but particular.

§ 788, part 3, Jus Nat.

§ 382, part 3, Jus Nat.

§ 789, part 3, Jus Nat.

The stipulative law of nations has its equivalent in the private law of citizens, which has its origin in their agreements. Therefore just as the private law for citizens, derived from agreements entered into between themselves, is considered as having no value at all as civil law for a certain particular state, so also the law that nations have derived from agreements with other nations, it seems, cannot be considered as the law of nations. Therefore it is plain that the stipulative law of nations is to be accepted only in a certain general sense, in so far as through stipulations nations can bind themselves to one another and acquire certain rights, and there is a certain proper subject-matter of these stipulations, so that therefore the stipulative law of nations has regard only to those things which must be observed concerning the stipulations of nations and their subject matter in general. For the particular stipulations and the rights and obligations arising therefrom as to the states stipulating, since they are simply factitious, do not belong to the science of the law of nations, but to the history of this law or of that nation, which it enjoys in respect of certain other nations.

§ 22. The general theory of the stipulative law of nations could have been referred to the voluntary law of nations; whoever desires so to do, will not have the least objection from us.

§ 24. *Of the customary law of nations*

The customary law of nations is so called, because it has been brought in by long usage and observed as law. It is also frequently called simply custom, in the native idiom *das Herkommen* [usage]. Since certain nations use it one with the other, the customary law of nations rests upon the tacit consent of the nations, or, if you prefer, upon a tacit stipulation, and it is evident that

§ 23. it is not universal, but a particular law, just as was the stipulative law.

What we have just remarked about the stipulative law must likewise be maintained concerning the customary law.

§ 25. *Of the positive law of nations*

That is called the positive law of nations which takes its origin from the
§ 22. will of nations. Therefore since it is plainly evident that the voluntary,
§ 23. the stipulative, and the customary law of nations take their origin from

the will of nations, all that law is the positive law of nations. And since §24.
furthermore it is plain that the voluntary law of nations rests on the
presumed consent of nations, the stipulative upon the express consent, §22.
the customary upon the tacit consent, since moreover in no other way §23.
is it conceived that a certain law can spring from the will of nations, the §24.
positive law of nations is either voluntary or stipulative or customary.

Those who do not have a clear conception of the supreme state,
and therefore do not derive from it the voluntary law of nations,
which Grotius has mentioned, and even wholly reject it, or refer some
part of it to the customs of certain nations, such recognize no other
positive law of nations at all, aside from the stipulative or customary.
But certainly it is wrong to refer to customs, what reason itself teaches
is to be observed as law among all nations.

§ 26. *General observation*

We shall carefully distinguish the voluntary, the stipulative, and the
customary law of nations from the natural or necessary law of nations,
nevertheless we shall not teach the former separately from the latter, but
when we have shown what things belong to the necessary law of nations,
we shall straightway add, wherever it may be, why, and in what manner
that must be changed to the voluntary, and here and there, when we
have carefully considered it, we shall add the stipulative and the customary laws, which are by no means to be confused with the voluntary,
especially since they have not been distinguished from it with sufficient
care by Grotius. And the method which we have thus far used, both in
the law of nature and in the other parts of philosophy already taught by
us, and which we shall likewise use in the other parts, to be taught by
us in their own time and order, this too we use in the law of nations,
although the particular laws peculiar to some nations, which either come
from stipulations or are due to customs, we do not consider, inasmuch as
they are at variance with our plan, with which only those things which
belong to science are in harmony. And why one must use such a method
is plain from our proofs and our notes in the Prolegomena to "The Law §§ 2 and fol.,
of Nature."   part 1, Jus Nat.

THE END OF THE PROLEGOMENA

✷✷ CHAPTER I ✷✷

Of the Duties of Nations to Themselves and the Rights Arising Therefrom

§ 27. *Definition of the duties of a nation to itself*

By the duties of a nation to itself I understand the acts which any nation is bound to do or omit for itself by nature or by force of the law of nature.

§ 9.

Here we consider a nation as a single entity, which is determined by certain essential characteristics of its own being and which is able to live in accordance with them. Now those are the actions of a nation as such, which are directed toward the interest of the nation itself as such and are consistent or inconsistent with those characteristics, so that for this reason it makes a difference which it does and which it omits. Therefore, it must be shown what sort of acts the nation ought to do or not do, in order that it may not be wanting to its own self.

§ 28. *On what the preservation of a nation depends*

§ 5, part 8, Jus Nat.

§ 497, part 8, Jus Nat.

The preservation of a nation depends upon the continuance of its union into a state; or as long as the union into a state endures, the nation is preserved. For a people or a nation perishes when its union into a state is broken up, therefore so long as this persists, it does not perish, and is therefore preserved. Therefore, the preservation of a nation as such depends upon the continuance of its union into a state.

§§ 349, 350, part 1, Jus Nat.

The preservation of the physical individual is one thing, that of the moral person another. The latter presupposes the former, but does not remain alive because the former is intact. Thus, although every man is bound to preserve his own body and his own life, without which the physical individual cannot exist; nevertheless it may not be inferred from this that a nation too as such is bound to preserve itself. For nature does not make a nation, but agreement. The preservation of the individuals who constitute the nation, as made up of physical individuals, belongs to universal public law; but the preservation of a nation as a nation belongs to the law of nations and must be here demonstrated. And hence it appears that there are duties of a nation to itself, which have to be considered separately from universal public law; and although the necessary law of nations consists in the law of nature applied to nations, nevertheless this application ought not to be made without caution, lest by confusing different things we may seem to have proved what was to be proved, and yet not have proved it at all. The same will be evident in other things which come later.

§§ 4, 5, part 8, Jus Nat.

§ 420, part 8, Jus Nat.

§ 4.

§ 29. *On what the perfection of a nation depends*

The perfection of a nation depends upon its fitness for accomplishing the purpose of the state, and that is a perfect form of government in a nation, if nothing is lacking in it which it needs for attaining that purpose. For every nation is a number of men united into a state, consequently, to accomplish that purpose on account of which the state was established. Therefore, since all perfection is to be estimated from the tendency of those things which are in harmony with an entity to realize the same in some respect; the perfection of a nation certainly depends upon its fitness for accomplishing the purpose of the state. Which was the first point.

§ 5, part 8, Jus Nat.

§ 4, part 8, Jus Nat.

§§ 503, 528, 529, Ontol.

For since the external condition of a nation is determined by those things which aid the nation as such; moreover since the accidental perfection, such as exists in a nation which depends upon its external condition, requires the harmony of those things which belong to it, together with those which make the essential perfection of a nation, consequently, the striving for the purpose of the state, as noted above in point 1; the perfection of its condition is to be determined from this, that nothing is lacking in it which the nation needs for attaining the purpose of the state. Which was the second point.

§ 706, Ontol.

§ 783, Ontol.

§ 528, Ontol.

The second point is also demonstrated as follows. If a nation is to be perfect, it is necessary that it shall be suited to accomplish the purpose of the state (as shown in point 1). Therefore it is further required that in its condition nothing should be lacking which it needs for accomplishing this. Therefore the perfection of its condition ought to have the same general reason as the perfection of the nation itself, through which reason it is understood why those things which belong to it are such and so great rather than otherwise, consequently suitable that by their aid

§ 505, Ontol.   the purpose of the state may be attained. Therefore the condition of a nation is then at last perfect, if nothing is lacking in it which it needs for attaining its purpose.

We can look upon a nation as a sort of composite entity, the different parts or organs of which are as it were groups of people living the same kind of life, which individual groups we look upon as a part or as one single organ. And so since this composite entity is perfect, if its several organs are adapted to the performance of their functions, and through this the entity becomes adapted to the attaining of its purpose, so likewise a nation is understood to be perfect if the particular combinations of individuals living different kinds of lives are adapted to the performance of their functions rightly, and through this the nation is adapted to the attaining of the purpose of the state. But a nation can scarcely be thought of as adapted to attaining the purpose of a state, if it lacks those things which it needs for attaining that end, when you wish to take into consideration not only the intrinsic, but also the extrinsic possibility, so that the purpose of the state can be actually accomplished. Therefore the perfection of its condition rests on the same basis as the perfection of the nation itself, and therefore it is necessary that nothing should be lacking in it which the nation needs for accomplishing the purpose of the state.

§ 30. *Whence those things are evident which are required for the perfection of a nation and its condition*

Since the perfection of a nation depends upon its fitness for attaining the purpose of the state, and since that is a perfect condition, if nothing is lacking in it which the nation needs for attaining that purpose, since,

§ 29.

§ 393, part 8,
Jus Nat.

§§ 394 and fol.,
part 8, Jus Nat.

moreover, the constitution of a commonwealth depends upon the determination of the method by which the purpose of the state is attained; from those things which have been proved concerning the establishing of a state, it is evident what things are required, both for the perfecting of a nation and for the perfecting of its condition.

But if you will properly consider those points which we have fully proved concerning the constitution of a state, you will see with perfect clarity that the whole nation may best be thought of in the likeness of a man, whose soul is the director of the state, but whose body is the subjects as a whole. It will likewise be plain with what mind and will, and with what subordinate powers the soul ought to be provided, and what kind of organs the body ought to have. Now the organs of this body are groups of men living various kinds of lives, as associations of scholars, workmen, artisans, numbers of farmers and workmen, troops of soldiers, and so on. If any one desires correctly to distinguish one from the other and properly enumerate the several kinds of lives which a properly organized state needs, he will give to us an adequate concept of the structure of this body, observing the analogy of the human body. And when he has considered further what things the superior ought to care for and what are his duties, he will give us a no less adequate concept of the soul also. It will also be plain what sort of a union there ought to be between soul and body, and how harmony may be established between soul and body, by determining the form of state, and that the bond of union is obedience of the subjects and mutual love of superior and subjects. If any one has sufficient intelligence, and has an adequate conception of the human soul and body, and also of a properly constituted state, he will not get a better conception of the perfection of a nation and its condition than by aid of this analogy. Nor in truth is it to be considered that this analogy is only a kind of play of the imagination. For it is a heuristic principle, which aids wonderfully in discovering those things which pertain to universal public law and the law of nations, and in confirming what is already plain in some other way, not to mention that by its aid men who cannot grasp a long course of proof may be persuaded of the truth of those things to which otherwise they would not easily assent. But it is not for us to pursue this argument at greater length.

§ 31. *Of a nation's duty of self-preservation*

Every nation is bound to preserve itself. For the people who make a nation, when they have united into a state, are as individuals bound to

§ 5, part 8, Jus Nat.

the whole for promoting the common good, and the whole is bound
to the individuals to provide for them those things which are required
as a competency for life, for peace and security. Furthermore it is self-
evident that this obligation cannot be satisfied, either on the part of the
individuals or of the whole, unless the union in a state should persist,
consequently, since the preservation of the nation depends on this union,
unless the nation should be preserved. Therefore every nation is bound
to preserve itself.

All obligation, by which the individuals in a state are bound to the
whole and the whole to the individuals, comes from the agreement by
which the state was established, as is evident from the proof given elsewhere. But since the obligation of self-preservation may proceed from
this, by force of the present proof; this obligation itself also comes
from the agreement, as we have already suggested above. But the obligation from the agreement ratified by the law of nature, receives its
force from the same source. Therefore every nation is bound to save
itself by the law of nature itself. It is no objection that agreements can
be dissolved by mutual consent, consequently it is permitted by nature
also to dissolve the union by unanimous consent, and when this occurs
the nation does not exist. For the obligation of self-preservation in a
nation belongs to the category of those which are called hypothetical, and rests on some human action as a basis. But this of itself is
not immutable, as being absolute, which comes from the essence and
nature of man, but in the present case it persists as long as the desire
to endure abides in the state. But with difficulty, and scarcely at all,
can it be conceived that the desire would fail all the inhabitants of any
district. Nay, unless there should be sufficient reason for its failure, as
is very unlikely, since states have been established in accordance with
natural law, those err especially who wish to end the union into a state
by common consent, therefore nations have besides the duty of preserving themselves. Individuals are bound to preserve themselves, and
they owe mutual assistance to each other in perfecting themselves and
their condition. But to destroy the union into a state, which is a means
of satisfying that natural obligation, is opposed to this. Nay, unless
you assume that the individuals who compose a nation are insane, or
so stupid that they do not recognize that it is to their especial interest

§ 28, part 8,
Jus Nat.

§ 28.

§ 28, part 8,
Jus Nat.

Note, § 3.

§ 26, part 8,
Jus Nat.

§ 789, part 3,
Jus Nat.
§ 840, part 3,
Jus Nat.

§ 28.

§ 19, part 1,
Jus Nat.

§ 26, part 8,
Jus Nat.

§ 349, part 1,
and § 144,
part 7, Jus Nat.

that the bond of civil society should not be removed, the spontaneous dissolution of the state is rightly considered as absurd or morally impossible.

§ 32. *Of the law of nations in regard to those things which are necessary for their preservation*

Since every nation is bound to preserve itself, since, moreover, the law of nature gives to men the right to those things without which they could not perform their obligation, every nation has the right to those things without which it cannot preserve itself.

§ 31.

§ 159, part 1, Phil. Pract. Univ.

It must be properly observed that we speak here concerning the preservation of a nation as such, which exists during its union in a state and consequently during the preservation of the state, in so far as it is regarded in general, and not in a particular form. Therefore we speak here of nothing except the right to those things which are necessary that the state may remain and the nation not perish. For those things which are necessary to the preservation of the individuals who make the state, belong to universal public law, and are evident from the things which we have abundantly proved concerning the constitution of a state, in the last part of "The Law of Nature."

§ 28.

§ 33. *Of averting the danger of destruction*

In like manner because each nation is bound to preserve itself; it ought also to avert from itself all danger of destruction, therefore it ought to avoid those things which can bring about its destruction, as much of course as is in its power, since no one is bound to the impossible.

§ 31.

§ 209, part 1, Phil. Pract. Univ.

The preservation of a nation and its destruction are mutually opposed to each other. Therefore, since it ought to preserve itself, it ought also to be on its guard lest it may perish of its own fault. For that which is to be imputed to bad fortune, and is not subject to our control, must be patiently endured and entrusted to divine providence. Association in a state is as it were the life of a nation. Therefore, just as a man ought to avoid every risk to his life so far as in his power, so also is a nation bound to avoid risk of destruction. But just as it is

§ 540, part 1, Theol. Nat.

§ 593, part 1, Jus Nat.

§ 1192, part 1, Jus Nat.

§ 371, part 17,
Jus Nat.

impossible for a man to resist a superior force, by which he is brought into peril of his life, or without his consent is deprived of life; so likewise it is not possible that a nation protect itself from destruction by a superior force threatening it, for example, from perishing by earthquake or extraordinary flood or from destruction by the wrongful act of a stronger nation or from dissolution of the union by force of internal war or by famine or pestilence, instances of which are found in the annals of the ancients, which it is not our plan to collect in this place. It is enough to have suggested those things which make for a better understanding of the present proposition.

§ 34. *Of the right to those things which are necessary for guarding against the risk of destruction*

§ 33.

§ 159, part 1,
Phil. Pract.
Univ.

Since a nation ought to ward off from itself all peril of destruction and avoid those things which can bring destruction to it, so far as it is within its power, and since the law of nature gives a right to those things without which we cannot perform our obligation, every nation has the right to those means by which it can, as far as possible, avert the peril of destruction and avoid those things which can bring destruction upon it.

§ 859, part 1,
Jus Nat.

§ 348, Log.

It is needful that the laws of nations be understood, that it may be plain in how many ways wrongs can be done to a nation; from which many other things may be derived which pertain to the law of nations. Moreover from the general principles which we have already proved, special conclusions will then be drawn, for whose sake these premises are here laid down. For general principles are very fruitful and in the sciences they are so to speak the seeds of truths.

§ 35. *Of a nation's duty to perfect itself and its condition*

§ 5, part 8,
Jus Nat.

§ 4, part 8,
Jus Nat.

Every nation ought to perfect itself and its condition. For since a nation is a number of men united into a state, and since men go into a state in order to accomplish a definite purpose by their combined powers; in order that this purpose may be accomplished it is undoubtedly necessary that the nation should be fitted to accomplish this purpose, nor should it lack those things which it needs to accomplish it. Therefore since the perfection of a nation consists in its fitness for accomplishing the purpose of the state, and since its condition is perfect, if there is nothing lacking in it which it needs for attaining its end, every nation ought to perfect itself and its condition.

§ 29.

How it may perform this duty is plain from those things which we have shown at length concerning the establishment of the state in the entire third chapter of the eighth part of "The Law of Nature." Hence it is plain that a nation errs, if in those things which have been mentioned in the same place, it is in any way remiss in diligence.

§ 440, part 1, Phil. Pract. Univ.

§ 36. Of the duty of being on one's guard and avoiding anything opposed to perfection

Since every nation ought to perfect itself and its condition, and the one bound to do this is at the same time bound not to do the opposite, every nation ought to be on its guard against and avoid those things which in any way interfere with its perfection and that of its condition, or which render it or its condition less perfect.

§ 35.

§ 722, part 1, Jus Nat.

Lucilius properly desired to make a distinction between guarding against and avoiding. To avoid is more than to guard against. He of course guards against, who takes care that a thing may not happen to him which he foresees can happen, although it is uncertain whether it will happen or not; while he avoids, who turns aside that for the producing of which some cause already actually exists. So he guards against a conflagration, who does not allow servants with lighted candles to go into a stable or granary filled with straw; he avoids a conflagration, who snatches himself betimes from a burning building. Therefore in the present proposition it is urged that we should not only look out for those things which can happen and take measures lest perchance they may happen, but also that in an emergency we should look out for ourselves and ward off evil from ourselves. Moreover it is quite plain that, in order to avoid, we must be on our guard, since no man can unerringly foreknow the future. We guard against what is uncertain, we avoid the certain. But since, as I have said, we cannot unerringly foreknow the future, we rightly fear in proportion to the degree of the probability of its occurrence that which is acknowledged as not impossible to occur. Nature herself leads us hither, who instills fear in the senses, and reason commands, in so far as the intellect reduces the confused notions which affect the senses, to distinct concepts, through which the will and the non-will are determined. But these points will become more manifest, if we are allowed to teach moral philosophy by the method which we use in metaphysics.

§ 37. *Of the right belonging to a nation to perfect itself and its condition*

§ 35.

§ 36.

§ 159, part 1, Phil. Pract. Univ.

Likewise since every nation is bound to perfect itself and its condition and must guard against and avoid those things which interfere in any way with its own perfection and that of its condition or render itself or its condition less perfect, and since moreover the law of nature gives a right to those things without which we cannot perform our obligation, every nation has the right to those things without which it cannot perfect itself and its form of government, nor guard against and avoid those things which interfere with its own perfection and its form of government, or render itself or its form of government less perfect.

Note, § 35.

Since from those things which we have shown concerning the establishment of the state, it is plain how a nation can perfect itself and its condition, and consequently also what things are to be guarded against and avoided to that end; from those also it is known in what respects a certain right belongs to it, so that it may be capable of perfecting itself and its condition, and capable of guarding against and avoiding those things which hinder its perfection or produce imperfection.

§ 38. *Of the duty of the ruler of a state in the preservation and perfection of the nation and its condition*

§ 42, part 8, Jus Nat.

§§ 4, 9, part 8, Jus Nat.

The ruler of a state has the care of perfecting and preserving his nation or people and likewise its condition, and also of guarding against and avoiding, so far as possible, all imperfection and destruction. For it belongs to the ruler of a state to exercise the civil authority, consequently to determine those things which are required to advance the public good, and therefore to accomplish the purpose of the state. Therefore it is necessary that he should see to it that the nation be fitted to attain the purpose of the state and that nothing be lacking which is needed for attaining that. Therefore since the perfection of the nation and its condition consists in this, moreover, since there is no perfection, unless the nation be preserved, as is evident of itself, the ruler of a state has the care of perfecting and preserving his nation and its condition, and also of guarding against and avoiding, so far as possible, imperfection and destruction.

§ 60, part 8, Jus Nat.

§ 29.

The care, of course, of saving and perfecting the nation and its condition belongs originally to the nation as a whole, to which originally belongs the civil sovereignty, or the right of the whole over the individuals, to be determined by the purpose of the state. When therefore this is transferred to another or others, on this same one or ones is imposed the care of saving and perfecting the nation and its condition. This same thing has already been made perfectly plain from those things which we have proved concerning the establishment of the state in the eighth part of our work on natural law.

§ 34, part 8, Jus Nat.

§ 31, part 8, Jus Nat.

§ 30, part 8, Jus Nat.

§ 39. *Of the character as representative of a nation belonging to the ruler of a state*

Since the care of preserving the nation and perfecting it and its condition belongs to the ruler of a state, whatever right belongs to the nation of preserving itself and of perfecting itself and its condition, the same resides with the ruler of a state, consequently the ruler of a state has the right which belongs to each nation, and therefore he represents his nation when it has dealings with others.

§ 38.

§§ 32, 37.

§ 70, part 1, Jus Nat.

The character as representative of the nation, belonging to the ruler of a state, presents no difficulty, if only you consider what a moral person is. The nation, in so far as there belong to it definite rights for the purpose of saving itself and perfecting itself and its condition, is a moral person, and so far as the nation rules itself, a thing which occurs in a democratic state, it is itself the ruler also of the state into which it has united. If, therefore, it has given over to another or others the care of preserving itself and perfecting itself and its condition, and consequently, if it has transferred to him or them the rights also belonging

§ 70, part 1, Jus Nat.

§ 131, part 8, Jus Nat.

to itself for that purpose, so that now the ruler of the state becomes a subject different from the nation, that moral person, which before existed in the nation as a whole, exists now in another physical individual. And so the ruler of a state represents the entire nation, so far as he is considered ruler of the state. But do not persuade yourself that the character as representative of the nation derogates in any respect from the dignity of the ruler of a state like the majesty of a monarch in a monarchical state. For this rather makes it the more conspicuous, because now one has that dignity which a large group of people has only when considered as a whole; from this, too, it follows, that this dignity is greater in a kingdom, in which one man has it, than in an aristocracy, in which it belongs to several together. And since none of this dignity will remain in the people, and none of it can belong to the individuals, since what belongs to the whole cannot be common to individuals, therefore the ruler of a state towers above the nation, nor can the dignity of any one of the nation be compared with his dignity. See what we have already proved and noted elsewhere.

§ 160, part 8,
Jus Nat.

§ 40. *Of the knowledge of itself*

§ 35.

§ 36.

Every nation ought to know itself and its condition. For it ought to perfect itself and its condition, and it ought to guard against and avoid those things which can hinder its perfection and that of its condition, or render itself or its condition less perfect. It is therefore necessary that it should know what sort of capabilities of mind and powers of body, and what things are needed for perfecting itself and its condition, what perfection it has already attained and with what imperfection it still suffers, both as regards itself and as regards its form of government. Therefore every nation ought to know itself and its condition.

This knowledge is especially necessary to a nation, unless it should wish to commit all to fortune and not to have knowledge except by its own hurt, or to trust simply to a blind imitation of other nations. Knowledge of its own self is enjoined for no other purpose than that a nation should, as far as is in its power, perform its duties to itself and strive to perform them fully. But if the care of perfecting itself and its condition is subjected simply to the power of fortune, a nation by no

means perfects itself and its condition as far as it can. Hence we see
that very many nations, which could have ascended to a high degree
of perfection, have always remained in a low degree.

§ 41. *The knowledge of a nation required of a ruler of a state*

The ruler of a state ought to know his nation and its condition. It is
plain from the proof of the preceding proposition that the care of perfecting itself and its condition demands a knowledge of itself and its
condition in a nation. Therefore, since the care of perfecting a nation   § 40.
and its condition belongs to the ruler of a state, the ruler of a state ought   § 38.
to know his nation and its condition.

When sovereignty is transferred to another, the ruler of a state
assumes the personality of the nation as a whole, and so all obligation
passes to him of perfecting the nation and its form of government,   Note, § 39.
consequently also the obligation of understanding perfectly the nation
which he represents and whose personality he bears, and its condition.
The care to be expended upon acquiring this knowledge is perpetual,
although generally among many nations this is neglected. For without
this knowledge it is impossible to administer the state properly.

§ 42. *Of the necessity of knowledge concerning the condition of the territory and of all places in it*

Since the ruler of a state ought to know the condition of his nation,   § 41.
since, moreover, this depends in great part on the condition of the territory, as is plainly evident, the ruler of a state therefore ought to know the
condition of the territory which his nation inhabits, and when this is not
the same everywhere, he ought to know the condition of all places in it.

It is impossible that the form of government of any nation should
be brought to that degree of perfection of which it is capable, unless
the condition of all the territory which it inhabits is accurately known
and understood; as this cannot be done, so that the nation itself may
be perfected, as far as possible, unless you examine carefully the natural gifts, the customs and the manner of life of all the inhabitants of
all places. Moreover, each form of knowledge is so closely connected

with the other that one cannot be separated from the other, whether you wish to perfect the condition of a nation, or the nation itself, or guard against imperfection, or remove blemishes from it. Whence it is plainly evident that for this knowledge is required an accurate geographical map of the whole territory and of the several parts, under whatsoever name they may finally come, an entire natural history of the whole territory, perfectly accurate measurement of all the fields, meadows, woods, cities, towns, villages, and so on, finally a trustworthy description of the inhabitants of all places and of those things which concern them in any manner. When this knowledge of the territory and inhabitants is prepared for the use of the ruler of the state and consequently of those whose advice and service he uses in administering the state, statecraft will readily tell what can be communicated safely to the public, and what ought to be concealed, lest it betray the country to others.

§ 43. Of those characteristics which are to be predicated of the nation by transfer from individuals

Those characteristics which are to be predicated of the greater part of a nation or the majority in some particular walk of life, pass from the individuals to the nation as a whole and consequently are to be predicated of it. For since every nation is a multitude of people, since moreover neither nature and fortune nor education, training and intercourse, even if they be very much the same, make individuals the same; it is altogether impossible for the things, which, as it were, are peculiar to individuals, to be predicated of them as a whole. Nevertheless, since every nation is to be considered as a single personality, the characteristics of individuals pass from them to the nation. But since contradictions cannot exist in one entity and it would in truth be absurd for the name to be taken from the smaller rather than the larger part, those things which are to be predicated of the greater part of the nation pass from the individuals to the nation as a whole and consequently are predicated of it. Which was the first point.

Now further, it is quite plain *a posteriori* that, if men are to pass their lives advantageously and pleasantly and live happily, all cannot follow the same kind of life, but, in order that all things may be done which ought

§ 5, part 8, Jus Nat.

§ 2.

§§ 28, 30, Ontol.

to be done in a well-established commonwealth, as we have fully shown in the entire third chapter of the eighth part of "The Law of Nature,"[1] some ought to do one thing, others another, just as in the human body there are different functions for different organs, fitted to accomplish one definite general purpose; the characteristics of the several groups of men living the same kind of life pass into the nation as a whole. But since, as before shown, it cannot happen that individuals who live the same kind of life should be the same, as likewise was before made plain, the characteristics which are to be predicated of the majority in some definite kind of life pass from them to the nation, and consequently are to be predicated of it. Which was the second point.

That the force and influence of the present proposition may be grasped, it must of course be illustrated by examples. We say, for example, that a nation is vigorous and industrious, if the majority found in it are vigorous men and the men generally are industrious. A nation is said to be vicious, if a very great number pollute themselves by every kind of vice; it is said to be intemperate, if it is a common custom to delight in excessive drinking; it is said to be licentious, if its common vice has been lust. Those who write of the customs of nations can use no other principle of distinction than that those characteristics pass from the individuals to the nation, which belong to the great majority. Likewise a nation is called rich, in which many are found who abound in wealth; that one is called educated and learned, which has many educated and learned men; the English are called excellent artisans, because manufactured articles are carefully fashioned in England; the Italians remarkable architects, because among them architecture has been cultivated and is to-day cultivated; the Dutch pre-eminent merchants, because merchandising flourishes among them in a singular manner. But it is to be observed that when a majority of those who are pre-eminent in any walk in life are to be considered, the number of those who are in one nation is customarily compared with the number of those who follow the same walk in life in other nations. But although that comparison may be especially attributed in general to

1. Christian Wolff, *Jus naturae, methodo scientifica pertractatum* (Halle, 1748), pt. VIII, chap. 3.

prejudice, nevertheless this does not prevent these general principles from having a basis also in truth. For prejudices act in no other way than that principles true in themselves may be wrongly applied, just as also is often done by those, who from one or two instances, draw a conclusion as to more, because they assume wrongly that, if not all, at least very many, ought to be such as they recognize the one or two to be. But he who avoids prejudice knows that it is to be proved and not assumed that those are in the majority, from whom some characteristic is to be transferred to the nation, before it can be attributed to the nation; nor in proving that does he assume what formerly was, but what now is, when a decision as to the present is to be given, and concerning that characteristic which he assigns to the majority, or to the very great number, he decides after very careful investigation. For unless those things are observed, his decision concerning the nation will be just as false as if, those points being ignored, he should decide concerning other things.

§ 44. *Of the duty of individuals arising therefrom*

Since those characteristics which are to be predicated of the greater part of a nation, or the majority in some definite kind of life, pass from the individuals to the nation as a whole and consequently are to be predicated of it; whoever belongs to a nation owes this not only to himself, but also to his nation, that, to his utmost ability, he perfect himself and his condition and so perform his work, that he may through that endeavour perfectly attain his purpose, and consequently may excel, so far as it can be done, in that kind of life which he follows.

§ 43.

§ 152, part 1, Phil. Pract. Univ., and §§ 522, 523, part 1, Jus Nat.

So we owe it not only to ourselves to acquire intellectual and moral virtues, but also to the nation to which we belong, lest we be to blame for its being styled less virtuous, or lest this or that intellectual or moral virtue come to be denied to it. Likewise the scholar is bound to his nation, that it may excel especially in learning, and that he may not detract from its reputation as a learned nation, and the artisan is bound to it, that it may be adorned by the art which he practices, and that he may not by his error diminish its reputation. It is in harmony with these general ideas that the characteristics of individuals pass from them to the nation, so that the individuals also who belong to the nation seem to share the reputation of the others who are of the same nation. Therefore contrary to common sense are the customs of that set of scholars in Germany who discredit the men especially deserving in the republic of letters and afterwards flatter and exalt to heaven with the highest praise those things in the works of foreigners which they have ridiculed in their own, as if by flattery they could share in the reputation of a foreign nation. But from this a new motive arises to perform with all our might all duties imposed by natural law, on which is based a new natural obligation, that we should not allow ourselves to be lacking in any effort or exertion to perfect ourselves.

§ 887, Psych. Emp.

§ 118, part 1, Phil. Pract. Univ.

§ 45. Of the necessity of not bringing disgrace on one's nation

Since each and every one owes it to his nation that, to his utmost ability, he should perfect himself and his condition and excel in the kind of life which he follows, as far as he can, and since he who is bound to do this, is bound at the same time not to do the opposite, each one ought to be on his guard, lest by doing those things which are wrong or less right, he may bring disgrace upon his nation; consequently since the ruler of a state ought to take care that citizens should not do the things which are opposed to the obligations prescribed by natural law, he therefore ought not to allow citizens to bring disgrace upon their nation.

§ 44.

§ 722, part 1, Jus Nat.

§ 395, part 8, Jus Nat.

Many particular conclusions follow from this, since this obligation is as widely extended as are the duties of a man and citizen. And hence also follows the right to punish the acts of subjects by whom disgrace is brought upon the nation, of which we have spoken elsewhere.

§§ 653, 654, part 8, Jus Nat.

§ 46. Of zeal for the reputation of one's nation

Because those characteristics pass from the individuals to the nation as a whole and are predicated of it, which come to be predicated of the greater part of a nation, or the majority in some definite kind of life, and consequently the good reputation also of the greater part, or of the majority in some definite kind of life passes over to the nation as a whole, those who are of the nation owe this not only to themselves, but also to their own nation, that its reputation should be good; consequently they

§ 43.

§ 554, part 1, Jus Nat.

ought to defend the reputation of their nation and country so far as in them lies.

The learned undoubtedly sin against their nation who revile with insult the men especially deserving in the republic of letters, preservers of the reputation of their nation, and who detract from their reputation or even strive with all their might to make public those things which ought rather to have been concealed, lest disgrace be imposed upon their nation. But those things which are said of the nation as a whole ought likewise to be understood of definite classes or groups of men. Now the duty of which we have already spoken, ought to be the more carefully observed when the welfare of the nation or of a definite class or group depends upon its reputation. Moreover, they err the more basely who do anything contrary to this duty, if it shall have been entrusted to their charge to protect the reputation of the class or group. I do not add examples lest they may be invidious.

§ 47. *What fame is*

§ 551, part I,
Jus Nat.

§ 552, part I,
Jus Nat.

Fame is the unanimous praise of the good and wise, or of those who judge properly. We call it in our native vernacular *ein grosser Nahme* [a great name]. Therefore since deeds arising from intellectual and moral virtues produce praise, and show that a man is worthy of that praise; without intellectual and moral virtues no one can attain real fame, and he excels especially in fame who is the most pre-eminent in virtue.

Fame does not differ from praise, except that praise is assigned by one, but many agree as to fame. Moreover the consensus of the many according to the laws of probability proves that praise is deserved. Still, it is needful that those who judge should judge well, consequently that they be wise, lest they fail in judgement, and that they be good, lest contrary to conscience they may honour some one with undeserved praise. For many, and often also the wise, praise in order that they may be praised, and are influenced either by the hope of some personal advantage or by the desire to promote the welfare of the one whom they praise. Hence, not rarely does it happen that some deserve fame, others have it. Now it is better to deserve than to have and not deserve. And since the reputation of a man is the common report of other men concerning his intellectual and moral habits, by force of the definition, fame without reputation is inconceivable. For those who are not able to judge for themselves follow the judgement of the wise, a course which at length becomes general. But because it happens that those are considered wise who are not, true and genuine fame differs from the false and empty.

§ 553, part 1, Jus Nat.

§ 48. *Of the fame of a nation*

Since fame is the unanimous praise of the good and wise, consequently since it depends upon the significance of the judgement concerning the perfection of some one, or the enumeration of his intellectual and moral virtues and the deeds arising therefrom, and since the reputation of those who belong to a nation passes to the nation itself, the fame of a nation consists in the praise which by the consensus of the good and wise is assigned to it, both on account of its own perfection and deeds, and on account of the deeds arising from the intellectual and moral virtues of those who belong to the nation.

§ 47.

§ 551, part 1, Jus Nat.

§ 43.

Of course fame is primarily and of itself attributed to the nation, because it is considered as a single person, which has its own actions dependent upon intellectual and moral virtues; but even more is it attributed to it, because the renown of individuals is passed over to it on account of acts or deeds which are considered as those of the individuals. So, for example, the good reputation of government is a part of its fame, likewise the customary keeping of faith in agreements with other nations; but it is no less a part of its fame if it should have learned men pre-eminent in the republic of letters, skilled artisans, industrious merchants and other things of this sort. The former of themselves point to the nation, and are not thought of without it, but the latter pass only from the individuals to the nation, and moreover of themselves belong to individuals and are thought of concerning them without regard to the nation. The condition is just the same as in man, or even in the human body, in which there are certain things which are referred to the entire man as such, or are predicated of him as such; and certain things, which come to him from definite organs or faculties of the soul, are predicated of them as such. So health is predicated of the whole body as such; but a man is said to have strong vision on account of the structure of the eye, from which keenness of vision comes to him. Since certain things are to be predicated of the nation, there is need of discrimination, lest those things which are of and belong to the individuals should be confused with those things which peculiarly belong to the nation as such, or rightfully come from the individuals to it. And although the discrimination may be aided, if you compare the nation with the human body, or with man as a whole, nevertheless there is need of caution here too, because a certain entire class of men, or a group leading the same kind of life, is compared with one organ of the body, inasmuch, of course, as the greater part represents the whole, because the things to be attributed to the group cannot under human conditions be discerned otherwise than from those belonging to the great majority.

§ 49. *Of the desire for fame*

§ 48.

§ 35.

Since the true and enduring fame of a nation depends upon its own perfection, since moreover a nation ought to perfect itself, it ought to strive to deserve fame.

§ 47.

§ 543, part I,
Jus Nat.

§ 542, part I,
Jus Nat.

Fame consists in praise. But although no one can bring it about that he be praised by others, it is at least within our power to deserve fame. Moreover we speak of true and enduring fame, which cannot be acquired except from the intelligent. There are indeed those who praise themselves under an assumed name, or even conspire for mutual compliments, so that they attain fame by deceiving others, who do not judge for themselves. Still this is not true and enduring fame, but false and empty, nor in the case of a nation does this come with the same ease. And, even if the pursuit of this especially empty sort of fame caused no difficulty, nevertheless we, who are devoted to truth, not to falsehood, and who do not teach how to deceive others by wicked devices, should not strive for it in the least.

§ 50. *How far this applies to individuals*

§ 48.

Likewise since the fame even of a nation depends upon the deeds of individuals which arise from intellectual and moral virtues, since moreover individuals owe this to their nation, that so far as possible they perfect themselves and excel in that kind of life which they follow, the

individuals, too, who belong to a nation, ought to strive to deserve fame §44.
and direct their actions to the glory of the nation.

Of course individuals ought to perfect themselves and do noble
deeds with the purpose that through those things which pass from
them to the nation, it may gain fame. If that is done with that idea,
one seeks not his own interest, but that of his nation, which he is
desirous of serving well; consequently he does nothing which can be
counted as evil, since he does not strive for his own fame as the ulti- §570, part 1,
mate object of his actions, which is characteristic of the ambitious Jus Nat.
man, much less does he aim at honours of which he is unworthy, §566, part 1,
which is characteristic of the arrogant, nor does he wish more perfec- Jus Nat.
tion attributed to himself than in very truth he has, which is character- §583, part 1,
istic of the haughty, nor forsooth does he indulge too much his desire Jus Nat.
for honour, which is opposed to modesty. §563, part 1,
Jus Nat.

§51. *How far this applies to the ruler of the state*

Because the fame of a state depends upon its own perfection, moreover §48.
because the care of perfecting his nation and its form of government rests §38.
on the ruler of the state; the ruler of a state especially ought to strive that
the nation over which he rules may deserve fame, and he ought to direct
the royal acts to the glory of his nation, consequently to do nothing §722, part 1,
which can diminish or destroy it. Jus Nat.

The desire for the fame of his nation is a part of the duty of the
ruler of a state, who deserves well of it, if in that he allows his diligence
to be in no respect lacking; but he deserves ill of it, if in that regard he
shows himself remiss. But when he strives for the fame of his nation,
he does nothing which can be blamed, and his acts remain untouched
by any imputation of evil. The things which we have just noted upon Note, §50.
the preceding proposition are to be applied likewise to the ruler of a
state. Moreover, it is quite plain that the ruler of a state can contribute
more to the glory of the nation than a private citizen can.

§52. *Of barbarous nations*

We call a nation barbarous, or in our native vernacular, *ein barbarisches*
§547, part 1,
Volck [a barbarian people], which cares but little for intellectual virtues, Jus Nat.

§§ 895, 896,
part 2, Phil.
Pract. Univ.
§ 687, part 2,
Phil. Pract.
Univ.
consequently neglects the perfecting of the intellect. Therefore, since barbarian nations do not develop their minds by training, in determining their actions they follow the leadership of their natural inclinations and aversions, and their uncivilized usages depend for the most part on these.

Even from the beginning those were called barbarians by the Greeks who used a less cultivated language, that is, other than Greek, and then by the Romans those were so called who did not speak Greek or Latin; but afterward the term was transferred from the speech and language to the method of living also and to the character of the usages. The perfection of speech and language depends upon the perfection of the intellect, consequently above all upon intellectual virtues, although it may happen that those may retain a rough and harsh pronunciation of words and an uncultivated speech, who prize the intellectual virtues and have cultivated manners. Therefore in our definition we do not depart from the received significance of the term, although we have retained in it the terminology usual in philosophy, so that the concept of a barbarous nation is resolved into the previous concepts, as ought to be the case in a system, lest it may lack the full light which it can and ought to have; for in definition one must use the terms previ-§ 162, Log.ously explained or made clear from general usage in speaking. But those who think that a barbarism is introduced, when any cultivate and teach studies in any other language than the Latin, because the Romans called those barbarians who did not speak Latin or Greek, are very greatly mistaken; for did not both the Greeks and Romans transmit their learning and arts in their native tongue? It is one question whether the knowledge of the Greek and Latin languages is useful to the scholar, quite another whether or not it is wise that scholars should use some common language, and whether that ought to be Latin. This is not the place for us to say what seems best concerning either point. But this concept of the barbarous nation, which we have given, is quite fruitful, provided only one shall have mentally grasped those previous concepts which lead up to it, and provided one is strong in the art of proof; for from this are to be derived the things which are to be predicated of barbarous nations, that we may not judge erroneously concerning their characteristics, as for example, by confusing natural manners with virtues, or by attributing to virtue the absence of vices, which is due to ignorance, or by counting civilized manners as uncivilized, because they may be different from those commonly received among other non-barbarous nations. Nevertheless, it is not our plan to follow up those ideas here; it is enough to have awakened the attention of others.

§ 53. *Of the cultured and civilized nation*

That is called a cultured nation which cultivates intellectual virtues, consequently desires to perfect the intellect, and therefore develops the mind by training. And that is called a civilized nation which has civilized manners or manners which conform to the standard of reason and politeness. We call it in our native vernacular, *ein gesittetes Volck* [a cultured people], just as with respect to their usages barbarous nations are called, *ungesittete Völcker* [uncultured peoples]. But since barbarous nations have uncivilized usages, therefore to a barbarous nation is opposed a nation cultured and civilized.

§ 547, part 1, Jus Nat.

§ 52.

If a cultured nation is assumed to cultivate the intellectual virtues without restriction, it will scarcely happen that it will not at the same time become civilized, since civilized customs develop from intellectual virtues, just as the uncivilized from the natural inclinations, unrestricted by reason. But there are indeed intellectual virtues also, which of themselves do not in the least correct morals and do not destroy barbarism. Hence it is not unusual that learned men exist, who have not undeservedly acquired fame of name, who are marred by bad and uncouth manners. Lofty genius and no ordinary shrewdness is required, if any one would excel in integral calculus and higher geometry. Therefore whoever does excel, has a name deservedly honoured. But to whatsoever extent at length integral calculus may be carried and to whatsoever height higher geometry, or the geometry of curves, may have been carried, nevertheless integral calculus and higher geometry do not refine the impulses even in the slightest degree, and consequently contribute nothing to the correction of manners. Nay more if any one uses up all his time in calculus alone

§ 888, part 1,
Jus Nat., and
§ 769, Psych.
Emp.

§ 583, part 1,
Jus Nat.

§ 566, part 1,
Jus Nat.

§ 570, part 1,
Jus Nat.

§ 43.

and in the application of it to geometry, when he thinks that he excels in this study and surpasses others, ambition, which controls his affection, brings forth pride and disdain, with ignorance as a midwife, and finally arrogance and ambition, by which vices he is led astray to do those things which are a disgrace to himself and to his class, and when he associates with strangers, he very greatly retards the growth of the sciences. If besides he lives to himself alone, and avoids association with men whom charm and grace of manners recommend, he either has no manners or uncouth ones, by which he brings the science which he cultivates into contempt with those who are not able to pass judgement on it for itself. Scholars of this sort, who neglect the studies fitted to refine the impulses and find pleasure only in those which do not destroy barbarism, are rightly considered semi-barbarous and, when they surpass others in number, make the nation semi-barbarous.

§ 54. *That nations ought to be cultured and civilized, not barbarous*

§ 35.
§ 199, part 1,
Jus Nat.

§ 53.

§ 53.
§ 895, part 2,
Phil. Pract.
Univ.

§ 131, part 1,
Phil. Pract.
Univ.

§ 259, part 1,
Phil. Pract.
Univ.

§ 204, part 1,
Phil. Pract.
Univ.

§ 53.
§§ 52, 53.

Nations ought to be cultured and civilized, not barbarous. For nations ought to perfect themselves and consequently their intelligence. Therefore, since a nation is cultured which perfects its intelligence and consequently develops the mind by training, nations ought to be cultured. Which was the first point.

Since a nation ought to be cultured, as proved above, in point 1, and therefore ought to develop the mind by training, in determining its actions, too, it ought not to follow the leadership of its natural inclinations and aversions, but rather that of reason, which the law of nature imposes as a sort of rule of conduct and also urges proper decorum. Therefore, since a nation is civilized which enjoys customs conforming to the standard of reason and politeness, nations ought to be civilized. Which was the second point.

Finally, since a cultured and civilized nation is not barbarous, moreover since nations ought to be cultured and civilized, as shown above, in points 1 and 2, nations ought not to be barbarous. Which was the third point.

It is indeed more to be desired than hoped for that all nations should be cultured and civilized; but it cannot for this reason be denied that it is the duty of a nation to seek to become cultured and civilized, developing the mind with the training which destroys barbarism. For there is no question here as to what sort nations are and why it happens that they are such, but what they ought to be. It happens that nations are barbarous through no fault of nature, as if she had refused them the dispositions necessary to the attainment of the training which destroys barbarism, but through the lack of the opportunity to raise the natural dispositions into a habit of life and through the presence of obstacles which divert and distract the mind from this desire and attempt. Who will persuade himself that the natural dispositions of the Greeks have been so changed that they to-day are so utterly unadapted to the learning in which they formerly excelled, and that training without natural gifts does not avail? But since a nation may be   Note, § 53. cultured, although it be not civilized, especial care must be used that it become civilized, namely by developing the mind by that training especially which removes barbarism. So the Chinese gave their best efforts to training in manners and to statecraft, and so from the most ancient times they have been prominent among the more civilized nations and are so to-day, yet it happens that few, nay, almost none of them have made advances in metaphysics or physics, much less have they acquired the fame of Europeans in mathematics. But on these points a greater light is shed by moral philosophy to be derived *a priori* from the nature of the human soul. It is sufficient for the present to add the following corollary.

§ 55. *What training is especially suitable to nations*

Since nations ought to be cultured and civilized and not barbarous, they   § 54. ought to develop the mind by that training which destroys barbarism, and without which civilized customs cannot exist.

Indeed there is no training at all which cannot contribute something towards correcting the will. Still not all training of itself tends to its correction. Therefore consideration must be given especially to that which of itself and directly conduces to this; further perfection, moreover, is to be expected from that which of itself has the least connexion with the appetite. But these things belong to a deeper inquiry, and of them we shall speak more properly in another place. Here is

Note, § 54.

pertinent the example of the Chinese of which we have already spoken. The correction of the will depends of course upon the perfection
of the intellect; nevertheless there is need of much caution, lest we
may pervert the will by perfecting the intellect. This is a point to be

§ 53.

considered among those things which we have suggested belong to a
deeper inquiry.

§ 56. *What purpose nations ought to set before themselves in perfecting the intellect*

§ 54.
§ 53.

§ 29.

Likewise because nations ought to be civilized, consequently ought to
perfect the intellect, moreover since the perfection of a nation consists
in its fitness for attaining the purpose of the state, and since the condition of a nation is perfect, if nothing is lacking in it, which it needs for
attaining that purpose; nations in perfecting the intellect ought always
to consider the purpose of the state and those things which they need for
attaining this purpose, consequently they ought to direct all their efforts
to this end.

§ 2.

  Inasmuch as the state is considered as a single person, to it belongs
also an intellect peculiar to the nation, or the human intellect is to be
looked at in its relation to the nation itself. Since, therefore, we are
here speaking of the perfecting of the intellect, what things are said
concerning it are not to be considered without regard to the nation,

Note, § 28.

which as a nation we argue ought to perfect the same. Those things
which we have said concerning the preservation of the nation, are
with proper variation to be understood also here and in regard to
other things which are said of the duties of nations. But just as it is
plain from those things which have been proved concerning the establishment of the state, what things are required both for the perfecting

§ 30.

of a nation, and for the perfecting of its condition, so likewise it is
understood from this, what sort of an intellect ought to be attributed
to a nation as such and consequently how it ought to be perfected,
in order that a nation be in itself reputed cultured, and in what sense
intellectual virtues must be applied to nations, that they may suit it
as a nation and that that, which belongs to a nation as such, may be
distinguished from that which comes from the individuals to it.

§ 57. *How we must look to a nation in the improving of the will*

Likewise since nations ought to be civilized, and therefore ought to have manners adapted to the rule of reason, and consequently to the law of nature, it is evident, as it was before, that in perfecting the will we ought to look to the purpose of the state and to those things which we need for attaining it, and therefore to direct all moral virtues to that end.

§ 54.

§ 57, part 2, Phil. Pract. Univ.

§ 53.

§ 56.

§ 321, part 1, Phil. Pract. Univ., and § 547, part 1, Jus Nat.

Just as in any nation we conceive an intellect peculiar to the nation as such, so also in it a will is thought of peculiar to the nation as such. Therefore just as by force of intellect it knows those things which are necessary to the perfection of itself and its form of government, so there ought to be produced a fixed and continual desire to strive after those things which produce this perfection and to avoid the things opposed to it. And hence we must decide what virtues are especially appropriate to a nation and what sort they ought to be, and in what way all other virtues may aid them. For a certain connexion exists between moral virtues, by which one is made dependent upon the other, so that therefore Christ will pronounce him a transgressor of the whole law who transgresses one precept. Just as the intellect of a nation, so also its will is in the ruler of a state, but it passes over into the intellect and will of the individuals in their various kinds of life as if to the organs of his body. And although these things may seem lofty, and those who decide hastily concerning things viewed as through a lattice may perchance include them among the Platonic ideas; nevertheless they follow, as it were spontaneously, when those things are given which we have proved concerning the establishment of the state in the eighth part of "The Law of Nature," so that there is need of nothing further, unless to urge that here the precepts are general. But since in this way the motives for virtues are redoubled, their cultivation likewise is facilitated, so that such arguments must not be considered to be rashly urged.

Note, § 30.

§ 58. *Of the right of a nation to purchase things for itself from another nation and to sell its own goods to the other*

To every nation belongs the right to purchase for itself at a fair price the things which it needs, from other nations, which themselves have no

§ 35.

§ 29.

§ 13, part 5, Jus
Nat.

§ 10, part 8,
Jus Nat.

§ 126, part 3,
and § 322,
part 4, Jus Nat.

§ 128, part 1,
Jus Nat.

§ 142, part 1,
Phil. Pract.
Univ., and § 23,
part 1, Jus Nat.

need of the same, but it has not the right to sell its products to another nation without its consent. For since a nation ought to perfect itself and its condition and therefore ought to be fitted to attain the purpose of the state, and since its condition is not perfect unless it has those things which make for the accomplishment of that end, and since a sufficient livelihood is part of the purpose of the state, that is, an abundance of those things which are required for the necessity, convenience, and pleasure of life; whatever it does not itself have, it is necessary for it to procure from others. Therefore, though every man has the right to procure for himself at a fair price from others the things that he needs, nevertheless no one has the right to procure from you the things which you yourself need, and since these natural rights on account of their immutability are not, as such, taken away because nations have arisen by bringing together civil societies, the right belongs to every nation to purchase at a fair price for itself the things which it needs, from those nations who themselves have no need of the same. Which was the first point.

§ 318, part 4,
Jus Nat.

But since no man can be compelled to purchase things for himself from others, or from one rather than from another, no nation has the right to sell its goods to another without its consent. Which was the second point.

§ 32.

§ 28.

§ 23, part 8,
Jus Nat.

§ 322, part 4,
Jus Nat.

The right indeed of purchasing goods for one's self from other nations at a fair price, it seems, can be inferred from the right to those things without which a nation cannot preserve itself because the union cannot endure unless the individuals are preserved; nevertheless since that right has reference to the property which belongs to other nations, there should also fall upon the other nations the obligation from which this right arises, such as is the obligation to share things one with the other at a fair price.

§ 59. Of forbidding the importation of foreign goods into a territory

§ 58.

§ 850, part 1,
Jus Nat.

Since no nation has the right to sell its goods to another nation without its consent, if any nation is not willing that certain foreign goods be brought into its territory, it does no wrong to the nation from which they come, consequently if the bringing in of foreign goods and their sale is prohibited, there are no just complaints by foreigners concerning this prohibition.

Foreigners complain on account of the loss of gain, which is not owed to them by another nation. If the complaints are poured forth upon the nation itself, they are unjust; if indeed they are limited to the loss of gain, they are free from injustice, although otherwise they may be subject to some imputation of wrong, inasmuch as they are opposed to some natural duty. But if the prohibition which causes loss of gain should have no legitimate reason, arising of course from the purpose of the state, or from the duties of the nation to itself; complaints are not unjust, because they are in regard to the duties of humanity due to one state from another. But a refusal to perform a duty of humanity must be endured. Investigation is difficult, however, as to whether complaints of this sort are just or unjust, because the reasons for the prohibition are rarely intimately known. Lest there may be some obscurity, consider the merchant, from whom you have for a long time purchased many wares; but you have reasons why you may wish to purchase such wares no longer. The merchant loses the profit, which he was to have had, if indeed you had continued your purchases. But who pray even in a dream will think that the merchant has just reasons for complaint against you, because you may not wish to make further purchases of wares of that sort, on the ground that he would lose his profit, which he could have had if the purchases had been continued. The things predicated of nations are in no other way more clearly and easily understood than by considering what under the same circumstances may be true of individual humans living in a state of nature; for that is to be applied to nations. But what we have said of the injustice of complaints and unfairness of the same, when merchandise is barred from some territory, the same in general holds good in regard to any complaints whatsoever arising from the denial of the duties of humanity, not only between nations, but also between private individuals.

§ 440, part 3, Jus Nat.

§ 2.

§ 3.

§ 60. *What commerce is*

Commerce is said to be the right to buy and to sell again anything whatsoever, movable and moving, that is necessary, useful, or pleasant.

So the objects of commerce are wine, oil, grain, cattle, wax, silk, cloth, linen. And where slavery is allowed, man servants and maid servants or slaves are bought and sold. This kind of commerce is called in our native vernacular, *der Sclaven-Handel* [slave trade].

§ 61. *Divisions of commerce*

Internal commerce is said to be that which those engage in who are subject to the same civil power, but that is called external which is transacted with foreigners. The former we call in the native vernacular, *einheimischer Handel* [domestic trade], the latter indeed we call *auswärtiger Handel* [foreign trade].

For among us likewise commerce is usually classified by the nature of its object and from this peculiarity names are assigned. So we speak of *Vieh-Handel* [cattle trade], if of herds and flocks; *Woll-Handel* [wool trade], if wool; *Eisen-Handel* [iron trade], if iron; *Wein-Handel* [wine trade], if wine is bought and sold, and so on. But these divisions at present have no utility, so that the varieties are not to be increased more than necessary.[2]

§ 62. *Of the advantage of internal commerce*

Since the practice of commerce consists in this, that whatever things are movable or moving, whether they are necessary, useful, or pleasurable, are bought and sold again, and those are engaged in internal commerce who are subject to the same civil power; internal commerce has this advantage, that every one can have those things which are required for the necessity, advantage, and pleasure of life, and since any labours

§ 60.
§ 61.

2. "[T]he varieties are not to be increased more than necessary" (Latin: "entia praeter necessitatem non sint multiplicanda"): a philosophical principle commonly associated in the early modern period with "nominalist" philosophers, who argued that universals had no real existence apart from particulars. Wolff's mentor, Gottfried Wilhelm Leibniz, used the phrase to characterize the "nominalist" school in his "De stilo philosophico Nizoli" of 1670; see G. W. Leibniz, "De stilo philosophico Nizoli," §28, in G. W. Leibniz, *Opera philosophica quae exstant Latina Gallica Germanica omnia*, ed. J. E. Erdmann (Berlin, 1840), p. 69.

can be purchased from another for money and things are bought and sold for money, internal commerce has this advantage also that the same money is continually transferred from one to another and is turned to the advantage of a very great number.

§ 293, part 1, Jus Nat.

§ 937, part 4, Jus Nat.

There is the greatest advantage in internal commerce, for it is the one means, as far as it goes, by which individuals may be provided with the things they need for the necessity, advantage, and pleasure of life. Experience teaches this fully, so that it seems superfluous to say more.

§ 63. Of the advantage of foreign commerce

Likewise since the practice of commerce consists in this, that whatever things are movable or moving, whether they are necessary, useful, or pleasurable, are bought and sold again, moreover since external commerce is transacted with foreigners, external commerce has this advantage, that the things which are lacking in one nation, but needed for the necessity, advantage, or pleasure of life, can be purchased from another nation, and since things are bought and sold for money, if more things are sold to other nations than are purchased from them, the nation grows in wealth, nay more it can attain to the greatest wealth.

§ 60.

§ 61.

§ 937, part 4, Jus Nat.

The advantage of foreign commerce is a double one. The one consists in that it procures a sufficiency for life; the other that it increases the wealth of the nation. The former is easily understood; the latter is proved by plain experience through the examples of nations among whom commerce flourishes.

§ 10, part 8, Jus Nat.

§ 64. Of the obligation of engaging in internal commerce

Nations are bound to engage in internal commerce. For since a nation is a multitude of men associated into a state, those who form a nation are bound to each other to gain by their combined powers those things which are required for the necessity, advantage, and pleasure of life. Therefore, since internal commerce has this advantage, that every one can have those things which are required for the necessity, advantage, and pleasure of life, nations are bound to engage in internal commerce.

§ 5, part 8, Jus Nat.

§ 4, part 8, Jus Nat.

§ 62.

There is no reason why you should object that necessity itself demands internal commerce and urges men to engage in it. For it is not enough that compelled by necessity men buy and sell again their property; but it is also required that they do this from a sense of duty, in order that they may not consider their own advantage simply, but likewise that of another, consequently that they may engage in commerce not without equity and justice. But although we have derived the obligation from agreement in the proof, which itself has already been confirmed by the natural obligation of observing agreements, nevertheless the obligation, which comes from an agreement, rests upon the natural obligation of mutual transfers of ownership in things. There is the added consideration, that the ruler both can and ought to promote internal commerce, if he wishes to satisfy his duty, and likewise that he is bound to see to it that nothing which is contrary to equity and justice should be allowed in commerce. It is not merely one thing, therefore, which must be laid down for the ruler with regard to internal commerce.

§ 4, part 8, Jus Nat.

§ 789, part 3, Jus Nat.

§ 123, part 3, Jus Nat.

§§ 420 and fol., part 8, Jus Nat.

§ 65. *How the wealth of a nation is determined*

The wealth of a nation is determined by combining the money of the individuals into one sum. For since a nation is considered as an individual person, the money which belongs to all together combined into one sum is the money of the nation. Therefore, since money itself is not used up, as is self-evident, although one is ever receiving it from another, the amount of it nevertheless is not on this account diminished in the nation, but the quantity of it remains the same. Therefore, since wealth is determined by the amount of extra money, the wealth of a nation also is determined by combining the money of the individuals into one sum.

§ 2.

§ 353, part 4, Jus Nat.

Of course the things that belong to the individuals, inasmuch as the individuals together ought to be considered as a single person, belong to the nation. For the nation has nothing except that which of itself belongs to the individuals. Therefore if the question arises as to the money of the entire nation, it is undoubtedly necessary that the money of the individuals combined into one sum be assigned to the nation. Nor is this at variance with common notions, for we all call a nation rich, if it has much money, without consideration as to how it is distributed among individuals; for it is not necessary that individuals be rich, for the nation to be rich, just as the individuals are not learned, if the nation is learned. Hence has arisen the proverb, or at least it is not inaptly transferred here: the poor man is found everywhere.

§ 66. *What nation is rich*

Since the wealth of a nation is determined by combining the money of the individuals into one sum, consequently since it matters little how the money is distributed among individuals, the nation is rich in which there are many rich families. §65. §43.

So the English and the Dutch are reputed rich nations, because among both nations there are many rich families. As long as we look at the nation itself as a nation, or even with respect to other nations, it makes no difference how the money is distributed among the individuals. But it is another proposition, if the individuals, who make up the nation, are considered with reference to each other, with the idea of imposing burdens on them, so that no one may be too heavily loaded. But since money can be stamped out of silver, silver vessels and any other things made of solid silver are on a par with coined money, since in case of necessity, when there is an extraordinary need of a great sum of money, they can be turned into money.

§ 67. *What things make a nation rich*

Likewise because a nation is rich which possesses very large amounts of money, since moreover money is increased by the aid of foreign commerce, external commerce can make a nation rich. §65. §63.

Indeed there is no other reason why maritime nations, as the Portuguese, the Spaniards, the English, the Dutch, have established trade with far away nations, and why other nations imitate them.

§ 68. *When commerce makes a nation poorer*

In like manner since the wealth of a nation is determined by combining the money of the individuals into one sum, and since money is diminished §65.

by external commerce, if more is bought from foreign nations than is sold to them—a fact which is self-evident—external commerce makes a nation poorer, if it buys more from other nations than it sells to them.

Of course more money is taken away than is received and therefore it is necessary that it should steadily decrease. Therefore in external commerce there is need of much caution, lest it be injurious to a nation. But this is to be more fully discussed in the "Politics."

§ 69. *Of the power of a nation*

A nation is said to be powerful which can resist the force of other nations by which either the nation itself or its property is attacked. Therefore the greater its power for resisting foreign attack, the more powerful the nation is. And since for resisting foreign attack, consequently for defending itself and its property against other nations, or even for obtaining by force its own right from another nation which refuses to concede it, both a number of soldiers, not infrequently vast, and enormous expenditures are required—a fact which is quite plain from experience—the power of a nation depends upon the number of men who can perform military service, and upon its wealth. And since it is just the same whether the soldiers are natives or foreigners hired for a price, a nation is still rated as powerful, if it is rich enough to hire for a price as many foreign soldiers as it needs.

§ 972, part 1, Jus Nat.

Nevertheless it is quite plain that the power of that nation must be considered greater, which has no need to purchase foreign aid, but is sufficient of itself alone, since in the case of hiring foreign soldiery, power is made dependent upon the consent of other nations, which cannot always be obtained nor obtained without delay, which quite often is harmful. But how many men are given up to utter destruction, when a war blazes up, and how great expenses have to be incurred for military affairs, the records of all times show and we have experienced in our own days. Indeed if one may believe recent announcements, the French alone in the present seven years' war have lost 146,000 able-bodied men and have spent 840,000,000 French livres or 280,000,000 [German] thalers—a thing which cannot be done except by a very powerful nation. From this too it is understood how great the power of a nation ought to be, if the war is to be continued through several years.

§ 70. *Of the obligation to strive for power*

Nations ought to strive as far as they are able to be powerful. For every nation ought to perfect itself, consequently to strive to be fitted to accomplish the purpose of the state. Therefore, since security also is required for the purpose of the state, consequently freedom from fear of force, especially external force, it ought also to strive to be able to resist the force of other nations by which it or its property is assailed. Therefore, since a nation is powerful, if it is strong enough to resist, nations ought to strive to be powerful. Which was the first point.

§ 35.

§ 29.

§ 15, part 8, Jus Nat.

§ 12, part 8, Jus Nat.

§ 69.

But since indeed no one can be bound to do that which is impossible, nations ought to strive as far as they are able to be powerful. Which was the second point.

§ 209, part 1, Phil. Pract. Univ.

> The power of a nation must be considered to be among those things which do not depend altogether upon itself, but are subject to the vicissitudes of fortune. The obligation therefore is not to be extended beyond that which can be done. But a nation errs if, when it can increase its power, it neglects to do so, and it pays the proper penalty of its weakness, if from this it suffers the loss which at length results.

§ 71. *Whether to attain a licit end one may use illicit means*

§ 170, part 1, Phil. Pract. Univ.

§ 350, part 1, Jus Nat.

To attain a licit end one may not use illicit means. For we are bound to forego that which is illicit. Therefore one may not use illicit means to attain a licit end.

§§ 519, 536, part 2, Jus Nat.

> For example, every man is bound to preserve his own life, consequently he is expected to look out for food and drink for himself. Nevertheless he is not therefore allowed to steal or to carry away what belongs to another, that he may have something to live on. For this is illicit, although the former is licit.

§ 383, part 1, Jus Nat., and § 170, part 1, Phil. Pract. Univ.

§ 72. *Of the illicit method of increasing power*

§ 71.
§ 70.
§ 1111, part 1,
Jus Nat.

§ 1109, part 1,
Jus Nat.

Since it is not permissible to attain a licit end by illicit means, nations, although they ought to strive as far as they are able to be powerful, nevertheless ought not to increase their power by an illicit method, consequently since an unjust war is illicit, and since there is no just cause of war unless a wrong has been done or threatened, a nation may not subject other nations to its control by force of arms simply for the sake of increasing its own power.

§ 55, part 8,
Jus Nat.

§ 858, part 1,
Jus Nat.

§ 859, part 1,
Jus Nat.

Every nation is naturally free. Therefore since liberty is an absolute right, he who simply for the sake of increasing his power subjects a nation to his control by force of arms, by taking away its right does it a wrong. Now there are many illicit methods of increasing one's own power, all of which cannot be named here in detail. But they are easily recognizable, because they consist in acts prohibited by the natural law, or which are contrary to the law of nations, as we show in the present volume.

§ 73. *Whether one nation must necessarily engage in commerce with another nation*

It depends upon the will of any nation whether it desires to engage in commerce with another nation or not, and upon what condition it desires to engage in it. For the right to purchase things for one's self from another is an imperfect right, consequently no one can be compelled to allow things to be purchased by us from himself, or to sell those things to us. Therefore, since commerce consists in the right of buying and selling certain things, and no nation is bound to allow that things be carried from another nation into its territory and sold there, no nation likewise can be compelled to engage in commerce with another nation; consequently it depends upon the will of any nation whether it desires to engage in commerce with another nation or not. Which was the first point.

§ 356, part 3,
Jus Nat.

§ 237, part 1,
Phil. Pract.
Univ.
§ 938, part 4,
Jus Nat.
§ 60.
§ 58.

§ 60.

§ 11, part 3,
Jus Nat.

For since by allowing commerce with a nation some right is granted to it, while it depends upon the will of the one transferring and consequently granting the right upon what condition it wishes to grant a certain right to another; likewise it depends upon the will of any nation upon what condition it wishes to engage in commerce with another. Which was the second point.

For no one has the right by nature to purchase for himself from another that which the other himself needs. Moreover by force of natural liberty the decision must be left to the other, as to whether he himself needs those things which you wish to purchase for yourself from him. And therefore that right is an imperfect one, as we have already shown elsewhere. Therefore in these matters the mere whim of the nation rules, in which one must acquiesce. Therefore likewise any nation can declare the condition upon which it desires to allow or bind itself to commerce with foreign nations.

§ 128, part 3, Jus Nat.

§ 156, part 1, Jus Nat.

§ 906, part 1, Jus Nat.

§ 356, part 3, Jus Nat.

§ 74. *How a perfect right to external commerce is acquired*

Since it depends upon the will of any nation, whether it desires to engage in commerce with another nation or not, and upon what condition it desires to engage in it, since moreover no one can bind himself perfectly to another except by a promise, that is, by agreements; a perfect right to engage in commerce with another nation cannot be acquired except by agreements, consequently that right is only a stipulative right.

§ 73.

§ 393, part 3, Jus Nat.

§ 788, part 3, Jus Nat.

§ 364, part 3, Jus Nat.

§ 23.

The ruler can impose internal commerce on his subjects and these are bound to obey him. But there is certainly another rule for external commerce, since nations are naturally free. Therefore since no private individual can bind another private individual to himself perfectly, and thus acquire a perfect right against him, except by a promise, so also no nation can acquire a perfect right to external commerce except by agreements. By agreements of course an imperfect obligation becomes perfect.

§ 1043, part 8, Jus Nat.

§ 55, part 8, Jus Nat.

§ 393, part 3, Jus Nat.

§§ 235, 236, part 1, Phil. Pract. Univ.

§ 788, part 3, Jus Nat.

§ 75. *Of the bare allowing of commerce*

Since a perfect right to engage in commerce with another nation, that is, in external commerce, is not acquired except by agreements, if one nation simply allows another to engage in commerce with it, from that fact a perfect right to this external commerce is not attained, therefore since it depends upon the will of the other whether it is willing or unwilling to

§ 61.

§ 74.

§ 73.

engage in it and upon what condition it wishes to engage in it, the one nation does no injury to the other, if it restricts commerce in any way whatsoever and arranges as to the manner of engaging in it according to its liking, however and whenever shall seem best to it.

§ 58.

§ 124, part 3, Jus Nat.

§ 268, part 4, Jus Nat.

§ 9.

§ 61.

§ 229, part 1, Phil. Pract. Univ.

Here is pertinent, what we have already shown above, although that may seem quite plain, that the transportation of foreign merchandise and its sale in his territories can be prohibited by the ruler. For although nations, like single individuals, are bound to give up their goods to each other in case of mutual need, although not *gratis,* nay although nations are understood to have united into a certain supreme state, whose individual members are single states, and in this respect external commerce may be likened to internal commerce, nevertheless it does not follow from this, that nations are bound by nature to engage in commerce with others, so that the freedom of determining according to their liking in these matters is taken away from them. So formerly the Chinese, for the purpose of preserving their own interests, did not wish to unite in trade with other nations. Nor did they err in that, because they do not need the goods of other nations; but even if the things which they themselves were able to do without had been of especial use to other nations, nevertheless the duty toward themselves was superior to the duty toward others. But if you think of nations as fellow citizens, and the commerce, in which they are engaged, as internal, no other conclusion follows from this than that it depends wholly upon the will of the nations, whether or not they wish to keep up trade with one another, and whether the practice ought to be a matter of liberty or of necessity. For is not any one in the state free to buy from and sell to any one he wishes, and may not the two as they desire make definite stipulation concerning buying or selling, in order that perfect rights may be acquired? No obstacle is presented by civil laws promulgated concerning commerce in general by which that liberty is hardly abridged. Moreover corresponding to these laws are natural laws, by which nations are ordered to engage in commerce one with the other, as will be proved a little later. So nothing is taught by us which involves a contradiction, but one point is accordant with all, there is one harmony, provided only all things are observed with keen insight. Therefore this concept of the supreme state clears up wonderfully all things which are to be maintained concerning the commerce of nations, nay, it leads us by the hand to the discovery of them.

§ 76. *What the rights of pure power and the acts of pure will are*

The rights of pure power are said to be those which any one may exercise or not as seems best to himself, free from all outside coercion. And from this, acts of pure will are said to be those which depend upon our will alone, as to go and to stay, and consequently acts of pure will are those which belong to the exercise of rights of pure power, as to buy or sell wine or whatever merchandise you choose, where you will.

The rights of pure power are not subject to definite laws, nor do they depend upon agreement, but in their case the mere will of the one exercising them rules. These rights therefore are altogether free, and in this respect they are even called *jura libertatis* [rights of freedom] by Grotius. Nor is there need with him to distinguish from the rights of freedom those which are not exercised daily, but only once when it shall be convenient, as the redemption of a pledge, if there has been no agreement concerning a definite time within which it ought to be redeemed. For then you are undoubtedly free to use that right when you will, nor can you be compelled to do contrary to your desire what must be done once for all, for example to redeem your pledge, when it shall seem best to another. The act, therefore, is one of pure will.

De Jure Belli ac Pacis, lib. 2, c. 4, § 15.

§ 77. *What sort of a right commerce between nations is*

Since a right of pure power is that which any one may exercise or not as seems best to himself, free from all outside coercion, moreover since it depends upon the will of any nation whether or not it wishes to engage in commerce with another nation, and upon what condition it wishes so to engage; commerce between nations is of itself, or naturally, a right of pure power, consequently acts pertaining to it are acts of pure will.

§ 76.

§ 73.

§ 76.

In order that no doubt may arise, those points must be considered fully which we have just noted. Moreover from what follows later, it is

Note, § 76.

plain that it is of no little importance to recognize what sort of a right commerce between nations is.

§ 78. *Of the prescription of rights of pure power*

The rights of pure power cannot be barred by prescription, and they are not lost, except from the time when a prohibition or order has intervened, and obedience has been given to it, with adequate evidence of consent. For you can use or not use the right of pure power, as shall seem best to you, nor can any other one compel you to use it or not use it. Therefore from the fact that you use it during a long period without any interruption, it cannot be understood that you wish always to use the same, and that you ought not to be free not to use it longer, if it shall seem best to you not to use it longer. And on the other hand, if you do not use this same right when you could, from that it cannot in the least be understood that you do not wish to use it, if it shall seem best to use it. Therefore, although by prescription a personal right may be lost by presumed consent, the rights of pure power cannot be barred by prescription or lost. Which was the first point.

But if another prohibits you from using a right which you were able to use and have used up to this time, or compels you to use the right which you have continuously used but do not wish to use further, and with adequate evidence of consent you obey the prohibition or order, assuredly it is understood that you agree in this, that you ought not to be free to use or not to use further, but that you wish to use constantly, or not to use the same, as the case may be, consequently you lose your right by the presumed consent. Therefore, since the loss of your right by presumed consent is prescription, the right of pure power is barred by prescription, from the time when the prohibition or order has intervened, and obedience has been given to it with adequate evidence of consent. Which was the second proposition.

For example, let us assume that you are free to use any mill-house whatsoever, but that for a long time you have used a certain definite mill-house, on that account your right to use any mill-house whatsoever, as may have been suitable, is not barred by prescription, nor does the master of the mill-house acquire by prescription the right to

§ 76.

§ 1024, part 3, Jus Nat.

§ 1024, part 3, Jus Nat.

compel you to use none except his mill-house. Therefore, although you have used that mill-house through a hundred and more years, this nevertheless in no way at all prevents you from using another, if it shall have so pleased you. But let us suppose that you do use another and that the master of the mill opposes it and forbids you to use any other than his, and moreover suppose you do this, although you are driven by no compulsion so to do, and do not oppose this in any way, although you might oppose it, it is rightly presumed that you agree to this, not to use any other mill than his. And therefore you lose your right of using any mill whatsoever, and the master of the mill from that time acquires the right of compelling you to use his mill alone. Moreover it is a matter of positive law that prescription requires a certain number of years, which it declares enough for presuming consent from silence.

§ 79. *Of the barring of commerce by prescription*

Since the rights of pure power cannot be barred by prescription, since moreover commerce between nations of itself, that is, if there is no agreement added thereto, is a right of pure power; commerce between nations cannot be barred by prescription, consequently since commerce consists in the right of buying and selling again, if through a hundred years two nations have united for trade, nevertheless on this account the one nation is not bound to allow the other to sell its goods to the former, or to buy its own goods from the other, nor is freedom in buying and selling its goods lost.

§ 78.
§ 74.
§ 78.
§ 60.

§ 1024, part 3, Jus Nat.

> For example, if a certain nation for however long a time has bought grain from a certain other nation, nevertheless the one cannot on this account compel the other to buy in the same way ever afterwards, if it desires not to do so. And on the other hand, if a certain nation has sold wine to a certain other nation, the latter is not bound to allow this nation ever afterwards to bring wine into its territories and sell it there. The same is understood of any other kind of merchandise whatsoever. Freedom in buying and selling always remains unimpaired to every nation.

§ 73.

§ 80. *Of the voluntary submission of a nation*

If one nation shall not be strong enough to protect itself against the wrongs done by other nations, it can submit itself to some more powerful nation, under definite conditions, upon which an agreement has been made, and the rights of each are to be determined in accordance with the compact of submission. For every nation has the right to those things without which it cannot preserve itself. Therefore, since it cannot preserve itself, unless it can protect itself against the wrongs done by other nations, consequently unless it is sufficiently powerful, moreover since the lack of power may be supplied by the power of another, and nations ought to strive as far as they are able to be powerful; if any nation shall not be strong enough to protect itself against the wrongs done by other nations, it can subject itself to some more powerful nation. Which was the first point.

For since it depends upon the will of any one, upon what conditions he wishes to transfer a certain right to another, it depends upon the will of nations also, upon what conditions one nation desires to submit itself to another, or to give itself into tutelage, and upon what conditions the other nation desires to receive it under its protection, consequently they must agree on these points. If therefore any nation is not strong enough to protect itself against the wrongs done by other nations, since it can submit itself to some other more powerful nation for the sake of protecting itself, as shown above in point 1, it can submit itself to it on definite conditions, upon which they shall have agreed. Which was the second point.

Finally, since agreements of this sort are stipulations, and since no one can acquire more right from another than that other wished to transfer to him, if any less powerful nation submits itself to a more powerful one for the sake of protecting itself, the rights of each are to be determined in accordance with the compact of submission. Which was the third point.

Every nation is free by nature. But in regard to this right it can determine to its liking, just as shall have seemed best to it, therefore can diminish its freedom for the sake of its own advantage; this is what happens, if a nation subjects itself to another upon certain definite conditions, or grants some right to another over itself, whatever indeed that may be. But whether a nation is not powerful enough to protect itself against the wrongs done by other nations, and whether it cannot provide for itself by some other agreement than by subjecting itself or giving itself into tutelage to another more powerful nation,

§ 32.
§ 28 h, and § 9, part 8, Jus Nat.
§ 69.

§ 70.
§ 159, part 1, Phil. Pract. Univ.

§ 11, part 3, Jus Nat.

§ 698, part 3, Jus Nat.

§§ 788, 361, part 3, Jus Nat.
§ 382, part 3, Jus Nat.

§ 55, part 8, Jus Nat.

§ 135, part 1, Jus Nat.

must be left to the decision of the nation itself in accordance with the principle of natural freedom. Therefore agreements entered into must be kept and there is no question as to whether the nation has acted wisely, which has subjected itself to another for the sake of its own protection, although it could have provided for itself in some other manner, but there must be acquiescence in that as to which agreement has been made.

§ 156, part 1, Jus Nat.

§ 81. *Whether by this act there is a derogation from the sovereign power*

Since any nation for the purpose of self-protection can submit itself to another nation under those conditions upon which they have agreed, and the rights of each are to be determined in accordance with the compact of submission; if a certain nation puts itself under the tutelage of another, this can be done either with or without diminution of its sovereign power.

§ 80.

So this happens without diminution of the sovereign power, if a definite tribute is to be paid annually; for then the nation which owes protection has no other right than that of demanding the tribute as due. And the obligation to pay to another nation annually a certain sum of money, which arises from a contract to pay for an act, does not affect the civil power itself, much less does it derogate from its sovereignty. But if indeed to the nation which owes the protection, is allowed the right of imposing new tributes, as shall seem best to it, or certain things pertaining to the exercise of civil power cannot be done without its consent, or the suzerain power itself can do such things on its own initiative; the submission has certainly been made with derogation from the sovereign power, because the exercise of power as to certain acts depends upon the will of the nation owing protection.

§ 60, part 8, Jus Nat.

§ 44, part 8, Jus Nat.

§ 82. *Of protection not furnished*

If the more powerful nation does not furnish the protection promised, it is allowable for the less powerful nation to put itself under the control of another, or to submit itself to such for the sake of self-protection. For if the nation which owes the protection does not

furnish it, it fails in its agreement, as is self-evident. But if one of the
contracting parties fails in his agreement, the other also may withdraw
from it. Therefore the less powerful is not bound to stand by its agreement, if the more powerful does not furnish the promised protection,
consequently since it is now free from its obligation, by which it was
bound under the agreement, nothing prevents it from putting itself
under the protection of some other nation or submitting to it for the
sake of self-protection.

§ 827, part 3,
Jus Nat.

§ 80.

There is no reason for objecting that the right exists to compel
due protection to be furnished. For the less powerful nation lacks
strength to coerce the more powerful; if it had possessed the strength,
it could have done this. With strength it could of itself have resisted
one wronging it, so that it would not have needed another's protection, if it had possessed sufficient strength to compel the more powerful nation to furnish the protection due to it. The situation is quite
different, if the nation to whom protection is owed does not pay the
annual tribute owed for it.

§ 83. *Of a nation which owes protection infringing upon the rights of the less powerful*

If a nation which owes protection assumes for itself a greater right against
one less powerful, than it has by the agreement, it is allowable to resist
it by force and to seek aid from another. For if a nation which owes protection assumes for itself a greater right against one less powerful than it
has by the agreement, this is contrary to the right of the less powerful,
consequently the one does a wrong to the other, and therefore injures it.
Therefore, since the right belongs to every one of demanding from any
one whomsoever, that he should not injure him, and of compelling him
not to do so when he attempts to injure him, if the nation which owes
the protection assumes for itself a greater right against one less powerful than it has by the agreement, it is allowable to resist by force. Which
was the first point.

§ 239, part 1,
Phil. Pract.
Univ.

§ 859, part 1,
Jus Nat.

§ 920, part 1,
Jus Nat.

§ 914, part 1,
Jus Nat.

§ 727, Ontol.

Moreover, since the less powerful cannot of itself resist the more powerful, as is self-evident, and since the right belongs to every one by nature
to defend another, nay more, it is bound to defend the other so far as lies

in its power, if of itself it is not capable of self-defence; it is allowable even to seek aid from another. Which was the second point.

§ 990, part 1, Jus Nat.

It would undoubtedly be better that a supplementary clause be added to the stipulation of submission that the stipulation should be void, if the nation which owes the protection assumes a greater right for itself than that which has been expressly agreed upon, for thus the right of resisting by aid of another rests on the credit of the stipulations and all objections are barred. This is perfectly in accord with the customs of the ancient Germans, who, since nothing was more time-honoured with them than the pledged word, desired that almost all their rights should rest upon agreements, and nothing was considered more disgraceful among them than to betray a pledge when given.

§ 84. Of prescription in favour of a nation owing protection against a less powerful nation

If the nation which owes protection assumes for itself a greater right against a less powerful nation than it has by the agreement and the weaker nation does not oppose it, the more powerful by the long acquiescence of the weaker at length acquires the right which it asserts, nay more, the weaker can utterly lose its supreme power and become subject to the more powerful. For if the nation which owes the protection assumes a greater right for itself against the less powerful than it has by the agreement, and the weaker does not oppose this, but allows the right to be assumed for a long time, from the long-continued silence it is presumed to relinquish its right and consent to the usurpation of it. Therefore, since he who gives up the property tacitly consents to the change of ownership, which includes incorporeal benefits, the nation which owes protection acquires at length, by long-continued acquiescence of the weaker nation, the right which it assumes for itself. Which was the first point.

§§ 1058, 1054, part 12, Jus Nat.

§ 1025, part 3, Jus Nat.

§ 216, part 2, Jus Nat.

But since the same thing is true in the same way of any right belonging to the supreme power, the less powerful nation can in the same way utterly lose its sovereignty and become subject to the more powerful, which formerly owed it protection. Which was the second point.

There will be no difficulty or obscurity in these matters, provided only there shall have been sufficient examination of those points which we have proved as to usucaption and prescription, in an entire chapter in the third part of "The Law of Nature." Occupation of course gets a new value from abandonment, so that the occupation, which was before illegal, when there is an abandonment by consent of the owner,

§ 1015, part 3, Jus Nat.

now begets a right, by force of the tacit consent of the owner. If there is doubt as to this, because it is generally said that what is not effective from the beginning cannot become effective after the fact, Grotius has already solved this doubt. Of course the rule has an exception in

De Jure Belli ac Pacis, lib. 2, c. 4, § 12.

the case where a new cause intervenes which is sufficient in itself to beget a right, as in the present instance is the added tacit consent of the weaker nation, against which the more powerful nation usurps some right.

§ 85. Of the occupation of sovereignty in uninhabited territory

If a certain nation occupies an uninhabited territory, it occupies the sov-

§ 5, part 8, Jus Nat.

ereignty over it at the same time. For since a nation is a number of people associated into a state, the civil sovereignty also belongs to it, whether

§§ 31, 32, part 8, Jus Nat.

it exercises that of itself or through another in some manner. If then it occupies some uninhabited territory, to dwell in it and hold its property

§ 37, part 8, Jus Nat.

in it, there is no doubt but that it desires to have sovereignty over it. But if it desires to have sovereignty for itself in that territory, it is understood not to wish to allow another to exercise in it some right belonging to sovereignty, or not to be subject to it. But since this is adequate for the

§ 219, part 3, Jus Nat.

occupation of sovereignty in an uninhabited territory, it follows that if a certain nation occupies an uninhabited territory, it occupies the sovereignty over it at the same time.

We are not yet speaking here of warlike occupation, which happens when a nation is expelled that had inhabited a territory already occupied. For of this we must speak in its own place. But it would be absurd for any one to wish to argue that sovereign power does in fact belong to a nation over those who are members of the state, but does not exist over the lands which are under the control of the nation. There is no one that does not readily see that this is opposed to the

§ 11, part 8, Jus Nat.

public tranquillity, which concerns the purpose of a state. Therefore, since civil authority is to be measured by the purpose of a state, the same undoubtedly is to be extended to all persons whomsoever, who sojourn in a territory for any reason whatsoever or enter into it. And so the people who inhabit a territory have sovereignty over the entire territory.

§ 13, part 8, Jus Nat.

§§ 30 and fol., part 8, Jus Nat.

§ 86. *Another case*

If families dwelling in the same territory unite into a state, they occupy jointly the sovereignty over the entire territory which was uninhabited. It is the same, whether families dwelling in the same territory unite into a state, after individual families have already beforehand occupied certain parts, that is, after occupation by estates has already occurred, or, as a whole, occupy the territory, after they have combined into a society; for the ownership of the estates always remains distinct from the sovereignty, nor does the sovereignty affect this ownership in any way. Therefore, in exactly the same manner as before, it is plain that, if families dwelling in the same territory unite into a state, they occupy the sovereignty over the entire territory which is uninhabited.

§ 196, part 2, Jus Nat.

§ 85.

> Occupation is assumed to have been made by estates, if separate families or free households are formed before the civil authority is; for the things which were not taken possession of were left in the original common holding. But when they come together into a state, the sovereignty is occupied in that territory and at the same time with it are occupied the places still without an owner, which were already subject to the ownership of the whole and therefore belong to the people.

§ 87. *Of the occupation of a territory*

If a certain entire territory is occupied by a certain nation, those things which are not apportioned to the individuals belong to the whole. For if a certain entire territory is occupied by a certain nation, those who constitute the nation jointly acquire ownership, and therefore the entire territory belongs to the nation. But since those things become the property of the individuals which are apportioned to the individuals, those things which are not apportioned to the individuals remain in the ownership of the whole nation, and therefore belong to the whole.

§ 189, part 2, Jus Nat.

§124, part 2, Jus Nat.

§ 191, part 2, Jus Nat.

§ 124, part 2, Jus Nat.

§ 2.

§ 175, part 2,
Jus Nat.

§ 129, part 2,
Jus Nat.

§ 126, part 2,
Jus Nat.

§§ 7, 9, part 2,
Jus Nat.

A nation is considered as a single individual. Therefore the things which it occupies are in its ownership, consequently if no other act is added to that of occupation, nothing belongs to all, other than the use of the things occupied in general, as of course any one shall have need. Therefore, since by the simple act of occupation nothing is introduced except a mixed common holding, from which there is no withdrawal except by agreement express or tacit, by which some things pass to the ownership of the individuals, others to a positive common holding,[3] and those things which are not subjected to the individual ownership, or to the positive common holding, are left in the mixed common holding. Now if certain things should be in the ownership of individuals, before sovereignty is occupied in the territory, that is, before families unite into a state, the other things which before had been in the original common holding are occupied with the sovereignty and are brought into a mixed holding, from which as before they either pass into the ownership of individuals, or into some positive common holding, or are left in the mixed holding. But if certain things should not be occupied, that they remain in the original common holding is evident of itself; in which case especially applies the right of occupation of things devoid of an owner, as wild animals and fish and likewise inanimate things, as treasures, metals, and minerals, and all things abandoned by the owner, or deprived of an owner by some accident. Of these we have spoken at length in the second chapter of the second part of "The Law of Nature."

§ 88. *Of the division of things*

Those things which were left in the original common holding when occupation occurred are called by the Roman jurists *res communes* [things common]; those which were brought into the mixed common holding of the entire nation and have continued in it, *res publicae* [things public]; those which came into the mixed common holding of definite groups or communities, *res universitatis* [things corporate]; finally those which

3. In positive common ownership goods are held in common by the members of a group; outsiders are excluded from ownership. In negative common ownership nobody has an exclusive right to any goods.

have become subject to ownership of individuals are called *res singulorum* [things of individuals].

This division of things made by the Romans is usually considered complicated, especially if things common are to be distinguished from things public. But if you consider those things which we have just said concerning the occupation of territory, by our definitions all those things are distinguished one from the other with sufficient clearness, just as they were divided by the Romans, so that no ambiguity remains. Moreover, it is quite plain that much must here depend upon the whim of those occupying, where the particular things belonging to this or that class are to be enumerated. Among the Romans things considered common were air, flowing water, the sea, shores, fish, birds, and wild animals; for all these things were left by them in the original common holding. Things public were all the rivers, which, seeing that they are under the control of the people, nevertheless as regards use were considered common to individuals, so that it was allowed any one to fish and sail in them as he liked. Things corporate were theatres, racecourses, and the like, as fountains, the forum, the curia, and open squares in cities. Here, too, to-day belong pastures in the country, forests fit for cutting, common groves. Here likewise are to be included temples and ecclesiastical property in city or country. All these things are in the mixed common holding of definite groups, inasmuch as the ownership is with a definite corporation, but the use is open to individuals who belong to the corporation. But since these rights can be changed by the act of men, by agreement between those to whom they belong, and because the use of the things belongs either to the whole or to the individuals, therefore things corporate can be still more minutely subdistinguished, and from this have arisen the difficulties which distract the interpreters of the Roman law. So by force of agreement there seem to be added to the positive common holding things which of themselves are to be referred to the mixed common holding, as when it is not allowed to individuals to drive into the common pastures more than a definite number of cattle, or hay growing in the common meadow is to be distributed to individuals in definite shares. But the mixed common holding suffers no change, if any one is allowed to hew down the quantity of wood which he needs, or mow down grass with a sickle in the common meadow in

Note, § 87.

accordance with his needs, or even drive into the common pasture as many cattle as he pleases. Likewise the common use of the temples has reference to the people as a whole, but the use of common meadows and pasture lands belongs to individuals. Nay, the use of those things also, which none except the people as a whole can have, belongs either directly or indirectly to the people as a whole. The temples are an example of the direct use, in which the people as a whole in general are free to attend sacred services; goods assigned to the support of the pastor of the church are an example of the indirect use, since the use of these goods only indirectly belongs to the people as a whole. A like distinction worthy of note occurs also in things public—a thing which we consider superfluous to pursue more at length. But now if you will really depend on our definitions, by which we have distinguished things occupied by a nation, no ambiguity or difficulty seems to be left. But if you shall be pleased to subdistinguish these more minutely, we shall not object. Nevertheless it will be difficult to find in the Latin language words suitable to characterize things so distinguished.

§ 89. *Of the derivative way in which a corporation acquires things*

Any one can turn his own property into the property of a corporation, either directly or indirectly, either simply or under a definite condition, as shall seem best to him. For any one can transfer the ownership of his own property to another, whomsoever he shall desire, and in whatever way he shall desire. Therefore he can likewise transfer the ownership of his property to a certain definite group of men, or community, as shall seem best to him; consequently since things belong to a corporation, which come into such a mixed common holding either directly or indirectly, any one can turn his own property into the property of a corporation, either directly or indirectly, either simply or under a definite condition, as shall seem best to him.

So an owner can give or sell, or when dying can bequeath his property to a corporation, nay, he can even appoint any corporation as heir. And so it is plain not only that the property of a corporation can be acquired by original acquisition, but also that a derivative method of acquiring the property of a corporation is allowed. Here, too, belongs

§ 12, part 3, Jus Nat.
§ 11, part 3, Jus Nat.
§ 88.

the case of some one providing for the building, at his own expense, of a fountain for common use in the forum or in another public square that belongs to a corporation.

§§ 176, 177, part 2, Jus Nat.

§ 90. *Of the alienation and pledge of property of a corporation*

The property of a corporation cannot be alienated from the corporation at will, nor can it be pledged, unless some pressing necessity exists or the evident advantage of the corporation recommends it. Since a particular church is a certain corporation or community, since, moreover, ecclesiastical property by nature belongs to a particular church in a certain definite place, that property belongs to a corporation. Therefore that the property of a corporation cannot be alienated or pledged at will is proved in the same manner as we have shown likewise in the case of ecclesiastical property. Which was the first point.

§ 484, part 8, Jus Nat.

§ 507, part 8, Jus Nat.
§ 88.
§§ 510, 516, part 8, Jus Nat.

That in case of pressing necessity it is allowable to sell or to pledge, is likewise plain in the same manner as we have proved the same in the case of ecclesiastical property. Which was the second point.

§§ 514, 516, part 8, Jus Nat.

Finally, if the evident advantage of the corporation recommends the alienation or pledge of the property of a corporation, when nothing is done to the disadvantage of the corporation for the future, but rather there is due consideration for it; nothing prevents the alienation or pledge from being made, since in fact nothing stands in the way of the alienation or pledge, such as a disadvantage which may come to the corporation in the future, as is evident from the proof of the limitation of the right of the church in ecclesiastical property. Which was the third point.

§ 511, part 8, Jus Nat.

Although we discussed ecclesiastical property in universal public law, nothing as yet had been said of public property, which we were obliged to postpone to the law of nations. Therefore it was not feasible first to prove the things which must be held concerning the alienation and pledge of the property of a corporation, and then apply those same things to ecclesiastical property; but the general demonstration had to be applied to the particular case. Nor is this wrong in any way. So Euclid, when in his "Elements" he discussed the circle as a certain sort of curve, makes plain in the instance of the circle what holds true of all curves, and, following his example, Apollonius proves the same things concerning particular conic sections.[4] Moreover they were able likewise to prove the same things in general concerning curves and then to apply them to the circle and to conic sections as to species included under a genus, just as afterwards Barrow gave general proofs in his "Geometrical Lectures."[5] If there should have been reasons why there ought to be a consideration of a certain species before there was a consideration of the genus, it cannot be otherwise than that the things which could be proved in regard to the genus, would likewise be so proved in regard to the species that the general demonstration would be applied just as to the species. And hence it happens that something can be proved in regard to the genus in the same manner in which it has been proved in regard to the species. We think it well advised that such cautions be given for the sake of those who have a special liking for accurate method, and in order that the captious criticism of the superficial may be avoided, who seem to themselves not even to have discovered what boys find in a bean, if they censure those things which because of a lack of intelligence they do not adequately understand.

§ 91. *Whether the consent of the ruler of the state is needed for alienation and pledge*

If necessity urges the alienation or pledge by a corporation of property belonging to it, or its evident advantage recommends it, that ought not to be done without the consent of the superior or ruler of the state. For since the right belongs to the ruler of a state to compel his subjects by force to regulate at least their external acts according to the law of nature, he also ought not to allow corporations to alienate or pledge corporate property at will, and since that may not be done except in case of extreme necessity or plain advantage, the ruler of the state ought to judge the necessity or advantage. Therefore if necessity urges or plain advantage recommends

§ 395, part 8, Jus Nat.

§ 90.

4. Euclid (fl. ca. 300 B.C.) and Apollonius (fl. ca. 200 B.C.) were Greek mathematicians.

5. Isaac Barrow (1630–77), mathematician and theologian, first incumbent of the Lucasian Chair of Mathematics at the University of Cambridge. His geometrical lectures were first published posthumously in Latin in 1683.

that the property of a corporation be alienated or pledged by it, it is necessary that this be done with the consent of the superior; consequently without his consent alienation or pledge ought not to be made.

§ 658, part 1, Phil. Pract. Univ.

Undoubtedly it is to the public advantage to take precaution lest the property of a corporation be alienated or pledged to the disadvantage of the corporation in the future, and lest those who now make up the corporation take some right away from those who shall constitute the corporation in the future, when they diminish their right. But the consideration of public advantage belongs to none other than the superior or ruler of the state, to whom likewise are subject the actions of those who form the corporation, so far as they have regard to the end of the state. Since corporations consist of individuals and therefore remain the same, even if some withdraw and others succeed to their places, and consequently even if all have died who are now in the corporation, in this respect they are like minors, who have need of a curator in the management of their property, consequently without the consent of their curator they cannot alienate or pledge their property. And so the superior or ruler of the state plays the part of a curator. This indeed is also the reason why the civil laws confer the rights of minors upon corporations. It is customary also to compare corporations to wards whose tutor is the ruler of the state. The natural obligation not to alienate or pledge the property of the state to the prejudice of the future is not sufficient to provide adequately for the future. Therefore it is necessary that there should be some external check in addition, as that the act of alienation or pledge may be invalidated at the will of the superior or ruler of the state.

§ 489, part 8, Jus Nat.

§ 494, part 8, Jus Nat.
§ 768, part 7, Jus Nat.
§ 842, part 7, Jus Nat.

§ 92. *Of eminent domain over the property of a corporation*

Eminent domain over the property of a corporation belongs to the ruler of the state. For eminent domain over the property of citizens belongs to the ruler of a state. Therefore since the property of a corporation is likewise the property of citizens, eminent domain over the property of a corporation belongs to the ruler of the state.

§ 111, part 8, Jus Nat.

§ 88 h, and § 6, part 8, Jus Nat.

Eminent domain is not to be confused with that right of the ruler of a state upon which depends his consent to alienation and pledge, as is apparent from its effect.

Note, § 91.

§ 93.

§ 93. *Of its effect*

Since eminent domain over the property of a corporation belongs to
the ruler of a state, moreover since by virtue of eminent domain he can
dispose of property belonging to citizens for the sake of the public good
in case of necessity; the ruler of a state also can dispose of the property of
a corporation for the sake of the public good in case of necessity.

> With respect to the advantage of the public the advantage of any
> corporation or community is considered as a private matter, just as
> the goods themselves of any corporation with respect to those of
> the whole state or commonwealth are considered as private goods,
> although in other respects they are and can be spoken of as public also.
> And hence is plain the difference we have just mentioned between
> eminent domain belonging to the ruler of the state over the goods of
> a corporation and the right otherwise belonging to him over them.
> Obviously, by virtue of eminent domain consideration is had for
> the public advantage or the advantage of the whole state, but by the
> remaining right only for the advantage of the corporation or of that
> group to which the goods belong. For example, let us assume that in
> some city there is a public granary, which must be destroyed for the
> purpose of saving the city. It is allowable to destroy that by virtue of
> eminent domain, since it is to the advantage of the commonwealth
> that the city should be defended in the best way.

§ 94. *Of the use of the property of a corporation*

Individuals who are in a corporation have the right to use and enjoy its
property, and the use is either open indifferently to the individuals, as shall
seem best to each one, or limited by definite conditions. For since the goods
of a corporation are in a mixed common holding of definite groups or communities, and since the ownership of the goods in a mixed common holding belongs to the corporation, but the use of them belongs indifferently
to the individuals, according of course as each one shall have need, the use
of the goods of the corporation also is open indifferently to the individuals
who are in it, as shall seem best to each. Which was the first point.

But if indeed the property does not admit of that use which shall seem
best to each, it is necessary that it should be limited by definite conditions

§ 92.

§ III, part 8,
Jus Nat.

§ 23, part 8,
Jus Nat.

N., § 92.

§ 88.

§ 129, part 2,
Jus Nat.

agreed upon between the individuals. And since the individuals can jointly dispose of the use of the goods of a corporation as of their own property according to their liking, they are able also to agree together for any reasons whatever as to the method by which the property is to be used and by this agreement to limit the use of the same by definite conditions. Therefore, since agreements must be observed, in this case the individuals are not able to use the property of a corporation except upon those conditions by which its use has been limited. Which was the second point.

§§ 118, 216, part 2, Jus Nat.

§ 789, part 3, Jus Nat.

So in forests fit for cutting which belong to some district, individuals can cut as great a supply of wood as they need, if indeed there shall be an adequate supply of wood. If, however, in the opposite case, it has been laid down by a definite provision, how much each one is allowed to cut, each one ought to be content with just that amount. But in a public theatre individual citizens may look on, as shall have seemed best to each. And in the same way individuals can hurl javelins on the field used for javelin practice, and bathe in the public bath.

§ 95. *Who are restrained from it*

No one can use the goods of a corporation who is outside the corporation, unless that be allowed him by the consent of the corporation. For the goods of a corporation are in the mixed common holding of the corporation. Therefore, since those who are in a mixed common holding may in their own right exclude all who are outside the corporation, in like manner no one can use the goods of a corporation who is outside the corporation. Which was the first point.

§ 88 h, and § 112, part 2, Jus Nat.

§ 130, part 2, Jus Nat.

Nevertheless, since all together can dispose of the use according to their liking, as we have just proved, it is not to be doubted that those who are in a corporation can by common consent grant to an outsider any use of the goods of a corporation. Which was the second point.

§ 94, Note 2.

So no one can feed cattle in a common pasture, or cut grain with a sickle in the common meadow, who is outside the corporation, unless that is allowed him by the corporation. But nothing stands in the way of granting this, since it concerns only those who now are in the corporation, that no one outside may feed his cattle in the common pasture or cut grain with the sickle in the common meadow.

§ 96. *Of the prohibition of the proper use of the property of a corporation*

No one who is in the corporation can without wrong be restrained from using the property of the corporation as it suits him. For suppose some one who is in the corporation is restrained from the use of the property of the corporation permitted by the provision which sets bounds to its use. Since the individuals who are in the corporation have the right of using and enjoying the property of the corporation, either in general, as shall seem best, or by that provision by which the use is limited, his right is taken from him without his consent. But one's right cannot be taken from him without his consent. Therefore no one who is in a corporation can be restrained from using the property of the corporation in the manner which seems best. Which was the first point.

Therefore, since if he is restrained, his right is taken from him, as demonstrated, consequently that happens contrary to his right, and since he who does what is contrary to his right, does him a wrong; if any one in a corporation is restrained from using the property of a corporation in a proper manner, that is a wrong to him. Which was the second point.

> So one cannot without wrong be restrained from cutting in a forest ready to cut the quantity of wood which the law allows to the individuals who are in the corporation, nor from cutting in accordance with his need, if it shall have been allowed generally to every one to cut that quantity of wood which he needs.

§ 97. *Whether a right in the property of a corporation can be transferred to another*

By nature nothing prevents any one from transferring, as he likes, the right which he has in the property of a corporation, to any other person whomsoever and in any way he pleases: it is still possible to reach a different agreement. For since any one can transfer any right whatsoever to any other person as he likes and in the way that shall seem best to him, nothing by nature prevents any one from transferring, as he likes, the right which he has in the property of a corporation, to any other person whomsoever, and in any way he pleases. Which was the first point.

§ 94.

§ 336, part 2, Jus Nat.

§ 239, part 1, Phil. Pract. Univ.

§ 859, part 1, Jus Nat.

§ 12, part 3, Jus Nat.

§ 11, part 3, Jus Nat.

But since what is allowed, we are not compelled to do, consequently § 170, part 1, Phil. Pract. Univ. it is not necessary that we should do it; it is left to our free will to do or not to do as shall have seemed best. Therefore, although nothing by § 118, part 1, Phil. Pract. Univ. nature prevents any one from transferring, as he likes, the right which he has in the property of a corporation, to any other person whomsoever and in any way he pleases, as shown above, nevertheless it can be agreed otherwise. Which was the second point.

So it is plain that by the law of nature a right in the property of a corporation can none the less be transferred to a stranger than to an associate, or another who is in the same corporation, as well by lucrative title, when given for nothing, as by onerous title, when granted on such terms that something should be given in exchange, both for a fixed time, and at will, either as a whole or in part. So if any one can pasture a hundred sheep in the common pasture, he can transfer to another the right to feed thirty, while he himself feeds seventy. Likewise he can sell or give to another hay due to him from the common meadow, or he can exchange it for something else. But if indeed it shall have been determined that he cannot feed more than a hundred sheep in the common pasture and none except his own; even if he have only fifty sheep, nevertheless he cannot grant to another permission to pasture fifty others in the same place, nor can he rent out his right of pasturing one hundred sheep. Moreover it is readily apparent in this case that the right of pasturing fifty sheep, which he does not use, by no means accrues to the others, who themselves in fact are not able to pasture more than a definite number.

§ 98. Of the ownership and use of public property

Public goods are in the ownership of the whole people, but the use of them belongs to the individuals without distinction, according of course as there shall have been need to any one of them. For the public goods have been brought under the mixed community holding of the whole §88. nation or people and have remained there. Therefore, since goods in a mixed community holding are in the ownership of the corporation, but the use of them belongs to the individuals without distinction, as of § 129, part 2, Jus Nat. course there shall have been the need of the same to each, public goods are in the ownership of the whole people, but the use of them belongs to the individuals without distinction, as of course each one shall have need of them.

So, for example, a river is in the ownership of the whole people, or is the property of the people, nevertheless any one of the people as he likes can sail or fish in it, unless the right of fishing shall have been appropriated and shall have come into the ownership of a certain private person, or corporation. But it is to be noted that the river is not to be confused with the water flowing in it. For although the river consists of the bed and the water, the water nevertheless is not looked at as flowing, but in so far as it fills the bed. Whence that is properly called running water which at any given time is in a certain part of the bed, while for instance it is being drawn, but it is not running water in so far as new water continually fills the same part of the bed. For in this regard it belongs to the river. And therefore this does not imply that running water is common, which is in the ownership of no one; while the river, which cannot be thought of without the water, belongs to the whole people, or is in the ownership of the same, by virtue of the present proposition, and because the use of the running water is open to all men, of whatsoever nation they are, while the use of the river is restricted to a definite nation. Obviously this is the difference between things common and things public, that the former are in the ownership of nobody, but the latter are in the ownership of some definite nation, the use of the former is common to all men, but the use of the latter is common only to some people. Likewise the difference is plain which exists between public goods and goods of a corporation. The public goods of course are in the ownership of the whole people and their use belongs in general to all, by virtue of the present proposition; but the goods of a corporation are in the ownership of some definite group or community, and their use is common to the individuals in that group or community. So public goods differ from the goods of a corporation, just as the more general from the special. But if you look at a certain group of men as a people, since each is a kind of corporation; by force of a principle of reasoning the things which we have proved of the goods of a corporation are easily applicable in their way to public goods.

§ 88.

§§ 88, 94.

§ 112, part 2,
Jus Nat.

§ 99. *Of the transfer of ownership of public property to the ruler of a state*

Since public property is in the ownership of the whole people; the people can transfer the ownership of public property to the ruler of the state, while all the use or at least some remains with the people.

§ 98.

§ 12, part 3,
Jus Nat.

So the ownership of a river can be transferred to the ruler of a state, while the use for sailing and fishing, for driving cattle to the river, and watering or washing them there remains with the people, or the right of fishing can be assigned to the ruler of the state, so that he can dispose of it, as seems best. In like manner the ownership of public roads can be transferred to the ruler of a state, their use for travelling and carrying remaining with the people.

§ 100. *Of the method of using public property*

Every one ought so to use public property that he may not in any manner impair the public use or that common to all. For the use of public property belongs to all without distinction, as of course each shall have need. If, therefore, any one so uses the public property that he in any way injures the public use common to all; this is contrary to the common right of all. Therefore, since no one ought to do anything contrary to the right of another, no one indeed ought so to use public property as to injure in any way the public use, or that common to all.

§ 88.

§ 239, part 1,
Phil. Pract. Univ.

§ 910, part 1,
Jus Nat.

So no one may build out a pier into the river, or build a mill on it, or draw the water into his own farm, because navigation is impaired, whether the river itself is navigable or makes another river navigable. To build in a public river is not allowed to a private individual for this reason also, that the bottom of the stream belongs to the whole people, and in it a private individual has no right, as to him belongs only a right to the use, not harmful to the other uses, which belong to the people. In like manner if any one desires to surround with a ditch a field adjacent to the public road, he ought to dig the ditch in his own land, nothing being taken from the public road, nor may he pile up a mass of earth, which he digs out, upon the public road.

§ 101. *Of the private right of fishing in a public stream*

If the right of fishing is subjected to private ownership, the river itself nevertheless remains public. For the uses of a public river, among which is the right of fishing, are such that one can exist without the other. Therefore nothing prevents any use from becoming private, while the rest remain common. Therefore, since the right of fishing can be subject to ownership, if the right of fishing is subjected to private ownership, it by no means follows from this that the river itself is under private ownership. Therefore if that alone is subjected to private ownership, the river itself remains public.

§ 216, part 2, Jus Nat.

§ 88.

Fish in a river are properly common property; but the right of catching them, that is, the right of fishing, can be subjected to ownership, and naturally it seems to have been acquired by the people with the river itself. And for this reason the right of fishing passes to the state just as does the river, and on this account fishing is related to the use of the river, just as is the taking of birds flying in the air to the use of the air, or, if it is done in the fields, you may relate it to the use of the fields. Therefore nothing prevents rivers from becoming public property, and the right of fishing remaining common, so that any one, even a foreigner, may fish in a public river. And in like manner the right of fishing can become private, the river itself remaining public. Fish of themselves do not belong to a river, just as birds do not belong to the air in which they fly, or to the fields on which they alight, nor do wild animals belong to the forests in which they wander about. Therefore the use of the river as such must be distinguished from that which it can have as regards things capable of appropriation in it.

§ 88.
§ 216, part 2, Jus Nat.

§ 88.

§ 102. *Of sovereignty and eminent domain over public property*

Sovereignty over public places and eminent domain over public property belong to the ruler of a state. Civil sovereignty which the ruler of a state exercises is properly the right to actions of individuals of the people, so far as concerns the common or public property of the state. And since the people have made a territory their own by taking possession of it, sovereignty must be exercised in every part of it, and in every place,

§ 42, part 8, Jus Nat.

§ 35, part 8, Jus Nat.

§ 175, part 2, Jus Nat.

whether the ownership has passed over into private hands or whether it has remained public. Therefore sovereignty belongs to the ruler of the state in every place which is to be considered as public property. Which was the first point.

But that eminent domain holds over public property is plain from the same argument by which we have proved that point concerning the property of a corporation. Which was the second point. §92.

So the ruler of the state has sovereignty over the rivers and public roads, in desert places, or those not yet under cultivation, although ownership of those places is with the people, and it is not held to have been transferred to the ruler of the state. For sovereignty always remains distinct from ownership nor are these two rights ever necessarily of themselves united. And so although ownership of public property may belong to the ruler of the state, nevertheless the sovereignty over public places does not therefore belong to him, which of itself is extended to all places, so far as in them individuals can do certain acts, the right to do which belongs to the one having sovereignty. But inasmuch as eminent domain is contained in this sovereignty itself as a potential part thereof, so it is not to be confused with the ownership of public property transferred from the people to the ruler of the state, and the things which by force of this he can do are rightly to be distinguished from those which are done by force of eminent domain, a thing which must be kept in mind, if you wish accurately to prove details and get at the true reasons for all those things which the ruler of the state does as concerns public property. For we desire that those things be drawn from the source whence they flow. But public rivers and public roads may be looked at from two standpoints, either in so far as men can do in them the things which have no bearing at all upon their use, for example, if any one should kill another in the river or on the road, or assault him with blows, or speak ill of him; or in so far as they serve a definite use, for example, sailing on the river, or driving cattle to it to be watered or washed, or walking or driving on the public road. With respect to the former, public rivers and public roads are properly speaking public places; but with respect to the latter, they are public property. And therefore over these the ruler of the state has sovereignty as over public places and the public places

§99.

§111, part 8, Jus Nat.

§99.

§88.

§166, part 8, Jus Nat.

belong to his territory. Since this distinction is based on the concepts
of property and sovereignty, by force of what has just been said, it is
properly made.

§ 495, part 1,
Jus Nat.

§ 103. *Of the effect of eminent domain over public property*

§ 102.

§ 111, part 8,
Jus Nat.

Since eminent domain over public property belongs to the ruler of the
state, since, moreover, by force of eminent domain disposition is made of
property for the public welfare in case of necessity, the ruler of the state
for the public welfare in case of necessity can dispose of public property,
as shall seem best to him.

So by power of eminent domain he can connect two navigable rivers by an artificial channel for the aid of commerce, or even direct the
waters of one stream into another, to make it navigable, even if there
should be some injury to the common use. And hence will be clearer
the difference which exists between eminent domain over public
property and ownership of the same, which is either with the people
or transferred to the ruler of the state.

§§ 98, 99.

§ 104. *Of the passing of civil laws concerning the use of*
public property and that of a corporation

The ruler of the state can pass laws concerning the use of public property and that of a corporation. For by civil law the ruler of a state can
make obligatory or forbidden what is allowed by nature; moreover he
can make a perfect obligation out of that which before was imperfect, as
is best for the purpose of the state, and if anything can be done in several
ways, he can direct that it be done in one way or another. Therefore,
since the use of public property and that of a corporation is allowed by
nature, and since that use can be exercised in several ways, as is plainly
proved before, the ruler of a state can make laws concerning the use of
public property and that of a corporation, by which a thing formerly
allowed may be made forbidden or obligatory, or by which an imperfect
obligation is made perfect and by which the use of that property is limited in a certain manner.

§ 977, part 8,
Jus Nat.

§ 978.

§§ 94, 99, and
§ 170, part 1,
Phil. Pract.
Univ.

So he can pass laws concerning fishing in rivers, for example, that
common fishing should be forbidden in a certain part of a river, or

that the smaller fish shall not be taken, and that one may not fish with nets, except such as allow the escape of fish not of a proper size, or that fishing should be forbidden at one time and allowed at another. Since still other methods may be given, by which civil laws may be made out of natural laws and which we have proved in the natural theory of the civil laws, besides those to which we have called attention in the discussion, it is plainly evident that very many laws can be passed, not only concerning fishing, but likewise concerning every use of any public property and that of a corporation. But while we speak of things public and those of a corporation, we are tarrying among generalities, and do not descend to particulars, which very often can be inferred from them by way of corollary, or without much difficulty be derived by proof. If we attempted to descend to public property and that of a corporation in detail, the treatment would be more extensive than the present plan demands. Likewise it ought not to seem strange, if we extend the legislative power to the use of things common or of those of the whole nation, or of some particular corporation. For that deals also with private ownership, or the use of private property. For all the actions of subjects are under the control of the civil power, so far as they are referable in any way to the purpose of the state, and laws are only the means through which the purpose of the state is attained, consequently they prescribe how subjects ought to direct their actions to the purpose of the state. And so it would be absurd, if any one should desire to remove the use of public property or that of a corporation from the legislative power, so that the free abuse of it would be left to any one, or that in its use the purpose of the state should be opposed.

§ 5, part 8, Jus Nat.

§ 105. *Of the prohibition of the proper use of public property*

No one of the people can be legally prohibited from using public property in a proper manner. This is shown in the same manner in which we have proved the same point in regard to the use of the property of a corporation.

§ 96.

So no one can be prohibited from going or driving on the public road or from sailing on a public river. We have already remarked above that public property can be made the property of a corporation, since even the whole people is a sort of a corporation.

Note, § 98.
§ 112, part 2, and § 5, part 8, Jus Nat.

§ 106. *Of a river separating two territories*

If a river separates two territories, the ownership and sovereignty over the river will belong to that nation which has first taken possession of it; ownership and sovereignty of either nation extend from either side to the middle of the river, if they take possession at the same time, and in a doubtful case this is presumed. But if the matter is decided by agreement, they must stand by it. For ownership is originally acquired by occupation, and if a certain nation occupies an uninhabited territory, it has sovereignty over it as soon as it occupies it. If then a river separates two territories and one nation gets possession of it first, ownership and sovereignty over the whole river belong to that nation. Which was the first point.

If two nations occupy at the same time the territories which a river separates, since the use of rivers serves the advantages of each, they are understood to have occupied this also at the same time. And therefore, since by nature the right of each is equal, the ownership and sovereignty of either nation extend from either side to the middle of the stream, as shown above. Which was the second point.

If it does not appear whether one nation has taken possession of the river before the other, or whether anything has been laid down by stipulations concerning the ownership and sovereignty over the river, that is presumed which is the most natural. Therefore, since nature gives precedence to no nation over another, moreover since by natural equity it is especially fitting that ownership and sovereignty reach from either side just to the middle, this is presumed in this doubtful case. Which was the third point.

Finally, since agreements must be observed, whatever shall have been determined by agreements concerning the ownership and sovereignty over a river must be observed. Which was the fourth point.

Since our times are very far away from the first occupation, the law of nations existing at the present time will scarcely be anything other than the stipulative. To be sure a case can be conceived, in which nations dwelling on either side of the same river have left the river in its original common holding, or have made it the common property of either nation, but since either case is scarcely consistent with

§ 178, part 2, Jus Nat.

§ 85.

§§ 78, 81, part 1, Jus Nat.

§ 94, part 1, Jus Nat., and § 2.

§ 789, part 2, Jus Nat.

sovereignty, as is easily understood, it will hardly be possible, and is easily considered as morally impossible. It more usually happens that a river is without ownership than without sovereignty, and positive common holding so far as regards the use of the river more usually happens than joint exercise of sovereignty. But since in either case very troublesome difficulties easily arise, the nations themselves take pains to make definite arrangements by agreements with each other. But it is evident, whether a river belongs to a single nation or the ownership and sovereignty of either extend from either side to the middle of it, that concerning the use of the river and the exercise of sovereignty over it various arrangements can be made, which then become matters of stipulative law.

§23.

§ 107. *Of the abandoned channel of a river*

If the river which separates two territories shall have left its channel and broken through another way, a nation retains the ownership and sovereignty over the channel which it had in the river, and the ownership and sovereignty extend from either side to the middle of the channel, if they extended to the middle line of the river. For the natural channel abandoned by a river flowing in another direction belongs to the one by whom it had been before occupied. Therefore if the ownership and sovereignty in a river which separates two territories belonged to one nation, when the channel is abandoned by the river, the ownership and sovereignty of this nation remains. Which was the first point.

§ 372, part 2, Jus Nat.

And in the same manner it is evident that the ownership and sovereignty of either nation ought to extend to the middle line of the channel, if before they extended to the middle line of the river. Which was the second point.

Grotius gives this reason, that the intention of the people must be considered to have been that if the river shall cease to be, then each should hold what it had held. But it does not seem to be necessary for us to seek a reason far away. For since a river consists of the channel and flowing water, the nation has such a right in the channel as it has in the river. Therefore, even if the river flowing in another direction should leave the whole channel and consequently should vanish so that there would be no river any longer where it had been before, nevertheless

De Jure Belli ac Pacis, lib. 2, c. 3, § 17.

there is no reason why this should destroy the right in the part which still exists. Indeed if a building burns, your right in the foundation is not taken away by its destruction, but you retain ownership in it. The case is certainly the same if a river abandons its entire bed.

§ 108. *Of territories having the river as their boundary*

§ 363, part 2, Jus Nat.

If the territories separated by a river have the river as their boundary, the nations on either side have the right of alluvium.[6] This is plain from the same proof which we have given in regard to land having a river as boundary.

§ 585, part 2, Jus Nat.

§§ 357, 358, part 2, Jus Nat.

Of course the land which is added by alluvium to either territory belongs to the territory to which it is added. The loss, which the nation dwelling on the opposite bank suffers, arises from the destruction of its own property, nor can it be said that the nation which has the right of alluvium is made the richer at the expense of the other, a thing which is opposed to the law of nature. See what we have noted concerning that point.

§ 109. *Whether any change is made in the right in a river by alluvium*

§ 108.

§ 362, part 2, Jus Nat.

Since nations whose territories have the river as their boundary have the right of alluvium, the right which they have in the river is not changed by alluvium; since the river, as the natural boundary separating their territories, does not disappear but remains, on which ever side the alluvium increases or decreases the territory. Therefore, if a river shall have belonged wholly to one nation, it retains the entire ownership and sovereignty after the alluvium is made; but if the ownership and sovereignty extend to the middle line from either side, they still will extend to the middle line of the river after the alluvium is made.

In a doubtful case territories which are separated by some river are presumed to have the river as their boundary, since for marking their boundaries nothing is better than that which is not easily crossed. And

6. Alluvium is land that has been formed by sediments deposited by a river or other body of water, usually over a long period of time. Alluvial rights refer to land of this kind.

those things which we have said of rivers are likewise understood of mountains which divide territories, but not with the same pertinence of forests, especially open ones, where the matter must be determined by agreements.

§ 110. *Of the building of a bridge on a river, belonging half and half to neighbouring nations*

If a river separating two territories belongs half and half to the nations dwelling on either side of the river, a bridge cannot be built upon the river without the consent of each nation, for since the owner by the right which he has in the property excludes all others who have not the right of ownership in it, a nation which has ownership only of half of a river, the other half of which belongs to the neighbouring nation, cannot build a bridge. If then a bridge is to be built upon the river, that cannot be done except with the consent of each nation.

§ 120, part 2,
Jus Nat.

The same is plain concerning any other thing which ought to be done in regard to the half which is understood to belong to the neighbouring nation, as e.g. the construction of a dam across the river for the purpose of building a mill.

§ 111. *Of the right of anticipation in the use of public property or that of a corporation*

If public property or that of a corporation does not admit of simultaneous use by all, he who is in fact using it cannot be deprived of this use by another, but the other ought to wait until the use shall have been ended. For if public property or that of a corporation does not admit of simultaneous use, it is impossible for all who have the right of use, to use the property at one and the same time. But he who is in fact using it is exercising his right. Therefore, since no man has the right of preventing another from using his own right, no one can prevent him from using it who is in fact enjoying the use; consequently although the right of using the thing belongs to one, nevertheless he ought to wait until the use of the other shall have been ended.

§ 180, part 1,
Phil. Pract. Univ.

Thus if any one is in fact drawing water from a common well, which is the property of a corporation, or shall have been the first to start to draw it, you cannot put him away so as to draw it first yourself, but you must wait until he has drawn the water and made place for you. In like manner if any one is in fact fishing in a public river, you cannot prevent him from fishing in that place, but you ought to wait until he has ended his fishing, if you wish to fish in the same place.

§ 112. *The same further considered*

If public property or that of a corporation does not admit of a use except such as consists in consumption, that is, if the use consists in the taking of things which are consumed in the use, he who is in fact taking the thing or is starting first to take it, cannot be restrained from taking it. For if the use consists in the taking of things of the sort which are consumed in the use, it is impossible that several who have the right of using take the same thing. Therefore then, as appears before, he who in fact is taking the thing or is starting first to take it, cannot be restrained from taking it, so that you may take it.

§ 111.

Thus if he who has the right of cutting timber in a forest ripe for cutting, is in fact cutting it, or is coming first to cut, you cannot prevent him from cutting this timber for the reason that you prefer to cut the same. The same thing is understood, if any one cuts grain with a sickle in a common meadow. The same law holds as in the original common holding. For the use of public property and of the property of a corporation, since it is common to the people as a whole and to the individuals of a corporation, imitates the use of things in the original common holding, nay, is in harmony with it.

§§ 35, 36, part 2, Jus Nat.

§ 88.

§ 113. *Laws and agreements to be made concerning the use and preservation of public property and that of a corporation*

The ruler of the state can pass laws concerning the use of public property and that of a corporation and concerning the preservation of the same, as far as this shall be to the advantage of the people or the corporation, and concerning the use of the property of a corporation and its preservation those who belong to the corporation can also arrange by agreements. For the use of public property pertains to the common good of the state, and since corporations belong to the state, the use of them also pertains

§ 9, part 8, Jus Nat.

to the good of the state. Therefore, since civil laws prescribe the means   § 88 h.
by which the good of the state is obtained, and legislative power belongs   § 969, part 8,
to the ruler of the state, the ruler of the state can make laws concerning   Jus Nat.
the use of public property and that of a corporation. Which was the first   § 813, part 8,
point.   Jus Nat.

But since the use cannot continue unless the substance of the thing
is preserved, it is thus plainly evident that the ruler of the state can pass
laws concerning preservation of public property and that of a corporation. Which was the second point.

And because public property ought to serve the advantage of the whole
state, and the property of a corporation the advantage of the corporation,   § 495, part 1, Jus
such laws ought to be passed concerning the use of public property and   Nat., and § 88 h.
that of the corporation as will be to the advantage of the people or of the
corporation. Which was the third point.

Finally, since the use of the property of a corporation belongs to the   § 94.
corporation, moreover, since any one can dispose of his own property as   § 118, part 2,
he likes, those who belong to a corporation can agree together concern-   Jus Nat.
ing the use of the property of the corporation, and that such use can be   § 698, part 3,
enjoyed, they can agree concerning the preservation of the same, and   Jus Nat.
since they are not able to bind themselves one to the other except by a   § 393, part 3,
promise, they can enter into agreements. Which was the fourth point.   Jus Nat.
                                                                               § 788, part 3,
                                                                               Jus Nat.

> In the particular case particular reasons are given why laws are to
> be passed, and of what sort, concerning the use and preservation of
> public property and of that of a corporation. But they are taken from
> general public law, which we have set forth in the eighth part of "The
> Law of Nature." So it is plain that it ought to be the concern of the
> ruler of a state that each should be saved from the wrong of others.   § 532, part 8,
> Therefore, if it is to be feared that in the use of public property or   Jus Nat.
> that of a corporation one may easily wrong another, the use must
> be limited by a law by which care is taken that wrong may not be
> done thereby, and a penalty sufficient for restraining a transgression   § 585, part 8,
> of the law must be added to the same. Here those same points are to   Jus Nat.
> be observed which we have proved in general concerning the theory of
> civil law or the method of rendering civil laws effective in accordance   § 966, part 8,
> with natural laws. In like manner the ruler of a state is also bound to   Jus Nat.
> care for a corporation for the future. Therefore he ought to provide   Cap. 5, part 8,
                                                                               Jus Nat.

lest anything may be done in the use at present which may injure the use in the future. If those who belong to the corporation at present should be negligent in preserving its property, they can be compelled by force to do those things which are necessary for the preservation of the thing and not to do those things which are detrimental to it. So if any one shall have been allowed to cut as great an amount of timber as he shall have desired in the forest ready to cut; for the sake of preserving the forests the ruler of the state can prescribe by law how much he may cut yearly and lay down those rules which are necessary for increasing the production of timber. Such things likewise could be determined by agreement provided only that all were sufficiently ready to do those things which are in harmony with natural equity and did not prefer their present advantage to the future welfare of posterity. Therefore civil laws ought to supplement the defect of the agreements.

§§ 395, 982, part 8, Jus Nat.

§ 114. *At whose expense the property of a corporation is to be preserved*

The property of the corporation is to be preserved at the expense of the corporation. Since a corporation is a number of men associated for a definite purpose, and therefore consists of individuals, the corporation continues even if those withdraw who now compose it and others take their places, consequently the use of property of a corporation belongs not only to present members but also to future members, so that as soon as any one comes into the corporation he has also the use. In order therefore that a property can have a use for future time also, the property must undoubtedly be preserved. Therefore, since it is plain of itself that a thing has to be preserved by the one who has the use and who cannot use the thing unless its substance is preserved, in order that its future use may not be prejudiced, the property of the corporation must be preserved at the expense of the corporation.

§ 112, part 2, Jus Nat.

§ 489, part 8, Jus Nat.

§ 494, part 8, Jus Nat.

§ 94.

The property of a corporation with respect to the entire state is considered as private property. Therefore since your private property has to be preserved at your expense so that you can have its use, and it would be absurd to pretend that it should be preserved at another's expense, for example, the state's, so also the property of a corporation is to be preserved at the expense of the corporation, nor can it be pretended that it should be preserved at the public expense of the entire people, or of any others who are outside of the corporation, unless there are adequate reasons why the benefit is sought by others, and if ever this shall have been necessary, the ruler of the state can change it to an absolute obligation.

§ 977, part 8, Jus Nat., and § 26, part 4, Jus Nat.

§ 115. *Of the repair of the property of a corporation*

Since the property of a corporation is to be preserved at the expense of the corporation, moreover since it cannot be preserved, unless it is restored to a better condition, when that is necessary, property is to be repaired at the expense of the corporation.

§ 114.

> For example, if a fountain in the market-place from which all who dwell in the city are allowed to draw water, is going to ruin with age, or some accident happens which renders it useless, it must be repaired at the common expense of the residents. And this is held to be done, if the municipal magistrate, who has charge of the property of the city, makes expenditures of those funds which the residents contribute for that purpose. But in the repair of the property of a corporation, the labour employed in it is also to be charged to the expense account. It is the same of course, whether those who belong to the corporation themselves perform the work, or whether they hire the services of others at a fixed price; for in the former case they save the expense to themselves.

§ 116. *Of imposing taxes for the benefit of the property of a corporation*

Since the property of a corporation is to be preserved and repaired at the expense of the corporation, the individuals who belong to the corporation ought to contribute proportionately to the preservation and repair of the property of the corporation, either ordinarily at a definite time or extraordinarily whenever the usual contribution shall not have been sufficient, consequently it is allowable to impose taxes for that purpose, and since what is contributed for that purpose must also be expended for the same, a thing which is evident of itself, those who control the property

§ 114.
§ 115.

§ 159, part 1, Phil. Pract. Univ.

of a corporation are bound to render an account of the administration to the corporation or even to the ruler of the state.

It is better for the individuals to contribute a moderate amount at a definite time rather than to contribute much in case of emergency. Taxes, therefore, imposed for the benefit of the property of a corporation are in accord with perfective law.[7] Moreover, it is quite evident with regard to the whole state that these taxes must be looked at as if they were private wealth, over which the entire people, consequently the ruler of the city, has no right, except in so far as he ought to take care that the money be rightly managed.

§ 193, part 1,
Phil. Pract.
Univ.

§ 395, part 8,
Jus Nat.

§ 117. *At whose expense the public property is to be preserved and repaired*

Public property is to be preserved and repaired at public expense. Since the use of public property belongs generally to all who are of the people, in like manner it is plain that the property must be preserved at the public expense, and it follows directly from this that public property is to be repaired also at public expense, a thing which we have proved of the property of a corporation, and this we have taken from that source.

§ 98.

§ 114.
§ 115.

Of course the one who has the use of a thing is also bound to preserve and repair it so that he can have the use.

§ 118. *Of taxes to be imposed for the benefit of public property*

Since public property is preserved and repaired at public expense, the entire people ought to contribute to the preservation and repair of public property, as shall seem best to the ruler of the state, and what is contributed to that end must also be expended for that purpose, nay more, the ruler of the state, for the purpose of lessening the taxes, may exact from the subjects the labours necessary for preservation.

§ 117.

§§ 777, 778,
part 8, Jus Nat.
§ 934, part 8,
Jus Nat.

7. A perfective law of nature, according to Wolff, is that "which imposes an obligation to do something that is better than another thing and is to be preferred to it." Wolff, *Philosophia practica universalis,* pt. I, chap. ii, §193.

It is usually the duty of the ruler of the state to provide for those things that pertain to the public good. If then some defect is found therein, it must be attributed to his negligence. But if he expends for another purpose the things which are contributed for the sake of preserving and repairing public property, that is to be counted as bad management. If contributions are made simply for the benefit of the public, in order of course that the necessary expenses for proper management of the state may not be lacking, it is quite plain that the expenses are to be borne from the public treasury.

§ 119. *Of the paying of the impost by those travelling on the public road*

Since the people in general ought to contribute to the preservation and repair of public property, moreover, since public roads are public property, and since he who in fact enjoys the use should be held especially to contribute, in order that he may be able to enjoy it, and since that which is paid as toll is called impost; it is allowable to exact an impost from those who travel on the public road, which impost, since it must be expended for that purpose for which it was imposed, must be expended upon the preservation and repair of the public roads.

§ 118.

§ 88.

§ 929, part 8, Jus Nat.

§ 934, part 8, Jus Nat.

See those things which we have discussed elsewhere concerning that matter. Here also is to be borne in mind what we have already noted with reference to the preceding proposition.

Note, § 934, part 8, Jus Nat. Note, § 118.

§ 120. *Of the use of the sea*

The use of the open sea consists in navigation and fishing, in occupation of things found on the beach near the shores, as shells, gems and in some places amber, and in extraction of salt from the sea-water. This is sufficiently plain from experience, so that it does not need further proof.

The former use of the sea is absolute, but the latter contingent. And he who has either the absolute or contingent use can exercise it without impairment of the substance.

§ 121. *Whether it is allowable to subject the sea to private ownership*

§ 120.

§ 195, part 2,
Jus Nat.

§ 201, part 2,
Jus Nat.

§ 199, part 2,
Jus Nat.

Since the use of the open sea consists in navigating and fishing, and because you navigate on the sea or fish in it, you do not therefore interfere with the possibility of another navigating or fishing, if he needs to navigate or fish; the open sea is a thing of unlimited use, consequently since no one is able to acquire ownership in property absolutely natural, subject to unlimited use, and no one is allowed to bring it under his ownership, no nation either is allowed to bring under its ownership the open sea, even if that were possible, nor can it acquire ownership of it without contravention of natural law. And the same thing in like manner is understood of several nations which cannot jointly subject the open sea to their ownership, consequently no nation is able to subject any great part of the ocean or open sea to its ownership. And since property is subjected to ownership for the sake of use, no nation can subject to its ownership the right of navigating and fishing in the open sea.

§ 156, part 1,
Phil. Pract.
Univ.

Grotius rightly calls this a moral reason, because it is derived from justice, which is a moral power, and is opposed to the physical power of action, which indeed the former presupposes, but which, on the other hand, is not presupposed in the latter, since you are able to do many things which nevertheless you are not allowed to do. So theft is an act physically possible, a thing which is unknown to none, nevertheless it is not morally possible, because one is not allowed to commit theft.

§ 122. *Whether any one can forbid navigation and fishing in the open sea*

§ 121.

Since the right of navigating and fishing in the open sea may be subjected to the ownership of no one, no one has the right of preventing another from navigating and fishing in the open sea, consequently it is allowable for any nation as it pleases to navigate and fish.

§ 119, part 2,
Jus Nat.

Of course each right ought to remain common for the entire human race, so that any man may use either, whenever and as often as he pleases. It is the right of an owner to exclude others from that right which he himself enjoys. But he who does not have an especial right cannot exclude others from it, much less from a common right.

§ 123. *Whether it is a wrong to restrain one from the use*

If one nation seeks to restrain another from the use of navigating and fishing in the open sea, it does a wrong to such other. For every nation is allowed as it pleases to navigate and fish in the open sea. If then some nation should seek to restrain another nation from the use of navigating and fishing, this is contrary to the right of such nation. Therefore, since he does a wrong to another, who does anything which is contrary to the right of the other, if any nation seeks to restrain another from the use of navigating and fishing in the open sea, it does a wrong to the other.

§ 122.

§ 239, part 1,
Phil. Pract. Univ.

§ 859, part 1,
Jus Nat.

Nor do we draw our conclusions from those things which either have been done in the past, or to-day are done. For the law of nature has a reason within itself, nor are the acts of nations a rule of law, but rather is the law a rule for the acts.

§ 124. *Whether that use gives just cause of war*

Since a nation which desires to restrain another from the use of navigating or fishing in the sea, does it a wrong, and since a wrong is a just cause of war, if any nation desires to restrain another from the use of navigating and fishing in the open sea, the latter nation has just cause of war.

§ 123.

§ 1109, part 1,
Jus Nat.

Of course the nation which wages war defends its right against another, which is striving to take that right from it without its consent. Therefore by nature the right of war belongs to the former against the latter.

§ 1104, part 1,
Jus Nat.

§ 125. *On whose part then a war is unjust*

On the other hand, because a nation, which does not desire to allow another nation free use of navigating and fishing in the open sea, does it a wrong, if by force of arms the nation seeks to restrain the other from this use, it does not have just cause of war. Therefore, since a war is unjust the cause of which is not just but unjust, if any nation desires to restrain

§ 123.

§ 1109, part 1,
Jus Nat.

§ 1110, part 1,
Jus Nat.

another by force of arms from the use of navigating and fishing in the open sea, the war which it brings upon the other is unjust.

One acts contrary to the right of nations, who seeks by force of arms to claim for himself the right to navigate and fish in the open sea to the exclusion of other nations, since, as it is to the advantage of nations to protect this right, it is allowable for any nations to oppose that action, nay more, since nations are understood to have united into a supreme state, they are bound by nature to protect the same. The laws of nations provide for the common welfare, and so he who injures that commits a wrong against all nations.

§ 10.

§ 12.

§ 126. *Of stipulative right in the use of the sea*

One nation can agree with another not to navigate or fish in the sea, or within certain limits in the open sea. For since the right belongs to any nation to navigate or fish in the open sea, wherever it pleases, if any nation agrees with another nation that the latter shall not navigate or fish in the sea, or within certain limits in the open sea, the latter renounces its right in favour of the former. Therefore, since by nature any one can renounce his special right, one nation can agree with another not to navigate or fish in the sea, or within certain limits in the open sea.

§ 122.

§ 103, part 3, Jus Nat.

§ 118, part 3, Jus Nat.

The exclusion therefore of any nation from free use of navigation or fishing in the open sea can be only a matter of stipulative right; when such agreements are lacking, exclusion has no place. Since navigation and fishing in the sea are matters of pure will, and the right itself one of pure power, moreover since rights of pure power cannot be barred by prescription, even if you shall have used them a very long time ago, or even never before; one nation cannot by prescription bar the right of another to navigate or fish in the sea, although the latter has never before navigated or fished in the sea. But the situation is different if one nation shall have prevented another from navigating or fishing, or compelled the other to refrain therefrom, and there has been compliance with the prohibition or order, with adequate evidence of consent. For the loss of the right rests in fact on tacit agreement, by which the same is tacitly renounced in favour of the one prohibiting or ordering, and consequently the nation, which obeys the prohibition or order,

§ 23.

§ 76.

§ 78.

§ 78.

§ 103, part 3, Jus Nat., and § 660, part 1, Phil. Pract. Univ.

binds itself to the one prohibiting or ordering, that it will not seek to use the right against the other, and the latter acquires the right not to allow it to use the right against itself.

§ 104, part 3, Jus Nat.

§ 127. *Whether the sea is of itself subject to occupation*

The open sea is of itself not subject to occupation. For let us suppose that the open sea is occupied by any nation, consequently that it can be subjected to its ownership. Since the right belongs to an owner to restrain any one not the owner from every act permitted by virtue of ownership, and not to allow that any other one may do anything without his consent which is allowable for him to do by virtue of ownership, and thus use his property; a nation which has occupied the open sea, or even a great part of it, is understood not to allow any other nation, or any one from any other nation, to navigate or fish at his will in the open sea or in a great part of it. But it is impossible to compel all nations, or any one from another nation, not to do whatever he wishes to, without the consent of the other, anywhere in the sea; a thing which no one can call in question, provided only he considers everything with sufficient care. Therefore it is inconsistent that any nation should have ownership in the sea, consequently the open sea is not among those things, the ownership of which can be acquired by occupation, therefore of itself it is not capable of occupation.

§ 175, part 2, Jus Nat.

§ 121, part 2, Jus Nat.
§ 136, part 2, Jus Nat.

§ 120.

It is absurd for any one to claim a right for himself which he cannot defend. Moreover, this reason why the sea does not belong to the category of things capable of occupation is a physical reason, not to be confused with the moral reason which prevents occupation, even if it were physically possible, of which we have spoken before. But do not persuade yourself that a nation can protect its ownership of the sea by the aid of a fleet or by forbidding descent to the sea from the shores adjacent to your territory; for it is not possible that all nations in general and any one from any nation anywhere can be restrained from navigating the sea or fishing in it anywhere. To act with an armed force against one nation or another, or to prevent access to the sea anywhere on the sea or at one place, is not the same as to exclude all nations in general from the use of the sea. The sea cannot be inhabited

§ 121.

as is the land; the case is quite different, in that the land can be divided
among nations and can all become subject to occupation, nor does the
sea have uses of the same sort as the land for individual men, of which

§ 120.

it is impossible to deprive them. The use of the sea is restricted to very
narrow limits, nor do all nations, much less single individuals, need
it, or if they should need it, nevertheless they are compelled for more
than one reason to refrain from it. Therefore the reasoning from land
to sea is not valid.

§ 128. *How far certain parts of the sea are subject to occupation*

Parts of the sea can be occupied by nations which dwell near it, so far as
they are able to protect the same. This is understood of bays and straits.
For the use in the parts of the sea of this sort near the shores, which
consists in fishing and collection of things produced in the sea, and not
in navigation alone, is not inexhaustible, nor is the use which consists in
navigation always innocent, since the sea furnishes a means of protection
to maritime countries, and therefore it is to the advantage of the inhabitants that no one should be allowed to remain there with armed ships.
Therefore there is no moral reason to prevent them from being occupied.

§§ 198, 199,
part 2, Jus Nat.

And since others can be excluded from this same use, and can be forbidden to remain there, there is according to the hypothesis no physical

§ 120, part 2,
Jus Nat.

reason that prevents them from being subjected to ownership. Since,
therefore, for the sake of advantage nations have occupied portions of
the earth, just as individuals have occupied farms, for the same reason
it cannot be doubted that nations dwelling on the shores of the sea can
occupy portions of the sea, so far as they can protect their ownership over
the same. Which was the first proposition.

It is plain for the same reason that the same thing is true concerning
bays and straits. Which was the second proposition.

Bays are recesses hollowed out in the earth like the backwaters of a
river in a private estate, and a strait is a narrow place in the sea. Hence

De Jure Belli ac
Pacis, lib. 2, c.
3, § 8.

the bay is open to the high sea, from which it enters the land, but it
has no exit; but a strait is open at either end. Grotius restricts the occupation of parts of the sea to the distance which can be seen from the

lands which nations have occupied. But no reason for this limitation is given, and it seems purely arbitrary. For the reason of the occupation is the advantage of the one occupying, so far as that is not limited by the necessary use of others, and it is absurd to desire to occupy more than can be protected, as will be perfectly plain from proof of the present proposition. How far the sea is subject to occupation, or can be subjected to ownership, presents no difficulty at all, provided only you should consider the matter without prejudice and partisan feeling. For there are no other reasons than those which are to be considered in the occupation of parts of the land by nations. If the sea could be inhabited as the land is, there would be no difference at all between occupation of tracts of the sea and of the land. And occupation of portions of the sea, as restricted in the proposition above, is altogether the same as occupation of rivers, so that, if any one presumes to deny that the sea can be thus occupied, he ought not to allow even the occupation of rivers. And hence Grotius says pertinently, in the passage cited, that bays and straits can be occupied as in the case of rivers. Hence two peoples who have a bay and a strait between them, can extend their ownership and sovereignty to its middle line, or in the bay according to their proportional share of the territory.

§ 180, part 2, Jus Nat.

§ 106.

§ 129. *Whether sovereignty over parts of the sea may be acquired at the same time*

Since nations occupying unclaimed lands acquire sovereignty over them together with ownership, moreover since certain parts of the sea can be occupied the same as lands, if any nation occupies a certain part of the sea, it acquires sovereignty over it together with ownership.

§ 85.

§ 128.

The right of restraining others from use of the sea cannot be attributed to the civil sovereignty, for this arises from ownership and is not comprehensible without it, although the civil sovereignty protects ownership, and consequently any rights arising from it.

§ 121, part 2, Jus Nat.

§§ 4, 32, part 8, Jus Nat.

§ 130. *Whether those parts belong to the territory*

Because the places over which a nation, or the ruler of a state, has sovereignty belong to the territory of the state, moreover since a nation, or

§ 166, part 8, Jus Nat.

the ruler of a state, has sovereignty over the occupied parts of the sea, the occupied parts of the sea belong to the territory of that nation which has occupied them.

Of course the situation is the same here as in the case of rivers, which, not less than the lands, belong to the territory.

§ 131. *What sort of a right in them belongs to the ruler of the state*

§ 130.

§ 167, part 8, Jus Nat.

Since the occupied parts of the sea belong to the territory of that nation which has occupied them, such a right belongs to the ruler of the state in the occupied parts of the sea as he has in his territory, and consequently those who frequent such parts of the sea are subject to the same laws as those who inhabit the lands or spend time there, including foreigners who have been allowed to enter.

If any prince had sovereignty over the whole ocean or a great part of it, he would have the same right over the whole ocean or part of it, as he has over his territory. But to aspire to a right of this sort is undoubtedly a foolish ambition.

§ 132. *Of laws imposed on the sea*

§ 131.

§ 813, part 8, Jus Nat.

§ 812, part 8, Jus Nat.

§ 969, part 8, Jus Nat.

Since in the occupied parts of the sea the ruler of the state has such a right as he has in his own territory, moreover, since in his own territory legislative power belongs to him, so that he can pass such laws as shall seem advantageous to the state, the ruler of the state can pass laws for the occupied parts of the sea, such as seem best to pass for the advantage of the state.

Therefore he can pass laws not only concerning the use of the sea and those waters which appertain to it, but also concerning the actions of those who dwell in them for any reason or sail through them, whether they are subjects or foreigners. Nay more, laws can be passed for the sea which differ from those which are passed for the land, in regard to the same actions. So offences committed on the sea can be punished more severely than the same offences committed on land.

§ 133. *Whether those born on the sea have the right of native born*

Those who are born of citizen parents either on the unoccupied sea, or an occupied part of it, are natives. For those who are citizens remain such, wherever they may live for the purpose of any business, consequently they do not lose the right of citizenship for the reason that they are spending time on the unoccupied sea or on an occupied part of it. Therefore, since a state is preserved through the children who are born of citizens, the children through their birth become members of the state, consequently citizens; and since therefore those are natives who are citizens of that region in which they dwell, those who are born of citizen parents either on the unoccupied sea, or on an occupied part of it, are natives.

§ 6, part 8, Jus Nat.

§ 411, part 8, Jus Nat.

Here are to be reconsidered the things which we have elsewhere discussed. As of course a citizen does not lose his right as native born, because he is absent from the territory on account of some business; so he does not lose the right of sharing this same right with his children by their birth, and consequently even when absent from the territory in some other place he shares it with his children when born. If it shall have been decided otherwise by some statute of a people, that is merely a civil enactment and is contrary to natural law, which decrees from the very nature of a state that children have the status which their parents have. That controversies have arisen concerning that matter, means nothing else than that generally by starting from different points of view no decision is reached. Disorderly concepts become the causes both of mistakes and also of confusion.

§§ 411, 414, part 8, Jus Nat.

§ 134. *What naturalization is*

Naturalization is the conferring of the right of a native upon an immigrant or foreigner. And he is said to be naturalized on whom the right of a native born is conferred. And so a naturalized citizen by a fiction of the law is considered as born of citizen parents, or native-born parents.

So that illustrious astronomer Dominicus Cassini, an Italian by nationality, was naturalized in France, and his descendants are now natives, as though they derived descent from French parents. Of course when one has received the right of a native born, certain rights belong to him as a native which strangers or foreigners do not enjoy. And it is quite plain that it depends upon the will of the people, consequently on that of the ruler of the state, who has the right of the people, or exercises it, whether or not he desires to make a stranger, or a foreigner, a participant in those rights which depend upon native birth. Moreover, although the rights of the native born have been conferred by the free will of the people, or of him who has the right of the people, the method nevertheless of acquiring the same through native birth, as far as the law of nature protects rights of that sort, is considered natural, and nature assigns them to those who in accordance with the laws of the country are born with capacity for them. But it is an extraordinary method of acquirement, for the rights to be conferred upon any one contrary to law; in order that the law may be kept intact, it is assumed that one is born of citizen parents, who is not so born. And so the law is not annulled, but is replaced by a legal fiction.

§§ 34, 42, part 8, Jus Nat.

§ 135. *Of the obligation of a nation to care for its own self, and of the love of country*

Every nation ought to care for its own self, and every person in a nation ought to care for his nation. For every nation represents a single person, and therefore to it are to be applied those things which by the law of nature are enjoined upon individuals, and in this the necessary law of nations consists. And so, since every person ought to care for his own self, every nation also ought to care for its own self. Which was the first point.

§ 2.
§ 4.
§ 607, part 1, Jus Nat.
§ 607, part 1, Jus Nat.

For if a state is established, consequently if a certain nation arises, individuals bind themselves to the whole because they wish to promote the common good, consequently the happiness of their nation. Therefore, since he cares for another who has the fixed and enduring desire to promote the other's happiness, or to do everything that he can that the other may be happy or to prevent him from becoming unhappy, the individuals who belong to a nation ought to care for their nation. Which was the second point.

§ 5, part 8, Jus Nat.
§ 9, part 8, Jus Nat.
§ 28, part 8, Jus Nat.
§ 617, part 1, Jus Nat.

Each kind of love is referable to the love of country as to its source. For he who loves his country, gains pleasure from the happiness of his country, and this pleasure itself is a stimulus to deserve well of his country. But if individuals are devoted to the happiness of their

§ 634, Psych. Emp.

nation, the nation loves itself and therefore also cares for itself, so that then it must be attributed to love of country if a nation cares for itself. Scarcely any nation exists which has not considered love of country an especially noble virtue, and therefore we see those are excessively praised by all, who have proved that they love their country, and their deeds are extolled, by which they have deserved well of their country.

§ 136. *Of not harming one's country*

Since any one who belongs to a nation ought to love his nation, therefore ought to take every care that she should not be made unhappy, no one ought to do anything by which he can in any way injure his nation.

§ 135.

§ 617, part 1, Jus Nat.

§ 722, part 1, Jus Nat.

Those who harm their country deservedly incur the reprobation of all good men. For this is ingratitude, the basest vice. There is no one indeed who is not loaded with many blessings, because he lives in the state, consequently he owes it to his nation that he enjoys those blessings. Therefore we ought to have a feeling of gratitude toward our country; and on this account love of country is especially becoming to humanity, and, on the other hand, he seems devoid of human nature who hates his country.

§ 137. *What domicile is*

Domicile is defined to be a fixed dwelling in some place with intention of remaining there permanently. In the native vernacular it is called *die Behausung* [the housing]. Since for establishing a domicile the intention is required of remaining permanently, a domicile is not understood to be fixed, unless the intention of remaining permanently is adequately declared, either expressly or impliedly, therefore one does not have domicile in a place where he lives for the purpose of some temporary business. Nevertheless, since any one is allowed to change his intention as long as he does nothing contrary to the right of another, a domicile can be changed, that is, it is not of itself unchangeable.

§ 377, part 2, Jus Nat.

So an ambassador, although he lives for many, nay, very many, years with his family at some court, and possesses his own home in the city, does not nevertheless on this account have a domicile there. Likewise, he who for the purpose of trade dwells anywhere for a long time does not nevertheless have a domicile there, but remains a foreigner.

§ 138. *Of natural and acquired domicile*

Natural domicile is defined as that which any one acquires by birth, in the place where his father has domicile. That is called acquired domicile which any one has established for himself of his own will. Therefore any one is supposed to retain his natural domicile as long as he has established none for himself by his own will, or has not abandoned it.

§ 139. *Of vagabonds*

§ 137.

§ 138.

A vagabond is defined as one who has no domicile anywhere. And so vagabonds live now in one place, now in another, nevertheless have no intention of remaining anywhere permanently. However, since a person is supposed to retain his natural domicile as long as he has established none for himself by his own will, vagabonds also are usually supposed to retain their natural domicile. But since nothing prevents any one from leaving his natural domicile and from being able to have the intention of remaining permanently in no particular place, vagabonds do not retain their natural domicile, if they leave it with the intention of remaining permanently in no particular place.

So swindlers, thieves, gamblers, actors, wandering doctors, and beggars are usually classed as vagabonds. Thence it happens that to the word vagabonds, in German, specifically *Landstreicher* [land-rovers] or *Landläuffer* [land-runners], some disgraceful significance usually attaches. Nevertheless there is no reason why even those who live an honourable kind of life, may not now and then be vagabonds. Indeed the Apostles, who established nowhere a domicile for themselves, were vagabonds. Likewise for the sake of trade a merchant can live now in one place, now in another, and have a domicile nowhere; then he is therefore enumerated among the vagabonds.

§ 140. *What a native country is*

A native country is defined as a place, namely, a land or city, in which one's parents have a domicile, when one is born, the reference being to the nation or some particular corporation of a nation, to which the land or city belongs. In the native vernacular, we say with the broader meaning *das Vaterland* [Fatherland], in the narrower *die Vaterstadt* [Father-city], as the land or city in which our fathers dwelt from whom we have derived our stock. Moreover, the place of birth, which is the place in which we have been born, differs from native country. When any one is born in his native country, a thing which usually happens, place of birth is synonymous with native country especially in the stricter significance, but if any one is born on a journey or in a foreign land, where his parents are living on account of some business, his native country differs from his place of birth. It is to be noted besides that the place of birth is to be considered without reference to the nation to which he belongs, and therefore it gives no right to one born in that place.

It is not without reason that the native land is discussed in the law of nations, since on it depend certain rights, which people do not enjoy unless they have this native land. Therefore, since these rights belong to any one because he is born of parents who have a domicile either in this territory or in this city or in this district, this is the reason why the term "native country" has a broader and a narrower meaning. Moreover, since those rights are established by the will of human beings, although they are in harmony with natural law, they are not natural rights but simply positive rights, and therefore they are not necessary rights nor are they the same among all nations. Indeed there is no reason why they should exist in any nation. Moreover, since the place of birth confers no right, of itself it deserves no attention at all in the law of nations, except in so far as it is considered a native country through a caprice of speech. In a broader sense Silesia is my native country, in the stricter, Breslau, the chief city of Silesia; from this I am styled Breslauer and Silesian, or Breslauer-Silesian and I feel in myself a certain love of my native country as natural, by force of which the advantages, as well as the disadvantages, which come to it, affect my feelings. Likewise he who is born of parents who have their domicile in London in England, is called a Londoner and an Englishman, even if his parents at the time of his birth have been living in some place outside of England, for example, if they were in Germany on account of military service or if the father was performing the duty of an ambassador in the court of the most Christian King.[8]

8. The "most Christian king" is the king of France.

§ 141. *Of the children of vagabonds*

§ 140.

§ 139.

Since a native country is a place where the parents have domicile at the time of one's birth, moreover, since vagabonds have no domicile anywhere, he who is born of parents who are vagabonds has no native country, except so far as vagabonds are supposed to have retained their natural domicile, consequently the native country of the parents is considered their native country also.

So those who are born of Gipsies have no native country, just as their parents do not.

§ 142. *Of what sort the love of country is*

§ 140.

§ 655, Psych. Emp.

Since the native country has reference to the nation or to a particular corporation of the nation, love of country (for we love even inanimate things) implies love of the nation or of some definite corporation of the nation.

§ 657, Psych. Emp.

We love inanimate things in so far as we receive pleasure from them, or the things which are innate in them or appertain to them. But these are such things as conduce to the advantage of people and promote their happiness. Therefore love of country has reference indirectly to those to whom it is beneficial if a territory and the cities in it abound in every sort of advantage. And consequently it happens that the term "fatherland" seems especially to be used of people, and not of the land.

§ 143. *Whether love of country is a part of natural law*

§ 142.

Since love of country involves love of a nation or of some definite corporation in a nation, consequently of the people living in it, moreover, since every one ought to care for his own nation, and therefore love it, every one ought likewise to love his native country.

§ 606, part 1, Jus Nat.

§ 135.

Love of country and love of the people thought of in general as living in the country cannot be separated the one from the other. Therefore, since love of one's nation is a part of natural law, love of country also is a part of natural law. And therefore he offends against the law of nature who does not love his country, much more he who hates it.

§ 144. *Of the immutability of one's country*

Since your native country depends upon birth, moreover, since what has been done cannot be undone, your native country remains your native country, even if you establish your domicile outside of it, or abandon it, or even if you are driven out of it.

§ 140.

So England or France remains the native country of an Englishman or a Frenchman, even if he has established a domicile for himself outside of England or France, intending never to return to England or France. And although those born of French parents in Germany or Holland are still called French, because they derive their stock from a Frenchman; nevertheless their native country in the narrower sense is Germany or Holland, or the city in which they were born. Of course one must determine whether the name of Frenchman is applied to any one from his native land, or from his ancestors and parents, from whom he takes his origin. The same is understood of the Jews. Therefore in German idiom, which is well suited to express all ideas, we say *Deutsche Juden* [German Jews], or *Polnische Juden* [Polish Jews], according as they have Germany or Poland as a native country. And in the same manner of Frenchmen born in Germany or in Holland, we can say *Deutsche* [German] or *Holländische Franzosen* [Dutch Frenchmen].

§ 145. *Of exile*

He is called an exile, who is driven out of the city or land where he has a domicile, or is compelled to depart without the stigma of disgrace. In our native vernacular he is said to be *ein Vertriebener* [banished], and *ein Exulante* [exile]. Since any right can be taken away by way of punishment, exile also can be a penalty. Exile is divided into voluntary, if one for the purpose of escaping a penalty or disaster departs of his own accord from the place where he has domicile, and involuntary, if he is compelled to depart by the decree of a judge or order of a ruler. In the former case, we say in the native vernacular, *er sey flüchtig worden* [he has] or *er habe müssen flüchtig werden* [had to become a fugitive]. If any one has a domicile in his native country, exile is a banishment from his native country, or a deprivation of the soil of his native country, and therefore

§ 589, part 8, Jus Nat.

an exile is one who is driven out of his native land, or deprived of the soil of his native land.

Cicero, in his "Pro Domo," says, What is an exile? the name itself is indicative of disaster, not of disgrace.[9] And therefore in the definition of exile we have taken away its stigma of disgrace. It is not now our purpose to describe more fully anything in the customs of the Romans. It is rather our purpose and desire that our notions should be adapted to our own custom, and be more universal and distinguishable from special peculiarities of certain peoples. In accordance with the custom of the Romans he was called an exile who was driven out of his native country, since a large number of foreigners did not, as among us, establish domiciles for themselves wherever they pleased. Among the Romans those went into exile who desired to escape some punishment, or even such as were not able to pay a fine, and it was necessary that those should depart who were forbidden water and fire, upon whom exile from home was thus imposed. But although even among us it may happen that exile is chosen instead of capital punishment or disgrace, nevertheless very often exile is accustomed to be inflicted; for example, when those are driven from the land, where they have domicile, who are unwilling to change their religion, or who hold to opinions not approved, or are thought dangerous to the magistracy, nay more, from any other cause whatsoever, either just or unjust. Indeed, some also go into exile on account of disaster of the times or adverse fortune which they experience, as on account of the conflagrations of war, unendurable famine or extreme poverty, into which they have fallen by some sad accident.

§ 146. Of the limitation of involuntary exile

§ 145.

§ 811, part 8, Jus Nat.

Since involuntary exile is imposed by decree of a judge, or by order of a ruler, even by way of penalty, moreover, since it belongs to the ruler to decide on those things which seem to him best to do for the public good and to determine the penalties from existing circumstances, and the

9. Marcus Tullius Cicero, *De domo sua*, xxvii. 72, in Cicero: *Pro Archia. Post reditum in Senatu. Post reditum ad Quirites. De domo sua. De haruspicum responsis. Pro Plancio*, trans. N. H. Watts (Cambridge, Mass.: Harvard University Press, 1923), p. 219.

right belongs to him likewise to abate and remit penalties, involuntary exile can be restricted to a definite place, both as regards the place from which he is bound to depart, and that in which he is bound to dwell as exile, and to a definite time.

§§ 636, 833, part 8, Jus Nat.

§ 842, part 8, Jus Nat.

Thus exile may be inflicted for a period of ten years. Any one may be expelled from a city and its territory, or from a certain province. He may be compelled to be an exile in some remote province, or in some place a certain distance removed from the city. Among the English they are sent to the East Indies, among the Russians into Siberia. Here the will of the ruler controls, because public safety, the supreme law of the state, governs. Therefore these are merely civil questions, to be determined from those points which we have proved concerning the theory of civil laws in the eighth part of "The Law of Nature." In the present case to be sure the order of the ruler makes the law, and it has the force of a statute as regards the person on whom exile is inflicted. It makes no difference that exile can be inflicted even without a just cause. For there are indeed civil laws that are unjust and unfair, because they have not been based on the natural theory of civil laws. When this happens, the ruler abuses his right. But this abuse has to be endured by subjects, and those things have to be endured by a private individual which he is not able to change.

§ 86, part 8, Jus Nat.

§ 1043, part 8, Jus Nat.

§ 147. Of the right of the exile to dwell anywhere in the world

By nature the right belongs to an exile to dwell anywhere in the world. For exiles do not cease to be human beings, because they are driven into exile, consequently compelled to depart from the place where they have domicile, a thing which is evident of itself. Therefore, since by nature all things are common, moreover since in primitive society any man is allowed to dwell anywhere in the world, and since by the introduction of ownership the necessary use of things, and consequently the right of living anywhere in the world cannot be absolutely taken away from any one, by nature the right belongs to an exile to live anywhere in the world.

§ 145.

§ 7, part 2, Jus Nat.

§ 66, part 2, Jus Nat.

§ 562, part 6, Jus Nat.

A right belonging by nature to a man or born in him could be taken away from no one, and for this reason ownership could not be

§ 64, part 2, Jus Nat.

introduced, nor consequently could definite tracts of land be subjected to ownership, except with this tacit restriction, that, if in a special emergency the necessary use of things should happen to be taken
completely from any one, some right would remain to him in those
things which are subject to ownership, consequently, that it should
be possible for him to dwell in a land subject to the ownership of
some nation, even if he should be restrained from living with his own
nation. Exiles are driven out or are compelled to depart from the place
where they have domicile, and so they are not allowed to dwell with
their own nation. Therefore by nature the right belongs to them to
dwell in any place in the world which is subject to some other nation.
He who is driven into exile cannot be driven out of the entire earth,
for this cannot be done in a physical sense, unless life is destroyed, nor
is it morally possible, since the ruler has no right over the lands not
under his sovereignty.

§ 563, part 6,
Jus Nat.

§ 145.

§ 148. *Of asking admittance*

Since by nature the right belongs to an exile to live anywhere in the
world, moreover since it depends altogether on the will of the people,
or on the will of the one who has the right of the people, whether or
not he desires to receive an outsider into his state, an exile is allowed to
ask admittance, but he cannot assuredly according to his liking determine domicile for himself, wherever he shall please, and if admittance is
refused, that must be endured.

§ 147.

§ 409, part 8,
Jus Nat.

Elsewhere already we have suggested that there may be several reasons on account of which admittance may be denied and that they
must be determined by the state. Therefore since in the entire third
chapter of the eighth part we have shown what things are to be considered in establishing a state, if any one shall desire to consider properly
the details, he will without difficulty recognize that there are legal
causes for the denial of admittance. Here properly belongs the fact
that the number of subjects is greater than can be provided for adequately from the things which are demanded for the needs, comforts,
and pleasures of life, both as regards the people in general and also as
regards the class of people who follow the same pursuit in life. Here
also belongs the reason that there is fear lest the morals of the subjects

§ 693, part 6,
Jus Nat.

§ 400, part 8,
Jus Nat.

may be corrupted, or lest prejudice may be aroused against religion, or even lest criminals be admitted, because of whom injury threatens the state, and other things which are detrimental to public welfare.

§ 456, part 8, Jus Nat.

§ 475, part 8, Jus Nat.

§ 149. *Whether exiles are to be admitted*

A permanent residence in its territory cannot be denied to exiles by a nation, unless special reasons stand in the way. For since exiles have been expelled from the place where they have a domicile, consequently dwell, they are allowed to seek admittance elsewhere. Therefore, since to these who, driven from their homes, seek admittance, a permanent residence in the territory subject to its control cannot be denied, unless special reasons stand in the way; permanent residence in its territory cannot be denied to exiles by a nation, unless special reasons stand in the way.

§ 145.

§ 137.

§ 148.

§ 693, part 6, Jus Nat.

We have already indicated what reasons prevent the admittance of exiles. Moreover, since nations are free, the decision concerning these matters must be left to the nations themselves, and that decision must be respected. The right belongs to an exile to dwell anywhere in the world, but no absolute right to settle in any particular lands belongs to him, a thing which in fact is opposed to ownership. And if this right should be claimed as regards these lands, it is imperfect, consequently no nation can be compelled to receive exiles.

Note, § 148.

§ 2.

§ 156, part 1, Jus Nat.

§ 121, part 2, Jus Nat.

§ 906, part 1, Jus Nat.

§ 237, part 1, Phil. Pract. Univ.

§ 150. *Of compassion toward exiles*

We ought to be compassionate toward exiles. For exiles have been expelled from the place where they had domicile or have been compelled to depart from it on account of offences, therefore they have no fixed abode so that they can dwell in any place and support themselves honestly. Wherefore, since they cannot free themselves from this evil with which they are afflicted, and we ought to be compassionate toward those who cannot free themselves from the evil with which they are afflicted, therefore we ought to be compassionate toward exiles.

§ 145.

§ 137.

§ 259, part 4, Jus Nat.

There is no reason why you should object that exile is also inflicted as a punishment, nay more, that certain ones even desiring to go into exile because of fear of punishment plan flight for themselves, and that these are not worthy of compassion. Compassion, indeed, is not

§ 652, Psych.
Emp., and
§ 256, part 4,
Jus Nat.

confined to those who have fallen into misfortune without fault on their part, but since it arises from love, which is extended to all men generally, it applies also to all who are wretched generally, whether they fall into wretchedness of their own fault or simply from misfor-

§ 619, part 1,
Jus Nat.

tune. Nor is it to be feared lest on this account we may approve crimes and offences, if any one is an exile on account of them; for we love the person, we hold in abhorrence the crimes or offences, which they have committed. Since the act cannot be undone by us or by them, it is rather incumbent on us that we bring them back to a better moral life, and that, if they should desire to reform of their own accord, we should not stand in the way to prevent it; a thing which would cer-

§ 256, part 4,
Jus Nat.

tainly occur, if there were no place for compassion. Nevertheless we do not therefore deny that those are more worthy of compassion who go into exile without fault on their part, or have been driven into exile for an unjust cause. This also is here properly to be noted, that when an

§ 642, part 8,
Jus Nat.

evil is such of itself that it ought not to be punished, no attention is to be paid to it by another nation, if any one has gone into exile for the sake of avoiding punishment; in order that this may be more plainly apparent, I propose to add the following proposition.

§ 151. *Whether any one can be punished by a nation against which he has not offended*

He who has offended against a nation or committed some crime against it cannot on that account be punished by another nation to which he has

§ 642, part 8,
Jus Nat.

§ 1061, part 1,
Jus Nat.

come. For since the evil is not such of itself that it ought to be punished, and by nature the right belongs to a man to punish one who has injured him; by nature also the right belongs to no nation to punish him who

§ 832, part 8,
Jus Nat.

has not injured it. Therefore, although the right to punish is a part of the civil power, and consequently belongs to the nation against which any

§ 34, part 8,
Jus Nat.

one has offended or committed some crime, nevertheless one nation can-not on this account punish him who has offended against another nation or committed some crime against it. And so it is plain that he who has offended against one nation or committed some crime against it, cannot be punished by another nation to which he has come.

§ 559, part 8,
Jus Nat.

Evil deeds are punished in a state because either some member of the state, or the corporation itself, has been injured. But he who for the purpose of escaping a penalty comes as an exile to another state, has not on that account injured any member of the state or any private citizen, nor the corporation itself. Therefore both reasons fail, as to why any one can be punished by a certain state, consequently a wrongful act committed in one state does not affect another state, nor from that thing itself does any right arise against an exile.

§ 579, part 8
Jus Nat.

§ 152. *Who should be called suppliants*

Those fugitives are called suppliants who beg another nation, or the one who has the right of the people, to defend them against their own nation, or the ruler of the state whence they come.

Suppliants of course are to be distinguished from exiles. For although exiles may be suppliants, nevertheless not all exiles are suppliants, whether they be voluntary or involuntary. So if one expelled from his native country on account of religion comes to another nation and seeks admittance there, he as a suppliant can entreat the ruler of the state to see to it that his property, which he has been compelled to leave, be delivered over to him. Likewise if any one is spitefully accused, without a cause, of fraudulent administration of the public goods, he can as a suppliant entreat the powerful ruler of another state to defend him against the threatened injuries. But what the rights of suppliants are will be more clearly evident when we have discussed the duties of nations toward each other and the rights arising therefrom. Of course this word is taken in the stricter meaning, although the broader meaning allows him to be called a suppliant who begs another that he defend him against some other.

§ 153. *What the right to emigrate is*

The right to emigrate is permission to go into voluntary exile.

So the right to emigrate belongs to subjects to whom permission is given to depart from the state, because they are devoted to a religion which the ruler of the state does not wish to tolerate. For it would not be necessary for them to depart if they consented to give it up. That the right to emigrate does not belong to every voluntary exile is readily evident. For exile is voluntary, when any one for the sake of escaping punishment becomes an exile, nevertheless he does not have the right to emigrate; for he goes into exile only in opposition to the will of the ruler, who cannot be said to permit it.

§ 154. *Of the source of this right*

§ 153.

§ 407, part 8, Jus Nat., and § 145 h.

§ 789, part 3, Jus Nat.

§ 77, part 8, Jus Nat.

Since the right to emigrate is permission to go into voluntary exile, moreover since the ruler of the state can allow this, either at his own discretion, or by virtue of the agreement entered into with other nations, or is understood to do this by virtue of the fundamental law; the right to emigrate arises either from agreement or from fundamental law, or depends upon the will of the ruler.

In a state of nature there is no right to emigrate; for this assumes that there are established states, consequently it depends upon the law of the state. Therefore the things which are to be maintained concerning the law of emigration are derived from that law as their source. At the same time the reason is to be considered, on account of which that must be granted. Moreover, that the law of a state can be changed by agreements and limited by fundamental laws is plain enough from the general principles of the law of nature and the special principles of universal public law.

§ 155. *Of wrongs done to those who have the right to emigrate*

§ 145.

§ 153.

§ 239, part 1, Phil. Pract. Univ.

§ 859, part 1, Jus Nat.

If the ruler of the state is unwilling to allow those to depart from the state who have the right to emigrate, he does a wrong to them. For he who has the right to emigrate may depart from the state, since that right consists in permission to go into voluntary exile. If then the ruler of the state is unwilling to allow this, that is contrary to his right. Therefore, since he does a wrong to another, who does what is contrary to that person's right, if the ruler of the state is unwilling to allow those to depart from the state who have the right to emigrate, he does them a wrong.

§ 77, part 8, Jus Nat.

This happens if the right to emigrate comes from agreement entered into with other nations, or from fundamental law. If you say that the right to emigrate can likewise exist by force of the agreement entered into with the ruler of the state at the granting of the sovereignty, it is easy to see that by this agreement a fundamental law was established.

∞ CHAPTER II ∞

Of the Duties of Nations toward Each Other and the Rights Arising Therefrom

§ 156. *What one nation owes others*

Every nation owes to every other nation that which it owes to itself, in so far as the other does not have that in its own power, while the first nation without neglect of duty toward itself can perform this for the other. For the law of nations is originally nothing else than the law of nature §3. applied to nations, which are considered as individual persons living in §2. a state of nature. Therefore, since every man owes to every other man that which he owes himself, in so far as the other does not have it in his power, while he without neglect of duty to himself can perform this for §608, part 1, the other, every nation also owes toward every other nation that which it Jus Nat. owes to itself, in so far as the other does not have that in its own power, while the first nation without neglect of duty toward itself can perform this for the other.

> This is a general principle, which of itself embraces within its scope all duties toward other nations. If therefore you have learned those things, which we have proved in the preceding chapter concerning the duties of nations toward themselves, it will not be difficult to recognize what they owe to other nations. But as we have cautioned above, the moral person is to be distinguished from physical individuals, that is, the nation as a nation is to be looked at, but not those who are of Note, §28. a certain nation, individually; so also this is to be guarded against, that the things which are due to individuals, who belong to another nation, as men, be not confused with those things, which are due to nations, in so far as all, who constitute the same, are looked at as a

§ 5, part 8,
Jus Nat.

§ 7, part 8,
Jus Nat.

whole. For he who is of another nation, member of another state, is a foreigner, and without respect to his nation he is looked at as equally a human being, consequently there are the same duties toward him as are due from one human being to another. Formerly an absurd belief obsessed many nations that only those are our friends who are members of the same state with us, and that all foreigners were enemies, and that we ought to love only the former but to pursue the latter with hatred. But it is evident that this is contrary to the law of nature,

§ 619, part 1,
Jus Nat.

§ 52.

which enjoins a universal love of all toward all in general, and Christ, the best interpreter of the law of nature, criticized that error in the Jews and corrected it. This error is rightly attributed to the barbarity of nations, although it may have occurred that the error was retained among other nations less barbarous; for that which smacks of barbarism does not forthwith make a nation barbarous, nor if there is some-

§ 53.

thing at variance with cultivated manners does this forthwith make a nation uncultivated. No nation can be conceived of so perfect that it is absolutely devoid of imperfection. But here must be re-examined

Note, § 618,
part 1, Jus Nat.

the points which we have already considered elsewhere concerning the same matter, in order that the error may be the more carefully investigated.

§ 157. *Who is judge as to whether one nation can do anything for another without neglect of its duty toward itself*

Since every nation owes to every other nation that which it owes to itself, in so far as the other nation does not have that in its own power, while the first nation without neglect of its duty toward itself can perform this

§ 156.

§ 2.

for the other, since, moreover, every nation is free and by virtue of natural liberty it must be allowed to abide by its own judgement in determining its action, every nation must be allowed to stand by its judgement,

§ 156, part 1,
Jus Nat.

as to whether it can do anything for another without neglect of its duty toward itself; consequently if that which is sought is refused, it must be

§ 906, part 1,
Jus Nat.

endured, and the right of nations to those things which other nations owe them by nature, is an imperfect right.

So when there is a scarcity of crops the nation which has an abundance of grain ought to sell grain to the other, which needs it. But if indeed it is to be feared that, if grain should be sold, it would suffer the same disaster, it is not bound to allow that the other procure grain for itself from its territory. But the decision as to whether it can be sold without risk, is to be left to that nation from which the other wishes to provide grain for itself, and the latter ought to abide by this decision. Therefore the right to buy grain from another nation on account of the scarcity of crops is an imperfect right. And in like manner the same thing is understood concerning any other duty of one nation toward others.

§ 158. *Whether one nation can coerce another nation to do those things which it ought naturally to do for it*

Since the right to those things which one nation naturally owes to another is an imperfect right, since moreover no one can compel another to perform those things to which he has only an imperfect right; no nation either can compel another to perform for it those things which nations are naturally bound to perform for each other.

§ 157.

§ 237, part 1, Phil. Pract. Univ.

So, when the price of bread is high, no nation can compel another nation to sell grain to it, even if it has ever so great a supply of grain, and is naturally bound to sell.

§ 159. *Of the disregard of a natural duty*

If one nation is unwilling to perform for another that which it is naturally bound to perform for it, when it can, that is unfair indeed, but it does no wrong to the other. For the right to those things which nations are naturally bound to perform for each other, is an imperfect right, and consequently if it is unwilling to perform, when it can, consequently when it ought, that is contrary to an imperfect right of the other nation. Therefore, since that is unfair which is contrary to an imperfect right of another, if one nation is unwilling to perform for another that which it is naturally bound to perform for it, when it can, that thing itself is unfair. Which was the first point.

§ 157.

§ 156.

§ 239, part 1, Phil. Pract. Univ.

Indeed it is plain of itself that what is contrary to an imperfect right of another is not contrary to his perfect right. Therefore, since he does no wrong to another who does anything which is not contrary to the perfect right of the other, if one nation is unwilling to perform for another that

§§ 235, 237, part 1, Phil. Pract. Univ.

§ 859, part 1, Jus Nat.

which it is naturally bound to perform for it, when it can, it does no wrong to it. Which was the second point.

It is against charity and not justice, if one nation fails in its duty toward another. Therefore although it does no wrong, nevertheless it sins.

§ 160. *Of the extent of duties toward other nations*

No nation is bound to perform for another that which is not within its own power. For no nation is naturally bound to perform anything for another, except in so far as that can be done without neglect of duty toward itself. Therefore, since that is not in your power which you cannot perform for another except by neglect of duty, no nation is naturally bound to perform for another that which is not within its own power.

§ 156.

§ 610, part I, Jus Nat.

That is not within our power which we cannot achieve by the use of our abilities, strength, and property. The obstacle is either physical, which renders the act physically impossible, so that we cannot even attempt it, however much we desire, or it is moral, which renders the act morally impossible, so that we can indeed attempt it, but ought not. It is quite plain that here we speak only of the moral impediment, since there is no obligation to do the impossible, and it is plain of itself that the things which exceed our ability and strength can by no possibility be done by us. But the moral obstacle, of which we are here speaking, reduces the morally impossible in a sense to a physical impossibility. For if the use of your ability, strength, and property is to be expended in service for yourself, this undoubtedly is the same as if you had no ability, strength, and property, the use of which you could expend in service for another. Therefore there can be no criticism to make, when that which is simply morally impossible is included by some in discussions of morals under the impossible. Of course in the statements we have just made, the morally impossible is made equivalent to that which is physically impossible.

§ 175, part I, Jus Nat.

§ 209, part I, Phil. Pract. Univ.

§ 161. *Of mutual love of nations*

Every nation ought to love and cherish every other nation as itself, even though it be an enemy. For every human being ought to love and cherish every other man as himself. Therefore, since the law of nations is

§§ 618, 619, part I, Jus Nat.

originally nothing else than the law of nature applied to nations, every §3.
nation too ought to love and care for every other nation as for itself.
Which was the first point.

And since we ought to love and cherish even an enemy as ourselves, §632, part 1,
it is evident in like manner that every nation ought to love and cherish Jus Nat.
another nation as itself, even though it be an enemy. Which was the
second point.

> Undoubtedly those are in error who limit the universal love of all
> for all to the circle of private individuals, as if nations were free to look
> out simply for themselves and to put aside absolutely consideration
> for other nations, nay more, to promote their own advantage to the §138, part 7,
> detriment of others. Just as the purpose of that great natural society, Jus Nat.
> which nature herself has established among human beings, is mutual §144, part 7,
> aid in perfecting themselves and their condition, so there is the same Jus Nat.
> purpose of that society which nature has established among all nations
> and which she binds them to cherish. But universal love includes both
> societies: love of individuals for individuals the former indisputably,
> but love of nations for nations the latter.

§ 162. *Of consideration for the happiness of other nations*

Since he who cherishes another has the fixed and lasting desire to promote the happiness of the other and does all he can to make the other
happy and avoids making him unhappy, since, moreover, every nation §617, part 1,
ought to cherish every other nation; every nation ought to have the fixed Jus Nat.
and lasting desire to promote the happiness of other nations and to do all §161.
it can to make them happy and avoid making them unhappy.

> As no human being is born for himself alone and as nothing ought
> to be more beneficial to man than other human beings, so also nations
> have united into civil societies not for themselves alone, and nothing
> ought to be more beneficial to one nation than other nations. No
> nation ought to care for its own happiness simply, but also for that of
> others. Just as the universal love of mankind looks to the happiness
> of all humans, so also the universal love of nations considers the hap-
> piness of all nations. It is inhuman for man not to love man, much
> more to hate him, but it is beastly for nation not to love nation, much

more to hate it. Love allows no man to be unhappy except by his own fault, so also it permits no nation to be unhappy except by its own fault. If nations were to look deeply into the meaning of that, all could be happy, and we should read much less frequently in history of one nation having made another unhappy.

§ 163. *Of charity of nations*

In like manner because charity is a virtue, by force of which we cherish others as ourselves, and since we are bound to it by the law of nature itself, since, moreover, every nation ought to cherish every other nation as itself; charity therefore ought to exist between nations, consequently that which is opposed to charity is contrary to the necessary or internal law of nations.

§ 620, part 1, Jus Nat.
§ 621, part 1, Jus Nat.
§ 161.
§ 4.

The place for charity between nations is rare. The perverse idea has taken possession of the minds of nearly everybody that the mainspring of the law of nations is personal advantage; from this it happens that this law is made equal to might. We condemn this in private individuals, we condemn it in the ruler of the state, but the same is to be equally condemned in nations. But charity of nations considers nations as such, and therefore differs from the charity of individuals, as we have already suggested before.

Note, §§ 28, 161.

§ 164. *Of the duties of humanity of nation toward nation*

Since every nation ought to promote the happiness of another nation, since, moreover, the duties of humanity are those by which the happiness of another is promoted; the duties of a nation also toward other nations, by which the happiness of those nations is promoted, are duties of humanity.

§ 162.

§ 655, part 1, Jus Nat.

Therefore it is plain that there are duties of humanity of nations toward nations, which generally are but little considered. Those duties originate from mutual love of nations. Therefore the fact that they are neglected arises from an erroneous idea that the duties of nations toward each other are to be measured by their individual advantage.

§ 161 h, and § 633, Psych. Emp.
Note, § 163.

§ 165. *What is to be held concerning them*

Because the duties of a nation toward other nations, by which their hap-   § 164.
piness is promoted, are duties of humanity, those things which have
been proved in "The Law of Nature" concerning the duties of humanity
are likewise true of the duties of nations toward other nations, by which
their happiness is promoted.

> It would be superfluous here to attempt to repeat those things,
> since any one for himself can readily apply them to nations. So we do
> not wish to be more prolix than necessary.

§ 166. *To what extent one nation is bound to preserve and perfect another*

Whatever one nation is able to contribute to the preservation and perfection of another nation in that in which the other is not self-sufficient, it
is bound by nature to contribute that to the other. For every nation is   § 31.
bound to preserve and perfect itself and its condition. Therefore, since   § 35.
every nation owes to every other nation that which it owes to itself, in
so far as the other does not have that in its own power, while the first
nation can perform this for the other nation without neglect of its duty   § 156.
toward itself; one nation is bound to contribute whatever it can to the
preservation and perfection of another in that in which the other is not
self-sufficient.

> It is a perverse idea, which nations frequently entertain, that the
> destruction of another nation helps in the preservation of itself. But if
> that could be eradicated from the minds of all nations, and each were
> content with its own lot, the preservation of one would by no means
> be harmful to the preservation of the others. The same thing is to be
> said of the perfecting of other nations and their condition.

§ 167. *The same is further considered*

Since one nation ought to contribute to the perfection of another what   § 166.
it can, in that in which the other is not self-sufficient, since, moreover,   § 666, part 1,
when you desire to promote the perfection of another, you have no right   Jus Nat.

§ 165.

to compel the other to allow you to do that; if some nation should desire to promote the perfection of another nation, it could not compel it to allow that to be done.

§ 156, part 1,
Jus Nat.

§ 665, part 1,
Jus Nat., and
§ 165 h.

Of course nations are to be looked on as free persons and consequently what each desires to be done must be left to its decision. The forcing of a benefit on one is opposed to natural liberty. A nation has performed its duty if it has offered to another its aid in perfecting the other.

§ 168. Of the duty toward barbarous and uncultivated nations

§ 54.

§ 156.

Whatever a learned and cultivated nation can contribute to make barbarous and uncultivated nations learned and more cultivated, that it ought to do. For nations ought to be learned and cultivated and not barbarous. Therefore, since every nation owes to every other nation that which it owes to itself, in so far as the other does not have that in its power, while the first nation can perform this without neglect of its duty toward itself, whatever a learned and cultivated nation can contribute to make barbarous and uncultivated nations learned and more cultivated, that it ought to do.

§ 664, part 1,
Jus Nat.

For example, let us suppose that some nation abounds in learned men and those endowed with cultivated manners. It ought to allow certain of them to introduce their learning and good manners in the nation that is barbarous and less cultivated. And since also we ought to offer our aid to another, even if he does not seek it, a nation also ought through envoys to make known its inclination [to offer its help] to another, and much more ought to accede to a request from it.

§ 169. Whether they admit of coercion

§ 168.

§ 167.

Since a learned and cultivated nation ought to do whatever it can to make a barbarous and uncultivated nation learned and more cultivated, but since, if any nation wishes to promote the perfection of another, it cannot compel it to allow that to be done; if some barbarous and uncultivated nation is unwilling to accept aid offered to it by another in removing its barbarism and rendering its manners more cultivated, it cannot be compelled to accept such aid, consequently it cannot be compelled by force to develop its mind by the training which destroys barbarism and without which cultivated manners cannot exist.

Barbarism and uncultivated manners give you no right against a nation. See what we have already remarked only a little while ago. Therefore a war is unjust which is begun on this pretext. Approval is not to be given to the opinion of Grotius, that kings and those who have a right equal to that of kings have the right to exact penalties from any who savagely violate the law of nature or of nations, nor is there need for correcting this, to employ the warnings which he puts forward in §§ 41 and following. The source of the error is found in the fact that the evil seems to him of such a nature that it can be punished and that it is quite in harmony with reason that it may be punished by him who is not guilty of it. Since in the first part of "The Law of Nature" we have shown the source of the right to punish, and besides have proved that the evil in itself is not such that it ought to be punished, it is not to be feared that the reasons of Grotius, which he brings in to the aid of his opinion, may cause us any difficulty; in fact it is not in the least consistent with the innate rights of man, so far is it from being deducible therefrom.

Note, § 167.

De Jure Belli ac Pacis, lib. 2, c. 20, § 40.

§ 642, part 8, Jus Nat.

§ 170. *Of the right of nations to seek the services of humanity*

Any nation has a perfect right to seek the services of humanity from another nation, if it itself cannot do what it desires. For no one has the right to seek from another some service of humanity, except when he himself cannot do the thing which he seeks. Therefore, since nations ought to perform for each other the services of humanity, when they have need of them, the right belongs to any nation to seek from another nation the services of humanity, if it itself cannot do the thing which it seeks. Which was the first point.

§ 661, part 1, Jus Nat.

§ 164.

§ 165.

The right of seeking from another the services of humanity is a perfect right. Therefore this right, which belongs also to nations, as proved above, is a perfect right. Which was the second point.

§ 904, part 1, Jus Nat.

§ 156.

The services of humanity are due from nation to nation in case of need. Therefore the nation which needs something is bound to indicate its need to the other. Nevertheless, since no man has the right to compel another to perform the services of humanity, one nation also may not exact from another the service of humanity, yet it may seek it.

§ 171. *Whether it can be obstructed without wrong*

§ 170.
§ 156, part 1, Jus Nat.
§ 859, part 1, Jus Nat.

Since a perfect right belongs to any nation to seek the services of humanity from another nation, if it itself cannot do the thing which it seeks, and the decision as to its need is with the one asking, and since what is contrary to the perfect right of another is a wrong, it is allowable for any nation to seek from another a service of humanity, nor without wrong can it be forbidden to seek, or even badly treated because it seeks.

We shall use this principle later in proving other points, lest a decision as to what the law of nature itself commands should be left to the mere whim of nations.

§ 172. *Of the friendship of nations*

§ 161.
§ 625, part 1, Jus Nat.

Nations ought to cultivate friendship with each other and every one ought to do its best not to make others hostile to itself. For nations ought to love one another as themselves. Therefore, since friendship consists in mutual love, nations ought to cultivate friendship with each other. Which was the first point.

§ 722, part 1, Jus Nat.

Therefore, since he who is bound to do a thing is at the same time bound not to do the contrary, every nation also ought to do its best not to make others hostile to itself. Which was the second point.

There are treaties of friendship, of which we shall speak below in their own place. But do not suppose that the friendship of nations rests on this basis alone; for it is a principle of natural law, and the law of nature is violated, if any nation does anything which is opposed to friendship.

§ 173. *On forbidding the injury of nations*

§ 166.

No nation ought to injure another. For every nation ought to promote the perfection of another as far as it can, consequently ought to do nothing by which the other nation or its condition is rendered less perfect.

Therefore, since one injures another who makes him or his condition less perfect, no nation ought to injure another.

§ 722, part 1, Jus Nat.

The same could be shown also in this manner. No one must be injured. Therefore likewise no nation ought to injure another.

§ 669, part 1, Jus Nat.

§ 695, part 1, Jus Nat.

Since an injury consists in acts, by which a nation or its condition is made less perfect, the prohibition that a nation must not be injured contains the general obligation concerning those things which a nation ought not to do to a nation.

§ 3.

§ 669, part 1, Jus Nat.

§ 174. *In what the perfection of a nation consists*

The perfection of a nation consists in fitness to attain the purpose of its state. For a nation is a number of people associated in a state. Therefore, since the perfection of society consists in its fitness for attaining the end of society, the perfection of a nation cannot consist in anything else than its fitness for attaining the end of its state.

§ 5, part 8, Jus Nat.

§ 171, part 7, Jus Nat.

We have often already warned, when we speak of a nation, that we are not thinking of the individuals singly who belong to a certain nation, but of all who constitute that nation taken as a whole, lest the duties which are due to man as man be confounded with the duties which are due to a nation as a nation. The nation is a moral person, and therefore ought to have a perfection of its own. Association turns a nation into a state, and since this is done with a definite end, the perfection of the nation must surely be determined from that. Just as the perfection of the human body depends upon its fitness to attain the purpose which can be attained by the concordant use of the several organs of the body, and the same thing is to be said of the perfection of the soul, from both of which combined arises the perfection of the entire human being, so also the perfection of a nation consists in its fitness to attain the purpose for the sake of which they have united into a state.

§ 5, part 8, Jus Nat.

§ 4, part 8, Jus Nat.

§§ 317 and fol., part 1, Jus Nat.

§ 201, part 1, Jus Nat.

§ 175. *How it may be promoted*

Since the perfection of a nation consists in its fitness to attain the purpose of its state, while what one nation is bound to contribute to the perfection of another nation in that in which the other is not self-sufficient,

§ 171.

§ 166. that it is bound by nature to contribute to the other; what one nation can contribute to this purpose, namely, that another may attain the purpose of its state, when it is not self-sufficient, that it ought to contribute.

For example, let us suppose that some nation is without civil laws, and it does not know how they can properly be fashioned, while another enjoys the best of laws. If then the former ask that those laws be shared with it, the request ought by no means to be denied. The same thing is to be said of other things which have been established to the advantage of the state, as, for example, the method of quickly and cheaply terminating lawsuits, or even of the proper administration of public affairs. Here likewise belongs what we have said before concerning the destruction of barbarism and of adapting manners to

Note, § 168. a standard of reason.

§ 176. *From what source the several things are attainable*

Since one nation ought readily to contribute what it can, that another
§ 175. nation, which is not self-sufficient, may attain the purpose of its state, and since what makes for the attaining of this purpose is plain from those
§ 393, part 8, Jus Nat. things which we have proved at length in universal public law concerning the establishment of a state, in what respects one nation is bound by
§§ 394 and fol., part 8, Jus Nat. nature to another nation is plain from what we have proved concerning the proper establishment of a state.

Of course from what we have proved concerning the establishment of a state, it is plain what a nation owes to itself. Therefore since what
§ 156. one nation by nature owes to another is not different from what it owes to itself; it is quite evident that these things must be derived from what has been proved concerning the establishment of the state.

§ 177. *The source of the duties of one nation*
toward another made plain

Since one nation ought to contribute whatever it can, that another nation
may attain the purpose of its state, when it is not self-sufficient, since
§ 13, part 8, Jus Nat. moreover the purpose of a state consists in a sufficiency for life, tranquillity and security, whatever one nation can contribute to the sufficiency

for life, tranquillity and security of another, that it ought to contribute, when the other is not self-sufficient; consequently since a sufficiency for life consists in the abundance of those things which are required for the necessity, advantage and pleasure of life, and in the means of happiness, since tranquillity consists in freedom from fear of injuries, and security in freedom from fear of violence, especially from the outside, whatever one nation can contribute, that the other may abound in those things which are required for the necessity, advantage and pleasure of life, and for the means of happiness, and that life may be free both from the fear of injuries and of violence, especially from the outside, that it ought to contribute, when the other is not self-sufficient.

§ 10, part 8, Jus Nat.

§ 11, part 8, Jus Nat.

§ 12, part 8, Jus Nat.

Just as we have derived from the purpose of the state those things which every nation owes to itself, so also from the same source can we derive those things which one nation owes another. If, then, some opportunity presents itself, when one nation can do another a service, from this it is easily seen whether one is bound by nature to do it. For the reason for the obligation is to be sought from that source. Nevertheless it is not necessary that we should always go back to this fundamental principle, if we may assume those things which have been derived from that source concerning the duties of a nation toward itself. Now it is evident from the general principles which are here proved, that the duties of nations toward each other extend much farther than is generally thought. And as the full extent of the law of nature with regard to individual human beings is not generally recognized, it is not remarkable if the full extent which the natural law of nations can have is not attributed to it. But if it could be brought about that all nations in general would recognize that and would strive with all their might satisfactorily to perform their duties, there would be abundant provision for the welfare of all nations, and that supreme state, which nature has established among men, would not be divided. But this is more to be desired than expected. But you should not on this account suppose that all teaching concerning the duties of nations toward each other is useless. For who, pray, would dare to argue that those duties are not to be insisted upon, which the law of nature enjoins, because men neglect them, and because all men cannot be made eager to perform them? Doubtless the love of enemies

§ 160.

§ 176.

is an exceedingly rare bird, but who, pray, objects to teaching love of enemies? And as it is rightly to be hoped of men, that some at least may perform their duties, if they know them, so likewise the same thing is to be hoped of some nations at least.

§ 178. *In what the imperfection of a nation consists*

The imperfection of a nation consists in its incapacity to attain the purpose of its state. For imperfection is opposed to perfection, and is contradictory to it, as is self-evident. Therefore, since the perfection of a nation consists in its fitness to attain the purpose of its state, so on the other hand its imperfection consists in its unfitness to attain the purpose of its state.

§ 174.

As a perfect nation is compared to a sound body, in which all the organs of the body are adapted to the proper performance of their functions, so an imperfect nation is to be compared to a sick body, in which certain organs are unfitted to perform their function, or are absolutely lacking, in which case it is compared to a maimed body. This is not a vague similarity, but, if you shall have learned to use it properly, particularly with the precaution added, that the simile is not to go beyond its third application, it is useful for discovery and proof. For true similarities are general notions, equally suitable to diverse things or including those attributes which exist at the same time in them, and therefore they furnish the most valuable assistance in the use of the principle of reduction, which is of the greatest importance in the art of reasoning.

§ 179. *In what injury to a nation consists*

Since he injures another, who makes him or his condition more imperfect, since, moreover, the imperfection of a nation consists in its unfitness to attain the purpose of its state, if a certain nation does that which renders another nation unfit to attain the purpose of its state, that is, that which is opposed to its purpose, it injures this nation, and therefore since no nation ought to injure another, no nation ought to do anything which is opposed to the purpose of another state, nor in any way prevent another nation from attaining the purpose of its state.

§ 669, part 1, Jus Nat.

§ 178.

§ 173.

He who injures a nation interferes with its perfection, or he deprives another nation of that which is necessary for its perfection. But he who neglects the perfection of another nation, and has no care for it, does not injure it; he refuses to perform a duty of humanity, the refusal of which is not an injury. The perfection of another nation is interfered with either directly, in so far as the act by which the interference is caused comes from the one himself who interferes, or indirectly, in so far as some one else is prevented from promoting the perfection of another. But it is a different thing to reinforce the obstacle which another puts in the way, for this belongs to direct interference. We have treated elsewhere of the aid to the action of another, and the arguments there given at very great length are easily applicable to nations. There is need also of this precaution: do not classify as an interference, that is, an injury to another nation, something resulting by accident from an action legal in itself, which prevents another nation from attaining that perfection which it otherwise could attain. For he who does what he ought either to himself or others, or exercises his own right, is neither directly nor indirectly aiming at the imperfection of another, and therefore cannot be said to interfere with the perfection of another. In morals all circumstances are to be carefully considered, the least of which alters the law, as has already been observed. But we have here a general principle, by force of which decision can easily be made concerning injuries of nations, provided only you are not ignorant of universal public law. And although the injuries of nations are not absolutely the same as injuries of the individuals who belong to a certain nation, nevertheless those things which we have independently proved from the civil status concerning the injuries of other individuals shed light on the injuries of nations also.

§ 170.

§ 671, part 1, Jus Nat.

§§ 106 and fol., part 2, Phil. Pract. Univ.

§§ 673 and fol., part 1, Jus Nat.

§ 5.

§ 180. *Of the performance by a nation of its duties to itself with a sense of duty toward other nations*

Every nation owes this duty, not only to itself but also to others, that it perfect itself and its condition. For every nation ought to contribute what it can to the perfection of another in that in which the other is not self-sufficient. Therefore, since it cannot do this, unless it perfect itself and its condition, it therefore ought to perfect itself also and its

§ 166.

condition, in order that it may be able to perform all parts of its duty

§ 35.

toward other nations. Therefore it owes this duty not only to itself, but also to other nations, that it perfect itself and its condition.

Man ought to be useful to man, a citizen to the state, nation to nation. Therefore, just as man ought to perfect himself, in order that he may be able to aid others also needing his assistance in perfecting themselves and their condition, and the same thing is understood of the citizen with respect to the state, so likewise a nation ought to perfect itself and its condition, in order that it may be able to aid other nations needing its assistance in perfecting themselves and their condition. Therefore, as it is incumbent upon a man to perform his duties toward himself with a sense of duty toward others, and upon a citizen, with a sense of duty toward the state, so also a nation ought to perform its duties toward itself with a sense of duty toward other nations. Perchance there will not be lacking some to whom this, which is here suggested, will seem paradoxical; but these will be the ones whose hearts are still void of the universal love of all toward all, and who have not yet realized in their hearts that there is a society which nature herself has established among humans, and much less do they recognize

§ 138, part 7, Jus Nat.

§ 7.

§ 9.

that society which this same nature is understood to have established among all nations. Since all nations are understood to have united into a state, the several members of which are the several nations, or individual states, if any one should not dare deny that it is incumbent upon every citizen to perform the duties toward himself with the sense of duty toward the state which is characteristic of a good citizen, such a one is understood to concede voluntarily that every nation ought to perform its duties toward itself with a sense of duty toward other

§ 934, part 1, Jus Nat.

nations. To perform what is one's duty toward oneself with a sense of duty toward others is assuredly a principle of universal justice, and since it has been enjoined by natural law, it is no less binding on every

§ 935, part 1, Jus Nat.

nation than on every man.

§ 181. *Of examples set by nations*

§ 180.

§ 275, part 2, Phil. Pract. Univ.

§ 277, part 2, Phil. Pract. Univ.

Since a nation owes this duty not only to itself, but also to others, that it should perfect itself and its condition, since, moreover, examples teach best the method of action and furnish motives for action, to say nothing of the further power of examples, which has already been demonstrated, every nation ought to teach others by its example, how they ought to perfect themselves and their condition, and consequently every nation is bound to offer good examples to others, and therefore also not to set bad ones.

§§ 259, 260, 265, 266, 269, 270, part 2, Phil. Pract. Univ. § 722, part 1, Jus Nat.

As every man ought to shape all his actions with reference to others in accordance with the principle of universal justice, so that he may aid them by his example and not injure them, so also one nation by its example ought to be an aid to others in perfecting themselves and their condition, since universal justice ought to flourish none the less among them, and it ought to be on its guard not to lead others astray by a bad example.

§§ 934, 935, part 1, Jus Nat.

Note, § 180.

§ 182. *The obligation of a nation with regard to the examples of other nations*

Every nation ought to adhere to the good examples of other nations, but ought not to follow bad examples, for every nation ought to offer good examples to others in perfecting themselves and their condition, but it ought not to set bad examples. Therefore, since every nation is bound to perfect itself and its condition, and consequently ought to protect itself from those things by which it itself or its condition is rendered less perfect, every nation ought to adhere to the good examples of other nations, but ought not to follow bad examples.

§ 181.

§ 40.

§ 722, part 1, Jus Nat.

The obligation to offer good examples and not to set bad examples would be in vain, unless nations also were bound to improve themselves by the good and not to follow the bad. Since by force of that obligation provision is made for the nations which of themselves cannot perfect those things which are needed for their welfare, it is necessary that the law of nature also, so far as it affects nations, should urge that these nations adhere to good examples and not follow the bad.

§ 181.

§ 183. *Of the perfection and imperfection of other nations*

Since every nation ought to adhere to the good examples of other nations, but ought not to follow the bad examples, every nation also ought to exert itself to learn both the perfection and imperfection of other nations and their condition.

§ 182.

Of course one must inquire, not only with what traits other nations are endowed, but also what institutions have been well or poorly established by them. And hence those deserve well of their own nation who describe the traits of other nations and those institutions which have been established in the state by them.

§ 184. *Of the imitation of nations*

§ 182.

§ 181.

§ 204, part 2, Phil. Pract. Univ.

§ 30.

Since a nation ought to adhere to the good examples of other nations, consequently ought to conform its actions in perfecting itself and its condition to their actions, and since he imitates another who conforms his action to the action of another, one nation ought to imitate another in those institutions which have been or are now well and properly established by it. Nevertheless, since one nation ought not to imitate another with any other purpose than that it may perfect itself and its condition, as proved above, therefore it ought not to inquire into the reasons for the actions of other nations and for those institutions which have been established by them in their state, nor imitate other nations, except in so far as their institutions are conformable to reason, and consequently

§ 208, part 2, Phil. Pract. Univ.

since imitation of that sort is rational and not blind, the imitation of nations ought to be rational, not blind.

§§ 508 and fol., Psych. Emp.

§ 208, part 2, Phil. Pract. Univ.

The imitation of other nations is not uncommon, especially in Europe; but usually it is a blind, not a rational, imitation. Since very many of those to whom the care of public property has been entrusted measure all things by utility or, if you prefer, by profit, therefore they are accustomed to imitate those things which they see have been established by other nations for utility. But oftentimes imitation is blind, because the particular circumstances on account of which a thing has been established for a useful purpose are not considered, so that there should not be imitation except in a similar instance—a thing which is required, if imitation is to be rational. Nay more, from this it also happens that one nation is contaminated by the depraved morals of other nations, especially if some preconceived opinion concerning some nation has spread a cloud over the mind. The perverse opinion of those who measure all things by the advantage of the prince, leads also to blind imitation, opposed to the interest of the state. These praise the institutions which have been properly and wisely established by other nations, but in order not to imitate them, they object that the advantage of the prince, if it is not contrary to them, at least does not recommend them.

§ 185. *Of the desire for the renown of other nations*

Every nation ought to strive, as best it can, that other nations also may deserve renown. For every nation ought to strive that it itself may deserve renown. Therefore, since every nation owes to another what it owes to itself, in so far as the other does not have that in its power, while the first nation without neglect of duty toward itself can perform this for the other, therefore it ought also to strive, as best it can, that other nations may deserve renown. § 49. § 156. § 160.

This can also be shown in this way. Every nation ought to contribute to the perfection of another nation what it can. Therefore, since true and substantial renown of a nation depends upon the perfection of itself, every nation ought to strive, as best it can, that other nations also may deserve renown. § 166. § 49.

Do not persuade yourself that we extend the law of nature to excess in reference to the reciprocal duties of nations toward each other; for we do not go beyond its limits, as long as nothing is admitted, except that which is evidently derived from its principles. But you must not think that the duties of a nation toward another are to be restricted to neighbouring nations; but if a nation be so far removed that you can contribute nothing to its perfection or that of its condition, however much you desire, that is not in your power, and you are consequently not bound to do so. The obligation is not terminated, if one look more deeply into the matter, but it is at least suspended, in so far as by an insuperable obstacle the act is rendered impossible upon which the obligation depends. Of course, if you can in any way care for a distant nation also, you are bound to it no less than if it were near by. Distance between places does not at all affect the right itself nor the obligation itself, since they flow from the nature of nations. Nay more, if all nations performed their duties toward others in every detail, however much neighbours cared for neighbours alone, yet in this way

§ 610, part 1, Jus Nat.

§ 166.

they would be caring for the most distant also. Since all nations are understood to have united into a supreme state, the several members of which are the several nations or individual states, this state itself is properly compared with the human body. Therefore, just as we observe in it, that, although the several organs in their function do not affect the function of the remote organs, but neighbours at least aid neighbours, yet by this provision is made for the functions of the remote organs also in the organs remote from them, so the same thing would hold among nations, if indeed all followed the law of nature. The latter suggests the same bond in the human body which it carefully guards in the universe, where there is nothing in one part, which does not depend upon those parts which are removed from it even at the greatest distance. The laws of nature which are prescribed to human beings are not out of harmony with those which are observed in the universe. Nature suggests the analogy between the universe and the supreme state established among nations, which would open up a very broad field for discussion, if we wished to consider it in detail, and if the plan of our present design did not forbid it.

§ 9.

§§ 8, 9.

§ 186. *Of the esteem and praise of other nations*

We ought to esteem every nation as highly as it deserves and give it as much praise as it deserves. For every one ought to esteem another as highly as he deserves and give him as much praise as he deserves. Therefore, since those things which belong to natural law are likewise to be applied to nations, we ought to esteem every nation also as highly as it deserves, and give to it as much praise as it deserves.

§ 647, part 1, Jus Nat.

§ 648, part 1, Jus Nat.

§ 3.

It is not necessary for us to explain more expressly how much esteem and praise any nation deserves; for since esteem consists in a judgement on the perfection of any one, and praise in the language by which that judgement is expressed, the amount of esteem depends upon the completeness of the perfection of a nation, and the praise must be proportioned to the esteem which is given to a nation. Since the perfection of a nation consists in its capacity for attaining the purpose of its state, which others cannot possibly come to know except through deeds, how much a nation deserves to be esteemed and how much praise is to be given it, is fully understood only by him who has

§ 538, part 1, Jus Nat.

§ 541, part 1, Jus Nat.

§ 174.

an intellectual appreciation of the things which have been proved concerning the proper establishment of a state, nay rather, of the general public law explained fully in the eighth part of "The Law of Nature." Genuine esteem for a nation and genuine praise are therefore not so readily attainable as it might seem. Therefore those who have learned to esteem another nation as highly as it deserves, and to give due respect to it, ought to extend the respect for it to others. This is particularly the duty of travellers and of scholars, who publish to the world and, as it were, make common to all what is worthy of respect even among remote nations. By this very means both the desire to imitate other nations in those things which have been or are well established by them in the state, is promoted, and good examples, otherwise far removed from our knowledge, become known. Of course duties owed to others are so closely connected with duties to oneself that they mutually influence each other.

§ 187. *Of the natural obligation to engage in commerce*

Nations are bound by nature to engage in commerce with each other, so far as is in their power. For whatever a nation can contribute that another may have an abundance of the things which are required for the necessity, advantage and pleasure of life, that it ought to contribute, and the §177. right belongs to every nation to procure for itself at a fair price the things which it needs from other nations and of which they themselves have no §58. need. Therefore, since commerce consists in the right to buy and sell in turn everything, movable and moving, as well necessaries as things useful and for pleasure, and consequently is the means of obtaining those things §60. which are required for the necessity, advantage and pleasure of life, but which nations do not have in their own territory, nations are bound by §§499 and fol., nature to engage in commerce with each other, so far as is in their power. part 1, Jus Nat.

If the original common holding existed among nations, all property would be held in common, consequently every nation could get from §§24, 29, part 2, every other nation the things, movable and moving, which it needs, Jus Nat. and which the other can do without. Since, indeed, civil sovereignty could not be introduced without ownership, at least without that mixed common holding in the hands of every nation which assumes §129, part 2, ownership—a thing which is readily evident from those arguments Jus Nat.

in which the meaning of civil sovereignty and ownership has been
sufficiently investigated;—in place of that right came the right to procure for itself at a fair price from another nation, which itself had no

§ 58.

need of them, the things which any nation needed for the necessity,
advantage and pleasure of life, as is made plainer by a discussion of
this right. And so it is plain that the source of the natural obligation
to engage in commerce which binds nations, comes as it were from
the fountain-head itself—that is, from the original common holding.
Moreover this common holding itself guarantees the ownership of
nations. For by virtue of the sanction of the original common holding
no one can take from another without his consent the thing which he
has taken possession of for his necessary use, consequently also that

§ 36, part 2,
Jus Nat.

which he has produced by his industry, or by his skill has fashioned for
his use. Therefore, since nations are considered to be like individual

§ 2.

persons, it is not allowable to take by force from any nation, without
its consent, things intended for its use. Therefore, since it has occupied territory for the sake of its permanent use and by its industry
raises a crop of natural products and prepares manufactured articles
for its own use, unless such an abundance of them is produced that it
itself does not need all, that right which comes from the original common holding, passes, as it were naturally, into the ownership of the

§ 5, part 8,
Jus Nat.
§ 4, part 8,
Jus Nat.

nation. And by the agreement from which nations arose ownership by
nations also came into existence along with sovereignty, though with
the reservation of the obligation established in the present proposition. But because in this proposition the obligation is thus restricted
to that which is in one's power, you must not think that nothing is to
be considered here, other than whether some nation can do without
that which another nation needs. For since it is not in our power to do

§ 610, part 1,
Jus Nat.

for another that which we cannot do except by neglect of duty toward
our own selves, here are also to be considered the other duties of a
nation toward itself, whatever they may be. So the Chinese, when they
wished to introduce the best possible form of a state, and therefore
to perfect the same perpetually more and more, and to preserve the
morals of their nation pure and uncorrupted, prohibited all commerce
with other nations; nor did they allow access to their lands by foreigners, although they had an abundance of the things suitable for engaging in commerce with other nations. Nor can it be said that therein

they violated the natural law of nations. For the obstacles had to be removed which could prevent them from perfecting themselves and their condition as it ought to be done. There is need of much caution, lest a hasty judgement be passed on the acts of nations.

§ 188. *Who decides whether commerce is possible*

Since every nation ought to engage in commerce with other nations, so far as is in its power, since, moreover, every nation is free, consequently must be allowed to stand by its own decision in determining its own business, it must be left to the decision of any nation itself whether or not it is in the power of such nation to engage in commerce with other nations. And in the same manner, further, it is plain that it is not bound to give to other nations the reason for this decision, consequently they must abide by its will alone.

§ 187.

§ 55, part 8, Jus Nat.

§ 156, part 1, Jus Nat.

Natural liberty is an inviolable right no less among nations than among individual humans. And this inviolability must always be observed in particular duties toward other nations, lest one nation arrogate to itself a greater right against another than the law of nature, always consistent with itself, allows. Nor is there reason why you should object that the case must be excepted in which it is plain that commerce can be engaged in by a nation without neglect of any duty toward itself. For since the decision as to this is difficult, nor by it can national integrity be made consistent with natural liberty, the will of any nation must be acquiesced in, however much it seems to abuse its liberty.

§ 189. *Of what sort the right of commerce is by nature*

Since the decision on the question, whether it is in the power of any nation to engage in commerce with another nation, must be left to the nation itself, and the right whose corresponding obligation depends upon the decision of another is an imperfect one; the right to engage in commerce with another nation is an imperfect one, and consequently no nation can compel another to engage in commerce with itself.

§ 188.

§ 906, part 1, Jus Nat.

§ 231, part 1, Phil. Pract. Univ.

Since the right to engage in commerce with another nation is a right by which another is bound to give or to do something for you

§ 60.

§ 355, part 3,
Jus Nat.

when you need his property or his labour, since, moreover, this right is an imperfect one, from this it can likewise be shown that the right to engage in commerce with another nation, which of course belongs by nature to nations, is only an imperfect right. Nay more, it is also immediately inferred from this, that after ownership of things has been introduced, the right to procure things for oneself from another

§ 356, part 3,
Jus Nat.

is only an imperfect right.

§ 190. *Of what sort the natural obligation of nations to engage in commerce is*

Since no nation can compel another to engage in commerce with itself,

§ 189.

§ 187.

§ 236, part 1,
Phil. Pract.
Univ.

although it may be bound by nature to do so, if it is within its power, since, moreover, no one is bound absolutely to another, if he does not have the right to compel him to perform his obligation, nations are not bound absolutely to engage in commerce with each other.

Therefore it is apparent that those things cannot depend upon the right alone which by nature belongs to nations in regard to commerce,

§ 409, part 3,
Jus Nat., and
§ 189 h.

since it must be endured, if some nation does not wish to engage in commerce with another. Since the obligation to engage in commerce is classified as a mutual obligation of giving and doing, moreover since

§ 60.

§ 354, part 3,
Jus Nat.

the mutual obligation to give and to do is by nature an imperfect one, it is evident from this also that the natural obligation of nations to engage in commerce is an imperfect one.

§ 191. *How a perfect right to commerce is acquired*

No nation can bind another absolutely to itself to engage in commerce except by stipulation, nor can a perfect right to engage in commerce be

§ 190.

otherwise acquired. For nations are bound only imperfectly to engage in commerce with each other, consequently that which is due on that obli-

§ 401, part 1,
Jus Nat.

gation is due only as an imperfect obligation. Therefore, since by mutual consent it may be brought about that what was due as an imperfect

§ 404, part 3,
Jus Nat.

obligation becomes due as a perfect obligation, nations are able to bind themselves absolutely to each other to engage in commerce by mutual

§ 698, part 3,
Jus Nat.

consent, consequently by agreeing with each other concerning such matters. But since no one can bind himself absolutely to another except by promises, no nation either can bind another absolutely to itself to engage in commerce except by stipulation. Which was the first point. § 393, part 3, Jus Nat.

Since from a perfect obligation a perfect right arises to that thing which another is bound to give to us, moreover, since nations are not able to bind themselves absolutely except by stipulation, as proved above, a perfect right to engage in commerce cannot be acquired otherwise than by stipulation. Which was the second point. §§ 235, 236, part 1, Phil. Pract. Univ., and § 23, part 1, Jus Nat.

Thence is obvious the necessity for stipulations between nations concerning commerce, which owes its stability to those stipulations alone. Therefore a perfect right to commerce between nations is a stipulative one, and consequently controversies which arise concerning that right are to be determined from the stipulation. § 23.

§ 192. *From what source the rule for agreements concerning commerce is to be taken*

Since no nation can absolutely bind another to itself to engage in commerce except by stipulation, and since a perfect right to it can be acquired in no other way, since, moreover, no one can bind another to himself to give anything or do anything without his consent, nor can one acquire from the other by his acceptance more right than the other wishes to transfer to him, it depends upon the will alone of the nations agreeing in regard to commerce, how they may wish to agree with each other concerning it, consequently all right of commerce is simply a stipulative one. § 191.

§ 382, part 3, Jus Nat.

§ 23.

Therefore the right of commerce between certain nations can be understood and interpreted only from their stipulations.

§ 193. *Of the limitation of commerce to purchase alone and to certain things*

Since it depends upon the will alone of nations agreeing in regard to commerce, how they may wish to agree with each other concerning it, since, moreover, commerce consists in the right to buy and sell movable and moving things, nations also can agree to this restriction, that it be allowed to one simply to purchase goods for ready cash, but not to sell its own goods on other terms to the same nation, or vice versa, or even to § 192. § 60.

purchase merely, or purchase and sell certain goods, but not everything in general, and consequently when the agreement has been restricted to certain things, the purchase and sale of other things can be prevented without wrong, since here no right is violated.

§ 859, part 1, Jus Nat.

For although generally commerce consists in the right to buy and sell, nevertheless those rights are not so united that they cannot be separated from each other. Therefore when agreements fix the law for commerce, nothing at all prevents the commerce from being limited to the right only to purchase or to sell, as shall seem best to either nation. And the same thing also is understood of the things which are the subject of commerce.

§ 60.

§ 194. *Of the method of entering into stipulations for the purpose of commerce*

In the same way it is evident that agreements for commerce can be entered into either without time limit, or for a definite time, and to them can be added any conditions, even definite provisions for rescission, as shall seem best for the interests of the contracting parties.

§§ 35, 36.

He who has understood the things which we have proved concerning the method of transferring a certain right to another—we discussed them here and there when we were talking about the contracts of private individuals—will have absolutely no difficulty in the present proposition. Nevertheless, since the law of nature ought to control also the stipulations of nations, consequently those which are made in regard to commerce, care must undoubtedly be taken lest anything may be done which is contrary to the duties of nations toward themselves and toward others. For although foreign commerce not only provides for our need, but also tends to increase our wealth, nevertheless one must not so strive after utility that he hinders his duties toward himself and toward others. That this thing may be avoided, those points must be well considered which we have proved concerning the proper establishment of a state. But in former sections we have already shown that it depends upon the will of any nation whether or not it wishes to engage in commerce with another nation, and upon what condition it wishes so to engage, and that a perfect

§§ 14 and fol., part 3, Jus Nat.

§§ 63, 67.

§ 176.

right to engage in commerce with another nation cannot be acquired otherwise than by stipulation. But what is true concerning individual nations viewed as such, that likewise is true concerning two or more nations mutually agreeing in regard to commerce.

§ 73.
§ 191.

§ 195. *Of the revocation of commercial arrangements*

If nations simply allow each other, either tacitly or expressly, to engage in commerce, but that arrangement is based on no agreement, it can be revoked, whenever it seems best. For if one nation simply allows commerce with another, either tacitly or expressly, from the bare permission the other nation, to which that is allowed, does not obtain a perfect right to commerce; consequently the same thing also is true concerning two nations allowing commerce reciprocally to each other. Therefore, since the right belongs to neither to compel the other nation to engage in commerce with itself, each one always remains free to exercise it or not, as it chooses. If then it does not wish to exercise it for a longer time, it is not bound to allow it further. Therefore, since any right, such as the right to engage in commerce, may be revoked, if he who bestowed it, or permits the use of it, declares that he is unwilling to allow it longer; if nations simply allow the right of commerce to each other tacitly or expressly, but that arrangement is based on no agreement, from which alone a perfect right arises—which cannot be taken from one against his will—it can be revoked whenever it seems best.

§ 75.

§ 235, part 1, Phil. Pract. Univ.
§ 73.

§ 60.
§ 741, part 3, Jus Nat.

§ 74.

§ 336, part 2, Jus Nat.

Commerce is tacitly allowed, if any nation carries its goods into a foreign territory and there sells them and then purchases other goods, or vice versa, and if when the opportunity is given the other nation also does likewise. But commerce is expressly allowed, if granted to a nation on its request, as it were by the bare agreement, which produces no obligation of itself, unless a promise is added, so that it is transformed into a stipulation. We have an example of tacit permission in the case of neighbouring nations, who sell their goods to each other, as it shall have pleased them, without any previous stipulation or even without express permission. Commerce, whether allowed tacitly or expressly, remains a right of pure power, and the exercise of it consists in acts of pure will, and therefore the freedom of the will always

§ 698, part 1, Jus Nat.

§ 701, part 3, Jus Nat.

§ 702, part 3, Jus Nat.
§ 788, part 3, Jus Nat.

§ 77.

§ 377, part 2,
Jus Nat.

§ 235, part 1,
Phil. Pract.
Univ.

§ 375, part 3,
Jus Nat.

§ 1125, part 5,
Jus Nat.

Note, § 1124,
part 5, Jus Nat.

§ 1141, part 5,
Jus Nat.

§ 23.

§ 187.

§ 75.

§ 427, part 3,
Jus Nat.

§ 73.

remains unimpaired, whether or not any nation desires to allow it or to engage in it, if allowed. Of course a change of will must be allowed, as long as there is nothing contrary to the right of another, a perfect right to be sure, although the change is devoid of intrinsic right. But from the commerce which rests on simple permission we must distinguish the *precaria*, given as revocable at will, as the meaning accepted among the Romans indicates, although this too may be called a *precarium*. The commercial *precarium*, since it is established by stipulations, belongs to the stipulative law of nations, while that [*precarium*] which is only permitted remains within the limits of duties to each other. And that is the reason why we wish to distinguish *precaria* from simple permissions, although they agree in this point, that they may be revoked at will. But lest doubt may arise in regard to the commerce reciprocally granted, it is to be understood that there can be two distinct permissions, whether they are given at the same time, as when the one asking offers to the other voluntarily the same thing which he asks, or, on the other hand, when the one granting uses the same right later, which up to this time it had allowed the other party, without opposition on the latter's part. Nay more, nothing stands in the way of permission being given under the condition that it be allowed to each in turn to sell his goods to the one asking, provided only this is kept within the limits of the real agreement. Nor indeed is it repugnant to the permission to add a condition of any sort, which can be performed at any time, even when the other party is unwilling; of course one must always conform to the will of the grantor. There will remain no difficulty in these matters for the one who has learned to distinguish obligatory acts from the non-obligatory, so that there is no need of further elaboration. An act is not understood to be obligatory, unless the intention of the one binding himself to the other shall have been adequately expressed. Since the presumption in a doubtful case is in favour of freedom, as this by nature belongs to nations, the same thing holds for a simple permission.

§ 196. *Whether contrary to the stipulations in regard to commerce anything can be granted to a third party*

Contrary to any stipulations, consequently also to stipulations in regard to commerce entered into with one nation, nothing can be granted to another nation in respect of which the nations are, apart from this, naturally bound to each other. For since stipulations must be observed, a nation, which for the sake of commerce or for any other reason has contracted with another nation, does not have it in its power to grant to a third nation anything which is opposed to the agreement entered into for the sake of commerce or anything else. But no nation is bound to perform for another nation that which is not in its power. Therefore contrary to any stipulations, consequently contrary to stipulations in regard to commerce entered into with one nation, nothing can be granted to another nation in respect of which the nations are, apart from this, naturally bound to each other.

§ 789, part 3,
Jus Nat.

§ 175, part 1,
Jus Nat.

§ 160.

To be sure in regard to the things which bind nations to each other by nature, there is this restriction, "if it be in their power." Every nation owes this also to itself, not to break its pledged word, so that it should observe its agreements not only because of necessity, but likewise from a sense of duty both toward itself and also toward other nations, with which it has contracted. The very preservation of its reputation demands this, which the law of nature enjoins both upon individual men, and also upon nations. But the things which we have proved here in regard to nations are likewise true in kind of every private individual. In order that this may in no way be called into question, I wish to add the following proposition.

§ 156 h, and
§ 610, part 1,
Jus Nat.

§ 553, part 1,
Jus Nat.

§ 557, part 1,
Jus Nat.

§ 3.

§ 197. *The same treated more at large*

Contrary to a stipulation entered into with another, no one can perform for any third party anything in respect of which he is, apart from this, naturally bound to him. For since stipulations must be observed, if any one has contracted with another, he does not have it in his power to perform for some third person anything which is opposed to the stipulation. For nobody is naturally bound to promote the perfection of another man and to guard against his imperfection, consequently to perform anything which he does not have in his own power. Therefore contrary to a stipulation entered into with another, no one can perform for any third party anything in respect of which he is, apart from this, naturally bound to such other.

§ 789, part 3,
Jus Nat.

§ 175, part 1,
Jus Nat.

§ 80, part 3,
Jus Nat.

§ 611, part 3,
Jus Nat.

To be sure all duties toward others have this limitation, that they should be performed, if it is in one's power. For otherwise natural

§§ 611 and fol.,
part 1, Jus Nat.
§ 79, Ontol.

§ 209, part 1,
Phil. Pract.
Univ.

obligation would be extended even to that which is impossible, which would certainly be absurd. The things, therefore, which we have just now suggested concerning nations, namely, that they observe their stipulations because of a sense of duty toward themselves and toward the nations with whom they have contracted—those things also must be understood of all private citizens. I am not indeed ignorant that this is usually not observed; nevertheless the natural obligation which comes from the law of nature does not on that account cease, nor indeed must one think so badly of the whole human race as to believe all men in general devoid of that sense of duty needed for the preservation of stipulations. Surely those do ill who separate the sense of duty from external obligation, or at least in the performance of those things which are in harmony with the latter think little of the former. This proposition could be set before the preceding, and from it the preceding inferred by way of corollary.

§ 198. Of the contract that certain things should not be sold except to one nation or bought from it

If one nation shall have contracted with another to sell certain things only to the other or buy from it, it cannot sell things of that sort to still another nation or buy from it, without the consent of the nation which has contracted with it. For let us suppose that a nation, which has contracted with another to sell certain things only to it, or buy from it, sells things of that sort to another nation or buys from it; there is no one that

§ 60.

does not see that this is done contrary to the stipulation entered into for the purpose of commerce. Therefore, since it is not allowable contrary to the stipulations entered into for the purpose of commerce with one

§ 196.

nation, to perform anything for another which is opposed to the interest of the former, although apart from this one is bound by nature to do that; if any nation has contracted with another to sell certain things only to the other or buy from it, it cannot sell things of that sort to any other nation or buy from it. Which was the first point.

And if one nation shall have contracted with another to sell certain things only to it or buy from it, it is evident that the right belongs to the

§ 235, part 1,
Phil. Pract.
Univ.

second nation in the former case to prohibit a sale to another nation, in the latter case not to allow a purchase. But since any one can waive his right, when nothing is done contrary to the right of a third person, it is not to be doubted that, contrary to the stipulation, a nation which has contracted with another to sell certain things only to it, or buy from it, can sell things of that sort with the consent of this nation to any other nation, or buy from it. Which was the second point. § 117, part 3, Jus Nat.

Many particular instances can be given, where a nation with whom the contract has been made readily consents, or is at least presumed to consent, that things may be sold to another nation or bought from it. Let us suppose, for example, that a certain nation has contracted with another to have the other sell grain only to itself. Suppose that it buys grain simply for its own use, but not for the purpose of engaging in commerce with its neighbours. No harm can then occur to it, if in case of necessity grain is sold also to a neighbouring nation, or when for the purpose of commerce with neighbouring nations it purchases to sell to distant nations, with whom the first nation can have no commercial dealing. Therefore, nothing prevents consensus from being presumed, nay more, exceptional cases of this sort are even tacitly recognized. §§ 515, 530, part 6, Jus Nat.

§ 199. *Of the natural right to commerce with nations*

By nature every nation has the right to engage in commerce with every other nation. For all nations are bound by nature to engage in commerce with each other, so far as is in their power. Therefore, since from the common obligation of one party a right arises for the other, by nature every nation has the right to engage in commerce with every other nation. § 187.

§ 23, part 1, Jus Nat.

By nature all nations are equal to each other, and therefore all have the same rights, and what is allowable for one is likewise allowable for the other. Therefore, by nature likewise, no nation can claim a certain right to commerce to the exclusion of any other, except in so far as it has acquired for itself some especial right through stipulations. § 16. § 17. § 18. § 194.

§ 200. *Whether the use of that right can be interfered with*

Since by nature every nation has the right to engage in any sort of commerce with another, moreover, since no one without his consent can lose a right which belongs to him by nature, no nation can prevent any other nation from engaging in commerce with a certain nation, for example, § 199.

§ 64, part 1, and § 336, part 2, Jus Nat.

§ 239, part 1,
Phil. Pract.
Univ.

a distant one, and consequently if it should desire to interfere, since it would violate the right of the other, it does the other a wrong.

§ 859, part 1,
Jus Nat.

A nation does not lose a right which belongs to it by nature, because it has not used it, while another has used it for a long time, especially indeed if the use of the right has been interrupted without pressing necessity. It is in accordance with the natural liberty of nations that they may desire or not desire to use the right which belongs to them by nature. Now a right of this kind which belongs by nature to nations is rightly compared to an innate right of human beings. For as we posit this innate right, based on the nature and the essence of man, so we posit a right naturally com-

§ 28, part 1,
Jus Nat.

§ 2.

§ 3.

Note, § cited.

petent to nations, based on the nature and the essence of a nation, each of which in itself is considered as a single person, so that those things can be applied to them which are proved in "The Law of Nature" concerning individuals, noting however the difference which exists between the essence and nature of a man and of a nation.

§ 201. *Of maritime commerce*

§ 200.

§ 122.

Since no nation can prohibit any other from engaging in any kind of commerce with some other distant nation, or from navigating the open sea, no nation can be prohibited from navigating the open sea to distant nations for the sake of commerce with any other nation.

§ 119, part 2,
Jus Nat.

No nation can make maritime commerce its special property by occupation, so that then by virtue of its own right it may exclude others; for that is opposed to a principle of the law of nature which is granted or at least should be granted by all, that no one's right belonging to him by nature can be taken from him without his consent. Particular rights are acquired only by stipulation, or by the intervention of some human act, fitted to produce obligations and rights, and they are conferred on no one by nature, in which they have a sufficient reason only as common rights.

§ 202. *Of negative stipulations in regard to commerce*

One nation can covenant with another not to engage in commerce with a certain nation, or to navigate to certain places for the purpose of commerce, or it can even restrict its own commerce in any way for the benefit of another. By nature the right belongs to every nation to engage in commerce with any other nation without any restriction, nor can any nation prevent navigation through the open sea for the purpose of commerce. Therefore, since it is possible for any one to waive his rights, consequently to bind himself to another, that he will not exercise his right against the other, since, moreover, we may be bound to another by stipulations, one nation can covenant with another, that it will not engage in commerce with a certain nation, or navigate to certain places for the purpose of commerce, or it can even restrict its own commerce in any way for the benefit of another.

§ 199.

§ 201.

§ 118, part 3,
Jus Nat.

§ 104, part 3,
Jus Nat.

§ 789, part 3,
Jus Nat.

> Negative stipulations of commerce depend upon this principle. Those of course are called negative stipulations which bind not to do, or even not to give, and are opposed to affirmative stipulations which bind to give or to do. Hence, moreover, arise mixed stipulations which are in part affirmative, in part negative. But since the negative stipulations of commerce rest on the renunciation of a right otherwise belonging to oneself, as is evident from the proof of the present proposition, while depending absolutely on the will of the one renouncing, in what way he may wish to renounce, whether indeed absolutely, or under a certain condition, whether altogether, or only in part; from this also it is readily understood upon what terms negative stipulations of commerce should be made. No one's right indeed can be taken from him without his consent; nevertheless any one can diminish his right as he pleases by stipulation.

§ 106, part 3,
Jus Nat.

§ 203. *What right arises therefrom*

Since one nation can covenant with another not to engage in commerce with a certain nation or to navigate to certain places for the purpose of commerce, or even can restrict its own commerce in any way for the benefit of another, since, moreover, stipulations must be observed or are binding by nature, from this obligation itself there arises for the nation with which the contract has been made the right not to allow that to be done concerning which there was an agreement that it should not be done; consequently from the negative stipulations of commerce the right arises for one party not to allow the other to engage in commerce with

§ 202.

§ 789, part 3,
Jus Nat.

a certain other nation or to navigate to certain places for the purpose of commerce or to extend commerce beyond the restriction agreed upon.

§ 1276, part 3, Jus Nat.

Those are mistaken who persuade themselves that by this stipulation a servitude is imposed on the sea. For the sea, so far as concerns its use indeed, is the common property of all, nevertheless the special property of none, while a servitude to another is established in one's own property. But it is one thing to bind yourself to another not to use a certain right of your own for the benefit of the other; it is another thing to establish a negative servitude in your own property for him.

§ 204. *In what freedom of commerce consists*

Freedom of commerce is defined as independence of the will of another in engaging in it. Therefore freedom of commerce between nations flourishes, if any nation can engage in commerce with any other nation as it pleases.

§ 153, part 1, Jus Nat.

Here we retain the general meaning of freedom, and we apply that to commerce in particular, in that respect not departing from the common usage of speech.

§ 205. *Whether it belongs to natural law*

§ 187.

§ 200.

Since nations are bound by nature to engage in commerce with each other, as far as it is in their power, and it is not possible for any nation to prohibit or prevent another nation from engaging in commerce with any other, by nature freedom of commerce between nations must be left untrammelled, as far as possible. And since in a state the liberty of individuals is indeed restricted, so far as concerns those actions which tend to promote the public good, while so far as concerns the others it remains untrammelled, freedom of internal commerce likewise ought to remain untrammelled, so far as possible, and ought not to be restricted beyond that which the public good demands.

§ 47, part 8, Jus Nat.

§ 61.

We have said that freedom of commerce between nations ought to be left untrammelled, as far as that is possible. But this restriction must not be taken as insufficiently determined. For from the preceding it is understood what ought to be considered in deciding it. For

nations are not bound to engage in commerce with each other, except
so far as that is in their power, consequently each nation ought to
measure this natural obligation by the purpose of the state. And since
by nature all nations are equal, one must guard also against injuring the general freedom of commerce. So far as internal commerce is
concerned, the decision is not difficult as to whether or not it should
be restricted beyond that which the public good demands, provided
only you turn your attention to the idea of the public good, and do
not oppose to it the advantage of the prince as distinct from it, as is
frequently done. Since all nations are understood to have united into
a state, and since these, like individuals united into a particular state,
are bound one to the other to promote the common good, the restriction imposed upon freedom of commerce among nations is defined
from the standpoint of the common good of all nations no less than
in internal commerce. In the supreme state the same duties naturally
exist between nations, as are found between citizens, or members of
some particular state.

§ 187.
Note, § cited.

§ 16.

§ 9, part 8,
Jus Nat.

§ 9.

§ 12.

§ 206. Of the conflict of the duties of nations toward themselves and toward other nations

If the duty of a nation toward itself conflicts with its duty toward another
nation, the duty of the nation toward itself prevails. For if duty toward
oneself conflicts with duty toward others, duty toward oneself prevails.
Therefore, since those things which are a part of natural law as between
private individuals, must be applied to nations also, if the duty of a
nation toward itself conflicts with a duty toward another nation, the
duty of the nation toward itself prevails.

§ 229, part 1,
Phil. Pract. Univ.

§ 3.

This general principle has great utility in the law of nations, since
it helps in the decision of many questions, which, if it were not considered, would seem beset with great difficulties.

§ 207. Of encroachment on the freedom of a third nation by stipulations of two in regard to commerce

It is not opposed to the natural freedom of commerce between nations,
that through stipulations the freedom of some third nation is encroached

upon. For a perfect right to engage in commerce with any nation cannot be acquired except by stipulations, and a certain nation can even covenant with another to sell definite things to it alone, nay more, can even agree not to engage in commerce with a certain nation. Therefore, since nations enter into stipulations in regard to commerce for the sake of their own advantage, and natural obligation itself leads them to promote it, if through a stipulation in regard to commerce between two nations the liberty of some third nation is encroached upon, duty toward itself conflicts with duty toward other nations. Therefore, since in a conflict of duties of nations toward themselves and toward others the duty toward themselves prevails, it is not opposed to the natural liberty of commerce between nations, that through stipulations in regard to commerce the liberty of some third nation is encroached upon.

The liberty of covenanting concerning commerce is no less natural than liberty of commerce. And since we have shown above that nations are not bound to engage in commerce with each other, except so far as it is in their power, it is readily evident, if a certain nation enter into a stipulation with another nation concerning commerce and for this reason cannot engage in commerce with some third nation, that this is not in its power. Indeed, if this were to be considered unfair between nations, it would not be allowed among private individuals to acquire for oneself through stipulations a perfect right to certain performances from another, for the reason that then it would no longer be possible to perform some duty of humanity for some third person seeking it, or even to one needing the same, nor in a particular case would it be allowable to sell your own property to one, because some third party might have been about to buy it. I do not deny that stipulations which are made between two nations concerning commerce frequently contain certain things which are unfair as regards some third nation, inasmuch as the stipulations could be made without prejudice to it; but who demands of the stipulations of men the highest rigour of equity? Therefore, since nothing is perfect in human affairs, it is sufficient that injustice may be removed from stipulations by understanding their force, that thus some perfect right of a third person may not be violated through them; otherwise the things which belong to the domain of charity must be left to the conscience of each and every one.

§ 192.

§ 202.

§§ 35, 63.

§ 206, part 1,
Phil. Pract.
Univ.
§ 206.

§ 187.

§ 208. *Whether it is allowable to divert gain from another nation*

Since it is not opposed to the natural freedom of commerce between nations, that through stipulations the freedom of some third nation is encroached upon as regards that commerce, and since commerce is profitable; it is allowable through stipulation in regard to commerce to divert gain from one nation to another, and since no perfect right of another is violated, it is devoid of any wrong.

§ 207.

§ 63.

§§ 189, 191.

§ 859, part 1, Jus Nat.

We have seen above that a nation can make a valid covenant with another nation, that it will sell certain things to it alone. If, then, some third nation cannot procure these things in any other way, except by buying them from that nation which has made the stipulation concerning the selling of them to the other alone, the gain is diverted from the latter to itself, especially if there are several nations which are bound by the same necessity. Since this is the consequence of a stipulation not in itself invalid, in fact resting upon ownership, and upon the duty of a nation toward itself, it cannot be considered illegal, if profit be diverted from some nation by this stipulation. What is here proved of nations, the same thing, it plainly appears, is also true of individual men, or of private persons. Of course the same reasons exist in either case, although they do not prevent monopolies from being granted in a state, and we have shown elsewhere when these are not illegal in themselves. It happens very often and in many ways, that profit may be diverted from one to another by stipulations, nor can it happen otherwise, unless you should wish to eliminate all stipulations, which, after ownership of things has been introduced, is certainly impossible.

§ 193.

§ 63.

§ 118, part 2, Jus Nat.

§§ 69, 70.

§ 3.

§ 875, part 7, Jus Nat.

§ 876, part 8, Jus Nat.

§ 209. *Of the taking away of gain*

If any nation by engaging in commerce, which it had not before engaged in, takes away the gain of another nation, it does it no wrong. For every nation by nature is bound to perfect its condition, and it ought to do its best to become powerful. Therefore, since foreign commerce makes a nation rich, consequently powerful, freedom of commerce naturally must be left untrammelled, as far as it can be done, consequently it is allowable for every nation to engage in commerce as it pleases, when and

§ 35.

§ 70.

§§ 67, 69.

§ 205.

§ 910, part 1,
Jus Nat.
however it desires, provided only it does nothing contrary to the perfect
right of another which is acquired only by stipulation, nay more, since
by nature the right belongs to every nation to engage in commerce with
§ 191. every other nation; if any nation engages in commerce, which before it
§ 199. had not engaged in, it uses its own right, which could not be barred by
§ 37. prescription, because beforehand the nation had not used the right at all.
Therefore, since through this the right of another is not violated, because
§ 79. you use your own right in doing what you are indeed permitted to do,
consequently you do no wrong to another, and, although the condition
§ 170, part 1,
Phil. Pract.
Univ. of other nations also must be perfected, as much as possible, nevertheless
in case of conflict the duty of a nation toward itself prevails over the duty
§ 859, part 1,
Jus Nat. toward others; if any nation, by engaging in commerce, which before it
had not engaged in, takes away gain from another nation, it nevertheless
§ 166.
§ 206. does it no wrong.

Not in one way alone, as by engaging in commerce, when beforehand that had not been done, does it happen that the gain of another
nation is taken away, either by stipulations in regard to commerce,
or without them. This happens, if some nation which had bought
certain things from another nation, for the sake of commerce with
that nation, from which such goods had come, or even with some
other nation, from which the same things could be had, itself enters
into a stipulation to buy goods, or even without previous stipulation buys them. Here also belongs the establishment of a market, to
which, because of advantage of position, or for some other reason,
buyers are attracted, who were accustomed to provide themselves
with certain things elsewhere from some nation. Although this dis-
pleases the nation whose gain is taken away, it has no just cause of
complaint in regard to it, nay more, its complaints are hardly fair.
The loss which a nation suffers in its profit is to be attributed to
unfavourable fortune, not to the nation which takes away its advantages by no illicit means. Nor is it of itself opposed to charity, if in
this manner the gain of another nation is taken away, unless other
acts are added which are opposed to it; for it has been abundantly
proved that acts allowable in themselves, or even good, can be affected
by others, illicit or bad, accompanying them, and be turned into illicit
or bad acts.

§ 210. *Of unfair monopolies of nations*

If any nation has contracted with another to sell certain things to it alone, which cannot be had elsewhere than from it, and it sells the same things to other nations which need them, at an unfair price, it sins, to be sure, but nevertheless does no legal wrong. For since nations are bound by nature to engage in commerce with each other, so far as is in their power, they ought to sell their own goods which they themselves do not need, but which others have need of, at a fair price, and it is not allowable to exact a price greater than is fair, or an unjust price. But if therefore a nation which has contracted with another to sell certain things to it alone, which cannot be had elsewhere, and then sells those same things to other nations which need them, at an unfair price, it does undoubtedly what is opposed to the law of nature, consequently it sins. Which was the first point.

§ 187.

§ 60.

§ 322, part 4, Jus Nat.

§§ 3 h, 323, part 4, Jus Nat.

§ 440, part 1, Phil. Pract. Univ.

Nevertheless, since it is wholly within the control of any one whether or not he desires to sell his property to another, and for what price he desires to sell, and the right to abuse his own right is also allowed him, although prohibited by the law of nature, as long as he does nothing contrary to the right of another, as here is not the case, by the hypothesis of the present proposition no legal wrong is done to the nation purchasing. Which was the second point.

§ 118, part 2, Jus Nat.

§ 170, part 2, Jus Nat.

§ 169, part 2, Jus Nat.

§ 191.

But do not persuade yourself that we argue that such things as we cannot prevent by law are done in accordance with law. For we have lately shown how great a difference there is between impunity in doing and the right to do. Many things are done with impunity by nations also, which are not done rightly, nor in accordance with any law. Grotius stated that any people might covenant with another people, that such people should sell to them alone fruits of a certain sort, which did not grow elsewhere, if the people that purchased them were ready to sell to others at a fair price. But indeed he adds a restriction, "in so far as it considers the duties which the law of nature prescribes for a nation toward nations"; from which he likewise concludes that such a purchase, made with the purpose which he mentioned, is not opposed to the law of nature. But if the question is asked, what is consistent with the duty which one nation owes to another, or every human

§ 859, part 2, Jus Nat.

§ 418, part 3, Jus Nat.

De Jure Belli ac Pacis, lib. 2, c. 2, § 24.

being to the human race; then assuredly the purchase of things made with the intention that they should be sold to others at a fair price contains nothing which is contrary to it, since, as Grotius rightly says, it makes no difference to other nations from whom they buy, moreover the one may lawfully divert gain from the other.

§ 208.

§ 211. *Of the desire to promote commerce between nations*

Whatever any nation can contribute to the promotion of commerce reciprocally between nations, that it is bound by nature to contribute. For nations are bound by nature to engage in commerce with each other, so far as that is in their power, and, because they are understood to have combined in a supreme state, to advance the common good. Whatever, therefore, any one of them can contribute to the promotion of commerce reciprocally between nations, that it is bound by nature to contribute.

§ 187.

§ 12.

Just as in a state no citizen ought to seek only that which is his own, but each is bound to promote the common good, as best he can; so also no nation ought to look out only for its own welfare, but each ought to provide, as best it can, for the welfare of all. But we have already noted above, that, if any nation would simply perform the duties owed by nature to neighbouring nations, that would conduce to the common good of all.

§ 28, part 8,
Jus Nat.

Note, § 185.

§ 212. *Of the removal of obstacles to commerce*

Since every nation ought to contribute what it can to the promotion of commerce reciprocally between nations it ought in no way to hamper commerce, but ought, as far as it can, to remove those things which can be obstacles to commerce.

§ 211.

§ 722, part 1,
Jus Nat.

Not in one way alone do nations err here, and from no other cause than that usually they measure everything simply by their own advantage, nor do they think that they are concerned with that which affects other nations, unless they themselves can gain some present advantage therefrom. Those who are influenced solely by their own interest put very many obstacles in the way of commerce, if they have also an insatiable desire for gain, and not rarely men of perverse character rend their own vitals. But such questions are left to civil prudence or the art of politics, to be more fully elaborated.

§ 213. *Of methods of promoting commerce*

Since every nation ought to contribute what it can to the promotion of commerce reciprocally between nations, and to remove, as far as it can, those things which may be obstacles to commerce, therefore every nation ought to see to it that the things which are subjects of commerce can be properly and safely imported and exported and readily exchanged each in its own locality, consequently that there should be safe approach and departure for ships and freighters, and that opportunity should not be lacking for exchange and selling and buying, and that importers and exporters and travellers should not be delayed, lest too great expenses should be incurred by them, that lawsuits arising between merchants should be ended without delay, that nothing should be done which is in any way contrary to the rights created by the stipulations of merchants, and many other things which are of this character.

§ 211.

§ 212.

If any case arises in which commerce can be promoted, or if some obstacle is thrown in its way, by force of the general principles from which we have derived certain particular applications, it will readily be recognized what ought to be done, what not, provided only that the selfish interest hostile to commerce which we have noted just previously does not cloud the mind of the judges.

Note, § 212.

§ 214. *Of imposing taxes on goods*

A tax can be imposed on goods either in transit, or when imported or exported, on the basis of the support of the burdens of commerce, and likewise on the basis of the profit received from the sale of goods. For since no one is bound to give to another for nothing, if the other is able to give in return; no nation either is bound to pay charges for forwarding without cost or for aiding commerce in any way. Therefore, since a tax is paid on goods and on transportation for the purpose of bearing the

§ 268, part 4, Jus Nat.

§ 929, part 8, Jus Nat.

burdens of the state, a tax can be imposed, either on goods in transit or when imported, on the basis of the support of the burdens of commerce. Which was the first point.

And since the advantage which citizens gain from the constitution of the state is also shared by foreigners, who sell their goods to citizens, a fact which can be assumed, since it is plainly evident, and since citizens are therefore bound to bear the burdens of the state; and furthermore, since the opportunity is given to foreigners of selling their goods, which need not be done for nothing; it is certainly not unfair, that on the basis of the profit received by foreigners from the sale of goods a tax may be imposed also upon the goods sold. Which was the second point.

> For no one is bound to do anything for another for nothing, if the other can give or do anything in return, and consequently no one is bound to increase the profit of another for nothing, if the other in any way can benefit him by way, to be sure, of return for what he has performed. And on this account it is quite in harmony with natural equity that because of the profit received from a sale some tax should be paid, nevertheless with this precaution, that the price of goods should not be too much increased, so that there would be no one who would want to buy or who would be able to buy, except at a loss to the seller.

§ 215. *What sort of burdens cannot be imposed on goods*

Burdens are not to be imposed on goods which are not appropriate to them. For although it is allowable to impose taxes for the purpose of bearing the burdens of commerce and for furnishing opportunity to sell goods, as is apparent by proof of the preceding proposition, if any burdens are imposed upon goods which are not appropriate to them, the reason fails altogether for allowing it to be imposed. Therefore the reason ceasing, the imposition ought also to cease. Therefore the burdens which are not appropriate to goods may by no means be imposed upon them.

> So the tribute which is paid for military purposes, or for any public disaster, or for any public business, is not appropriate to goods, and therefore cannot be imposed on goods, or exacted from those whose goods are in transit, or who import or sell them. Therefore, from the

§ 775, part 8, Jus Nat.

§ 268, part 4, Jus Nat.

§ 268, part 4, Jus Nat.

§ 931, part 8, Jus Nat.

§ 213.

§70, Ontol.

purpose for which burdens are imposed on citizens, it is readily recognized whether or not they are appropriate to goods. But whether taxes are imposed on goods on the basis of bearing the burdens of commerce, is readily known by determining whether more is asked for than the burdens demand; and whether they are imposed on the basis of profit received, the opportunity for sale and the promised security must be considered, which indeed seem difficult to calculate, nevertheless it can be calculated from this, that the seller willingly pays, that he may be able to sell his goods. The Massilians, according to Strabo, having dug a canal from the Rhone to the sea, demanded toll from those who ascended or descended in ships. Since the canal could not possibly be dug and kept in repair without expense, the toll was just, because it was equal to the interest on the amount paid out on the canal and the expenses incurred in its preservation.[1] In like manner the Corinthians received toll on the goods which were transferred by land from the Aegean to the Ionian Sea and return, that they might not have to go around the Peloponnesus and that the risks of the Malean promontory might be avoided. For in this way they provided for the security of their goods and facilitated commerce. Here too belongs the case of channels made in rivers for the purpose of navigation, through which a passage is open for ships, which would otherwise be closed up by rubbish piled up in the channel. In our native idiom we call them *Schleussen* [sluices].

§ 216. *Definition of an emporium*

Emporia are defined as places intended for continuous commerce between nations, consequently one may at any time import goods for sale into them and export goods purchased from them.   § 60.

> In emporia commerce between nations flourishes daily, and is not restricted to a certain time of year. Goods for sale are collected in them, so that at any time they can be purchased and exported by foreigners, and on the other hand foreign nations are allowed at any

1. Strabo, *The Geography of Strabo*, trans. by Horace Leonard Jones and J. R. Sitlington Sterrett, 8 vols. (London: William Heinemann; New York: G. P. Putnam's Sons, 1917–32), vol. 2, bk. IV, 1.8, p. 189.

time to import their goods and likewise to sell them. The meaning here is a little more restricted than the Latin usage allows, or than our word *Handel-Stadt* [commercial city]; but it is that which applies to the commerce of nations in modern practice, and consequently to our present purpose. In the broader meaning it denotes any place in which goods are exposed for sale.

§ 217. *Of the obligation to establish emporia*

Since in emporia the stock of goods for sale to a foreign nation is set out and into them goods from foreign nations are likewise imported for sale or exchange, and consequently emporia promote and facilitate commerce between nations, since, moreover, every nation is bound to contribute what it can to promote and facilitate commerce between nations; nations ought to establish emporia.

§ 216.

§ 66.

§§ 211, 212.

In establishing emporia nations consider the interest not only of others, but likewise of themselves; for commerce tends to mutual advantage. Therefore emporia ought to be established, not only from necessity, in so far as a nation goes into a business useful to itself, but also in consideration for the advantage of other nations. Nevertheless you ought not to think that a sense of duty toward other nations is superfluous, because personal advantage leads to establishing emporia. For to say nothing of the fact that it is scarcely in harmony with the law of nature that a sense of duty toward other nations be ignored, as we have already shown above; if we get down to those points, which are to be considered in establishing emporia for the purpose of commerce, it will be plainly evident, if there should be consideration simply of personal advantage, that there would not be equal provision for nations engaged in commerce with each other.

Note, § 180.

§ 218. *What things are to be considered in establishing them*

Because emporia are designed for commerce between nations, since, moreover, nations ought to promote commerce in every way and to remove all impediments to it; not only must care be taken, that in emporia goods can readily and safely be imported and exported, and likewise readily exchanged, that approach and departure may be safe for ships

§ 216.

§§ 211, 212, 213.

and freighters, that opportunity may not be lacking to exchange and purchase goods, that importers or exporters or transients may not be delayed, that excessive charges may not be imposed upon them, that disputes arising between merchants may be ended without delays, that nothing may be done which in any way is opposed to the rights created by a stipulation of commerce; but also that privileges useful in promoting commerce be bestowed upon foreign nations, such as, that permanent residence be allowed there to foreigners, possession of immovable property, free exercise of religion, the use of their native law with each other, exemption from tax on imported or exported goods, or at least tax at a rate less than that which is ordinarily paid, and many other things of this sort. But since a perfect right to those things which pertain to commerce is not acquired except by stipulation, and since the things which are not ratified by stipulation, but indeed are merely allowed by a nation, can be revoked whenever it shall seem best, one nation, when it wishes to engage in commerce with another, ought to bind the other to itself by stipulation in regard to those things which seem to it suitable for promoting commerce in emporia, or facilitating it. And because promises are to be kept, if any nation in order to facilitate commerce makes certain promises to foreign nations, it also ought to keep them.

§ 853, part 8, Jus Nat.

§ 191.

§ 195.

§ 431, part 3, Jus Nat.

When indeed we here speak of law, the points are not considered which prudence may have suggested as pertinent in politics, to which belongs all consideration as to whether or not this is advantageous to the state. But here for the sake of brevity we have as it were heaped together those things which in entering into stipulations in respect to commerce in emporia must be considered, or which even of their own free will nations ought to allow, since they flow naturally from general principles proved by us.

§ 219. *What a port is*

Ports are defined as enclosed places near the shores of a sea, where goods are imported and from which they are exported in ships. And therefore it is plain that ports are made for the sake of maritime commerce.

Ports have also this accidental use, that, when a storm is raging on the open sea, safety may be afforded ships carried into them, and that likewise ships may be able to pass the winter in them.

§ 220. *Of the making and fortifying of ports*

§ 213.
§ 219.

Since nations are bound to facilitate commerce, since, moreover, ports tend to facilitate commerce by sea, nations are bound to make ports for the sake of maritime commerce and to fortify them, in order that they can be defended against a hostile force, and security be thus furnished to merchants.

§ 8.

§ 941, Ontol.

Note, § 180.

The natural obligation to make ports comes from the law of nature, which enjoins upon nations the promotion of the common good, and from this common good are derived the arguments in regard to those things which pertain to ports; but aside from natural obligation, physical necessity suggests the making of ports, inasmuch as he who desires an end must necessarily desire the means also, and the arguments in regard to those things which pertain to ports are derived from their purpose, and the will is moved by personal advantage, which in case of a conflict between desire and aversion brings it about that desire prevails. Therefore, although nations make ports without a sense of duty, and arrange and establish everything in accordance with their purpose, nevertheless on this account it is not to be believed that this is not done from a sense of duty, as if the law of nature cared not for this, or that the sense of duty is altogether useless.

§ 221. *To what extent one may argue from emporia to ports*

§§ 216, 219.

Since ports are made for the same purpose for which emporia are established, those things which are proved concerning emporia are to be applied to ports also, in so far as their condition allows.

§ 218.

Perfect rights for foreign nations in ports also arise from stipulation, just as in emporia, but certain things rest on the bare concession of a nation to whom the ports belong, and therefore depend on the will alone of the one granting.

§ 222. *What markets are*

By markets [*nundinae*] we understand the transaction of business restricted to a certain time, or also at the same time to merchantable goods, as to certain days of the week and to things necessary to live on, or to a certain time of the year and any kinds of goods. In the former case they are called in our native vernacular *Marckt-Tage* [market days]; in the latter *Jahrmärckte* [yearly markets], and, if they have been established especially for the benefit of merchants, *Messen* [fairs].

The markets were so arranged by the Romans that the peasants worked for eight days in the field, but on the ninth day they resorted to the city for trade. Hence Festus says that the peasants were accustomed to come together every ninth day [*nundinis*] for the purpose of buying and selling.[2]

§ 223. *Of the natural obligation to establish markets*

Since markets tend to promote both internal and external commerce, since, moreover, nations are bound to engage in both internal and external commerce, they are also bound by nature to establish markets.

§§ 62, 63, 222.
§§ 64, 187.

Necessity itself leads to the establishment of markets, because they serve the internal advantage of the state and by them a sufficiency for the life of the individuals is provided. Nevertheless this necessity does not destroy the natural obligation, as we have just now suggested, and as we have already so often inculcated.

Note, § 217.

§ 224. *How those things are to be determined which are to be established in regard to markets*

Since markets consist in the transaction of business, consequently aid in providing everything movable and moving, the necessary as well as

§ 222.
§ 60.

2. See Verrius Flaccus and Sextus Pompeius Festus, *De verborum significatione libri XX ex editione Andreae Dacerii cum notis et interpretatione in usum delphini*, 2 vols. (London, 1826), vol. 1, s.v. "nundinis," footnote z: "[Nundinae] [a] nono die dictae, quia nono quoque die fiebant, ut cum rustici octo diebus in agris opere faciendo versati essent, nono die intermisso rure ad mercatum et leges accipiendas Romam venirent." ("The *nundinae* are named after the ninth day, because they occurred on the ninth day. For after the farmers had been occupied with laboring on their fields for eight days, on the ninth day they left the countryside and came to Rome to go to market and settle legal matters" [my translation]). Festus was a Roman grammarian in the second century A.D., who made an epitome of the encyclopedic *De verborum significatione* of Verrius Flaccus.

the useful and agreeable, since, moreover, in every state public welfare
is the supreme law, the things which are to be established concerning
markets are to be determined from their tendency to further the welfare
of the state.

§ 86, part 8,
Jus Nat.

He who considers carefully the purpose of markets and keeps constantly in mind the welfare of the state, which consists in the unhin-
dered attainment of a sufficiency for life, its tranquillity and security,
will have no difficulty in any case in defining what is allowable by
nature in regard to markets, nor is it to be feared that he will do
anything which is out of harmony with the duties of nations either
toward themselves or toward other nations; in what manner indeed
an exception is to be made in case of conflict of these duties is plain
from what precedes.

§ 17, part 8,
Jus Nat.

§ 206.

§ 225. *What a* propolium *is*

A *propolium* (in the native vernacular *der Vorkauf* [a forestallment]) is
usually defined as a privilege by which citizens or certain definite individuals are allowed to purchase imported goods before foreigners or
other persons are allowed to purchase them. Since, therefore, goods
are imported into emporia, ports and markets, to be sold, *propolia* are
granted in emporia, ports and markets. Akin to this right is the privilege
conceded to any one, that a purchaser may be bound to release in favour
of another purchaser his own right acquired from a contract of purchase
and sale and give up to the same person the property purchased, if such
person is willing to pay the same price as the other agreed upon with the
vendor. Akin also is the right by which in markets, or even in emporia
or in ports, citizens or certain other individuals are allowed to sell certain goods before that privilege is allowed to foreigners or to everybody
generally.

§§ 216, 219,
222.

We take *propolium* with that meaning which is to-day assigned to it
as a recognized technical term. By the Romans he was called a *propola*,
who, before others bought, purchased a thing at a less price or bought
in advance, that he might afterwards sell at a higher price, the one
who in our native speech is called ein *Aufkäuffer* [a forestaller]. Since
propolae increase prices of things more than is necessary, it is plainly

evident that they are not to be tolerated in the state, especially in the
weekly markets.

§ 226. Propolia *not to be granted*

Propolia are not to be granted, unless the public good for some special reason suggests it. The same is understood of the rights which are
akin to *propolia*. For the one to whom a *propolium* has been granted has
the right of purchasing imported goods before others are permitted to
purchase, consequently since freedom of commerce consists in engag- §225.
ing in it independently of the will of another, freedom of commerce
is restricted through *propolia*. Therefore, since commerce is to be left §204.
untrammelled, as far as that can be done, nor is internal commerce to be
restricted beyond that which the common good of the state demands,
and the same is understood of foreign commerce, because nations are §205.
known to have united into a supreme state, but also because nations
ought to facilitate commerce in every way, and ought not to hinder it in §12.
any way, but ought to remove, as far as possible, those things which can §211.
injure it; *propolia* are not to be allowed, unless for some especial reason §212.
the public good suggests it. Which was the first point.

Since the kindred rights consist in this, that a vendor is compelled
to deliver the thing purchased to another purchaser, if he pays the same
price, or that certain persons are allowed to sell their goods before it is
permitted to others; in the same way as before it is understood that rights §225.
of this sort are not to be granted, unless on account of some special reason the public good suggests it. Which was the second point.

> Special reasons must be sought from the public good, that *propolia*
> be granted, and the rarer the former are, the more reluctantly also
> the latter are to be granted; for it is not permitted to detract from the
> equality of citizens and nations, except in case of conflicts of duties,
> on account of which an exception is to be made.

§ 227. *What the right of staple is and of what sort it is*

The right of staple, in the native vernacular *Stapel-Recht*, is the privilege
of arresting those who are passing by with goods on a public river and
compelling them to sell, or, if they are unwilling to sell, to pay tribute,

as Wachter defines it in his "Glossarium Germanicum."[3] But the meaning is also extended, so that it includes the right by which certain goods are to be imported into a certain locality and likewise sold there, or even that goods are to be carried to other ships or freighters for transportation. Therefore it is plain that the right of staple is decidedly opposed to

§ 204.   freedom of commerce.

> Staple is a word Germanic in origin: it was received by the jurists in the subject of law, there being no Latin word which indicates the same thing, as occurs in many other cases of the same sort, for example, in Saxon law, *gerada, heergewettum, wehrigeldum.*[4]

§ 228. *Whether it may be allowed*

§ 227.   Since the right of staple is especially opposed to freedom of commerce, it
§ 226.   is shown in the same way as before that it must not be allowed, unless very special reasons derived from consideration of the public good suggest it.

> So there is no injustice in this, if all the wool from a certain entire province at a definite time of year is to be brought into a certain

---

3. Johann Georg Wachter, *Glossarium Germanicum: Continens Origines & Antiquitates Totius Linguae Germanicae, Et Omnium Pene Vocabulorum, Vigentium Et Desitorum* (Leipzig, 1737), col. 1587.

4. *Gerada* is the inheritance of a deceased woman's possessions, which pass to her nearest female blood-relation. See, for example, Benedict Carpzov, *Jurisprudentia forensis Romano-Saxonica. Editio V.* (Leipzig, 1668), pt. II, constit. XIV, definit. 22, p. 572: "Bona utensilia jure Saxonico non solum praemortuo marito ad uxorem superstitem pertinent; Sed & si uxor ante maritum decesserit, bona illa ad proximam cognatam devolvuntur." ("According to Saxon law, not only do utensils belong to the wife if her husband predeceases her, but if the wife dies before the husband these goods also pass to the closest blood-relation" [my translation]). *Heergewettum*, also *res expeditoriae*, "are those things, which are required for arming a soldier and providing for one person going on a military campaign" ("sunt eae, quae ad armandum militem, & ad expeditionem militarem unius hominis requiruntur"), which were to be inherited by the male heir of the deceased (Carpzov, *Jurisprudentia forensis Romano-Saxonica. Editio V.*, pt. III, constit. XXXVIII, definit. 23, p. 1275). *Werigeldum* or *Wergeldum* was the payment by a person responsible for the death of another to the heirs of the victim (Carpzov, *Jurisprudentia forensis Romano-Saxonica*, pt. IV, constit. XI, definit. 1, p. 1331).

emporium by the merchants and there sold; for this tends to promote commerce, and certainly throws no obstacle in its way, as is quite plain by force of what precedes.

§ 229. *What consuls in maritime emporia are*

Consuls are defined as persons to whom in maritime emporia or ports is entrusted the duty of guarding the privileges and rights of their people or nation, and of ending disputes of merchants.

> In our time, when European nations dwelling on the sea engage in maritime commerce with foreign nations, they have their own consuls also in foreign emporia.

§ 230. *Of the appointment and acceptance of consuls*

Consuls are to be appointed in maritime emporia or ports by nations engaging in maritime commerce with distant nations, and are to be received by the latter. For consuls are appointed for the purpose of guarding the privileges and rights of their nation and ending the disputes of merchants. Since, therefore, perfect rights to commerce are acquired only through stipulations, and since privileges are special rights conceded to merchants, which they otherwise lack, and for the sake of facilitating commerce it is allowed that foreign merchants may reside permanently in emporia, likewise that they may use native law in contracts with each other and in other matters, which have no effect on the state of the nation granting, consequently controversies arising between them are to be settled in accordance with the same law, since, moreover, stipulations must be observed, and consequently rights as well as privileges derived therefrom are to be protected, consuls are to be appointed by nations engaging in maritime commerce with distant nations in their maritime ports and emporia. Which was the first point.

Since consuls are appointed for the purpose of facilitating commerce, as is plain from what has been proved, since moreover every nation ought to contribute what it can to promote, consequently to facilitate commerce, and to remove the things which could hinder it, nations are

§ 229.

§ 191.

§ 853, part 8, Jus Nat.

§ 213.

§ 789, part 8, Jus Nat.

§ 211.

§ 212. bound by nature to receive consuls in their maritime emporia or ports. Which was the second point.

Experience speaks clearly of the use and necessity of commerce, and Conring explains that fully in his "Treatise on Maritime Commerce."[5] From this too it will be plain how much their appointment and acceptance aid in facilitating commerce.

§ 231. *How the perfect right of appointing consuls and the obligation of receiving them are acquired*

Since consuls are appointed and received in maritime emporia for the

§ 230.

sake of commerce, since, moreover, a perfect right to those things which affect commerce can be acquired only through stipulations; a perfect

§§ 191, 192.

right also to appoint consuls on the one side and the obligation corresponding to that on the other side, consequently also a perfect right to those things for the sake of which consuls are appointed, can be acquired only through stipulations.

There is no reason why you should think that the appointment and acceptance of consuls are necessarily implied in stipulations entered into concerning commerce; for only those things without which commerce cannot exist are necessarily implied; but not those things which simply facilitate it. But here also come in for distinction bare conventions, which only imply a permission on the part of the recipient, but do not produce a perfect right on the part of the one appointing. If then nothing is said concerning consuls in the stipulation of commerce, and no perfect stipulation is afterwards added concerning them, a perfect right of appointing also and the obligation of receiving those appointed do not exist. Therefore the acceptance is a duty of mere human kindness.

§ 232. *Whether consuls remain subjects of the nation appointing them*

Consuls remain subjects of the appointing nation. For consuls are appointed for no other purpose than to guard the privileges and rights of

5. Hermann Conring, "De maritimis commerciis," theses ii ff., in *Opera* (Brunswick, 1730), vol. 4, pp. 858–70.

their nation in maritime emporia and to end the disputes of merchants coming from the territory of the appointing power, and those remaining or dwelling there, and consequently he who receives them consents to this. Therefore they perform a public duty conferred by the appointing nation upon them, and on this account, if they perform it negligently or fraudulently, they can be removed by the appointing nation. Therefore they are subject to the law of the appointing nation, at the behest of which they are bound to perform the duty required of them. For since any one is subject to another, to whom a right over his acts belongs, consequently to whose right he is subject, consuls who were subject to the appointing nation at the time of appointment also remain such, after they have been appointed.

§ 229.

§ 884, part 8, Jus Nat.

§ 915, part 8, Jus Nat.

§ 141, part 8, Jus Nat.

§ 134, part 8, Jus Nat.

The duty of a consul cannot be understood apart from the civil power of the appointing nation over him. For let us suppose that he is subject to the receiving nation. Since he is held to obey this one, consequently to do those things which it orders, and not to do those things which it forbids; if he acts contrary to the privileges and rights of the nation by which he was appointed, or even desires to end the disputes of merchants according to his pleasure, that nation will have to abide by his will. Therefore his duty, which consists in guarding the privileges and rights of that nation and in ending the disputes of merchants, will in very truth be non-existent. Consequently it would be absurd to imagine a consul who would be the subject not of the appointing, but of the receiving state. And the one who receives them cannot receive them otherwise than as subjects of the appointing state.

§ 1043, part 8, Jus Nat.

§ 105, part 7, Jus Nat.

§ 229.

§ 233. *What right over consuls belongs to the appointing nation*

Since consuls remain subjects of the appointing nation, the appointing nation has the same right over consuls as over other subjects, consequently the right even to punish them in accordance with national laws, and it is possible to impose on them the burdens to be borne by other citizens, both ordinary and extraordinary.

§ 232.

§§ 832, 833, part 8, Jus Nat.

§ 775, part 8, Jus Nat.

The right belonging to a superior over one who is performing a public service, in one respect is general, in so far indeed as he is a

§ 925, part 8, Jus Nat.

subject, in another it is special, in so far as he is performing a particular duty. And therefore also a right belongs to the appointing nation over the consul as a subject, and likewise a right over him as a consul. The former is evident from the common principles of general public law, but the latter is to be measured from the duty of the consul, or from the purpose for which he was appointed. Therefore also the appointing state can punish him, both if he offends against the laws of his country, and also if he performs badly the duty required of him. For example, let us suppose that in that nation where some consul has been appointed, polygamy is allowed, or even that incest is tolerated, while according to the laws of his country both polygamy and incest are restrained by a specific penalty. If a consul takes several wives, or commits incest, he can be punished by the appointing nation in accordance with the laws of his country.

§ 234. *Of the recall of a consul by way of punishment*

§ 233.

Since a nation appointing a consul can punish him in accordance with the laws of his country, it can recall him, when he is accused, so that his offence may be inquired into, and proper punishment exacted from him.

All processes are undoubtedly permissible against a consul which are permissible against a fugitive defendant, except that he can be taken away from an emporium, where he is living, without the consent of the one who has jurisdiction over that place. For since such a one has received the consul as the subject of the state appointing him, his own jurisdiction is not at all infringed upon, if the consul is arrested as a defendant and taken away, since it is understood that the state receiving him has allowed this right to the state appointing him. He who consents to this, that any one may remain subject to another and be punished by such other, also consents to those things without which punishment cannot be exacted.

§ 235. *What sort of a right against consuls belongs to the nation receiving them*

§ 232.

In like manner, since consuls remain subjects of the nation appointing them, in the territory of the nation receiving them they are considered as foreigners living there to manage their own business, consequently the same right against consuls belongs to the nation receiving them, as against foreigners living in its territory, except in so far as there is a derogation therefrom through stipulations or the very nature of consular duties.

Since a little later there must be a discussion of the right against foreigners who live in alien territory, the right against a consul of the nation receiving him will be left until then.

§ 236. Of the protection of consuls

Since consuls remain subjects of the one by whom they are appointed, the one appointing them is also bound to protect them.

§ 232.

§ 532, part 8, Jus Nat.

Of course they are protected both against the wrongs of those by whom they are received and against the wrongs of merchants, for whose sake they are appointed. For what is due to citizens or to individual subjects, that also is due to consuls.

§ 229.

§ 237. Whether prerogative belongs by nature to nations

By nature no prerogative belongs to any nation. For nations are considered as individual free persons living in a state of nature. Therefore, since by nature no prerogative belongs to any man, by nature no prerogative belongs to any nation.

§ 2.

§ 94, part 1, Jus Nat.

Individual nations as nations are individuals of the same species. Therefore, since they are included under the same definition, and their attributes must be derived from it, there is assuredly no reason why a certain prerogative can belong to one nation. By nature nations in their relations with each other use a common law, just as do humans as humans. Therefore, since it is absurd for any man to desire to assume a certain prerogative, as if one human being were not equal to another, so it is no less absurd for any nation to dare to assume a prerogative, as if one nation were not equal to another nation. And just as no man by nature can assume a certain prerogative because he is larger, or stronger, or richer, or excels in a certain virtue either intellectual or moral, so also no nation by nature enjoys a certain prerogative because it is more powerful or cultured, or for any other reason.

§ 238. *Whether one nation can assume for itself a certain right before another*

§ 237.

§ 93, part 1,
Jus Nat.

Since by nature no prerogative belongs to any nation, since moreover a prerogative consists in a right which belongs to some one before others who in other respects use the same law, no nation by nature can assume to itself a certain right, which does not belong to other nations, and the right which belongs to one nation against others is also common to the several others.

§ 16.
§ 17.
§ 225, part 1,
Phil. Pract. Univ.

This of course flows from the natural equality of all nations, by force of which all have the same rights and the same obligations to all, and consequently all have the same duties to all.

§ 239. *How prerogatives are acquired*

§ 17.

§ 117, part 3,
Jus Nat.

§ 698, part 3,
Jus Nat.

§ 393, part 3,
Jus Nat.

§ 788, part 3,
Jus Nat.

Prerogatives can be acquired by nations through stipulation. By nature all nations have the same rights. Nevertheless, since any one by nature is able to waive his right, one nation also can waive a certain right of its own in favour of another nation, that right being preserved as regards other nations. And the same thing is understood of several nations at the same time. Therefore, since it is necessary that they agree concerning that, and one nation or several bind themselves to another, in that they are willing to grant a certain privilege to it, a thing which cannot be done otherwise than by a promise, since, moreover, agreements of this sort are stipulations, prerogatives can be acquired by nations through stipulations.

§ 23.

§ 24.

§ 1054, part 3,
Jus Nat.

Therefore prerogatives of nations, if they exist, are matters of pure stipulative right. There is no reason why you should take the exception, that those can be or even are matters of customary right; for it is quite plain that customs of that sort cannot be introduced among nations otherwise than by a certain tacit stipulation, because in truth they are tacitly presumed to consent when some nation assumes some prerogative for itself.

§ 240. *Whether precedence belongs by nature to a nation*

§ 106, part 1,
Jus Nat.

By nature precedence belongs to no nation. Since by nature precedence belongs to no human being, in like manner it is quite plain that by

nature precedence belongs to no nation, as a little while ago we showed   § 237.
that no privilege belongs to a nation.

> Of course precedence of a nation is opposed to equality of nations,   § 16.
> and destroys that, just as it does equality of men.   § 107, part 1,
> Jus Nat.

§ 241. *Of precedence in assemblies or in stipulations expressed in writing*

Since by nature precedence belongs to no nation, that is, priority in the   § 240.
order to be observed by several, since, moreover, in assemblies some   § 104, part 1,
order must necessarily be observed, as also in agreements, which are   Jus Nat.
expressed in writing, it is undoubtedly necessary that nations in assembly or in making covenants should agree with each other concerning
precedence.

> That, concerning which agreement is made, holds for the present,
> but it is quite evident that it cannot be extended to the future. Nor is
> it less plain that it is a matter of mere whim as to how they may desire   § 95, part 3,
> to meet together. For the coming together implies a purely arbitrary   Jus Nat.
> waiver of their right. But it is prudent that they depart as little as   § 117, part 3,
> possible from equality, a condition which is attained in assemblies,   Jus Nat.
> if that order is observed in which each has come or if, in reducing
> agreements to writing, now one and now another is given the prece-
> dence. It is perfectly in accord with nature, that he precede who first
> has deserved the dignity, or even that regard be had to the age of the
> nation.

§ 242. *How precedence is acquired by nations*

Precedence can be acquired by a nation by stipulation. This is proved in
the same way as we have before shown that prerogative is acquired by
stipulation.   § 239.

In fact since precedence is a kind of prerogative, and since prerogatives
can be acquired by a nation through stipulations, it is quite evident that   § 108, part 1,
precedence also can be acquired by a nation through stipulations.   Jus Nat.
§ 239.

> What we suggested a little while ago concerning prerogative is like-   § 239.
> wise to be understood concerning precedence.   § 108, part 1,
> Jus Nat.

§ 243. *Whether precedence or order of nations is changed when the form of the state is changed*

If a democracy be changed into a monarchy or kingdom, or into an aristocracy, the monarch or king, or the nobles have that place among the nations which the nation had as a democracy and vice versa. For in a monarchy the monarch, that is, the king, and in an aristocracy the nobles taken together represent the people in relation to other nations. Therefore, if precedence belongs to a certain nation, it also ought to belong to the monarch or king, or to the nobles, and consequently if a democracy is changed into a monarchy or kingdom, or into an aristocracy, the monarch or king, or the nobles have that place among the nations which the nation had as a democracy. Which was the first point.

But if indeed in place of a monarchy or kingdom, or an aristocracy, a democracy is introduced, the right of the people which the monarch or king had, or which the nobles had, returns to the people. Nay more, because these persons represent their nation, as proved above, the precedence also, which belonged to them among nations, was the right of the nation which they represented. If then a monarchy or kingdom, or an aristocracy, is changed into a democracy, the precedence which belonged to the monarch or king, or to the nobles, now belongs to the nation, and consequently the nation will have the place among other nations which before the monarch or king had, or the nobles had. Which was the second point.

By nature nations are free and therefore the civil power, consequently the mode of exercising it, or the form of the state, is quite independent of other nations. Therefore the form of the state has no bearing on those things which belong to the nation, nor do they depend in any way on it. Therefore, if anything has been determined concerning the precedence of some particular nation, or concerning the place which it ought to have among other nations, that will be the same whatsoever the form of the state may then have been, and since the ruler of a state has a right over the nation which he governs, it makes little difference how much right the people shall have bestowed on him, or reserved for itself, or in what manner the exercise of it shall have been limited. Here are to be reconsidered those things which we

§ 160, part 8, Jus Nat.

§ 139, part 1, Jus Nat.

§ 160, part 8, Jus Nat.

§ 55, part 8, Jus Nat.

§ 153, part 1, Jus Nat.

§ 39.

have discussed above concerning the representative character of rulers   Note, § 39.
of a state.

§ 244. *Of the name of ruler of a state and of titles of honour to be assigned him*

Every nation is free by nature to call the ruler of its state by any name
it wishes and to assign any titles of honour to him. For since it depends
solely upon the will of a people on what condition it may desire to trans-   § 36, part 8, Jus Nat.
fer sovereignty to a ruler of the state, and since the ruler of a state is a
corporate person which is determined by the rights conferred upon it,   § 70, part 1, Jus Nat.
since, moreover, the names by which corporate persons are designated   § 959, Ontol.
are arbitrary, every nation is free to call the ruler of its state by any name
it pleases. Which was the first point.

And since a people is bound to recognize as ruler of its state the one to
whom it has transferred sovereignty, as is evident of itself, consequently   § 841, part 1, Jus Nat.
to signify by its outward acts also that it recognizes him as such, and
therefore honours him as ruler of its state, and since among these tokens   § 959, Ontol.
of respect belong also the titles of honour which are likewise arbitrary
tokens, it depends upon the will of the people also what titles of honour
for indicating his dignity it may wish to assign to him. Which was the
second point.

Since the name by which the ruler of a state is addressed indicates
the corporate person which he represents, while his dignity is determined by the right which belongs to him over the people, the name
by which he is addressed neither increases nor diminishes his dignity,
but in so far as in the opinion of men some addition or subtraction
is supposed to be made to his dignity, the name is useless. The same
certainly must be believed of titles of honour which have no value
beyond that which they indicate. But in so far as the words are empty,
indicating nothing definite and fixed, and nevertheless are supposed
to effect an increase in the dignity of the ruler of a state, the struggle
is for naught. The same thing holds here which holds in titles and
names of other public persons who perform some particular duty for
the state, or even in those of other private persons. Therefore we, who
consider things, and not words, have been content with the general

name of ruler of the state. Whether you call one who has absolute sovereignty over a great and powerful people an emperor, or a king, or a prince, or a duke, or a master, or by whatsoever other name you call him, the words will always have the same meaning, nor will it add anything to his dignity, nor detract from it, by whichever of those names he is called. If you should desire to rate the dignity of a ruler of the state by names of this sort, it will frequently happen that he may be thought greater than he really is, and that may be attributed to him which belongs in no way to him. But this world, as the common saying goes, is much ruled by opinions.

§ 245. *Whether the ruler of a state can determine the name and titles to be assigned to himself*

If the ruler of a state should order that he be addressed by a certain name by his subjects and that certain titles of honour be assigned to him, his subjects are bound to address him by this name and to assign these titles to him, unless a fundamental law prevents. For a people is bound to obey the ruler of the state, so far as he does not command things opposed to the fundamental laws. Therefore, since names by which certain corporate persons are called and titles of honour have an arbitrary meaning, since, consequently, it would be just the same whether a ruler of a state is addressed by one name or another and whether some titles or others are assigned to him, if the ruler of a state should order that he be addressed by a certain name by his subjects and that certain titles of honour be assigned to him, his subjects are bound to address him by this name and to assign these titles to him, unless a fundamental law prevents.

§§ 1043, 1046, part 8, Jus Nat.

§ 995, Ontol.

Through the name by which the ruler of a state is addressed and the titles of honour which are assigned to him, he acquires no more right over the people than he has, consequently if you look at the truth and not the foolish opinion of the ignorant, he is honoured neither more nor less, whether he be addressed by one or by another name and whether these or other titles be assigned to him. Therefore there is then no reason why subjects should be allowed to refuse obedience.

§ 246. *Of the law in regard to the name of the ruler of a state and his titles of honour*

Whether other nations wish to address the ruler of any state by the same name by which his subjects address him and attribute to him the same titles of honour, depends entirely upon the will of those nations, and their consent must be obtained that they may do this. For it is a matter simply of free will, by what name nations may wish to address the ruler of their state and what titles of honour they wish to assign to him, or the ruler of a state can even command his subjects to address him by this name and assign to him these titles of honour. But since all nations are free, consequently no nation in acting depends upon the will of another, therefore other nations are not bound to address the ruler of any state by the same name because it pleases his subjects to address him by this name, nor to assign the same titles of honour to him because it pleases his subjects to assign them to him. Since the ruler of a state may exercise the sovereignty which he has only over his own people, in like manner it is understood that he cannot command other nations that they address him by this name by which his subjects are bound to address him and assign the same title of honour to him which his subjects are bound to assign. Therefore it is plain that whether other nations may wish to do this, depends entirely upon the will of those nations. Which was the first point.

§ 244.

§ 245.

§ 55, part 8, Jus Nat.

§ 153, part 1, Jus Nat.

§ 42, part 8, Jus Nat.

Since every nation is free to determine whether it may wish to address the ruler of any state by the same name by which his own people address him, and assign the same title of honour to him which this people assigns to him, as proved above; that other nations may be bound to do this, it is necessary that they bind themselves to do it, consequently their consent must be obtained. Which was the second point.

For example, let us suppose that a certain ruler of a state possessing sovereign powers wishes to be called king and that the title majesty be assigned to him. He can give this order to his subjects, and they are bound to call him king and to assign the title majesty to him. But that other nations should do the same and a perfect right be acquired from them, their consent must be obtained either by petition or by stipulation. If the petition is denied, this is accomplished on the proper occasion by means of stipulation, a thing which can be done in several ways, even so that an agreement should not be entered into, except under this condition, namely, that beforehand the name of the ruler of the state and the title belonging to him are recognized. These methods are in harmony with practice, and are easily established by examples from history. We have, indeed, examples from our own time, by which these statements are verified. But in a plain case there is no need of appealing to them.

§ 247. *When the denial of name and titles is wrong*

If any nation has acquired a perfect right that the ruler of the state should be called by this name by another nation and that these titles of honour should be attributed to him, and afterwards that state fails to perform those things, it does a wrong. For since the omission occurs contrary to a perfect right (as is clear from the hypothesis), and that which is contrary to the perfect right of another is a wrong, it is plain that, if, in accordance with the hypothesis of the present proposition, the name is not attributed to the ruler of any state and the titles belonging to him are not attributed to him, a wrong is committed.

§ 859, part 1, Jus Nat.

Since it is a matter of free will whether or not any nation wishes to address the ruler of another state by that name by which he wishes to be addressed, and to assign these titles which he wishes to be assigned to him, when it refuses this to a nation on its request, it does no injury at all to it. But after it has promised one who requests it or has entered into a stipulation concerning it, since then it is bound to do, it does a wrong by not doing. Since it is in harmony with the customs of nations that names and titles indicate the dignity of the ruler of the state, if the name belonging to the ruler of a state, together with the titles before assigned to him, is not assigned, that can be done only from contempt. For when any one binds himself to assign name and titles, it is understood that he thinks the one to whom he binds himself is worthy of the name and title. If then he is unwilling to bestow them, it is undoubtedly the same as if he should declare that he holds him unworthy, nor does he think him of sufficient worth to ascribe them to him, a plain evidence of contempt.

§ 246.

§ 787, part 1, Jus Nat.

§ cited.

§ 248. *Of the meaning of names and titles derived from usage of speech among nations*

If usage of speech received among neighbouring nations assigns to certain words, which are included in the name and titles of the ruler of a state, a meaning which assumes certain characteristics in the ruler of the state; in case these are lacking, that name and those titles cannot be assigned to him by other nations, nor can he assume that name or those titles for himself without temerity. For since words were invented to signify things, if a usage of speech received among neighbouring nations assigns to certain words a certain meaning they seem to have tacitly agreed with each other that any name or a certain title should not be assigned except to the one to whom those characteristics belong. Therefore when a name or a title is assigned to any one, by that very fact it is indicated that he has these characteristics. Therefore it is in fact absurd to desire to assign a name or a certain title to any one contrary to the usage of speech received among nations, consequently when the characteristics fail which the usage of speech assumes, the name cannot be assigned by other nations. Which was the first point.

§ 349, Log.

And since that is done rashly, which is done with no purpose, it is plain in like manner that when the characteristics are lacking, of which we have spoken, no one can assume a name or title for himself without temerity. Which was the second point.

§ 277, part 3, Jus Nat.

§ 249. *Whether a denial in that case is contrary to the duty of humanity*

When, according to the hypothesis of the preceding proposition, the name and titles of honour which the ruler of the state aspires to are denied to him who asks for them, nothing is done which is contrary to a duty of humanity. For when that name which he asks to be attributed to him, together with the titles of honour which he aspires to, cannot be attributed to him, it is not opposed to the law of nature which orders the honour which he deserves to be bestowed on every one, if the request is refused to the one who asks that it should be attributed to him. Since, therefore, an act not opposed to the law of nature is not contrary to a duty of humanity, nothing is done contrary to a duty of humanity, if

§ 248.
§ 648, part 1, Jus Nat.
§ 224, part 1, Phil. Pract. Univ., and § 655, part 1, Jus Nat.

according to the hypothesis of the preceding proposition the name and titles, which one aspires to, are denied to him on his request.

Inappropriate names and titles are rightly refused when the characteristics are lacking which the significance of words introduced by usage of speech assumes. Nay more, if from this the dignity of the one to whom they are attributed should be determined and if they should be attributed to one who does not deserve them, they are then worthless, their significance having been changed by this very use of them; a thing which is just as true of the titles of private individuals, if they become abused. Undoubtedly the French are to be commended in this respect because they strive very little for the vanity of titles, as is the custom with us; but they use a few words by which every distinction in civil dignities is expressed and the usage of which they keep unchanged. But in order that the honour which they deserve may be bestowed upon rulers of states, those things are not to be confused which ought to be distinguished from each other. For the ruler of a state bears a double personality, inasmuch as he is looked at as the person who rules the state, and inasmuch as he is considered a private person in regard to those acts which have nothing at all to do with government. Now in the former case the honour which is due to him as the person to whom civil sovereignty has been transferred, is to be further distinguished from the honour which he deserves because he administers the state well. Moreover, virtues enter into his acts of government which are peculiar to his own private personality. The names and titles which are attributed to rulers of a state properly indicate only the dignity which they derive therefrom, because they have been endowed with civil sovereignty. (Consequently these names and titles do not give rise to renown, but simply indicate the rulers' status. Renown comes at last from good government, which assumes kingly virtues, and from private virtues contributing to it. If those would properly consider these things who assume to judge for themselves concerning the bestowing of honour on rulers of a state, they would determine nothing which would be far from the truth. It is characteristic of flatterers to confuse everything for the sake of their own advantage. But as soon as one departs from the truth, there is no further certainty, and very many wicked and absurd things follow therefrom.

§ 250. *How the ruler of one state ought to regard the ruler of another state*

Every ruler of a state ought to consider the ruler of another state as his equal by nature. For by nature all nations are equal. Therefore, since the ruler of a state represents his nation, when he is dealing with others, all rulers of states also are by nature equal. Therefore every one ought to consider the other as his equal by nature.

§ 16.

§ 39.

Lest the equality of rulers of a state should be subject to doubt, and lest it become abused, one must not only carefully consider that the civil power, through which the person of the ruler of the state was established, is the same in every nation, and consequently that the natural dignity, which belongs to the concept of the ruler of the state, is the same in all; but care must also be taken lest the things that arise from accident may be confounded with those things which exist of themselves in the ruler of the state. Therefore, although all rulers of a state are equal to each other, and for that reason every ruler of a state is bound to recognize another as his equal, and consequently to assign the honour to him which belongs to any ruler of a state as such; nevertheless it does not follow from this that the superior excellence of one in comparison with another, which arises from accident, is not to be recognized and consideration given to that in bestowing honour. For since every one ought to honour another as much as he deserves, since, moreover, in bestowing honour on rulers of a state those things also must come in for attention which arise from accident, as is abundantly understood from what we have already noted; from the recognition of equality, identity in bestowing of honour does not flow. But from this there cannot be inferred any prerogative and precedence of a nation. Nay more, the things which come by accident, since they do not remain always the same, cannot give rise to any permanent right, even if it were considered simply as an imperfect right. But if there are things so much a part of the person of the ruler of the state that they cannot be changed with him, but remain even to his successor, for example, that he is a ruler over a very powerful nation and a vast realm, it is not to be doubted but that this may be taken into account in the

§ 42, part 8, Jus Nat.

§ 60, part 1, Jus Nat.

§ 648, part 1, Jus Nat.

Note, § 249.

name by which he is to be addressed and in the titles to be assigned to him and in the prerogatives and precedence to be granted through stipulations. Nevertheless we must not get away from equality by nature, when the duties are to be considered which one ruler of a state owes to another ruler of a state, and as long as the honour is considered which is due to the ruler of a state as such. But there is nothing peculiar in this, which is not to be observed equally in the case of any private persons, because of the natural equality of men, which in bestowing honour does not reject those things which by accident exist in one man in preference to another.

§ 251. *When a wrong is committed by pursuing the opposite course*

Since every ruler of a state ought to look at the ruler of another state as equal to himself, all acts are illegal by which any ruler of a state indicates that he does not look upon another as equal by nature to himself, that is, as equally a ruler of a state, consequently much more illegal are the acts by which he shows that he judges another unworthy to be considered as ruler of a state and therefore as one to whom the duties are owed which a ruler of a state owes to a ruler of another state. But since acts of this sort verge on contempt and scorn of another, all acts are illegal which verge on contempt and scorn of the ruler of another state, and consequently since contempt and scorn are wrong, he who is guilty of acts of that sort does a wrong to another.

This proposition, as well as all others which discuss a wrong committed by nations against other nations, must be considered carefully on account of its value in connexion with others that follow. But lest it may seem strange to any one that, although only an imperfect right belongs to any person to the duties of humanity such as is the bestowal of honour, a wrong, which consists in a violation of a perfect right, is done by acts contrary to those duties; it should be carefully noted that there is a distinction to be made between privative acts contrary to duties, which consist in a bare omission, and positive acts contrary to duty, which are prohibited by natural law, and in which therefore there is no place left for natural liberty.

§ 250.

§ 722, part I, Jus Nat.

§ 787, part I, Jus Nat.
§ 812, part I, Jus Nat.
§ 860, part I, Jus Nat.

§ 859, part I, Jus Nat.
§ 722, part I, Jus Nat.
§ 912, part I, Jus Nat.

§ 252. *Of the right not to allow an injury*

The right belongs to every nation not to allow that it should be injured by another, and that is a perfect right. For no nation ought to injure another. Since, therefore, from a passive obligation on one party a right arises for the other party, and since, of course, if one party is bound not to do a thing, the other has the right not to allow it to be done; the right belongs to every nation also not to allow itself to be injured by another. Which was the first point.

§ 173.

§ 23, part 1,
Jus Nat.

For nations are regarded as individual persons living in a state of nature, consequently just as a right belongs to every man by nature not to allow himself to be injured by another, so also a right belongs to every nation not to allow itself to be injured by another nation. Since, therefore, the right not to allow himself to be injured by another is a perfect right belonging by nature to every man, the right also, which belongs to every nation, not to allow itself to be injured by another nation, is a perfect right. Which was the second point.

§ 2.

§ 3.

§ 913, part 1,
Jus Nat.

In the Corpus Juris Civilis only a perfect right is discussed, and therefore, in the sources of this law the principle is laid down by the emperor: Injure no one. Therefore, just as from this source flows a perfect right not to allow an injury between individuals in the law of private persons, so also from the same source flows the same right between nations to which the law forbidding injury applies no less than it does to individuals.

[*Institutes* 1. i,
§ 3.]

§ 253. *Of the right to resist one who injures and to guard against the injury*

Since the right not to allow an injury is a perfect right, since, moreover, a perfect right involves the right to compel another party not to do injury, any nation is entitled not only to resist by force another nation intending to injure it, but also, after it has injured, to compel it by force not to dare to injure it again.

§ 252.

§ 235, part 1, Phil.
Pract. Univ.

The right not to allow an injury involves also the right to the means of attaining that purpose, and therefore one legally uses the force which is necessary to avert and prevent a wrong.

§ 170, part 1, Phil.
Pract. Univ.

§ 254. *Of the right of security*

§ 252.

§ 917, part 1,
Jus Nat.

In like manner because a perfect right belongs to every nation not to allow itself to be injured by another, since, moreover, the right not to allow any one to injure you is a right of security, the right of security belongs to every nation, and if any nation injures another, or tries to injure it, it does this contrary to the right of security, and every injury is opposed to the right of security.

§ 170, part 1,
Phil. Pract.
Univ.

This right is not to be confused with the execution of one's right which involves no obligation, so that therefore the permissible is to be distinguished from the obligatory. Therefore, although the right not to allow an injury admits of no restriction, since the law of nature could not otherwise simply forbid injury, nevertheless it does not follow from this that no injury is to be endured; for not only does a lack of power often render impossible the execution of a right, but also prudence suggests that it may be right not to do that which it is permissible to do. It is quite plain that the things which are here said concerning the right of security of nations are true concerning any right. The physical impossibility which arises from lack of power is easily recognized, provided only that our mind is not disturbed by force of passion, and that with calm mind we employ circumspection and careful consideration; but prudence requires that, while you enjoy your right, you may not fail in some duty to yourself or even to others; consequently a deeper examination of duties makes plain the things which are prudent.

§ 255. *Of the right to an act which belongs to the exercise of the sovereignty of another nation*

§ 57, part 8,
Jus Nat.

§ 44, part 8,
Jus Nat.

By nature no nation has the right to any act which belongs to the exercise of the sovereignty of another nation. For sovereignty, as it exists in a people or originally in a nation, is absolute. Since, therefore, the perfection of sovereignty consists in its exercise independently of the will of any other, all the acts of any nation which belong to the exercise of civil sovereignty are altogether independent of the will of any other nation.

§ 156, part 1,
Phil. Pract. Univ.

Therefore, by nature no nation can have the right to perform any act which belongs to the exercise of the sovereignty of another nation.

§ 34, part 8,
Jus Nat.

Civil sovereignty is originally a thing belonging to the people, so that therefore the right to any act which belongs to the exercise of that

sovereignty is opposed to the natural liberty of nations. Therefore, a
right of that sort, since it involves a contradiction, is impossible, and
consequently is void. Therefore, by nature nations have no right to
acts which belong to the exercise of the sovereignty of another nation;
but just as by force of natural liberty it must be allowed to everyone
that he abide by his own judgement in acting, consequently also in the
exercise of his right, as long as he does nothing which is contrary to
your right, so likewise by force of the natural liberty of nations it must
be allowed to any one of them to abide by its own judgement in the
exercise of sovereignty. Nay more, since civil sovereignty arises from
the stipulation by which men have united into a state and by force of
which individuals have bound themselves to the whole, because they
desire to promote the common good; the obligation of individuals has
regard only to the whole; and the right of the whole over individuals,
which is sovereignty, belongs only to the whole, who have contracted
one with the other, consequently there is absolutely no natural reason
why a certain nation should share any of this right with another nation.

§ 55, part 8, and
§ 153, part 1,
Jus Nat.

§ 43, Ontol.

§ 79, Ontol.

§ 156, part 1,
Jus Nat.

§ 4, part 8,
Jus Nat.

§ 28, part 8,
Jus Nat.

§ 31, part 8,
Jus Nat.

§ 256. Of the wrong done to a nation by interfering with the exercise of its sovereignty

Since by nature no nation has a right to any act which pertains to the
exercise of the sovereignty of another nation, if any nation dares to do
anything which belongs to the exercise of the sovereign power of another
nation, it does this without right and contrary to the right of the other
nation, and consequently does a wrong to it.

§ 255.

§ 859, part 1,
Jus Nat.

To interfere in the government of another, in whatever way indeed
that may be done, is opposed to the natural liberty of nations, by virtue of which one nation is altogether independent of the will of other
nations in its action. Besides, whatever nations as such do, that they
do by virtue of sovereignty.

§ 153, part 1,
Jus Nat.

§ 257. Of not interfering in the government of another

Since by nature no nation has a right to any act which pertains to the
exercise of the sovereignty of another nation, since, moreover, the ruler
of a state exercises the sovereignty of a state, and since government consists in the exercise of sovereignty; no ruler of a state has the right to
interfere in the government of another, consequently cannot urge that

§ 255.

§ 42, part 8,
Jus Nat.

§ 218, part 7,
Jus Nat.

another should establish anything in its state or do anything, or not do anything, and the government of the ruler of one state is not subject to the decision of the ruler of any other state.

If any such things are done, they are done altogether without right. And although the less powerful may be compelled to yield at length to the more powerful, nevertheless might confers no right which the latter does not have from another source.

§ 258. *If the ruler of a state should burden his subjects too heavily or treat them too harshly*

§ 257.

If the ruler of a state should burden his subjects too heavily or treat them too harshly, the ruler of another state may not resist that by force, nevertheless he may intercede in their behalf. For no ruler of a state has the right to interfere in the government of another, nor is this a matter subject to his judgement. If, therefore, he does interfere in the government of another when the ruler of another state burdens his subjects too heavily or treats them too harshly, he himself resists the other by force, as is self-evident; according to the hypothesis of the present proposition he may not resist the other by force. Which was the first point.

§ 162.
§ 160.

Since every nation ought to do all it can to make other nations also happy, but since it is not bound beyond that which is in its power, and since it may not resist by force the one who rules badly, as shown above, consequently, since nothing is left except that it should endeavour by its prayers to persuade him to change his mind, or that it should intercede in behalf of the subjects too heavily burdened or too harshly treated, there is no doubt that it can rightly intercede in their behalf. Which was the second point.

We omit those points which in intercession are matters of prudence; for they have to do with civil prudence, of which we speak in politics. Since consideration is to be given to prudence, it frequently happens that even intercession is not in one's power, consequently it may rightly be refused to those who ask it.

§ 160.

§ 259. *Whether any nation can be compelled to embrace the religion of another nation*

§ 458, part 8,
Jus Nat.

No nation by force may compel another nation to introduce its religion into its own territory or to embrace it. For since the ruler of a state

ought to take care that his subjects worship God, and since religion is
the method of worshipping God; to regulate those matters which pertain
to religion belongs to the exercise of civil sovereignty or to government.
Therefore, as no nation has a right to any action which pertains to the
exercise of the sovereignty of another nation, so no nation can compel
another nation by force to introduce its religion into its own state or to
embrace it.

§ 512, part 2,
Theol. Nat.
§ 218, part 7,
Jus Nat.
§ 255.

The question is not now whether religion can be propagated by force:
we are discussing the right of nation towards nation. Nor is the distinction here to be considered between true religion and false, so that in
case of conflict in the law of nations, duty towards God may be said to
conquer; for there is no nation which does not consider its own religion
to be the true one. But force is a means not suited to inculcate truth.

§ 260. Whether on account of religion it is permissible to subject a nation to one's sovereignty

Since no nation by force may compel another nation to embrace its
religion, it has no right to subdue another nation and subject it to its
sovereignty on account of religion.

§ 259.

Here we are speaking of the right which by nature belongs to
nations. Therefore we do not make our own the quarrel of the theologians concerning religious propaganda, who do not argue this
question from principles of reason, which is the teacher of the law of
nature, but from the principles of revelation.

§ 259, part 1, Phil.
Pract. Univ.

§ 261. Of the duties of a nation in regard to the true worship of God

Whatever one nation can contribute to persuade other nations to the
true worship of God, that it is bound by nature to contribute. But if
nevertheless the other nation cannot be induced to embrace it, that must
be endured. For since men are bound to worship God, so too are nations;
and since, on the one hand, superstition is to be avoided, which arises
from erroneous beliefs concerning God and Divine Providence with
reference to those things which can result for good or ill to humans,
and, on the other hand, idolatry is to be avoided, which consists in the

§ 1231, part 1,
Jus Nat.
§§ 2, 3.
§ 1256, part 1,
Jus Nat.
§ 1255, part 1,
Jus Nat.

§ 1262, part 1,
Jus Nat.
§ 1258, part 1,
Jus Nat.
§§ 156, 160.

§ 259.
religions worship of false gods; and since what each nation owes to itself, that also it owes to every other nation, as far as is in its power; it follows that whatever one nation can contribute to the promotion of the true worship of God among other nations, that it is bound by nature to contribute. For no nation can compel another nation by force to embrace its religion, consequently nothing is left, except to persuade others to do so. Therefore, whatever a nation can contribute to persuade to religion or to the true worship of God, that it is bound by nature to contribute. Which was the first point.

§ 164.

§§ 655, 665,
part 1, Jus Nat.
But the duties of a nation towards other nations by which their happiness is promoted are duties of humanity. Therefore, since you have satisfied your obligations in regard to the duties of humanity, if you have offered to perform them, though the other refuse that offer; if any nation should attempt to persuade another to accept the true worship of God, but that other nation can in no way be induced to embrace that worship, that must be endured. Which was the second point.

When you have rejected force, no means exist for promoting the true worship of God, other than that men should be taught it, either through living teachers, who, if sent to foreign nations, are called missionaries, or through inanimate ones, which are books written concerning the true worship of God. But persuasion may be by arguments, by which in part the truth is asserted, or the falsity of the opposing errors are shown, and in part motives for embracing religion are furnished. But as, in the former case, the arguments vary, to suit the different capacities of those who are to be won to the truth, so, in the latter, they vary to suit the variety of inclinations and customs of those who give their assent, where also prejudices have great weight. But since a nation in those things which have to do with embracing religion depends entirely upon itself, and cannot be coerced, if it is unwilling to admit and tolerate missionaries in its territory, or to allow books to be brought to it in which a divine worship, other than the one received by it, is taught and inculcated, that must be endured. But there is need of no little caution, if any nation wishes to induce another to embrace its religion. For natural obligation, of which the present argument speaks, assumes that a divine worship is a true one; otherwise there is no natural obligation; nay more, since no man

§ 708, part 1,
Jus Nat.

ought to instil errors into the minds of others, if any nation desires to promote a false worship of God in other nations, it errs, and injures it. But since a decision is difficult as to a true worship of God or a true religion, one must not attempt to impose this on others except with all proper precautions; in a doubtful case, one must refrain from the attempt. Here also must be considered what are the dictates of prudence, that we may not harm ourselves by not acting. And therefore there is need of much circumspection, as every one admits when the thing is treated among private individuals. But the law of nations does not differ from that which private individuals use one with the other. As elsewhere, so here also we make such notes in passing, since this discussion in accordance with our plan has no relation to the law of nature and nations.

§ 440, part 1, Phil. Pract. Univ.

§ 693, part 1, Jus Nat.

§ 3.

§ 262. *Of the right of nations in regard to missionaries*

No nation has the right to punish missionaries or to treat them badly, unless they have disturbed the public peace or are obstinate and unwilling to leave; if it does not wish to tolerate them, it simply has the right to order them to depart from its lands. For no nation can be compelled to embrace the religion of another nation, and if it cannot be persuaded to embrace it, that must be endured; consequently it depends upon the will of every nation whether or not it wishes to tolerate missionaries, that is, those who desire to persuade it to adopt a religion different from that which it practises. But since, if it is unwilling to tolerate them, it is sufficient to order them to depart, as is plain of itself; no nation has the right to punish them or to treat them badly, but simply to order them to depart from its territory. Which was the first point.

§ 259.
§ 261.

For if missionaries disturb the public peace, since that must be preserved in a state, and since those who disturb it injure the state and are liable to be punished, missionaries also can be punished, not as missionaries, but as disturbers of the public peace or tranquillity. Which was the second point.

§ 19, part 8, Jus Nat.

§ 579, part 8, Jus Nat.

Finally, since missionaries ought to bear it if a nation does not allow itself to be induced to embrace a religion to which they wish to convert it, if they are ordered to depart from the territory, they ought so to depart, in obedience to the order. Therefore, since an order of that sort

§ 261.

§ 205, part 7, Jus Nat.

§ 131, part 1,
Phil. Pract. Univ.
has the sanction of the law, and penalties must be affixed to the laws

§ 585, part 8,
Jus Nat.
which are adequate to restrain transgression of the laws as far as possible, it is not to be doubted, that obstinate missionaries, who when ordered are unwilling to depart from the territory, can be punished, on account, namely, of the refusal to obey, as they ought. Which was the third point.

Note, § 29.
We have already suggested above that here the distinction between a true and a false religion has no weight. For since every nation, unless convinced or persuaded to the contrary, thinks its religion is the true one; the truth of a religion is no criterion for determining the law of nations in regard to a diversity of religions, when the parties disagree among themselves. But he who is not willing to tolerate missionaries has no more right over them than simply not to tolerate them. And therefore any one easily sees that by no law at all can they be restrained by penalties, much less can capital punishment be inflicted upon them, unless a wrong is committed deserving to be restrained by as severe a penalty as is decreed against them. But here must also be considered what we have noted a little while ago, that here we do not go beyond
Note, § 260.
those things which can be proved from the principles of natural law, nor make that our argument which belongs in the realm of the theologians.

§ 263. *Whether difference of religion interferes with the duties of nations towards each other*

On account of difference of religion no nation can deny another the duties of humanity which nations owe to each other. For the duties which nations owe to nations do not assume identity of religion but are proved without any respect to it, as is perfectly plain from proof of individual cases. Consequently nations are bound to perform those duties for each other without any regard to religion. Therefore on account of difference of religion no nation can deny another the duties of humanity which nations owe to each other.

Here there is nothing peculiar included in the law of nations which does not likewise prevail among private individuals. For the love of
§ 620, part 1,
Jus Nat.

§ 654, part 1,
Jus Nat.

§ 618, part 1,
Jus Nat.
mankind, or charity, which embraces all duties of one human being towards others, extends to all humans generally, without any regard to religion. And there is no one of us who does not recognize this, and who does not condemn the perverse belief of the ancients, which bids us hold in scorn those devoted to another religion. But he who

recognizes this among individual men is likewise bound to admit the same among nations.

Note, § 618, part 1, Jus Nat. § 3.

§ 264. *The foundation of justice between nations*

Every nation ought to allow to another nation its right. For his own right is to be allowed to every one. Therefore, since by nature nations are bound to each other in the same way as individuals are bound to individuals, every nation also ought to allow to another nation its right.

§ 922, part 1, Jus Nat.

§ 3.

Neither does the law of nature give rights to nations in vain, nor do they acquire them in vain from each other. For there would be no advantage in law if it depended upon the whim of another whether or not he wished to allow to you your right, and whether you ought to acquiesce in his decision. From this it is readily understood that there is a perfect obligation of nations for each to allow the other its own right.

§ 265. *Of the practice of justice by nations*

Since every nation ought to allow to another nation its right, since, moreover, the virtue by which his own right is allowed to every one is justice, nations ought to practise justice with each other, consequently ought to be very careful not to do anything which is opposed to justice.

§ 265.

§ 926, part 1, Jus Nat.

§ 722, part 1, Jus Nat.

Although justice is not to be practised for the sake of its advantages, but with a sense of obligation and duty, nevertheless great advantage comes to a nation, if it shows itself just to others and does not allow itself to be led away from the path of justice. It would also be greatly to the advantage of the human race if all nations in general and their rulers were lovers of justice, just as on the other hand injustice is the cause of very many evils.

§ 266. *Of avoiding offences to nations*

Every nation ought to be on its guard that it may not really offend other nations. For since no one ought really to offend another, it is plain, just as before, that every nation ought to be on its guard that it may not really offend other nations.

§ 939, part 1, Jus Nat.

§ 264.

Nothing is more opposed to the society which nature herself has established among all nations and which she binds them to cherish, than wrong and injustice. Therefore we have considered it appropriate

§7.

to discuss clearly each of those points, so far as through them could now
be made plain what we have generally proved above. But not without

§§ 3, 165.

reason have we said that nations ought to guard against real offence.
For only this is illegal; but a nation cannot guard against that which
is wrongly considered as illegal by a nation, and which is not a real
offence, nay more, not rarely, if it could, it ought by no means to do so,
as is sufficiently plain from those things which we have elsewhere laid

§ 936, part 1,
Jus Nat.

down concerning the difference between a true and an alleged offence.
Everyone knows that many consider themselves offended by another,
even when there is no cause for real offence. But just as it is a matter of
prudence to avoid this also, as far as the consideration of duties allows,
so there is special opportunity for it among nations, which nevertheless
themselves by acting rightly ought to fear no one.

§ 267. *Of taking away the right of nations*

The right belongs to every nation not to allow some other nation to take

§ 264.
§ 922, part 1,
Jus Nat.
§ 23, part 1,
Jus Nat., and
§ 24, part 1, Phil.
Pract. Univ.

away from it any of its rights. For every nation ought to allow its own
right to another, consequently ought by no means to take it away. Since,
therefore, from this obligation of the one party the right of one comes
into existence to a negative act of the other, that right can be nothing else
than that of not allowing your right to be taken away from you. Therefore the right belongs to every nation not to allow some other nation to
take any right away from it.

Note, § 252.

We have already indeed shown above that a perfect right is established by a prohibitive law, nevertheless it does not seem ill-advised to
prove that in general, since this principle is by far the most useful of
all in defining just causes of war and in distinguishing a perfect from
an imperfect right.

§ 268. *Of the right which arises from an*
obligation established by a prohibitive law

From the obligation of one party, which is established by a prohibitive
law, the right arises for the other party not to allow the first party to do
that which it is bound not to do, and that is a perfect right. For from the
obligation of one party a certain right is brought into existence for the

other party. Therefore, since a prohibitive law binds one not to do, since it is to the advantage of the other party that he should not do, the right which arises from the obligation established by this law can be nothing else than the right not to allow the party obligated to do what he is bound not to do. Which was the first point.

§ 23, part 1, Jus Nat.

§ 163, part 1, Phil. Pract. Univ.

Since the right belongs to you not to allow the other party to do what he is bound to you not to do (as proved above); and the means are also permitted, without which the other party could not be prevented from doing what he is bound to you not to do, consequently the right belongs to you to compel that party not to do. Therefore, since a right which is bound up with the right to coerce another, if he is unwilling to perform his obligation, is a perfect right, the right, established by a prohibitive law, which arises from the obligation of one party to the other, is a perfect right. Which was the second point.

§ 235, part 1, Phil. Pract. Univ.

Since all prohibitive natural laws belong to this general category, namely, that we must not do that which renders ourselves or our condition less perfect, but as we have proved that a man has a perfect right not to allow another to do that which renders himself and his condition more imperfect, or to do that by which the perfection of himself and his condition is interfered with; if you should examine the thing itself more closely, what we here point out has been in truth already proved in that place, as is also understood from those points which we noted in the same place. Nevertheless it is not devoid of its own utility, that a thing announced in general terms be proved from the connotation itself of those terms, because otherwise it cannot be applied easily or without ambiguity to particular cases. Indeed, not only can those things be brought under the present proposition, which we have hitherto proved in regard to the right not to allow that another may do anything in particular cases, but it is also allowable to use the same principle in other particular cases. Nay, if that which is true must be told, those general principles are in truth natural laws, by the application of which particular cases are resolved, and they increase wonderfully our knowledge and greatly assist our memory. Indeed, if doctrines are to be adequately developed, the effort will have to be made to reduce everything to general principles, which are contained in the particular, or, if you prefer, special [principles], when they are more deeply understood.

§ 152, part 1, Phil. Pract. Univ.

§ 912, part 1, Jus Nat.

§ 269. *Of the right not to allow any nation to interfere in the government of another*

A perfect right belongs to every nation not to allow any other nation to interfere in any way in its government. For if any nation interferes with the government of another, it does this in contravention of the other's right. Therefore, since no one ought to do anything which is contrary to the right of another, since, moreover, from the obligation of one party, which is established by a prohibitive law, the right comes into existence for the other party not to allow the first party to do that which it is bound not to do, and that is a perfect right; a perfect right belongs to every nation not to allow any other nation to interfere in any way with its government.

From the present demonstration it is quite plain how the right not to allow another to do anything to us, may be inferred by virtue of the preceding general principle, so that the same thing may be proved with the same ease in other cases. But here, just as in all other cases when we are talking of our right against another, those points must be noted which we have suggested above. For it is a general principle, that one must not use one's own right when duties towards ourselves or towards others or even towards God, demand another course.

§ 270. *Of the right of a nation against another, which is subject to it by a definite stipulation*

If any nation is subject by a definite stipulation to another nation, the right of the nation to which it is subject, cannot be extended beyond the acts agreed upon. For if any nation is subject to another, a certain right over it belongs to the other. But since, indeed, every nation is free by nature, no other nation has any kind of right over it. The same thing is evident from this, that by nature no nation has a right to any act which concerns the exercise of the sovereignty of another nation. Therefore, since by the acceptance no one can gain more right from another than he has desired to transfer to him, if any nation is subject by a definite stipulation to another nation, no more right belongs to this nation over the other than shall have been agreed upon in the stipulation, consequently this right is not to be extended beyond the acts agreed upon.

§ 256.

§ 910, part 1,
Jus Nat.

§ 268.

Note, § 254.

§ 211, part 1,
Phil. Pract. Univ.

§134, part 1,
Jus Nat.

§ 55, part 8,
Jus Nat.

§ 135, part 1,
Jus Nat.

§ 55.

§ 382, part 3,
Jus Nat.

Therefore the right of one nation over another is to be measured by the stipulation of subordination. Every stipulation which is accompanied with diminution of the sovereignty of one of the two nations is in accord with this; for then certain acts belonging to the exercise of civil sovereignty are made subject to the right of the other nation, but this nation has no right except in regard to those acts. A right of that sort is, that one nation cannot choose a king for itself, except with the consent of another nation, and without the consent of this nation it cannot begin a war, that it may be compelled to tolerate subjects devoted to a certain definite religion, and so on. Rights are so limited by stipulations, that certain acts may become illegal, which before were permissible, and obligatory, which before were simply permissible, so that they could be both committed and omitted.

§ 271. *Of the right to obtain one's right by force*

The right belongs to every nation to obtain its right against another nation by force, if the other is unwilling to allow that right. For the right belongs to every nation not to permit any other nation to take away its right, consequently also not to permit it not to allow that right. Therefore it is necessary, when one does not wish to allow a right, that the other compel it by force to allow it. Therefore the right belongs to the one nation against the other nation to obtain its right by force, if the other does not wish to allow it.

§ 267.

This right is really the right of war. Therefore we shall fully consider this subject later, when we are ready to discuss the right of war. For example, if one nation has caused loss to another, it is bound to make reparation to it. But if it is unwilling to make reparation, the right belongs to the other nation to compel it by force to make reparation. In like manner if one nation has been made tributary to another, but is unwilling to pay the tribute, the other nation can obtain payment of the tribute by force.

§ 1103, part 1,
Jus Nat.

§ 580, part 2,
Jus Nat.

§ 272. *Of the right of punishment among nations*

The right belongs to every nation to punish another nation which has injured it. For by nature the right belongs to every man to punish the one who has injured him. Therefore, since the same right must be applied to

§ 1061, part 1,
Jus Nat.

§ 3.

nations also, the right belongs to every nation to punish another which has injured it.

§ 252.

§ 288, part 1,
Phil. Pract.
Univ.

This is likewise proved in this way. The right belongs to every nation not to allow that it be injured by another. Therefore, since we bind others by penalties to omit actions, the right belongs to every nation to punish another which has injured it.

> The present proposition has no little utility in developing more fully the right of war, so that therefore it ought not to be passed over. This could in fact be proved in many other ways besides, but there is no need of piling up proofs. The right of security belongs to every nation and every injury is opposed to that. If then some nation pun-

§ 253.

§ 271.

> ishes the one injuring it, it pursues its right of security against the other by force; a thing which undoubtedly it can do.

§ 273. Of the right of defending oneself and one's right

§ 973, part 1,
Jus Nat.

The right belongs to every nation to defend itself and its right against another nation. For the right of self-defence belongs to everybody. Therefore, since the same right is to be applied to nations also, the right belongs to every nation also to defend itself against another nation. Which was the first point.

§ 3.

§ 267.

But now the right belongs to every nation also not to allow any other nation to take any right from it. Therefore, if another nation intends or attempts to take away the right which a nation has in fact, it may resist it by force. Therefore, since its right to defend its right consists in that, the right belongs to every nation to defend its right against another. Which was the second point.

§ 727, Ontol.

§ 972, part 1,
Jus Nat.

§§ 4, 5, part 8,
Jus Nat.

§ 26, part 8,
Jus Nat.

> This proposition is the basic principle of defensive war, as we shall see in its proper place. Self-defence itself might be reduced to defence of one's right. For the compact by which the nation had united into a state makes the nation; and since this compact has been in accordance with the law of nature, it has accomplished this by virtue of its own right. If then a certain nation attacks another as a nation, it infringes upon its right, consequently when the other nation defends itself, it is defending its right. Nay more, when a nation defends itself against another, it defends also its right of security. But in these matters we do not wish to be too prolix.

∞ CHAPTER III ∞

Of Ownership by Nations and the Rights Connected Therewith

§ 274. *What things are originally subject to the ownership of a nation*

If a nation has occupied a certain territory, all the land and the things which are in it are subject to its ownership. For if several jointly occupy the same thing, they acquire joint ownership over it. Therefore, since a nation is a number of human beings united into a state, if a certain nation occupies a certain territory, all who make up the nation occupy it jointly, consequently all jointly, that is, the entire nation, acquire ownership over those things which are occupied. Since, therefore, when a territory is occupied, all the land and the things which are in it are occupied, those things are subject to the ownership of the nation.

§ 189, part 2, Jus Nat.

§ 5, part 8, Jus Nat.

The original method of acquiring ownership is occupation. Therefore a nation also could not originally acquire ownership in certain lands and in those things which are in the same, except by occupying them. But just as, when the primitive joint holding is abandoned, the right to occupy a certain thing belongs to all without distinction who need it, so also nations were able to occupy lands not subject to ownership for the purpose of permanent use, and in this way to acquire ownership over lands and over the things which are in them. But there are two cases. For either men who had not yet a settled abode, or were not content with their abode, united into a civil society and, seeking a settled abode, occupied a certain territory, just as in times past is understood to have happened in the migration of nations, or separate families dwelling in the same territory can form a civil society and thus occupy the entire territory. In the former case, by division

§ 178, part 2, Jus Nat.

§ 179, part 2, Jus Nat.

§§ 86, 87.

§ 175, part 2,
Jus Nat.

§ 174, part 2,
Jus Nat.

certain parts of the land and certain things become the property of individuals; but in the latter case, things remain as they had been and the things which still belonged to nobody pass under the control of the nation. We have already distinguished those cases above. Of course the nation which occupies a territory for the purpose of its perpetual use, is understood to desire to hold for itself, not only all the land, but likewise all the things which are in it; this intent to occupy is necessarily required, where ownership is acquired. For although on account of ignorance or for some other reason a nation should make no use of a certain thing, or not care for that use for the present, nevertheless the use which things might have belongs likewise to that nation, and because it occupies the territory for the purpose of permanent use, it is assumed to have intended that use also which perchance those things might have for the future. Besides, it is certain that no one loses his ownership in his property for the reason that he handles it carelessly and does not make every use of it which it can have.

§ 275. *Of places desert, sterile and uncultivated, in a territory inhabited by a nation*

§ 274.

§§ 118, 120,
part 2, Jus Nat.
§ 77, part 8,
Jus Nat.

Since all lands and all things which are in a territory occupied by a nation are subject to its ownership, if there are in any territory, which a nation inhabits, desert and sterile, or uncultivated places, those belong to the nation, consequently no one can dispose of them except the nation or the ruler of the state, if indeed the state has transferred its right to him; which it is understood to have done, if sovereignty has been transferred without any restriction or limitation, consequently without any fundamental law.

Places of that sort are vast forests, which are of no use to a nation, uncultivated lands, to the cultivation of which no need drives the inhabitants, sterile lands which no one wishes to cultivate on account of the excessive labour and expense required, great lakes, marshy places, and others which are akin to these.

§ 276. *Whether one may occupy at pleasure desert, sterile, and uncultivated places in an uninhabited territory*

§ 275.
§ 338, part 2,
Jus Nat.

Since desert and sterile, or uncultivated places are the property of the nation which inhabits the territory, no one, either foreign or native, can occupy those places and make them subject to his ownership.

Ownership of things was introduced and is desired for the sake of their use; but whether the owner wishes or does not wish to enjoy the use, is left to his will, and for this reason another is not allowed to take away his property or to use the same. But what no one calls in question among private individuals must be allowed among nations also. The force of ownership with a nation is the same as with a private individual.

§ 277. *How ownership is acquired by private individuals in those places*

Likewise, since no one can dispose of desert, sterile, and uncultivated places in an inhabited territory, except the nation or someone who has its right, such as the ruler of the state, the ownership of those places cannot be transferred to private individuals except by the consent of the people or of one who has the right of the people, such as the ruler of the state.

§ 255.

Ownership of things which are already subject to ownership cannot be acquired from another except by the consent of the owner, when he transfers his right to the one accepting. Therefore, since the nation has ownership of desert, sterile, and uncultivated places, the same cannot pass to any private individual without its consent. For when the ruler of a state transfers ownership to a private individual, that is supposed to be done by the will of the people. But because nations occupy the sovereignty and ownership at the same time, and these rights are distinct the one from the other, what is said of one right, such as ownership, is not to be transferred to the other.

§ 13, part 8, Jus Nat.

§ 275.

§ 158, part 8, Jus Nat.

§ 278. *Of ownership in desert and uncultivated places*

Since a nation has ownership of desert, sterile, and uncultivated places, and since sovereignty is occupied at the same time as ownership by nations, a nation, and consequently the ruler of the state, has sovereignty over the desert, sterile, and uncultivated places which are in its territory, and although ownership may be transferred to private individuals, nevertheless sovereignty over those places is retained.

§ 275.

§ 85.

We are not speaking here of the alienation which occurs between nations and includes alienation of sovereignty also in a certain part of the territory, such as the places of which we speak, a thing which is readily understood from the underlying meaning. Ownership can be transferred without transfer of sovereignty; both rights can also be transferred at the same time. Nevertheless a transfer of ownership to a private person, even a foreigner, is not understood as made along with the transfer of supreme sovereignty, so that sovereignty itself ought to be considered as alienated.

§ 279. *Of conveyance to aliens of uncultivated places for cultivation*

Desert and uncultivated places should be granted to aliens, that they may cultivate them. For if desert and uncultivated places are transformed by cultivation from sterile or at least useless places into fertile and useful places, since in this manner products of labor are multiplied and a crop of natural products is developed by industry and exertion, that assuredly tends to the perfecting of the condition of a nation. Therefore, since every nation ought to perfect its condition, desert and uncultivated places should be granted to aliens, that they may cultivate them.

§ 30 h, and
§ 421, part 8,
Jus Nat.
§ 35.

That concession can be made in more than one form, for example, a usufruct may be given for a certain time for labour and expenditure, or ownership may be transferred for nothing to those who have wished to cultivate, nay more, certain privileges may even be given to those undertaking cultivation, as immunity from burdens for a certain time, or that a fief or an emphyteusis be established in the lands, and by still other methods, as circumstances may have suggested. If the aliens are exiles, there is a benefit in the grant, since thus they have that by which they may support themselves. If sterile and uncultivated places be cultivated, the land can also support more, and consequently if they are transferred to aliens for cultivation, that tends to increase the power of the nation, for the increase of which nations ought to provide.

§ 69.

§ 280. *Of the right to occupy things which as yet have become subject to the ownership of no one*

It will depend upon the will of a nation, whether it desires that the things which as yet have become subject to the ownership of no one be left in

the primitive joint holding or whether it desires that the right of occupation belong to itself. In a doubtful case it is presumed to have desired
the latter. But if it has assumed the right of occupation, then it depends
upon its own will whether it desires to make the property public or the
property of a corporation or the property of individuals. It is no secret
that there are things which as yet have become subject to the ownership
of no one, which nevertheless can be made subject to it by occupation.
Such things are indeed fish, birds, and four-footed wild animals. Such
also are pearls, shells, corals, amber, which are collected on the occupied
shores of the sea. Nay, here are to be included also fruits of trees and wild
shrubs. Therefore, since the ownership of those things is to be acquired
originally, it is acquired by occupation. But since the right of occupation
of things still lacking an owner can be subjected to ownership, since,
moreover, the act of occupation is a voluntary one, as is evident of itself,
it certainly depends altogether upon the will of a nation occupying a
certain territory, whether or not it wishes to assume also the right of
occupying the things which as yet have become subject to the ownership
of no one, or whether, that is, since the same remains common to all
men, if the nation does not occupy the things which as yet have come
under the ownership of no one, to leave it in the primitive joint holding.
Which was the first point.

For since a nation occupies a territory for its own advantage, as is evident of itself, and it is to its advantage if the right to occupy things which
have as yet come under the ownership of no one is subject to its ownership, so that it may not only dispose of that right as it pleases among its
subjects but also may exclude outsiders from an exercise of this right, in
order that they may not acquire those things for themselves in its lands;
in a doubtful case the nation is presumed to have subjected the right to
occupy things to its ownership. Which was the second point.

But if a nation in its own territory has assumed the right to occupy
things which have as yet come under the ownership of no one, that
right is under its ownership. Therefore, since an owner can dispose of
his property as shall seem best, if a nation has assumed the right to
occupy, it depends upon its will whether it desires that to be common
to the whole nation or wishes to transfer it to certain corporations or
even to individuals, consequently whether it desires to make that public

§ 176, part 2,
Jus Nat.
§ 178, part 2,
Jus Nat.

§ 316, part 2,
Jus Nat.

§ 9, part 2,
Jus Nat.

§ 118, part 2,
Jus Nat.
§ 120, part 2,
Jus Nat.
§ 244, part 2,
Jus Nat., and
§ 578, Log.

§ 175, part 2,
Jus Nat.
§ 118, part 8,
Jus Nat.

§ 88.

property or property of a corporation or of individuals. Which was the third point.

The presumption in favour of occupation is a perfectly natural one. For unless by express law, such as existed among the Romans, it has been provided that whoever thinks best may be allowed to occupy the things which have not yet become subject to ownership, and if the right has not been made subject to the ownership of corporations or individuals, there will be scarcely any one who would not consider it unjust, if any foreigner should take fish, birds, or other wild creatures. But when a nation does dispose of the right of occupation, wisdom suggests that what is especially to the interest of the state should be considered.

§ 281. Of the power of eminent domain over the right of occupation belonging to individuals

If the right to occupy the things which have as yet come under the ownership of no one should belong to individuals, and if it shall be to the advantage of the state that it should not belong to individuals, the ruler of the state can take that right away from the individuals. For the ruler of the state has eminent domain over the property of subjects, consequently also in the right belonging to them to occupy the things which as yet have come under the control of no one. Since, therefore, by the power of eminent domain he can dispose of the property belonging to citizens for the sake of public safety in case of necessity, by force of this power he can also take away from them the right to occupy the things which have as yet come under the ownership of no one, if it should be to the advantage of the state that the right should not remain with individuals.

§ 111, part 8, Jus Nat.

§ 111, part 8, Jus Nat.

There is a case of necessity of this sort, if individuals should carry that right to excess, so that it would be more harmful to them than beneficial, and loss would manifestly come upon the state from promiscuous use of such a right; it is recognized without difficulty that this is a thing which could happen in more than one way. Then undoubtedly the public welfare prevails, the supreme law of the state, and makes a place for the exercise of eminent domain.

§ 86, part 8, Jus Nat.
§ 110, part 8, Jus Nat.

§ 282. *Whether it is allowable to expel a nation from the territory which it inhabits*

The right belongs to no nation to expel another nation from the territory which the other inhabits in order that it may fix its abode in the same place. For a nation which inhabits a territory has not only ownership but also sovereignty over the lands and the things which are in it. If then it is driven from the territory which it inhabits, its right is taken from it. Therefore, since no nation ought to take its right from another nation, the right belongs to no nation to expel another nation from the territory which the other inhabits, in order that it may fix its abode in the same place.

§ 85.

§ 274.

§ 264 h, and § 722, part 1, Jus. Nat. § 170, part 1, Phil. Pract. Univ.

There is no reason why you should take the exception that this is then permitted, if the nation which is expelled has before done the same thing. For then this is just the same as if you were to desire to carry off a thing taken by theft or robbery from its possessor or quasi-possessor with the intention that it should be your own. But everyone knows that ownership in a thing cannot be acquired in this manner. Nor does the illegal act of another make your act legal, as by the law of retaliation, for which nevertheless there is no place in the present instance, even if the law of retaliation be admitted to the uttermost. But here it must be noted that, although sovereignty properly speaking is a right to control the actions of men, nevertheless the same is applied to places in which men live who are subject to sovereignty. If then the union of a nation is not destroyed when it is driven out, which however necessarily happens if it cannot find vacant territory which it may occupy, still there is taken from it even as far as sovereignty is concerned the right to exercise the same in those localities from which it is expelled. Therefore nothing is assumed in this proof which might not be assumed, whatever possible case you may imagine. The law of nature protects no less the rights of nations, consequently also their ownership and sovereignty, than the rights of individuals. Just as any private citizen ought to be content with his own lot, and ought not to covet the goods of others because they are better than his, so also every nation ought to be content with its own abode, nor oust another from its abodes because it is better off. This is diametrically opposed to justice which wishes to assign to every one

§ 194, part 7, Jus Nat.

§ 3.

§ 926, part 1, Jus Nat. § 722, part 1, Jus Nat.

his own right, and consequently forbids that to be done which cannot be done without infringing the right of another.

§ 283. *Whether it is allowable to extend the limits of sovereignty*

§§ 85, 274.
§ 282.

No nation has the right to extend the limits of sovereignty. For the nation which extends the limits of sovereignty, extends the sovereignty beyond its boundaries into the territories of a neighbouring nation. Therefore, since the neighbouring nation has ownership and sovereignty over those territories, it is clear in the same way as before, that no nation has the right to extend the limits of sovereignty.

The present case can be looked on as falling under the preceding, although there is some difference between them, inasmuch as those who inhabit places over which sovereignty is extended are not expelled from their abode. Although, indeed, private ownership over their estates is not taken from them, nevertheless the ownership which belongs to the nation over that part of the earth is taken away. Here the same law prevails which obtains between possessors of neighbouring estates.

§ 284. *Of determining the boundaries of territories*

§ 283.

§ 166, part 8,
Jus Nat.

Since no nation has the right to extend the limits of its sovereignty or to enlarge its sovereignty beyond the boundaries of its territory, and consequently it is necessary that these boundaries should be certain, the boundaries of territories, or, if you prefer, of domains, are to be fixed between neighbouring nations.

Thus disputes are prevented which can arise between neighbouring nations. But since we are talking here of not extending the limits of sovereignty, anyone can see that our discussion is not now of those cases in which for some just cause that is taken from another which is his own. We shall have to discuss this at length when we treat of the law of war.

§ 285. *Of harmony of nations*

Nations ought to live in harmony with each other. For they are members of the supreme state into which they are understood to have united, consequently they are to be regarded as citizens. Therefore, since citizens ought to live in harmony with each other, nations also ought to live in harmony with each other.

§§ 9, 10.

§ 6, part 8, Jus Nat.

Nothing is more useful to nations than harmony, nevertheless it is well enough known that the same rarely exists.

§ 1083, part 8, Jus Nat.

§ 286. *Of avoiding dissension*

Since nations ought to be harmonious with each other, they are bound to use every effort to avoid those things which give cause for dissensions or tend to stimulate them.

§ 285.

Therefore harmony also enjoins upon nations that they define the boundaries of the territories between neighbours and that each nation keep its sovereignty within those boundaries. Harmony contributes not a little to the happiness of neighbouring nations, as, on the other hand, discord is the cause of many troubles and produces much harm.

§ 722, part 1, Jus Nat.

§ 287. *In what harmony of nations consists*

Since nations ought to live in harmony with each other, since, moreover, they are in harmony whose likes and dislikes are the same, the likes and dislikes of nations also, especially neighbouring nations, ought to be the same: of what sort these ought to be, their duties, which have been proved above, indicate.

§ 285.

§ 132, part 7, Jus Nat.

Identity of likes and dislikes, in which harmony consists, has its own rules, that it may be a real identity. It is not sufficient to will and not to will the same thing, since we are not free to will and not to will anything, but we ought to will one thing and ought not to will another. Harmony is not a virtue enjoined by nature, except in so far as likes and dislikes are in harmony with the law of nature, consequently with our duties. And from this too is determined what is the cause of discord. Of course if you will what you ought to will but another does not will it, you are not the cause of the discord, but rather the other who ought to conform his will to yours. But if each wills what he ought not to will, and their wills are mutually opposed, as when each intends to create trouble for the other, the fault indeed belongs to each.

§ 288. *The general law of the preservation of harmony*

§ 287.

Since the likes and dislikes of nations ought to be such as their reciprocal duties require, what any nation wishes to be done to itself by another in conformity with its duties, that also it ought to do to the other, but what it does not wish to be done to itself, that it ought not to do to the other.

§ 225, part 1, Phil. Pract. Univ., and § 3 h.

§ 263, part 1, Phil. Pract. Univ.

§ 265, part 1, Phil. Pract. Univ.

§§ 98, 99, part 1, Jus Nat.

If nations were to perform all parts of their duty towards other nations, there would be no dissension, but steadfast and permanent harmony. Since the law of nature prescribes the duties of nations towards each other, both positive and negative, that is, both those things which they ought to do the one to the other and the things which they ought not to do, since, moreover, the same law provides for the advantage of nations; no other way exists by which harmony may be more readily preserved and, on the other hand, dissension avoided, than if one nation does not do to another the things which it does not wish done to itself, utility of course producing volition, and detriment, nolition. But since utility is not a sufficient reason for right, in order that volition and nolition may not wander from the path of righteousness, they ought to be in accord with our duties. See how we have limited these duties elsewhere and what we have noted concerning the same. Since no one wishes that his property be taken away from him by another or that he be disturbed in any way in the exercise of his ownership, one preserves that right in no way more easily than by holding to the purpose of not doing to another that which he does not wish to be done to himself. Therefore, since at present we are discussing the question as to how ownership and sovereignty of nations may be safely established, this has been the place especially in which present duty should be insisted upon and the harmony of nations, which is preserved thereby, should be discussed.

§ 289. *How foreign nations ought to regard the property of individuals*

With respect to foreign nations all property of individuals taken as a whole must be considered as property of the nation, or property of citizens must be considered as property of the state. For nations in relation

to each other are regarded as individual persons. Therefore, since all §2.
together who make up a nation are regarded by foreign nations simply
as one person, their property also taken as a whole cannot be regarded
otherwise than as the property of this person, that is, of the nation.
Therefore, it is plain with respect to foreign nations that all the property of the individuals taken as a whole is to be considered as property
of the nation, or, what is just the same, since individuals who make
up the nation are members of that same state, the property of citizens
with respect to foreign nations must be considered as the property of §4, part 1,
the state.   Jus Nat.

Private ownership is not considered except as between private
persons, but as between nations the question concerning it is, what
belongs to the nation? But that it may be more readily understood,
that as between nations the property of citizens must be considered
as the property of the state, suppose that such a community of goods
existed in the state as Campanella desired in his "Respublica [Civitas]
Solis."[1] There will certainly be no one who doubts that this property,
which is under the control of citizens taken together, is the property
of the state. But does it not depend upon the will of a nation whether
it wishes to introduce community of property in the state or indeed §129, part 1,
to leave place for private ownership? Therefore, since no nation has Jus Nat.
the right to any act which affects the exercise of sovereignty of another
state, no nation also ought to consider what another nation has established concerning the ownership of things in the state, whether it has §255.
desired that they be held in common or indeed as the property of
individuals. Therefore, however much the latter form shall have been
preferred, nevertheless foreign nations cannot look at the property
of individuals otherwise than as the property of the nation. But the
things which are said of nations cannot be extended to the individuals who belong to the nation, so that some private individual of one

---

1. Tommaso Campanella (1568–1639) was a Dominican friar who wrote the uto-
pian *City of the Sun* while he was a prisoner. On the community of goods in Campanella's work, see Tommaso Campanella, *La città del sole: Dialogo poetico / The
City of the Sun: A Poetical Dialogue*, trans. Daniel J. Donno (Berkeley: University of
California Press, 1981), p. 65.

nation can look on the property of some private individual of another
nation as the property of this nation; for the individuals who make
up a nation do not have the right of the nation, which in fact belongs
to the whole, or to the one to whom it has been transferred. Now, we
shall use the present proposition as a fundamental principle in proving
other things to follow.

§ 290. *Of the right to the property of another nation*

§ 289.

Since with respect to foreign nations the property of citizens must be
considered as the property of the state, if any nation has a right to certain
property of another nation, it has the right to the goods of any citizen at
all within the limits, of course, of the debt.

Of course, if a nation wishes to use its right against another, it does
not inquire whether a thing belongs to this or that private citizen, but
whether it belongs to the nation against whose property it has some
right. Nevertheless, on this account it has no more right to the private
property of a citizen than it has to the property of the other state or, if
you prefer, of the other nation. For this right is to be determined from
the debt of the other state, or other nation. These points will become
the clearer when, in what follows, they shall be applied to particulars.

§ 291. *Of the occupation of uninhabited lands*

§ 6, part 2,
Jus Nat.

§ 7, part 7,
Jus Nat.

§ 175, part 2,
Jus Nat.

§ 179, part 1,
Jus Nat.

Islands arisen or discovered in the ocean, and other lands not subject to
ownership and sovereignty or uninhabited by any nation, can be occupied
and colonies established in them. For islands arisen or discovered in the
ocean and other uninhabited lands, or those not subject to ownership and
sovereignty, since a special right to them belongs as yet to no nation, are
the property of nobody, consequently by nature they are still common
to all men. Therefore, since the ownership of things which are subject
to the primitive joint holding is acquired by occupation, and when one
gets away from that, as has already occurred by introducing ownerships
and sovereignties, the right of occupation belongs indifferently to all who
need a certain thing; islands that have arisen in the ocean or lands that
have been discovered uninhabited, or not subject to ownership and sovereignty, can be occupied by any nation. Which was the first point.

But since ownership is acquired by occupation, and if a certain nation occupies an uninhabited territory, it occupies at the same time the sovereignty of it; a nation has ownership and sovereignty in an island arisen or discovered in the ocean and in other land not subject to ownership and sovereignty, which it has occupied. But because either right is of no use, unless the island and occupied lands are inhabited, a thing which is self-evident, it is necessary that colonies be established in them. Therefore, since any nation can occupy an island and lands of that sort, as shown in the first point, after it has occupied them it can also establish colonies there. Which was the second point.

§ 175, part 1, Jus Nat.
§ 85.

Colonies were said by the Romans to be lesser cities, and for peopling them citizens were sent from the greater cities. Therefore also in the same sense the word can be applied to entire districts of the earth, for peopling which citizens are sent from a certain nation. Nay more, it makes little difference whether those who are sent thither are residents or foreigners. For as soon as foreigners subject themselves to the civil sovereignty of the nation by which they are sent, they become equal to citizens. It is well known that in former times the Romans in this manner cleared the city of the poor, who were not able to pay taxes, and thus at the same time provided for their need, since to those who were willing to be taken away to the new colony, they would give two, four, six, or seven acres of land, and sometimes more.

§ 292. *Whether they belong to the territory of the nation*

Since any nation is able to occupy islands and other uninhabited lands, and since if any nation occupy a certain territory, all the land and the things which are in it are subject to the ownership of it, and the sovereignty in that land is occupied at the same time; the nation which first has occupied an island, or uninhabited land, has ownership and sovereignty over it, and consequently the uninhabited islands and lands into which colonies are brought by the nation occupying them become an accession to the territory of that nation, however far removed they be from it, so that then it is just as if they were adjacent to it or included within the same boundaries.

§ 291.
§ 274.
§ 85.

The distance of the places is not considered. For territory is determined by the civil sovereignty. Therefore those places belong to the same territory over which there is the same civil sovereignty, or they are considered as parts of the same. And here we are talking of the territories of nations. Concerning ownership there is no doubt but that it can be held in things separated from each other by any distance whatsoever. Therefore lands over which a nation has sovereignty, although they are widely separated, are subject to its ownership with the rest, and are included by a common name under the ownership of the nation. Now you must not think that these suggestions are devoid of any utility, for their use will be plain in what follows, especially when we come to discuss the right of war.

§ 166, part 8, Jus Nat.

§ 293. *Of a right not belonging to outsiders in the territory of another*

No nation nor any private person who is a foreigner can claim any right for himself in the territory of another. For a territory is subject to the peculiar right of a nation or ruler of a state, since the nation whose land is inhabited, or the ruler of the state, has sovereignty and ownership over it. Therefore, since all others, whoever they may be, may be excluded by force of the peculiar right from all right belonging thereto, no nation nor any private person who is a foreigner can claim any right for himself in the territory of another.

§ 34, part 8, and § 118, part 2, Jus Nat.

§ 274.

§ 42, part 8, Jus Nat.

§ 119, part 2, Jus Nat.

We have already suggested above that there is the same force in the ownership of a nation as in that of a private individual. Therefore, just as a private citizen is not bound to allow another to do anything on his estate without his consent, so also no nation is bound to allow any other nation to do anything on its territory without its consent, consequently claim for itself any right whatsoever in that territory—a thing which is understood quite as readily of any foreign private person.

Note, § 276.

§ 156, part 1, Phil. Pract. Univ.

§ 294. *Of a criminal fleeing into the territory of another*

Since no nation can claim any right for itself in the territory of another, it is not allowable to enter with an armed force into the territory of another and take therefrom a fugitive criminal or one hiding there.

§ 293.

There is no reason why you should object that criminals hiding in the homes of private citizens are taken therefrom without their consent. For this has to do with the ownership of a nation, which by virtue of its sovereignty it has in the estates of private persons. For to a nation and consequently to the one who has the right of a nation, or to whom the exercise of the same is entrusted, belongs all the use in the estates of private individuals, without which the civil sovereignty cannot be exercised and which was either reserved in the grant of private ownership or to which those have tacitly agreed, who as possessors of private estates have united into a state.

§ 295. *Of the prohibition of entrance into the territory of another*

In like manner because no foreigner can claim for himself any right in the territory of another, no foreigner is in any way permitted, contrary to the prohibition of the ruler, to enter the latter's territory, no matter whether this is for some definite purpose or not, as the prohibition may have set forth.

§ 293.

> A nation has the same power of ownership as a private person. Therefore, just as the owner of a private estate can prohibit any other person from entering upon the same, a thing which no one denies, so also the ruler of a territory can prohibit any foreigner from entering upon it.

Note, § 276.

§ 296. *Of the prohibition of entrance into the territory of another under a definite penalty*

Since no foreigner is permitted to enter a territory contrary to the prohibition of its ruler, and since the effect of a prohibition is void, unless those who are forbidden to do something are bound by penalties not to do it; if the ruler of a territory forbids any foreigner to enter the territory, he can impose a penalty upon the one entering or forbid it under a definite penalty.

§ 295.

§ 292, part 3, Phil. Pract. Univ.

> So formerly the Chinese, who had adequate reasons for forbidding any foreigners to enter their territory, decreed capital punishment for

him who should dare to enter. But it is quite plain that the prohibition ought to be known to those who are forbidden to enter, together with the penalty by fear of which they ought to be deterred from entering. Otherwise, if they attempt an entrance or desire to enter, they should only be warned to withdraw, and the prohibition with the penalty which is affixed to it should be made plain to them. He who attempts to enter contrary to the prohibition known to himself, should blame himself, if the penalty imposed on that act is inflicted.

§ 297. Of prohibiting under penalty the approach of missionaries

§§ 295, 296.

Note, § 261.

Because the ruler of a territory can under definite penalty prohibit any foreigner from entering it for a definite purpose, and since missionaries enter a territory for the purpose of urging their religion upon the inhabitants, it cannot be doubted that the ruler of a territory can under definite penalty prohibit missionaries from entering it.

§ 262.

§ cited.

We have already seen above that it depends upon the will of any nation whether it wishes or not to tolerate missionaries. If it does not wish to tolerate them, it can even prohibit them from entering its territory, and that under penalty, lest the prohibition fail of its effect, a thing which we have also already indicated above, when we proved that missionaries could be punished as obstinate, if they were unwilling to depart when ordered. Here also is to be reconsidered what we there noted.

§ 298. Of the immigration of foreigners to the territory of another

§§ 118, 136, part 2, Jus. Nat.

The conditions under which the ruler of a territory desires to permit immigration to foreigners depend altogether upon his will. It is self-evident that immigration to a territory is a part of the use of a place, the civil sovereignty over which belongs to the ruler of it. Therefore, since an owner can dispose of the use of his property according to his liking, the conditions under which the ruler of a territory desires to permit immigration to foreigners, depend altogether upon his will.

It is scarcely necessary to observe, lest some injustice may be committed here, that the duties of humanity are not to be violated. For this is to be considered in every transfer of one's special right and in the allowance of acts belonging to it: even the abuse of his right is to be allowed to an owner, so long as he does nothing contrary to the perfect right of another. And from this it is easily decided whether the condition under which immigration is allowed is unjust. But however unjust the condition may be, nevertheless one cannot complain of injury if one enters the territory of another under that condition, since it depends upon his own will whether he desires to enter under that condition, and he is not allowed to enter contrary to the prohibition of the owner.

§ 169, part 2, Jus Nat.

§ 295.

§ 299. *Under what condition immigration of foreigners is understood to be allowed*

The ruler of a territory is not understood to allow foreigners to dwell in his territory nor stay there, except under this condition, that their actions are subject to the laws of the place. For he has civil sovereignty in the territory and by virtue of the legislative power which belongs to the same he can make laws concerning those things which he wishes or does not wish to be done in his territory or in certain places belonging thereto. But since the contrary desire which produces the exception is not presumed, the ruler of a territory is not presumed to desire that the actions of foreigners should be exempt from the law. Therefore it is understood that he does not allow foreigners to dwell in his territory nor stay there, except under this condition, that their actions are subject to the laws of the place.

§ 166, part 8, Jus Nat.

§ 813, part 8, Jus Nat.

In alien territory no right belongs to any foreign nation nor to the ruler of another state. Therefore, when your citizen dwells in alien territory, he is not subject to your law there. But it would be absurd that then he ought to be free to do what he wishes. Every one is bound to recognize in this situation that the local civil sovereignty holds, consequently if he should wish to live in that place or stay there, he ought also to submit to the law of that place. There is no reason why you should urge that civil laws bind only members of that state in which they are promulgated; for that holds, as long as someone is outside of

§ 967, part 8, Jus Nat.

the territory with his own nation, where no right over him belongs to the ruler of the territory. But entrance into alien territory produces a certain right over him which elsewhere belonged to his ruler.

§ 300. *How foreigners in alien territory are subject to the laws of the place*

§ 298.

§ 299.

§ 363, part 3, Jus Nat.

Since the condition under which the ruler of a territory desires to permit immigration to foreigners depends altogether upon his will, and since it is understood that he does not allow foreigners to dwell in his territory nor to stay there, except under this condition, that their actions are subject to the laws of the place; if foreigners enter alien territory and dwell or stay in it, they are understood to promise tacitly, consequently they bind themselves that they wish their actions to be subject to the laws of the place and consequently the laws have the same force over them as over citizens.

§ 288.

There is nothing in that of which any nation can complain. For this right is common to all nations. And just as one nation wishes that foreigners should be subject to its laws as long as they dwell in their territory or stay there, so also it ought to wish that, if its subjects dwell or stay in the territory of another nation, they should be subject to its laws.

§ 301. *Whether foreigners committing offences in alien territory are to be punished there and in what manner*

§ 300.

Because the actions of foreigners, as long as they dwell in alien territory or stay there, are subject to the laws of the place in which they are, if foreigners commit an offence in alien territory, they are to be punished in accordance with the laws of the place.

Therefore it is not necessary that they should be sent to their own nation for punishment by it, although I do not deny that such a course might be agreed upon between neighbouring nations; for is there any one who does not know that rights can be changed by stipulations? Nevertheless it is scarcely to be believed that any example of that kind of agreement exists. For it does not lack difficulties of its own, if one

had to stand by an agreement of that sort, as certainly one ought to
do. Hence if your citizen has committed a theft in alien territory and
is arrested there, you ought to allow that he be hung from a gibbet,
or if he commits murder, that he be beheaded, or that, on account of
some less offence, he be fined.

§ 789, part 3,
Jus Nat.

§ 302. *Of settling disputes of foreigners in an alien territory*

In like manner because foreigners in an alien territory are subject to the
laws of the place in which they dwell or stay, if between themselves and
citizens or even between two foreigners certain legal disputes arise, they
are to be settled by a judge of the place in accordance with the laws of
the place.

§ 301.

Nor does it make any difference that their native civil laws differ
from those laws; for there is no place for their laws in the territory in
which they are dwelling, since the ruler of the territory is not bound
to consider their laws, but in promulgating laws in his own territory
he is certainly independent of any other nation or of the ruler of any
other state, as is quite plain from arguments given above and from
universal public law.

§ 303. *Of temporary citizens*

Foreigners, as long as they dwell in alien territory or stay there, are temporary citizens. For when they enter an alien territory they tacitly bind
themselves that they wish to subject their acts to the laws of the place,
and the laws have the same force over them as over citizens. Since the
condition under which the ruler of a territory desires to permit foreigners
to enter depends altogether upon his will, he can also pass laws which
bind foreigners alone. Therefore, since civil laws bind only the members
of that state in which they are passed, foreigners, as long as they dwell in
alien territory or stay there, are to be considered as members of that state to
which the territory belongs; consequently, since members of a state are
citizens, foreigners, as long as they dwell in alien territory or stay there,
are temporary citizens.

§ 300.

§ 298.

§ 967, part 8,
Jus Nat.

§ 6, part 8,
Jus Nat.

He who dwells in alien territory or stays there, since that cannot
be done without the consent of the ruler of the territory, associates

§ 295.

himself with citizens, not indeed permanently, but only for a certain time. And he cannot be considered otherwise than as one received into the state on a certain condition for a certain time. Therefore the idea

§ 409, part 8,
Jus Nat.

of a temporary citizen, such as we conceive foreigners to be as long as they dwell in the territory of another or stay there, contains nothing absurd, and everyone knows that foreigners staying in alien territory are called temporary citizens.

§ 304. *To what foreigners in alien territory are bound*

Since foreigners, as long as they dwell in alien territory or stay there, are

§ 303.

temporary citizens, they are bound only to do and not to do the things which must be done or not done by citizens at the time under the same circumstances, except in so far as particular laws introduce something

§ 298.

else concerning foreigners.

Temporary citizens certainly differ from permanent ones and consequently this difference also must come into consideration in measuring the obligation of foreigners and in measuring the right of the ruler of a territory over foreigners. For example, if at the time a citizen had injured another citizen, he should be punished. Therefore also

§ 651, part 8,
Jus Nat.

a foreigner can be punished on account of an injury inflicted on a citizen or another foreigner. In like manner if a citizen had contracted with another citizen, the unwilling party could be compelled by a judge to perform his part of the contract. Therefore, if a foreigner has

§ 540, part 8,
Jus Nat.

contracted with a citizen or another foreigner, the unwilling party can also be compelled by the judge to perform his part of the contract. In the same manner it is evident, if citizens selling certain goods at that time are bound to pay certain taxes, those also must be borne by foreigners intending to sell goods of that sort, unless special laws passed in regard to foreigners enjoin the contrary. But if any taxes which are imposed upon citizens have no relation to the business for which foreigners are dwelling in alien territory or staying there, those cannot be demanded of them. So the taxes which are imposed for the purpose of defence of the state cannot be imposed upon foreigners. Just as in a state the right of the ruler of the state is to be measured by the purpose

§§ 4, 30, part 8,
Jus Nat.

for which the individuals have united in the state, so the right against foreigners is to be measured from the purpose for which they have associated themselves temporarily with citizens. Between foreigners and the ruler of the state there exists a certain tacit stipulation, whose object is that for which the foreigner is dwelling in his territory or staying there and, if any special laws have been passed concerning foreigners, they have the force of conditions added to that stipulation. Therefore a foreigner can be compelled to do those things which a correct interpretation of that stipulation directs. Moreover, as special laws have the force of conditions added to a tacit stipulation, it is plainly necessary that they should be known to foreigners entering an alien territory, lest they labour under hopeless ignorance, for which they cannot be blamed. It is altogether contrary to equity that a foreigner should suffer loss from that which he could not possibly have known. Therefore, if foreigners are not to be allowed to bring certain goods to market, such as they might sell elsewhere, certainly care must be taken by the ruler of the state that his will in regard to those things should be announced in good time. From those things which we have said it is perfectly plain that, from the source which we have opened up, many particular cases can be drawn which, in order to avoid prolixity, we do not desire to enumerate at present. This especially is to be noted, that from temporary citizens, which we have shown foreigners dwelling in alien territory or staying there to be, those are to be distinguished who enter into a territory with the intention of doing harm. For a right arises against them from the right of self-defence against the injuries of strangers, a thing which flows from the very purpose of the state.

§ 466, part 6, Jus Nat.

§ 28, part 1, Phil. Pract. Univ.

§ 550, part 1, Phil. Pract. Univ.

§ 303.

§§ 12, 13, part 8, Jus Nat.

§ 305. *Of the connexion between ownership and sovereignty of a nation*

Ownership of a nation is connected with sovereignty. For in that territory which a nation has occupied, all the land and the things which are in it are subject to the ownership of the nation, and the things which have not been distributed to individuals remain subject to the ownership of the whole or of the entire nation, and if any have been distributed to individuals, nevertheless over them eminent domain is retained. But since a nation occupies the sovereignty at the same time that it occupies the territory, and since eminent domain must be considered as a potential part of sovereignty, the reason why it has sovereignty over all places

§ 274.

§ 87.

§§ 110, 111, part 8, Jus Nat.

§ 85.

§ 111, part 8, Jus Nat.

which belong to the land inhabited by the nation and why it has eminent domain over the estates of private persons, is none other than that all those things are subject to the ownership of the nation and that eminent domain over the estates of private persons has been reserved. Therefore, since things are connected one with the other and one of them contains a sufficient reason for the co-existence of the other, ownership by a nation is connected with sovereignty.

§ 56, Ontol.
§ 10, Cosmol.

Therefore there is a natural connexion of the ownership by a nation with sovereignty, so that if ownership is established, sovereignty is likewise established, but if sovereignty is taken away, ownership also is taken away. If, indeed, sovereignty belongs to some foreign nation, for example, over the public roads, the nation inhabiting the territory in which the public roads are, cannot dispose of them as it pleases and consequently it does not have ownership of them.

§ 118, part 2,
Jus Nat.

§ 306. *Of the transfer of the ownership from the nation to the ruler of the state*

§ 305.

Since the ownership of a nation is connected with sovereignty, when the sovereignty is transferred to the ruler of a state, the ownership of the nation is transferred at the same time and it is understood to have been transferred by the same law as was the sovereignty, unless some special provision has been made. Hence then it follows, if the sovereignty is only in usufruct, that the things also which are subject to the ownership of the nation are only in usufruct, whether they are corporeal or incorporeal, and if the sovereignty shall have been subject to complete ownership then these also are subject to complete ownership, and so on.

The fundamental laws concerning sovereignty pertain likewise to the ownership by a nation. From those laws, therefore, and from the method of holding the sovereignty, is determined the right of the ruler of a state in the things which are subject to the ownership of the nation, with respect of course to that nation. Certain acts directed toward the exercise of this ownership are so closely connected with acts pertaining to the exercise of sovereignty that they cannot be separated from each other; from this the connexion of the sovereignty and ownership of a nation is most clearly evident. For example, public

roads are subject to the ownership of a nation. But the care of repairing public roads and the collecting of tolls for carriage belong to the
civil sovereignty. The ruler, therefore, can make laws for public roads,
concerning acts which are subject to the will of the owner. Nay more,
it flows from the ownership of a nation that by virtue of sovereignty
the ruler of the state has a right over certain acts relating to the ownership of individuals. Sovereignty brings acts of that sort into relation
with itself, just as in turn the ownership of individuals does the acts
of sovereignty. And from this it happens that sovereignty, which is
properly a right over a person or certain actions of persons, exists
over estates of private persons. Therefore the keener minds will readily
recognize how necessary it is that he who desires to investigate more
deeply universal public law ought to turn his attention to those things
which we have said.

§ 307. *Why the ruler of a state is called lord (or owner) of the territory*

It is now understood in what sense the ruler of the state may be called
the lord (or owner) of the territory, in our native vernacular *der Landes-
Herr* [the territorial lord], because, of course, he has ownership over the
nation.

From this the name lord (or owner) is properly united with the
name of the ruler of a state by his subjects, so that, for example, he is
called king and lord, although he is not the owner of estates which are
subject to private ownership. By the name king it is at once recognized
that the right belongs to him to direct the actions of his subjects as
shall seem to him best for the interest of the state. If, then, the title
lord ought not to be a sound without sense, it is necessary that by it
should be indicated some right over things which belong either to the
people as a whole or to individuals. But this right can be no other than
the ownership of a nation, a certain part of which is eminent domain,
therefore included under sovereignty, so far as sovereignty affects the
acts of ownership of a nation, and the one right is connected with
the other. These points might be expressed more elaborately, but lest
we may be more prolix than the reason of the case warrants, we leave
those things to the private meditation of each and every one.

§ 308. *Of uninhabited land occupied by several nations at the same time or by a private individual*

If two or more nations at the same time should occupy an island or other uninhabited land, each of them will have sovereignty and ownership over that part which it has occupied, nevertheless it is wiser that they should agree with each other concerning the division. Nay more, by nature it is possible even for a private citizen to occupy, provided there is a sufficient number of men who wish to submit to his authority and fix an abode there. Since the right of occupying an island or other uninhabited land belongs in general to all nations, if two or more nations occupy together, or at the same time, they have the same right, nor can one nation interfere with the other in the exercise of its right. Therefore, since a nation occupying an island acquires ownership in it and in all the things which are in it, and with ownership acquires at the same time sovereignty, each nation has ownership and sovereignty over that part of the island or of the land which it has occupied. Which was the first point.

Since, indeed, disputes may easily arise from this, and since nations ought to be in harmony with each other, it is wiser that they should agree with each other concerning the division. Which was the second point.

Finally, since the union of human beings into a state depends upon their free will, since, moreover, an island and an uninhabited territory may be occupied both as regards ownership and as regards sovereignty, as proved above, and since a private person is deprived of the right of occupancy so far as concerns sovereignty alone; if any private person can influence a sufficient number of men, so that they desire to submit to his sovereignty and fix their abode in the occupied land, it is not to be doubted but that he can occupy it and acquire ownership and sovereignty over it. Which was the third point.

Neither nation can be compelled to agree concerning the division of an island or other land occupied at the same time by two nations, although the interests of harmony may suggest it. Therefore we have said that it is wiser that they should agree with each other concerning division than that either should desire to hold for itself what it has occupied. For that agreement is, as it were, a kind of compromise to which no one can be forced against his will. If two unite to occupy a

§ 291.

§ 85.

§ 285.

§ 3, part 8, Jus Nat.

§ 179, part 2, Jus Nat.

§§ 882, 883, part 5, Jus Nat.

thing belonging to nobody, the Germans have decided that the thing should belong to each, half and half; hence two who unite in the act of occupying are wont to say *Halbpart* [the half part], which means the same as "half to me." And it is understood that the Athenians had the same custom. But although in the occupation of movable things, or even of immovables, for private use that custom seems to be quite in harmony with equity, nevertheless in the occupation of territories and uninhabited islands, in which not only ownership but also sovereignty is acquired, it does not seem that the same may safely be declared, since various circumstances may present themselves on account of which division into unequal parts is to be preferred to division into equal parts; in other words, division of lands into equal parts is not to be compared with division into such parts of movable things, which certainly as a matter of fact are rated at a fixed price, so that one may receive as much as the other. The right of a private citizen to occupy an island or other land not inhabited is no less clear, provided only that everything be carefully considered. For since states are established in accordance with the law of nature, the intention to establish a state is allowable. But since this cannot be done, unless land is available in which a number of men uniting together into a state can dwell, he who occupies uninhabited land with the intention of establishing a state does not occupy it, except for the reason that he needs the same. From this it is quite plain that a right of occupying belongs to him. But if indeed he cannot find a sufficient number of people who desire to submit to his authority and fix an abode there, it is no less plain that the occupation would be foolish, which can produce no effect in law.

§ 26, part 8, Jus Nat.

§ 178, part 2, Jus Nat.

§ 277, part 3, Jus Nat.

§ 278, part 3, Jus Nat.

§ 309. *Whether territories inhabited by a nation may be occupied, because they are unknown*

Unknown lands inhabited by a nation may not be occupied by foreign nations. For since a nation which inhabits a land has occupied it, the land is subject to its ownership and also the sovereignty over it is its own property. Therefore, since no one may be deprived of his own property, it is not allowable to take from a nation the ownership and sovereignty which it has in the land that it inhabits. Therefore, since he does this who occupies land before unknown to himself but inhabited by a nation,

§ 174, part 2, Jus Nat.

§ 274.

§ 85 h, and § 34, part 8, Jus Nat.

§ 519, part 2, Jus Nat.

§ 174, part 2,
Jus Nat.

unknown lands inhabited by a nation may not be occupied by foreign nations.

§ 174, part 2,
Jus Nat.

§ 3.

§ 5, part 8,
Jus Nat.

§ 31, part 8,
Jus Nat.

§ 288.

§ 17.

The notion itself of occupation, which assumes that a thing capable of occupation belongs to nobody, is opposed thereto, nor can ignorance give a right to that to which otherwise you would have no right. Suppose it is not known to you that Sempronius is living somewhere with an abundance of wealth. Who, pray, would dare to assert that you had the right to take away his wealth from Sempronius? But do not nations by nature enjoy the same right in their relations with each other as private individuals? But it is to be noted that we take the term nation with the fixed meaning which we have assigned to it, because of course it denotes a number of men who have united into a civil society, so that therefore no nation can be conceived of without a civil sovereignty. For groups of men dwelling together in certain limits but without civil sovereignty are not nations, except that through carelessness of speech they may be wrongly so called. Certainly separate families dwelling in the same land are to be distinguished from nations, nor can those things be applied to them which we have proved concerning the right and duties of nations. But if the desire for gain cloud your mind, so that you recognize less clearly the truth of the present proposition, recall to yourself that which we have proved above, that no nation ought to do to another what it does not wish to be done to itself. Indeed, if it is allowable for one nation to occupy lands inhabited by another nation, because they have been hitherto unknown to it, by the same reasoning it will be allowable also for the second nation to occupy the lands of the first, or for any other foreign nation to do so. But since the first nation does not concede such a right to the other, what reason, pray, is there why this right ought to belong to it, since by nature the rights and obligations of all nations are the same? And so it is absurd to assume a right to occupy lands inhabited by a nation for this reason alone, because they have hitherto been unknown to you; this is undoubtedly the same as considering things the property of nobody which have been unknown to us, although they are owned by somebody, because we are ignorant that they exist.

§ 310. *Of separate families dwelling together in a certain territory*

If separate families dwell together in a certain territory and possess private lands, they have ownership in them, but the other places are the property of nobody or are still left in the primitive community-holding. But if, indeed, those families have no settled abode but wander through uncultivated wilds, the lands which can be subject to their use are subject to a mixed community-holding, the rest remaining in the primitive community-holding. For if separate families have fixed abodes for themselves in a certain territory, the lands which they possess they have occupied undoubtedly from the beginning, and consequently have acquired ownership in them, which afterwards has passed over to their successors. [§ 174, part 2, Jus Nat.] Therefore the private lands which they possess are subject to their ownership. Which was the first point. [§ 175, part 2, Jus Nat.]

And since by nature all things are common, but each of them is the property of nobody, consequently they remain subject to the primitive community-holding, and since the original method of acquiring ownership is occupation, the things which have not been occupied by those families are still left in the primitive community-holding or are still the property of nobody. Which was the second point. [§ 7, part 2, Jus Nat.] [§ 9, part 2, Jus Nat.] [§ 178, part 2, Jus Nat.]

But if the families have no settled abode but wander through the uncultivated wilds, in that case, nevertheless, they are understood to have tacitly agreed that the lands in that territory in which they change their abodes as they please, are held in common, subject to the use of individuals, and it is not to be doubted but that it is their intention that they should not be deprived of that use by outsiders. Therefore they are supposed to have occupied that territory as far as concerns the lands [§ 174, part 2, Jus Nat.] subject to their use, and consequently to have jointly acquired ownership of those lands, so that the use of them belongs to all without distinction. Therefore those lands are subject to a mixed community-holding. Which was the third point. [§ 175, part 2, Jus Nat.] [§ 129, part 2, Jus Nat.]

But that the other places besides these lands remain in the primitive community-holding is evident by precisely the same method of proof as we have used for the second point above. Which was the fourth point. [Note, § 2.]

Things are occupied for the sake of their use. Therefore only those things are subject to individual ownership by separate families whose use cannot be free to all generally at any time, but the things which can have a use of that sort, nay more, ought of necessity to have it by virtue of the primitive community-holding, a right belonging to all equally, would be subjected to individual ownership, not only to no purpose, but also not without wrong, nay more, the others, who need this use, would certainly not endure it. But occupation accomplished through a corporate body cannot be imagined in the case of separate families, who are united in no way except by joint habitation of the same territory. But if, indeed, separate families should be accustomed to wander about after the manner of the Scythians through uncultivated wilds, particularly for the purpose of pasturing cattle or for some other purpose, the intention of wandering, which is governed by that intended use, gives sufficient evidence of the occupation of the lands subject to their use, although they have not established a permanent abode on them. Therefore nothing is more natural than that the mixed community-holding of separate families should be assumed in regard to them. Nay more, let us suppose that outside families wish to subject some of those lands to individual ownership, it is not to be doubted but that the separate families who wander here and there would resist, and so would adequately prove their intention of holding those lands in common for themselves to the exclusion of outsiders. Therefore the present proposition is quite in harmony with the principles of the law of nature, provided that you know how properly to investigate the details.

§ 311. *Of the occupation of uninhabited lands in a territory where separate families possess property*

Since separate families dwelling together in a certain territory own the lands which they have occupied, but the other places are the property of nobody; if in a district in which separate families hold their own lands there are still other lands the use of which can be private or individual, those lands can be occupied by anybody.

§ 310.

§ 173, part 2, Jus Nat.

In this case the right of no one is violated by occupying, consequently the occupation occurs without wrong to anybody, nay rather, the one who occupies exercises his own right, the same, to be sure, which the separate families dwelling there used, when they made the lands subject to their ownership. And since a nation, properly speaking, is not a number of men who live without civil sovereignty, no one who comes into that territory, properly speaking, can be called a foreigner, consequently the things which we have proved concerning foreigners coming into another territory cannot be applied to them. All the earth is open to everybody as long as sovereignty over it has been assumed by no one, and every one who needs them can occupy things in it which have no owner.

§ 859, part 1, Jus Nat.

§ 179, part 2, Jus Nat.

§ 4, part 8, Jus Nat.

§ 7, part 8, Jus Nat.

§ 312. *Of separate families wandering hither and thither*

Since lands subject to private use or to the use of individuals in that territory in which separate families wander hither and thither are subject to the mixed community-holding of those families, and consequently, since those who are not in the number of those families are excluded from the ownership which they have in those lands, those lands can be occupied by no one coming into the territory inhabited by these families, even if at the time those who inhabit the territory are not using those lands.

§ 310.

§ 130, part 2, Jus Nat.

> Ownership is not lost by non-use. And if separate families wander through uncultivated places, they intend a use of the places only in alternation, a thing which is readily evident, if only you turn your attention to the reason which impels them to wander through uncultivated places.

§ 313. *Whether separate families can be subjected to civil sovereignty*

In either hypothesis no one has the right to subject separate families to civil sovereignty. By nature all men are free and by the introduction of ownership the status of freedom is not destroyed. Therefore, since a right born with him can be taken from no man, but since it certainly is taken away in part, if any are subjected to civil sovereignty against their will; in either hypothesis no one has the right to subject to the civil sovereignty separate families dwelling in a certain territory or staying there.

§ 146, part 1, Jus Nat.

§ 147, part 1, Jus Nat.

§ 64, part 1, Jus Nat.

§ 152, part 1, and § 28, part 8, Jus Nat.

There is no reason why you should object, that if separate families should be formed into a state, they become more civilized and provide better for their welfare than if they dwell together without civil sovereignty, and that therefore it is quite in accordance with their duties towards others that they should be subjected to sovereignty. For from this no right arises to deprive another of his natural liberty without his consent or to restrict it for his benefit as much as the purpose of the state demands; for where you desire to promote the perfection of another, you have no right to compel him to allow that to be done by you. Nor is there any reason why you should urge further that, if lands

§ 666, part 1, Jus Nat.

do not remain uncultivated, the advantages of foreign nations could be promoted, which they are compelled to relinquish without any advantage to those men who without civil authority have occupied those lands as far as concerns the estates subject to their use; for no right is created for you in regard to that which belongs to another, because he does not use and enjoy his own property as much as he could, however much it would have helped you, if he used it and enjoyed it in another way. But a thing which every one admits concerning individuals, that also he is bound to admit concerning entire families living separately in any territory without civil sovereignty. And how, I ask, can you show

§ 265, part 1, Phil. Pract. Univ.

that for the sake of your advantage or that of another nation families may be made subject to sovereignty without their consent, when from that which is useful to you no right arises? Indeed, if these reasons were to prevail, it would even be allowable to subject barbarous and uncultivated nations to your sovereignty, in order that they might experience what is better for them. For although in this case the fact that the sovereignty is taken away either from the nation or its ruler may seem to prevent this result, nevertheless no difference arises therefrom, because in case of the present assumption liberty is taken from

§ 859, part 1, Jus Nat.

those who are unwilling. Therefore, in either case the subjection is not devoid of wrong. But it comes back to the same point, if any one wishes to derive a right from the fact that it is to the advantage of nations to have civilized neighbours. For as long as your neighbours do not injure

§ 252.

you, no definite right arises in your favour against them. That it is not allowable to subject others to your sovereignty on account of religion,

§ 260, 261.

is plain from those things which we have proved above. For the things which we have proved with reference to religion as affecting nations are readily applicable also to separate families inhabiting a certain territory. It is quite another thing if you should persuade them to submit to civil sovereignty. For then the state is established by the compact which is the origin of states and the source of civil sovereignty.

§ 3, part 8,
Jus Nat.

§§ 31, 32, part 8,
Jus Nat.

§ 314. *Of the private wrongs of citizens of different nations*

If a citizen of one nation injures the citizen of another nation of his own intent or does him harm in any way, that cannot be imputed to the nation, unless the ruler of the state ratify or approve the act of the one doing the injury or committing the wrong. For because the citizen acts of his own intent, with respect to the nation of which he is a citizen, the act is that of a stranger, for the reason that one citizen and an entire nation are not one and the same person, as is self-evident. Therefore, since the deed of a stranger can be imputed to no one, except in so far as the same depends on his will, if a citizen of one nation injures a citizen of another nation of his own intent or does wrong to him in any way, that cannot be imputed to the nation. Which was the first point.

§§ 528, 650, part
1, Phil. Pract.
Univ.

But since the act of another is imputed to one approving of it, if the ruler of a state ratifies the act of one doing an injury or committing a wrong, the act itself is imputed to him also, consequently, since he represents his nation when he is dealing with others, it is imputed to the nation itself also. Which was the second point.

§ 673, part 1,
Phil. Pract. Univ.

§ 39.

In the law of nations it is of the greatest importance that the injuries of private individuals should not be confused with the injuries of nations. Therefore it is necessary that it should be understood when a nation is supposed to have injured the citizen of another nation, or if you prefer, an alien subject, when some private citizen has inflicted the injury. For from the wrong, rights arise against the offender in regard to which nothing can be determined, unless it is definitely known who is to be considered the offender.

§ 315. *When on account of such injury a nation cannot be said to have injured another nation*

Since, if a citizen of one nation injures the citizen of another nation of his own intent or does him harm in any way, that cannot be imputed

§ 314.

to the nation; the one nation cannot be said to have injured the other nation or done it a wrong.

The acts of a private citizen are not the acts of the nation to which he is subject, since they are not done as by a subject or so far as he is a subject. Therefore they have no relation to the state of which the doer of the deed is a member. The situation is different if he acts by order of the ruler of the state, whom he obeys as a superior.

§ 316. *When it is to be said*

§ 314.

On the other hand, because the act by which a citizen has injured the citizen of another nation or done a wrong to him is imputed to the nation, if the ruler of the state ratify or approve; if the ruler of a state, whose member is the offending party, ratifies or approves the act of the one doing the injury or committing the wrong to the citizen of another nation, the nation, to which the offending party belongs, is itself to be considered to have committed the injury or done the wrong.

§ 39.

Of course, then, the ruler of the state, and consequently the nation itself, concurs in the act of the citizen, and so the act which beforehand was the act of a private person becomes the act of the nation. Of course the ratification coming after the act is equivalent to a command, since the one ratifying or approving would also have ordered it, if the intention of the one acting had been beforehand communicated to him, so that then it is just as if the nation itself through its citizen had done that which he did, and consequently it is rightly considered to have done the same thing itself.

§ 317. *Of not allowing subjects to do wrong to subjects of other nations*

§ 533, part 2, Jus Nat.

§ 911, part 1, Jus Nat.

The ruler of a state ought not to allow any of his subjects to cause a loss to a citizen of another nation or do him a wrong. For no one ought to cause a loss to another or do him a wrong. Therefore, since the ruler of a state ought to compel his subjects by force at least to conform their outward acts to the law of nature, consequently he ought not to allow them to perform acts contrary to it; he ought not to allow any of his subjects to cause loss to a citizen of another nation or do him a wrong.

§ 395, part 8,
Jus Nat.

In order that doubt may not arise, on the ground that an observance of the law of nature to be encouraged by the ruler of the state applies only to citizens, but is not to be extended to foreigners, as it seems might be understood from the proof before given, and from this also it might be inferred that civil sovereignty cannot be extended beyond those actions which have to do with the attainment of the common good of the state; it must be duly observed that it is to the interest of nations that the rulers of states should not allow the subject of one to injure the subjects of another. If, indeed, injuries of that sort had to be endured by either party, as they would have to be endured if it were permissible for the ruler of one state to allow his subjects to injure the subjects of another without punishments; then he could not keep his subjects safe from the wrong of others: a thing which certainly is opposed to the common good of the state. It is likewise the fact that individual nations also, because they are understood to have united in the supreme state, may be assumed to have bound themselves to the whole, that they desire to promote the common good. But who does not see that it belongs to this very obligation also that the ruler of a state should not allow his subjects to cause loss to the subjects of another or do them injury? Therefore, if the proof which we have given does not satisfy, it is possible easily to prove the same thing in another way besides from this very principle.

§ 395, part 8,
Jus Nat.

§ 35, part 8,
Jus Nat.

§ 9, part 8,
Jus Nat.

§ 12.

§ 318. Of repairing the loss caused to subjects of another nation and of punishing a subject on account of a wrong done to the subjects of another nation

Since the ruler of a state ought not to allow any of his subjects to cause a loss or do a wrong to a citizen or subject of another state, and since he who has caused a loss is bound to repair it and he who has injured another is rightly punished and those who do things which are not to be allowed in a state must be restrained by penalties, if any one of his subjects causes a loss to the subject of a foreign state or does him a wrong, the ruler of the state in the former case ought to

§ 317.

§ 580, part 2,
Jus Nat.

§ 1071, part 1,
Jus Nat.

§ 647, part 8,
Jus Nat.

compel him to repair the loss caused, and in the latter case ought to punish him.

If your subject be injured by the subject of another, you do not desire that he do that with impunity, and if loss is caused, you certainly desire that it should be repaired. Therefore you ought not to allow your subject to injure the subject of another, and when he has caused a loss you ought to see to it that it is repaired. By the introduction of states the duties of men towards each other are not destroyed, but it is rather demanded that they should perform all parts of them more faithfully than if they had remained independent individuals.

§ 288.

§ 142, part 1,
Phil. Pract.
Univ.

§ 319. *Of the right against a nation whose established custom it is to injure the subjects of another nation*

If a certain nation shall have the established custom of injuring the subjects of other nations as it pleases and of causing loss to them, other nations have the right to compel it by force to change the custom. For no nation ought to permit its subjects to injure the subjects of another nation as they please and cause loss to them, nay rather, it is bound to punish offenders and to see to it that the loss caused should be repaired. Therefore, since the right belongs to nations in general to coerce individual nations, if they are unwilling to perform their obligation or if they show themselves negligent in that respect; if a certain nation has the established custom of injuring subjects of other nations as it pleases and of causing loss to them, other nations have the right to compel it by force to change the custom.

§ 317.

§ 318.

§ 13.

It is understood that there have been in the past, and to-day also still are, some nations that persuade themselves that anything is permissible with impunity against another nation; for example, that it is permissible to invade the territory of another, drive away cattle and carry away any property they please, nay more, to carry off the subjects of another state into slavery. That this is an evil custom we have already shown above, as well as elsewhere. No one who has considered the principles of the law of nature and nations will deny that it is not to be endured by nations. Nay more, that custom is diametrically opposed to the idea of a supreme state, which is the basis of

Note, § 156.

Note, § 618,
part 1, Jus Nat.

the happiness of the whole human race. Therefore, if certain nations uniting their powers should compel by force a nation following that custom to change it, they exercise in this their right, nay more, they do only that which is in conformity with their duty towards themselves and other nations.

§ 320. *Of a right created for another nation in its own territory*

Any nation can create a certain right for another in its own territory. For a nation in that district which it has occupied has the ownership of all the land and things which are in it, and over the estates of private individuals it retains eminent domain, while they are subject to the right of the individuals. And since it has sovereignty also over that district, consequently that district becomes its territory; the territory, therefore, is subject to the ownership of the nation, consequently is the peculiar property of it, or, if you prefer, is its own property. Therefore, since any one can create any right for another in his own property, of whatsoever sort he may desire, any nation also can create a certain right for another in its own territory.

§ 274.
§§ 110, 111, part 8, Jus Nat.

§ 85.
§ 166, part 8, Jus Nat.
§§ 132, 736, part 2, Jus Nat.
§ 124, part 2, Jus Nat.
§ 982, part 3, Jus Nat.

It is frequently to the advantage of a neighbouring nation that it should have some right in the territory of another. Therefore it is in accordance with the duties of nations towards each other that one should create in its own territory some right for the advantage of the other, so that then the creation of a right of that sort cannot be regarded as an abuse of the ownership of nations.

§ 984, part 2, Jus Nat.

§ 321. *Examples of rights of that sort*

Since any nation can create a certain right for another in its own territory, it can grant to the other the right of fishing in its own river or even in a part of the sea which is under its ownership, the right to have a fortress on its own soil or a garrison in a certain fortification, jurisdiction over certain places within its territory or even in certain cases or against certain persons, nay more, it can subject certain cities or parts of the earth to its ownership and sovereignty, and any other rights which can be considered useful to any neighbouring or distant nation.

§ 320.

If you should consider these examples of rights established for a foreign nation in your territory, you will no longer doubt that it is to the advantage not only of neighbouring nations but also of distant ones that certain rights may be created for them in the territory of another. But the things which are to be further maintained concerning those rights are plain from what we have proved concerning rights created in the property of another in general and concerning servitudes in particular; for that rights of that sort are considered as servitudes on territories is plain from the definition of servitudes. There is no need, therefore, for us to go into particulars.

C. 6, part 3, Jus Nat.

C. 6, part 5, Jus Nat.

§ 1267, part 5, Jus Nat.

§ 322. *Of the original method of acquiring rights of that sort*

If any nation has occupied in a certain district certain places as yet uninhabited or certain rights, another nation afterwards occupying that district cannot occupy those places or rights. For as long as a district is still uninhabited, any nation may occupy in it what things it will, and what things it has occupied belong to it, and consequently the right acquired in those things no other nation can take away from it without its consent. Therefore, although another nation can occupy a district as yet uninhabited, and when it occupies it, it acquires ownership over all the land and all the things which are in it together with the sovereignty; nevertheless it cannot occupy those places or even the rights which have been already occupied beforehand by another nation.

§ 291.

§§ 124, 175, part 2, Jus Nat.

§ 336, part 2, Jus Nat.

§ 291.

§ 274.

§ 85.

For example, let us suppose that a certain nation has constructed a fortress in an uninhabited island or has occupied the right of hunting certain wild animals; this in no way prevents the island from being subject to occupation by another nation, both as regards ownership and as regards sovereignty. Nevertheless it is bound to allow the outside nation to have a fortress in that island or to exercise the right of hunting certain wild animals to the exclusion of itself. And hence it is plain that rights of that sort, which have the character of a servitude, can also be originally acquired. But nothing prevents similar rights also from being acquired by a nation in that district in which are dwelling separate families possessing private estates, so that then there is no need of a further proof of that.

§ 310.

§ 323. *Of the right arising therefrom*

Since a nation occupying an uninhabited district cannot occupy places §322.
and rights in it already occupied beforehand by another nation; if a certain
nation in a certain uninhabited district occupies certain places and rights,
and afterwards another nation occupies the entire district, those places
and rights remain the property of the nation which first occupied, both as
regards the ownership and as regards the sovereignty, nor does any right
over them belong to the other nation, and consequently the places are not
a part of the territory of the other nation, and it is bound to allow the first
nation to exercise the rights belonging to it within its territory as it pleases
and to dispose of them, and since it cannot exercise these rights, unless it
enters upon the territory of the other, free access also to the territory of
the other belongs to it, and because the exercise of its right is altogether
independent of the will of the owner of the territory, so far as concerns the
acts affecting the exercise of its rights, the nation which exercises them is
not subject to the laws of the place, but since as regards other acts it cannot be regarded otherwise than as a foreigner dwelling in alien territory or
staying there, for the reason that its right is not extended to them, so far as
concerns them it is subject to the laws of the place, and, if it offends, is to §300.
be punished in accordance with the laws of the place. If a dispute should
arise between itself and citizens, it is to be determined by a judge of the §301.
place in accordance with the laws of the place, and so far as concerns doing §302.
and not doing, the same obligation binds it which binds other foreigners. §304.

> The rights of both nations are to be kept unimpaired. Therefore the
> acts required for the exercise of any rights are to be accurately distin-
> guished from others to which that right is not extended, lest one party
> may infringe upon the right of the other and distinct rights may be
> confused with each other. Nevertheless in order that controversies may
> not easily arise which are hostile to the harmony that must be preserved
> by nations, it is wiser that those rights be defined by stipulations. §285.

§ 324. *Whether he remains a citizen who dwells in alien territory*

Foreigners dwelling in alien territory or staying there remain citizens
or subjects of their own nation. For since foreigners dwelling in alien

territory or staying there have not departed from their own nation with
the intention of changing their domicile, since rather they have the
intention of returning to their own nation, they remain members also
of their own state, consequently citizens or subjects of their own nation.

It is undoubtedly one thing to depart from a society, even such as a
state is, and to declare by that deed itself that one does not desire to be
a member of that society, but it is another thing to go away for some
time from a place in which the society has its abode. Absence from
the place of domicile can deprive no one of the right which he has in
it, nor free him from the obligation by which he is bound therein.
Nor does it make any difference that a foreigner, so long as he dwells
in alien territory or stays there, becomes a temporary citizen; for the
obligation by which one is bound as a temporary citizen in alien territory is limited to certain actions alone for a certain time, and this
detracts in no respect from the obligation by which any one is bound
as a citizen to his nation and from the right which belongs to him in
it. For example, let us suppose that it is a matter of accepted custom in
a state that certain citizens ascend to a certain dignity in their order. If
the succession falls to one who is absent, his absence does not prevent
him from becoming capable of that dignity, however long he stays in
alien territory. In like manner, if any one dies for whom an heir exists
according to the laws of the place, he does not lose the inheritance
because he is dwelling in an alien territory and is regarded as a temporary citizen there. In like manner let us suppose that a poll-tax is
assessed; he is bound to pay the tax assessed on him when absent just
as if he were present, although he may be dwelling in alien territory or
staying there for the purpose of special business. The obligation of a
foreigner in alien territory is consistent with the obligation by which
any one is bound to his own nation, nor does one contradict the other,
provided you examine each closely.

§ 325. *Of the obligation and right of citizens who are staying in alien territory as foreigners*

Since foreigners living in alien territory or staying there remain citizens, or subjects of their own nation, the obligation by which they are
bound to their own nation is not terminated, nor are citizens or subjects

deprived of the right which they enjoy with the same, for the reason that they live for some time in alien territory or stay there on account of some business, and consequently if a citizen injures a fellow citizen in alien territory and the offender returns to his own people, he can be punished there according to the laws of the place and compelled to repair the loss.

Indeed, the things which are expressed in the present corollary are already plain enough through those things which we have added as a note to the preceding proposition; nevertheless we have not considered it unwise to include that in the number of the propositions. Take such an example as the one of punishing him who has killed a fellow citizen in an alien territory and has taken to flight in order that he might not be punished there. If he should return to his native country, it cannot be doubted that he can be punished on account of the murder committed. But the situation is quite different if one freed from the ordinary penalty in the place of the offence returns to his native country; for one cannot be punished twice on account of the same offence, and every nation is bound to recognize the jurisdiction of another nation in its own territory, consequently to acquiesce in the decision which the other, following its own law, has reached. For since a nation is not conceivable without civil sovereignty, if one nation should be unwilling to recognize the jurisdiction of another nation in its own territory, this would be just the same as if it should be unwilling to consider it as a nation, a thing which assuredly is directly opposed to the respect which one nation owes another.

Note, § 324.

Note, § 309.

§ 186.

§ 538, part 1, Jus Nat.

§ 326. *Of a will made in alien territory*

Since a foreigner dwelling in alien territory still remains a citizen of his own nation, since, consequently, his acts which have no relation to the alien territory are subject to the laws of his own country, if he makes a will, he is held to do that according to the laws prescribed in the place of his domicile, nor can it be valid otherwise. Nevertheless, inasmuch as one nation is bound to recognize the jurisdiction of another nation, it is valid as a judicial will, if it shall have been deposited in a court of justice in the place where it was made.

§ 324.

Note, § 325.

So a will cannot be made without the solemnities which the laws of one's native land require for the validation of a will, even if the same are not required in accordance with the laws of the place in which the will is made, nor can the statutory portion of the widow be diminished, even if the laws of that place define it otherwise. For a will ought to be good in the place of domicile. Therefore nothing is more in harmony with reason than that its validity should be determined in accordance with the laws of that place.

§ 327. *Of the goods of a foreigner dying in alien territory*

§ 324.

§§ 326, 332.

§§ 299, 304 h,
and § 35,
part 8, Jus Nat.

§ 289.

If a foreigner dies in alien territory, naturally the goods which he has there belong to the one who becomes his heir in his native land; they do not indeed fall to the treasury, nor can the power of making a will be taken from him. For if a foreigner dwells in alien territory or stays there, he remains a citizen of his own nation, consequently either he becomes heir of the deceased, who succeeds according to the laws of the place in which the deceased has domicile or by intestate inheritance, or he is heir whom the testator has so appointed in a will legally made. Since, therefore, a right belongs to the ruler of the state over a foreigner who dwells in his territory or stays there, only in regard to those acts which have some relation to the purpose of the state, the foreigner is the owner of his own goods which he has with him or possesses there, and they are regarded as goods belonging to a foreign nation. Since, therefore, they come into the same category with the other goods which he has in the place of his domicile or in his native land; if he dies in alien territory, naturally the goods which he has there belong to the one who becomes his heir in his native land. Which was the first point.

Since the goods of which a foreigner dying in alien territory is possessed belong to the one who becomes his heir in his native land, as proved in the first point, it is plain that by nature they cannot fall to the treasury. Which was the second point.

§ 999, part 7,
Jus Nat.

Finally, since a foreigner who dwells in alien territory or territory of a foreign nation or stays there is owner of his own goods which he has there or possesses, as proved in the first point, nor can they by nature fall to the treasury if he dies, as proved in the second point, moreover, since by nature it is allowable for an owner to make a will, the power of making a will cannot by nature be taken away from a foreigner dwelling in alien territory or staying there, so far as concerns the goods which he has or possesses there. Which was the third point.

However much you consider a foreigner dwelling in alien territory or the territory of some foreign nation, or staying there, as a temporary citizen, nevertheless you may not therefore infer that his goods after his death are to be considered the property of nobody, which by right of occupation that has been transferred to the ruler of the state fall to the treasury. For the power of making a will is not taken from a citizen, consequently there is no reason why it ought to be taken from him who is the equivalent of a citizen for a time. Therefore from this the contrary rather is inferred. Furthermore, we must hold that the power of making a will is a right belonging to man by nature, which it is understood cannot be taken from him, for the reason that he dwells for some time in the territory of some foreign nation or stays there. We do not argue that there are other duties of nations towards each other with which it is not in harmony that the goods of a foreigner dying in alien territory should fall to the treasury.

§ 303.

§ 999, part 7, Jus Nat.

§ 328. *What the law of alienship is*

That is called the law of alienship by which aliens or foreigners are excluded from the right of succession in the goods of a deceased citizen, and consequently cannot be appointed heirs in a will nor can legacies be left to them.

For example, let us assume that you have a brother who has a domicile in England, and that he dies there without issue. You would succeed him as an intestate, if he were to die in the place of your domicile. If the English exclude you as an alien from the right of succession, this is said to be done by the law of alienship. In like manner, if the same brother, or even some Englishman, were to appoint you his heir, or leave a legacy to you, but the will were declared void, and you were not permitted to take the inheritance or even a legacy, this likewise would be said to be done by the law of alienship. It is known that the law of alienship has been received among certain nations, even the more highly civilized. Therefore the plan of our undertaking demands that we show whether it is in harmony with natural law or is in truth opposed to it.

§ 329. *Of the succession of aliens to the goods of a deceased citizen and to a legacy left to aliens*

§ 999, part 7, Jus Nat.

§ 994, part 7, Jus Nat.

§ 1021, part 7, Jus Nat.

§ 975, part 7, Jus Nat.

§ 1034, part 7, Jus Nat.

§ 994, part 7, Jus Nat.

§ 1031, part 7, Jus Nat.

§ 562, part 7, Jus Nat.

§ 111, part 8, Jus Nat.

§ cited.

§ 165.

§§ 620, 654, 655, part 1, Jus Nat.

§ 702, part 1, Jus Nat.

§ 1004, part 7, Jus Nat.

§ 1003, part 7, Jus. Nat.

Aliens can by nature succeed to the goods of a deceased citizen, both by intestate inheritance and if they should be appointed heirs in a will, nay more, legacies also can be left to them. Since by the law of nature a will may be made, he succeeds by nature to the goods of the deceased, who has been appointed heir, or he succeeds without a will by intestate inheritance, as is the case with children, or, if there are no ascendants or descendants among the living, those in a certain fixed order, who are in the family of the father, or the mother, or the parents of higher grade. Succession, therefore, to the goods of the deceased depends upon the expressed or presumed wish of the deceased, consequently upon kinship. Therefore, since only eminent domain belongs to the ruler of a state over goods of citizens, by force of which in case of necessity he can dispose of them for the sake of the public welfare, as, it is self-evident, is not the case in the present instance, and since besides one nation is bound to perform the duties of humanity for another nation, and thus also for the citizens of another nation, and therefore not to prevent even a foreigner from acquiring those things which aid him in living comfortably and happily; by nature undoubtedly aliens can succeed to the goods of a deceased citizen both by intestate inheritance, and if they should be appointed heirs in a will. Which was the first point.

Since legacies are left in accordance with the law of nature, and are gifts of some thing, or even of a certain sum of money made by the last will, consequently it is just as if the legatee were to succeed to a certain part of the goods of the deceased; but since aliens also by nature can succeed to the goods of the deceased citizen, as proved in the first point, legacies also can be left to them. Which was the second point.

§ 118, part 2, Jus Nat.

§§ 3, 31, part 8, Jus Nat.

Ownership is a right over things belonging to us, but sovereignty is a right over the actions of a man belonging by virtue of a compact to the nation as a whole, in so far as those actions are directed to attaining the common good of the state. By nature ownership was conceived of before sovereignty, which was introduced for the sake of protecting it, and therefore of itself is altogether independent of sovereignty. Therefore, although when ownership has been introduced sovereignty is conceived of as added, nevertheless the rights derived from ownership remain unaffected, and sovereignty will not be exercised over acts of an owner, except in so far as they are opposed to the public good, or in so far as the public good cannot be promoted without them. For sovereignty does not destroy the duties of men towards each other prescribed by the law of nature, because of the immutability of this law. Human beings remain equally human beings, to whatsoever civil sovereignty they are subject. Therefore those things which are in harmony with their duties toward each other are naturally not changed by civil sovereignty. And for that reason—since it is plain that succession to the goods of a deceased is sufficiently founded in ownership and in the duties of men toward each other, as is perfectly evident from what we have proved concerning that point in the seventh part of "The Law of Nature"—succession to the goods of a deceased, which the law of nature approves, is certainly not destroyed by the introduction of sovereignties. Therefore nothing is more natural than that citizens of different states should mutually succeed each other in the same way as they would succeed if they were fellow citizens. There is no reason why you should object that, if that succession to the goods of a deceased were allowed, the goods of one nation would come to another nation; for the reason that with respect to nations the goods of individuals are the property of the nation. For since nations, because they are understood to have united into a supreme state, are assumed to have bound themselves as a whole to the individual nations, because they wish to provide for their good, and since also by the necessary law of nations one nation ought to promote the advantages of another, so far as that can be done without neglect of its duty towards itself, it is not to be considered absurd that some goods of one nation should go to another nation. Those who can persuade themselves of any such thing seem to have a mind filled with that perverse error, that civil sovereignties have limited the universal friendship of humankind to a certain number, and have made those enemies who ought by nature to be friends, or at least they would limit the law of charity to that bad interpretation generally accepted: that a well-ordered charity begins with oneself,

§ 35, part 8, Jus Nat.

§ 1, part 8, Jus Nat.

§ 142, part 1, Phil. Pract. Univ.

§ 289.

§ 12.

§ 156.

§ 229, part 1,
Phil. Pract.
Univ.
when the only place for it is where the conflict of duties toward oneself and toward others produces an exception.

§ 330. *Whether the law of alienship belongs to the law of nations*

The law of alienship is not in harmony with the law of nations. For by the law of alienship foreigners are excluded from the right of succession in the case of the goods of a dead citizen or even of a foreigner who dies in alien territory, nor can they be appointed heirs in a will nor can legacies be left to them, and consequently if there is no one who can become heir by virtue of the laws of that place, the goods of the deceased, as goods of nobody, go to the treasury, according to the ruler's right of occupation. But if a foreigner dies in alien territory, by nature the goods which he has there belong to the one who becomes his heir in his native land, and do not go to the treasury, nor can the right of making a will be taken from such a foreigner, and even aliens can by nature succeed to the goods of a citizen, both by intestate inheritance and if they are appointed heirs in a will, nay more, legacies also can be left to them. Therefore the law of alienship is not in harmony with the law of nations.

§ 328.

§ 327.

§ 329.

Therefore, when a law of that sort has been accepted, it comes only from ordinance, and is opposed to equity. For although civil law is made out of natural law, in so far as something is added or taken away; nevertheless that which is to be added or subtracted ought to have sufficient reason either in the condition of the state in general or of that state in which the law is passed in particular. Therefore the law of alienship can be admitted only by way of exception in particular cases of conflict of duties of nations towards themselves and towards others, which nevertheless are very rare and difficult to find among nations, so that they are not worthy of consideration in law derived from the idea of a supreme state.

§ 239, part 1,
Phil. Pract.
Univ., and
§ 156 h.

§ 991, part 8,
Jus Nat.

§ 987, part 8,
Jus Nat., and
§ 22 h.

§ 331. *Of immovable property which a foreigner possesses in alien territory*

If a foreigner in alien territory possesses immovable property, it is under the jurisdiction of the place in which it lies, and the laws or statutes in regard to it bind the owner. For since the ruler of a territory has sover- § 166, part 8, Jus Nat. eignty over his territory, if he allows a foreigner to possess immovable property in that territory, it is understood that he allows that on no other condition than that it should remain under the jurisdiction of the place in which it lies, and also that its owner should be subject to the relevant laws or statutes of the place. Therefore, since a foreigner is able to acquire ownership in property only under this condition, it is under the jurisdic- § 382, part 8, Jus Nat. tion of the place in which it lies, and the laws or statutes bind the owner, just as if he were a citizen or a subject of the ruler of the territory and had his domicile there.

> For example, if a subject of Brunswick possesses immovable prop-
> erty in the Electorate of Saxony, the Saxon laws and statutes bind him
> as far as this property is concerned, if there are such laws for the place
> in which the property is situated, and as far as it is concerned he is
> bound to recognize the jurisdiction of the place. It certainly would be
> absurd to change the laws which affect immovables, in favour of aliens
> who are allowed to acquire property in your territory, and subject
> them to alien law; a thing which is not conceivable without diminu-
> tion of civil sovereignty, which belongs to the ruler of a state indepen-
> dently of every other nation.

§ 332. *Of particular laws in regard to the same*

Since immovable property possessed by a foreigner in alien territory is subject to the jurisdiction of the place in which it lies, and since laws or § 331. statutes in regard to it bind the owner; the heirs of one who has immovable property in alien territory can succeed to it only according to the laws of the place in which it lies, the burdens which affect it must be borne by its owner, and all acts which are in any way referred to it are subject to the jurisdiction of the place.

> Of course the condition of the citizen is the same as that of the
> foreigner with regard to that property. Therefore, whatever is true of
> a citizen, the same is also true of a foreigner. Consequently a subject
> of Brunswick cannot succeed to immovable property which is situated
> in Saxony, except according to the law of Saxony, without considering
> the difference, if any exists, between the law of Saxony and the law of

Brunswick. Hence it happens that he who is excluded in the place of his domicile, nevertheless can succeed as regards immovables in the place where the thing is situated. Foreign laws cannot be valid in alien territory; for since legislative power relates to sovereignty, that could not occur except with diminution of the sovereignty. But who can persuade himself that by a private act, by which ownership of an immovable thing is acquired in alien territory, the sovereignty of the ruler of the territory is diminished, so that he would be compelled to allow in regard to that, things which are opposed to his sovereignty? The burdens which are imposed on immovable things are paid by their possessors, because they possess. Immunity is a privilege, which, since it can be granted only by a superior, on whose will it depends altogether whether he may wish to grant it, can therefore belong to no one on the ground that he has a domicile elsewhere than in the place where the thing is situated. The domicile of the possessor is not considered in the imposition of burdens of that sort. He who acquires an immovable thing upon which certain burdens have been imposed, or can be imposed by a superior, acquires that thing not otherwise than with its burden, actual as well as possible. Nay more, it would undoubtedly be absurd that foreigners acquiring immovable property should be exempt from burdens which would have to be paid by citizens, if they possessed it. Burdens inhering in the things (in fact the right of imposing a burden on a thing is even looked on as a burden) pass with the things to any possessor. In like manner if a contract of purchase and sale or a security needs to be confirmed by judicial authority to be good, the confirmation can be obtained only from one who has jurisdiction over the place where the thing is situated, nor can an action against a captious debtor, who has pledged a security to another, be brought elsewhere than in the court relevant to the location of the property, even if he has a domicile elsewhere. Unless these things were so, ownership and sovereignty of nations would be prejudiced in many ways, contradictories to which cannot co-exist with them.

§ 813, part 8,
Jus Nat.

§ 853, part 8,
Jus Nat.

§ 855, part 8,
Jus Nat.

§ 856, part 8,
Jus Nat.

§ 333. *Of the right to possess immovable property in alien territory*

It depends on the will of the ruler of a state, whether or not he desires to permit foreigners to possess immovable property in his lands. No

foreigner can claim any right for himself in alien territory, and consequently not the right of possessing immovable property. Therefore he   § 293.
cannot acquire this right, except by permission of the ruler of the territory or the ruler of the state. Therefore it depends on the will of the ruler
of the state, whether or not he desires to permit foreigners to possess
immovable property in his lands.

It makes no difference, that by nature aliens can succeed to the
property of a citizen, and that the law of alienship by which they are
excluded from succession is not in harmony with the law of nations.   § 327.
For if it should happen that a foreigner acquires an immovable thing   § 328.
by right of inheritance, since he cannot possess it, he is bound to sell
it. Nor is there reason why you should think that the prohibition   § 330.
that any foreigner, or he who has domicile elsewhere, may not possess immovable property is opposed to the natural law of nations. For
since access to his territory can be forbidden to foreigners by a ruler
in accordance with the law of nature, if it should be to the advantage
of the state; so for the same reason he can also forbid any foreigner   § 295 h, and
to possess immovable property. For although it cannot be denied that   § 30, part 8,
the permission to possess is in harmony with the duties of nations   Jus Nat.
towards each other; nevertheless if these are in conflict with their
duties towards themselves, the conflict makes an exception. Reasons
are not lacking derived from the purpose of the state, why possession
is to be allowed, nor are reasons lacking, why at times it is not to be
allowed. But the decision on these points is with the ruler of the state
and his decision must be followed, so that the natural liberty of the   § 50, part 8, and
state may not be violated.   § 156, part 1,
   Jus Nat.

§ 334. *Whether the right of possession can be granted on a definite condition*

Since it depends upon the will of the ruler of a state, whether or
not he desires to permit foreigners to possess immovable property in   § 333.
his lands, since, moreover, the right to transfer something to another
depends on his will, as to how and under what condition he may desire   § 11, part 8,
to transfer it; the ruler of the state also can lay down the condition on   Jus Nat.
which the possession of immovables in his lands ought to be granted to
foreigners.

For example, he can impose a burden upon a foreign possessor, from which his citizens are exempt, and on the other hand can also grant certain immunities or other rights which the citizens do not enjoy, as he may think best for the state or commonwealth. The reasons suggesting either course belong to civil prudence; but in this place we are talking simply of law, and the reasons of equity are discussed, which frequently are at variance with strict law or external law, because to be sure even the abuse of his right must be allowed a ruler, in order that natural liberty may not be violated. For we have already quite often given warning, that such rules must be observed in the exercise of one's right, in order that we may exercise it with a sense of duty.

§ 335. *Whether that is allowed except to those devoted to a certain religion*

§ 334.

Since the ruler of a state can lay down the condition on which possession of immovables ought to be granted to foreigners, he can also restrain any one who is devoted to a religion other than that which is received in his territory, from possessing immovable property; consequently if a foreigner shall be devoted to another religion, he is restrained, not as a foreigner, but because he is devoted to another religion.

So in the Saxon Electorate there is a provision that none other than a Lutheran can possess immovables. Therefore if a foreigner, or one having domicile in alien territory, purchases a farm, the contract is not ratified, unless he shall have proved beforehand that he is devoted to the religious beliefs of the Lutherans. Nor is it an objection to a law of that sort, that those opposed to these religious beliefs are tolerated, nay more, that the exercise of their religion is allowed them. For to have a domicile in any place and enjoy the exercise of religion and to possess immovable property do not depend upon each other, nor are there reasons lacking in harmony with the purpose of the state, in accordance with which the former may be allowed, even if the latter is not permitted.

§ 336. *Of contracting marriages in neighbouring nations*

By nature it is allowable for foreigners to seek and contract marriages in neighbouring nations, unless it shall be to the advantage of the state that that should not be allowed by a particular nation. For it is self-evident that by nature it is allowable for any man to contract marriage with any woman. But when, indeed, individuals enter into a state, sovereignty belongs to the whole over the individual, and the liberty of individuals is restricted as far as concerns those actions which tend to promote the public good. Therefore, if it shall be to the advantage of the state, that it should not be allowed by a certain nation that foreigners should seek and contract marriages with its people, it is not bound to allow this privilege to them: but if that privilege brings no detriment to the state, by nature then it is not restricted. Therefore it is allowable for foreign nations to seek and contract marriages with neighbouring nations, unless it shall be to the advantage of the state that that should not be allowed by a certain nation.

§ 31, part 8, Jus Nat.

§ 47, part 8, Jus Nat.

In regard to those things which affect nations, natural reasons are to be derived from the purpose of the state, from which is to be measured the right of the whole against individuals. Therefore that which by nature is free for everybody, that by nature also remains such in the state, unless it is opposed to the purpose of the state. But the law of nature, which makes the public welfare the supreme law of the state, restricts natural liberty also in regard to those things which are opposed to the purpose of the state, however much that should be allowed by the ignorance or carelessness of the nation, or of the one who has the right of the nation. Of course the nation is remiss in its duty toward itself, and does not use its right, as it could, just as on the other hand it abuses its right, if the purpose of the state does not demand that natural liberty should be restricted, yet that is not allowed which is free for every one by nature.

§ 30, part 8, Jus Nat.

§ 86, part 8, Jus Nat.

§ 337. *Of the law of nations as regards marriages*

Since by nature it is allowable for foreigners to seek and contract marriages in neighbouring nations, unless it shall be to the advantage of the state that that should not be allowed by a certain nation, since, moreover, it belongs to the civil sovereignty to decide concerning that point, and since by nature no nation has any right over this act, it depends upon the will of any nation, whether or not it wishes to allow, and under what condition it wishes to allow, foreigners to seek and contract marriages with its people, and in regard to those matters other nations must acquiesce.

§ 336.

§ 60, part 8, Jus Nat.

§ 255.

But if you shall desire to determine in accordance with the law of nature the reasons for the prohibition, your attention must also be called to the conflict of the duties of the nations towards themselves and towards others, and especially must the particular reasons be worked out on account of which marriages are sought by foreigners. Since circumstances may vary greatly in particular instances, there is frequently need of much discussion, in order that a decision in no respect faulty may be reached concerning the righteousness of the act.

§ 338. *Of the right of necessity of nations*

By nature some right belongs to an outside nation over those things which are subject to the ownership of another nation, if in case of emergency it should happen that the necessary use of those things is absolutely denied any nation. For it is understood that rights of ownership were introduced with this tacit restriction, that, if in case of emergency it should happen that the necessary use of things should be absolutely denied any nation, it would have some right over those things which are § 563, part 6, subject to ownership. Therefore, since the same thing must be understood concerning those things which have become subject to the ownership of nations; by nature therefore some right belongs to an outside nation over those things which are subject to the ownership of another nation, if in case of emergency it should happen that the necessary use of them is absolutely denied it.

§ 563, part 6,
Jus Nat.
§3.

In order that the right of necessity of nations may not be extended beyond its limits to an excess, those points must properly be considered which we have brought out concerning the same matter elsewhere.

§§ 564 and fol.,
part 6, Jus Nat.

§ 339. *Of what sort the right of necessity of nations is*

Since by nature some right belongs to an outside nation over those things which are subject to the ownership of another nation, if in case of emergency it should happen that the necessary use of those things is absolutely § 338. denied it, since, consequently, only extreme necessity, which cannot be avoided in another way, makes a place for this right, since, moreover, § 599, part 6, this necessity itself turns the right of seeking into a right of compelling

§ 338.

§ 599, part 6,
Jus Nat.

another nation to do or to give; the right of necessity of nations is a perfect right, consequently the force is legal, whether it be secret or open, which is employed for obtaining that which is denied the one asking it, or which cannot be asked for on account of imminent danger.

§ 235, part 1, Phil. Pract. Univ.

This right of necessity frequently has application in war; but this must be investigated when we speak concerning the law of war and the law in war. Nevertheless instances can occur in time of peace also, although more rarely, one or two examples of which may be brought in among those which follow immediately.

§ 340. *Of the right to the grain of another neighbouring nation in case of unendurable famine*

Since by nature some right belongs to an outside nation over those things which are subject to the ownership of another nation, if in case of emergency it should happen that the necessary use of those things is absolutely denied it, and since this is a perfect right, if there should be such great want of grain that very many would have to perish of famine, unless a supply of grain should be furnished it by a neighbouring nation, this nation can be compelled to sell grain to it at a fair price, nay more, it is allowable to carry away the grain by force, if the other is unwilling to sell.

§ 338.
§ 339.

But it is readily evident that extreme necessity is not yet at hand as long as the ruler can look after his subjects. So the custom of the emperors of China is to be approved, who from their own granaries relieve the need of their subjects, if their subjects in any province suffer from famine. For that which can be had from your own nation may not be taken by force from another. Still other suggestions could be made here, but they are such as more than one reason bids us pass over in silence and leave to the personal consideration of each one. But the things that we have proved of grain are readily understood also of other things serving for food.

§ 341. *Of the right of necessity as to the seizure of maidens*

From the same reasoning it is evident that if the right is denied to the men of one people to contract marriages with the women of neighbouring nations, since a people cannot preserve itself without marriage, there is a legal necessity of making a seizure of maidens.

We have an example in the Romans, who at the beginning were a people of men, and were not able to preserve themselves without a seizure of maidens.[2]

§ 342. *Of the use of ships, wagons, horses, and labours of foreign nations*

From the same reasoning also it is understood that, if any nation needs ships, wagons, horses, or labours of foreign nations to ward off imminent danger, the necessary use of them belongs to it by nature. Of course the goods of a state, in which category after the introduction of ownership labours also are included, with respect to a nation, are considered as things which are subject to the ownership of a nation.

§ 437, part 2, Jus Nat.

§ 289.

Nay more, since in extreme necessity the common right to things revives, nothing prevents you from regarding as individuals still living in a state of nature those who are citizens of different nations; nay more, even those who rule over them, since nations in their relations with each other are looked on as free persons living in a state of nature. Indeed, for no other reason those things come to be applied to entire nations which we have proved concerning the right of necessity with respect to individuals. Let us suppose, for example, that a fire is raging in some place and horses are needed to carry sufficient water for extinguishing it, it cannot be doubted that passers-by can be compelled to allow the use of their horses. If likewise on a river, which is a boundary line, danger of flood should threaten, there is no reason why we should doubt that it is allowable to use the ships which are along the shore of the territory of another, for saving men and goods, without the owner's knowledge, or even without his consent.

§ 600, part 6, Jus Nat.

§ 2.

§ 3.

2. The story of the rape of the Sabine women by the Romans which led to the integration of the Sabines into the Roman community under the joint rule of Romulus and Titus Tatius is one of the central legends surrounding the early history of Rome. See Livy, *From the Founding of the City*, trans. B. O. Foster, 14 vols. (London: Heinemann; Cambridge, Mass.: Harvard University Press, 1919–59), vol. 1, I.ix.9–16, pp. 35–39.

§ 343. *Of the right of harmless use by nations*

By nature the right belongs generally to nations to the harmless use of things which are subject to the ownership of another nation. For this right is a right of harmless use. Therefore, since ownership of things could not have been introduced unless the right of harmless use had been reserved, and since nations use natural law one with the other; by nature, therefore, there belongs generally to nations the right to the harmless use of things which are subject to the ownership of another nation.

§ 685, part 6, Jus Nat.

§ 686, part 6, Jus Nat.

§ 3.

Since we have already discussed at sufficient length the particular rights of harmless use, as that of passage for proper causes over lands and rivers, of the right of remaining in lands which are subject to the ownership of a nation, of the admittance of those who have been expelled from their own homes, of the right of purchasing for oneself at a fair price things which other nations do not need, and the rights which are akin to these; it would be superfluous to rehearse the same things here. Nevertheless we desire to add some things not mentioned there, that it may be evident in what way general principles are to be applied in cases which arise.

§§ 689 and fol., part 6, Jus Nat.

§ 344. *Of the admission of foreigners to our academies*

Foreigners should be allowed to stay in our schools and academies for the purpose of study, regardless of their religion. For whatever a learned and cultivated nation can contribute, to make barbarous and uncultivated nations learned and cultivated, that it ought to do, consequently it ought not to prevent the sciences and liberal arts and virtues from flourishing among other nations. Therefore, since in schools and academies those things are learned which are necessary and useful for wisdom and knowledge, and if entrance to them is open to foreigners also, by that very fact it would be brought about that the sciences also and liberal arts and virtues would be increased among outside nations, as is self-evident, and since the right to stay in our land for the purpose of study is a right of harmless use, not to be denied to outside nations; certainly foreigners must be allowed to stay in our schools and academies for the purpose of study. Which was the first point.

§ 168.

§§ 433, 434, part 8, Jus Nat.

§ 692, part 6, Jus Nat.

§ 259.
§ 263.

And since no nation can compel another nation by force to embrace its religion, nor on account of a difference of religion can any nation refuse another the duties of humanity, which they owe to each other, much less deprive them of the right belonging to them of sending their boys, lads and young men to our schools and academies for the purpose of study, as proved above; foreigners must certainly be allowed admission to our schools and academies for the purpose of study, regardless of their religion. Which was the second point.

Let us suppose that some foreigner comes to our academy for the purpose of learning mathematics, philosophy, or medicine. He is to be received among the number of the students, from whatever nation he may come and to whatever religion he may then be devoted, however firmly it has been established by the fundamental law that none other than the accepted religion will be tolerated, and that only he who professes that religion publicly can possess immovable property. For it is one thing to stay in these lands for the purpose of certain definite studies which have nothing in common with religion, but it is another thing to have free exercise of religion and possess immovable property there. The former of course belongs to the right to stay for reasonable cause in alien territory, which is included under the right of harmless use; but the latter has no connexion therewith.

§ 345. Of the right to stay for the sake of health in alien lands

Foreigners must be allowed to stay with us for the purpose of recovering health, without giving any consideration to a difference in religion. For in lands subject to foreign ownership one may stay for some time for reasonable causes. Therefore, since every one is bound to do his best to recover his health, consequently he has the right to do the acts without which he cannot recover his health, and since this is a perfect right, there undoubtedly is reasonable cause for staying in alien territory or in lands subject to the ownership of another nation for the purpose of recovering health. Therefore foreigners must be allowed to stay with us for the purpose of recovering health. Which was the first point.

And that no consideration is here to be given to a difference of religion, is proved by a method not dissimilar to that by which we have

§ 692, part 6,
Jus Nat.

§ 413, part 1,
Jus Nat.

§ 159, part 1,
Phil. Pract.
Univ.

§ 905, part 1,
Jus Nat.

§ 240, part 1,
Phil. Pract.
Univ.

shown the same thing in the preceding proposition. Which was the second point.

There are various reasons why one may be compelled to stay in alien lands for the purpose of recovering health, for example, if he falls ill on a journey, if he shall have desired to use the counsel and assistance of some wise and skilful physician in getting rid of disease, if he shall have such great confidence in mineral waters or baths that he believes that he cannot recover without the use of them. In the first case the right of necessity concurs with the right of harmless use, in which case it would be so much the more shameful to be unwilling to allow a foreigner to remain in our lands, nay more, would be very unjust.

§ 758, part 1,
Jus Nat.

§ 748, part 1,
Jus Nat., and
§ 159, part 1,
Phil. Pract. Univ.

§ 346. *Of passage allowed to persons and goods for the sake of commerce*

Those who desire commerce with a distant nation must be allowed passage for themselves and their goods over the lands, rivers, and parts of the sea which are subject to the ownership of any nation. For by nature every nation has the right to engage in commerce with any other nation, nor can any nation prevent any other nation from engaging in commerce with a distant nation. Therefore, since commerce cannot be engaged in with a distant nation unless passage be allowed over the lands, rivers, or parts of the sea which are subject to the ownership of any other nation, since, moreover, by virtue of the right of harmless use belonging generally to nations by nature, passage must be allowed for reasonable causes over lands and rivers, and consequently over parts of the sea which are under their ownership, both to persons and to goods, unless just fear of loss may exist, such as in case of the present proposition does not exist; those who desire commerce with a distant nation must be allowed passage for themselves and their goods over the lands, rivers, and parts of the sea which are under the ownership of any nation.

§ 199.

§ 200.

§ 343.

§ 689, part 6,
Jus Nat.

§ 690, part 6,
Jus Nat.

When in a particular case the question arises concerning the granting to outside nations of passage over lands, rivers, and parts of the sea which are under the ownership of any nation, it is readily evident from the proof of the present proposition that two points are to be determined; namely, Does a reasonable cause for passage exist? and, is there no loss to be feared from the passage by the nation through whose territory passage is allowed?

§ 347. *Likewise to the one going to an academy for the purpose of study*

If any one goes to an academy of a distant nation for the purpose of study, passage is to be allowed him over the lands which are subject to the ownership of any nation. For since in academies young men are instructed in the knowledge of things necessary and useful to know, since, moreover, no one ought to prevent another from attaining intellectual virtues, consequently from learning things necessary and useful to know, there is undoubtedly reasonable cause why any one should go to an academy. Because, therefore, by virtue of the right of harmless use belonging generally to nations by nature, passage must be allowed for reasonable causes over lands subject to ownership, unless reasonable fear of loss exists, such as evidently does not exist in the present case; if any one goes to an academy of a distant nation for the purpose of study, passage must be allowed to him over the lands which are under the ownership of any nation.

There is no reason why you should take the exception, that it can happen that it would be to the advantage of the nation, through whose lands one must pass, that the neighbouring nation, whence he comes who has the intention of going to an academy, may remain barbarous and uncultivated. For since every nation ought to contribute whatever it can, that any other nation which is barbarous and uncultivated should become learned and more cultivated, one may not prevent knowledge of things necessary and useful from being disseminated to such a nation. There are, indeed, still other reasonable causes on account of which passage must be made over lands which are under the ownership of another nation; but concerning these the decision will not be difficult in cases that come up, provided only any one should have comprehended the duties both of men and of nations towards themselves, and should consider also that the law of nature gives to us a right to those things without which we could by no means satisfy those duties. For any one to interfere with the use of

§ 434, part 8, Jus Nat.

§ 696, part 1, Jus Nat.

§§ 220, 547, part 1, Jus Nat., and § 275, Psych. Emp.

§ 343.

§ 699, part 6, Jus Nat.

§ 168.

§ 722, part 1, Jus Nat.

§ 159, part 1, Phil. Pract. Univ.

this right is certainly opposed to justice. There is therefore no need of our descending to more particular cases.

§ 926, part 1, Jus Nat.

§ 348. *Of the supposition concerning the common right of nations to perform certain acts*

If any nation allows a certain right to definite acts in its lands to other nations generally, that cannot be denied to one nation unless there has been a precedent offence. For if any nation allows the right to definite acts in its lands to other nations generally, it allows them that right under no other condition than because they are nations to which the same thing is due which is due to itself, inasmuch as the other nation does not have that in its power, while the nation itself can perform this for the other without neglect of duty towards itself. If, then, it should wish to deny the same to one nation, this is undoubtedly just the same as if it should not consider that nation as a nation, or although indeed all nations are by nature equal to each other, it should not put that nation on an equality with others. Therefore, since this inclines towards contempt of the other, and since no nation ought to despise another, nay rather, each nation ought to rate the other as highly as it deserves, consequently on the hypothesis of the present proposition ought to consider it as equally a nation; if any nation allows a certain right to definite acts in its lands to other nations generally, that cannot be denied to one nation. Which was the first point.

§ 156.

§ 16.
§ 787, part 1, Jus Nat.
§ 790, part 1, Jus Nat., and § 3 h.
§ 186.

But if, indeed, a certain nation has wronged the nation granting, since the right belongs to it to punish that nation, it may as a punishment rescind those rights; if, therefore, there is a precedent offence, the right to definite acts, which is allowed to other nations generally, can be denied to that nation. Which was the second point.

§ 272.
§ 589, part 8, Jus Nat.

Grotius calls this "the common right by supposition to commit certain acts" because he supposes an act of the nation, namely a general permission, in opposition to "the common right to acts simply as such," which by nature belongs to nations without any act of a nation, such as is the right to those acts which procure the means, without which life cannot be lived comfortably. The former could be called "hypothetical," but the latter "absolute." Grotius cites examples of the

De Jure Belli ac Pacis, lib. 3 [2], c. 2, § 22.

See loc. cit., § 19.

former in the place cited; that foreigners may hunt anywhere, fish, catch birds, collect pearls, take by will, sell property, contract marriages even if there is no lack of women.

Loc. cit., § 22.

§ 349. *Of a right to acts granted by way of privilege*

If a right is granted by a certain nation to certain other definite nations, to certain definite acts, for certain special reasons, the nation can deny that right to other nations. For if there are special reasons, on account of which a certain nation has granted to certain other definite nations a certain right to definite acts, these nations are no longer regarded as nations simply, nor the right which is granted to them as the right of harmless use, which as a residue from the primitive joint holding remains common to nations after the introduction of ownership, since by virtue of natural liberty belonging to nations any one may determine a matter of harmless use and others must acquiesce in that decision. If, then, a right is granted by a certain nation, to certain other definite nations, to certain definite acts, for certain special reasons, the nation can deny that right to other nations.

§ 687, part 8, Jus Nat.

§ 686, part 6, Jus Nat., and § 3 h.

§ 55, part 8, Jus Nat.

§ 156, part 1, Jus Nat.

Here we are speaking of the right of harmless use which, since it belongs by nature to nations generally, can be denied to none, except in case of conflict of duties of a nation towards itself and towards other nations. But since in that case one must abide by the decision of the nation refusing, by virtue of natural liberty, therefore one must see how the nation may declare its will. If, then, a nation grants a right to other nations generally to certain definite acts of harmless use; by that very act it declares that no duty towards itself conflicts with a duty towards other nations, consequently no right belongs to it to deny to any nation any right of harmless use. For, indeed, if it should be unwilling to grant that right generally, it certainly indicates the contrary by that very act, and other nations must abide by its decision. Therefore in the former case the natural liberty of nations is in force, by virtue of which they can avail themselves of the right of harmless use as they please; but in the latter case natural liberty cannot be extended to acts of that sort which are no longer thought to be of harmless use, the right of harmless use having been taken away. Therefore Grotius rightly says that in the former case by virtue of natural liberty a right has been

§ 343.

§ 206.

§ 156, part 1, Jus Nat.

§ 472, part 3, Jus Nat.

§ 157.

allowed to nations generally to definite acts, which exists of course so long as the right of harmless use remains; but in the latter case that right is allowed by way of privilege, when it is no longer available to other nations to use it as they please, and consequently in the former case the right existing by nature is violated, also the right of liberty, by virtue of which each nation can use that right as it pleases, in which case assuredly wrong occurs; but in the latter case, since the refusal of the privilege must be endured and it must be left to the will of the grantor, to whom he may wish to grant it, no wrong is done. But it must be noted that as long as the right to occupy a thing belonging to nobody has not been exercised by a certain nation in its own territories, or even in an occupied part of the sea, the right to occupy belongs by nature to all nations, but access to alien territory is part of the right of harmless use, so that they can use that right; a point which therefore must be held in mind, in order that the examples before cited from Grotius may not confuse any one. When certain acts are allowed to nations generally, we are not speaking of that which belongs to the grantor, but of that which by nature belongs to the nations themselves, and ought not to be denied, except in case of conflict of duties towards itself and towards other nations, and liberty in granting has no place, except in so far as concerning that conflict one must abide by the decision of the nation allowing or refusing to allow. Frequently in the law of nature and nations things must be distinguished sharply, which elsewhere are easily confused, lest something in conformity with the truth may be considered as erroneous, or vice versa.

§ 859, part 1, Jus Nat.

§ 28, part 4, Jus Nat.

§ 29, part 4, Jus Nat.

Note, § 348.

§ 350. *Of lodging-houses and inns*

Provision must be made by nations that houses should not be lacking in which those making a journey and foreigners to whom the right of transit is allowed can pass the night comfortably and safely with their goods, and enjoy healthful food and drink, and that fodder be supplied for the horses and that the services which they need should be furnished at a fair price. For foreigners in travelling through countries are to be received into a house for the purpose of proper rest, where they can conveniently be received, and healthful food and drink, together with services which they need, ought to be furnished at a fair price.

§ 699, part 6, Jus Nat.

Therefore, since it is not possible for foreigners to determine in what houses they can conveniently be received and those things be furnished them which they need, nay more, since the decision in regard to that rests with the owner, by virtue of natural liberty, it is necessary that for that purpose special houses should exist. Therefore in order that nations may not be remiss in their duty, provision must be made by them that such houses may not be lacking in which foreigners to whom the right of transit is allowed can pass the night with their property comfortably and, what is understood of itself, also securely, and enjoy healthful food and drink, and that the services which they need should be furnished them, and that fodder for their horses be supplied at a fair price. Which was the first point.

§ 156, part 1, and §§ 118, 121, part 2, Jus Nat.

But since any persons making a journey, whether they shall be foreigners or residents or those dwelling in the same land, who with respect to the inhabitants of a certain locality can be considered as foreigners, have need of reception into a house for the sake of proper rest, and in it they need healthful food and drink and the services of others, as is evident of itself; no one will call in question that the same holds good concerning any persons making a journey which we have proved concerning those passing through the territory of another nation. Which was the second point.

Houses of that sort, into which those making a journey and foreigners passing through our territory are received, are called lodging-houses and inns, in the native speech, *Gasthöffe, Wirthshäuser*. The need of them so far as citizens are concerned is a matter belonging to general public law, but so far as foreigners are concerned, to whom transit is allowed, this belongs to the law of nations. In the former case the purpose of the state demands them, by virtue of which nothing is to be neglected which in any way satisfies the needs and comforts of life; but in the latter case the right surviving from primitive society requires them, a right not to be carelessly ignored by nations, as is fully understood from what has gone before. Therefore the state does not deserve to be considered well established which is without comfortable lodging-houses and inns, and where the expense for travel or transit is excessive.

§ 4, part 8, Jus Nat.

§ 351. *Of courtesy towards foreigners*

We ought to be courteous towards foreigners living among us, or passing through our lands, and the ruler of the state ought to see to it that we are. For we ought to be courteous to all. Therefore, since he is courteous who is always ready to perform the duties of humanity to any others, consequently performs readily any duty, so far as it is in his power; therefore we ought to be courteous also towards foreigners living among us or passing through our lands. Which was the first point.

§ 899, part 1, Jus Nat.

§ 898, part 1, Jus Nat.

§ 156.

Since in establishing the state we must see to it that the subjects make at least their outward acts conform to the law of nature, since, moreover, subjects ought to be courteous towards foreigners, as proved in point 1; the ruler of the state, to whom the exercise of sovereignty in the state belongs, ought also to see to it that subjects should be courteous towards foreigners living in their lands or passing through them. Which was the second point.

§ 395, part 8, Jus Nat.

§ 42, part 8, Jus Nat.

> Duties towards others are due for no other reason than because they themselves are equally human beings. Therefore the duties do not cease, although they are not subject to the same civil sovereignty as we are; hence only in a case of conflict of duties to be performed for others, other things being equal, does a preference arise for a fellow-citizen. Otherwise courtesy prevails between fellow-citizens and foreigners without any distinction, nor is there any other reason on account of which it is to be manifested, except the need of the one to whom it is to be manifested.

§ 668, part 1, Jus Nat.

§ 667, part 1, Jus Nat.

§ 352. *How the reputation for courtesy towards foreigners is acquired by a nation*

If a large number at least are courteous towards foreigners dwelling among them, or to those passing through their lands, the nation gains a reputation for courtesy. For the things which are to be asserted of the greater part of a nation are transferred to the nation itself and are to be asserted of it. If then very many shall have been courteous towards foreigners dwelling among them, or to those passing through the lands which they inhabit, the reputation for courtesy is acquired by the nation itself also, and it is said to be courteous towards strangers.

§ 43.

§ 51.

Courtesy towards foreigners recommends a nation most highly and extends its fame to foreign people. Therefore, since the fame of his nation ought to be an object of solicitude also to the ruler of the state, on this ground too he is bound to be solicitous that his subjects show themselves courteous to foreigners.

§ 353. *Of courtesy of nations*

§ 899, part 1,
Jus Nat.

§ 3.

Nations ought to be courteous towards each other. For human beings are bound by nature to be courteous towards each other. Therefore, since nations enjoy the same law in their relations with each other as by nature exists between individuals, nations also ought to be courteous towards each other.

§ 352.

§ 39.

The courtesy which is exercised by a nation as such is not to be confused with that which passes from individuals to it. For by virtue of the latter citizens of different nations perform the duties of humanity to each other; but by virtue of the former one nation as a whole does this to another nation as a whole, or, what is just the same, the rulers of states which represent nations, to each other as rulers of states, or in so far as they represent their nations.

§ 354. *In what that consists*

§ 353.
§ 898, part 1,
Jus Nat.

Since nations ought to be courteous towards each other, and since courtesy consists in readiness to perform the duties of humanity to another, courtesy of nations consists in readiness to perform for each other those duties which nations by nature owe to each other.

§ 328, part 1,
Phil. Pract.
Univ.

§ 225, part 1,
Phil. Pract.
Univ.
§ 39.

Therefore, since in the preceding chapter we have fully shown what duties a nation owes a nation, since, moreover, virtue requires a steadfast and permanent desire to do acts in conformity with the law of nature, which are natural duties; of what sort the desire of nations ought to be, and that of the rulers of a state who represent them, is understood therefrom. Nor is the external act sufficient in the case of nations, although from it one nation is bound to gather the will of the other, but it is required that the outward act be in harmony with the inner acts, particularly with the rightly determined will. For nations ought to be virtuous, even as nations, so that what they do, they do with the sense of duty each to the other. For although one nation does not benefit another nation otherwise than by external act; nevertheless more regard is paid to the happiness of nations, if the external act originates from virtue, than if it is determined by extrinsic reasons, which are not present in every case in which one nation needs the aid of another, nor are they always the same. The virtue of nations resides in the rulers of states, who represent those nations.

§ cited.

§ 355. *Of the right to navigate occupied seas*

Every nation has the right freely to navigate even the occupied seas, unless there should exist just fear of loss. Since by nature the right belongs to nations to things of harmless use which are subject to the ownership of another, the right freely to navigate occupied seas belonging to any nation is proved in exactly the same way as we have shown that the passage for reasonable causes through lands and rivers subject to ownership cannot be denied. Which was the first point.

§ 343.

But if, indeed, a nation, in whose ownership a part of the sea is, shall have had reasonable fear of loss from permission to navigate; in the same manner also, by which we have shown that passage through rivers subject to ownership can be forbidden, it is shown that the nation is not bound to allow navigation. Which was the second point.

§ 689, part 6, Jus Nat.

Since, indeed, no difference exists between the passage through rivers subject to ownership for just causes and navigation through occupied seas, it seemed that there was no need that the right of freely navigating occupied seas by nations should be proved at length in detail. Nevertheless, since it is certain that controversies have arisen among nations concerning that matter and can to-day arise, we have considered it wise that definite mention of that be made, in order that we may not seem to pass over anything which helps to resolve disputes of nations. And here must be reconsidered the things which we have elsewhere noted concerning the harmless passage through lands and rivers subject to ownership.

§ cited.

Note, § 689, part 6, Jus Nat.

The right of another is not taken away except in case of conflict of a permissive with a mandatory or prohibitive law. Therefore your fear does not take away my right, unless it combines either with a

§ 211, part 1, Phil. Pract. Univ.

duty towards yourself, or towards others, so as to avert loss or danger from yourself, or even from others; a thing which is none the less to

§ 493, part 2, Jus Nat.

be understood of nations than of single individuals. Therefore, since fear may arise, if we imagine some evil as liable to occur to us, this

§ 495, part 2, Jus Nat.

fear will then be reasonable, when it is at least probable that loss, which we are bound to avoid, will be caused to us or others, if passage of ships through occupied seas is allowed. For it is well known

§ 3.

that some men are timid by nature, so that they are troubled by

§ 822, Psych. Emp.

groundless fear. Reasonable fear is to be measured by the probability of the occurrence of evil, which demands that it should be proved that certain requisites are present for determining the effect of it. The logic of probabilities would shed more abundant light, if it had been sufficiently cultivated and reduced to the form of an art. Thus far therefore we ought to be content with the seeds which we have sown in logic. Already quite often have we appealed to the logic of

§§ 578 and fol., Log.

probabilities, from which the utility of it is understood, even more the necessity of reducing it to the form of an art. Nevertheless it is not to be supposed that so difficult a thing can be worked out by slight effort; for the logic of probabilities is more unapproached than demonstrative logic, which produces a science, and has already been reduced to the form of an art.

§ 356. Of the method of allowing passage through occupied seas

§ 355.

Since the right freely to navigate even occupied seas belongs to every nation, unless there should be reasonable fear of loss; if any nation should wish to prohibit some other nation from navigating a sea occupied by itself, it ought naturally to allege reasons why it does not wish to allow that, and, where reasonable fear exists, it can demand a warranty that the passage be harmless, nay, can even prescribe the condition under which that ought to be granted, consequently, if there should be suspicion that the navigation may be harmful, for example, if it shall be with armed vessels, permission must be asked.

§ 55, part 8, Jus Nat.

For although by force of natural liberty, which belongs also to nations, one must abide by the decision of that nation under whose control the part of the sea is, so long as nothing is done contrary to the right of the other; nevertheless this does not apply in the present instance, because the prohibition of harmless navigation is contrary to the right of the navigator. And he who is using his own right is not bound to allow that without reasonable cause, such as reasonable fear of loss is in this case, he should be interfered with in that use. Since it more easily happens that passage through lands and rivers included within a territory is harmful, than that through the sea, the right of control also is broader in the former case than in the latter, and consequently passage may be more readily denied.

§ 156, part 1, Jus Nat.

§ 355.

§ 336, part 2, Jus Nat.

§ 357. *Of the sea occupied merely as regards the sovereignty*

If a part of the sea is occupied merely so far as regards the sovereignty, the use of it remains common to nations. Since sovereignty and ownership are two distinct rights, one of which can exist without the other, the sovereignty of the sea can be occupied without the ownership. The use of things belongs to ownership, and by nature the necessary use of things is open to every one, as he has need, because all things exist in common. If, then, in a certain part of the sea the sovereignty alone should be occupied, the use remains common to nations.

§ 136, part 2, Jus Nat.

§ 27, part 2, Jus Nat.

§ 24, part 2, Jus Nat.

Hence any one is allowed to navigate there as he pleases, to fish, to collect corals and shells. Nor can any one be forbidden the use of the sea without wrong. And this right is not to be confused with that which still exists in the occupied sea, as a remnant of the primitive joint holding and of which we have before spoken. Moreover, Grotius rightly observes that sovereignty is acquired over a part of the sea as well on account of persons—as when a fleet, which is a naval army, takes its place in some part of the sea, since whatever is within the limits of the sovereignty is subject to the sovereignty of the one occupying—as on account of territory, inasmuch as those who are operating in a part of the sea can be coerced from the land or even by a fleet, no less than if they were found on the land itself. But it is plain that the sovereignty of the sea by a fleet is a temporary occupation, as long of course as it is operating there. But see what we have proved above.

De Jure Belli ac Pacis, lib. 2, c. 3, § 13, n. 2.

§§ 131, 132.

§ 358. *Whether usucaption and prescription have a place among nations*

§ 1023, part 2, Jus Nat.

Usucaption and prescription also have a place among nations. Usucaption belongs to natural law. Therefore, since nations use natural law in their relations with each other, usucaption also has a place among nations. Which was the first point.

§ 3.

§ 1024, part 3, Jus Nat.
§ 1021, part 7, Jus Nat.
§ 497, part 1, Jus Nat.
§ 216, part 2, Jus Nat.

Since prescription is a loss of right from presumed consent, while usucaption is the acquisition of ownership from presumed abandonment of a thing, and since rights, as incorporeal things, are also subject to ownership, rights are lost by prescription from presumed abandonment, no less than ownership is acquired. Therefore, since usucaption has a place among nations, as proved in point 1, prescription also has a place among them. Which was the second point.

§ 1021, part 3, Jus Nat.

We have explained with sufficient clearness the distinction between usucaption and prescription. Therefore, recognizing that distinction, the right is barred by prescription which he who is presumed to have abandoned it, had in a thing, and the possessor acquires it, consequently he gets the thing by usucaption. But if then you should consider rights as an incorporeal thing which can be owned, the same thing also is readily understood of a right, as of sovereignty, which, barred by prescription to the one abandoning, is acquired for the possessor, because of course in that case the intention of abandoning and the agreement in the acquisition by the possessor are presumed.

§ 359. *Whether among nations usucaption and prescription arise from long-continued silence*

Usucaption and prescription on account of long-continued silence are not so readily presumed among nations as among private persons. Of course usucaption depends upon the presumed abandonment of a thing, and on this also prescription depends, by the presumed consent, of course, to the loss of the right from the presumed intention to abandon it. Therefore, since abandonment of a thing is presumed from long-continued silence, unless manifest reasons to the contrary exist, and since therefore the silence, from which consent is presumed, ought to

§ 1021, part 3, Jus Nat.

§ 1024, part 3, Jus Nat.
§ 1058, part 3, Jus Nat.

be that of one knowing and consenting, so that he is silent when he could and ought to speak; but since nations cannot pursue their right except by force of arms, a thing which is not always in their power, nor is it wise, usucaption and prescription on account of long-continued silence do not occur as easily among nations as among private persons.

§ 1055, part 3, Jus. Nat.

§ 1054, part 3, Jus Nat.

He who is not ignorant how great expenditures war demands and what a mass of evils it draws after it, and how little strength avails against one more powerful, will not doubt that one must frequently keep silent, because it is not wise to speak, and that the favourable occasion must be awaited, on the coming of which one is allowed to seek one's right by force against one unwilling to allow it. There is also the consideration, that the silence of one knowing and consenting cannot injure others, from whom he cannot take away a desired right by his own act; a thing which applies especially to sovereignties, since the possessor of the sovereignty cannot abandon the kingdom without the consent of the people and of those who have the right of succession in their order. Prescription, therefore, among nations, if it is to proceed from long-continued silence alone, is certainly exposed to the greatest difficulties, especially since there is no judge to decide the question whether or not the silence has been that of one knowing and consenting.

§ 368, part 8, Jus Nat.

§ 360. *What immemorial prescription is*

That is called immemorial prescription which rests upon immemorial possession, that is, if there is no remembrance of the beginning of the present possession, consequently, if there shall have been immemorial possession, it cannot be proved whether the possession has come down to the present possessor from an owner or a non-owner.

Grotius properly suggests that a time exceeding the memory is plainly not the same as a century, for memory of a fact can be preserved by writing more than one hundred years. When therefore writings worthy of credence exist, by which the beginning of a present possession can be proved, this is not immemorial possession, since now it is plain from what time it has continued to the present possessor.

De Jure Belli ac Pacis, lib. 2, c. 4, § 7.

§ 361. *Whether it belongs to the law of nature*

§ 1033, part 3,
Jus Nat.

§ 360.

Immemorial prescription belongs to the law of nature. For by nature every possessor is presumed to be owner of the thing, unless probable reasons to the contrary exist. But if, indeed, the prescription shall have been immemorial, it rests on immemorial possession, and consequently it cannot be proved whether it has come down from an owner or a non-owner to the present possessor, and therefore probable reasons cannot exist that the present possessor is not the owner, consequently he may not rightly be presumed to be so. Therefore immemorial prescription belongs to the law of nature.

§ 545, part 2,
Jus Nat.

The effect, of course, of immemorial prescription is that the thing is left as it was, or that he who possesses remains in possession. But even if it should really happen that possession has come down to the present possessor from a non-owner, from whom nevertheless it cannot come, according to the hypothesis; the possession nevertheless is not opposed to the law of nature, since no one is bound to restore a thing possessed by himself, unless he who seeks restitution shall have adequately proved ownership, and such proof is here lacking, according to the hypothesis. But the case is different if it is plain that the possession has come down from a robber or a non-owner to the present possessor; for then it is no longer doubtful that the beginning of the possession is defective, consequently that there is no immemorial possession. And then the right of the owner is assured, or that of the one to whom ownership belongs, and time, however long, can in no way take this away from him, since time in fact has no power to transfer ownership and rights of any sort.

§ 362. *Whether it has a place among nations*

§ 361.
§ 3.

Since immemorial prescription belongs to the law of nature, and since the law of nature prevails among nations, immemorial prescription also has a place among nations.

§ 545, part 2,
Jus Nat.
§ 360.
§ 153, part 2,
Jus Nat.

I do not see what difficulty exists in that, provided only the meaning of immemorial prescription be not changed and limited to a certain number of years. For not he who possesses, but he who seeks a thing, is obliged to provide sufficient proof of ownership. And since in

case of immemorial prescription it cannot be ascertained that possession has come down from a robber or a non-owner to the present possessor, the present possessor consequently is not in the wrong, since
there is no one to whom he is bound to restore the thing.

§ 471, part 8,
Jus Nat., and
§ 440, part 1,
Phil. Pract. Univ.

§ 363. *When long-continued silence does no harm*

Prescription does not avail against him who adduces reasons for his long-
continued silence. For since the silence ought to be that of one knowing
and consenting, in order that abandonment, upon which depends the
consent to the loss of the right, can be presumed; from long continued
silence abandonment is therefore presumed, for the reason that it is not
credible that in so great a space of time the other party should not have
obtained knowledge of its right, or that no opportunity of questioning
it had arisen. If, therefore, reasons for long-continued silence are alleged,
the reason for the presumption fails, consequently also the prescription,
and it does not avail, therefore, against him who adduces reasons for
long-continued silence.

§ 1055, part 3,
Jus Nat.

§ 1024, part 3,
Jus Nat.

No one is so foolish as to think that simply by lapse of time the right
can be transferred without the consent of the owner. Therefore he who
presumes an intention of abandonment by another ought to have probable reasons for his presumption. But if then these are refuted by showing
the contrary, the presumption certainly falls; nay more, if the opposite
party can adduce reasons even more probable, on account of which can
be presumed either ignorance of his own right or lack of opportunity
to pursue it, or at least to call in question the possession, the stronger
presumption overcomes the weaker. That presumption is certainly of the
least weight which rests on lapse of time alone. And therefore it is plain,
as we have already noted above, that prescription among nations, which
has to arise from long-continued silence alone, is beset with the greatest
difficulties, so that it is scarcely ever of any use. But may you be far from
confounding that with immemorial prescription.

§ 244, part 2,
Jus Nat.

Note, § 359.

§ 360.

§ 364. *Of the one who by some sign indicates that he does not wish to give up his right*

If any one sufficiently declares by any sign that he does not wish to give
up his right, even if he does not pursue it, prescription does not prevail

against him. For what any one sufficiently declares, when he is bound to
speak the truth, that is held against him as the truth. Therefore if any one
sufficiently declares by any sign that he does not wish to give up his right,
it cannot be held as true against him, indeed, that he wishes to give it up,
because he does not pursue it. Therefore, since no one loses his right, and
consequently against him prescription does not avail, unless consent to
the loss of his right can be presumed; if any one sufficiently declares by
any sign that he does not wish to give up his right, even if he does not
pursue it, prescription does not avail against him.

§ 427, part 3,
Jus Nat.

§ 28, Ontol.

§ 1024, part 3,
Jus Nat.

> Here, indeed, belongs the case when any one protests against any-
> thing done contrary to his right. Hence it is generally said that one's
> right is saved by protesting. Here likewise belongs the case of one
> who, being unwilling to give up the sovereignty, claims the title and
> royal insignia, although he does not possess the kingdom. Lest hope-
> less quarrels arise between nations, to be ended only by force of arms
> "(and sometimes not even by that)," it is undoubtedly wise that the
> one who wishes to preserve his right, and does not wish to give it up,
> should give plain indications of his desire, so far as is in his power. For
> controversies concerning causes of long-continued silence between
> nations, whose disputes are subject to no judge, and involve questions
> exceedingly hard to prove, are ended with the greatest difficulty, nor is
> war a suitable method of ending them, although to it at last they may
> have to turn as to a last resort.

§ 365. How the right of another is barred by prescription, by doing or not doing

If any one does or does not what he could by no means do or not do,
unless he should give up his right, prescription avails against him. For
if any one does or does not what he could by no means do or not do,
unless he should give up his right, he declares properly that he does not
wish to preserve his right; but if indeed he were to wish to preserve it,
he would undoubtedly need to say that he does this or does not do it
with a reservation of his right. Therefore, since what any one properly
declares, when he is bound to speak the truth, is held against him as the
truth; if any one does or does not what he could by no means do or not
do, unless he should give up his right, it is held against him as the truth

§ 427, part 3,
Jus Nat.

that he wishes to give it up, and consequently consents to the loss of his right. Therefore prescription avails against him.

§ 1024, part 3, Jus Nat.

Of course it cannot be argued that he did this or did it not with a reservation of his right. For since the mind of another is open to no one, unless it should be indicated by plain signs, it was undoubtedly necessary that one should plainly indicate that the doing or not doing ought by no means to injure one's right. Otherwise mental reservations would have to be allowed by which all certainty in human affairs would be taken away, and which are prohibited as illegal by the law of nature, since we are bound to indicate the thoughts of our mind to another. Nay if tacit exceptions of that sort were to be allowed in words and deeds, it could not be ascertained what should be held as true against the speaker or doer. Therefore one who does not properly express his intention, when he ought to express it, should charge up to himself any injury done to his own right. Presumption of abandonment from overt act we have already explained elsewhere.

§ 231, part 3, Jus Nat.

§ 237, part 3, Jus Nat.

§ 1053, part 3, Jus Nat.

§ 366. Whether prescription for a very long time is in harmony with the voluntary law of nations

Prescription on account of silence for a very long time is in harmony with the voluntary law of nations. For since individual nations, inasmuch as they are understood to have united into a supreme state, are understood also to have bound themselves to the whole, because they wish to promote the common good, and all are bound to the individuals because they wish to provide for the special good of themselves, in this also they ought to agree, that every nation may quietly enjoy its own right, consequently that sovereignty and other rights should at length be certain, and not always remain uncertain. Therefore, since the law of nature gives a right to those acts without which certainty of ownership cannot be attained, consequently also of any other rights which not less than corporeal things are subject to ownership, since, moreover, if prescription on account of silence for a very long time were not acknowledged among nations, sovereignty and other rights of nations would be subject to uncertainty, which after a very long time could give cause for war, than which nothing is more opposed to the welfare of nations, as no one would dare to doubt; nations ought to agree to prescription on

§ 12.

§ 4, part 8, Jus Nat.

§ 1050, part 3, Jus Nat.

§ 216, part 2, Jus Nat.

account of silence for a very long time, inasmuch as they are understood to have united into a supreme state. Therefore, since the law of nations is voluntary, because it is derived from the idea of a supreme state, pre-

§ 22.

scription on account of silence for a very long time is in harmony with the voluntary law of nations.

Grotius refers prescription among nations to the voluntary law of nations, and he proves from the annals of history that nations have appealed to it. Since he derives the voluntary law of nations from the

Note, § 20.

consensus of the more civilized nations, and by other authorities it is therefore held to be a fiction, because the express consensus of nations cannot be proved, and furthermore because the consensus of some cannot bind others; prescription, therefore, is not admitted among nations, which nevertheless we have proved exists even by nature in

§§ 358 and fol.

certain cases. But if you perchance object to the law of nature, because prescription on account of silence for a long time is difficult to prove, if it should rest on this case alone; nevertheless Grotius does not miss the truth when he asserts that the voluntary law of nations is not opposed to it. For the reasons of those things which are referred to the voluntary law of nations are not intrinsic, such as are required in the law of nature, being derived from the concepts themselves of ownership or property and sovereignty, but extrinsic, as derived from the purpose of the supreme state, nor different from those by which

§ 14.

civil law is derived from natural law. Therefore just as there are reasons

§ 22.

for civil laws, which, depending on the common purpose of the state in the category of states in general, give rise to civil laws suitable for any state, and through which their fitness is to be determined; so also are there reasons depending on the purpose of the supreme state, into

§ 9.

which nature herself has united nations—because in fact the law of nature itself prescribes certain duties to nations, as has been shown before—which give rise to a law of nations, as a thing which is to be admitted for the purpose of securing that supreme state, however much, like the civil law, it may depart from the law of nature. Of course, since the supreme state is no less in harmony with the law of nature than are the individual states, the law of nature itself binds

§ cited.

nations to attain the purpose of the supreme state, consequently it

§ 26, part 8, Jus Nat.

confers the right to establish those things without which the purpose of the state cannot be attained in accordance with human conditions, although they may depart from a strict understanding of the law of nature. Therefore, since it does not seem unfitting that prescription should apply among citizens in a well-established state, since it is to the advantage of a state that ownership should not remain uncertain, neither can it be considered absurd that there should be a place for long-time prescription among nations, since it is much more to their advantage that their ownership and sovereignty should not always be uncertain. The obligation which binds individuals not to be negligent, but rather diligent in inquiring after their things which perchance have come into the power of another, likewise after the rights belonging to themselves, and which binds them to do their best that the ownership of others may not remain uncertain, binds nations also, consequently even the law of nature gives to nations a right to those things without which certainty of ownership and sovereignty could not exist among them. And therefore nations are rightly presumed to have agreed to those things, because they ought to have agreed, as is already quite plain from the notes given above. The law of nature considers no less the happiness of nations than of individuals, even to the extent that the less evil is to be endured that the greater may be avoided. The voluntary law of nations therefore no more deserves to be called a fiction than do laws merely civil deserve to be classed as untenable fictions. No sane human being denies that the voluntary law of nations is opposed to the strict understanding of the law of nature; but it by no means follows from this that it is not to be tolerated among nations that one should depart from the law of nature even by a finger's breadth, if it happens, in case of emergency, to come into conflict with the well-being of nations.

§ 1046, part 3, Jus Nat.

§ 1047, part 3, Jus Nat.

§ 1052, part 3, Jus Nat.

§ 3.

§ 159, part 1, Phil. Pract. Univ.

Note, § 9, and Note, § 12.

§ 367. *Of the stipulative law of nations as regards prescription*

If neighbouring nations agree with each other concerning prescription, prescription will apply in the manner agreed upon. Since stipulations must be observed, or are binding by nature, if neighbouring nations agree with each other concerning prescription, they give to each other reciprocally the right to require that prescription and those rights, concerning which they have agreed, should be effective. And since one transferring any right to another can define, as shall have seemed best to him, how it

§ 789, part 3, Jus Nat.

§ 430, part 3, Jus Nat.

§ 11, part 3,
Jus Nat.
is to be transferred, if neighbouring nations agree with each other concerning prescription, prescription will apply in the manner agreed upon.

By the agreement of nations concerning prescription not only is the quasi-stipulation, upon which the voluntary right of nations rests, changed into a perfect stipulation; but also things can be added to it which are not defined in that law, or at least are defined with the greatest difficulty, or cannot be defined because of unknown or uncertain facts in the given case. Therefore, since prescription among nations § 359. on account of long-continued silence is presumed with difficulty and § 244, part 2,
Jus Nat. the entire presumption rests only on probable reasons, to which other probable reasons can be opposed, since, moreover, the estimation of the grades of probabilities is subject to dispute; it is certainly wise for § 578, Log. neighbouring nations to agree with each other concerning prescription, and so it is in harmony with stipulative law that, just as by the civil law, prescription should be limited to a certain number of years, although not to the same number as the civil laws demand; for those things which depend upon human impulse are not destitute of reason for determination one way or another, and this is not exactly the same among nations and among individuals. For the disinclination of men to admit a right, even when not unknown to them, unless it arises from plain stipulations, suggests agreements concerning prescription also. For it is customary with most men to desire that any right be effective against others but not against themselves. For although the ruler of any state, when prescription is disadvantageous to him, rules that he recognizes no prescription among nations, nevertheless it cannot be inferred from this that he rejects it in general. For if prescription were useful to him, it is scarcely to be doubted that he would assert it for himself. Therefore it is foolish to desire to prove, by examples of that sort, that among nations prescription is effective neither by nature nor by the voluntary law of nations. And if one must abide by the opinion of the rulers of a state, why, pray, ought his testimony to be of more weight, against whom prescription is asserted, than his, who asserts it in his own behalf? Therefore it is plainly evident that nothing can be determined by examples of that sort, but that doubtful points are brought into discussion. We suggest, in passing, that those who consider the voluntary law of nations a fiction, nevertheless admit many things which can be referred only to this law, as will be plainly evident when we discuss the law of war.

Of Treaties and Other Agreements of Nations, and of Promises

§ 368. *What are called sovereign and minor powers*

Authorities simply, or, in contrast with minor authorities, sovereign authorities, are defined as persons to whom the supreme sovereignty in a state belongs. Therefore sovereign authorities are rulers of a state, who have supreme sovereignty, and in a democracy they are the free people. In the native vernacular they are called *die Gewaltigen* [the Powerful]. Those persons are called minor authorities who exercise a certain part of the sovereignty, dependent upon a sovereign authority and acting in its name, as magistrates, and leaders in war, of whom we shall speak later. In the native vernacular they are called *die Obern* [the Superiors].

§ 42, part 8, Jus Nat.
§ 131, part 8, Jus Nat.

§ 162, part 8, Jus Nat.

> Since the meaning of the word *potestas* is adapted to Latium[1] and is used in Grotius and other authors who discuss the law of nations, therefore in the present treatise also we desire to use the same term. But although the word *potestas* without an adjective is applied indifferently to the rulers of states and free peoples and to magistrates by Roman writers, a thing which also occurs with the German word *die Obern;* since nevertheless in the present argument sovereign authorities are to be distinguished from minor authorities, we too, with Grotius, shall use the word only with the adjective.

§ 369. *What treaties are; what compacts are*

A treaty is defined as a stipulation entered into reciprocally by supreme powers for the public good, to last for ever or at least for a considerable

1. Latium: a region in Italy which was originally the land of the ancient Latins.

time. But stipulations, which contain temporary promises or those not to be repeated, retain the name of compacts.

For example, if two nations reciprocally agree to furnish troops to each other in time of war, this stipulation is called a treaty; but if one nation permits another, on account of the high price of grain, to purchase in its territory, this will be a compact. A compact of that sort, also, is the truce made after a battle for the purpose of burying the dead.

§ 370. *Who are able to make treaties*

§ 369.
§ 368.
§ 131, part 8,
Jus Nat.
§ 133, part 8,
Jus Nat.

§ 135, part 8,
Jus Nat.

§ 139, part 9,
Jus Nat.

Since a treaty is made by the sovereign powers, consequently by those who have supreme sovereignty, and since in a democracy the supreme sovereignty is with the people, in a monarchy with the monarch, in an aristocracy with the aristocrats; since, moreover, it can be limited or diminished in a certain manner in a kingdom, so that the king cannot do certain things, or at least cannot do them without the consent of the people or of certain others; in a democratic state treaties can be made only by the people, in a monarchy by the monarch, in an aristocracy by the aristocrats, in a kingdom either by the king—with the consent of the people or of certain others, or without it—or by the people, or by some certain others, as may have been determined by the fundamental laws.

§ 33, part 4,
Jus Nat.

§ 36, part 8,
Jus Nat.

The forms of mixed states are limited by fundamental laws, and therefore from these it is plain to whom the right of making treaties belongs, or if the right has been transferred to the king or the aristocrats on a certain condition, it is plain how the king or the aristocrats ought to exercise that right. Just as originally the civil sovereignty is with the people as a whole, the right also of making treaties is originally with the same people. But since the people can transfer the sovereignty to one person or to several jointly as it pleases, and since it depends on its will on what condition it may wish to transfer the same, it is to be decided from the method of transfer how great a right belongs to the ruler of the state in making treaties.

§ 371. *What sort of consensus of the people is required for a treaty in a democracy*

Because in a democracy or a popular state treaties can be made only by the people, but since in this form of state that is to be considered the will of the whole people which shall have seemed good to the majority, unless it shall have been expressly agreed otherwise concerning some things, for example, that only a unanimous vote is conclusive, or that a certain number of votes prevails; in a popular state a treaty is valid to which a majority of the people agrees, unless it shall have been expressly agreed that for making a treaty there should be a unanimous vote, or that a certain number of votes should prevail.

§ 370.

§ 157, part 8, Jus Nat.

Although in a popular state the full and supreme sovereignty is with the people, nevertheless the method of exercising the sovereignty can be limited by certain conditions. And therefore in a popular state fundamental laws can also exist, from which a decision must be reached concerning the right of making treaties.

§ 131, part 8, Jus Nat.

§ 77, part 8, Jus Nat.

§ 372. *Of a mandate to make a treaty*

Since treaties are stipulations which are made by sovereign powers, and since it is just the same whether one acts of himself or through another, so that he has a mandate to make a treaty to whom the sovereign power has entrusted it to be done in his name, they can make treaties who have a mandate from the sovereign power.

§ 269.

§ 640, part 4, Jus Nat.

Nations themselves cannot meet in order to make treaties, nor can their rulers easily meet for this purpose. Therefore they entrust this matter to others, such as envoys, of whom we shall speak below. Hence Livy says that treaties are made by the order of the sovereign power. But how great their right may be to whom this matter is entrusted is to be determined from their mandate, the limits of which he who has the mandate cannot overstep. Since these points concerning the mandate have been proved at length elsewhere, that is, in the fourth part of "The Law of Nature," they are to be applied to the present matter also.

§ 373. *Of private stipulations of sovereign powers*

§ 369.

Furthermore, because treaties are made for the public good, if sovereign powers, such as kings, agree with each other as to private matters, or as to things affecting their own personal advantage, or even if the sovereign power agrees with some private foreign person, this stipulation is not a treaty.

It is required for a treaty, of course, both that the parties should be sovereign powers, and that the subject-matter concerning which the stipulation is made, should affect the public good. If it be lacking in either respect it will not be a treaty, but is considered a private stipulation. So if a certain king should agree with another king to sell him a certain quantity of wine at a certain price, this will be only a private stipulation. Here is to be considered the difference which exists

§ 284, part 8,
Jus Nat.

between the royal acts of the king and his private acts, since as far as regards his private acts he is looked at as a private person, nor does he enjoy any other law than the law of private persons. Likewise if

§ 285, part 8,
Jus Nat.

some king makes a contract with some subjects of another, that they may bring certain goods into his territory, this is a private stipulation, although entered into for public advantage.

§ 374. *What things are to be maintained concerning treaties*

§ 369.

§ 788, part 3,
Jus Nat.

§§ 32, 33, part
8, Jus Nat.

§ 3.

Finally since treaties are stipulations containing promises, moreover since nations and their rulers, to whom the right of the people has been transferred, use natural law in their relations with each other, the things which have been proved in the law of nature concerning stipulations and promises are true concerning treaties also.

§ 788, part 3,
Jus Nat.

Therefore it would be superfluous to repeat those things which have been proved at length, in the third part of "The Law of Nature," concerning stipulations and the promises which stipulations contain.

§ 375. *Some comments on their interpretation*

§ 374.

§ 461, part 6,
Jus Nat.

Since those things are true concerning treaties which have been proved of stipulations in the law of nature, since, moreover, no one can be an interpreter of his own words in stipulations, nor is the promisee allowed to interpret the words of the promisor in the sense in which he wishes them to be understood, but has the right to compel the promisor to do that which a proper interpretation warrants; in treaties also neither party can be an interpreter of his own words, nor is the promisee allowed to interpret the words of the promisor in the sense in which he wishes them to be understood, but he has the right to compel the promisor to do that which a proper interpretation warrants, that is, that interpretation which is made through the rules of interpretation, discussed in chapter six of "The Law of Nature."

§ 463, part 6, Jus Nat.
§ 466, part 6, Jus Nat.

§ 465, part 6, Jus Nat.

Since treaties are made for the sake of public advantage, with which the advantage of the ruler of the state is connected by the closest bond, even if the silly opinion of pseudo-politicians is to the contrary, namely that the people should be for the benefit of the ruler of the state and therefore all things in the state should be measured by his private advantage; nothing happens more easily than that either party to treaties should wish to interpret both his own words and those of the other party as may be more useful to himself. Therefore it cannot happen otherwise than that controversies should arise between parties to a treaty concerning that which has been promised in the treaty, or excepted from it, to be terminated in no other way than by admitting the interpretation made in accordance with rules, which each party to the treaty is bound to admit as true. In fact he who rejects this interpretation does the other party an injury; but for this reason it cannot be said that interpretation of treaties is useless, and that controversies are not to be terminated except by force of arms. In the law of nations the question is, what is right and what ought nations and their rulers to do, but not what it is necessary to do if they are unwilling to submit to the truth; otherwise all law of nations would have to be called useless, and privilege would have to be given to nations to act as if in their position war of all against all should prevail, so that each one may do what it can do, such justice as is demanded of citizens being held superfluous among nations and their rulers.

§ 369.

§ 464, part 6, Jus Nat.

§ 466, part 6, and § 859, part 1, Jus Nat.

§ 376. Of treaties and promises to be observed by nations and their rulers, and of not violating a promise given

Nations and their rulers are bound to observe treaties and promises, and are bound by nature not to violate a promise given. For treaties are stipulations and stipulations contain promises. Therefore, since we

§ 369.
§ 788, part 3, Jus Nat.

§ 789, part 3,
Jus Nat.
§ 431, part 3,
Jus Nat.
§ 765, part 3,
Jus Nat.

§ 369.
§ 368 h, and
§§ 33, 42,
part 8, Jus Nat.

are bound by nature to observe stipulations and promises, and not to violate a promise given; and since the things which have been proved in the law of nature concerning stipulations and promises are true concerning treaties also which are made by sovereign powers, that is, by nations and their rulers; nations therefore and their rulers are bound by nature to observe treaties and promises and not to violate a promise given.

§ 49.

§ 51.

§ 766, part 3,
Jus Nat.

Nothing contributes more to the glory of nations and their rulers than complete and perfect good faith, since it is of the greatest importance that a promise given should not be violated, if treaties have been made. Therefore, since not only nations, but also in particular their rulers, ought to desire that they be worthy of fame, and do nothing which can diminish or weaken it, nations therefore and their rulers ought to take care to be full of faith, steadfast, and persistent. Nothing tarnishes the reputation of a nation or of the ruler of a nation among outside nations more than treachery. Foolish is the ambition of those who desire to be pre-eminent among other nations and strive for glory of name, and, relying on their power, consider it not at all opposed to their religion to violate a promise. They object to the name of treachery, deservedly despised among nations, just as if forsooth he is not treacherous who does an act contrary to what he has promised to do. But that is the foolishness of men, by which also sovereign powers are contaminated, that they are not ashamed to be what they are unwilling to be called.

§ 377. *What sort of an obligation is incurred and what sort of a right is acquired from treaties*

§ 369.

§ 788, part 3,
Jus Nat.

§ 363, part 3,
Jus Nat.

§ 364, part 3,
Jus Nat.

A perfect obligation arises from treaties and a perfect right is acquired. For treaties are stipulations, consequently they contain promises made by one party, accepted by the other. Therefore, since a promisor binds himself absolutely to the promise, and a perfect right belongs to the promisee to that which has been promised; from treaties a perfect obligation arises and a perfect right is acquired.

Stipulations and consequently treaties between nations were introduced with no other purpose than that one human being might bind another and one nation bind another absolutely to do anything which is necessary, so that since he now rejoices in a perfect right to that which is to be performed, he can demand it and need no longer beg for it, and by force can coerce one who is unwilling to perform his promise. Therefore treaties between nations are of the greatest advantage, but this advantage nevertheless goes for naught if presumptuous power may violate a promise.

§ 235, part 1,
Phil. Pract.
Univ.

§ 378. *Whether the violation of a treaty is wrong*

Since a perfect right is acquired from treaties, he who violates a treaty violates a perfect right of the other party. Therefore, since the violation of a perfect right is a wrong, he who violates a treaty does a wrong to the other party.

§ 377.

§ 859, part 8,
Jus Nat.

This is to be noted, that it may be understood what right belongs to a party to a treaty against the violator of a treaty. It is plain without my saying it, that a treaty is violated if anything is done which is contrary to it, or if anything is not done which is to be done by virtue of it.

§ 379. *What allied nations are*

Those are called allied nations which have entered into some treaty. And with the same meaning the rulers of states also are called allies. In our native vernacular they are called *Bundsgenossen*.

Frequently the word is taken in a narrower meaning, for those who have been united under a treaty to protect themselves, or have made a treaty to furnish troops to each other in war.

§ 380. *To what extent allied nations are bound to each other*

Since allied nations have entered into a certain treaty, inasmuch as a perfect obligation arises from treaties to observe what has been promised in the treaty; allied nations are bound absolutely to each other to perform those things which they have agreed upon in the treaty, consequently, since they ought not to violate a promise given, in order that they may not seem to desire to violate it, they ought promptly to perform those things for each other.

§ 379.

§ 377.

§ 376.

§ 430, part 3,
Jus Nat.

§ 376.

Good faith gains glory for nations and their rulers. But this shines out most clearly by promptness in performing those things which they have agreed upon in the treaty. Therefore, since this very promptness proves that the nation has full and complete good faith, the nation which performs those agreements most perfectly excels especially in glory, and on the other hand it loses much of that glory, if it is brought with reluctance and difficulty to a performance. Moreover it is understood that performances are of a twofold nature, affirmative and negative, the former of which consists in giving and doing, the latter in not doing.

§ 381. *Whether it is allowable to make treaties contrary to those already made beforehand*

It is not allowable to enter into treaties contrary to treaties already contracted with another nation. For, if treaties are entered into contrary to treaties already contracted with another nation, things are promised in them which, by virtue of the treaty contracted beforehand, may not be performed. Therefore, since treaties are to be observed, consequently those things are to be performed which have been promised in the treaty; it is impossible that both treaties should be observed, consequently the promise given must be violated: since this is illegal, it is not allowable to enter into treaties contrary to treaties already contracted with another nation.

§ 376.

§ 430, par. 3, Jus Nat.
§ 376.

For example, let us suppose there has been an agreement in a former treaty that you would sell certain goods to me alone; it is not allowable to enter into a treaty with another that he also may purchase goods of the same sort from you. In like manner if you shall have promised not to send troops to some third person if he should be involved in war, you may not make a treaty with him concerning the sending of troops to each other, if either of you should be assailed in war. For if the former stipulation is to be observed, in the former case the goods agreed upon are to be sold to no one except myself, in the latter case troops are not to be sent to a third person if he is assailed in war; in either case, therefore, the later treaty cannot be entered into without the intention of violating the promise given in the earlier treaty, nay more, without a violation of the earlier treaty. When any one enters into a treaty, since he binds himself absolutely to perform that which he promises, by the promise he alienates his liberty so far as regards the contrary act. Therefore it depends no longer upon his will whether or not he should wish to promise the contrary to some third person.

§ 377.

§ 360, part 3, Jus Nat.

§ 382. *What are called earlier treaties, what later treaties*

If treaties should be made at different times with different nations, those which are first entered into are called the earlier; those which after others have already been made are then at length made are called the later.

Although it may seem that these things could be understood without explanation, nevertheless they had to be explained for the sake of conciseness, that no ambiguity may exist in what follows. We also have need of such terms in the sciences, that concise statements may not seem inadequately expressed.

§ 383. *Of later treaties which are contrary to earlier ones*

Later treaties contrary to earlier ones are illegal, and they are invalid by the law of nature. For a perfect right is acquired from treaties. If, then, treaties are entered into which are contrary to earlier ones, since that which is promised in the later treaties cannot be performed unless the earlier treaties should be violated, the later treaties are made contrary to the perfect right of the one with whom the earlier ones were entered into. Therefore, since that is illegal which is contrary to the right of another, later treaties contrary to earlier ones are illegal. Which was the first point.

§ 377.

§ 239, part 1, Phil. Pract. Univ.

§ cited, part 1, Phil. Pract. Univ.

And if later treaties shall have been contrary to earlier ones, in them things are promised which cannot be promised without impairing the earlier treaties, consequently this would be just as if he who enters into the later treaty should promise a thing which he no longer has. Therefore, since a promise would be invalid, if any one promises a thing which he knows that he no longer has, later treaties which are contrary to earlier ones are invalid by the law of nature. Which was the second point.

§ 637, part 3, Jus Nat.

It is plain from the comments that have been made a little while ago, that when the earlier treaty is entered into, the liberty to promise the contrary of that which has been promised in the treaty has been

Note, § 381.

§ 386, part 3,
Jus Nat.

alienated, since the promisor promised the same things beforehand. Therefore it ought not to seem paradoxical, that what there is in the later offer contrary to that which was promised in the earlier treaty is equivalent to what we no longer have. For it could also be equivalent to a thing, if you prefer, which has already been promised to another; in which case the later promise also is invalid. Of course when I prom-

§ 681, part 3,
Jus Nat.

ise you that I will do one thing, I certainly at the same time promise that I will not do the opposite, which cannot be done if the first is done. Therefore, if I promise the opposite to another, it is undoubt-edly just the same as if what I have promised to give to you I were to desire rather not to give to you but to another. But since this does not seem so plain as it would if the opposite to the earlier promise should be compared to a thing which we no longer have, we have preferred rather to use this aid in the proof. But if that is contained in the later treaty which cannot be performed without impairment of the earlier, the promise then is understood to have been made concerning that which is morally impossible, and therefore it renders the treaty invalid.

§ 384. *Of treaties which are good in part and bad in part*

§ 383.

Since later treaties contrary to earlier ones are invalid by the law of nature; if a later treaty should contain many promises, some of which are not contradictory to the earlier treaty, but others are, so that both treaties as regards the latter provision cannot be observed at the same time, the treaty holds good as regards the former, but as regards the latter is invalid.

Of course the later treaty labours under a defect only as regards the later promises, but not as regards the earlier. Therefore there is no reason why it ought not to hold good as regards the earlier, although it cannot hold good as regards the later. The later treaty is opposed to the right of a third party only in so far as it contains anything which cannot be performed without impairment of the right of a third party.

§ 385. *Of a treaty entered into with two parties for the same purpose*

Treaties for the same purpose may be entered into with two parties, if the same thing can be performed for two parties. For if a treaty is made for the same purpose with two parties, since a treaty is a stipulation, and therefore contains a promise, the same thing is promised twice. Therefore, since each promise is valid if the same thing is promised twice and can be performed twice; treaties may be entered into for the same purpose with two parties, if the same thing can be performed for two parties.

§ 369.

§ 788, part 3, Jus Nat.

§ 682, part 3, Jus Nat.

So a treaty for the purpose of commerce may be entered into with two parties, if that can be done without prejudice to the earlier ally, since the goods to be sold to foreigners may be sufficient for either of the allies, or possibly nothing may have been said in the earlier treaty by which the right of the ally is extended to a certain quantity of goods. In like manner troops can be promised to two parties in war, if either they can be sent to the two at the same time, or it should not happen that each of the allies is involved in war at the same time. Since the latter is not presumed, the later treaty is not illegal for the reason that it can happen that each of the allies may be involved in war at one and the same time. But this particular case will have to be worked out more carefully in what follows.

§ 386. *Which is to be preferred in case of conflict*

But if on the hypothesis of the preceding proposition a case should occur in which that which has been promised cannot be performed for each of the allies at the same time, the earlier ally is preferred to the later. For since it is not allowable to enter into a treaty contrary to a treaty contracted beforehand with another nation; when a treaty for the same purpose is made with two parties, the latter has this tacit provision, if that which is promised can be performed without impairing the right of the earlier treaty, or, what is just the same, as long as the same thing can be performed for each ally. If, then, a case should occur in which that which has been promised cannot be performed for each of the allies at the time, since an exception must be made, moreover, since through the later stipulation the right created by the earlier cannot be taken away, as proved above, the earlier ally is to be preferred to the later.

§ 381.

§ 539, part 6, Jus Nat.

The promise made to the later ally is equivalent to one made on condition, since this tacit exception exists, if it may be allowed to be done in accordance with the right of the earlier ally, or unless the right

§ 859, part 1,
Jus Nat.

§ 546, part 6,
Jus Nat.

of the earlier ally should be opposed to it; but that which has been made to the earlier ally is absolute and bars every tacit exception. If, then, the later ally should be preferred to the earlier, that would be contrary to the right of the earlier and therefore a wrong would be done him, which in the other case, in which the later is subordinate, is not to be apprehended. Compare what we have elsewhere proved.

§ 387. *If a later treaty should be contrary to an earlier one which has already expired*

If an earlier treaty has already expired, it does not stand in the way of making a treaty with another contrary to it. For if the earlier treaty has expired, all right also claimed under it is at an end, a thing which is self-evident. Therefore if a treaty should be made with another contrary to an earlier treaty, this is not automatically contrary to the right of the party with whom a treaty had previously been concluded. Therefore if an earlier treaty has already expired, it does not stand in the way of making a treaty with another contrary to it.

§ 239, part 1,
Phil. Pract.
Univ.

For example, let us suppose there has been an agreement that certain definite goods should not be sold to a certain definite nation for a period of ten years. If this period of ten years shall have elapsed, the treaty containing the prohibition has expired, consequently you are now free to sell those goods to this nation. If, therefore, when you enter into this treaty that you will sell those goods to itself alone, nothing is done contrary to the earlier treaty, but rather this does not prevent you from entering into the later treaty, then I say, not without reason, that the earlier treaty which has expired does not prevent the later one, which is made with another party, from being made contrary to it; for the question is not now of what is in conformity to equity. This to be sure is determined by other reasons based on the duties of nations towards each other in a particular case. Here the only question is, what can be done without impairment of the right derived from the earlier treaty; since this is a nullity as soon as the treaty has expired, it deserves indeed no attention, nor has it any weight in stipulating a later treaty. So it can happen that he who was an ally in war, by the termination of the treaty becomes an enemy instead of an ally, by entering into a treaty with an enemy.

§ 388. *When, because of the non-performance of what is contained in a treaty, the same is not violated*

If that which is due by a treaty is in the category of duties of nations toward nations and you yourself need it for the preservation of your nation, you ought to prefer your nation to another nation, nor is the treaty violated if you should not perform that which has been promised. For in case of the present proposition the duty of the nation towards itself conflicts with its duty towards other nations. Therefore, since by nature the duty of a nation towards itself prevails over its duty towards another nation, if there should be an agreement with a certain nation that that should be performed for it which by nature nations owe each other by way of duty, there is in this agreement the tacit provision that the case should be excepted in which you necessarily need for the preservation of your own nation that which is to be performed for the other nation. Therefore in spite of the treaty you prefer your own nation to the other with whom the treaty was made, and since in this case of conflict the other nation has been able to acquire no right from the treaty, if that should not be performed which has been promised, the treaty has not been violated.

§ 206, part 1, Phil. Pract. Univ.

§ 206.

Let us suppose that a provision is contained in the treaty that the allied nation should purchase grain of you. If there shall have been such lack of grain that there is hardly enough of it for your own nation, the treaty does not stand in the way of prohibiting sales of grain to the allied nation. Of course no one is understood to promise a thing which is not in his power. Therefore in treaties of that sort the case is undoubtedly to be excepted as to which there can be no doubt that the one making the treaty would have made an exception if he had been asked whether he wished that case to be excepted or to be included under the treaty.

§ 389. *Of treaties which are made concerning a thing which is due by nature*

If treaties are made concerning a thing which is due by nature, a perfect right is acquired to it. The right of nations to those things which are due by nature to each other is an imperfect right, but by treaties a perfect

§ 157.

§ 377.

right is acquired to that which is contained in them. If then treaties be made concerning a thing which is due by nature, a perfect right is acquired to it.

Hence the reason is plain why treaties are made concerning those things which are already due by nature, namely, that a special right may be acquired to it, and that it may be possible to demand what beforehand might only be asked for. There is added to the natural obligation through the treaty a positive obligation by which liberty is alienated as far as regards the promises agreed upon, so that what was a matter of liberty now becomes a matter of necessity. For example,

§ 187.

nations are bound by nature to engage in commerce with each other so far as is in their power, but the right to commerce is only an imper-

§ 189.

fect right, and nations are not bound absolutely to engage in it with

§ 190.

each other. A perfect right to it can be acquired only through stipula-

§ 191.

tions. Since treaties are such stipulations, if treaties are made for the

§ 369.

purpose of commerce, the right to engage in commerce with another nation will be a perfect right. But it is readily evident that here we are talking only of affirmative treaties, which contain affirmative promises, such as is the grant of commercial rights, just as also above we understand those things which nations owe to each other by nature to relate to positive acts, and only concerning these is this common saying true, that no one can be bound beyond what is possible, or, as we have said above, no nation is bound to perform for another that

§ 160.

which is not in its power; this restriction of obligations by nature, in so far of course as they consist in positive acts, is otherwise a matter of imperfect right in regard to them.

§ 390. *Of the purpose of those treaties*

§ 389.

Since through treaties a perfect right is acquired to that which one nation owes another by nature, since, moreover, a perfect right involves the right

§ 235, part 1, Phil. Pract. Univ.

to compel one to perform who is unwilling to perform what has been agreed upon; treaties concerning a thing which is already due by nature are to be made in order that the performance may become certain.

§ 157.

For if a thing is denied which by nature nations owe to each other, that is to be endured, even if there is injustice in the denial. But if then one is to trust to equity alone, there will be no certainty in those things which depend upon the co-operation of other nations. Therefore, although you assume a thing which nevertheless it is certain cannot be assumed, that all nations are conscientious, consequently perfectly ready to perform any duties of humanity towards each other, as they ought to be, and that they love and cherish each other, as they ought, so that the natural obligation which, when it is effective, produces a steadfast and permanent desire to promote the happiness of other nations and to do one's best that they may be happy, and look out that they may not become unhappy, would need no new force to be gained from a positive obligation; nevertheless treaties would not be superfluous, since not even under that condition would the affairs of nations be assured which depend upon the co-operation of other nations. For duties, in so far as by nature they are due from one nation to another, are not restricted to a certain nation as to an individual, nevertheless the powers of no nation are inexhaustible, so as to be sufficient for all in general which need its aid, and of course are not extended beyond that which is in its power. Therefore, since you do not know whether or not that which you seek can be performed for you by a certain nation without neglect of its duty towards itself or not, and if, under the treaty, it is in its power, in regard to which the decision is made by the nation itself, the performance is limited to you as to an individual, so that it is no longer in its power to perform the same thing for some other nation, to whom it is equally bound by nature, consequently this may properly be denied to one asking it; certainty in those things in a state which depend upon the co-operation of other nations, in that situation which we have assumed, could in no way be attained except through treaties. Therefore you should not try to persuade yourself that only in this is natural obligation to be strengthened by contract, because hatred of treachery and fear of present vengeance is more effective than a sense of shame and respect for the divine will, or love of virtue, although we may not deny in the present condition of nations, in which love of equity and virtue is not effective against the violence of the passions, which force many nations and their rulers towards their selfish interests, that the opprobrium of treachery and fear of present vengeance hold nations much more closely to their duty than a sense of shame and respect for the divine will. But from this is

§ 159.

§ 898, part 1, Jus Nat.

§ 353.

§ 161.

§ 162.

§ 160.

§ 157.

§ 156.

proved only a greater need for treaties in this condition of nations than in that which we have assumed and which is in harmony with natural law, so that then treaties have been introduced not only in accordance with the present condition of nations, but also of natural law, in so far as nations are regarded as they ought to be in accordance with this law, not in so far as they are driven in the opposite direction by depraved passions. It is undoubtedly to the interest of nations, that in regard to that which is to be expected from other nations they should definitely be assured, and this is the especial reason why treaties ought to be made and why the law of nature gives the right to make them, even if you should not assume that nations are wicked.

§ 391. *Of the adding of things which have not been determined by natural law*

If treaties are made concerning that which is due by nature, it is allowable to add things which have not been determined by natural law. For through treaties one nation transfers to another a certain right which it had not had before. Now it will depend on the will of the one transferring, how he may wish to transfer a certain right to another. Therefore nations, when making treaties, are able to agree by what condition they may wish to be bound to perform that concerning which the agreement is made. If, then, they make treaties concerning that which is due by nature, it is allowable to add things which have not been determined by the law of nature.

§§ 377, 157.

§ 11, part 3, Jus Nat.

Since the law of nature controls all human acts, it is not to be doubted that it also controls acts as regards things to be added in treaties made concerning that which by nature is already due by way of duty. For although those things have not been determined in general, nevertheless they can be defined from the particular circumstances which arise in a given instance for each contracting party, and because the law of nature binds every one to righteous conduct, they ought to be defined. Nevertheless, since that determination is a difficult one, nay more, is very often beyond the capacity of the contracting parties, and since, moreover, in that case the particular decision of each nation is to be followed, in making treaties the will of the contracting

§ 189, part 1, Phil. Pract. Univ.

parties controls, and one party cannot acquire from the other a greater right than such other has wished to transfer to it, nor is one party able to bind the other against its will to perform anything for itself. And hence it is evident why in treaties, just as in stipulations, many things are to be admitted which are not altogether in harmony with duty, and on this account they are not devoid of every taint of injustice, and they do not have that rectitude which reason prescribes. This indeed is to be attributed in part to human weakness, which undoubtedly is to be considered, but in part it is to be endured, in order that human affairs can have an end, and that the rights which are acquired may not be subject to never-ending disputes.

§ 157.

§ 382, part 3, Jus Nat.

§ 392. *What things can be added*

Since in treaties which are made concerning that which by nature is owed by way of duty it is allowable to add those things which have not been determined by the law of nature in general, all details of a transaction can be determined by the mutual consent of the contracting parties as shall seem best, or as is agreed, and consequently treaties can be restricted to the persons contracting, to a certain time, to certain acts, and conditions can be imposed under which something is to be performed concerning which there is an agreement, exceptions of certain cases, certain burdens, limiting clauses, penalties for non-performance of the treaty, warranties against the violation of the treaty, and any other things besides of this sort.

§ 391.

So if a treaty for purpose of commerce is entered into, this certainly can be made with the existing king, so that it may expire at his death. The same can be restricted to a certain number of years, as to ten years, and to certain things, such as grain, wool, sheep, or cattle. It can be agreed that certain goods may be imported, and for the goods which are imported, or even exported, a certain duty may be paid, or that imported goods may be exchanged for exports on agreed terms, that for certain imported goods no duty may be paid; that, if the one permitting the commerce should be involved in war, during the continuance of war that should cease, as for example, if it has been allowed in the treaty to buy up grain and horses. In like manner it can be agreed that the purchased goods may not be sold to another outside nation, and when this has occurred, that the treaty should be void immediately, or that a definite sum of money should be paid by way of penalty. Since treaties are made for the sake of the public advantage, which

§ 393, part 8, Jus Nat.

is to be determined by the purpose of the state, hence those things are to be determined by the contracting parties which are to be included in a treaty; in order nevertheless that utility may be kept within the limits of justice, consideration is to be given to the duties of nations towards each other. And hence it is quite plain, at least to the more keen-sighted, that the will of the contracting parties is controlled by the law of nature in conscience, and that things can be unjust which by virtue of the treaty are considered lawful, although the same thing also is already plain from the fact that natural liberty, upon which

§ 159, part 1, Jus Nat.

depends the free disposition of that which is your own, does not destroy natural obligation, although it must be left to the conscience of each one what he may wish to do, provided only he does not do

§ 157, part 1, Jus Nat.

that which is contrary to your perfect right. Not all things are right which are to be allowed to another by virtue of natural liberty, and to which want, weakness, or the harsh law, necessity, compels another

§ 156, part 1, Jus Nat.

party to consent, so that therefore perfect rights which are acquired are not rarely opposed to equity, and if you should observe the strict rule of natural law, which avails in conscience alone, they deserve nothing less than they do the name of right. Therefore, as is commonly said, no state is ruled without great wrong; so likewise it is rightly said that very often a perfect right is not acquired without injustice, especially among nations. Nor indeed is this so at variance with common sense as at first it would seem. For if any have regard for conscience in their dealings with others, in so far forsooth as they grant a place to the duties flowing from the universal love of human beings towards each other and of nations towards nations, they receive very little respect from those who consider it not necessary to excuse the passion for gain by a pretence of right. I add no more, lest something too harsh may seem to be said in regard to others who are considered good persons. Let those who wish to be so considered see whether they are so in very

§§ 967 and fol., part 5, Jus Nat.

truth. But from this also the reason is plain why it is that the more thoroughly skilled one is, especially in the laws, the more harm he

§ 971, part 5, Jus Nat.

may do in the administration of justice, unless he be a good man, and consequently a lover of truth.

§ 393. *Of treaties not to injure*

It is not necessary to enter into treaties not to injure; but if nevertheless this perverse idea has permeated the mind of any nation, that it
is allowable to injure foreign nations at will, treaties not to injure are
rightly made. For to a human being, consequently also to every nation,
belongs a perfect right not to allow that he should be injured, and if any
one should attempt to injure him, he has the right to compel him not
to do it. Therefore, since treaties are made with no other purpose than
to acquire a perfect right, since, moreover, perfect rights are acquired in
order that you may be able to compel one who is unwilling to give you
the right, it is not necessary indeed to enter into treaties not to injure.
Which was the first point.

But if indeed this perverse idea has penetrated the mind of any nation,
that it is allowable to injure foreign nations at will, since you cannot root
out that idea from its mind, and since it is not always wise to avenge
wrongs by force of arms, you can protect yourself in no other way than
by treaties which that nation has not the least doubt should be observed.
Therefore, since every one, consequently also every nation, ought to
avoid every loss to himself as far as he can, it is not to be doubted that
treaties not to injure are properly made, if this perverse idea has penetrated the mind of any nation, that it is allowable to injure foreign
nations at will. Which was the second point.

> Since a perfect right belongs to every nation not to allow that it
> should be injured by another nation, from a treaty not to injure a
> nation acquires no right, except that which it already has. Nevertheless
> on this account a treaty not to injure is not to be considered useless.
> For if indeed the contract obligation should be considered more bind-
> ing than the natural one, it renders the nation more secure against
> wrong than it would to use the right by force of arms to avenge the
> wrong, or to ward it off, if attempted. And although treaties of that
> sort may properly be called shameful, because the nation ought to
> be ashamed to injure another nation; nevertheless there is no sense
> of shame in a nation whose mind has become permeated with the
> perverse opinion that it is allowable to injure foreign nations at will,
> although it may believe that treaties are to be observed. Therefore as
> long as you are not able to root out that error from its mind, some

Margin notes:
§ 3.
§ 913, part 1, Jus Nat.
§ 914, part 1, Jus Nat.
§ 377.
§ 235, part 1, Phil. Pract. Univ.

§ 3.
§ 493, part 2, Jus Nat.

§§ 252, 253.

consideration indeed must be given to it—for example, that wrongs may be atoned for by a definite payment in accordance with the treaty that has been made, or by some other useful guarantee which can furnish a motive for observing a stipulation.

§ 394. *What treaties of friendship are*

Treaties of friendship are defined as those which are contracted for the performance of the duties of humanity, or not to do injury.

What is to be understood concerning those treaties is plain from those things which have been proved and more elaborately explained in what immediately precedes.

§ 395. *What equal treaties are*

Treaties are said to be equal, when the contracting parties promise to each other the same things or equivalent things. Therefore, since those things are the same which can be substituted one for the other in every particular, in equal treaties the promise of one party can be put in the place of the promise of the other, the value of equivalents of course having been observed, and the condition of those promising not having been changed, and consequently the condition of the parties entering into an equal treaty is the same, and the condition of neither party is rendered worse by it.

§ 181, Ontol.

A treaty is of that sort in which there is the provision that engaging in commerce should be free for each party, nor should a greater duty be paid by one than by the other, or that no duty should be paid by either party. Such also is the one in which there is an agreement that fortifications may not be built within certain limits, or that those already built should be razed. Here also include the one in which there is an agreement that one nation should not allow passage through its territories to the enemy of another, or should not give aid to an enemy.

§ 396. *Upon what the diversity of treaties depends*

Since there are different public matters in which one nation can help another, which is well enough known from experience, equal treaties which are made between nations vary in proportion to the variation in public matters.

Grotius divides equal treaties into equal treaties of peace and equal treaties of alliance. Among the former he includes those which are made concerning the return of prisoners, captured property, and for security, concerning which we shall have to speak below in their proper place. But in the latter he reckons those which relate to commerce, as that no duty should be paid, or no greater duty should be paid than at present, or up to a certain amount; those that apply to common warfare, as that like forces of cavalrymen should be furnished, or of footmen, or of ships, either for every war, or for a certain one, or against certain enemies, or against all indeed, but with allies excepted. Nevertheless he does not deny that the term treaty applies to other things also, as the examples cited a little while ago show. Since it is not our purpose to treat in detail of the several species of treaties, and since the plan of our undertaking orders us to stop with generalities, we have therefore not considered it necessary to divide the genera into their species, but it is sufficient for us to have indicated that the specific difference is to be sought from the object or the subject-matter of treaties.

De Jure Belli ac Pacis, lib. 2, c. 15, § 6.

Note, § 395.

§ 397. *When equal treaties are to be entered into*

If it shall be in the power of the nations entering into a treaty to perform equivalents for each other, by nature they ought to enter into an equal treaty, unless some special reason exists why they should depart from equality. For since no one is bound to give to another or do for another without compensation, if the other can do or give anything in return, nations also are not bound by nature to gratuitous performances for each other, if it shall be in their power to perform equivalents for each other. Because treaties are stipulations, and consequently cannot be made except for giving or doing, or for definite performances, if it shall be in the power of nations entering into a treaty to perform equivalents for each other, by nature they ought to enter into an equal treaty. Which was the first point.

§ 268, part 4, Jus Nat.

§ 3 h, and § 80, part 3, Jus Nat.

§ 369.

§ 797, part 3, Jus Nat.

But if indeed there shall be some special reason why they should depart from equality, it is necessary that one nation should be bound to another for a different cause, either by nature in the way of duty, or by a perfect right, to perform something, even if nothing should be performed by the other by way of compensation. Therefore it is plain that it is not opposed to natural equity, which orders that equality be observed in a treaty, as proved above, that in making such a treaty there should be a departure from equality. Which was the second point.

§ 240, part 1,
Phil. Pract.
Univ.

For example, let us suppose that a military alliance is made. Now if the nations shall have been equally powerful, so that they may furnish equivalent forces to each other in war, it is quite in accordance with natural equity that the treaties should be equal. But let us suppose that one nation at a time of the greatest scarcity of food had furnished grain to another nation at a fair price, although it did not have an excess of grain. If after this a military alliance should be entered into, since nations also are bound to each other to return a favour when there is an opportunity, it cannot be said to be unfair if the nation which has received the favour should bind itself to furnish a greater number of soldiers in the war than the nation which granted the favour. Another case is possible, namely, if one nation cancels the debt of another on this condition, that the soldiers which the first nation sends the other should support at its own expense, while the first nation should be free from this burden. Everyone knows that in onerous contracts equality is to be observed, so that one of the contracting parties should receive from the other just as much as he himself gives; nay more, as Grotius properly suggests, even in beneficial contracts a certain equality of fact is regarded according to the presumed intention, that no one, of course, should suffer loss from his beneficence—for example, that the borrower should be bound to repay the loss to the lender if the thing loaned shall have deteriorated or have been completely destroyed, that the loss should fall on the mutuary, if the thing given by way of *mutuum*[2] should have perished, or deteriorated before use, that the depositor should repay to the depositee expenses incurred in the preservation of the thing deposited, that the agent should suffer no

§ 41, part 4,
Jus Nat., and
§ 3 h.

§ 898, part 4,
Jus Nat.
De Jure Belli ac
Pacis, lib. 2,
c. 12, § 13.

§ 446, part 4,
Jus Nat.

§ 574, part 4,
Jus Nat.

2. *Mutuum* in Roman law is a contract for the loan of a commodity which will be consumed or used up by the borrower and is to be repaid in kind. *OED Online*, March 2016. Oxford University Press, http://www.oed.com/view/Entry/124398?red irectedFrom=mutuum.

disadvantage, and other things of this sort which are not to be passed over without violation of equity. Therefore, since nations by nature use no other law with each other than the natural law which belongs by nature to individuals, every one is bound to recognize that nations in their treaties ought to observe equality with the same conscientiousness which is observed in the contracts of private individuals, in so far as that is in their power. Nay more, if there is a departure from equality for some special reason, even if it were in their power to perform mutual equivalents, when one is pleased to look more deeply into the matter, equality itself is observed, because what is performed in excess by one party is compensated for by that which has already been performed beforehand by the other party, or is either performed in some other way at the present, or the hope is that it is to be performed in the future apart from the treaty.

§ 592, part 4, Jus Nat.

§ 682, part 4, Jus Nat.

§ 398. *What treaties are unequal*

Those treaties are unequal in which the same things or equivalents are not promised by each of the contracting parties. Hence it is evident that in unequal treaties one party promises something to the other and the same or what is equivalent is not promised in return to it, or it promises more than is promised to it in return. Therefore, moreover, it follows that the condition of one of the contracting parties is made worse by the treaty, or the conditions of those entering into an unequal treaty are not equal. Unequal treaties are divided into treaties unequal as regards the more worthy party and treaties unequal as regards the less worthy party. A treaty unequal as regards the more worthy party is one in which he who is the more powerful, or who can perform more, promises performances that are either gratuitous or greater. But a treaty unequal as regards the less worthy party is one in which he who is less powerful is either loaded too heavily by some promise, or promises performance either gratuitous, or greater, or such as burden him excessively.

So a treaty unequal as regards the more worthy party is one in which the more powerful ally promises troops to the other and there is no promise in return, or promises a greater number of troops, or promises troops to be supported at his own expense, while an equal number of troops is promised in return to him, to be supported at his own personal expense. Here likewise is included this case, if the more powerful grant commercial rights without payment of duty, while the less powerful stipulates a certain duty for itself. On the other hand, a treaty unequal as regards the less worthy party is one in which some-one is bound to promise that he will not make war on any nation without the consent of the other party, that he will consider as enemies and friends those whom the other party should wish, that he will not construct fortifications in some place, that he will not recruit soldiers in certain localities, and other things which are of this sort, mentioned by Grotius, or to be added to the same from other sources.

Loc. cit., § 7.

§ 399. *Of treaties with diminution of sovereignty, and without diminution of it*

Some treaties unequal as regards the less worthy party are made with diminution, others without diminution of sovereignty. Of course it can be agreed that some acts affecting the exercise of the sovereign power may be subjected to the right of the other contracting party, or that they may be dependent on his consent, or that a certain part of potential sovereignty may pass to the other party. In either case, indeed, it is evident that the sovereign power is diminished, since in either case certain acts affecting the exercise of sovereignty can be made of no effect by the other party, which certainly impairs the perfection of sovereignty, and especially in the latter case the people or the ruler of the people is bound to allow the other party to intrude upon its own government, a thing which by virtue of the sovereign power, which depends upon the natural liberty of nations, it is otherwise not bound to allow. Therefore it is plain that treaties unequal as regards the less worthy party can be made with diminution of sovereignty. Which was the first point.

§ 44, part 8, Jus Nat.

§ 269.

Nevertheless not all things concerning which an agreement is made in an unequal treaty and which burden excessively the less worthy party are necessarily acts affecting the exercise of sovereign power, if they merely bind the less worthy party to do certain things for the advantage of the more worthy, or not to do them; for example, if it is bound not to allow passage through its own territories to an army with which the other party is at war, or not to furnish it supplies, or not to attack the allies of the other party, or if walls are to be torn down, or a certain sum of

§ 398.

money paid. For that these and similar acts do not affect the exercise of civil sovereignty is plain from the very definition of it. Therefore it is evident that not all treaties unequal as regards the less worthy are made with diminution of sovereignty, but that there are even very many others which are made without diminution of it. Which was the second point.

§ 32, part 8, Jus Nat.

An example of a treaty with diminution of sovereignty is that the less worthy party may not make war upon any one without the consent or without the order of the more worthy party. But a treaty will be one without diminution of sovereignty, if the less worthy party without the consent of the more worthy party may not make war upon a particular nation. In the former case of course all exercise of any right affecting the civil sovereignty is subject to the right of another, by which certainly civil power is diminished; but in the latter case the less worthy party to a treaty simply binds itself not to do some particular thing, which otherwise by virtue of its sovereign power it could do, in which case civil power is impaired in no respect. Those do not consider this difference who think that every treaty unequal as regards the less worthy diminishes the sovereign power, or at least they include very many treaties of that sort in the category of those by which the sovereign power is diminished, although nevertheless they simply make some act of a sovereign nation either forbidden, or obligatory, which was otherwise left to its discretion, whether the burden shall have been temporary, as that a wall is to be torn down or that they must depart from certain localities, or permanent, as that they may not found a city or recruit soldiers in certain localities or sail to a certain location. That this confusion may be avoided I wish to submit definitions of unequal treaties with diminution of sovereignty and without it.

§ 400. *Definitions of those treaties*

A treaty unequal as regards the less worthy with diminution of sovereignty is one in which a certain right pertaining to civil sovereignty, or a certain potential part of the sovereignty, as far as regards its exercise or even its substance or ownership, is transferred to the more worthy party, or at least the right to all acts affecting the exercise of that right. But, on the other hand, an unequal treaty without diminution of sovereignty is

one in which the less worthy party binds itself simply to do some definite
thing, or not to do it, which otherwise by virtue of the supreme power,
or of natural liberty, or of the right belonging to a nation itself as such,
it was allowable not to do or to do.

The truth of these definitions is evident from those things which
have been said for the purpose of demonstrating the truth of the preceding proposition, and the examples which we have there given illus-
trate the same definitions. He who has mentally grasped those things
which have been fully explained concerning the civil sovereignty in
universal public law, in the eighth part of "The Law of Nature" and
concerning promises and stipulations in the third part of the same,
for him no ambiguity will remain as regards the present definitions.
From this it is evident that if the full civil sovereignty, or, if you prefer,
the entire civil sovereignty, should be transferred to another, it can be

§ 39, part 8,
Jus Nat.

transferred either as regards its exercise, or as regards the substance
itself. And the same is understood concerning any potential part.
Therefore nothing stands in the way of transferring to an ally even

§ 64, part 8,
Jus Nat.

by treaty a certain potential part of the sovereignty as far as regards its
substance, although that should not be presumed, since in stipulations
not the greater but the lesser burden should be presumed, lest any one
should be more heavily burdened than he has wished to be, and not
improperly may it be doubted whether a treaty of such a sort has ever
been entered upon, that a certain potential part of its sovereignty has
been transferred to the more worthy ally by the less worthy, so that
it could have disposed of this at its liking and could have alienated it
freely. But since in the law of nations one speaks not of that which
has been done or to-day is done, but what can be done, in order that
in the definition of a treaty with diminution of sovereignty there may
be a consideration of its transfer as regards substance or ownership, it
certainly is enough that this transfer is possible. The keener-sighted
also readily recognize that cases can arise in which the advantage of
the one holding urges alienation, if that is legally possible. But since

§ 65, part 8,
Jus Nat.

sovereignty divided into potential parts can be supreme for each separate part, the sum total of sovereignty is certainly diminished, if some
potential part is withdrawn from the sovereignty: a thing which is
so plain, that he who would dare to deny it may be held to concede
that the greater part of a whole divided into two quite unequal parts

is equal to the whole. The sum total of full sovereignty is certainly greater than the sum total of the less full. But here must be considered especially the difference as regards the transfer of a potential part of the sovereignty itself, or as regards the exercise of it only, or as regards the substance itself and as regards the transfer of a right to acts affecting the exercise of a right. For in the former case the right belongs to the more worthy ally at its pleasure to command the less worthy to act, and to order it not to act, and then it is said that the less worthy cannot act without the order of the more worthy; but in the latter case the right certainly belongs to the more worthy ally not to allow the less worthy to do anything without its knowledge and consent and without a request for its consent, or even not to allow it to act. But since there are several potential parts of a sovereignty into which the supreme power can be divided and which are called rights of sovereignty, so also several treaties can be made which are made with a diminution of sovereignty. Thus, for example, it can be provided in a treaty that not without the consent of the more worthy party can the less worthy make new laws, or change old ones and impose new taxes, or even that by order of the more worthy it is bound to pass a new law, or abrogate some old one, or impose a new tax. We suggest, by the way, since the intrinsic possibility is proved *a priori*, as is usually done by us and as science commands should be done, that there is no need of examples taken from history, nevertheless they still have this use, that it may be evident that the case is supposable, which we have recognized as possible, since it may be presumed that that can be done again, which has already been done once or several times. Therefore we do not disapprove of the bringing in of examples from the records of the ancients and more modern records, particularly in universal public law and the law of nature, although we do not consider it wise that examples already collected from other sources be heaped together, lest we may be more tedious than necessary and may not have the time to collect new examples.

§ 62, part 8, Jus Nat.

§ 207, part 8, Jus Nat.

§ 401. *Of the variety of rights from an unequal treaty with diminution of sovereignty*

Since in an unequal treaty with diminution of sovereignty a certain right pertaining to the exercise of sovereignty is transferred to the more worthy ally either as regards its exercise, or as regards its substance, or at least a certain right to single acts affecting the exercise of some sovereign right, and when the sovereignty, consequently also merely a certain right belonging to it, is transferred to another as far as regards its exercise, he has the same in usufruct, but if as regards substance, he holds the same by right of ownership, and when the right is granted to some one merely to single acts pertaining to the exercise of some sovereign right, so that indeed there is need of his consent to those acts, the right of sovereignty is limited; if in an unequal treaty a certain sovereign right is transferred as regards its exercise to the more worthy ally, he has the same in usufruct, if as regards the substance, he holds the same by right of ownership; but if it is a right merely to single acts affecting the exercise of some sovereign right, so that indeed the consent to them of the more worthy ally is required, that sovereign right is limited, and consequently in the first case those things are true which have been proved in universal public law concerning the usufruct of sovereignty, in the second case those things which have been proved concerning the ownership of sovereignty, in the third case those things which have been proved concerning the limitation of sovereignty.

Civil sovereignty is a combination of many rights, which taken together compose it, just as the parts taken together constitute the whole. If, therefore, the complete sovereignty or all those rights are transferred at the same time to some one, or at least one of them, the right of the one receiving is to be measured by the manner in which the one transferring that right has wished to transfer it to him. Therefore the things which have been proved of the civil sovereignty when transferred to another, those things also are certainly true of any sovereign right transferred to another. Those who argue that the diminution of sovereignty through an unequal treaty does not affect the sum total of sovereignty, do not turn their attention to the idea of the sum total of sovereignty, which consists in the exercise of sovereignty independently of the will of any other, so that no right over acts pertaining to it belongs to anybody, nor can any of these acts be made void by another.

§ 402. *The effect thereof*

Because in an unequal treaty with diminution of sovereignty either a certain sovereign right is transferred to the more worthy ally, or a certain

right to single acts affecting the exercise of some sovereign right, and
consequently in the former case the more worthy ally can direct the less
worthy as to those things which the less worthy ought to do, or not do, in
the latter case the consent of the more worthy ally is required to do those
things which ought to be done; in an unequal treaty with diminution of
power certain acts affecting the exercise of the civil sovereignty are made
dependent upon the will of the more worthy ally.

§ 400.

§ 851, Ontol.

And hence the reason is plain why those treaties are said to be
made with diminution of sovereignty, because of course the one ruling cannot command certain things which by virtue of the civil sovereignty can be commanded, or at least he cannot command them
at his pleasure. Therefore there is truth in the combination of words
by which those treaties are designated and distinguished from others,
nor is there need of departing from the received meaning of the word
diminution. For is not his right diminished, who can do less than he
could do by virtue of that right?

§ 403. *How far that is extended*

Since no one can acquire more right from another than the one transferring has desired to transfer to him, since, moreover, in an unequal treaty
with diminution of sovereignty there is transferred to the more worthy
ally either some sovereign right, or a right to single acts affecting the
exercise of that right, and through this certain acts affecting the exercise
of civil sovereignty are made dependent on the will of the more worthy
ally, consequently there is a diminution of the sum total of the sovereignty on the part of the less worthy ally; all remaining sovereign rights,
which the unequal treaty with diminution of sovereignty does not affect,
remain unimpaired, consequently the civil sovereignty remains entire as
regards all those things on the part of the less worthy ally, nor beyond
that which has been agreed can the more worthy ally infringe upon the
government of the other.

§ 382, part 3,
Jus Nat.

§ 400.

§ 402.

§ 44, part 8,
Jus Nat.

§ 269.

For example, if it shall have been agreed that the less worthy ally
may not make war upon any one without the order or consent of the
more worthy ally, nevertheless the less worthy ally can defend himself
against an aggressor, without consultation with the more worthy ally,
because the treaty is understood to be only concerning offensive, not

defensive war. Likewise, if it shall have been agreed that the less worthy must make war by order of the more worthy ally, he is not bound to make a war that is manifestly unjust, since a stipulation entered into for an illegal purpose is not valid, consequently the treaty can be understood to apply only to a just war. But if there has been an agreement only in regard to the right of war, the more worthy ally cannot claim any right for himself to acts pertaining to the exercise of any other sovereign right; for example, he cannot prevent the less worthy ally from imposing some new taxes upon his subjects, or from burdening them too heavily in another manner, even if the subjects implore his aid. Although, indeed, he may rule badly, the treaty nevertheless does not subject the government of the less worthy ally to the control of the more worthy, much less does it assign to him the right to coerce the other who is ruling badly.

§ 404. *When treaties unequal as regards the more worthy are just*

If any nation can perform more for another than the other can perform for it in return, treaties unequal as regards the more worthy are in perfect harmony with the law of nature. The same thing is understood, if any nation can perform something for another, even if nothing can be performed by the other in return. For every nation owes to every other nation that which it owes to itself, in so far as the other does not have that in its power, and it without neglect of its duty towards itself can perform this for the other. Therefore, since treaties are to be made,

§ 156.   concerning that which is due by nature, so that the performance may
§ 390.   be certain, and since we are not bound to perform anything for another without compensation if it can perform in return, if any nation is able
§ 268, part 8,   to perform more things for another than that nation can perform for it
Jus Nat.   in return, it ought by nature to perform more things. Therefore, since treaties are unequal as regards the more worthy, if the nation which is able to perform more things for another than that nation can perform for itself in return, promises more things than are promised in return to it; if any nation can perform more things for another than that nation
§ 398.   can perform for it in return, treaties unequal as regards the more worthy are in perfect harmony with the law of nature. Which was the first point.

In the same way it is shown that a treaty unequal as regards the more worthy nation is in perfect harmony with the law of nature, if any nation can perform something for another nation, for which this nation can perform nothing for it in return. Which was the second point.

The question here is concerning the equity of treaties unequal as regards the more worthy, when they are made with the sense of duty and nothing is done which can in conscience be criticized. Therefore the reasons are to be derived from the duties of nations towards each other and from the way in which they are owed, that no lack of righteousness may be observed. For although treaties are made for the sake of advantage and there must be consideration of that also in making them; nevertheless regard for internal right ought to take precedence and consideration of advantage follow it, which without a consideration of right puts a certain blemish on a treaty, and gives just cause of complaint to either party, or just censure of the one who looks less to the perfection of his own condition than he could and ought. Let us suppose that a treaty of alliance for war is contracted by a more powerful nation with one less powerful. That properly becomes unequal as regards the more worthy, because the powerful nation can furnish greater forces than the less powerful. Let us suppose further that the less powerful nation is fearful, not without reason, lest it may be overwhelmed by a very powerful neighbouring nation. An unequal treaty with another powerful nation is properly contracted, in order that forces may be furnished it in war, even if it itself can promise none in return. But to this treaty there is an advantage added as regards the more worthy nation, if it should be to its interest not to have a very powerful nation as neighbour, and therefore not to allow the less powerful nation to be oppressed by it. And hence it is plain in what way there must be regard for utility in making treaties, even if beforehand their equity should be considered, that nothing may be done except that which is quite in harmony with duty. If any one should object that a solicitous over-nicety of that sort will hardly be approved by nations and their rulers, we do not tarry over that objection, since in struggling solely for the truth we inquire what is right, and not what is pleasing to those who, since they measure all things from their personal advantage, destroy the common welfare of nations, and finally overturn the bulwarks of their own safety. For men and especially rulers of states are the creators of misery, in so far as they are not persistent in the duties which the law of nature imposes and which are means of happiness both for individuals and nations, and for the entire human race.

§ 405. *Of the equity of a treaty unequal as regards the less worthy nation*

If any duties of a nation towards itself, or even towards another, demand that certain things should be performed for it by another nation, for which it itself may perform nothing in return, although it could perform, or that more things should be performed, or that it itself should do this for another; an unequal treaty is not opposed to the law of nature, nor will it be unjust. For since duties are prescribed by the law of nature, which nations also are bound to observe, the law of nature therefore gives to us a right to those things, without which we are not able to satisfy those duties. If, then, the duties of a nation towards itself demand that certain things should be performed for it by another nation, for which it performs nothing in return, or even, that more things should be performed; to make such an agreement concerning those things is not opposed to the law of nature. Therefore, since stipulations of that sort are treaties unequal as regards the less worthy, treaties unequal as regards the less worthy are not opposed to the law of nature, consequently are not unjust, if any duties of a nation towards itself demand that certain things should be performed for it by another nation, for which it itself should perform nothing in return, even though it could do something, or that more things should be performed. Which was the first point.

In a way not dissimilar it is shown that a treaty unequal as regards the less worthy is not opposed to the law of nature, or is not unjust, if some duty towards another nation should demand that certain things should be performed for it gratuitously, or that at least more things should be performed, although the other nation could perform equivalents. Which was the second point.

Of course in either case there exists a special reason approved by the law of nature why equality should not be observed in a treaty, although it could be observed, and ought to be observed, if that reason

§ 225, part 1,
Phil. Pract.
Univ.

§ 3 h, and
§ 136, part 1,
Phil. Pract.
Univ.

§ 159, part 1,
Phil. Pract.
Univ.

§§ 369, 398.

§ 240, part 1,
Phil. Pract.
Univ.

failed. There is an example of the former case, if it should be peril-
ous for one nation that another nation have fortifications in a certain
place; since that nation ought to avoid loss for itself, as far as it can, it
properly stipulates in a treaty that the fortifications should be razed,
or that they should not be built in that place. There is an example of
the latter case, which we have given above, in that which is done to
indicate a grateful spirit.

§ 493, part 2,
Jus Nat.

Note, § 397.

§ 406. *Of the equity of an unequal punitive treaty*

If any injured nation agrees with another that by way of penalty the other
should perform some definite thing within the limits of justice, a treaty
unequal as regards the less worthy nation is allowable. For every nation
has the right to punish another which has injured it. Therefore, since a
penalty is exacted for the purpose of avoiding further injury, and may be
allowed against the offender only so far as is sufficient for avoiding it, if
any nation has been injured by another, it is allowable for it also to agree
with the other that by way of penalty the other should perform some
definite thing, but because a heavier penalty is illegal, when a lighter one
is adequate, this must be within the limits of justice. A treaty of that sort
is unequal as regards the less worthy nation. Therefore a treaty unequal
as regards the less worthy nation is allowable, by which an injured nation
agrees with another that by way of penalty the other should perform
some definite thing.

§ 272.

§ 1062, part 1,
Jus Nat.

§ 1059, part 1,
Jus Nat.

§ 1065, part 1,
Jus Nat.

§ 240, part 1,
Phil. Pract. Univ.

§ 400.

There is no reason why you should think that the present proposition is not adequately limited, when it is said of that which is to be
performed by way of penalty that there must be an agreement within
the limits of justice. For the right of punishing is of itself unlimited,
consequently limits cannot be prescribed for it except from the particular circumstances. From these indeed a decision ought to be reached
as to what is sufficient to guard against further injury, beyond which
the penalty may not be extended. Of course for exemplary punishment, in so far as it allows anything further, there is scarcely a place
among nations. And when there seems to be need of it, it can suffice
that a permanent, not a temporary, burden shall be imposed by way of
penalty, that remembrance of the penalty may persist, although even
among the temporary burdens there frequently may be those which

§ 1063, part 1,
Jus Nat.

§ 977, part 1,
Jus Nat.

§ 1059, part 1,
Jus Nat.

§ 1068, part 1,
Jus Nat.

serve the same end, for example, if the walls of a certain city are to be razed, or if a place on the sea is not to be fortified on the side which looks towards the sea.

§ 407. *What is required for the validity of treaties between nations*

Treaties between nations are valid, if there is no inherent defect in the method of agreement, without consideration of the equity or inequity of the treaty. For from treaties are acquired perfect rights which of course one nation transfers to another when it binds itself to perform those things in regard to which the agreement is made, and since those things are true of treaties which in the law of nature are proved of stipulations and promises, those things which invalidate stipulations and promises on account of a defect inherent in the method of agreement, also render treaties between nations invalid. It depends upon the will of one who transfers some right to another whether he wishes to transfer that right to another and in what manner or on what condition he wishes to do so, and whether the promisor has properly considered everything which he should consider, before he promises, is not to be determined by the promisee. Therefore treaties between nations are valid, if there be no inherent defect in the method of agreement, nor is there then a question of their equity or inequity, consequently this is not considered.

For the validity of a stipulation and its equity are to be properly distinguished from each other. The former is determined from the method of agreement, for which the mutual consent of the contracting parties adequately expressed is sufficient. For that which the promisor adequately declares, is considered as true against him, and the promisee by acceptance acquires the right which the promisor has desired to transfer to him, to whom even the abuse of his right must be allowed, when he arranges for the transfer of it. But the equity of a stipulation is determined from duties, both those to oneself and especially those to others. It cannot occur, especially in the state of nature in which nations live, that equity should be rigorously observed, although in a civil state provision can be made by positive laws that one may not depart too far from equity. Therefore, lest stipulations may be lacking

§ 377.
§ 380.
§ 374.

§§ 21, 12, part 3, Jus Nat.

§ 422, part 3, Jus Nat.

§ 428, part 3, Jus Nat.

§ 381, part 3, Jus Nat.

§ 169, part 2, Jus Nat.

in permanence, especially among nations, which recognize no superior, we must abide by the free disposition of their own property by owners, whether they dispose of it rightly or not, when the manner of disposal is considered in relation to their duties. And hence it is, as is commonly said, that the will of parties agreeing makes law. But you must not think that those things are therefore useless which have been proved concerning the equity of unequal treaties, because their validity does not depend upon equity. For parties promising are bound in conscience to pay attention to equity, that in agreeing concerning that which is to be performed they may not depart from it. The good man, since he is a lover of the truth, in an agreement also observes the truth, lest he himself may do something or lest he may allow something to be done by the other party through his fault, which is not in harmony with duty, and lest he may therefore be censured. The good man wishes to seem neither unjust nor dishonourable to others, and therefore he omits even those things which he could rightly do, if indeed it is to be feared that he may arouse in certain ones hostile criticism of his reputation. Nor ought the rulers of a state to be unacquainted with the duty of a good man, because when they act they most of all consider their own renown and that of their nation, which passes from them to it. Undoubtedly it would be desirable that rulers of a state from their early life should be trained in those principles, just as individual men ought to be trained. If, indeed, good men in making treaties should desire as far as possible to perform their duty in all respects, it would promote the happiness of nations. But this is more to be desired than hoped for.

§ 971, part 5, Jus Nat.

§ 968, part 5, Jus Nat.

§ 408. *Whether treaties can be rescinded on account of injury*

Since treaties between nations are valid, if no defect inheres in the method of agreement, without consideration of the equity or inequity of the treaties; no treaty between nations is rescinded on account of injury, if no defect inheres in the method of agreement.

§ 407.

For although no nation ought to injure another nation, and consequently would err if it should do this; nevertheless an injury, to which

§ 173.
§ 430, part 1, Jus Nat.

§ 117, part 3,
Jus Nat.

the other party has consented, is to be endured, nor is it considered
as such, because any one can waive his own right as far as he wishes,
even if he should prefer not to waive it, but is obliged to submit to
the occasion. Nor does the validity of the treaty affect the complaints
of the injured party and render them unjust, and the offending party
incurs the censure of the good and right minded. Not all the things
which among individual men and among nations must be done without punishment are also rightly done. Things unfair and unjust are to
be endured as the lesser evil, lest there should be an opportunity for
great wrongs as the greater evil, especially among nations, in order that
wars may be avoided, which are so deadly to the human race.

§ 409. *Of observing equity in making treaties*

§ 165.

§ 162.
§ 173.
§ 179.
§ 240, part 1,
Phil. Pract.
Univ., and
§ 157 h.

Nations ought to observe equity in making treaties. For by nature
nations are bound to perform the duties of humanity for each other,
and every nation ought to have a fixed and lasting desire to promote the
happiness of other nations and to do all it can to make them happy and
avoid making them unhappy, and no nation ought to injure another, nor
ought it to do anything which is opposed to the purpose of another state.
Therefore, since these things are in harmony with equity, nations ought
to observe equity in making treaties.

§ 142, part 1,
Phil. Pract.
Univ.

Note, § 408.

Although the law of nature does not formally prescribe duties to
nations, as proved by us above, who, pray, but a man of contradictory
spirit will doubt that it desires that treaties should be made in accordance with a sense of duty? Therefore, although treaties are valid, if
nothing is lacking in the form of agreement which the law of nature
requires for a valid stipulation, natural obligation as regards duties is
not therefore destroyed, which is immutable, since the duties come
from the law of nature. There are certain things tolerably just, which
are necessarily done without punishment, but nevertheless have no
excuse in conscience. They are pseudo-politicians who throw conscience out of court and banish it to the provinces to private individuals, substituting in its place, under the specious title of wisdom,
a desire for utility divorced from equity, and make cunning, which
imitates wisdom, a proper characteristic of nations also. They may
laugh at conscience and the sense of duty which we recommend to

the ruler of a state in all his acts, and to his ministers, and therefore
also to the nations whose right the rulers of a state exercise; it fully
suffices us, that the truth is with us, to which every good man ought
to be devoted, and without which no possible happiness exists for
nations regarded as individuals or in relation to each other. He who
has a mind hostile to the truth, is in no respect a lover of the human
race, and is deservedly considered its enemy. Undoubtedly it is to be
deplored, that truth and a sense of duty are an unknown, or at least
an unfamiliar name, among those who ought to rule the earth. Hence
those tears of the people.

§ 971, part 5,
Jus Nat.

§ 410. *What a tributary nation is*

A tributary nation is defined as one which is bound to pay a certain yearly
tribute to another. Since by nature all nations are free, consequently to
none belongs any certain perfect right against another, the right of exact-
ing tribute is to be acquired by making a treaty, and consequently one
nation is tributary to another by force of treaty.

§ 55, part 8,
Jus Nat.

§§ 134, 135,
part 1, Jus Nat.

§ 377.

§ 411. *Whether it has supreme sovereignty*

A nation does not lose supremacy of sovereignty by becoming tributary.
For if a certain nation becomes tributary, it is bound to pay a certain
yearly tribute to another nation, nor does any right belong to the other
by virtue of the treaty except to demand that tribute. But since, indeed,
civil sovereignty consists in the right to determine those things which
are required for promoting the public good in the state, by virtue of the
treaty by which it is made tributary the other nation has acquired no
right to acts affecting the exercise of sovereignty. Therefore, since he in
no way loses supremacy of sovereignty, who gives to another no right
over acts pertaining to the exercise of sovereignty, a nation does not lose
supremacy of sovereignty by becoming tributary.

§ 410.

§§ 35, 60, part 8,
Jus Nat.

§ 44, part 8,
Jus Nat.

By virtue of the treaty by which a certain nation is made tributary
the other nation, to whom tribute is to be paid, is not allowed to
interfere in its government, and if it should dare to do this, it does
it a wrong, nor is the tributary nation bound to allow that. It is one
thing to be debtor to another, quite a different thing to be his subject.

§ 256.

§ 269.

The former derives its origin from ownership, the latter from sovereignty. But ownership and sovereignty are two distinct rights, the one of which is not dependent upon the other.

§ 412. *Of personal and real treaties*

§ 369.
§ 801, part 3,
Jus Nat.

Treaties are either personal or real. For treaties are stipulations. Therefore, since stipulations are either personal or real, treaties also are either personal or real.

It makes a great deal of difference whether a treaty is only personal or in fact real, since the effects of the two treaties are different.

§ 413. *What things are true of those treaties, and how long the personal treaty lasts*

§ 412.
§ 369.
§ 801, part 3,
Jus Nat.

Since treaties are personal or real, since, moreover, both are stipulations, those things which are true of personal and real stipulations are likewise true of personal and real treaties, and therefore by virtue of a personal treaty only the persons are bound who have entered into it, and if one of them dies, the treaty is terminated.

§ 803, part 3,
Jus Nat.

Personal treaties are understood to have been entered into under this condition, that they should terminate, when one of the contracting parties dies, so that the contracting parties are bound to each other for their lifetime.

§ 414. *Of determining the end of a personal treaty*

§ 413.

Since a personal treaty is terminated if one of the contracting parties dies, and since this is just as true if he should die, or if for any reason he should cease to reign, a personal treaty comes to an end if one of the contracting parties for any reason ceases to reign, and the treaty does not extend to his successors.

§ 284, part 8,
Jus Nat., and
§ 369 h.

The making of a treaty is a royal act. Therefore it is understood to have been made with the king as king. For the king is a corporate person, which is determined by the sovereignty which he holds. Therefore when he ceases to have sovereignty, the king as king dies.

Therefore the condition under which a personal treaty is understood to have been made can also be thus explained, namely, that it should stand until one of the contracting parties ceases to rule; a thing which happens not only by a natural death, but also by a moral death, by which the moral person[3] dies which has been combined with the natural person, if, for example, he should deliver the sovereignty to his son, or to his successor, if he should be deposed. It is self-evident that such a condition can also be expressed in a treaty, in which case it is self-evident that the treaty is ended as soon as one of the contracting parties ceases to reign. So if troops have been promised in war, they need not be sent to a successor, nor is he bound to send troops to the other party.

§ 70, part 1, and § 2, part 5, Jus Nat.

§ 415. *Of the names of the contracting parties added to a treaty for the purpose of proof*

Personal treaties are personal stipulations. But stipulations are not personal, if in the stipulations mention should be made of the persons who enter into it, simply that it may be plain by whom the stipulation has been made; a treaty is not a personal one, if the names of the contracting parties shall have been added simply to prove by whom the treaty has been made.

§ 413.

§ 802, part 3, Jus Nat.

Not from the person of the contracting parties, but from the intention with which they enter into a treaty, whether adequately expressed in words or to be gathered from the subject-matter of the agreement, is it to be determined whether a treaty is personal or real. Therefore, since it is important to know whether a treaty is personal or real, and since, especially in a doubtful case, controversies can arise between nations concerning it, we must carefully explain whence the intention of the contracting parties is made evident.

§ 416. *Of a treaty made with a free people*

If a treaty should be made with a free people, it is real, and continues to exist, although the form of the state is changed, unless the treaty has

---

3. A moral person, as distinct from a physical person, is either an individual or a group of individuals as defined by legal or moral status or office.

been made for a purpose peculiar to a democratic state. For a people remains the same, even if on the death of some men others should succeed to their places. Therefore, even if all shall have died who were living at that time when the treaty was made, nevertheless a treaty made with a free people is understood to have been made with these who are now living, and consequently does not terminate on the death of those who have made it. Therefore, since a treaty is not personal but real, which is not limited to the persons of the contracting parties, but in which there is consideration not so much of the persons as of the things to be performed; a treaty made with a free people is real. Which was the first point.

§ 495, part 8, Jus Nat.

§ 801, part 3, Jus Nat.

But a people remains the same even though the form of the state is changed. Therefore, since a treaty made with a free people would continue to exist as long as the people remains the same, as proved in point 1, a treaty made with a free people continues to exist, although the form of the state is changed. Which was the second point.

§ 505, part 8, Jus Nat.

But if indeed there should have been an agreement in a treaty, which is proper only to a democratic state, it is self-evident that if the democratic state is destroyed, the treaty also is destroyed, and consequently by changing the form of the state, the treaty is terminated. Which was the third point.

Hence it is plain how necessary it is to know how long a people remains the same, since it is of the greatest importance that real stipulations be distinguished from personal ones. Nor indeed is there reason why you should object, that if sovereignty is transferred either to a king or to nobles, this is just the same as if he who has ruled to this time should cease to rule, since the physical individual in whom the corporate person exists would be changed and consequently the ruling power would as it were die; for from king to people in the present case the consequence does not follow. For although sovereignty is originally a thing belonging to the people, nevertheless it does not cease to belong to the people, for the reason that it is exercised by king or nobles. Nor would it cause difficulty if the sovereignty should have been patrimonial, consequently the king should possess it by right of ownership. For since sovereignty returns to the people, if there be no one who could claim right to it, the sovereignty transferred to the king

Note, § 414.

§ 34, part 8, Jus Nat.

§ 42, part 8, Jus Nat.
§ 40, part 8, Jus Nat.

with power of alienation nevertheless does not cease to belong to the people, who, as long as it remains a people, cannot be conceived of without sovereignty. The power to alienate the sovereignty and consequently to change the form of the state certainly does not bring it about that the sovereignty does not belong to the people just because it is exercised through another, or others, as a king, or nobles. For the power of alienation implies nothing else than that the one exercising the sovereignty can at his pleasure designate the one who should exercise it after him.

§ 304, part 8, Jus Nat.

§ 31, part 8, Jus Nat.

§ 417. *Of a treaty made in perpetuity, for a certain time, and with successors*

If a treaty be made in perpetuity, or for a certain time, or with the one with whom the agreement is made and his successors, the treaty is not personal but real. For in each case it is readily understood that the treaty is not restricted to the person of those contracting it, so that one only desires to be bound for himself to another to the performance of that which has been agreed, but rather consideration is given to the things to be performed. Since, therefore, the treaty is then real, not personal if a treaty be made in perpetuity, or for a certain time, or with the one with whom the agreement is made and his successors, the treaty is not personal but real.

§ 801, part 3, Jus Nat., and § 413 h.

If a treaty is extended to successors, the intention of the contracting parties is declared in express words, that it is not to be restricted to the person of the makers. The same also would be plainly indicated, if the treaty be said to have been made in perpetuity or for a certain time, both because it is certain that the contracting parties will not be forever among the living, and also because it is uncertain how long a time they are going to live.

§ 418. *Of treaties made for the good of the kingdom*

If it should have been added to a treaty, that it has been made for the good of the kingdom, the treaty is real. For if it should be said that a treaty has been made for the good of the kingdom, it undoubtedly is plainly indicated that in making the treaty, particular consideration is

paid to that which is to be performed. Therefore, since a stipulation of
that sort, consequently also a treaty, is real, if it should have been added
to a treaty that it has been made for the good of the kingdom, the treaty
is real.

§ 369.
§ 801, part 3,
Jus Nat.

For every ruler of a state ought to promote the public good or that
of his state, for which he ought not only to look out in the present, but
also to provide in the future, as far as he is able. If then one entering
into a treaty should say expressly that he does this for the good of the
kingdom, it is understood that he does not restrict it to the days of his
life, nay rather that the intention which he has, he adequately declares
in these very words, namely, that the treaty should be permanent, so
that then this would be just as if he were to say that the treaty ought
to be made in perpetuity, or with himself and his successors; and if he
should have said either of these things, the treaty is real.

§§ 85, 995,
part 8, Jus Nat.

§ 417.

§ 419. *Of a treaty made for the permanent benefit of the state*

If a treaty is made for the permanent benefit of the state, it is real. For if
a treaty is made for the permanent benefit of the state, it is plain enough
that in it particular attention is paid to that concerning which there is
a promise of performance in the treaty, and not to the persons entering
into the treaty. Therefore it is plain, as before, that the treaty is real.

§ 418.

I speak designedly of a treaty made for the permanent benefit of
the state, for there are also temporary benefits, or those lasting only
for a short time, which are properly also restricted to the person of
the contracting parties, if indeed it should appear that the benefit has
some bearing upon their person. But such things are to be decided
from particular circumstances. But if it should be plain that the benefit to the state on account of which the treaty is made remains the
same, even if the present king should die, and another should succeed him, there is no good reason why the treaty should be restricted
to the person of the contracting parties, and consequently should be
considered as personal. Thus treaties of commerce are real, since in
them the permanent benefit of the state is considered, nor are they to
be considered as personal, unless they should be expressly restricted to
the life or person of the contracting parties.

§ 420. *What is to be presumed in a doubtful case*

In a doubtful case a treaty is presumed to be personal as regards its unfavourable, real as regards its favourable characteristics. For in stipulations, consequently also in treaties, those characteristics are favourable which look towards the common benefit and provide equally for either party, but those are unfavourable, which burden one party too much or burden one more than the other. If in the latter case the treaty should be extended to successors, and should not be restricted to the life of the contracting parties, in a case where it is doubtful whether the treaty be personal or real, one would have to fear lest the burden of one party be increased much beyond the intention of the contracting parties, which certainly would be opposed to justice. But in the former case no such thing is to be dreaded, nay more, there would be no injury to either of the contracting parties, even if the stipulation should not be restricted to their person. Therefore, in a doubtful case treaties as regards unfavourable characteristics are presumed to be personal, but as regards favourable ones, real.

§ 369.

§ 495, part 6, Jus Nat.

§ 496, part 6, Jus Nat.

The case is doubtful if there are arguments on both sides of the controversy, as well for a personal treaty as for a real one, so that then we may properly hesitate as to what is to be presumed. Therefore nothing remains but to make a conjecture from the subject-matter itself of the treaty in regard to the intention of the contracting parties, who are supposed to have desired to provide in the best way for their nation, and to burden it in no way beyond what is necessary. Therefore they are supposed to have desired that which is in harmony with this intention. Although, for example, a doubt may arise whether a treaty of commerce entered into unqualifiedly, or with no limitation added which renders the condition of either party unequal to that of the other, is personal or real, since commerce certainly is to be considered among things favourable, the treaty is to be considered as real, so that when the king is dead who has made the stipulation, the treaty still exists. But the situation is different if the conditions of the treaty are very harsh, as if one party on account of the concession of commercial rights cannot make war without the order of the party granting, or is bound absolutely to make war by its order. Here the question is usually asked whether war is to be included among the things unfavourable, or whether it can be included among the favourable also. Those who include all war without qualification among things unfavourable are undoubtedly hasty in their judgement. For since without doubt it may be for the advantage of the public to defend the state against enemies, a defensive war is undoubtedly favourable. And for this reason, treaties entered into to furnish troops to each other in a defensive war, in a doubtful case are presumed real rather than personal. But the situation is different if troops should be promised for offensive war, since no one willingly would involve himself in the quarrel of another. There are those indeed who argue that in a doubtful case every treaty without exception is to be considered as real, lest perchance it may happen that treaties are not observed which were to be observed. This reasoning is properly followed in those treaties which are favourable. But it certainly seems too hard to be compelled to perform a duty which burdens excessively, to the performance of which we have not been bound. Therefore it has seemed wiser to us in the present position to prefer the doctrine of Grotius. If the presumption should be erroneous, by the admission of the former doctrine we must perform that which we are not bound to perform, and which burdens us excessively in the performance; while if the latter doctrine is approved, one party does not perform that which it had been bound to perform, but the other party is equally relieved from its performance. But it is to be carefully observed, that the favourable and the unfavourable in distinguishing the real from the personal stipulation are not admitted, except in a doubtful case, such as is presumed in the present proposition, where, on account of the fact that there are arguments on both sides, the mind is at a loss what to decide. For when the reasons to be deduced from the words by the cause or nature of the transaction fail, one must undoubtedly take refuge in the extrinsic facts, so that something certain may be determined, since otherwise there would be no end to the strife among the disputants, who nevertheless are bound to admit that which a proper interpretation suggests. For you should not suppose that Grotius and we are so silly as to believe that the unfavourable and the favourable have any effect in stipulations. We willingly agree that right arises only from declared intention, but when that is not plainly expressed, the question is what ought to be presumed concerning it. But no one will criticize if that should be presumed which is in perfect accord with equity, which is to be determined by a sense of duty. But if the logic of probabilities had been

De Jure Belli ac Pacis, lib. 2, c. 16, § 26.

§ 466, part 6, Jus Nat.

Note, § 415.

reduced to a formal art, the presumptions would be more evident, since in them nothing would be assumed except that which had been adequately proved in logic as sufficient for presumption.

§ 421. *Whether a treaty is to be considered real, until the contrary be proved*

Since in a doubtful case a treaty is presumed personal as regards unfavourable characteristics, real as regards its favourable ones, not every § 420. treaty is to be considered as real, until the contrary should be proved from its words, or from the subject-matter of the agreement.

For if like arguments are brought in on either side, that is, both for the personal treaty and for the real, there certainly is no reason why the treaty should be presumed to be real rather than personal, and therefore, as we have said, we must turn to the extrinsic reasons which may deter- Note, § 420. mine the presumption concerning the will of the contracting parties. Of course there ought to be a reason why one of two contesting parties must yield to the other, but since in a doubtful case the arguments brought in on either side are equal, by definition, there is no reason why those ought to prevail which are brought in for the real treaty. But the decision must be otherwise, if stronger arguments have been brought in on either side, for then the stronger presumption prevails; nor then is there doubt as to what is to be understood from the words or from the subject-matter of the agreement. But here the question is not who ought to settle a controversy between nations, since they have no arbiter other than that which is in harmony with the truth. Who will compel contesting parties to admit that a treaty is to be considered as real, until the contrary may be proved from the words or subject-matter of the agreement? Nations as well as private individuals who are ruled by the impulse of their passions, and not by reason, do not admit many things which nevertheless on that account do not cease to be true.

§ 422. *Of the treaty existing with a king driven from his kingdom*

If a treaty should have been made for the defence of a king and the royal family, it continues to exist, even if the king or his successor should have been driven from the kingdom. For if the king be driven from his kingdom, he loses possession of it, but not his right to it, which cannot be taken away without his consent. Therefore, since, by definition, the treaty has been entered into for his defence and that of the royal family, and belongs consequently to his successor also, and since, then, there is an especial need of defence, if the king, with whom a treaty has been made, or his successor, should have been driven from the kingdom; it is not to be doubted that his right is to be protected by his ally, and therefore the treaty continues to exist.

§ 336, part 2, Jus Nat.

It is undoubtedly just the same, whether the king should be driven from his kingdom by rebellious subjects or by an invader. The allied king none the less properly defends him against his subjects than against an invader and, since treaties are to be observed, he ought to defend him.

§ 390 h, and § 789, part 3, Jus Nat.

§ 423. *A treaty entered into by a king affects the nation*

If the king enters into a treaty, it is understood to have been made with the nation. For a treaty is entered into for the sake of the public good by virtue of the sovereignty, consequently the stipulation of a treaty is included among royal acts. Therefore since the king has the right of the people, or of the nation, and since he represents his nation when he has business with others, of course for the benefit of the state, if he enters into a treaty, the nation must be said to have made it through the king, and therefore it is understood to have been made with the nation itself.

§§ 368, 369. § 284, part 8, Jus Nat.

§ 39.

Supreme sovereignty is originally with the people, and it remains the property of the people, even if it shall have been transferred completely to the ruler of the state as regards substance. Therefore all treaties are made by the right of the people, or of the nation, and the king is understood to have made the treaty, not in his own name, but in the name of his nation. But if he agrees concerning his own private affairs, that is not a treaty, but is a private stipulation.

§ 34, part 8, Jus Nat.

Note, § 416.

§ 369 h, and § 284, part 8, Jus Nat.

§ 424. *Of the obligation and rights from a treaty*

Since a treaty entered into by a king is understood to have been made with the nation itself, it binds the nation also and, at least if it is not

§ 423.

§ 414.

personal, it binds also his successors, and the right acquired from the treaty passes over to these also.

Even personal treaties, although they may be restricted to the person of the king, bind the nation itself, and a right based on it is sought from the nation. For when they are said to be restricted to the person of the king, that must be understood as meaning that the treaty should continue, or last, as long as the king shall live, or remain king. But this by no means prevents it from being understood that the treaty was entered into with the nation itself: for it is a temporary treaty. In fact it is just the same, whether the time should be determined by a certain number of years or by an event certain to happen, although the day is uncertain on which it is to happen.

§ 413.

§ 425. *Of a treaty confirmed by an oath*

Since an oath does not impose a new obligation to perform anything for the person to whom the oath is addressed, but the one taking the oath simply asserts that he will not change the intention to perform, which he has, consequently since the oath changes nothing in the treaty itself, and since real treaties bind successors also and the nation, and a right is sought from them based on the treaty, a treaty confirmed by an oath binds also successors and the nation, and the right sought from it passes over to them, although the oath does not extend beyond the person of the one taking it, and therefore with respect to the nation and his successor the treaty is to be considered as one not established by an oath.

§ 903, part 3, Jus Nat.

§ 902, part 3, Jus Nat.

§ 424.

Treaties are confirmed by an oath only for the sake of greater security, because it is considered more disgraceful to break a pledge sanctioned by an oath than one not so sanctioned, and it is presumed that the one taking the oath will not so readily fail to observe the treaty, on account of fear of divine vengeance. But this security fails when the king who took the oath is dead, since he cannot swear by the soul of the people, nor of his successor, unless he have an express mandate; consequently such an oath cannot be said to have been made tacitly, nor can it be presumed.

§§ 941, 942, part 3, Jus Nat.

§ 426. *If a people should become free by the death of a king*

§ 423.

If a king enters into a treaty, it is understood to have been made with the nation; therefore, if a people becomes free by the death of a king, the treaty continues. The same is also true if the nation should become free by the expulsion or deposition of a king, or should choose another king,

§ 421.

unless the treaty has been entered into for the purpose of defending the king's person.

Note, § 414.

§ 55, part 8,
Jus Nat.

§ 156, part 1,
Jus Nat.

§ 39.

See what we have noted above concerning a natural and moral death. Nor does it make any difference whether he shall have been expelled or deposed for an unjust cause. Since every nation is free, one must abide by its decision expressed in a treaty. The king is not to be recognized as an ally by an allied state, except in so far as he represents his nation and it exercises its right through him; if then it exercises its right either through itself, or through another, no consideration is given to a king expelled or deposed by the treaty, if the treaty does not affect his person; for he has not acquired from the treaty the right of intruding himself upon the interests of the nation not included in the treaty.

§ 427. *Whether a later treaty confirmed by an oath is to be preferred to an earlier one not confirmed by an oath*

§ 902, part 3,
Jus Nat.

§ 386.

A later treaty is not preferred to an earlier one because it has been confirmed by an oath. For an oath establishes no other obligation than that which arises from the treaty. Therefore, since in case of conflict an earlier treaty should be preferred to a later, the same is still to be preferred, even if the later shall have been confirmed by an oath, consequently the later cannot be preferred to the earlier because it has been confirmed by an oath.

§ 386.

§ 425.

The right of preference belongs to the earlier treaty. Therefore it cannot be taken from it by an oath. If a case of conflict should arise only when he is dead who has given the oath, it is already plain from the preceding argument that the treaty confirmed by an oath is changed into one not confirmed by an oath, and then the question is utterly useless, as to whether the treaty is to be preferred, because it is confirmed by an oath.

§ 428. *Whether an oath makes valid a treaty contrary to an earlier one*

A later treaty contrary to an earlier one does not therefore become valid because it is confirmed by an oath. For later treaties contrary to earlier ones are invalid by the law of nature, consequently its provisions are in no respect obligatory. Therefore, since a non-obligatory provision would not become obligatory through an oath, a later treaty contrary to an earlier one does not become valid because it is confirmed by an oath.

§ 383.

§ 904, part 3, Jus Nat.

That oath is certainly illegal, and in the present instance the more so for this reason, because it is offered with the intention of breaking faith pledged to the former ally. The right acquired from the treaty for the former ally, which cannot be taken away from him without his consent, cannot be taken away by an oath. Otherwise an ally could free himself from any obligation at will; how absurd that would be, is evident. Since stipulations must be observed, an oath added to a later stipulation which is contrary to an earlier one is made for an illegal object, and therefore does not bind one to performance and is itself illegal.

§ 915, part 3, Jus Nat.

§ 758, part 3, Jus Nat.

§ 674, part 3, Jus Nat.

§ 789, part 3, Jus Nat.

§ 429. *Of treaties entered into with a nation devoted to another religion*

§ 913, part 3, Jus Nat.

It is allowable to enter into a treaty with a nation devoted to any other religion. For treaties are made for the sake of the public good, consequently nations bind themselves to each other through them, that the one may contribute to the other that which tends to its preservation and perfection. Therefore, since every nation is bound by nature to contribute what it can to the preservation and perfection of the other in that in which it is not self-sufficient, so that it may attain the purpose of its state, since, moreover, a perfect obligation to perform such things arises from a treaty and a perfect right to performances of that sort; in making treaties no consideration is to be given to the religion to which the nations are devoted. Therefore it is allowable to enter into a treaty with any nation, to whatever religion indeed it may have been devoted.

§ 914, part 3, Jus Nat.

§ 369.

§§ 9, 23, part 8, Jus Nat., and § 174 h.

§ 166.

§ 175.

§ 377.

That treaties may be legal, it is necessary that they should be made for that which is not illegal. If then there is no defect inherent in

the subject-matter nor in the form in which it is made, the treaty is
valid by nature. Other mistakes on the part of the contracting parties, which belong to their understanding, or defects which invalidate
their intention, since they do not affect a stipulation, have no influence also upon the contract, but it is just as if they were non-existent.
Since religion is a certain method of worshipping God, it has nothing
in common with a stipulation, nor does a stipulation depend upon it
in any way. It is simply to the interest of the contracting parties that
stipulations should be observed. The obligation to observe stipulations arises from the promises which the stipulations contain, not
from a method of worshipping God, nor from religion. But if you
assume that a certain nation is persuaded by force of its religion that
it may break its pledged word, if the one with whom the contract was
made is a stranger to its religion, then religion does not vitiate a treaty,
so that it cannot legally be made, but the treaty certainly will be useless or not safeguarded, inasmuch as the one who has contracted with
the nation is not sure that the pledged word may not be broken. Nor
is there any reason why you, in company with Grotius, should make
a distinction between treaties which are made for non-offensive purposes, as treaties of commerce, and those which are made for offensive purposes, as they are hastily called, or those which cannot be
fulfilled, except with a loss to others, such as are treaties of war, no
less the defensive than the offensive, although Grotius restricts them
to the latter. For since wars are legal, treaties for war are also legal.
And it makes no difference whether one by whom unavoidable losses
are inflicted in war is devoted to one religion or another, whether he
is Turk or Christian. The effect of war depends upon force of arms,
not upon religion. It is generally asked whether one may enter into
a treaty with a nation hostile to true religion. But since any nation
may think its religion is true, and may consider any other nation, not
devoted to the same religion, as hostile to true religion, it has seemed
wiser to us to prove that it is allowable to enter into a treaty with a
nation devoted to any other religion. Hence, indeed, it naturally follows, if any nation has the true religion, it can enter into any treaty
otherwise legal with any other nation hostile to the true religion. So
nothing prevents a nation devoted to the sacred rites of the Christians
from entering into a treaty with a nation Mohammedan in religion,

§ 393, part 3,
Jus Nat.

§ 788, part 3,
Jus Nat.

as, for example, with Turks or Persians. There are those who restrict the question to idolatrous nations or to blasphemers of the true God. But from the proof of the present proposition it is evident that there is no need of this restriction. On account of a difference in religion no nation can deny to another the duties of humanity, which nations owe to each other, and therefore it is not forbidden by nature that one nation should bind itself absolutely to another by treaty to perform those duties, even if the other should be devoted to another religion. No nation can compel another to embrace its religion. Therefore in matters which concern one in its dealings with another, there is no question as to what their religion may be, nor must there be conformity in religion before there can be conformity in any other thing. But if particular circumstances prevent a treaty from being made with a nation of another religion, it is not diversity in religion, but that which is added to this from some other source which invalidates it. Here belongs that which Grotius warns must be avoided, in the passage cited, that excessive commingling may not cause contamination to the weak, that is, to those not sufficiently instructed in religion, or endowed with less force of intellect. For not to guard against this, is opposed to the duty of the ruler of a state, who ought to take care that his subjects may worship God in the way certainly in which He wishes to be worshipped, and that they may be pious. But when the question is asked whether it is allowable to contract treaties with profane nations, strangers to our religion, it must be understood that the question is one concerning their intrinsic morality, lest forsooth anything may be done in making the treaties that is contrary to natural obligation which is to be observed in the court of conscience, but there is no question concerning that which can be done without impairing the natural liberty of any nation, upon which also depends the free disposition of one's own right. Those who do not consider this, bring forward many arguments which are not to the point. But no one can doubt that this ought to be considered, because all willingly grant that treaties entered into with a profane nation are valid, and are therefore to be observed; for I suppose there will be scarcely any one to contend that they are not to be observed. Hence Grotius in the passage cited says rightly that here there is no innate defect.

§ 263.

§ 259.

De Jure Belli ac Pacis, loc. cit., c. 15, § 11.

§ 458, part 8, Jus Nat.

§ 457, part 8, Jus Nat.

§§ 156, 157, part 1, Jus Nat.

De Jure Belli ac Pacis, loc. cit.

§ 430. *Of a treaty violated by one party*

§ 827, part 3,
Jus Nat.

§ 374.

If one party shall have violated a treaty, the other party also can withdraw from it. This is true concerning stipulations. Therefore, since those things which have been proved concerning stipulations are true also of treaties, if one party shall have violated a treaty, the other party also can withdraw from it.

§ 826, part 3,
Jus Nat.

§ 827, part 3,
Jus Nat.

We do not say that one party ought to withdraw, but that it is allowed to withdraw, if that shall have seemed best. Those who deny that one can withdraw, and argue that the other at all events ought to be compelled to fulfil his promise, do not consider that every obligation which arises from an agreement containing mutual promises is a conditional obligation. See what we have noted elsewhere. But that there may be no misgiving, these points ought to be a little more carefully examined. Let us suppose, for the sake of greater clearness, that the contracting parties are Sempronius and Gracchus. Sempronius has promised that he will perform what he has agreed to, if Gracchus will perform what he has promised in return, who in turn has promised that he on his part will perform what he has agreed to, if Sempronius will stand by his promises. Therefore as long as Sempronius has the intention of standing by his promises, Gracchus cannot free himself from his obligation, consequently he has the right to compel Gracchus to fulfil his promise, if he should be unwilling to stand by it. Nevertheless, since he is not bound to stand by his promises if Gracchus should not stand by his, he has the right to withdraw from his stipulation, consequently the right not to perform for him what he has promised. And so Sempronius is free to use whichever right he chooses, whether he prefers to compel Gracchus by force to perform his promise, or to withdraw from the stipulation. The right to compel Gracchus to perform his promise, Sempronius acquired from the stipulation, as it arises from the obligation of Gracchus, who bound himself to it by promising, and from which he cannot free himself at will; but he has the right to withdraw from a conditional promise, so that he is not bound to perform if Gracchus should not perform on his side what he has promised in return. Therefore the stipulation, even when Sempronius withdraws from it, is not dissolved by the dissent of Gracchus alone, which he has disclosed by his act, nor even by his words, but by the added dissent of Sempronius also, who decides it to be wiser to dissolve the stipulation than to seek to compel Gracchus to fulfil it: and since this cannot be done between nations otherwise than by force, frequently it can be advantageous to withdraw from the stipulation, or abrogate it, rather than to make war upon the one who first withdraws. Reciprocal promises, one of which assumes the other by way of condition, are to be distinguished from a simple promise on condition, to which either party agrees. Therefore the one does not operate in the same way as the other, as is plain enough from those things which have just been said. But certainly it is one thing, if the stipulation should cease to operate, as happens in the latter case, when the condition ceases to exist; but another thing, if the stipulation exists indeed, and one is free, either to withdraw from it, or to compel the other to observe it. Any one can give up his right gained by a stipulation. But when he does this, the thing promised ceases to exist so far as he is concerned, because it assumed the fulfilment of the stipulation on the part of the other by way of condition. For then only the condition is in fact realized, when one consents to the other not observing his promise; which consent he certainly manifests clearly when he puts aside the intention of compelling the other to perform that which he has promised, and declares it plainly by withdrawing from the stipulation.

§ 117, part 3, Jus Nat.

§ 431. *If an ally has broken faith in another treaty*

If one ally has been unwilling to do what he ought to do in accordance with one treaty, the other ally is not allowed to withdraw from another treaty. For if one ally has been unwilling to perform what he ought to perform, he has broken faith. But if any one has broken faith in regard to one stipulation, consequently in regard to one treaty, you are not allowed to withdraw from another stipulation. Therefore, if one ally has been unwilling to do what he ought to do in accordance with one treaty, the other ally is not allowed to withdraw from another treaty.

§ 790, part 3, Jus Nat.

§ 369.

§ 834, part 3, Jus Nat.

Two or more treaties can be entered into between two nations at different times, the earlier of which is continuous with the later. It also can happen that, when the earlier treaty is temporary, the later one may be made when the time determined for the earlier has already

elapsed. If one ally should be unwilling to observe either of these treaties, or has not observed the earlier treaty, the other party has no right
to withdraw from the treaty not violated. The obligation which has
arisen from one treaty does not depend upon the obligation which
has arisen from the other, in the way that reciprocal obligations in
the same treaty depend upon each other. It is undoubtedly plain that
those things which have been explained quite fully concerning the

Note, § 430.   same treaty cannot be applied to two different treaties.

§ 432. *Of the violation in one particular of a treaty entered into in regard to various matters*

Since, if one ally has been unwilling to do what he ought to do in accordance with one treaty, the other ally is not allowed to withdraw from

§ 431.   another treaty, since, moreover, treaties which have been entered into
concerning different matters, the one of which depends in no way upon
the other, are to be considered as different treaties entered into at the
same time; if one ally violates a treaty as regards one term, the other ally
has no right for this reason to withdraw from the entire treaty, but is
either allowed not to perform that which on his part has been promised
in return, or the other ally can be compelled to perform, if performance
is still possible, or, when this cannot be done, to repair the loss caused
by violation of the treaty, and consequently can be compelled to do this
under threat of withdrawal from the entire treaty, and since the violator of the treaty agrees to this, if, ignoring the threat, he is unwilling to
perform that which he owes by virtue of the treaty, or to repair the loss
caused, when he does not wish to satisfy the injured party and ignores

§ 840, part 3,   the threat, it is allowable to withdraw from the stipulation or treaty.
Jus Nat.

Whatever things are here said are in harmony with the principles
of the law of nature. For damages caused are to be repaired, and he

§ 580, part 2,   who has a perfect right, such as is acquired by a treaty, can compel the
Jus Nat.
§ 377.   other party to perform what he ought, if he should be unwilling to
§ 235, part 1,   perform of his own accord. But this right of itself is readily understood
Phil. Pract.
Univ.   to be limitless. Therefore, since there is need of some means for con-
§ 677, part 1,   trolling the will of the violator, it cannot be doubted that a threat of
Jus Nat.   withdrawing from the entire treaty is allowable. But this threat would

have no effect, unless also it should be allowable to withdraw from the entire treaty, if it were ignored. If from this a treacherous ally suffers a greater loss, he should charge it to himself, because he has been willing to incur a greater loss by causing a smaller loss to another, which he could and ought to have avoided. In the law of nature there is one harmony, one agreement, provided only you have closely examined the interrelation of natural law, which we have made plain in our work. But here we do not repeat more of the observations which we have already proved elsewhere in regard to stipulations.

§ 889, Psych. Emp.

§ 890, Psych. Emp.
§ 493, part 2, Jus Nat.
§§ 829 and fol., part 3, Jus Nat.

§ 433. *Of a treaty tacitly renewed*

When its time is expired a treaty is not understood to be tacitly renewed, except by acts which are open to no other interpretation. For no stipulation is renewed without mutual consent, but if nevertheless that should be done by one of the contracting parties to an expired temporary stipulation, which could be done only by virtue of it, with the knowledge and consent of the other, that is, such acts are committed as admit of no other interpretation than that there is an agreement to the renewal of the stipulation, it is understood that the stipulation is tacitly renewed. Therefore, since the same is true of treaties, when its time is expired a treaty is not understood to be tacitly renewed, except by acts which are open to no other interpretation.

§ 819, part 3, Jus Nat.

§ 820, part 3, Jus Nat.

§ 374.

When the time is expired for which a treaty has been made, the treaty comes to an end. Neither party therefore is any longer bound to the other to perform anything which has been agreed upon in the treaty. If then the obligation is to be continued, it is necessary that each should declare his consent. But the intention can be declared both by express words and by such acts as are open to no other interpretation than that the treaty has been renewed. But even without my saying it, it is evidently wiser that the treaty should be renewed at the proper time, in order that difficulties in regard to interpretation may not arise, causing controversies not easily settled. I say at the proper time, for it can happen that one ally may make a treaty contrary to that made with another before all the time has elapsed, although it will not be effective until the time has elapsed, in which case nothing

§ 844, part 3, Jus Nat.

§ 382, part 3, Jus Nat.

is done contrary to the earlier treaty; or it can happen that he makes a treaty contrary to the other immediately on the termination of that treaty, and this he may do, without any delay, as soon as the first one is ended.

§ 434. *Whether any one can be compelled to enter into a treaty*

§ 369.

§ 788, part 3, Jus Nat.

§ 386, part 3, Jus Nat.

No one can be compelled to enter into a treaty. For treaties are stipulations, consequently they contain promises. Therefore, since it is dependent upon your will whether you wish to promise anything to another or not, consequently no one can be compelled to promise; no one then can be compelled or driven by force to enter into a treaty.

§ 858, part 1, Jus Nat.

§ 859, part 1, Jus Nat.

It is contrary to the natural liberty of sovereign powers that they should be compelled by force to enter into a treaty; since this is a perfect right, the one that dares to infringe upon it, does the other a wrong. So a power commits a wrong, which brings war upon a nation to make it enter into a treaty of commerce with itself.

§ 435. *Or to renew it*

§ 826, part 3, Jus Nat.

§ 434.

Since a treaty is renewed, if each ally agrees to a continuation of the treaty, consequently if a treaty is renewed, it is as though such a treaty as before existed should be made a second time, and since no one can be compelled to make a treaty, no one can be compelled to renew a treaty.

In fact there seems to be no need of proving these things, which are sufficiently plain of themselves; nevertheless it is not to be considered superfluous, since it is plain that there are not lacking examples of nations which have considered it not against their consciences to compel other nations by force of arms to make and continue treaties. And that this can easily happen is not doubtful, since nothing happens more frequently than that very powerful nations measure their right by their advantage, considering that that is legal which is useful to themselves, provided only they can obtain it by their own might. Therefore in the law of nations the truths opposed to this most deadly error are to be proved, and not to be passed over in silence.

§ 436. *Of a treaty cancelled in respect of the people*

If a people perishes, the treaty disappears. For treaties, although they may be stipulated with the king, are understood nevertheless to have been made with the people, by virtue of the sovereign power, and bind the nation no less than the king, who promises by virtue of the right of the people. If, therefore, the people should perish, and consequently the sovereignty, which is the right of the whole over individuals, should disappear, and therefore he who had been ruler of the state and represented the people should cease to be ruler of the state and could no longer represent the people, no one longer exists who can be bound to another contracting party. Therefore the treaty cannot exist, but disappears.

§ 423.

§ 369.

§ 42, part 8, Jus Nat.

§ 32, part 8, Jus Nat.

§ 39.

§ 42, part 8, Jus Nat.

Since nations are considered in the law of nations as individual persons, treaties also as regards the nations are assimilated to personal agreements, being restricted to the nation by whose right they have been made, as are personal treaties to the person of the king. Therefore, just as at the death of the king a personal treaty is extinguished, so also any treaty is extinguished when the people perishes. The performances, concerning which the agreement in a treaty is made, are personal which become impossible of performance when the person bound ceases to be. When indeed a people perishes, we have proved in universal public law.

§ 2.

§ 369 h, and § 34, part 8, Jus Nat.

§ 413.

§§ 497 and fol., part 8, Jus Nat.

§ 437. *Whether a nation bound by a treaty can put itself under tutelage by a law contrary to the treaty*

One nation cannot put itself under the tutelage of another nation, unless it leaves unimpaired the treaty made with some other nation. For let us suppose that it puts itself under tutelage to another on the condition that the treaty is abrogated; since it is bound by that treaty to its ally, it frees itself from its own obligation, and takes away the right gained by the treaty without the consent of the other party. Either of which is absurd.

§ 424.

§ 674, part 3, and § 336, part 2, Jus Nat.

As long certainly as the nation remains the same, it is bound to observe its treaty. Therefore it must not violate it, if it puts itself under the tutelage of another nation. Since it cannot put itself under the tutelage of another nation, except by a stipulation by virtue of the

sovereign power which belongs to it, consequently by a treaty entered
into with that nation under whose tutelage it puts itself, that would
be done upon a condition with which the treaty cannot co-exist,
therefore it would contract a treaty contrary to the former treaty, a
thing which it is not allowed to do. A treaty for protection, so far as
regards those things which are repugnant to the former treaty, would
be unjust and invalid by nature.

§ 381.

§ 383.

§ 438. Whether an ally is not bound to observe a stipulation because the other ally puts itself under the tutelage of a third nation

If one of two allied nations puts itself under the tutelage of some third
nation, the other ally remains bound to it. For let us suppose as before,
that the other ally does not wish to be bound further to it. It will be
plain, as before, that it wishes to free itself from its own obligation and
to take away the right of the other without its consent; either of which is
absurd, as is before evident.

§ 437.

§ cited.

We have seen before that a nation which puts itself under the tutelage of another is bound to observe its treaty. Therefore, since a stipulation, consequently a treaty, may not be dissolved by the contracting
parties except by mutual dissent, and not by the dissent of one, a
nation also, which although allied to another nation puts itself under
tutelage, is still bound to observe the treaty.

Note, § 437.

§ 369.

§§ 839, 840,
part 3, Jus Nat.

§ 439. Whether a treaty continues if an allied nation puts itself under the tutelage of a third nation

If one of two allied nations puts itself under the tutelage of some third
nation, the treaty continues. For in spite of this, allied nations remain
bound to each other. Therefore, since a treaty continues as long as the
obligation incurred by it is not destroyed, so that it is to be observed by
either of the contracting parties, a treaty also continues if one of two
allied nations puts itself under the tutelage of some third nation.

§§ 437, 438.

§ 340, part 3,
Jus Nat.

If a treaty ought to continue, when one of two allied nations puts
itself under the tutelage of a third, it certainly is necessary that allied

nations should remain bound to each other as they had been before. Therefore, in order that this may be plain, we certainly had to prove that it was not allowable for a nation putting itself under tutelage to withdraw from a treaty, nor was this allowable for the other nation. But that neither party is allowed to withdraw from a treaty, without the consent of the other, is more than manifest from this, that no one can free himself from his own obligation, nor can he take away the right of another without his consent. If then an allied nation should agree that the other nation may put itself under the tutelage of a third nation, then the treaty is dissolved by mutual dissent, which certainly is an allowable thing to do.

§ 839, part 3, Jus Nat.

§ 440. Of the right of a nation to make treaties, which has put itself under the tutelage of another

If any nation puts itself under the tutelage of some other nation, any treaty can be entered into with another nation which is not contrary to the treaty of protection, unless in it the right of making treaties shall have been restricted or taken away. For since a nation can put itself under the tutelage of another nation, either with diminution or without diminution of sovereignty, and the rights of each are to be measured by the stipulation of subjection, or, what is just the same, by the treaty of protection; if nothing shall have been said in this treaty concerning the right of making treaties, any treaty can be entered into with another nation. Which was the first point.

§ 81.
§ 80.
§ 369.

Since, nevertheless, a later treaty cannot be contrary to an earlier one, neither can a nation which has put itself under the tutelage of some other nation enter into a treaty with a third nation which is contrary to the treaty of protection. Which was the second point.

§ 381.

But since it is repugnant to a treaty of protection, if a nation which has put itself under the tutelage of another nation should make a treaty, if it should have been expressly agreed that it would not make it, or if it should extend the right to make treaties beyond the condition by which that has been limited or restricted, which is self-evident, and since a nation which has put itself under the tutelage of another cannot enter into a treaty with a third nation, which is contrary to the treaty of protection, as proved in point 2; a nation which has put itself under the

protection of some other nation can enter into any other treaty whatsoever with another nation not contrary to the treaty of protection, unless
the right of making treaties should have been restricted or taken away.
Which was the third point.

A treaty which is entered into with a third nation by a nation
which has put itself under the tutelage of another nation, can be
repugnant to the treaty of protection in a double fashion, either
because that concerning which there has been an agreement in it is
repugnant to that concerning which there has been an agreement in
the treaty of protection, or to that which is in every treaty of protection as such, or because the making of a treaty has been prohibited in
the treaty of protection, either absolutely or to a certain extent. So if
there has been an agreement in the treaty of protection that certain
goods should be sold to the allied nation alone, it is not allowable
to enter into a treaty of commerce with another nation, by which
permission is given to it to purchase goods of that sort. For it belongs
to every treaty of protection as such, that the nation which is under
tutelage may not do anything which can in any way whatsoever be
injurious to its protector. So it cannot allow passage through its territories to its enemy with an army, nor furnish it with grain, arms,
and horses. But if it shall have been plainly specified in the treaty of
protection that without its order or without its consent the nation
cannot make a treaty with another nation, or that it may not make
a treaty of commerce with some particular nation, it is allowable to
do neither.

§ 441. *The obligation arising from the promise of a third party that the agreements in a treaty are to be observed*

If some third party promises to each ally, or to either of them, that agreements will be observed, he ought to omit nothing which can secure the
performance. For if some third party promises to each ally, or to either of
them, that agreements are to be observed, he promises an act of another,
as is self-evident. But he, indeed, who promises the act of another ought
to omit nothing which can aid in obtaining the performance. Therefore, if some third party promises to each ally, or to either of them, that

§ 602, part 3,
Jus Nat.

agreements are to be observed, he ought to omit nothing which can secure performance.

The third party is accustomed to interpose his assurance that provision may be made for the security of the allies, if by chance each or one of them may fear lest the treaty be violated.

§ 442. *What a guaranty or a guarantee is*

This promise made to each ally, or to either of them, that agreements are to be observed, is usually called a guaranty or by others a guarantee, in the native vernacular *die Gewähr* [the warrant]. And he who promises that the agreements are to be observed by others is called a guarantor.

The jurists use this barbarous word. It is a certain kind of surety which can be called the surety of a treaty. And then guarantors are to be called sureties for a treaty. But since the truth of things is our especial anxiety and desire, we are not particular as to words. And that truth may be more easily understood by those who are interested in examining it, we care little for the barbarism of the jurists, although it is bolder than the barbarism of the scholastics.

§ 443. *The obligation of the guarantor*

Since a guaranty is a promise made to each ally, or to either of them, that agreements will be observed, and a guarantor ought to omit nothing which can secure the performance, a guarantor is bound to give assistance against him who does not wish to observe agreements, if there is need thereof.

§ 442.

§ 441.

Of course an ally has acquired from the treaty a perfect right, consequently the right to compel another by force to observe the agreements in a treaty. If then one does not wish to observe them, the other can compel him by force to observe them. If he alone is not sufficient for himself, he needs the aid of another. Therefore, since a guarantor ought to omit none of those things which he can do, that the agreement may be observed, he is bound to give assistance. And therefore it is plainly evident that a guarantor is not bound to give assistance, if the one to whom the promise was made does not need the same. Of

§ 377.

§ 225, part 1, Phil. Pract. Univ.

§§ 440, 441.

§§ 353, 354.

course the guarantee of itself is considered a duty of humanity which one nation does not owe another by nature, except when the latter needs a stranger's aid. Therefore a guarantor is understood not to have bound himself to give assistance, except when the promisee may have need of it, since he has bound himself absolutely to that which was due by nature.

§ 156.
§ 363, part 3, Jus Nat.

§ 444. *When he is bound to give aid*

§ 443.

Although a guarantor is bound to give assistance against him who does not wish to observe agreements, if there is need thereof, he is not bound to give assistance unless it is asked for.

Of course the one for whom the guaranty has been assured is bound to decide whether he has need of the assistance of the guarantor. But in regard to that the latter cannot be certain unless the former should ask his aid.

§ 445. *Of the tacit treaty contained in a guaranty*

Since a guarantor is bound to give assistance, if there is need thereof, against him who does not wish to observe agreements, consequently, since it is understood that he has agreed with the other to furnish aid if he should have need thereof for acquiring that which is due from his ally, and since agreements of that sort are stipulations, and therefore are treaties between nations; a guaranty contains a tacit treaty to give assistance against him who does not wish to perform agreements in a treaty, on the condition that there shall be need of his aid.

§ 443.

§ 788, part 3, Jus Nat.
§ 369.

The guarantor interposes his assurance that provision may be made for the security of the allies, consequently he agrees to those things which are needed to furnish security. Therefore, since security cannot be furnished otherwise than by giving assistance against the one unwilling to observe agreements, if the other alone cannot compel him to do this, that certainly is understood to have been agreed upon, when the guaranty was made. If then you shall have included it among treaties, that ought not to seem in any way incongruous. It is, of course, a treaty added to a treaty for the purpose of strengthening

Note, § 441.

it. For it is intended that because of fear of the guarantor, he should be compelled to observe agreements, who otherwise would be unwilling to observe them because of the weakness of the other ally. For a greater force is more feared than a less one.

§ 446. *Guaranty general and special*

A guaranty is said to be general, if it is made in regard to all things agreed upon in a treaty: but that is called special which is made in regard only to some or to one or two agreements. Since a guaranty is a promise, since, moreover, it depends upon the will of the promissor as to what he may wish to promise, and because a guaranty is made for the sake of greater assurance that agreements will be performed, and it depends upon the will of him for whom it is made, as to what he may desire it to be made for him, a guaranty, both general and special, can be added to a treaty, as seems wise to him for whose sake it is made.

§ 442.

§ 386, part 3, Jus Nat.

§ 442.

In proving the reality of definitions of moral entities it is not sufficient to show the physical possibility, but it is needful that the moral possibility also should be put in a clear light. Therefore, although the former is evident of itself, nevertheless in spite of this the latter is still to be worked out.

§ 447. *A guaranteed treaty*

A stipulation or treaty is said to be guaranteed, to which a guaranty either general or special is added.

If good faith were assured, guaranteed treaties would be useless; but the fact that good faith is nowhere assured makes a place for them. Since he is treacherous who does not observe his promises, consequently breaks faith, on account of fear of treachery a guaranty is exacted, which is a remedy against treachery, because it produces fear of the power of the guarantor, which joined with the power of the one for whose sake the guaranty is made, is superior to the power of the one against whom it is made or whose good faith is suspected. And hence those things are easily understood which statecraft requires concerning a guaranty.

§ 268, part 3, Jus Nat.

§ 759, part 3, Jus Nat.

§ 448. *Whether the consent of the one against whom the guaranty is made is required in order to make a guaranty*

To make a guaranty, the consent of the one against whom the guaranty is made is not required. For a guaranty contains a treaty which is entered into between the one who makes it and the one for whom it is made, to give assistance against him who does not wish to observe agreements in a treaty. Therefore, since a treaty, as a stipulation, is made by the mutual consent of those entering into it, to make a guaranty, the consent of the one against whom the guaranty is made is not required.

§ 443.

§ 788, part 3, Jus Nat.

He who seeks a guaranty does it for the purpose of defending himself against him whose good faith he doubts. Therefore it is to the interest of the one asking it that it should be made, not of the one against whom it is made, although it also may happen to be to the interest of the one making it, in order that agreements in treaties should be observed. If then these should agree to a guaranty for the sake of their own advantage, since by virtue of the liberty belonging to them they can enter into treaties at their pleasure, and since, when they agree to a guaranty, they do nothing which is contrary to the right of him against whom it is made, they are not bound to require his consent also.

§ 442.

§ 449. *Whether it can be made without his knowledge or consent*

Since to make a guaranty the consent of the one against whom it is made is not required, a guaranty can be made without the knowledge and consent of the one against whom it is made.

§ 448.

But although a guaranty can be made without the knowledge of one against whom it is made, nevertheless it is necessary that, when it has been obtained by the one seeking it, this should come to his knowledge, on account of the effect which it ought to have. Nevertheless it is not an absolute necessity. For let us suppose that a case arises in which it may seem wise to the guarantor that he against whom the guarantee is made should not be aware of that fact, since the treaty to give assistance which it contains is valid, even if no one is aware of it except the contracting parties; certainly nothing prevents the guaranty from remaining secret.

§ 443.

§ 450. *Whether there can be several guarantors of the same treaty*

Several can make a guaranty at the same time concerning the same thing, or there can be several guarantors of the same treaty. For a guaranty is made for the purpose of assurance that the agreements in a treaty will be §442. observed, and guarantors are bound to give assistance against him who §443. refuses to observe agreements. Therefore, since there is greater assurance that agreements are to be observed, if several make a guaranty at the same time, several can make a guaranty of the same treaty.

The fear of the power of the guarantors ought to be a remedy against treachery, and the greater this is, the greater is the assurance that agreements will be observed. Therefore several guarantors are   Note, § 447. properly added to the same treaty, as either the ally may be very powerful whose good faith the other party doubts, or as his good faith may have been otherwise under suspicion, or that concerning which an agreement has been made may have been such that the fear is not vain that the ally could easily be induced to break faith. Since every one should properly care for his own security, as far as possible, because he ought to avoid every loss to himself, as far as he can; he also, who needs the same, properly desires a guaranty for himself   §493, part 3, to be made by many when circumstances suggest it. The necessary   Jus Nat. means are to be selected for accomplishing this purpose, as is the part of wisdom, to which we are also bound by nature, that there can be no censure of the righteousness of the act. Certainly it were best that   §678, Psych. the good faith of rulers of a state be unimpaired, for whom, since they   Emp. represent entire nations, nothing is more unbecoming than to break   §254, part 1, faith. And every suspicion of treachery ought to be as far as possible   Jus Nat. from Christians. Nevertheless experience teaches that often among Christian nations good faith is less observed than among others, even the most barbarous.

§ 451. *Of a guaranty given by allied nations for each other*

If several enter into a treaty, the whole number can give a guaranty for the individuals. For since a guaranty contains a stipulation to give assistance against him who does not observe his agreements, if several should enter into a treaty, and the whole number give a guaranty for the individuals,   §445.

all agree with each other, that if one does not observe the agreements, the others in a body will seek to compel him by force to observe them, or, if by the violation of the treaty it should be no longer possible to perform that concerning which an agreement has been made, to repair the loss occasioned. Therefore, since a guaranty is made for the purpose of assurance that the agreements will be observed, and by this stipulation all look out for the security of the individuals, it is not to be doubted that they can so agree. If, therefore, several should enter into a treaty, the whole number can give a guaranty for the individuals.

§ 442.

Let us suppose that Gaius, Seius, Sempronius, and Gracchus enter into a certain treaty at the same time; it is undoubtedly just the same as if each one of them should enter into a treaty with the three separately, as Gaius with Seius, with Sempronius, and with Gracchus. But if then the whole number should give a guaranty to the individuals, it is just as if Sempronius and Gracchus should give a guaranty to Gaius and Seius, Seius and Gracchus a guaranty to Gaius and Sempronius, Seius and Sempronius to Gaius and Gracchus. Therefore if Gaius should break faith, Sempronius and Gracchus are bound to give assistance to Seius against Gaius, and so Gaius will find the other allies of the treaty opposed to himself. And the same thing in the same manner is understood of Seius, and of Sempronius and Gracchus, if they break faith. Therefore the guaranty has the same effect then as it has if it is given by others who are not allies in the treaty. But it makes no difference whether the agreement is in regard to the same thing, or whether the individuals agree in regard to a thing peculiar to themselves, provided they do not agree concerning a common matter, so that by virtue of the alliance contracted the whole is bound to the individuals, and the individuals to the whole; in which case the guaranty to the individuals by the whole would be useless.

§ 452. *Of an outside guarantor uniting with the allied guarantors*

§ 450.

§ 451.

Since there can be several guarantors of the same treaty, so many of course as it shall have been expedient and possible to obtain, and if several enter into a treaty, the whole number can give a guaranty to the individuals; to a treaty, for the guaranty of which the allies mutually bind themselves, the guaranty of others also, whom the treaty does not affect, can be added; nay more, nothing prevents an outsider from giving a guaranty to one only of the allies in a case affecting himself.

The more guarantors any one has, the better his security is provided for. Therefore it is to be left to the decision of every one how he may adequately provide for his security; every one must also be allowed, even if he has allied guarantors, to try to get the guaranty of others besides. But if a guaranty of an entire treaty is to be given by an outsider, it is self-evident that it is to be obtained by all who have entered into the treaty, since otherwise the guarantor would not be bound to the individuals.

§ 156, part 1, Jus Nat.

§ 453. *Of a guaranty inserted in a treaty for the sake of any one*

If those entering into a treaty, in addition to the other things for the sake of which the treaty is made, also agree with each other to give a guaranty to some other one who does not contract the treaty with them, the individuals are bound, not only to this one, but also to all entering into the treaty, to give assistance against him who is not willing to observe his agreements. For since it is self-evident that a guaranty is not inserted in a treaty except on the petition of the one whose interest it is that it be performed, it is also evident, when individuals agree with each other that it should be inserted, that it is in fact given by them for the one whose interest it was that it should be inserted. Therefore, since a guarantor is bound to give assistance against him who is unwilling to observe his agreements to the one for whom the guaranty has been made, the individuals also who have made the treaty are bound to him in whose favour the guaranty has been inserted in the treaty, to give aid against him who is unwilling to observe his agreements. Which was the first point.

§ 443.

But since those who have entered into a treaty give promises to each other, that they are willing to perform those things concerning which they have agreed with each other, consequently the individuals bind themselves in this respect to the whole body; and since by hypothesis besides other things they agree with each other in regard to giving a

§ 363, part 3, Jus Nat.

guaranty for some other one who does not contract with them; the individuals also are bound to all entering into the treaty to give assistance against him who is unwilling to observe his agreements. Which was the second point.

Let us suppose that Gaius, Seius, Sempronius, and Gracchus enter into a treaty in regard to something, and they also agree in it to give a guaranty for Florens against Celsus. Gaius, Seius, and Sempronius are bound to Florens to give assistance to him if Celsus should refuse to perform for him what he has agreed to perform, then too all are bound to each other to give assistance with their united powers; this latter obligation has this effect, that one can exact from another the fulfilment of a promise, and may give assistance after counselling together.

§ 454. *Of assistance promised against him who dares violate the right of another*

If any one promises assistance to another against the one who attempts to take from him some right, he makes a treaty with him. He does not properly speaking give a guaranty. For that agreement contains a promise, consequently it is a stipulation. Therefore, when the same thing is done by sovereign powers, it is a treaty. Which was the first point.

But since a guaranty properly speaking is given in regard to that concerning which there is an agreement in some treaty, a thing which is not assumed in the hypothesis of the present proposition, the promise made in the present case is not a guaranty. Which was the second point.

If that concerning which an agreement is made in a treaty is not observed, the right of the ally is violated. Therefore a guaranty is given against him who can violate the right of any one. Consequently the inconsistency of speech easily arises, that we define as a guaranty also a promise made to give assistance against him who attempts to take some right from some other one, or to violate it in some way. Nay more, if a guaranty should not be restricted to agreements in a treaty, but should be extended generally to any rights which can be violated by another, and, where the fear of its violation is not vain, so that it may not be given in vain, that promise can be called a guaranty in its proper signification. We have decided in the law of nations to retain

§ 788, part 3, Jus Nat.
§ 369.

§ 442.

§ 349, Log.

the more familiar meaning, by which a guaranty is said to be made in regard to treaties. Therefore we have not considered the meaning of the guaranty which the plaintiff in Saxon law is bound to give, at the request of the defendant, both in civil and criminal cases, and in regard to which see Carpzovius, in "Processus Juris in Foro Saxonico,"[4] tit. 9, art. 4, where in § 4 he reviews the double effect of the guaranty; namely, (1) that the plaintiff may not later amend the petition, (2) that it defends the accused in court if he is afterwards brought to trial by another in regard to the same case.

§ 455. *Surety of a nation for another nation*

If any nation promises that it will perform what another nation ought to perform, if the nation itself cannot or is unwilling to perform, it becomes surety for it. This is plain from the definition of suretyship.

§ 782, part 4, Jus Nat.

This act also is by some usually included under guaranty. But since it is nothing else than suretyship, no reason indeed compels us to prefer to describe it by a barbarous word rather than to call it by its own proper name. There is the further consideration that if this promise should be included along with guaranty, two quite different acts would in fact be described by the same name, in regard to which the same things are not true, so that they would have to be held different species of guaranty which would have to be defined in more general terms. But it is useless to descend into these ambiguities, since in regard to suretyships of nations we must maintain the same things which we have proved concerning this subject elsewhere in the law of nature, nor is there need of repeating them under another name. Expromission can also have a place among nations, which, since it gives security to a creditor just as does suretyship and guaranty understood in the stricter sense, could, in the same way as suretyship, be classed under guaranty. Of course, in general, guaranty would have to be defined as the act through which one nation makes another sure of the performance of that which is due to it from some third nation; a

§ 783, part 4, Jus Nat.

§ 865, part 4, Jus Nat.

4. See Benedict Carpzov, *Processus juris in foro Saxonico* (Leipzig, 1708), tit. IX, art. 4, §4, p. 233.

thing which it is plain can be done both by suretyship and by expromission, as well as by a promise to give assistance against him who refuses to satisfy his obligation.

§ 456. *Whether by a guaranty a right can be taken away from a third person*

Any right which a third party has cannot be taken from him by a guaranty. For no one can take away any one's right without his consent. Therefore any right which a third party has cannot be taken from him by a guaranty.

§ 336, part 2,
Jus Nat.

If, then, it should happen that a right belongs to any third person to that, or in that, for which a guaranty has been made, his right remains unimpaired in spite of it. In so far as a guaranty is made against him to whom a certain right belongs, it is illegal; consequently is not valid by natural law, although the guarantor does no wrong if he is ignorant of the right of a third party, or if that has not been fully ascertained by him.

§ 457. *When it is known to have been given*

§ 456.

Since any right which a third party has cannot be taken away from him by a guaranty, it is understood that a guaranty is given only without prejudice to the right of a third party.

A nation is not presumed to wish to do injury to a third nation for the sake of another. Therefore a guaranty is not understood to have been given by it on other terms than that the right of a third party should be unaffected.

§ 458. *When it is not binding*

§ 457.

Since a guaranty is understood to have been given only without prejudice to the right of a third party, if he who has a right to that for which a guaranty has been given should wish to obtain it, since this case has been tacitly excepted; the guarantor is not bound to give assistance against him.

No one ought to do anything which is contrary to the right of another. Therefore if a case should arise in which a promise cannot be observed by a guarantor, unless he should wish to do that which is contrary to the right of a third party, he is not bound to observe it. Of course a promise is wrongfully extended to this case which the law of nature itself excepts, so that then it may rightly be understood that this is tacitly excepted. But it is self-evident that the right of a third party ought either to be plain or at least ought to have very probable reasons, which the other party cannot really refute.

§ 910, part 1, Jus Nat.

§ 459. *Of a guaranty added to a treaty in which the agreements affect the contracting parties individually*

If several enter into a treaty in regard to things affecting the parties individually, and a guaranty is given in regard to all included in the treaty, the guarantor is bound to each one of the allies in regard to that which affects him. For if several enter into a treaty in regard to things affecting the parties individually, it is understood that there are as many treaties entered into as there are things dealt with in them which affect the contracting parties individually. If, then, the guarantor pledges his faith in regard to the whole treaty, or in regard to all included in it, the guaranty is understood to have been added to the several treaties, just as if each one had been made individually. Therefore it is plain that the guarantor is bound to each one of the allies as regards that which affects him.

§ 460. *Of assistance denied by a guarantor*

If the assistance of a guarantor should be asked, it cannot be refused without wrong. For a guaranty contains a tacit treaty. Therefore, since from a treaty an absolute right arises to that in regard to which there has been an agreement, if a guarantor denies assistance when asked, he violates an absolute right acquired by him to whom the guaranty was given. And a violation of another's absolute right is a wrong. Therefore, if the assistance of a guarantor should be asked, it cannot be denied without wrong.

§ 445.

§ 377.

§ 859, part 1, Jus Nat.

It is one and the same thing not to observe a treaty and to refuse assistance to the one to whom a guaranty has been given. In either case pledged faith is violated. Nevertheless the case is to be excepted in which a third party claims his right, since the guaranty was given only without prejudice to that right. But it is self-evident that here that is assumed as to which the guarantor has power to give assistance, for he cannot bind himself beyond that which is in his power. But concerning that we shall have to speak more fully below.

§ 457.

§ 461. *When a guaranty is ended*

When a treaty is ended, the guaranty is ended. For a guaranty is made for the sake of assurance that the agreements in a treaty will be observed, consequently there is no further need of it, if a treaty shall have been ended. Therefore, when a treaty is ended, the guaranty also is ended.

§ 442.

§ 462. *How broad a guaranty is*

A guaranty is either personal or real, nevertheless a personal guaranty is not presumed. For the giving of a guaranty is a sort of treaty entered into with him for whom it is given. Therefore, since treaties are both personal and real, a guaranty also is either personal or real. Which was the first point.

§ 445.
§ 412.

And he who seeks to have a guaranty made for himself, does it with the intention that he may be assured that the agreements will be observed, consequently special attention is given to the subject-matter, and not simply to the persons agreeing on the guaranty. Therefore, since a guaranty is not personal, unless the stipulation is restricted to the persons of the contracting parties, so that in the present case the guarantor is bound only for himself to the one to whom it is given, or only to the person of the one to whom it is given, a guaranty is not presumed to be personal. Which was the second point.

§ 442.

§ 801, part 3,
Jus. Nat.

In a presumption, attention is given to what the intention may have been of the one seeking a guaranty in a doubtful case, and to what extent the guarantor has bound himself thereto. But there is no doubt that he who seeks a guaranty wishes to have made provision for assurance that the agreements will be observed so long as the treaty continues. If, then, there should be no other express statement, the promise of guaranty is certainly to be continued during the life of the treaty, and on no ground can it be restricted to persons who have agreed concerning the guaranty. A guaranty is therefore never presumed to be personal.

§ 463. *In how many ways a guaranty can be personal*

Since a guaranty can be personal, and since a personal stipulation is restricted to the persons of the contracting parties, a guaranty can be restricted either to the person of the guarantor, or to the person of the one to whom it is given, or to either person; consequently in the first case the guaranty expires when the guarantor dies, in the second, when the one dies to whom it was given, in the third, when either of them dies.

§ 462.
§ 801, part 1, Jus Nat.

> Of course in the first case the guarantor promises assistance as long as he shall live, in the second case as long as the one to whom the guaranty was made shall live, in the third finally, as long as either shall live.

§ 464. *Of stipulations of nations*

Stipulations are made either by the sovereign powers or by subordinate powers, either on the mandate of the sovereign powers, or within the limits of their authority, in so far forsooth as the nature of the business over which they have been placed allows it. For nations and their rulers can enter into stipulations which are distinguishable from treaties. This can be done by their orders, as when the envoy of one, in the name of the one sending him, enters into a stipulation with the ministers of the one to whom he is sent. And then the stipulation is said to have been made by the sovereign powers. But minor powers, such as magistrates and leaders in war, are also able to make stipulations in regard to public matters, by right of the one by whom they have been placed over some public business. But then, indeed, they have a mandate, either general or special, to make stipulations of that sort, or, from the nature of the business over which they have been placed, it follows that they can make them, especially in the case when the consent of the sovereign power cannot be asked for, as when a leader in war agrees with an enemy concerning the surrender of a besieged city. And in these cases stipulations are made by subordinate powers, either on the order of the sovereign powers, or

§ 369.

within the limits of their authority, in so far of course as the nature of the business over which they have been placed allows it.

Since stipulations by subordinate powers are made most often in war, we shall speak fully of them also below, where we are going to discuss the law of war and law in war. Therefore we add no more concerning them at present. It seems wiser, indeed, that the generalities be discussed in the place where the special applications are to be deduced from them and added to them.

§ 465. *What a sponsion is*

A sponsion is a stipulation made concerning a public matter without the mandate of the sovereign power, and not within the limits of its authorization. It is readily understood that the sponsor promises that he will bring it about that the sovereign power will ratify that which is promised, since otherwise no one would contract with him.

Sponsions of that sort can be made by legates and by leaders in war, and they are made with the hope of ratification.

§ 466. *The obligation contained in a sponsion*

Since the sponsor promises that he will bring it about that the sovereign power, or the one in whose name he promises something, will ratify it, he binds himself to bring it about that the thing promised by himself will be ratified, or that the consent of the one whom the agreement affects will be added.

It can indeed happen that the sponsor may believe that more lies within his power than is actually the case, but the determination of that lies with himself, not with the other with whom he contracts, and who therefore has not unwarranted confidence in the words of the sponsor. But if, indeed, the sponsor is himself uncertain, he could and should have promised only on condition of ratification. Therefore it is to be charged to him, if he shall have believed that more lay in his power than was actually the case, and shall have induced another to contract with him. But from this it is understood that a sponsion is not a simple promise for the performance of another, and therefore it produces a much more binding obligation.

§ 467. *Of the subject-matter of sponsions*

The subject-matter of sponsions can be as varied as that of treaties. For since treaties are stipulations which are made by supreme powers in regard to matters affecting a state, or on the mandate of those powers, since, moreover, sponsions are stipulations which are made concerning the same things without the mandate of the sovereign power, and not within the limits of its authorization; sponsions do not differ in their subject-matter from treaties, but only in the respect that the latter are made by right of sovereign power, and of the one having its mandate, but the former are made without this right and without a mandate. Therefore the subject-matter of sponsions can be as varied as that of treaties.

§ 369.

§ 372.

§ 463.

§ 368.

> Let us suppose that a stipulation is entered into by a minister concerning some public matter. Now if he should do that by order of the supreme power, or within the limits of his mandate, it will be a treaty; if outside of his mandate, a sponsion. Therefore the subject-matter of a stipulation makes no difference, nor the person contracting, but the right by which the contract is made, which in a treaty is the right of the sovereign power, while in the case of a sponsion there is no right. Therefore the subject-matter of a treaty and a sponsion can be the same.

§ 468. *Whether a sponsion binds the sovereign power*

A sponsion does not bind a sovereign power, unless it should ratify the same either expressly or tacitly, by doing, after the sponsion has become known to it, that which cannot with probability be referred to another cause. For a sponsion is made without a mandate, consequently without the will, of the sovereign power. Therefore, since no one can bind another to himself, consequently much less to a third party, without his consent, a sponsion does not bind the sovereign power. Which was the first point.

§§ 640, 642, part 4, Jus Nat.

§ 465.

§ 382, part 3, Jus Nat.

If indeed the sovereign power ratifies it, that is, declares that it wishes to perform what the sponsor has promised, since now the consent of the sovereign power is added to the sponsion, that is, the stipulation is understood to have been entered into with its consent, the sponsion is transformed into a treaty. Therefore, since a perfect obligation arises from a treaty, a sponsion expressly ratified by the sovereign power is binding on it. Which was the second point.

§ 369.

§ 377.

§ 660, part 1,
Phil. Pract.
Univ.

Finally, if after a sponsion has become known to the sovereign power, it does that which cannot with probability be referred to another cause, it tacitly declares its consent; consequently, since a tacit consent is a true consent, the consent of the sovereign power is added to the sponsion.

§ 662, part 1,
Phil. Pract.
Univ.

Therefore, since a sponsion binds the sovereign power when its consent is added to it, as proved in point 2, a sponsion tacitly ratified, that is, by doing, after the sponsion has become known to it, that which cannot with probability be referred to another cause, binds the sovereign power. Which was the third point.

The agreement of a minister does not become valid until the time when the sovereign power ratifies it, if it has been made on condition of ratification; for his promise is in this case conditional. Nay, more, as long as the condition is unfulfilled, that is, as long as the sovereign power has not declared its will in regard to that which has been agreed upon, nothing seems to have been done on his part. When, indeed, the ratification has been made, and therefore the consent of the sovereign power is added, then only his act is completed and made effective. Since a minister promises nothing of his own, his promise also, however it may be made, has no effect of itself as regards the sovereign power. But it is just the same whether the consent of the sovereign power is given to the agreement immediately or after an interval, and whether in the latter case it should be expressly or tacitly declared. And a sponsion as regards the sovereign power is equivalent to an agreement made on condition of ratification. Therefore on the part of the sovereign power the same things are true of a sponsion as of an agreement made on condition of ratification.

§ 469. *If the sovereign power expressly declares its dissent*

§ 468.

Since a sponsion does not bind the sovereign power, unless it should ratify the same, but since that does not occur if it should expressly declare its dissent, if the sovereign power expressly declares its dissent to the sponsion, the sponsion does not bind it.

Note, § 466.

For a sponsion is not transformed into a treaty, so that the act becomes obligatory on the part of the sovereign power, before its consent is added to the same. But the opposite of this happens if the sovereign power declares its dissent.

§§ 658, 659, part 1, Phil. Pract. Univ.

§ 470. *Whether from knowledge and silence ratification may be assumed*

In like manner, since a sponsion does not bind a sovereign power, unless it should ratify the same, consequently there is no obligation to be destroyed by a declaration of dissent, for no obligation is present, but since he only is presumed to consent who is silent when he could and ought to speak; from knowledge and silence alone it cannot be assumed that the sovereign power ratifies a sponsion.

§ 468.

§ 1054, part 3, Jus Nat.

Hence the reason is plain why an act ought to be added to knowledge and silence, from which consent can be assumed, unless the same should be expressly declared. But certainly it is wiser that, when a sponsion comes to the knowledge of a sovereign power, the dissent should be expressly declared, for in every case certainties are to be preferred in those matters which can perchance become subject to doubt; but this does not belong to the law of nations, but to statecraft.

§ 468.

§ 471. *Of what special character the promise of a sponsor is*

A sponsor promises an act of his own, not simply that of another. For a sponsor promises that he will bring it about that the sovereign power will ratify his agreement, not simply that it will perform what has been agreed upon, although the second promise may be tacitly included in the first, or expressly added to it. Therefore, since it is an act of the sponsor to bring it about that the sovereign power ratify the promise made by him in its name, a sponsor promises an act of his own, not simply that of another.

§ 465.

Therefore, although a sponsion is a conditional promise as regards the sovereign power whose validity is dependent on the outcome, nevertheless it is absolute as regards the sponsor, and produces a present obligation, namely, of fulfilling his promise, and is immediately effective.

§ 468.

§ 472. *Whether a sponsor is relieved by the use of diligence*

§ 471.
§ 465.
§ 602, part 3,
Jus Nat.

Since a sponsor promises an act of his own, namely, to bring it about that the sovereign power will ratify his agreements, he is bound by the promise of an act of his own to the one to whom the sponsion has been made, not by the promise of the act of another, consequently it is not sufficient for him to have used every effort that the sovereign power should ratify his agreements.

§ 789, part 3,
Jus Nat.

§ 430, part 3,
Jus Nat.

Of course, since agreements are to be observed, that is to be performed which has been promised. But the sponsor promises that he will bring it about that the sovereign power will ratify his agreements. But to use diligence and to bring it about that something shall be done, are not one and the same thing. Therefore the sponsor has not yet satisfied his promise by the use of diligence, as one who has simply promised the performance of a third party.

§ 473. *To what the sovereign power is bound by an unratified sponsion*

If the sovereign power should not ratify a sponsion, it is bound in no respect to the one to whom the sponsion has been made, except to restitution, if perchance it should happen that it had been made richer by the sponsion. For if the sovereign power does not ratify the sponsion, it is not bound thereby. Therefore it is not necessary that on account of the sponsion it should perform anything for him to whom it was made, consequently it is then bound in no respect to him. Which was the first point.

§ 468.

§ 118, part 1,
Phil. Pract.
Univ.

§ 585, part 2,
Jus Nat.

§ 586, part 2,
Jus Nat.

But since, indeed, no one can be made richer with loss to another, that is, if the thing which he has accepted should be restored, when the thing from which he has been made richer no longer exists, he is bound to restore only in so far as he has been made richer; if perchance it should happen that the sovereign power has been made richer by the sponsion, it is bound to make restitution. Which was the second point.

§ 640, part 4,
Jus Nat.
§ 465.

The former point is also proved in this way. Whereas a sponsion is made without a mandate, consequently without consent of the sovereign power, when it does not ratify the sponsion, nor give its consent after the event; the sovereign power also then has promised nothing to the one

to whom the sponsion was made. Therefore, since we cannot be bound
to another, except by a promise, if the sovereign power should not ratify
a sponsion, it is bound in no respect to the one to whom the sponsion
has been made.

§ 393, part 3,
Jus Nat.

Of course a sovereign power is bound in no respect by a sponsion,
which is an act not affecting it as long as its consent is not given. When
indeed we said that the sovereign power is bound to restitution if perchance it should happen that it has been made richer by the sponsion,
that comes not from the sponsion, but from a natural obligation. Therefore the proposition that the sovereign power is bound in no respect by
an unratified sponsion is not restricted by this. A natural obligation does
not come from a sponsion, although a sponsion may have given rise to
it, in so far as without it the obligation would not have existed.

§ 474. Whether it is bound to that which a thing is worth, or to restore it to its former condition

Since the supreme power is bound in no respect by an unratified sponsion, therefore it is not bound to that which the ratification was worth
by virtue of the transaction, nor to restore the thing to the condition in
which it had been before the sponsion.

§ 473.

The sovereign power, without whose mandate the sponsion has
been made, is not responsible, if the one for whom the sponsion has
been made should incur some loss by failure of its ratification, or
should fail of some gain which he could have had if it had been ratified. And therefore it is plain that there is no reason why the sovereign
power should be bound for that which it was worth, so as to make an
estimate of the advantage which he to whom the sponsion was made
would have had from the result, or of the loss which arises from the
non-ratification of the sponsion. We are bound by our own act, not
that of another, for what it is worth. But it is easy to see that the valuation of its worth is often quite uncertain.

§ 465.

§ 622, part 3,
Jus Nat.
§ 625, part 3,
Jus Nat.

§ 623, part 3,
Jus Nat.

§ 475. To what the sponsor is bound

If a sponsion has not been ratified, the sponsor is bound to him to
whom he has promised for the loss sustained. For since the sponsor

promises that he will bring it about that the sponson shall be rati-

§ 465

fied, and by the promise of his own act is bound to him to whom the

§§ 471, 472.

sponson has been made, he certainly is understood to promise that he wishes to keep him harmless, if he should not bring it about that the sponson is ratified. If then the sovereign power does not wish to ratify

§ 625, part 3,
Jus Nat.

the sponson, the sponsor is bound to him to whom he has promised for the loss sustained.

Of course it is one thing to promise on condition of ratification, another to promise that one will do his best that a sponson will be ratified, and still another that one will bring it about that it will be ratified. In the first case he has fulfilled the promise which he tacitly gave, if he shall have ascertained the desire of the sovereign power; but in the second, if he shall have used every effort to have the spon-son ratified. In the third case, since the consent of the sovereign power has been assumed as a certainty, and therefore the agreement is absolute, the sponsor is properly understood to have promised that he will pay the loss sustained if the sponson should not be rati-fied, since otherwise he to whom the sponson was made would not have contracted with him. Nor is there any injustice in that, since the sponsor is already by his own act naturally bound for the loss sustained, because forsooth he has contracted without a mandate, however faulty it may have been.

§ 476. How a sponsor satisfies his obligation if the sponson is not ratified

§ 475.

Since a sponsor is bound to the one to whom the sponson is made for the loss sustained, if ratification does not follow, and since the spon-

§ 135, part 1,
Jus Nat.

sor has nothing except his own goods and his power over himself and

§ 146, part 1,
Jus Nat.

therefore the liberty belonging to him by nature; if the sponson is not

§ 1094, part 7,
Jus Nat.

ratified, the loss sustained must be paid to him to whom it was made out of the sponsor's goods, or he himself must be given up, even into absolute slavery.

Since it was formerly thought that the right to his own life belongs

§ 351, part 1,
Jus Nat.

to man, which nevertheless is not true, not only the goods and liberty of the sponsor were believed to be bound to him to whom a sponson has been made, but also his life. Therefore they thought that a sponsor could rightly be killed if the sponsion was not ratified. But this false doctrine is properly rejected.

§ 477. When a sponsor is bound to perform some definite thing

If a sponsor shall have promised some definite thing to him to whom he has made the sponsion, if the sovereign power shall have refused to ratify the sponsion, the sponsor is not bound to him beyond that. For since no one can bind himself to another except by a promise, nor by the acceptance of the promise can any one bind the promisor to himself beyond his intention, if a sponsor shall have promised some definite thing to him to whom he has made the sponsion, when the sovereign power has refused to ratify the sponsion, the sponsor is bound to perform nothing for him beyond that which he has promised, consequently he is not bound to him beyond that.

§ 393, part 3, Jus Nat.

§ 382, part 3, Jus Nat.

Since the valuation of what the sponsion is worth is quite difficult, and since there is no one to determine it between the sponsor and the other one to whom the sponsion was made, consequently one must yield to the superior force; it would certainly be better that an agreement be made concerning that which is to be done if the sponsion is not ratified. But if the sponsor offered this condition, he would appear to be still in doubt concerning the ratification, and then the one to whom the sponsion is made, and who contracts with the sponsor in reliance on the ratification, would not readily accept it. Although it is not impossible that he would accept it, we had to pass over this case in silence.

Note, § 474.

§ 478. Of a stipulation by the ruler of a state with private individuals for the sake of the state

A stipulation by the ruler of a state, entered into with private individuals for the sake of public advantage, binds the nation also and his successors. In the same manner it is plain that if a ruler of a state enters into a stipulation with private individuals, from what we likewise have shown above concerning a treaty, that stipulation is understood to have been

§ 423.

made with the nation itself. Whence, further, it follows that it binds the
nation also and his successors who represent the nation.

Here there is no difference whether the ruler contracts with foreigners or with his subjects. Take this example: if a ruler of a state,
for the purpose of paying the expenses of war, incurs a debt to private
citizens. Hence debts of that sort are debts of the state, called in our
native vernacular *Staats-Schulden* [national debts].

§ 479. *Of debts of the state that are to be paid*

Since a stipulation by the ruler of a state, entered into with private individuals for the sake of public advantage, binds the nation also and his successors; if the ruler of a state, for the benefit of the state, incurs a debt with
private individuals, his successors also and the people are bound to satisfy
it, and to pay the interest agreed upon so far as that is not in itself illegal.

§ 478.

§ 1406, part 4,
Jus Nat.

Not every rate of interest is allowable by nature, as is clearly evident
from those things which we have proved elsewhere. But since it is
extremely difficult to determine the amount of interest in accordance
with natural equity, a definite sum must be fixed by the civil laws. And
if some nation incurs a debt with another nation, since each nation
is free, consequently neither is subject to the laws of the other, and
since by virtue of natural liberty it must be left to each one what it
wishes to do, it is necessary that they should agree as to the amount
of interest. But the question is asked, what is allowable if a nation
or a ruler of a state who has the right of a nation incurs a debt with
private individuals, either subjects or foreigners? If money should be
taken from subjects as a loan, since these are bound by civil laws, the
amount of interest it seems is to be determined by them, and what is
unconditionally promised is deemed to be neither more nor less than
the laws allow. Nevertheless nothing prevents them from agreeing on
a lesser amount, since even a private individual can agree with a private individual upon a smaller rate, since the law merely forbids that
they should exact a greater one. Nevertheless, since it can happen that
a higher rate would not be repugnant to natural equity, as is clearly
evident from those things which we have proved elsewhere concerning
the amount of interest, and since the ruler of the state can dispense
from the civil laws, it is not contrary to law to make an agreement for a

§§ 1047 and
fol., part 4,
Jus Nat.

§§ cited.

§ 986, part 8,
Jus Nat.

§ 55, part 8,
Jus Nat.

§ 156, part 1,
Jus Nat.

§ 512, part 6,
Jus Nat.

§§ 1407 and
fol., part 4,
Jus Nat.

higher rate also. But if finally money should be accepted as a loan from private individuals of a foreign state, since these are not subject to the civil laws of the nation to which the loan is made, nor is the nation bound by the laws to which the creditors are subject, the agreement is subject to the provisions of natural law. Therefore it is evident as before, that it is necessary that they should agree on the rate of interest. When civil laws do not prevent, each one is free to dispose of his property as he pleases, and the agreement determines the law, however much that should depart from natural equity. Such things of course are to be endured, that business may go on, and in the disposition of one's property even an abuse of natural liberty is to be allowed.

§ 824, part 8, Jus Nat.

§ 480. Of taxes imposed for the purpose of payment

Since if the ruler of a state for the benefit of the state incurs a debt with private individuals, the people are bound to satisfy it, and to pay the interest agreed upon; for the purpose of satisfying it and of paying the interest agreed upon, the ruler can impose taxes.

§ 479.

If the right of declaring a new tax has been taken from the ruler of the state by the fundamental laws, it is plainly evident that this ought to be done either with the consent of the people or of those whom such laws designate.

§ 481. Of strengthening treaties and stipulations by a pledge

In a treaty or in another stipulation it can be provided by means of pledges that agreements will be observed. For a pledge is made as security of a debt. Therefore, since nations are bound to perform those things in regard to which they have agreed in treaties or in other stipulations, and since a thing which is to be performed is a debt, provision can be made by means of pledges in a treaty or in another stipulation that agreements are to be observed.

§§ 1142, 1143, part 5, Jus Nat.

§ 377.

§ 401, part 3, Jus Nat.

Indeed, between private individuals pledges and hypothecs are frequently made by way of security, on a *mutuum*,[5] as for money loaned, so that if the debtor should not pay, or should be stubborn,

5. *Mutuum*: See above, p. 296, n. 2.

§ 1194, part 5,
Jus Nat.

the creditor may be satisfied from the thing pledged; nevertheless they can as such be added to every stipulation, since they furnish a security no less for any debt than for a thing, or for money given as a loan. Nor are pledges of this sort unknown among nations.

§ 482. *Whether that is allowed between nations by the law of nature*

§ 481.

§§ 493, 495,
part 2, Jus Nat.

Since provisions can be made by pledges in a treaty or in another stipulation that agreements will be observed, and since by nature we are bound to avoid losses both for ourselves and for others, a pledge is by nature lawfully added to treaties and any stipulations between nations.

§ 377.

§ 235, part 1,
Phil. Pract.
Univ.

§ 3.

From treaties a perfect right arises to that which has been agreed therein. And the same is plain in regard to any other stipulations. That, therefore, which has been agreed we can exact and by force compel one to perform who is unwilling to perform. Therefore those means are permissible by which we can most easily of all obtain that which has been agreed upon, if the debtor does not pay, or an estimate of what it is worth if loss is caused us by failure to perform. Hence it is plain that, not indeed by the customs of nations has the pledge been introduced, but by natural law, which nations use with each other, and that the same thing can be added to treaties and to other stipulations of nations, when it is important that the promises agreed upon should be kept faithfully, especially those which are transitory. Since the law of nations has to be demonstrated by us, it is not sufficient to enumerate those things which can be done and are regularly done; but from the principles of the law of nature that is to be derived which is allowable for nations, for physical possibility does not make right, nor can that be allowable for nations which is contrary to duty.

§ 483. *What sort of a right a nation has in a thing pledged*

§ 3.

The right belonging to a nation in a thing pledged is to be determined both from those things which are proved concerning a pledge in the law of nature, and from those things which have been agreed in particular concerning it. Nations use natural law in their relations with each other. Therefore the things which we have proved in "The Law of Nature," concerning the law of pledge and hypothec, or of pledging, to have a Part 5, chap. 5, Jus. Nat. bearing on private individuals, affect nations also. Nevertheless, since nations are able to dispose of their property as shall seem best to them, §§ 1, 12, part 3, Jus Nat. in regard to pledging also they can especially agree on certain things, and then no more right belongs to the nation to whom the thing has been pledged than has been granted to it. The right therefore belonging to a § 382, part 3, Jus Nat. nation in a thing pledged is to be determined both from those things which are proved concerning a pledge in the law of nature, and from those things which have been agreed in particular concerning it.

If pledges are made between nations, it is usual to agree concerning the right also which ought to belong as regards them to the one to which the thing is pledged, unless that is plain of itself from the very nature of the pledge. But provision is also made in that for the security of the one which pledges the thing, lest perchance the thing pledged may deteriorate, and that all difficulties may be provided against which could be brought up in regard to restoration of the pledge. But the special discussion of these things belongs to civil jurisprudence. That universal love of all towards all, which is prescribed even to nations by § 161. the law of nature, demands that in agreements one nation should have no less consideration for the advantage of another than for its own; so it happens that this may seem perchance paradoxical to some, who measure the rights of nations only by utility and power.

§ 484. *What can be pledged by nations*

Cities can be pledged by nations, certain parts of their territory, entire provinces, rights belonging to themselves and valuable things which belong to the state: moreover, the ruler of a state can pledge even his own private property for the debts of a nation. For since no one can pledge anything except his own property, only what is its own can be pledged by a nation also, consequently what is its own can be pledged. § 1164, part 5, Jus Nat. Therefore, since the lands which nations inhabit are subject to their ownership, together with all things which are in them, as are the rights belonging to them, and since in regard to valuable things which belong to the state the same thing is evident of itself; cities can be pledged § 274.
§ 216, part 2, Jus Nat. by a nation, certain parts of their territories, entire provinces, rights belonging to themselves, and valuable things which belong to the state. Which was the first point.

But since an owner can pledge his property for the debt of another, but the debt of a nation is not the private debt of the ruler of a state, although it is contracted by him by the right of the nation, consequently it must be looked at as the debt of another as regards his own private property; the ruler of a state is able to pledge his own private property also for the debts of the nation. Which was the second point.

§ 1164, part 5, Jus Nat.

> As security for a debt, cities, districts, and provinces are transferred to the one to whom they are pledged, or else indeed by a written instrument the right is established in them, as either shall have been more suitable to the nature of the business concerning which an agreement has been made. But rights cannot be pledged otherwise than by entrusting to another the exercise of them. But valuable things as movables are always to be handed over.

§ 485. *Of the stipulation of antichresis of nations*

If an entire province, or a certain part of a territory is transferred as security for money loaned, or for a debt of any other sort, the stipulation of antichresis is added to that of pledge. For if a province or a part of a territory pledged as security for money loaned, or for a debt of any other sort, is transferred, that nation to which it is transferred acquires possession. But since as a security for a debt it is sufficient that an hypothec should be established in the pledged lands, and if that should not be believed to be sufficient, the creditor may have soldiers as guards in them; pledged lands are transferred for no other purpose than that the returns from the domain lands, the taxes and imposts, may be taken in lieu of interest. Since, therefore, the stipulation of antichresis is one by which the right is conferred on the creditor to use and enjoy the thing pledged in lieu of interest, if an entire province or a certain part of a territory is transferred as security for money loaned, or for debt of any other sort, the stipulation of antichresis is added to that of pledge.

§ 23, part 5, Jus Nat.

§ 1143, part 5, Jus Nat.

§§ 926, 927, 929, part 8, Jus Nat.
§ 1205, part 5, Jus Nat.

> The stipulation of antichresis is added to the contract of pledge, that provision may be made for the security of the interest, just as

by the pledge provision is made for security of the debt. But doubt
could arise as to whether in a stipulation of antichresis the taxes and
imposts should be included, since they ought to be paid for that
use for which they have been imposed. Therefore, since burdens
are imposed on the subjects of a state, in order that the expenses
incurred for the purpose of administering and defending the state
may not fail to be paid, it does not seem that the taxes and imposts
can be ceded to another in lieu of interest. But indeed expenses also
are to be paid by the subjects to the ruler of the state to support himself and the royal family and to assure the splendour of the royal dignity. Therefore the things which are contributed for this purpose can
be pledged no less than the returns from the domain lands. And if
indeed the ordinary tributes exceed the expenses incurred in administering the state, it is understood that this surplus is contributed to
that purpose. If, then, the taxes and imposts should not be put into
separate treasuries, which have their own administrators, it certainly
is the duty of the ruler of the state that, from those which are contributed, he should pay the necessary expenses for administering the
state, and then with this burden they also pass over to the creditor
by virtue of the stipulation of antichresis. Such taxes therefore are to
be determined from the particular circumstances, and concerning
them agreement is to be made in the stipulation of antichresis which
is added to the contract of pledge: in such cases nevertheless, in
accordance with the law of nature, one must look out that subjects
should not be too heavily burdened by the pledging, nor extraordinary burdens imposed beyond what is necessary. Nor would I deny
that over-nicety of that sort is very little expected from nations and
their rulers. But several times already we have given warning that
here we are not speaking of that which is a matter of fact, but of
that which is a matter of law, according to the immutable law of
nature. For already it has been observed that no state is ruled without wrong, nor are all things which are, nay, should be, considered
as law among nations in harmony with internal justice, which flows
from the immutable law, for the same reasons that civil laws cannot
be altogether in harmony with natural law, by virtue of what we have
proved concerning the natural theory of civil laws in Part 8, ch. 5, of
"The Law of Nature."

Note, § 1205,
part 5, Jus Nat.

§ 934, part 8,
Jus Nat.

§§ 774, 778,
part 8, Jus Nat.

§ 784, part 8,
Jus Nat.

§ 778, part 8,
Jus Nat.
§§ 779, 780,
part 8, Jus Nat.

§22.

§ 486. *From what the right of a nation is to be determined in that case*

If an entire province or a certain part of a territory is transferred to a nation as security for money loaned, or for a debt of another sort, its right is to be determined both from those things which have been proved concerning antichresis in the law of nature, and from those things concerning which there has been a special agreement. This is shown in the same manner in which we have proved the same thing concerning the right of a nation to which a pledge has been made.

§ 483.

Do not persuade yourself that we wish to define the transactions of nations from the principles of the civil law. For here we do not appeal to those things which are related in the civil law in regard to antichresis, but to those things which are proved concerning it from the principles of the law of nature; a thing which is also to be understood concerning the law of pledge. For although we would not deny that there are very many similarities to those things which are found in the civil law, nevertheless we do not here appeal to those things, as far as they occur in the Roman civil law, which are the same as in the law of nature. There is no one who does not know this if he has a knowledge of either law, and it is at once plain by a comparison of the law of nature, so very fully explained by us, with the Roman law.

§ 483.

§ 487. *Of the pledging of sovereignty*

If an entire province or a certain part of a territory is transferred to a nation as security for money owed, the sovereignty can be put in pledge at the same time, or not. For since sovereignty is a certain right belonging to a nation, and since rights also can be put in pledge by nations, and the right of a nation to which a pledge has been made is to be determined from the agreement, if an entire province is transferred or a certain part of a territory as security for money owed, the sovereignty can be put in pledge at the same time, or not.

§§ 32, 34, part 8, Jus Nat.

§ 484.

§ 483.

In the hypothesis of the present proposition the sovereignty is indeed usually put in pledge at the same time; nevertheless this is not absolutely necessary, since even without it the stipulation of antichresis

can exist, of which we have spoken. But in this case there is very great   § 484.
need that there should be an agreement, to what extent the exercise
of sovereignty should be entrusted to a creditor, and it is in harmony
with the law of nature that provision should be made for the benefit of
the subjects over whom the creditor exercises sovereignty. For although
it can also be shown, from those things which belong to the law of
nature in regard to pledge and the stipulation of antichresis, what is
proper in case of a pledge of sovereignty, nevertheless, since this is not
so plain to everybody, it is wiser to make an agreement in regard to its
exercise. Certainty is always to be preferred in cases which can be called
in question.

§ 488. *How sovereignty put in pledge is to be exercised*

If sovereignty is put in pledge at the same time with lands transferred as
security for money owed and the interest, and there has been no special
agreement concerning it, the sovereignty ought to be exercised in the
same way that the ruler of the state was accustomed to exercise it, and
all things ought to remain in the condition in which they are. It is self-
evident that if sovereignty is put in pledge at the same time with lands   § 1152, part 5, and § 662, part 2, Jus Nat.
transferred as security for money owed and the interest, the sovereignty is
not transferred, but simply the exercise of it is given up. If, then, no special agreement shall have been made which must certainly be observed,
the exercise of sovereignty is understood to have been allowed in the
same way as was customary at the time of the grant. Therefore he to   §§ 382, 789, part 3, Jus Nat.
whom it is granted ought to exercise it in the same way that the ruler of
the state was accustomed to exercise it, and all things ought to remain in   § 512, part 6, Jus Nat.
the condition in which they are.

Therefore on the pledging of the sovereignty no right belongs to
him to whom it has been pledged to change anything in the state
without the consent of the pledgor. Nay, more, if complete sovereignty without exception shall have been in the hands of the pledgor,
the same remains with him. Therefore if he himself should desire to
change anything, without prejudice to the creditor, the creditor cannot oppose it. For although the subjects are bound to obey the creditor and have been subjected to his control, so far as the exercise of
sovereignty over them has been granted to him, nevertheless they are

still subjects of the pledgor, who exercises his right over them through the creditor. But there are many things which can be agreed upon in regard to the exercise of the sovereignty put in pledge, in so far indeed as the pledgor reserves for himself certain rights belonging to the civil sovereignty, as the right to confer public honours, legislative power, the right to make treaties, the right to enrol soldiery; or the exercise of those rights is limited, or restricted to certain conditions, as that he cannot confer any public honour upon a foreigner, that he may not grant a monopoly to any one, that he may not allow certain goods to be imported or exported, that he may not have more than an agreed number of garrison soldiers, that he may not allow the public exercise of religion to a certain sect, and more things which are of this kind.

§ 489. Of the method of exacting the taxes and imposts allowed by virtue of the stipulation of antichresis

If there should be an antichresis without pledging of the sovereignty, the creditor in the antichresis cannot exact the taxes and imposts from stubborn debtors, except by the aid of the magistrate who has jurisdiction; he can assume no act of jurisdiction for himself. For since no one can acquire from another more right than the transferor has wished to transfer to him, and since, by virtue of the stipulation of antichresis, taxes and imposts are granted simply by way of compensation for interest, since, moreover, the jurisdiction which belongs to judges and other magistrates comes from sovereignty, if an antichresis should be made without pledging of the sovereignty, the creditor in the antichresis cannot exact the taxes and imposts from stubborn debtors, except by the aid of the magistrate who has jurisdiction, and he can assume no act of jurisdiction for himself.

§ 382, part 2, Jus Nat.

§ 1205, part 5, Jus Nat.

§§ 162, 538, part 8, Jus Nat.

Of course, since by force of the antichresis the one to whom a certain province or certain lands have been pledged without the sovereignty certainly has the right over them to demand the returns from the domain lands, the taxes and imposts, he can indeed appoint certain persons to collect them, but as often as a case arises in which there is need of the aid of a judge or of another magistrate, he is bound to ask it. For it is understood that no more is granted than that the creditor in the antichresis may receive what is paid to him. But in no way

Note, § 485.

can he intrude himself upon the control of the debtor which neither
belongs to him by natural law nor has been granted by virtue of the
stipulation.

§ 256.

§ 490. *Of the farming-out of the incomes from domain lands, the taxes and imposts in the pledged territory*

If a stipulation of antichresis is added to a pledge, the incomes from the
domain lands, taxes and imposts can be farmed out to others. For the
creditor in an antichresis can grant to another also the right to use and
enjoy the pledge. Therefore, since this right, if the stipulation of antichresis is added to the pledge of a province, or of a certain part of the
territory, consists in the taking of the incomes from the domain lands,
the taxes and imposts, according of course to the agreement made; if a
stipulation of antichresis is added to a pledge made with a nation, the
creditor in the antichresis, that is, this nation itself, can farm out to others the returns from the domain lands, the taxes and imposts.

§ 1217, part 5, Jus Nat.

§ 485.

It is assumed, of course, that there has been no agreement otherwise. But if there shall have been agreement that the returns from the
domain lands, the taxes and imposts, should not be farmed out, there
is then no possibility for the farming them out. But if the subjects
shall have had any complaints in regard to the hirers, since the creditor
in the antichresis has no power of jurisdiction, the complaints are to
be referred to the judge who has jurisdiction in that place, and he is
bound to take cognizance of them; and if he should favour one party
more than is fair, complaints against him can be referred to the superior from whom he holds jurisdiction, so that indeed the hirers can be
assured of impartiality.

§ 486.

§ 489.

§ 547, part 8, Jus Nat.

§ 491. *Of the stipulation akin to antichresis*

If a certain province or a certain part of a territory together with the
sovereignty should be transferred to a nation with the provision that
it should possess it for a definite time in place of money owed, or of
another debt, the same things would be true as in case of antichresis with
pledging of sovereignty. For although this stipulation by which there is
an agreement that a creditor may enjoy the things pledged, until there

§ 1215, part 5,
Jus Nat.

shall have been enough made by taking of the fruits to pay both principal and interest is not properly an antichresis; nevertheless, since it differs from it only in the respect that in antichresis the incomes are taken from the domain lands, the taxes and imposts in lieu of interest simply, but in the stipulation akin to it, by hypothesis, in lieu of capital as well, no difference in right arises from it. Therefore those things which are true of an antichresis made with pledging of sovereignty are also true of the present stipulation.

Note, § 1215,
part 5, Jus Nat.

Indeed, when we were speaking of this stipulation akin to antichresis, we suggested that if it should not be restricted to a definite time, but should be arranged until satisfaction should have been given to the creditor for principal and interest, an account would have to be rendered of the fruits taken; nevertheless it will not be so easily arranged between nations, for the reason that the business of rendering an account would be beset with many difficulties. Moreover the very greatest care would have to be exercised between nations lest material should be furnished for controversies not easy to be terminated. The present stipulation is to be likened to the contract for hiring of territory for a certain time, in which the entire price of the rent is paid at the very beginning, and consequently should be less than if it were paid specifically on a certain day. For just as the incomes from domain lands, the taxes and imposts can be let to private individuals, so nothing stands in the way of their being let to a nation also, nor is it then absurd that the letting should be joined with a grant of sovereignty.

§ 492. *When pledges between nations are ended*

§ 1244, part 5,
Jus Nat.

As soon as that has been performed for the sake of which a certain province or part of a territory or some definite locality or a definite right has been pledged, the pledge is released and the antichresis which had been added to it is extinguished. For when that has been performed for the sake of which a certain province or part of a territory or some definite locality or a definite right has been pledged, it is self-evident that the debt has been paid. Then indeed, if the debt has been paid, the pledge is released. Therefore also it is paid as soon as that has been performed for the sake of which a certain province or part of a territory or some definite place or a definite right has been pledged. Which was the first point.

§ 3.

As soon as the pledge is terminated, the antichresis is extinguished. Since, therefore, when the debt is paid, that is, when that has been performed which was due, the pledge is terminated; as soon as that has been performed for the sake of which the pledge was made the antichresis which had been added to it is extinguished. Which was the second point.

§ 1218, part 5, Jus Nat.

§ 659, part 5, Jus Nat.

§ 1159, part 5, Jus Nat.

When the debt is paid, the reason for the pledge is at an end, and the reason for the antichresis is also at an end. Therefore, since there is no further reason why a certain right ought to belong to one nation in the property of another, none can belong to it. Therefore it is plain that without difficulty those things can be derived from the fundamental principles of basic philosophy which are proved more at length in the law of nature. It is likewise to be noted that the principle of sufficient reason is no less dominant in the law of nature than in other sciences, as a principle which can be violated by nobody, unless you should desire to forswear reason, consequently to become insane. But although I should prefer that those things should not be proved from the first principles of ontology, which can be derived therefrom, for the reason that demonstrations sought from proximate principles afford us greater light and show the connexion of truths (a thing which is the peculiar virtue of a system), nevertheless I think a deduction from the principles of ontology is useful for investigation, and there ought also to be this use of them, since they are guiding concepts which point out the way by which one must go in an investigation. Ontology has this use besides, that you can bring the cognition of many things under your control by burdening the memory very little.

§ 3.

§ 170, Ontol.

§ 493. *Of the restoration of a thing pledged*

Since a pledge is released, and the antichresis which has been added to it is extinguished, as soon as that has been performed for the sake of which the pledge has been made, consequently no further right in it belongs to the nation to which the property of another has been pledged; as soon as that has been performed for the sake of which a pledge has been made, the provinces, parts of territories, or other places pledged are to be restored, and the use of the right pledged ought to cease immediately.

§ 492.

Since on payment of a debt the reason for the pledge and for the antichresis ceases, those things which belong to another nation are now without reason in the hands of the nation to which they had been pledged and the antichresis given. Therefore they are to be restored. Since rights are not transferred, except in so far as the owner allows them to be exercised by another, they also can be restored in no other way than that the one who has exercised them ceases to do so.

Note, § 492.

§ 467, part 2,
Jus Nat.
§ 39, part 3,
Jus Nat.

§ 494. *When a pledge which has been paid can be retained*

A pledge which has been paid can be retained for another debt by the nation to which the pledge was made, unless it shall have been expressly agreed otherwise. For if a pledge is paid, by natural law it can be retained for another debt. Therefore, since nations use with each other no other law than natural law, if a pledge is paid it can be retained for another debt by the nation to which the pledge was made. Which was the first point.

§ 1239, part 5,
Jus Nat.
§ 3.

If indeed it should be expressly agreed that it cannot be retained for another debt, he who receives the pledge renounces the right belonging to him according to natural law, as has been proved. Therefore, since by natural law any one can renounce his right, as long as he does nothing contrary to the right of a third party, as in the present instance is evidently not the case, and since he who renounces his right binds himself to the one for whom he renounces it, that he does not wish to use his own right against him; if it shall have been expressly agreed that a pledge cannot be retained for the debt of another, when the pledge is terminated the thing pledged must be immediately restored, nor can it be retained for the debt of another. Which was the second point.

§ 103, part 3,
Jus Nat.

§ 118, part 3,
Jus Nat.

§ 104, part 3,
Jus Nat.

The retention of a pledge for the debt of another is not contrary to the preceding proposition. For there it is tacitly assumed that there is no other existent reason why the pledge which is satisfied ought to remain with the one for whom it was established. Hence the utility of general principles is evident, which frequently make it plain to us that those things should not seem to us self-contradictory which are both true at the same time. But it is advisable that in those pledges which are made by nations an agreement should be made in regard

§ 493.

Note, § cited.

to restoration, in order that the thing which has been pledged cannot be retained for another purpose. For then the nation to whom the pledge is made renounces the involuntary pledge belonging to it by nature, and consequently by force of the present proposition renounces the right acquired by itself from the same, and therefore it cannot use the right against another.

§ 1118, part 5, Jus Nat.

§ 104, part 3, Jus Nat.

§ 495. *Of property of citizens bound for debts of the state*

The property of citizens or subjects is bound by nature for the debts of the state or nation. For by nature the property of a debtor is bound to a creditor for his debt. Therefore, since with respect to foreign nations all property of individuals taken together is to be considered as the property of the state, the property of citizens or of subjects is bound by nature to the nation for the debts of the state or of another nation.

§ 1177, part 5, Jus Nat.

§ 289.

See what we have noted elsewhere, and compare what has been noted above.

Note, § 1177, part 5, Jus Nat.

Note, § 289.

§ 496. *Whether the same is true of the private property of the king*

Since the property of citizens is bound by nature for the debts of the state or nation, and since the private property of the king, who so far as regards that property is considered a private person, is on an equality with the property of citizens, which likewise is private property, the personal property of the king also is bound by nature for the debts of the state or nation.

§ 496.

§ 23, part 8, Jus Nat.

Here and in the present proposition debt is used with the general signification of all that which we are bound to perform for another, from whatsoever source the obligation may come.

§ 170, part 3, Jus Nat.

§ 497. *What hostages are*

Hostages are defined as persons who are delivered as security for a debt, namely, that an agreement will be performed or a debt will be paid. Since a pledge is given as security for a debt, hostages are in fact given as pledges; consequently the things which have been proved in the law of

§§ 1142, 1143, part 5, Jus Nat.

nature in regard to pledges can be applied also to hostages, as far as the difference existing between things and persons permits.

As things are pledged so also are persons, consequently hostages are given where the good faith of the one who is bound to perform anything is suspected. But wherever good faith is assured there will be no need of hostages, since there will be no advantage in them.

§ 498. *How long hostages are to be retained*

§ 497.

Since hostages are given as security for a debt, they are retained until that shall have been performed which was due.

By hostages, of course, provision is made for the observance of an agreement or for the performance of what is due. There is need of the proviso "until it shall have been performed." And therefore they are to be retained until the debt shall have been paid. But here we speak only of the right; but he who has received hostages is not bound to retain them for so long. If indeed the good faith of the giver ceases to be suspected, since any one can give up his right, he can dismiss them; nay more, if so it shall seem good, he can dismiss them for any other reason.

§ 117, part 3,
Jus Nat.

§ 499. *Of the right to guard hostages*

§ 498.

In like manner, since hostages are given as security for a debt, since, therefore, it is to the interest of the one accepting them that they should not escape, the right of guarding them belongs to the one accepting them, so far as is adequate to prevent their escape, consequently a harsher guarding of them is illegal.

So it is not allowable to put hostages in chains and imprison them, for there is no reason why their flight is to be prevented in this way. There is the further consideration that, if they are not too harshly and severely treated, a thing which ought not to be done, there is no reason why it should be suspected that they will escape. But the guarding of a thing pledged is different from the guarding of hostages. For the creditor is bound to the debtor to guard the pledge carefully, that it may not be destroyed or deteriorated, and he is bound to compensate him

§ 1184, part 5,
Jus Nat.

for the loss, if by his fault or error the thing pledged should have been destroyed or deteriorated; but hostages are guarded for the advantage of the one who has received them. The guarding of the former is necessary, the guarding of the latter is at least allowable.

§ 1185, part 5, Jus Nat.

§ 500. *Whether hostages can be compelled to perform services*

Hostages cannot be compelled to perform any services, for hostages are pledged to the one who accepts them. Therefore, since a creditor is not allowed to use a pledge, and, since it is not possible to use hostages otherwise, except insofar as they are to perform certain services, they cannot be compelled to perform any services.

§ 1182, part 5, Jus Nat.

The giving of hostages assigns no other right to the one receiving than that they should be retained until the debtor shall have given satisfaction for them, and consequently the right to use the means without which they cannot be retained, such as custody. Therefore he has no right to the performance of services, nor to treat the hostages harshly and too severely, while they are in the place of a pledge.

§ 498.

§ 499.

§ 501. *What is pledged in the giving of hostages*

If hostages are given, their natural liberty is pledged, but their life cannot be put in pledge. For men are free by nature. Therefore, since anything can be put in pledge, and since liberty is included in the number of incorporeal things, if a hostage is given, his liberty is put in pledge. Which was the first point.

§ 146, part 1, Jus Nat.
§ 498, part 1, Jus Nat.

But no man indeed has any right over his own life, nor does this right belong to any other. Therefore a life cannot be put in pledge, and consequently, if a hostage is given, his life cannot be put in pledge. Which was the second point.

§ 351, part 1, Jus Nat.
§ 743, part 1, Jus Nat.

A man has nothing except his property and liberty belonging to him by nature, since no right over his life belongs to him. When a hostage is given, a right of pledge in his goods is not established in the one accepting, for they are not transferred, nor is anything said of them. The right is in the person who is transferred. Therefore not his goods

§ 351, part 1, Jus Nat.

Note, § 476.

but his liberty is put in pledge, but his life cannot be put in pledge. We have already said above, that formerly there was an opinion that by nature a right belonged to a man over his own life also. And then it was believed that the lives of hostages were put in pledge. But that doctrine is at variance with the law of nature.

§ 502. *Of the dismissal of hostages*

§ 1159, part 5, Jus Nat.

§ 659, part 5, Jus Nat.

§ 1160, part 5, Jus Nat.

§ 497.

§ 498.

§ 499.

As soon as that has been performed for which hostages have been given, they are to be dismissed. For as soon as a pledge is terminated—that is, the debt is paid, and that is performed which was due—the pledge must be restored. Therefore, since hostages are put in pledge, and ought to be retained only until the debt is paid, as soon as that has been performed for which hostages have been given, they are to be dismissed.

Therefore at that very moment at which payment is made the hostages are also freed; consequently the custody of them ends, and free departure is to be allowed them.

§ 503. *Whether hostages can be retained for another reason*

§ 497.

§ 1159, part 5, Jus Nat.

§ 494.

Hostages given for one reason can be retained for another, unless it shall have been expressly agreed that they should be returned when that shall have been performed for the sake of which they have been given. For since hostages are given in place of a pledge, and the pledge is terminated when that is performed for the sake of which they have been given, and since, when a pledge is terminated it can be retained for another debt even among nations, unless there shall have been an express agreement otherwise; hostages also can be retained for another debt, although that may have been performed for the sake of which they have been given, unless it should be expressly agreed otherwise, namely, that they should be returned when that for the sake of which they have been given should have been performed.

§ 1239, part 5, Jus Nat.

There are indeed those who think that it is merely a rule of civil law that a pledge can be retained for another debt when the pledge right is terminated. Nevertheless we have already proved the contrary elsewhere. But in the same place we have already observed, a thing which the proof itself also plainly shows, that the right to retain the pledge for another purpose does not come from the contract of pledge, to which alone those turn their attention who look upon it as merely a rule of the civil law, but from the right of involuntary pledge belonging to every one by nature. Therefore there is no need that the controversy concerning the right to retain hostages for another purpose should be determined from the interpretation of the stipulation, since it is plain enough that the one accepting could not acquire from that a greater right against the hostages than the one giving has desired to transfer to him, but against him that only can be considered as true which he has plainly declared, namely, that hostages should be held for that purpose for which they are given; for that the contrary is to be presumed, not even interpretation admits. Indeed, when it is evident what has been agreed upon, there is no place for interpretation. But Grotius himself allows the retention of hostages in accordance with that law by which, through the act of sovereigns, subjects can be detained by the right of *androlepsy*, or, as Gronovius interprets it, through a seizure as pledge.[6] Thus he refers this right to the voluntary law of nations. But it matters little whether you should say they are retained as hostages or deny that they are retained as hostages and assert that they are retained only as subjects of the one giving them. For the question here is, whether those who had been given as hostages for one purpose can be retained for another purpose, or as security for some other debt. Nevertheless they are not less properly said to be retained as hostages, when in fact they are retained by way of pledge; not as hostages, which they cease to be as soon as the debt is paid for which their freedom was pledged, but as captives by virtue of the right of pledge, as has just been said. But *androlepsy*, by the meaning of the word itself, suggests the seizure of a man, which was allowed by law among the Athenians. If an Athenian citizen had been killed in foreign territory, then the right belonged to the nearest of kin of the murdered man to hold not more than three men until punishment should be inflicted for the murder,

§ 1118, part 5, Jus Nat.

§ 382, part 3, Jus Nat.

§ 427, part 3, Jus Nat.

§ 512, part 6, Jus Nat.

§ 460, part 6, Jus Nat.

De Jure Belli ac Pacis, lib. 3, c. 20, § 55.

§ 501.

6. Johannes Fridericus Gronovius (1611–71), German classical scholar who produced an annotated edition of Hugo Grotius's *De Jure Belli et Pacis* (see Hugo Grotius, *De Jure Belli ac Pacis Libri Tres*, ed. J. F. Gronovius [Amsterdam, 1712], bk. 3, chap. xx, 55, p. 874, n. 54).

or the murderer should be surrendered. Nevertheless, in order that there should be no further difficulty, the right of involuntary pledge, or, if you prefer, the right of seizure as pledge between nations, could be extended also to individuals themselves, as will be shown later. But from what we have said it is plain, when there is an express agreement that hostages cannot be retained for another purpose, the right of seizure as a pledge existing by nature is renounced.

§ 164, part 3, Jus Nat.

§ 504. *Of the expenses for the support of hostages and of debts contracted by them*

He who has given hostages is bound to repay the expenses incurred for their support, and the hostage must pay the debts which he has contracted before he is dismissed. For the debtor is bound to repay the expenses necessarily incurred for the pledge. Therefore, since hostages are given in place of a pledge, and since no one can live without food, and consequently, since expenses incurred for the support of hostages are equivalent to the expenses necessarily incurred for a pledge, he who has given the hostages is bound to repay the expenses incurred for their support. Which was the first point.

§ 1199, part 5, Jus Nat.

§ 497.

Since we are bound to repay a debt, it is beyond all possibility of a doubt that a hostage ought to pay the debts which he has contracted in the place in which he has been detained as hostage. For payment ought to be made in that place in which it was agreed it should be made; and if in fact nothing has been expressly stated concerning the place of payment, the place of making the contract is considered the place of payment. Therefore, whether the hostage shall have expressly promised payment before his departure, or whether nothing shall have been said concerning the time and place of payment, the hostage nevertheless is bound to pay in that place where he has been detained as hostage. And since interpretation must be made in accordance with that which has probably been thought, he who contracted with the hostage, although nothing has been expressly said concerning the place and time of payment, is nevertheless understood to have contracted on no other condition than that he would pay before his departure. Therefore a hostage is bound to pay the debts which he has contracted before he is dismissed. Which was the second point.

§ 604, part 2, Jus Nat.

§ 170, part 2, Phil. Pract. Univ., and § 659, part 5, Jus Nat.

§ 693, part 5, Jus Nat.

§ 512, part 6, Jus Nat.

There is no one who does not know, or who would dare deny, that it is to the advantage of a creditor that the hostage should pay before he is dismissed. But from that which is to your interest no right arises for you to that which you do not have otherwise. Therefore in the proof we have not considered the reasons which are derived therefrom.

§ 265, part 1,
Phil. Pract. Univ.

§ 505. *That a hostage can be held for those things*

Since he who has given a hostage is bound to repay the expenses incurred for his support, and the hostage also is bound to pay the debts which he has contracted before he is dismissed, as long as the expenses incurred for support have not been repaid, or the debts which the hostage has contracted have not been paid, the hostage can be retained as a debtor.

§ 504.

The right to retain a hostage, although that has been performed for the sake of which he was given, comes from a double source; namely, from the fact of delivery, to which belong the expenses incurred for support, and from the contracts which the hostage has entered into with citizens of the place where he has been retained. In the former respect he could be said to be retained as hostage, unless you should desire the giving of a hostage to be strictly interpreted; but in the latter he can be retained in no other way than as a debtor on a contract, and his retention is equivalent to an arrest. But it seems to make little difference indeed whether the hostage should be said to be retained as hostage or as debtor; nevertheless it is necessary that one's attention should be directed to this distinction, lest asserting the right of retention may be thought contrary to the dismissal of hostages before proved, and in order that we may not state an exception to the rule, as if it were not universally true, if there be added no cause calculated to beget a right contrary to the former one. Therefore, although we may often say that something is true, unless another thing should be true or should be done, nevertheless that is not to be understood as if what is asserted is not universally true, but restricted by that which is added, or, as is commonly said, that the rule has this exception, but it is simply asserted that a new reason can be added which begets a right contrary to a former one, by which the execution of the former is either deferred or suspended, or the earlier right is altogether destroyed. This is sufficiently evident from the demonstration itself of those propositions which determine the nature of the

§ 502.

restriction. For the proposition itself is universally proved, a thing which could not be done, unless it should be in fact universally true; but what is added by way of restriction is especially proved as a different proposition from the earlier one, inasmuch as in it assumptions are made different from those in the present one. And therefore the latter also as a special proposition can be separated from the other and demonstrated apart from it, as has indeed been done frequently by us.

§ 506. *Of the effect of hostages*

The giving of hostages does not produce a new obligation, but it makes the good faith of the giver more secure for the one to whom they are given. For hostages are given as security for a debt—namely, that an agreement is to be performed, or a debt to be paid. Therefore, since the giving of hostages does not bind one to perform anything except that which the giver was already beforehand bound to perform, it is plain that the giving does not produce a new obligation. Which was the first point.

§ 497.

Since, indeed, hostages are given as security for a debt, and consequently they are demanded of the one whose good faith is suspected, or when he who demands them fears that the other may break faith, he who gives a hostage binds himself to the other to observe good faith. Therefore, since he makes secure the good faith of another, who binds himself to observe good faith, the giving of hostages makes the good faith of the giver more secure for the one to whom they are given. Which was the second point.

§ 758, part 3, Jus Nat.

Of course the freeing of the hostages ought to be the motive for performing that for the sake of which they are given. And therefore it is plain that by the giving of hostages the giver binds himself to perform that for the sake of which they are given, for him who receives them. But since the giving of hostages does not produce a new obligation, but simply secures the obligation for the sake of which they are given, hostages are described as simply an accessory to an obligation.

§ 118, part 1, Phil. Pract. Univ.

§ 507. *Of the personal obligation of citizens for the debts of the state*

The persons of citizens are bound by nature for the debts of the state, or nation. For the property of citizens is bound by nature for the benefit of the state. Therefore, since the rights also belonging to a man are included in his property, consequently also the liberty belonging to him by nature, and since this right itself is so closely connected to the person that it cannot in any way be separated from it, the persons also of citizens are bound by nature for the debts of the state.

§ 495.

§ 451, part 2, Jus Nat.

§ 146, part 1, Jus Nat.

And thus we have shown that which we promised to prove a short time ago. Hence, indeed, there arises for the nation for which another nation is unwilling to perform that which it owes, a right against the persons of its citizens, just as against its goods, as will be more plainly evident in its own place.

Note, § 501.

§ 508. *Who may be given as hostages*

Those persons are given as hostages in regard to whom there is the greatest hope that they will be redeemed, women and children no less than men. Since the persons of citizens are bound by nature for the debts of the state or nation, and since the natural liberty of the one who is given as a hostage, consequently the personality with which that is inseparably connected, is bound for the debt of the nation, and since women and children are understood to be included in the number of citizens no less than men; by nature any person, women and children no less than men, can be given as hostages. But hostages are given as security for a debt— namely, that an agreement will be performed, or that what is due will be paid. Therefore, since it is to the interest of the one receiving that not all persons generally should be given as hostages, it is undoubtedly necessary that those should be given in regard to whom there is the greatest hope that they will be redeemed.

§ 507.

§ 508 h, and § 1163, part 5, Jus Nat.

§ 6, part 8, Jus Nat.

§ 497.

In the giving of hostages the security of the one receiving them is alone considered, who without them does not wish to trust the debtor. But the one who suspects the good faith of another in abiding by his promises, is for that reason none the less likely to suspect that the other will not redeem a hostage. And this suspicion can be removed in no other way than by giving as hostages those persons in regard to whom there is the greatest hope that they will be redeemed, a thing which is to be determined from their character and is easily decided according to the given circumstances.

§ 509. *Of the rank of hostages*

§ 508.

Because those persons are given as hostages in regard to whom there is the greatest hope that they will be redeemed, therefore the most beloved persons are given as hostages, those pre-eminent in the state in dignity or merit, or those possessed of very great wealth; and if such cannot be had, dependence is placed on a great number of hostages.

Indeed, kings and princes themselves have given their own children as hostages, as Francis I to Charles V. But not only upon the will of the one to whom hostages are given, and who is especially interested in their being given, will it depend as to what sort he wishes to accept or to ask; but also just as much does the giver, as evidence of his sincerity and persistence in keeping faith, offer such hostages as can inspire the greatest confidence: a thing which is in harmony with the duty of a good man who desires as far as he can to avert from himself all suspicion of injustice and dishonesty. Therefore you should be far from censuring any one who voluntarily offers as hostages the persons most dear to him, as his own children, if the circumstances so demand.

§ 968, part 4,
Jus Nat.

§ 510. *To whom belongs the right to give hostages*

The right to give hostages belongs to sovereign powers and to subordinate powers within the limits of their authority. For hostages are given as security that state agreements will be adhered to, or that what is otherwise due will be paid, consequently for the sake of the stipulations of the state, and since he to whom they are given is unwilling to trust bare promises without them, necessity demands them. Therefore, since the supreme sovereignty in a state belongs to the sovereign powers, and therefore also eminent power over the person of citizens, by virtue of which for the sake of the public welfare in case of necessity they can dispose of the persons of citizens, to them also belongs the right to give hostages. Which was the first point.

§ 497.
§ 369.

§ 368.

§ 114, part 8,
Jus Nat.

And subordinate powers exercise a certain part of the sovereignty in dependence upon the sovereign power and in its name. Therefore, since within the limits of their authority they can do the same thing which the sovereign power itself ought to do, and since the sovereign power, when necessity demands, can give hostages, as proved above, subordinate

§ 368.

powers also within the limits of their authority can give hostages. Which was the second point.

Of course only so much right is understood to have been granted by the sovereign power to subordinate powers as they need, so that they can attend to the matters over which they have been given control. In war, in which the giving of hostages is especially important, the cases are not rare in which it is necessary that hostages should be given by subordinate powers; for in war particularly is good faith accustomed to be called in question. Nevertheless cases are not lacking also in which apart from war hostages are properly demanded and given to those demanding them, though these cases occur more rarely.

§ 511. *Whether any one is bound to go as a hostage*

Since the right to give hostages belongs to sovereign powers and to subordinate powers within the limits of their authority, he who is given as a hostage is bound to go as a hostage, nor does it depend upon his choice whether he may wish to go or not.

§ 510.

The giver would have no right, if it should depend upon the choice of him who is given as hostage whether he should wish to go as hostage or not. Therefore the obligation to go is bound up with the right to give, and derives its origin from the stipulation by which states have been established, and by force of which individuals have bound themselves to the whole, that they are willing to promote the common good, from which source arises state sovereignty, which contains the eminent power by virtue of which it is plain from the preceding proposition that hostages are given.

§ 4, part 8, Jus Nat.
§ 28, part 5, Jus Nat.

§§ 29, 32, part 8, Jus Nat.

§ 114, part 8, Jus Nat.

§ 512. *Whether any one may be given as a hostage without his consent*

Since he who is given as a hostage is bound to go as a hostage, and since it does not depend upon his choice whether he may wish to go or not, he can be compelled to go.

§ 511.

It is self-evident that it is extremely disagreeable to go as a hostage, consequently that there will be very few who would desire to go as hostages, and who would not rather prefer to be relieved from this burden. But since this is their duty, they therefore can be compelled by the sovereign power, which has the right of the people or of all the individuals in the state, and by the subordinate powers in its name, to satisfy their obligation, if they should be unwilling to do so.

§ 29, part 8, Jus Nat.

§ 513. *When it is to be determined by lot who ought to go as a hostage*

If there should be several, any one of whom may go as hostage without any difference to the state, the matter should be determined by lot. For if indeed there should be several, any one of whom may go as hostage without any difference to the state, a reason for choice is lacking, consequently there is no reason why one rather than another should be compelled to go. Therefore, since it may be decided by lot what is to be chosen from two or more options, and only those things are not to be decided by lot which can be determined by proper consideration, a thing which cannot be done in the present instance, as proved above; if there should be several, any one of whom may go as hostage without any difference to the state, the matter is certainly to be determined by lot.

§ 512.

§ 297, part 5, Jus Nat.

§ 296, part 5, Jus Nat.

It must be carefully noted that it is necessary, if the matter is to be determined by lot, that it would make no difference to the state which of them should go as hostage. For in the opposite case a reason for choice is not lacking, and this allows no place for the lot.

§ 296, part 5, Jus Nat.

§ 514. *When a vassal may not be given as a hostage*

The right does not belong to the lord of a fee to give his vassal as a hostage, if he is not a subject. For the right of giving a hostage belongs to the sovereign power, consequently a hostage is given by virtue of the supreme sovereignty, which also includes eminent power, or the right to dispose of the person of citizens for the sake of the public welfare in case of necessity. But if a vassal should not be a subject, the lord of the fee does not have eminent power over him. And since the right of the lord of a fee is to be determined from the feudal contract, and since in this there is merely an agreement concerning certain performances which are not included in the fee itself, which merely requires that fealty be given

§ 510.

§ 368.

§ 114, part 5, Jus Nat.

§ 172, part 6, Jus Nat.
§§ 173 and fol., part 8, Jus Nat.

the lord, consequently that he should not fail to avoid losses for him and to promote his interests, and that he should perform those things which have been especially agreed; the lord of the fee cannot assert any right over the vassal which belongs to the exercise of eminent power, nor does his right extend so far. If, then, the vassal is not a subject, the right does not belong to the lord of the fee to give the vassal as a hostage.

§ 155, part 6,
Jus Nat.

§ 154, part 6,
Jus Nat.

> To be a subject is one thing, to be a vassal is another, nor does the right of the lord of a fee over his vassal flow from the same source as the right of supreme power over a subject. Therefore the rights belonging to a supreme power over a subject cannot be given to the lord of a fee. And if it should happen that a certain right belongs to the lord of a fee over a vassal, which a supreme power also has over a subject, that is accidental and it is not for the same reason that it belongs to both, and therefore what belongs to each is to be determined from different principles.

§ 515. Whether one given as a hostage may escape

It is not allowable for one given as a hostage to escape. For hostages are given by the right of supreme power, and since they are already bound by the law of nature for the debts of the state, all the more must they abide by its will. Moreover, since they are given by way of assurance that agreements will be performed, or a debt will be paid, they are understood to have been given with no other intention than that they ought to remain until that should have been performed for the sake of which they have been given, and therefore they ought to remain, and it is by no means allowable for them to escape.

§ 511.

§ 507.

§ 497.

> Since a subject ought to consent to those things which the supreme power does by virtue of its eminent power, a hostage given by the supreme power or by virtue of its right is never considered to be given without his consent. Therefore it makes no difference whether the hostage has given himself of his own free will, or whether he has been given by the supreme sovereignty or by virtue of its right, so that in the first instance he may not escape because he is bound by his own act, and in the latter instance he may not, because in so far as regards his private rights he is merely to be considered a captive, the state transferring only its right of sovereignty over him, leaving his private rights

intact. For this does not accord with eminent power, which if the superior exercises it, is none the less to be obeyed than when it commands other things by virtue of its ordinary right. But what Grotius says, namely, that it does not seem to have been the intention of the state to bind a citizen not to escape, but to give the enemy the power to guard him as he chooses, is opposed to that fair dealing by which affairs of nations are to be conducted, and it undoubtedly would make the position of hostages more difficult, who since they should rightly be suspected of planning escapes, would properly be guarded even cruelly and with excessive harshness.

Loc. cit., c. 20, § 54.

§ 516. *Whether an escaping hostage can be received and retained by a state*

A state cannot receive and retain an escaping hostage. For the state has given the hostage by way of assurance that agreements will be performed, or that the debt will be paid, for which the hostage is given, consequently since the security would be destroyed, unless the hostage should remain, the state has given him with the understanding that he ought to remain. If, then, the state should receive and retain the fugitive, it would approve his act and would break faith. Therefore, since it is not allowed to break faith, the state cannot receive and retain an escaping hostage.

§ 497.
§ 758, part 3, Jus Nat.
§ 765, part 3, Jus Nat.

In the giving of hostages there is the tacit promise that the escaping hostage will not be received or retained, by which the giver not only binds himself to the receiver not to receive him, but he also furnishes a motive to the hostage for remaining and not escaping, when he knows that he will not be received by his state. And so the giving of hostages is accomplished with perfect good faith, and scarcely anything is more becoming to nations than this.

§ 517. *Whether another hostage is to be given in place of one who has died*

If a hostage dies, another is not to be given in his place. For hostages are given in place of a pledge. Consequently, if a hostage should die, the situation is the same as if a pledge should be destroyed. But if indeed a pledge should be destroyed, the pledge obligation is terminated. Therefore, if a

§ 497.
§1255, part 3, Jus Nat.
§ 1249, part 5, Jus Nat.

hostage dies your right also, which you had in him, is extinguished. But since in giving a hostage there has been no agreement that, if he who is given as a hostage should die, another would be given in his place, since, moreover, no one can acquire more right than another has wished to trans- §382, part 3, fer to him, nor can anything be held as valid against him, unless he has Jus Nat. properly declared it; if a hostage dies, another is not to be given in his place. Jus Nat.

§ 382, part 3, Jus Nat. § 427, part 3, Jus Nat.

There is no reason for urging that by the death of a hostage the security is destroyed which you wished to give to the one receiving him. For it is not destroyed by your fault, but by a superior force, which you can in no way resist. Therefore the accident, which has happened by no fault of yours, you are in no way bound to repair. Certainly, if a pledge is destroyed, the security also disappears which the creditor had in it. Nevertheless you are not on this account bound to give another pledge. There has to be trust without the pledge. But the situation is otherwise if there should be an express agreement that, in case the hostage should die, another should be given in his place, for then the obligation to give another is derived from the agreement, not from the giving of the pledge.

§ 518. *Why several are to be given*

Since if a hostage dies another is not to be given in his place, and since §517. the hour of death is uncertain, the security of the one receiving is better attained, especially if the hostage should be given for a considerable period, if several hostages are given, therefore also he who suspects the good faith of the debtor properly asks that several hostages be given.

Several hostages are given for the sake of greater security; but there is not one invariable reason for attaining security through a plurality of persons. For the worth of a person is balanced by it, or there is a §509. provision for security in case of death, as in the present instance, or finally the excessive mistrust of the one seeking security demands it.

§ 519. *If the hostage given should succeed to the throne of the giver*

If the hostage given should succeed to the throne of the giver, before that is performed for the sake of which he is given, he himself is freed on condition that another suitable person is substituted in his place. Since he who is given as a hostage is not himself a sovereign power, it is self-evident that it was not intended that the king himself should be in the position of a hostage, and consequently one to whom he is given cannot claim that he should be a hostage. Therefore it is understood that the tacit exception has been made that, if it happens that the hostage succeeds the king, some other suitable person should be substituted in his place. Therefore in the present instance, if some other person is substituted in his place, he who had been given at the beginning is freed.

He to whom the hostage has been given cannot assume a greater right to himself than has been transferred to him by the giver in the act of giving itself; what this may have been is to be decided from that which was at the time sufficiently expressed. Therefore, since there has been no agreement that the king himself should be a hostage, the one receiving him cannot claim, when the hostage given assumes the personality of the king, that he should remain a hostage. Full satisfaction is given him, if another suitable person is substituted in his place, by which of course his security would be just the same as it had been before. There is the further consideration that if the question had been asked at the beginning whether he who is given as hostage ought to remain, if he should succeed the king before that was performed for the sake of which he was given, the one giving would by no means have consented to this. Therefore it must be considered a proper interpretation of the agreement, that in that case the hostage should be freed, if another suitable person is substituted in his place.

§ 382, part 3, Jus Nat.

§ 427, part 3, Jus Nat.

§ 515, part 6, Jus Nat.

§ 520. *Whether any one can give himself as hostage*

Any one can give himself as hostage for his own debt. For the natural liberty of one who is given as a hostage is put in pledge as security that the debt is to be paid. Therefore, since nothing stands in the way of any one pledging his natural liberty for his own debt, because a pledge has been established in that which is his own, nothing stands in the way of his giving himself as a hostage for his own debt, consequently he can do so.

§§ 501, 497.

§ 1142, part 5, Jus Nat.

It is readily evident that this cannot be extended directly to subordinate powers: for example, if it cannot be done without prejudice to the sovereign power, then it cannot be done within the limits of their authority. For there is then the further objection that it takes away the natural liberty of deciding as one pleases concerning oneself. Nor is a hostage here given for his own debt. But the case is very rare in which any one is compelled to give himself as hostage. But here the question is, what can be done, not what often is done. Nevertheless there is no doubt in regard to that in the case of private individuals.

§ 521. *Whether at the death of the king who has made the treaty the hostage should be freed*

On the death of the king who has made the treaty the hostage is freed, if the treaty was a personal one; he is not freed, if it was a real one. For if, indeed, the treaty was a personal one, it expires on the death of the king who made it. Therefore, since the hostage has been given as a security $\quad$ § 414. for a treaty, for which there is no further need on the death of the king, $\quad$ § 497. as proved above; on the death of the king who had made the treaty there is no need of a hostage, consequently on his death the hostage is freed, if the treaty was a personal one. Which was the one point.

But if, indeed, the treaty was real, it binds his successors also. There- $\quad$ § 424. fore, since on the death of the king the treaty still exists, for securing $\quad$ § 497. which the hostage has been given, if the treaty was real, on the death of the king who had made it the hostage is not freed. Which was the third point.[7]

Of course the hostage is not freed before the time when that has been performed for the sake of which he is given. If the treaty was $\quad$ § 498. personal, on the death of the giver there is nothing which ought to be done, consequently there is nothing for the sake of which the hostage is to be retained. But the situation is different when the treaty is real, because then his successor is still bound to perform that which is to be done by virtue of the treaty. It makes very little difficulty, in what we said above, that a personal treaty binds the nation also; for that is $\quad$ § 424.

7. The Latin text has "tertium." This should probably be "alterum."

Note, § 424. understood to mean so long as the treaty exists, that is, so long as the king who made it is among the living. See what we have noted above.

§ 522. *Whether on the death of a hostage for whom any one has given himself as hostage the latter is freed*

If any one should give himself as a hostage for another hostage until the other should return, and the other should die, the one who had given himself as hostage is freed. For if any one should give himself as a hostage for another hostage until the other should return, he is in place of a

§ 497. pledge as security for the return of the other hostage. But it is self-evident indeed that the other cannot return if he is dead, and it is plain that the

§ 700, part 6, Jus Nat. obligation of returning is extinguished by his death. Therefore, since that is gone for the sake of which the one has given himself as hostage for the other, on the death of the other he is freed.

> For this is not to the prejudice of the one to whom the hostage has been given; for his condition is not made worse by this, because the other gave himself as a substitute hostage for the first. The substitute hostage was not given for that purpose for which the other was given. On him depends the security for the return of the one who acted as security for the debt. Of course it is just the same as if the other on the return of a pledge should in the meantime give another pledge, as security that the pledge which is returned is to be restored, which therefore is understood to have been given as security for the pledge bound by the debt. But the reasoning is different, if it should be expressly agreed that the hostage should remain, if he should die who was given at the beginning; for then he is bound by the promise, not by the vicarious substitution.

§ 523. *Of the death of the king to whom a hostage has been given*

If the king should die, to whom a hostage has been given, the hostage is freed, when the treaty was personal; he is not freed if it was real. It is shown in the same manner, as we proved a little while ago, that the hostage is not free, if the king who has made it dies and the treaty was real;

§ 521. but he is freed if the treaty was personal.

The hostage given as assurance that the treaty is to be observed remains bound so long as the treaty continues. Therefore it is not the lives of those who have agreed concerning the hostages that are considered, but the performance for the sake of which the hostage is bound. Hence if the performance should have been on condition, by the termination of the condition the hostage is freed; if it was for a certain time as the term to which it was restricted, when the time has elapsed the hostage is freed. A personal treaty is on the same basis as the latter case, for in it the performance has been limited to the life of either of the contracting parties. But here also the distinction is to be considered which exists between transitory and permanent promises; and affirmative and negative transitory promises are not on the same basis: for example, those things which ought not to be done, or can be done only within a certain space of time, or within all time to come. The obligation of the hostage is an accessory one which follows the principal obligation, and when this is extinct the accessory itself is also of no force. The addition of a hostage to a treaty changes it in no respect, and therefore it cannot make a real treaty out of a personal one.

Note, § 414.

§ 524. *Whether one hostage is liable for the act of another given at the same time*

If one of the hostages should commit an offence, or should escape, the others are not liable for his offence, or in general, one hostage is not liable for the act of another, unless they all shall have expressly bound themselves for each. For on account of the act of another, by which any one has been injured, consequently on account of the offence of another, no one can be punished, and in general, the deed of one cannot be imputed to another, except in so far as it in some way depends upon his will. Therefore the act of one hostage cannot be imputed to the others who are given at the same time, and if one should commit an offence, or should escape, or should have done anything, the rest are not liable for his offence or act. Which was the one point.

§ 581, part 8, Jus Nat.

§ 1084, part 1, Jus Nat.
§ 650, part 1, Phil. Pract. Univ.

But if, indeed, all should bind themselves for the individuals to the one to whom the hostages have been given, as that no one of them should escape, or that they would be willing to pay the debt contracted by the other, if he should not pay it; then for that which has been agreed upon the rest are liable not as hostages, but as debtors, by the stipulation. Which was the other point.

§ 789, part 3,
Jus Nat.

The obligation of hostages which comes from the giving of hostages is not to be confused with that which arises from another source, either from contract or delict. For the one is absolutely distinct from the other, nor as regards the latter are those considered as hostages who have been given as hostages. Lest indeed the application of the definition of delict, which we have given elsewhere, may offend some one, it is to be understood that nations in their relations with each other are to be looked at as private persons, and consequently also one nation with respect to the subjects of a foreign nation is not to be considered otherwise than as a private person, and therefore in case of giving of hostages the nation to whom the hostage is given cannot be considered otherwise than as a private person. But those things which do not arise because of the giving of hostages are to be determined from the principles of the law of nature which are in harmony with them: for example, if hostages contract a debt, from the contract by which they have been made debtors, and then hostages are looked at as foreigners dwelling in the territory of another.

§ 581, part 8,
Jus Nat.

§ 525. *Of the obligation of a hostage as a surety and as an expromissor*

If a hostage should promise that he will perform that for the sake of which he is given, either absolutely, or upon the condition that the other for whose debt he is given has not performed, in the former case he is held as an expromissor, in the latter as a surety. When he is an expromissor he so binds himself for another that he himself in his own name will perform as principal debtor that which the other was bound to perform, but a surety is one who so binds himself for another that he himself is willing to perform if the other does not perform; if a hostage should promise absolutely that he will perform that for the sake of which he is given, he is held as expromissor, but if under the condition that the other has not performed, he is held as surety.

§ 865, part 4,
Jus Nat.

§ 784, part 4,
Jus Nat.

In the former case, of course, the expromission, in the latter the suretyship, is added to the giving of a hostage. But in either case he who is given as a hostage represents a double personality, that is, in the former case he is looked on as a hostage who is given in place of a pledge, so far as the giver is concerned, as an expromissor, so far as he himself is concerned; while in the latter case he is likewise looked on as a hostage, so far as the giver is concerned, and as a surety, so far as he himself is concerned. Therefore the obligation of the giver to free the hostage, on performance of that for the sake of which he is given, is left unimpaired; however, as regards the one to whom the hostage has been given, it is not on the same basis, on account of the difference which exists between expromission and suretyship by virtue of those things which we have proved elsewhere in the fourth part of "The Law of Nature."

C. 3.

§ 526. *Of the principal obligation of the hostage*

Since the hostage is bound as expromissor, if he should bind himself absolutely that he will perform that for the sake of which he is given, and since an expromissor assumes the personality of the principal debtor, in that case the obligation of the hostage is a principal obligation, not simply an accessory one.

§ 525.

§ 867, part 4, Jus Nat.

§ 527. *Of what sort the obligation of a hostage as surety is*

Since a hostage is bound as surety, if he promises that he will perform that for the sake of which he has been given, unless he who has given should perform, and since the obligation of a surety is only an accessory one; in that case the obligation of the hostage remains accessory, nevertheless it is a different one from that which comes from the giving of hostages.

§ 525.

§ 784, part 4, Jus Nat.

Not without reason is the obligation of the hostage, which arises from suretyship and expromission, distinguished from that which comes from the giving of hostages, since the one produces a legal effect, which the other does not, as will become clearer later.

§ 528. *If a hostage should promise that a debt is to be paid*

If a hostage promises that he will bring it about that the thing for the sake of which he has been given shall be performed, he is obliged to provide that which is at stake. For when a hostage promises that he will bring it about that the thing for the sake of which he has been given shall be performed, by hypothesis he promises, as sponsor, that he will bring it about that the sovereign power will ratify the agreement, consequently will perform. Therefore, since each promise concerning the debt of another is made in the same manner, the promise of the hostage is equal to a sponsion. Therefore, since a sponsor is obliged to provide that which is at stake, a hostage also, if he should promise that he will bring it about that the thing for the sake of which he has been given shall be performed, is obliged to provide that which is at stake.

§ 465.

§ 475.

Of course he is obliged, as principal debtor, to provide that which is at stake, from the promise of his own act; but there remains also the accessory obligation, which comes from the giving of hostages, by virtue of which the natural liberty of the hostage is put in pledge. And this is really the case of which Grotius speaks, when he says that hostages are sometimes in fact the principal part of the obligation. But if, indeed, he should be an expromissor, the whole obligation is transferred to him and he himself assumes the personality of the principal debtor. But undoubtedly the obligations are dissimilar by which one is bound to pay that which another owes, and that by which he ought to pay the loss sustained when the principal debtor has not performed what he ought to have performed. Besides, it must be noted that it is just the same whether a hostage should promise that he would bring it about that the thing should be done for the sake of which he has been given, through himself, or through others, as for example his kinsmen or friends.

§ 501.

De Jure Belli ac Pacis, lib. 3, c. 20, § 58.

§ 867, part 4, Jus Nat.

§ 529. *When the property of a hostage is bound for the loss sustained*

Since a hostage is bound for the loss sustained, if he promises that he will bring it about that the thing for the sake of which he has been given as hostage shall in fact be performed, since, moreover, besides his liberty and his property he has nothing which he can put in pledge, and his liberty is already pledged in so far as he is a hostage; if a hostage promises that he will bring it about that the thing for the sake of which he has been

§ 528.

§ 501.

given shall be in fact performed, his own property is put in pledge, so far as that is sufficient for paying what is at stake.

There is no reason why you should say, that if he who has given a hostage breaks faith, he will not deliver the goods of the hostage, or give satisfaction from them to the one with whom he has not kept faith; for other means are not lacking among nations of collecting that which is due to one from another, of which we must speak in their own place.

§ 530. *When and in how many ways the property of a hostage is pledged for the amount for which he is given as hostage*

If a hostage becomes an expromissor, or a surety, his property in the former case absolutely, or as principal, in the latter case as security, is put in pledge to the one to whom he is given. For if a hostage should become an expromissor, he assumes the personality of the principal debtor. And the property of a debtor is bound by nature for his debts. Therefore, also, the property of a hostage is bound to the one to whom he has been given for that debt for which he was given. Which was the first point.

§ 867, part 4, Jus Nat.
§ 1177, part 4, Jus Nat.

The principal debtor must be sued before the surety can be compelled to pay the debt, consequently he is not rated as a debtor unless the principal debtor has been sued, and therefore he is held only as security for the creditor. Therefore, since by nature the property of a debtor is bound to the creditor for his debt, the property of a surety is bound by nature as security for the debt of the principal debtor. If therefore a hostage shall have been a surety, his property is bound by nature to the one to whom he has been given for the amount for which he was given. Which was the second point.

§ 805, part 4, Jus Nat.

§ 1177, part 4, Jus Nat.

It seems indeed to make little difference in the case of hostages whether a hostage is looked at as an expromissor, or as a surety, especially since the principal debtor would be bound in no respect to the surety if he goes security for him without his consent and pays, just as an expromissor cannot demand from the principal debtor what he has paid for him, unless it shall have been so agreed; nevertheless it is not

§ 799, part 4, Jus Nat.

§ 869, part 4, Jus Nat.

useless to consider this difference. For in the case of the expromissor, he to whom the expromission has been made can urge immediately, upon the breaking of faith, that the property of the hostage should be surrendered to him; but in the latter case, since there is doubt whether or not he who gave the hostage would ratify the giving of security, the alternative is to be urged that he should either satisfy himself or the property of the hostage should be delivered to him.

§ 531. *Whether hostages are slaves*

§ 501.

§ 1145, part 5, Jus Nat.
§§ 137, 138, part 1, Jus Nat.

§ 1096, part 7, Jus Nat.

Hostages are not slaves of him to whom they are given. For if any one is given as a hostage, his liberty alone is put in pledge, consequently since a pledge contains only a conditional right of alienation, no right over the actions of the hostage is in fact transferred to him to whom a hostage has been given, when he is given, except in so far as the liberty of the hostage to stay in a particular place and to act as restricted by the nature of the matter. For since a man is not the slave of another, if the other has no power of control over his actions, hostages are not slaves of him to whom they are given.

§ 499.
§ 859, part 1, Jus Nat.

From the right to hold him, which by virtue of eminent power has been taken away from him who has given the hostage, arises the obligation of the hostage to remain in that place in which he to whom he is given detains him. And therefore no other right belongs to him over the hostage than that he should guard him, in order that he may not escape, if he should not wish to satisfy his obligation. He cannot claim for himself a further right over the actions of the hostage without wrong. If he should reduce him to the condition of a slave, he certainly does wrong.

§ 532. *If he who has given a hostage breaks faith*

§ 501.

If that for the sake of which a hostage has been given should not be performed, the hostage either becomes a slave or is retained as a captive, but he cannot be killed. For the natural liberty of a hostage is put in pledge. Therefore, since if that for the sake of which a hostage has been given should not be performed for the one to whom he has been given, he cannot be satisfied out of the pledge otherwise than by acquiring a right over the free actions of the hostage, consequently by reducing him to slavery, or by detaining him as a captive in prison; if that, for the sake of which a hostage has been given, should not be performed, the hostage either becomes a slave or is retained as a captive. Which was the first point.

§ 153, part 1, Jus Nat.

§ 1096, part 7, Jus Nat.

But since the life of a hostage cannot be put in pledge, therefore he to whom he has been given can acquire no right over his life, even if that should not be performed for the sake of which he was given, and consequently the hostage cannot be killed. Which was the second point.

§ 501.

> The condition of the hostage is harsh enough, if indeed he is reduced to slavery, or thrown into lifelong imprisonment. Because of that therefore the motive is undoubtedly strong that he who has given him should not break faith, but should be most steadfast in preserving it. Prison is substituted in place of slavery, not only where the latter is not practised, but also on account of the rank of the person. For no other act seems possible in the other case than that the hostage should be detained in prison if he who has given him breaks faith. But as to the fact that hostages have been killed in former times, or that they may be slain to-day by barbarous nations; this is to be attributed to the error that a right belongs to a man to his own life, consequently a ruler can dispose of this also by virtue of eminent power. Nay more, even if an absolute right should belong to a man over his own life, nevertheless a superior would abuse his sovereign power if he should pledge the life of an innocent man as security for good faith, and nevertheless should not hesitate to break it.

Note, § 501.

§ 533. *Of the performance of that for which a hostage is bound by his own act*

If that for the sake of which a hostage has been given is not performed, the hostage is bound to perform that for which he is bound by his own act. For he is bound by his own act to the person to whom he has been given as hostage, either as an expromissor, or as a surety, or as a sponsor, and in every case his property has been put in pledge to him to whom the hostage has been given. If then that should not be performed for the sake of which a hostage has been given, since promises are to be observed, and therefore those things are to be performed which have been promised, a hostage certainly is bound to perform that for which he is bound by his own act.

§ 525.

§ cited.

§ 528.

§§ 529, 530.

§ 431, part 3, Jus Nat.

§ 430, part 3, Jus Nat.

Since this debt does not come from the giving of hostages, although it may have been contracted on the occasion of their giving, it is not to be confused with the right which, from the giving of hostages, belongs to him to whom the hostage has been given, and in regard to that a decision must be made from the peculiar principles of the act by which it was contracted. But there is no cause to speak here of the method of collecting a debt. For of that we shall speak in its proper place, when we shall show in general how a nation may acquire from a nation what is due to it, so that nothing is done which is not in harmony with its right.

§ 534. *Of the wrong done to a hostage if faith is broken*

§ 510.

§ 789, part 3, Jus Nat.

§ 765, part 3, Jus Nat.

§ 532.

§ 501 h, and § 858, part 1, Jus Nat.

§ 859, part 1, Jus Nat.

If he who has given a hostage should break faith, he does the hostage a wrong. For he who gives a hostage, has indeed a right to give a hostage; nevertheless since that, for the sake of which he is given, ought to be performed, and since one may not break faith that has been given, no right belongs to him to deliver an innocent citizen into slavery, or to lifelong imprisonment, a thing which happens if he should break faith. If then he should break faith, that undoubtedly would be done contrary to the right of the hostage, from whom liberty is taken without a cause. Therefore, since that is wrong which is done contrary to the right of another, if he who has given a hostage should break faith, he does the hostage a wrong.

Note, § 532.

§ 118, part 1, Phil. Pract. Univ.

Since the condition of the hostage is rendered very hard, if the giver should break faith, it is no slight wrong which he inflicts on the hostage. And because therefore this could and ought to have been a most potent motive for not breaking faith, he who gives by way of hostageship is bound as firmly as possible to keep faith, that therefore it may become the established custom to have confidence in hostages, because such great and disgraceful treachery is not readily presumed, which is coupled with the greatest wretchedness to innocent people, whose welfare the traitor ought to consider. The violation of good faith secured by hostages is in itself so extraordinarily base, that it is dreadful treachery for one to break faith who has given a hostage.

§ 535. Of the redemption of a hostage if good faith should not have been observed

If he who has given a hostage shall have broken faith, he is bound to redeem the hostage. For if that for the sake of which a hostage has been given should not be performed, consequently if he who has given him should have broken faith, the hostage either becomes a slave or is retained as captive, and therefore, since the giver causes a loss of his liberty, which had been put in pledge, the greatest loss is inflicted upon him, and that indeed by the wrong of the one giving him as hostage. Therefore, since loss caused by a wrong is to be repaired, if he who has given a hostage shall have broken faith, he is bound to restore to the hostages the loss caused, and since it is apparent that this can be done in no other way than by restoring his liberty, that is, by redeeming him, he is bound to redeem him.

§ 758, part 3, Jus Nat.
§ 532.
§ 501.
§ 488, part 2, Jus Nat.
§ 534.
§ 580, part 2, Jus Nat.

> Of the redemption of captives we shall speak later in its proper place. Therefore, since hostages are put on an equality with captives, if he shall have broken faith who has given them, the things which will be proved later concerning the redemption of captives are to be applied to hostages also; when this is done those doubts will also be removed which could still be suggested to the minds of one or another in regard to the right over hostages.

§ 536. Of the restoration of the loss which a hostage suffers

The state or its ruler is bound to restore to the hostage or to his next of kin the loss which he suffers. To go as a hostage is undoubtedly a burden which is borne for the sake of the public good, since the right is taken from the hostage of staying where he wants to be and doing as he pleases what may seem best to him. Therefore, since all are jointly bound to promote the public good, the hostage alone is not bound to undertake that for nothing. Therefore the state or its ruler is bound to restore the loss which he suffers. Which was the first point.

§ 497.
§§ 498, 499.
§ 28, part 8, Jus Nat.

But since benefit can be repaid for benefit in the persons of those whom we love, moreover, since every one is presumed to love his next of kin, if the inconvenience which the hostage himself has suffered cannot

§ 716, part 6, Jus Nat.

conveniently be made good, it must be made good to his next of kin. Which was the second point.

Compensation can consist of rewards, of promotion to public office, of conferring of dignities and privileges, as the occasion shall have suggested and as shall have seemed best to the one making recompense. But it seems foreign to our plan to descend to particulars of that sort.

§ 537. *If it has been introduced by custom that hostages may be killed*

If it has been introduced by the custom of nations that it is allowable to kill hostages, this is a customary right and cannot be referred to the voluntary law of nations, and it really consists only in the absence of punishment. For if it has been introduced by the custom of nations that it is allowable to kill hostages, since that is a customary law of nations, which has evidently been introduced by long usage and is observed as law, it must be referred to the customary law of nations. Which was the first point.

§ 24.

§ 532.

Note, § 50.

§ 22.

§ 992, part 8, Jus Nat.

The killing of hostages is contrary to the law of nature, and was only introduced into the custom of nations in former times from the mistaken idea that a man has a right to his own life. Therefore, since the voluntary law of nations, as we have said, is developed from the necessary law of nations in the same way as civil law from natural law, and since if civil laws are to be made from natural laws, general errors ought not to be taken as the law of nature; if it has been introduced by the custom of nations that it is allowable to kill hostages, that cannot be referred to the voluntary law of nations. Which was the second point.

§ 532.

§ 418, part 3, Jus Nat.

Finally, if it has been introduced by the custom of nations that it is allowable to kill hostages, that is simply permitted by the other party by whom the hostage is given, although it is illegal by nature. Therefore, since he goes unpunished who is permitted by others to act, although he is bound by nature to do the opposite, if it has been introduced by the custom of nations that it is allowable to kill hostages, that is not properly speaking a right, but only an absence of punishment. Which was the third point.

Grotius asserts that by the external law of nations, which he calls the voluntary, hostages can be killed; but the reason for this statement is, that he does not derive the voluntary law of nations from the concept of a supreme state, as he ought, but from the acts of nations, from which he contends their consent is to be presumed, so that for that reason he does not distinguish the customary law of nations from the voluntary. The former contains errors, nor does it give a true right to the one acting, but only an absence of punishment. The latter rejects the errors, which are opposed to the imperative and prohibitive law of nature, nor does it tolerate anything save what by virtue of natural liberty is to be tolerated in any man. The voluntary law of nations rests on definite principles from which it can be proved, but errors exist in connexion with it no less than in connexion with natural law. Therefore, although those errors may be assumed as law, nevertheless they do not belong to the law of nations any more than errors contrary to natural law belong to the law of nature. So fornication is not permissible by the law of nature, for the reason that even civilized nations have considered it as legal, or that even now certain ones may so consider it.

De Jure Belli ac Pacis, lib. 3, c. 20, § 53.

§ 22.

§ 538. *If faith is broken, whether hostages remain such*

When faith is broken in that for the sake of which hostages have been given, those given as hostages cease to be such. For when faith is broken the hostages either become slaves or are retained as captives. Therefore, since hostages are not slaves, nor are they retained as captives, but are simply guarded, that they may not be able to escape; when faith is broken, those given as hostages cease to be such.

§ 532.

§ 531.

§ 499.

When he who has given a hostage has broken faith, the reason for which the hostage was given ceases to exist, consequently there is no further need of a hostage. When therefore they are retained either as slaves, or as captives, since hostages are in place of a pledge, it is undoubtedly just as if the pledge has been sold or has taken the place of the debt. Since, therefore, the pledge then ceases to be a pledge, so also a hostage ceases to be a hostage, if he who has given him has broken faith. The right over a hostage, which belongs to the one to whom the hostage has been given, after he who had given him has broken

§ 497.

§ cited.

his pledge, is quite different from the right which he had before. But if you except his life, the one to whom the hostage had been given can do as he pleases in regard to him who had been the hostage, just as he could to his own human being.

§ 539. *Whether they can be dismissed*

He to whom hostages have been given can dismiss them, on whatever condition he may please, after he who has given them has broken faith. For any one can give up his own right provided he does nothing contrary to the right of a third party, as here is not the case. Therefore, since he to whom hostages have been given, gives up his right to them when he dismisses them after he who has given them has broken faith, he can dismiss them. Which was the first point.

§ 117, part 3, Jus Nat.

§ 532.

If hostages are dismissed when he who had given them has broken faith, the one dismissing them disposes of his own right. Therefore, since any one can dispose of his own property, consequently also of his own right, as shall seem best to him, hostages can be dismissed on that condition which may seem best to the one dismissing them. Which was the second point.

§ 498, part 1, Jus Nat.
§ 118, part 2, Jus Nat.

Undoubtedly the condition of hostages is very hard, if he who has given them has broken faith, since they are deprived of their liberty, certainly an inestimable good, especially with regard to persons who have been given as hostages. Hostages as such are in fact innocent, since in them there is no blame for the broken faith, but they are merely unfortunate. Therefore it is characteristic of a generous spirit to dismiss hostages uninjured when faith has been broken, unless they are redeemed by their own nation. But they can be dismissed on the condition that they shall not return to their own people, or that they remain with the nation to whom they have been given and hold their property there, as circumstances may suggest, which are for prudence to consider. Those who are cruel to hostages certainly have the customs of barbarians, and they do injury to them.

§ 532.

§ 509.

§ 532.

§ 540. *What sort of pledges hostages really are*

Hostages are not so much pledges of a debt, as of good faith. For hostages are given as security for a debt indeed, but not with the intention that, unless the debt should be paid, satisfaction should be given from them to the creditor or to the one to whom they are given, but that through them provision may be made that agreements will be observed, or a debt will be paid. Therefore it is plain that hostages are not pledged for a debt as things are pledged, but for the good faith of the debtor.

§ 497.
§ 1142, part 5, Jus Nat.
§ 757, part 3, Jus Nat.

And this is the reason why the points which have been proved of pledges cannot be applied generally to hostages, but we have said that the difference must be considered which exists between persons and things. There is indeed no valuation of a free person as there is of things, and therefore for a debt which admits of valuation hostages cannot be pledged, but in fact only for the good faith of the debtor, so that, if he should break faith, they may be retained either as slaves or as captives, as a penalty for violated faith; when this happens they themselves are not punished for the act of another, a thing which is certainly unjust, but they feel the evil occasioned by the act of another and they suffer wrong from their own nation, or its ruler. Therefore the injustice, of which they properly complain, is not at the hands of him to whom they are given, but at the hands of him who gave them. And this injustice ought to deter the giver from treachery, who in this very manner is bound to avoid treachery. That hostages are in fact nothing but pledges of good faith is seen with perfect clearness from the fact that they are given either by him whose good faith is suspected, or by him who desires to avert from himself all suspicion of treachery. See what we have noted above.

§ 1084, part 1, Jus Nat.
§ 534.

§ 118, part 1, Jus Nat.

Note, §§ 508, 509.

§ 541. Of the determination of the price of redemption

Since hostages are pledges, not so much of a debt as of good faith, therefore there is no valuation of the act, for the sake of which they are given, a thing which very often has no valuation, nor of the loss sustained, and consequently when they are redeemed, there must be an agreement as to the price of redemption.

§ 540.

Therefore, although they be made slaves, which undoubtedly is a harsher thing than if they should only be detained as captives, and slaves, when they are sold, may be valued at a certain price; nevertheless the price of redemption is not calculated in this way. When they

§ 532.

§§ 501, 540.
are redeemed their liberty is to be restored, which had been pledged for the good faith of the giver; and that is incapable of valuation. Therefore on failure of any intrinsic standard for determination of value one must turn to extrinsic standards, which reduce the determination to that which seems most expedient to the acceptor.

§ 542. *Of hostages given by each of the contracting parties*

§ 540.

§ 99, part 1,
Jus Nat.

§ 497.

If there has been an agreement for mutual performances, and one of the contracting parties demands hostages, the other party can likewise demand them. For since hostages are in truth pledges of good faith, they are demanded by him who suspects the good faith of the other. But if you suspect my good faith, you cannot object if I suspect yours also. Therefore if one of the contracting parties demands hostages as security for that which is to be performed for him, the other party also, as security for that which is to be performed for him, can likewise demand hostages.

§ 761, part 3,
Jus Nat.
§ 47.

§ 49.

§ 3.

§ 39.

Note, § 509.

It is also in harmony with the custom of nations that in the circumstances of the present case hostages should be reciprocally given. Certainly it would warrant that the good faith of nations would be secure everywhere, as ought to be the case, and that would greatly conduce to the glory of nations, to pursue which they are bound; but just as individual men are not such as they ought to be, nor is the good faith of many assured, so also nations are not what they ought to be. There is the added consideration that a good man, whose duty is extended to the nations themselves also, and to their rulers who represent them, ought also to avert from himself all suspicion of treachery, as we have already observed above.

§ 543. *Of hostages given in return for hostages given*

§ 497.

§ 499.

Hostages also can be given as security for those given, that is, that nothing harsh may be done to them, and that when that object has been accomplished, for the sake of which they were given, they may be restored without delay. For hostages are given as security for that which ought to be performed. Therefore, since nothing harsh ought to be done to them, and they ought to be restored without delay as soon as that has been performed for the sake of which they are given, they can be given as

security for this also. Therefore it is plain that hostages can also be given   § 502.
as security for those received, that is, that nothing harsh may be done to
them, and that when the object has been accomplished for the sake of
which they were given, they may be restored without delay.

That has especial pertinence, when there has been an express agreement that hostages given for one purpose may not be retained for
another; or when it has been expressly declared how hostages are to   § 503.
be held. For if he who receives ought to give hostages in return, the
recipient is assumed to be bound to perform some particular act; for
otherwise he cannot break faith, consequently the suspicion that he
may break faith ceases. We do not desire to add more concerning
hostages, for if cases arise in regard to which nothing has been said,
they are determined without difficulty, by an understanding of those
things which we have said depending upon the principles of the law
of nature and nations.

§ 544. *Of the strengthening of a treaty by affirmation*

Treaties are strengthened by affirmations. For an affirmation is proof of
the truth of statements with conscience as a witness. Therefore, if nations   § 851, part 3,
affirm that they will faithfully keep the agreements in a treaty, they call   Jus Nat.
their conscience to witness that they will do that, and consequently one
pledges his faith to the other. Therefore, since this is done for no other   § 757, part 3,
reason than that one party may be certain that the treaty will be observed,   Jus Nat.
  § 760, part 3,
and the promisor pledges his faith to the promisee concerning it, treaties   Jus Nat.
are strengthened by affirmations.

It is readily evident, if you consider the present proof, that a man
proves himself devoid of good faith, who does not consider it a matter
of religious duty to do those things which he has not only promised
but also affirmed that he will do. For in whom are we to have confidence if he breaks faith who calls his conscience to witness that he will
keep his promises? The same also is understood of him who does not
do what he has affirmed he will do. It is plain, furthermore, that it is
much more disgraceful to break faith if an affirmation is added to a
promise, than if there is a bare promise. And therefore, affirmations
ought to be a motive for much greater concern that nothing should be

done contrary to the treaty. They are formulas of this sort: "by sacred faith," "under the royal pledge," "by our majesty we promise"; likewise "we promise that we will preserve this treaty inviolate," and other formulas of the sort which have been introduced in our customs for that purpose, on which the signification as introduced by usage depends. If all nations were insistent on preserving good faith, good faith could never be suspected, and consequently there would be absolutely no need of affirmation, since it would be inadvisable, and also certainly illegal. But since it not infrequently happens that even nations and their rulers break faith, there is need of affirmations in order that what natural obligation, or the law of nature from which it is derived, cannot effect, a sense of shame may effect, and that a good man consciously persisting in the observance of his good faith may avoid all suspicion as far as possible. But although several formulas of affirmation have been accepted in common usage among nations, nevertheless all these formulas do not indicate exactly the same thing, certainly some by virtue of the proper signification of words, from which one must not depart in the interpretation of treaties unless reason suggests it, indicate a stronger affirmation than others. Affirmations of course differ in degree. But would that all who add an affirmation to promises would notice the signification of words, and that it were sufficiently deliberated, so that there would be truth in their words, and that they would not simply speak thus because it is the custom so to speak. But deliberate intention is rightly presumed in affirmations, and what one has said is considered as true against the speaker.

§ 276, part 3,
Jus Nat.
§ 856, part 3,
Jus Nat.

§ 469, part 6,
Jus Nat.

§ 387, part 3,
Jus Nat.

§ 424, part 3,
Jus Nat.

§ 427, part 3,
Jus Nat.

§ 545. *When that is allowable by nature*

If your good faith should seem suspected by any one, or if it should be to your interest that he to whom you promise certain things should not perchance doubt your good faith, it is allowed by nature to strengthen treaties by affirmations. For if your good faith is suspected by any one, he doubts that you will perform what you promise that you will perform, consequently that you speak the real truth. And in the same way it is plain that he who doubts your good faith, doubts whether or not you speak the real truth. But if any one should doubt that you are speaking the real truth, or cannot determine this from that in regard to which the words are spoken, as in the present instance when the question is as to

§ 758, part 3,
Jus Nat.

§ 150, part 3,
Jus Nat.

the fulfilment of a promise, and if it is to his advantage that he should
be certain of the truth of the words, or to your interest that he to whom
you are speaking should not by any chance doubt the truth of the words,
affirmations are allowable. Therefore if your good faith should be suspected, or if it should be to your interest that he to whom you promise
certain things should not perchance doubt your good faith, affirmations
are allowable, and consequently because treaties are strengthened by affirmations, it is allowable by nature to strengthen treaties by affirmations.

§§ 854, 855,
part 3, Jus Nat.

§544.

> As the law of nature controls all human acts, consequently also
> the acts of nations, so also it controls affirmations, which are useless
> as soon as they are withdrawn from its control. Therefore it is our
> purpose to show what that immutable law may enjoin upon them.

§ 546. *What is sacred among nations*

A thing is said to be sacred which the public or common welfare of
nations commands should be exempt from every violation. Therefore
sanctity is the inviolability of a thing, or a person, demanded by the
public welfare or by the common welfare of all nations.

> Sanctity is attributed to things as well as to persons. So the per-
> son of the ruler of a state is sacred because the public welfare, or the
> welfare of the entire state, demands that he should not be injured.
> Likewise the walls by which cities are surrounded, and which the need
> of public security makes inviolable, are called sacred. That anything
> should be considered sacred by the law of nations, it is necessary of
> course that it should be to the interest of nations that it be considered
> inviolable, and consequently that very need of safety of nations should
> protect and defend it from injury by humans. Therefore there is a
> certain moral quality which is understood to be inherent in the thing,
> or person; as rights are thought to be inherent in the thing or person,
> or as the moral person, which is determined by the rights, is supposed
> to exist in the physical individual.

§ 547. *Of the sanctity of treaties*

Since treaties are stipulations entered into by sovereign powers for the
sake of the public good, consequently the public safety and common

§ 369.

welfare of all nations demand that they should be perfectly observed and should not be violated in any way at all, and since that is sacred which the public or common welfare of nations commands should be exempt from every violation, treaties are sacred, and they are to be considered sacred by nations.

§ 546.

No one will doubt that the common safety of all nations requires that treaties should be violated in no way, unless one is either ignorant or does not care what those things may be as to which a nation binds itself to another nation, and how much difference it makes that a nation to which another nation has bound itself to do something, should in fact do it, and not break the good faith pledged. Therefore, since nations, in so far as they establish a certain supreme state, are bound to recognize the public welfare, the supreme law in a state, in the supreme state too they ought undoubtedly to agree to that which is the means of preserving and promoting the public safety of nations. The public welfare of nations, like the public welfare of a particular state, consists in the unhampered enjoyment of sufficient means of life, of tranquillity and of security, and all treaties are directed to this end. Therefore, since the public safety of nations is promoted if individual nations are steadfast in observing treaties, they ought to agree to this, that treaties by their nature should be considered inviolable, and that nothing should be considered more disgraceful than the violation of treaties. And so it is evident, even by the voluntary law of nations, of which we have spoken, that treaties are to be considered sacred.

§ 9.
§ 86, part 8, Jus Nat.

§ 17, part 8, Jus Nat.

§ 22.

§ 548. *That the violation of a treaty is contrary to the law of nations*

§ 547.
§ 546.

Since treaties are to be considered sacred, and since he who violates a treaty destroys or impairs the sanctity of the treaty by not doing that which by virtue of the treaty he ought to have done, or by doing that which by virtue of the treaty he could not have done, the violation of a treaty is contrary to the law of nations, and he who violates a treaty violates the law of nations.

Hence it is properly said, as is also commonly said by sovereign powers, when there is an open complaint of the violation of treaties,

that it is done contrary to all law of nature and nations, in our native vernacular, *wieder alle Rechte der Natur und der Völcker* [contrary to all laws of nature and of peoples]. For nations are not only bound by the law of nature itself to observe stipulations, but as nations they are bound in addition in an especial manner to observe the same. There- §3.
fore he errs in two respects, who violates a treaty, both in so far as he Note, §547.
acts contrary to that which the law of nature demands, and in so far as he disregards the sanctity due to treaties by the common consent of nations, and offends against the human race itself, which has been united into a supreme state by nature herself. These things are to be §§7, 8.
properly considered, in order that the innate baseness of the violation of treaties may be completely understood, which sullies especially the reputation of nations. And this innate baseness itself ought to be a motive for the most perfect observance of treaties, since nations and their rulers ought to do nothing which can diminish or undermine their glory. Hence too it is understood why it may be said of him who has no religious scruple about the violation of a treaty, that there is nothing too sacred for him to despise.

§ 549. *What things are to be observed in the making of treaties*

Since treaties ought to be considered sacred among nations, conse- §547.
quently, since nothing ought to be done which seems to be done con- §546.
trary to them, the details concerning which there is an agreement in treaties are to be exactly determined and expressed in plain words, so that all ambiguity may be removed, and that no room may be left for disputes on either side.

There is no reason for saying that there is no need for so much concern as to the expression of the idea in your mind, since he to whom something has been promised in a treaty has the right to that §466, part 6,
which a proper interpretation suggests. For a proper interpretation Jus Nat.
is not so easy as it might seem to be, as is abundantly evident from those things which we have proved in regard to interpretation, nor is §§468 and fol.,
it so evident that all dispute can be avoided, and that on this pretext part 6, Jus Nat.
he will not violate the treaty, who desires it to seem that the treaty has been considered sacred by him. And since it is the custom of those

who especially respect the sanctity of treaties, since they are unwilling to appear to be what they are, intentionally to use ambiguous words and vague expressions; therefore he who is especially interested in the observance of a treaty ought to be much more solicitous that this should not happen.

§ 550. *Of the sanctity of the good faith of treaties*

§ 757, part 3, Jus Nat.

§ 1062, part 1, Theol. Nat., and § 788, part 3, Jus Nat.

§ 369.

§ 548.

§ 546.

The good faith of treaties is sacred. For good faith is a fixed desire expressed to another concerning that which we wish to perform, and therefore in treaties it denotes an unchangeable intention to perform those things which are promised, in treaties as well as in stipulations, consequently not to violate treaties in any respect. Therefore, since it is contrary to the law of nations to violate treaties, and since he who violates them violates the law of nations, consequently since the common welfare of nations demands good faith in treaties, the good faith of treaties is sacred.

§ 546.

§ 547.

§ 369.

§ 368.

§ 39.

§ 51.

The inviolability of a treaty and the inviolability of good faith are inseparably connected, so that the former cannot be inviolable unless the latter is also. Therefore the inviolability of a treaty is just the same as the inviolability of good faith. Since, therefore, the sanctity of a treaty consists in its inviolability, the sanctity to be attributed to good faith also consists in its inviolability. Therefore, just as treaties are to be considered sacred, so also the good faith in them ought to be considered sacred. It is disgraceful in the common people to break faith, it is much more disgraceful if sovereign powers, which make treaties, should break faith. For since sovereign powers, or the rulers of states, represent the entire nation, if a sovereign power should break faith, it is just as if there were not even one person in the entire nation who would keep faith. Hence it is easy to compare the extent of the turpitude of this fault in the sovereign power to its turpitude in a private individual. And since the ruler of a state ought to use royal actions to further the glory of his nation and do nothing which can diminish or undermine it in any way, so much the more ought he to consider the sanctity of good faith entrusted to him.

§ 551. *Whether the sanctity of good faith has any relation to the religion of the allied nation*

The sanctity of good faith has no relation to the religion of the nation with which the treaty is made. For the sanctity of good faith depends upon the common welfare of nations, in so far, that is, as they are understood to have united into a state: since this consists in the unobstructed enjoyment of adequate means of life, of tranquillity, and of security, it has no relation to the method of worshipping God, and hence to religion. Therefore the sanctity of good faith has no relation to the religion of the nation with which the treaty is made.

§ 546.

§ 9.

§ 17, part 8, Jus Nat.

§ 512, part 2, Theol. Nat.

> No treaties or stipulations between nations would rest on good faith if they were to depend upon the truth of religion. For every nation, whatsoever its religion may be, thinks that religion is the true one which it professes. If then it were admitted that it were allowable not to preserve good faith toward a nation that was a stranger to true religion, every nation would think that a violation of good faith is allowable for it, if it had made a treaty with a nation devoted to another religion, consequently no nation could trust another which was devoted to a religion different from its own. Nothing, therefore, can be more absurd in the law of nations than to make the sanctity of good faith dependent upon the truth of religion.

§ 552. *Of the identity of the sanctity of good faith among nations*

Since the sanctity of good faith has no relation to the religion of the nation with which a treaty is made, and since it is allowable to make treaties with a nation devoted to another religion, good faith ought to be sacred in the same way whatsoever may be the religion of the nation with which the treaty is made, consequently the sanctity of good faith is the same among all nations without regard to their religion.

§ 551.

§ 429.

> Whether a treaty should be made with Christians, or with Turks, or with pagans, there is certainly no difference in the sanctity of good faith. Nay more, he who thinks that his religion is true but another's is false, ought so much the more to indorse the sanctity of good faith,

lest the defect may be charged to the religion which belongs only to him who confesses it. For true religion surely does not tolerate vices, especially so foul a one as the violation of good faith, which ought to be considered sacred. Here those things are to be reviewed, which we have discussed at length above.

§ 550.

Note, § 429.

§ 553. *A manifestly false interpretation of treaties is opposed to the sanctity of good faith*

A manifestly false interpretation of treaties is utterly opposed to the sanctity of good faith. For if the interpretation of treaties is manifestly false, nothing else is aimed at thereby than that he should break faith who wishes to seem to observe treaties. But good faith is not considered sacred by the one who does this, and since he wishes to seem to observe treaties, he shows plainly enough that it is not unknown to him how disgraceful it is to break faith. Therefore nothing is more opposed to the sanctity of good faith than a manifestly false interpretation.

§ 546.

§ 759, part 3, Jus Nat.

Examples of sophistries of this sort occur in ancient history, some of which Grotius mentions. So the Plataeans, when they had promised they would return the captive Thebans, returned them, not living, but dead. When the Romans agreed with Antiochus that they would return the half part of his ships, cut all the ships in two, that they might despoil the king of his whole fleet. And Alexander the Great himself, when he had promised a free departure from the city, asserted that it was not guaranteed that the road was safe. Here also belongs the case cited by Tacitus, where he tells that Rhodamistus swore to Mithridates that he would not do violence to him by poison or sword, but afterwards slew him by smothering him in a pile of clothing.

De Jure Belli ac Pacis, lib. 2, c. 16, § 5.

Annals, XII.

§ 554. *Likewise if one with such a purpose expresses his intention badly, so that there may be opportunity for false interpretation*

Since a manifestly false interpretation of treaties is utterly opposed to the sanctity of good faith, this also is utterly opposed to it, that any one inaccurately defines the agreements in a treaty, and does not express them in plain and unambiguous words, with the purpose that, if it seems to

§ 553.

his advantage, there may be an opportunity for false interpretation and sophistries.

He who does this, has not the intention of keeping faith, and consequently he does not consider it sacred.

§ 546.

§ 555. *Of the granting of a right to transitory acts*

Both express and tacit concessions of a right to certain transitory acts in their territory are equivalent to stipulations of nations. For if a certain nation expressly grants to another some right to certain transitory acts in its territory, this concession is made to the one asking either absolutely or on a certain condition, consequently they agree one with the other concerning that which is granted, and the grantor is understood to have promised all things which are necessarily required for the use of this right, since the right would be granted to no purpose unless at the same time those things were granted without which it is not possible to use that right. Therefore, since agreements which contain promises are stipulations, express concessions of nations of a right to certain transitory acts in their territory are equivalent to stipulations of nations. Which was the first point.

§ 698, part 3,
Jus Nat.

§ 788, part 3,
Jus Nat.

And since tacit consent is true consent, consequently, since it would be just the same whether the concession should be made expressly or tacitly, since, moreover, an express concession is equivalent to a stipulation, as proved above, a tacit concession ought also to be equivalent to a stipulation. Which was the second point.

§ 662, part 1,
Phil. Pract. Univ.

Here belongs the concession of the right of passage to an army through one's lands, or even to a king making a journey, the right to tarry in one's territory for some just cause, as for the use of mineral springs for the sake of health, or the right of purchasing certain crops, which a neighbouring nation needs because of the high price of grain, and other things which are of this sort. For although those things which are granted can be referred either to the duties of humanity or to the rights surviving from the primitive joint holding, if nevertheless reasons should arise, dependent upon the public welfare, which is the supreme law in the state, they are rightly denied, and therefore, since the decision concerning the matter rests with the one granting them, his consent is required.

§ 86, part 8,
Jus Nat.

§ 156, part 1, Jus
Nat., and § 55,
part 8, Jus Nat.

§ 556. *Whether sanctity should be allowed them*

Since both express and tacit concessions of a right to certain transitory acts in their territory are equivalent to stipulations of nations, and since treaties, and consequently all other stipulations also, are to be considered sacred by nations, and since the good faith in them ought to be sacred, concessions also of any right to certain acts in its territory, granted either expressly or tacitly by one nation to another, ought to be sacred, and the good faith in them ought to be sacred.

§ 555.
§ 369.
§ 547.
§ 550.

The good faith of nations ought to be the same in all matters which arise between them. For the reasons which demand sanctity for treaties have a place in all of them. Good faith is always the public good faith; but the good faith of the public ought to be sacred, since it is a baser thing to break public faith than private.

Note, § 550.

§ 557. *Of the customary law in regard to them*

If certain things have been introduced by the customs of nations in regard to concessions of some right to transitory acts in their territory, those things belong to the customary law of nations. This is evident from the definition itself of the customary law of nations.

§ 24.

This customary law is not to be confused with that which in cases of that sort one nation makes of its own accord with another, although if the same thing should be done in turn in a similar case by the latter to the former, customary law can be introduced by repeated acts.

§ 558. *Whether an act contrary to customary law is a wrong*

Any act which is contrary to customary law is a wrong. For the customary law of nations has been introduced by long usage and is observed as law. Therefore what is done contrary to that law is understood to have been done contrary to the absolute right belonging to a nation. Therefore, since that which is done contrary to the absolute right of another is a wrong; whatever is done contrary to customary law is a wrong.

§ 24.

§ 859, part 1, Jus Nat.

§ 662, part 1, Phil. Pract. Univ.

Customary law rests upon the tacit consent of nations, and since this is a real consent, it is undoubtedly just as if nations had expressly agreed with each other concerning that which belongs to custom. And therefore the customary law of nations as regards its effect is equivalent to the stipulative law.

§ 559. *What tacit good faith is*

Tacit good faith is defined as that which rests upon the tacit consent of nations, and consequently it exists in regard to those things concerning which there is a tacit agreement or those which are tacitly promised.

Many tacit agreements exist in the affairs of nations. Therefore tacit good faith ought not to be thought of as a term unknown among nations. But even if indeed the term should not be used at all, nevertheless the thing itself which is indicated by it is not unknown, so that therefore in the law of nations it is just as if it were proclaimed under this very name.

§ 560. *What is to be observed*

Since tacit consent is true consent, and consequently as regards its effect is equivalent to express consent, which is declared in words; good faith also, which rests on the tacit consent of nations, that is, tacit good faith, is equivalent to that expressly given, consequently is no less to be observed than this, and he is guilty of treachery who acts contrary to that to which he has tacitly pledged his faith.

§ 662, part 1,
Phil. Pract. Univ.
§ 660, part 1,
Phil. Pract. Univ.
§ 765, part 3,
Jus Nat.
§ 766, part 3,
Jus Nat.

He who rejects tacit good faith makes a place for fraud, all of which nevertheless by the law of nature is illegal, and it is understood that it ought to be absent from every stipulation. Since fraud is of itself exceedingly disgraceful, so much the more disgraceful ought it to be considered when it is contrary to good faith, which ought to be sacred.

§ 147, part 5,
Jus Nat.
§ 148, part 5,
Jus Nat.

§ 149, part 5,
Jus Nat.

§ 561. *Of those things which are tacitly included in agreements*

Note, § 147,
part 5, Jus Nat.

That is understood to have been tacitly agreed upon, without which that in regard to which there has been agreement cannot occur. For every business includes all the actions positive as well as negative that are necessary to obtain or cause something. If, then, there should be an agreement

§ 550.

§ 68, part 7,
Jus Nat.

§ 24, part 1,
Phil. Pract.
Univ.
concerning some business, whatever be its nature, not only is the agreement made in regard to those things expressly mentioned, but also in
regard to all others which are necessary in order that the thing in regard
to which there has been an agreement can be accomplished, and conse-
§ 698, part 3,
Jus Nat.
quently those things are understood to have been tacitly agreed upon.

De Jure Belli ac
Pacis, lib. 3,
c. 24, § 1.

Part 4, Jus Nat.

    Grotius says that certain things belong by nature to an act and he
asserts that those are tacitly agreed upon. So in every contract of beneficence there is indemnity for him who does something for another for
free, as we have shown in its own place. Therefore he is understood to
have tacitly agreed to that for whom something has been performed
for free. For no one will enter into a contract of beneficence unless it
can be done without loss on his part; consequently without indemnity
for the one who performs something for free contracts of beneficence
cannot exist, and therefore indemnity belongs to every contract of
beneficence. Likewise he who either demands or allows a conference,
tacitly promises that it will be without risk to the participants; for one
will not go to a conference unless he is assured that it will be without
risk to him, and therefore a conference cannot exist without this, consequently the promise of security to the participants belongs by nature
to the agreement for a conference. But those things are rightly said to
belong by nature to a certain act, which can be derived from it by way
of demonstration; for those things belong to a thing which are derived
from the idea of it by direct reasoning.

Of the Method of Settling
the Controversies of Nations

§ 562. *What the controversies of nations and rulers of a state are*

The controversies of nations and rulers of a state are their disputes concerning the rights belonging to them or concerning a wrong done.

> Rulers of a state dispute with each other, if one of them asserts that a certain right belongs to him, but the other denies it, the one alleging reasons, on account of which it belongs to him, the other denying them, or alleging others in opposition. This dispute is called a controversy. Learned men dispute with each other concerning the truth of dogmas, or of facts, and these disputes are called the controversies of the learned, in the native vernacular, *gelehrte Streitigkeiten* or *Streitigkeiten der Gelehrten* [scholarly disputes or the disputes of scholars], which differ from the controversies of nations only in their subject-matter. Moreover it is evident of itself that there are controversies of private individuals, which correspond to the controversies of nations and rulers of a state, and consist in disputes concerning the right belonging to themselves or wrong done to them.

§ 563. *What grievances are*

Grievances of nations and rulers of a state are defined as complaints concerning the denial of their plain right by another nation, or by another ruler of a state, or concerning a wrong done to them or likely to be done. In our native vernacular they are called *Beschwerden* [complaints].

Thus if a certain nation does not pay what it cannot deny that it ought to pay, the complaint which is offered by another nation concerning the non-payment is a grievance. If any nation has violated the right of ambassadors, or allows it to be violated by its subjects without punishment, the complaint which the other nation offers concerning it is a grievance. It frequently happens that the grievances of one nation are called into controversy by another, if the other is not ready to remove them. Of course it is plain, even without my saying it, that there is a place for grievances even between private individuals.

§ 564. *Of unjust grievances*

§ 563.

Since grievances are complaints concerning the denial by one nation of the plain right of another nation, or concerning a wrong done to one or likely to be done; if in fact no right to be allowed by another belongs to you, or if the act of another is not a wrong, which you claim is such, you have no grievance, and therefore the grievance is said to be not just, or unjust, as based on no right.

The judgements of men are not always accurate in a matter which affects themselves. And therefore they consider plainly proved a thing which is not only doubtful, but even absolutely non-existent. Therefore they complain of a thing which does not exist. And therefore their grievances are of themselves nothing, or they are unjust. Frequently also grievances are assumed where none exist. But such belong in the category of false pretences.

§ 565. *Whether interfering with the government of another is a just cause of grievance*

§ 563.

§ 269.

§ 859, part 1, Jus Nat.

Since a grievance of the ruler of a state is a complaint concerning injury done him, since, moreover, every ruler of a state has an absolute right not to allow any other nation to interfere in any way in its own government, if the ruler of another state does this, it does a wrong to him; consequently if the ruler of a state interferes with the government of another, that is a just cause of grievance.

This can be done by ambassadors in different ways depending upon the different forms of government, also, if some ruler of a state seeks to forbid another to do that which he can do by virtue of his sovereign power.

§ 566. Of the method of removing grievances

Because grievances are complaints concerning the denial of a plain right, or concerning a wrong done or likely to be done, since, moreover, it is self-evident that those complaints cease if the complainant is allowed his right, or the wrong is repaired, or if it cannot be repaired, satisfaction be made for it, and further wrong avoided; grievances are removed, if a nation which has given cause for grievances should restore to the other its right, repair the wrong done, or give satisfaction for that which cannot be repaired, and moreover should cease from wrongdoing, or when its good faith has been under suspicion should give adequate security.

§ 563.

> Of course, when the reason for complaint ceases, the complaints end, since they cannot be supposed unless a reason is supposed. And when the complaints cease, the grievances no longer exist.

§ 118, Ontol.
§ 563.

§ 567. Of the duty to remove grievances

If any nation has grievances against another, the other is bound to remove them. For every nation ought to allow to another its right, consequently also to repair a wrong done, or give recompense for loss caused, or if the wrong cannot be repaired, to give satisfaction for it, and since no nation ought to injure another, but each one ought to guard against offending another, it ought to refrain from the wrong which it intends to do. For if a nation against which grievances exist should do this, the grievances are at an end. If then any nation has grievances against another, the other is bound to remove them.

§ 264.
§ 923, part 1,
and § 580,
part 2, Jus Nat.

§§ 252, 253.
§ 173.
§ 266.
§ 566.

> This is especially in harmony with the friendship which nations ought to cultivate with each other and with the care which they are bound to exercise, that they may not make other nations hostile to themselves, nay more, it is also in harmony with justice, which nations are bound to cultivate towards each other. Just as in a state the grievances of private citizens are to be removed, as is plainly understood from those things which have been proved in the eighth part of "The

§ 172.

§ 265.

§ 9.

Law of Nature" concerning trials, so also in the supreme state, into which nations have united, it is of the greatest importance that grievances should be removed in order that a nation which has grievances

§§ 271 and fol.

should not be compelled to attain its right and remove wrong to itself by the use of force.

§ 568. *Whether it is allowable voluntarily to renounce grievances*

Every nation is free, if it wishes, to renounce grievances for the benefit of

§ 567.
§ 23, part 1,
Jus Nat.
§ 117, part 3,
Jus Nat.
§ 95, part 3,
Jus Nat.

another. If any nation has grievances against another the other is bound to remove them, consequently the former has the right to demand that from the latter. But since, indeed, any one can give up his right, and since he does this, who plainly signifies that he does not desire another to do for him what he is bound to do, a nation which has grievances against another can give up the right to have them redressed, consequently it is free, if it wishes, to renounce grievances for the benefit of another.

It is often the part of wisdom to present grievances indeed, but nevertheless not to press that they be removed, but with generous spirit to declare that you wish to renounce them. Just so also it is the part of prudence to conceal them, or at least to dissimulate for the present. But then indeed they are not renounced, nor is the right lost to demand that they be removed. There is no one who doubts, unless he is absolutely ignorant of all law, that every nation can dispose of its right as may seem best or as prudence suggests.

§ 569. *Of the method of settling controversies of nations*

Controversies between nations can be settled in the same manner as those between private individuals living in a state of nature. For nations

§ 2.
§§ 538, 540,
and fol., part 8,
Jus Nat.
§ 145, part 1,
Jus Nat.

are to be looked at as free individual persons living in a state of nature, consequently they have no judge to give and enforce an opinion on a disputed right, nor do private persons living in a state of nature, which is a condition of liberty, have such a judge. Therefore, controversies between nations can be settled in no other way than are those between private individuals living in a state of nature.

Nations use no other law than natural law. The right, therefore, which belongs to private individuals as to the method of settling controversies in a state of nature belongs likewise to nations.

§ 3.

§ 570. *Those methods are reviewed in greater detail*

Since controversies between nations can be settled in the same manner as those between private individuals living in a state of nature, and since by natural law they can be settled either amicably, or through compromise, or through mediation, or finally through arbitration or submission to arbiters, controversies between nations also can be settled either amicably or through compromise, or through mediation, or arbitration.

§ 569.
§ 878, part 5,
Jus Nat.
§ 885, part 5,
Jus Nat.
§ 923, part 5,
Jus Nat.
§ 945, part 4,
Jus Nat.

The duel and the lot are also cited indeed as methods of settling controversies in a state of nature; nevertheless the duel is not a method suited to decide controversies, nor is it allowed by the law of nature, while the lot, although it is not illegal, nevertheless will scarcely recommend itself to litigant nations.

§ 1092, part 5,
Jus Nat.

§ 1091, part 5,
Jus Nat.
§ 1099, part 5,
Jus Nat.

§ 571. *Of assemblies and conferences of nations*

Since controversies between nations are to be settled either amicably, or through compromise, or through mediation, or through arbitration, and since controversies cannot be settled through an amicable adjustment, or compromise, or mediation, or arbitration, unless the disputants come together and confer, a thing which is sufficiently evident of itself, therefore nations are bound to hold meetings and to come into conference, consequently to agree concerning the place, the time, the persons to be admitted to the conference, and concerning other things to be observed in these matters according to the nature of the case.

§ 570.

These are the true means of settling controversies among nations, which the law of nature prescribes, as is plainly evident from those things which have been proved concerning the natural method of settling controversies, in the fifth part of "The Law of Nature." What the duel is between private individuals, war is between nations. Therefore, just as the duel is not a suitable method to decide a controversy, so war is not suitable for deciding a controversy between nations. The

§ 1092, part 5,
Jus Nat.

outcome of a war is not less doubtful and uncertain than that of the
lot, so that in either case the German proverb fails according to which
God is said to assist the one having a just cause. Therefore, just as
those things are not to be decided by lot which can be settled by plain
reasoning, so much the less by war. Nay more, war does not, like a
duel, arise from an agreement that the disputed right is to be settled
in favour of the one who conquers, that is, that the controversy may
be decided by force of arms, but the purpose is that the parties may
at length come to a compromise which may put an end to the war.
The way is open to a compromise without arms; but the parties do
not wish to come to it by that way, because each party, trusting in
his arms, promises victory to itself, and since the victor can impose
conditions on the vanquished, he hopes to obtain better conditions
in the compromise. That war, therefore, is preferred to meetings and
conferences, and that the controversy is not settled without the blood
of many and without pillaging and devastation, does not come from
the law of nature, but is to be attributed to the passions by which the
minds of the disputants are distracted. Those decide too hastily who
simply announce that the controversies of nations are to be ended by
force of arms and that this right has been given to them by God and
nature, because they have no judge and they themselves are the vindi-
cators of their own right. In a civil state, indeed, in which actions in
court take the place of war, there is no trial in court unless the parties
are unwilling to settle the controversy amicably, or through compromise, mediation, or submission to arbiters, that is, unless they refuse
to use the means in harmony with the nature of men prescribed by
the law of nature, which in no way favours war, nor does it allow it
except as a means of defence, as we have already suggested elsewhere
and as will be more evident from what follows. But that it is in accordance with natural law, that in a doubtful case or when there is a
controversy on a disputed point, either that a conference should be
held for settling amicably the matter in dispute, or that a compromise
should be reached concerning it, either by bringing in mediators, or
without them, or that the thing should be submitted to arbitration,
or finally, that the settlement of the dispute should be committed to
the lot, we have already proved elsewhere, and this is understood no
less of nations than of private individuals. Nay more, as in a state of

§ 296, part 5,
Jus Nat.

§ 561, part 8,
Jus Nat.

§ 1102, part 5,
Jus Nat.

nature the right of war as such belongs to no man in a doubtful case, §3.
but it is illegal for you to harass another by war, in order to extort by
force of arms what you claim; so likewise for nations which live in a §1100, part 5, Jus Nat.
state of nature, and use no other law with one another, that cannot §1101, part 5, Jus Nat.
be allowed which is not allowed to individuals in a state of nature,
or is not permitted by nature. But do not persuade yourself that by
this the right is diminished which belongs to nations and to rulers of §2.
states who have that right. For to nations and to their rulers also are §3.
to be applied those things which we have proved elsewhere concerning
the right of private war allowable in a disputed case. For private war
allowed by nature in the case of individual men is the norm of public
war, since nations in relations with each other are regarded in the same §2.
way as private persons.

§ 572. *Of the right of war on account of the controversies of nations*

If in a doubtful case one nation is not willing to accept a conference for
an amicable adjustment or compromise, or to accept a submission to
an arbiter, the one making the offer has the right of war against the one
unwilling to accept, by which the former is driven to a settlement by
force of arms. For nations are bound to hold meetings and to come into §571.
conference for the sake of settling their controversies, that their disputes
may be determined amicably or by compromise, either with mediators
or without them, or through arbiters. But if, indeed, any one is unwilling §570.
to accept a conference for an amicable adjustment or compromise in a
doubtful case, or a submission to an arbiter, the one making the offer has
the right of war against him, so that he is driven to a settlement by force. §§1103, 1104, part 5, Jus Nat.
Therefore, also, if in a doubtful case one nation is not willing to accept
a conference by an amicable adjustment or compromise, nor to accept
a submission to an arbiter, the one making the offer has the right of war
against the one unwilling to accept, by which it is driven to a settlement
by force of arms.

Therefore it is evident that the right of war does not arise from the
fact that nations do not have a judge, but are themselves defenders
of their own right; but from the wrong of the nation in refusing the

Note, § 1104,
part 5, Jus Nat.
method properly offered it by the other party for settling the controversy by the law of nature. Here are to be reconsidered the points
which we have already noted elsewhere. But if you should object that
those things which have been said by us concerning the method of
settling disputes of nations and concerning the right of war in cases
of controversies between them are opposed to the general opinion of
nations and to their customs, that objection affects us but little; for
it was not our purpose to recount those things which are in harmony

§24.
with the general opinion of nations, but to teach those things which
are in accord with the truth. And although the customs of nations
make customary law, nevertheless we do not recognize as true law that
which is observed as customary law among nations, except in so far

§ 22.

§ 975, part 8,
Jus Nat.
as it is in harmony with the natural theory of civil law, and therefore, as
we have said, deserves a place in the voluntary law of nations. Just as
a legislator cannot make an illegal thing legal by positive civil law, and
ought to be on his guard lest certain errors prevailing generally may

§ 992, part 8,
Jus Nat.
be taken for the law of nature, so that same thing is to be understood
concerning the customary law of nations.

§ 573. When the right of war exists, even though a conference or submission to arbiters is not attempted

Since the right of war belongs to the nation offering a conference for an
amicable adjustment, or compromise, or for a submission to arbiters,
against the nation unwilling to accept, so that the nation may be driven

§ 572.
to a settlement by force of arms, and since it is just the same whether the
refusal is express or tacit, if it can be easily foreseen that a conference or
arbitration is not going to be accepted, or that, if it should be offered,
there is no other outcome to be expected than delay harmful to the one
offering, the one foreseeing such results has a right of war against the
other nation, even though the conference or arbitration is not attempted.

§ 258, part 1,
Jus Nat.

§ 256, part 1,
Jus Nat.
The law of nature also obligates us to be prudent, therefore it
enjoins us to be prudent, that we do nothing rash, especially if the
rash action should be accompanied by loss to ourselves, which we are
bound to avoid. Therefore you see that we do not absolutely disapprove of one taking up arms in a doubtful case, when a conference

or arbitration has not yet been attempted, concerning which it seems there is no hope left, although, when delay is useful to the one accepting, the conference may be accepted not with the idea that the controversy is to be settled, but that delay is to be interposed.

§ 278, part 3, Jus Nat.

§ 493, part 2, Jus Nat.

§ 574. *What is here in harmony with the voluntary law of nations*

By the voluntary law of nations it is not unjust to take up arms in a doubtful case for the purpose of obtaining a settlement, even if a conference or arbitration has not been attempted. For even in certain matters, especially those of great importance, the good faith of nation with nation has always hitherto been open to suspicion, and to-day is usually suspected, so that therefore guarantors of treaties and hostages are demanded as security for good faith. Therefore, in disputed matters of great importance among nations, since it is scarcely to be hoped that the controversy can be settled by a conference and arbitration accepted, on account of fear of the zeal of the parties, and since the acceptance of a conference may not be above suspicion, when indeed it can be easily foreseen that a conference or arbitration is not going to be accepted, or, if it should be offered, that there is no other outcome to be expected than delay harmful to the one offering, arms may lawfully be taken up without attempting a conference or arbitration, and since by virtue of the natural liberty belonging to each nation, all must abide by the decision of each in these matters; by the voluntary law of nations, in order that a controversy may have an end, arms are not unjustly taken up in a doubtful case for the purpose of obtaining a settlement, even if a conference or arbitration has not been attempted beforehand.

§ 443.

§ 540.

§ 575.

§ 55, part 8, Jus Nat.
§ 156, part 1, Jus Nat.
§ 22 h, and § 983, part 8, Jus Nat.

If good faith were as sacred to nations as it ought to be, and if it were not for the fact that they prefer to be ruled by their impulses rather than by their reason, or if their glory, which they ought to cherish, restrained them from being compelled only unwillingly to agree to that to which they did not wish to agree, their controversies could be settled as the law of nature prescribes, nor would there be need of settling them by force of arms. And then there would be no voluntary law of nations, which is created only by the perverse

§ 550.

§ 49.

customs of nations, and which a nation is bound to use even against its will and its more enlightened judgement. But since it is not to be hoped that all nations will be what they ought to be, there will always be a place for the voluntary law also, with this distinction, that the nation which sees and approves the better course, uses the voluntary law only unwillingly, if it is not to do damage to its conscience, but other nations, with whom truth is an unknown or disregarded name, carried away by a vain hope, abuse it. Just as every man is said to be the maker of his own fortune, so likewise nations are the makers not only of their own fortunes, but also of the fortunes of other nations, which are favourable as long as they pursue the better course, but unfavourable when they follow the worse. But do not persuade yourself that the nation which follows the guidance of reason, and does not stray from the pathway of truth, will be in a worse condition than other nations which seek all protection from the voluntary law. For no more is permitted to the latter than to the former, but what the latter do with impunity among nations by virtue of the voluntary law

§ 47.
§ 49.

§§ 572, 573.

§ 47.

is nevertheless not free from censure by those who think more rightly, and it is a blot on their glory, which they ought to cherish; but the former act in accordance with law given to them by nature, nor do they lack the commendation of those who think rightly and regard their honour as they ought. The same things are to be noted in other instances in which the voluntary law departs from the strict rule of the law of nature.

§ 575. Of the right of war in a doubtful case considered in general

Those things which have been proved concerning the right of war existing by nature in a doubtful case are true also among nations. For

§ 3.

nations in their relations with each other use no other law than natural law. Those things, therefore, which have been proved concerning the right of war existing by nature in a doubtful case are true also among nations.

Therefore there is no need in this place of proving them at length, nor of repeating what we have said concerning them, although they may be reviewed with profit.

§ 576. *Considered in detail*

Since those things which have been proved concerning the right of war existing by nature in a doubtful case are true also among nations, if any nation in a doubtful case should offer fair terms to another nation with which it has a controversy, and the other should be unwilling to accept them, it has a right of war against the other, and if, after arms have been taken up, fair conditions should be offered by either party, the same are to be accepted and the war ended, and each party is bound to seek conditions on which war may be avoided, nor can the nation which seeks them compel the other to withdraw from possession, and a war is unjust which is undertaken for the purpose of getting possession.

§ 575.

§ 1105, part 5, Jus Nat.

§ 1106, part 5, Jus Nat.

§ 1109, part 5, Jus Nat.

Since the right of war existing by nature in a doubtful case has especial significance among nations, after civil sovereignties have been introduced, therefore it seems especially pertinent that the things proved elsewhere concerning the right of war in a doubtful case should be reviewed here and applied to nations, lest in the law of nations, which is here laid down, those things should seem to be lacking which claim a place for themselves therein.

§ 1110, part 5, Jus Nat.

§ 577. *Of the right of retaliation between nations*

Retaliation is not allowable between nations, nor does the right of retaliation exist in the voluntary law of nations; but if retaliation has been introduced by custom, it must be referred to the unjust customary law of nations. For retaliation has been forbidden by the law of nature, consequently it is illegal. Therefore, since nations use natural law in their relations with each other, consequently that cannot be legal between them which is illegal by the law of nature; retaliation, therefore, cannot be allowed between nations. Which was the first point.

§ 640, part 8, Jus Nat.

§ 170, part 1, Phil. Pract. Univ.

§ 3.

Now the voluntary law of nations is established in the same way as civil law in a state. But if, indeed, civil law rests on natural law, legality cannot arise from illegality. Therefore, since vengeance is illegal by the law of nature, as proved above, the right of retaliation does not exist in the voluntary law of nations. Which was the second point.

§ 22.

§ 975, part 8, Jus Nat. Note 1.

But if, then, retaliation has been introduced among certain nations by custom, by some common error, as though it were legal, it certainly will belong to customary law. But since that is unjust which is opposed to the law of nature, moreover as retaliation is opposed to this law, as proved above, the right of retaliation is unjust customary law. Which was the third point.

§ 24.

§ 239, part 1,
Phil. Pract.
Univ.

We have already suggested elsewhere that a common error formerly existed and to-day exists, that retaliation is perfectly fair, because nothing is considered more in harmony with justice than that one should suffer as much wrong as one has inflicted, and how far this mistaken opinion is from the truth, we have already shown. Of course retaliation owes its origin to vengeful passion, to which nations no less than individual men ought to have an aversion. Nor should you object that the passion for vengeance does not affect a nation, and therefore the right of retaliation could be exercised by it without that. For the law of nations is enforced by rulers of a state, who indulge their passions no less than private individuals, and relying on their power they are usually more inclined to vengeance than private persons, who are frequently restrained from vengeance by their weakness. Righteousness in act is none other in the ruler of a state than in a private person, and the law of nature requires the same purity of mind in the one as in the other. Therefore, just as a private individual ought to control his actions by reason, by yielding in no way to his passions, so the more ought this to be done by the ruler of a state, who represents the entire nation.

Note, § 640,
part 8, Jus Nat.
§ 3.
§ 948, part 1,
Jus Nat.

§ 39.

§ 578. *Whether irreparable injury makes a place for it*

§ 577.

§ 639, part 8,
Jus Nat.

Since retaliation is not allowed by nature even among nations, since, moreover, retaliation consists in this, that one should suffer as much wrong as one has inflicted, if irreparable injury has been done to any nation by another, or that which it cannot be hoped will be repaired, it is not allowable to do the same thing to that nation which it itself has done.

Those who defend the law of retaliation are accustomed very often to extend it beyond the limits which it has by its own nature. Thus if any nation has murdered the ambassadors of another nation, or

has returned them with nose and ears cut off to the nation sending
them, they think it is also allowable for this nation in its turn to slay
the ambassadors of the other nation, or send them away with nose
and ears cut off. But it is plainly evident that then retaliation is not
made between the same persons, that is, between the one injuring
and the injured, as the nature of retaliation demands. Therefore, even
if the right of retaliation were perfectly fair, as is generally thought,
nevertheless there would be no place for it in cases of that sort, and
on this account there would rarely be use for it among nations. Nevertheless, it is not to be supposed that, if the right of retaliation were
taken away, there would be no remedy for irreparable injury; for that
other remedies exist, if the offending nation should be unwilling to
assume responsibility for the wrong, as it ought, will be plain from
what follows.

§ 639, part 8,
Jus Nat.

§ 567.

§ 579. *When retaliation becomes the more illegal*

Since retaliation is not allowable, it will be much more illegal if it consists
in an act disgraceful by nature.

§ 577.

> For example, let us suppose that soldiers have been promised that
> they may publicly rape honourable women; since rape of that sort is
> by nature disgraceful, however much the right of retaliation may have
> been introduced by the custom of certain nations, it will not be allow-
> able to permit it to their soldiers in turn; and if, nevertheless, it should
> be done, such retaliation would be much more illegal than that which
> consists in some physical wrong which is not considered illicit in itself.

§ 335, part 7,
Jus Nat.

§ 580. *When an injured nation can use the right to punish*

If a nation should be unwilling to give satisfaction for an irreparable
injury to another nation injured by itself, or there should seem to be
no hope of satisfaction being given, the injured nation can use its right
to punish within fair limits. For if an irreparable injury has been done,
satisfaction ought to be given to the injured nation for it. If, then, the
offender is unwilling to give satisfaction to the injured nation, or there
seems to be no hope that satisfaction will be given, since the injured
nation has the right to punish the offender, and since the offender is

§§ 566, 567.

§ 272.

§ 1071, part 1,
Jus Nat.

bound to submit to the punishment, the injured nation can use its right to punish the offender. Which was the first point.

§ 1063, part 1,
Jus Nat.

§ 977, part 1,
Jus Nat.

§ 1065, part 1,
Jus Nat.

Note 1.

But since the right to punish has no limit, consequently limits to it have to be determined beforehand from existing circumstances, and a more serious punishment is not permissible when a lighter one is adequate, the injured nation, if the offender should be unwilling to give satisfaction for an irreparable injury, can indeed use its right to punish, as proved above, but nevertheless only within fair limits. Which was the second point.

§ 13, part 8,
Jus Nat.

The fair limits are to be determined from the purpose of the punishment and from the circumstances which render that easy or difficult to achieve. Punishment is intended for no other purpose than that the injured nation may be secure from fear of wrong in the future; but it cannot be secure if it should permit itself to be injured with impunity. Security is part of the purpose of the state, to protect it is the same thing as to punish, so that then the right to punish is to be referred to the right of defence.

§ 581. *In how many ways a nation can be punished*

§ 2.

§ 589, part 8,
Jus Nat.

By way of punishment of a nation its property, both corporeal and incorporeal, can be taken away, for example, its rights to certain acts in the territory of the injured party; nay more, war also is righteously undertaken against the offender unless provision can be made for security in some other way. For nations are looked at as individual persons living in a state of nature. Therefore, since any property, corporeal and incorporeal, or any rights, can be taken away from private persons by way of punishment from a nation also its property, both corporeal and incorporeal, can be taken by way of punishment, for example, its rights to certain acts in the territory of the injured party. Which was the first point.

§ 1071, part 8,
Jus Nat.

§ 1063, part 1,
Jus Nat.

And since, indeed, he who injures another is bound to pay the penalty; if the penalty, by which sufficient provision is made for security, cannot be secured otherwise, because the right to punish has no limit, even war is properly undertaken against the nation which has offended. Which was the second point.

In truth to give satisfaction for an irreparable injury is nothing else than to pay a penalty. Therefore, the things which are either proffered by the offender, or demanded by the injured party, have the nature of a penalty. Therefore, it is plain that it is not absurd that by way of punishment corporeal property may be taken from the offender, or that the offender may be deprived of some right which it has to acts in the territory of the injured nation, as the right of commerce, or the right of having protection, and other things which are of the same kind. Nay more, the offending nation can be deprived of a right which belongs to it against the injured nation, as that the latter may not be bound to pay duty on the goods passing through the territory of the other, which before it had to pay. Nor indeed is it absurd that by way of penalty a certain sum of money should be paid, just as a fine is included in the list of private penalties. If the penalty should be voluntarily paid, there is no need that he who is to be punished should be compelled by force to pay. But if he should refuse to pay there is need of coercive measures. Since, nevertheless, this is to be kept within fair limits, it is to be determined from the circumstances how great a force must be applied that the purpose of the punishment may be attained. Therefore, when other means are not adequate, it is undoubtedly allowable to take up arms against the offender. Indeed, he who applies force for securing a penalty seems to be waging war; nevertheless no one can be said to wage war on a nation except he who with armed force assails the nation itself which refuses to pay the penalty, as is plainly to be recognized from the discussion concerning the taking of a penalty in war, and is understood from the proposition itself. For he who takes a penalty from an offender, applies force to him who refuses the same. But no force, except armed force, can be applied to a nation.

§ 590, part 8, Jus Nat.

§ 580.

§ 1114, part 1, Jus Nat.

Loc. cit.

§ 582. *When it is allowable to bring war by way of penalty*

Before war is brought on a nation for an irreparable injury, one should try to find out whether an agreement can be made concerning the payment of a penalty or whether it can be taken in some other way from the offender. For the right to punish must be used within proper limits, consequently if the penalty can be imposed without force, there is no right

§ 580.

to use force; if a penalty can be taken without the use of armed force, by which a nation itself is attacked, there is no right to bring war against the nation itself. Therefore, it is plain that before war is brought against a nation for an irreparable injury, one should try to find out whether an agreement can be made concerning the payment of a penalty, or whether it can be taken in some other way from the offender.

§ 1071, part 1,
Jus Nat.

Since he who has done a wrong is bound to pay the penalty, the nation which has done another an irreparable injury ought of its own accord to give satisfaction for it, much more ought it not to refuse to pay the penalty on demand. But just as there are very few people who are willing to submit themselves of their own accord to a penalty, so also to nations penalties are hateful. If, however, gentler measures are tried, before proceeding to harsh ones, a nation should blame itself that harsher measures must be used against it. War drags a great mass of evils after it, and its result is doubtful. Therefore, since every means must be sought to avoid it, war is not readily to be undertaken for the purpose of collecting a penalty. Nay more, it is frequently advisable to remit the penalty, putting in protests, if need be, rather than to take up arms.

§ 583. *What a retorsion of law is*

A retorsion of law is defined as an enactment, by which there is passed against the subjects of another nation a law, either positive or negative, which that nation uses against our subjects, or briefly it is the use of a law against another nation which that nation uses against our nation.

For example, it is a retorsion of law if a law of confiscation is opposed to a law of confiscation, namely, if you take from your citizens intending to come to me a tenth part of their goods, and I in turn take from my citizens who are going to subject themselves to your sovereignty a tenth part, or if you take from my citizens a tenth part of the inheritance which comes to them in your territory, and I use the same device against your citizens. Nay more, here belongs the case of my not allowing your citizens to take an inheritance or legacy from my citizens, because you do not allow the same to mine. Here also belongs the enactment, that the right of paraphernalia or of war-pledge[1] does not apply in the case of subjects of a nation in which this right is not acknowledged. Here likewise is further to be included the case of your prohibiting the export of certain merchandise, as grain, wool, or cloth, into my territory, and in turn my prohibiting the export of the same things or others into your territory. This retorsion of law is not to be confused with the retorsion of wrongs, which consists in repayment for injuries, and is approved in the last "Electoral Decision,"[2] in so far indeed as verbal injuries are repaid with verbal injuries, for as it is not allowable to repay verbal injuries with real injuries, such retorsion has no place among nations, and if real injuries are repaid with real, retorsion will be reduced to retaliation, which itself is illegal among nations, and if indeed it has been introduced by custom, it must be referred to unjust customary law. Therefore, there is no place left for the retorsion of wrongs in the law of nations. But retorsion of wrongs and retorsion of law agree in this respect, that any one may use the same law against another which the other has decreed against him, except that what is done in retorsion of wrongs the opponent was bound not to do in return, consequently he claims a certain right for himself who has none. But in retorsion of laws each one uses the right which he has.

No. 81.

§ 639, part 8, Jus Nat.

§ 577.

§ 584. *Whether retorsions of law between nations are illegal*

Retorsions of law between nations are not illegal. Since each nation is free to determine concerning those things which are to the advantage of the state, as may seem best to it, it can also determine without wrong how much right it may wish to allow another nation in its territory or with itself, consequently the other nation is bound to acquiesce in its

§ 55, part 8, and § 156, part 1, Jus Nat.

---

1. On *gerada* and *heergevettum*, see above, p. 170, n. 4.

2. See Christian Heinrich Breuning (ed.), *Verordnungen, und Constitutiones, den rechtlichen Prozess und andere streitige Faelle betreffende. Wie auch des Durchlauchtig-sten Hochgebohrnen Fuersten und Herrn, Herrn Johann Georgen des Andern, . . . Decisiones Electorales Saxonicae, oder Erledigung derer Zweifelhafften Rechts-Faelle* (Leipzig, 1746), pp. 223–24.

§ 563.
§ 16.
§ 18.

desire, and therefore it has no grievance. For since all nations are equal to each other, and what is allowed to one is also allowed to the other, the other nation also can decide, as seems best to it, concerning those things which are of advantage to the state, and consequently can use the same law towards it which it uses towards itself. Therefore, since it would be

§ 583.

a retorsion of law, if it should do this, retorsions of law between nations are not illegal.

Indeed, it frequently happens that by a retorsion of law the nation which has made a place for it feels more loss from it than it receives gain from the law which it has decreed against the other nation; then indeed that can be a reason why the matter should be returned to its former state. When that, indeed, is no longer possible the nation may censure itself, because it has not bargained more carefully. In a particular instance special reasons also are frequently given, which make a retorsion legal. So if the right of paraphernalia and war-pledge[3] are not in use somewhere, as it is unknown outside Saxon territories and some few other localities in which Saxon law is retained, retorsion of law rests on this principle, that you are bound to give no one anything for free who can give you something in return, consequently to give

§ 268, part 4,
Jus Nat.

profit to a nation from which in a similar case or the same case it is not allowable to hope for something in return. For nature, which makes all nations equal, does not bind you to make the condition of another better than the other makes yours. There is no reason indeed why any privilege ought to belong to one rather than to another.

§ 585. *Whether retorsion of law is obligatory*

§ 584.
§ 170, part 1,
Phil. Pract.
Univ.

Since retorsion of law is not illegal, consequently, since the right to the same certainly belongs to nations, and since any one is able to waive his right, every nation is free to decide whether or not it desires to make retorsion.

§ 117, part 3,
Jus Nat.

Nay more, adequate reasons are frequently not lacking, because of which it is better not to make retorsion of law than to make it; for example, if your subjects feel no loss from the restriction imposed by

3. See above, p. 170, n. 4, for *gerada* and *hergevettum*.

another nation, but a similar restriction would impose loss on them. Likewise also there may be especially cogent reasons for a restriction, so that you cannot complain of it, but ought rather to approve. Sometimes retorsion is necessary, as when exportation of grain is forbidden by a neighbouring nation, lest if exportation should be allowed by us grain would be forced to a high price among us. Therefore prudence especially limits retorsion; nor in it does anything come from either party which can be considered a wrong, although on the occasion of its exercise one or the other party or even both may experience some disadvantage, which nevertheless is sought by neither party, as each one of course enjoins what seems to the advantage of its own state. This is perfectly plain in the case in which we do not allow a certain right to foreigners which our citizens enjoy, because foreigners do not use a right from which our citizens in turn could hope for any advantage, an example of which we have seen in the right of paraphernalia and of war-pledge.

Note, § 583.

§ 586. *Of the satisfaction of a right and of pledge between nations*

If any nation cannot obtain its property or that of its citizens from another nation which detains it, or anything which is due to it in any other way, or if one nation refuses to do justice to another nation or to its citizens, the nation, in place of its property or debt, or of the property of its citizens or debt due to them, can take away any goods of the citizens of the other state, which are just as valuable; but it is bound to restore any excess of value, or not to return the goods seized, until it shall have received its own property or that of its citizens, or the debt due to itself or its citizens. For if I cannot obtain my property from one who detains it, or from a debtor what he owes me, by the law of nature it is allowable for me to take from him in place of my property or my debt another thing just as valuable. And the property of citizens is bound by nature for the debts of the state, and also the private property itself of the ruler of the state. Therefore, if any nation denies the right of another nation or its citizens, so that the nation cannot obtain its property or that of its citizens, or what is due to it or its citizens, it is allowable for it to take away any goods of the citizens of the other state, or even the goods of the ruler

§ 1112, part 5, Jus Nat.

§ 495.

§ 496.

of the state, in place of its property or the debt due to it, or of the property of its citizens or the debts due to them. Which was the first point.

But if one who cannot obtain anything from the detainer or debtor in place of his own property or the debt owed him should take another thing

§ 1115, part 5,
Jus Nat.

of greater value he is bound to restore the excess to the detainer or debtor. Therefore, if the goods of the citizens of another nation, or of the ruler of a state, are taken away for the satisfaction of a claim, whatever excess of value they have is to be restored to that nation. Which was the second point.

But since also it is allowable to take property from its detainer or from one's debtor by way of pledge, not to be returned until you shall have received

§ 1118, part 5,
Jus Nat.

your property, or what is due to you, the property of citizens of another state, or the private property of the ruler of a state can be taken by way of pledge, to be restored, if the nation shall have received its property or that of its citizen, or what is due to it, or its citizen. Which was the third point.

We made a distinction between the involuntary satisfaction of a right and an involuntary pledge, when we were discussing the methods of obtaining one's right in a state of nature, although usually there

§§ 1112, 1118,
part 5, Jus Nat.

is no distinction made between them, and in the law of nations they are included in the one category of pledge. Nevertheless, both from what was there proved and from the notes appended, it is evident and more than evident that they are different. But each is allowable

§ 3.

among nations, because in a state of nature, in which individuals as well as nations exercise only the right belonging to them by nature, each is allowable for everyone. And only in this way does the necessary or natural law of nations appear in the clearest light, if that which by nature is allowable for individuals is applied to nations, and care

§ 4.

is taken that nothing should be carelessly incorporated in the law of nations which comes from the civil law. But since we have proved in the place cited what things are to be understood concerning the involuntary satisfaction of a right and an involuntary pledge, it is not necessary to repeat them here.

§ 587. *How far that extends*

Since if a right is denied, it is allowable to take the property of citizens of another nation or the private property of the ruler of a state in satisfaction

of a right or by way of pledge, and since the right is denied not only if a   § 586.
judgement cannot be obtained within a proper time against the detainer
of a thing or against a debtor, but also if in a matter not doubtful a decision has been made plainly contrary to law, which is assumed to be clear
of itself, it is allowable to take the property of citizens of another nation
or the private property of the ruler of a state in satisfaction of a right or
by way of pledge, if in a matter not doubtful a decision has been made
plainly contrary to law.

A right is denied you if you cannot acquire by a judgement that
which is your own or ought to be made your own. It is plain then that
this can be brought about in two ways, either if the judge refuses to
hear you, or if he gives an unjust decision. It is in accord with civil law
that a decision made by a judge ought to be considered just, if either
within a certain time it should not be appealed against to a higher
court, or should have been affirmed by it. Therefore, since civil laws
bind only members of the state in which they are promulgated, among   § 967, part 8,
nations the decision of a judge whether properly or improperly made   Jus Nat.
is not considered correct and just, even if it shall have been confirmed
by a higher court. If then in a matter not doubtful a decision has been
made plainly contrary to law, the decision is considered a nullity, and
therefore the right denied is properly taken.

§ 588. *The same is further considered*

Likewise, since he who delays a right or postpones restoration by various
devices may properly be assumed to be unwilling to give it to you, since,
consequently, this would be the same as denying your right to you, and
when a right is denied, it is allowable to take the property of citizens of
another nation in satisfaction of the right or by way of pledge; if a right is   § 586.
delayed, it is allowable to take the property of citizens of another nation
or even the private property of the ruler of a state in satisfaction of a
right, or by way of pledge.

He who has the intention of allowing another his right, allows it
promptly, since nothing prevents him from doing without delay that
which he is ready to do. And this promptness is especially in accord
with the justice which nations ought to cultivate in their relations

§ 265.

with each other with solicitude, that nothing may be done which is opposed to it. If then a nation which hears the grievances of another, and promises that they will be removed, delays the right beyond limit and justifies the delay by frivolous reasons, it is undoubtedly properly understood that it has no intention of allowing the other his right. Therefore, it is the same whether it openly denies a right or delays it beyond limit. Many things are endured in a state which are not to be endured from strangers.

§ 589. *What reprisals are and whether they are legal*

Reprisals are defined as the taking away of the goods of citizens of another nation or even of the ruler of a state in satisfaction of a right or by way of pledge. This is also called a pledge among various peoples, the "Withernam" of the Saxon jurists, from the Germanic word *Wiedernehmen* [recapture], because in place of that which has been taken away another thing

§ 586 and fol.

just like it is taken. Since taking away of this sort is allowable among nations by the law of nature, reprisals are legal. But it is evident from what

§§ cited.

has been proved before, that there is no place for reprisals, except when another people does an injury to us or to our citizens, and, when asked, is unwilling to repair it within a proper time, that is, without delay. Furthermore, it is also plain that the right of reprisal belongs only to nations and to those who have the right of nations, namely, to rulers of states.

There is no reason why you should object that this right belongs in a state of nature to individuals, and consequently the same also exists between citizens, or subjects of different peoples. For in a state of nature only the property of one who detains my property or of my

§§ 1112, 1118,
part 5, Jus Nat.

debtor can be taken in satisfaction of a claim or by way of pledge. But that the goods of citizens are bound for the debts of a state, comes

§ 495.

from the law of nations, consequently also the right of reprisal, by which the goods of any citizen are taken for any debt of the nation or of any other citizen, can belong only to nations.

§ 590. *Whether the right of reprisal belongs to private individuals*

§ 589.

Since the right of reprisal belongs only to nations and to their rulers, the same cannot belong to the subjects of different nations in their relations with each other, consequently a private individual cannot use the right of reprisal unless this should be allowed him by the ruler of a state.

If, then, private individuals should desire to exercise the right of reprisal, it is necessary that they should obtain beforehand the consent of the ruler. Moreover the express consent is required, the implied consent is not enough. For the decision as to a matter which affects the interest of the state belongs to the superior, and not to a private individual. But it is not always advisable to use coercive remedies, or to use the same ones at every time and place. Besides it may happen that the superior by his authority may persuade the ruler of another state to render justice to his citizen, so that there would be no need of coercive remedies, however much private complaints should be disregarded.

§ 591. *Whether subjects of another nation can be taken by way of pledge*

If a right is denied, even the subjects of another nation can be taken by way of pledge. For just as the property of citizens is bound, so too their persons are bound for the debts of states. Therefore, since it is allowable § 495. among nations to take the goods of any citizen of another nation if it § 507. denies justice to us or to our citizens, it must also be allowable among § 586. nations, if justice is denied, to take the subjects of another nation by way of pledge.

We have seen above that hostages are in fact put in pledge, nor can they be looked at otherwise than as pledges of good faith. Therefore, § 497. just as men can be put in pledge as evidence of good faith, so it is § 540. not absurd that they should be pledged for debt. And as is plain from the case of reprisals, involuntary pledges of property are made; therefore it is also not absurd that there should be involuntary pledges of persons.

§ 592. *Androlepsy or viricaption*

Androlepsy or viricaption is defined as the taking, by way of pledge, of the citizens of a state which denies justice to us or to our citizens. Therefore it is evident that androlepsy is a certain sort of reprisal, and that is allowable by the law of nature among nations.   § 589.

Note, § 503.

We have already above made mention of androlepsy, when we observed that hostages when freed can be retained as captives by way of pledge. And now it is evident that that comes from the right of reprisal belonging to nations.

§ 593. *The purpose of androlepsy*

§ 592.

Since by the right of androlepsy men are taken by way of pledge, because a nation is unwilling to do justice as it ought, androlepsy has the purpose that a nation which is unwilling to do justice to us or to our citizens may be compelled to do so, consequently citizens of a foreign state may be retained as captives until justice shall have been done.

§ 887, Psych. Emp., and § 497 b.

§ 591.

The liberation of captive citizens ought, therefore, to be a motive for which a nation which refuses to do justice should do it, just as the liberation of hostages is a motive for performing that for the sake of which they have been given. We have before suggested that androlepsy is akin to giving of hostages, except that in the latter, citizens are given by way of pledge, but in the former they are taken by way of pledge. Therefore, the giving of hostages and androlepsy have many things in common, so that what things have been proved concerning hostages may easily be applied to androlepsy, and therefore in explaining the right of androlepsy it is allowable for us to be briefer.

§ 594. *Of androlepsy in case of a demand for a penalty*

Because in androlepsia the subjects of another nation are taken by way of pledge, for the reason that it refuses to do justice to us or to our citizens, and since justice is refused if the nation is unwilling to punish its citizen who has offended against us or our citizens, the right of androlepsia is allowable, if any nation is unwilling to punish its subject who has offended against us or our citizens.

Note, § 503.

§ 982, part 8, Jus Nat.

We have already noted above, that in this case the right of androlepsia was formerly exercised among the Athenians, a little more narrowly, however, since it was restricted to the case of the murder of an Athenian citizen in a foreign territory, and under certain limitations was transformed into a civil right.

§ 595. *The effect of androlepsy, if justice cannot be secured*

If by right of androlepsy a nation cannot be persuaded to do justice, those who have been taken by way of pledge are either to be kept in prison forever as captives, or where slavery is practised, become slaves, but they cannot be killed, nay more, they cannot even be made to suffer a serious corporeal punishment, even if judgement cannot be obtained against the offender. Since a man is not the master of his own life, nor of his own body, nor any of his members, when he is put in pledge neither his life nor his body can be pledged, consequently nothing remains which can be put in pledge except the natural liberty belonging to him, or control over his own actions, under which also it is self-evident that there is included the right to be wherever one pleases. Therefore, if the right cannot be obtained, for the denial of which the citizen of the foreign state was taken, the one who has taken him by way of pledge acquires a right over his actions, and consequently a right to detain him, and therefore he can either keep him in prison forever as a captive or, where slavery is practised, can reduce him to slavery, but he cannot be killed, nor can any physical violence be inflicted upon him. Which was the first point.

§ 351, part 1, Jus Nat.

§ 374, part 1, Jus Nat.

§ 146, part 1, Jus Nat.

§ 153, part 1, Jus Nat.

§ 1096, part 7, Jus Nat.

When we use the right of androlepsy, because we are seeking the punishment of the guilty, he who is seized is put in pledge, not for the wrong of the offender but for the purpose of obtaining a right, namely, to inflict punishment on the guilty. Therefore, since it neither follows from the nature of the act that he who has been seized by way of pledge should suffer the same punishment as was to be inflicted on the offender, nor is it allowable to punish any one on account of the act of another by which any one has been injured; if a judgement cannot be obtained against an offender, the penalty which was to be inflicted upon the offender cannot be imposed upon the one seized, consequently, because the offender is not punished, he cannot be killed nor can any serious corporeal punishment be inflicted upon him. Which was the second point.

§ 593.

§ 1084, part 1, Jus Nat.

In former times not only nations whose minds were obsessed with the perverse idea that human beings had a right over their own life and body, believed that the life and body of innocent subjects were bound for such a reason, since they had transferred to the state the right belonging to themselves by nature. But even those who are unaffected by this error, nevertheless do not hesitate to argue that the right to kill captured citizens, consequently also to inflict other serious bodily penalties upon them, if justice should not be done, is included under the right of reprisal. For they assume that they are punished not for the act of another but for their own, and therefore they are not innocent. For citizens approve or are understood to approve of the act of their state, namely, the fact that, by denying justice, the state is unwilling to repair the wrong, and therefore they are bound to make reparation for their own wrong. But in the first place it is plainly evident that it cannot be thought of a captive citizen that he approves of the act of his state, for since his liberation, of which it cannot be doubted but that he is especially desirous, depends upon the redress of the injury, he cannot approve of the ruler of the state, whose subject he is, being unwilling to redress it. For the obligation of a citizen does not extend so far that he is bound to approve of the illegal act of the ruler of the state, much less of his fellow-citizen. But individuals are bound to the whole only in that they seek to promote the common good, and from this obligation it by no means

§ 28, part 8, Jus Nat.

follows that one is bound to approve and defend an illegal act of the state, for example, that it is unwilling to pass a sentence of death on a criminal; nay more, one cannot bind himself to this, since no one can bind himself to approve and defend an illegal act, because of the unchanging natural obligation which directs otherwise. Therefore, it is improperly assumed that the wrong is that of the captive, which makes him subject to capital punishment or to serious corporeal pun-

De Jure Belli ac Pacis, lib. 3, c. 2, § 5, Note 2. § 24.

ishment. But less properly Grotius asserts that the right of reprisal was not introduced by nature, but was received here and there by custom, so that it would be only customary law; for we have seen in what precedes that that is not without natural reasons.

§ 596. Of that which is allowable against one who resists execution of the right of reprisal

Against one who resists the execution of the right of reprisal all measures are allowable which are allowed to a defender against an aggressor. For since a nation to which justice is denied by another has the right of reprisal against the nation denying it, when there is resistance to the execution of this right that is contrary to the right of the one to whom such a right belongs, consequently it tends to injure him. Therefore, since he who resists one intending or attempting to injure him defends himself, and since the right of self-defence belongs to a man by nature, the right of self-defence belongs to nations also against one who resists the execution of reprisals, consequently all measures are allowable against him which are allowed to a defender against an aggressor.

§ 589.

§ 239, part 1,
Phil. Pract. Univ.

§ 920, part 1,
Jus Nat.

§ 972, part 1,
Jus Nat.

§ 973, part 1,
Jus Nat.

There is no reason for thinking that, if any one should desire to carry away by force from another person his own property or even to seize that person, the latter is defending his own property or himself, nor consequently that he who attempts to carry away such property or to take such a person is not to be looked at as a defender; for it is self-defence on your part only if the one attempting to carry away your property has no right to it or the one wishing to take you has no such right. But when one is using his own right, no one ought to interfere in any way with the exercise of that right, consequently it is not allowable to resist the execution of the right of reprisal. He who resists attempts an injury, or tries to harm you, and therefore is the same as an aggressor.

§ 655, part 2,
Jus Nat.

§ 727, Ontol.

§ 979, part 1,
Jus Nat.

§ 597. *That is further considered*

Since against the one who resists the execution of the right of reprisal all measures are allowable which are allowed to a defender against an aggressor, and since only so much is allowable against an aggressor as is sufficient to avoid injury, if any one resists an act of reprisal, only so much is allowable against him as is sufficient to make it possible to capture him or his property, consequently any force is allowable without which that purpose cannot be attained, and if it should happen that he is killed in resisting, he is not killed under the right of reprisal, but from accident under the right of defence.

§ 596.

§ 980, part 1,
Jus Nat.

§§ 589, 592.

He is killed by his own fault who happens to be killed while resisting the execution of reprisals, for he ought not to have resisted. Therefore, his death is to be imputed to himself, not to him who was defending the execution of his right. For self-defence with killing of the aggressor is allowable, if the illegal force cannot be otherwise

§ 1013, part 1,
Jus Nat.

repelled. But what might be further explained here is plain from those things which have been proved at sufficient length concerning the right of self-defence.

§§ 982 and fol., part 1, Jus Nat.

§ 598. *Of those who give cause for reprisals*

Those who have given cause for reprisals ought to repay the loss to those by whom anything is lost from that cause. For by the law of nature every one is bound to repay the loss which he has wilfully or negligently caused another. Therefore, since he who has given cause for reprisals causes a loss to his fellow-citizens, those who have given cause for reprisals ought to repay the loss to those by whom anything is lost.

§ 580, part 2, Jus Nat.
§§ 589, 592.

It is in perfect harmony with natural equity that those who have wilfully or negligently caused a loss should repay it. And there is no reason why that ought not to apply in case of reprisals. For although in regard to foreign nations any property of citizens may be considered the property of the state, nevertheless in a state in which there is individual ownership of private property the property of one citizen is not considered the property of other citizens in general. And although the act of a citizen ratified by the ruler, as is the case in the present instance, would be considered the act of the nation, as regards foreign nations, if the citizen refuses to do justice; nevertheless in a state the acts of one citizen cannot be imputed to another who in no way participates therein.

§ 289.

§ 316.

§ 599. *Of the duty of a ruler of a state as regards the restoration of loss caused by reprisals*

Since those who have given cause for reprisals ought to repay the loss to those by whom anything has been lost from that cause, and since the ruler of a state ought to see to it that every one should be allowed his right, he therefore ought to take care that those who have given cause for reprisals should repay the loss to those by whom anything has been lost from that cause.

§ 598.

§ 535, part 8, Jus Nat.

It is self-evident that no other course can be taken in a state to repay the loss caused to a citizen than for the ruler to provide that this

be done through judges appointed for that purpose. For although he
himself by denying justice has also given cause for reprisals, nevertheless on this account the obligation is not terminated of those who
were the original cause of the reprisals, nor does his duty cease with
regard to those who have suffered loss through reprisals because of no
fault of their own. For since he ought not to have allowed any one of
his subjects to cause loss to a citizen of another nation, or to do him
a wrong, but in the former case ought rather to compel repayment
of the loss, and in the latter case ought to punish the offender; when
he refuses justice asked for, he defends the bad cause of his citizen
or subject, certainly not without his connivance, at least tacit. But
when the defence fails, the loss caused to an innocent citizen through
reprisals ought to be charged, not so much to the defender of the bad
cause, but rather to the one who did the wrong. But the situation is
otherwise if the ruler of the state by his own act has given cause for
reprisals, or private citizens have been acting on his command. What
is here in harmony with the law of nature is proved in the following
proposition. But for that purpose must be prefixed the lemma which
immediately follows.

§ 538, part 8, Jus Nat.
§ 539, part 8, Jus Nat.

§ 317.

§ 318.

§ 600. *Of the act of a ruler of a state to be assumed by the people*

The act of the ruler of a state as such, by which injury is caused to outsiders, the people is bound to assume as its own. For since the people
has originally transferred its sovereignty to the ruler of the state that
he may exercise it, whatever he does as ruler of the state he does by the
right of the people, or the people is understood to have done through
him. Therefore, since he represents his nation when he deals with other
nations, if by some act of his own he does a wrong or causes a loss to
some nation, or to its citizen or citizens, the people subject to him is
understood to have done this. Therefore, the people is bound to assume
as its own the act of the ruler of a state as such, by which injury is caused
to outsiders.

§ 34, part 8, Jus Nat.
§ 42, part 8, Jus Nat.
§ 39.

Undoubtedly it is true in general that the people ought to
assume as its own the act of the ruler of a state, as is understood

§ 158, part 8,
Jus Nat.

§ 424.

from the present proof also. And in truth the same thing is already evident from the fact that the will of the ruler of a state is to be considered the will of the whole people. Therefore, just as the obligation which is derived from treaties binds the nation also, so also the obligation which arises from a wrong extends to it. There is surely no reason why a distinction is to be made between other acts and a wrongful act.

§ 601. *Of repaying the loss caused by reprisals, to which the act of the ruler of a state has given rise*

§ 600.

§ 598.

If the ruler of a state by his own act, or a private individual by his order, has given cause for reprisals, the loss must be paid from the public funds to those by whom anything is lost from that cause. For the act of the ruler of a state as such, by which injury is caused to outsiders, the people ought to acknowledge as its own. If then the ruler of a state by his own act, or, what is just the same, a private citizen by his order, has given cause for reprisals, the whole people is understood to have given cause for the same. Therefore, since those who have given cause for reprisals ought to repay the losses to those by whom anything is lost thereby, if the ruler of a state by his act or a private citizen by his order has given cause for reprisals, the loss must be repaid to those by whom anything is lost from that cause by the people, consequently from the public funds.

Note, § 600.
§ 598.
§ 1043, part 8,
Jus Nat.

§ 586.

§ 600.

The obligation which is derived from the wrongful act of the ruler of a state as such binds the entire people. But from his wrongful act the obligation arises to repay the loss caused by reprisals. Therefore, that obligation also binds the entire people. Therefore, although any citizen is bound patiently to obey his ruler, even if he rules badly, nevertheless it does not follow therefrom that the innocent citizen alone ought to bear the loss which he has suffered in the name of his nation, and that indeed for an act which concerns the whole people. Nor here is there anything exceptional admitted which does not hold equally in other cases. Indeed, if disposition is made of the property of individuals by the power of eminent domain, satisfaction must be made therefore from the public funds, as far as is possible, and the owner should bear only his share of the loss. Likewise the state either through itself or through the ruler of the state is bound to compensate the hostage or his kinsmen for the injury which he suffers. There is no reason why one citizen ought to suffer loss for the wrongdoing of the ruler of the state, which has given cause for reprisals.

§ 119, part 8, Jus Nat. § 536.

§ 602. *Of ownership acquired through reprisals*

The ownership of things taken by reprisals is acquired by those for whom they were made, unless something is left over which is to be restored. For things are taken by reprisals either in satisfaction of a right, or by way of pledge. Now in satisfaction of a right ownership of a thing is acquired in place of one's own, or of a debt due to one, and when a pledge is made, if the pledge is not redeemed within a proper time, satisfaction must be given to the creditor from the price of it. Therefore it is plain that the ownership of things taken by reprisals is acquired by those for whom they were made. Which was the first point.

§ 589.

§ 1119, part 5, Jus Nat.

§ 1145, part 5, Jus Nat.

But that the excess of value, or what is left over, is to be restored, we have already proved above. Which was the second point.

§ 586.

Since all fraud is illegal, in civil law it usually is determined what is to be observed about the manner of acquiring property by reprisals, in order that all fraud may be guarded against. Since a pledge cannot be redeemed, unless the pledging should come to the notice of the one whose things have been taken by way of pledge, and sufficient time allowed him, within which he can express his desire, what may be sufficient time, within which he ought to redeem the pledge, is to be determined by particular circumstances.

§ 148, part 5, Jus Nat.

§§ 978, 982. part 8, Jus Nat.

§ 603. *Whether reprisals are war*

Reprisals are a certain kind of war, but one which is more akin to private war. For by reprisals things are taken by force which belong to subjects of another nation, and by androlepsy, which is a certain kind of reprisal, persons are taken who are subjects of another nation, with the purpose that we may acquire the right which another nation refuses to give us,

§ 589.

§ 592.

§ 593.

§ 1102, part 1, Jus Nat.

consequently we pursue by force our right against one who does not wish to give it to us. But the violent pursuit of our right against one who does not wish to give it to us is war. Therefore reprisals are a certain kind of war. Which was the first point.

But when reprisals are made the whole people is not assailed by force, but individuals rather contend by force. Therefore, since this war is carried on as if between individuals, although reprisals have been allowed by the authority of the state, reprisals are more akin to private war. Which was the second point.

§ 586.

Reprisals certainly have taken the place of private war, which under like circumstances exists in the same case. Therefore, if reprisals are allowed private citizens by authority of the state, it is understood that private war, the right to which belongs by nature to every one, is allowable for individuals. But although it may also happen that the ruler of the state may use reprisals, or the nation itself in a public cause, nevertheless he does not use this right otherwise than in so far as it belongs to individual men in a state of nature, so that there is no difference in the execution of it.

§ 604. *Whether reprisals and androlepsy are a just cause of war*

§ 592.

§§ 589, 592.

§ 975, part 1, Jus Nat.
§ 1109, part 1, Jus Nat.

Reprisals and androlepsy do not give to the other party a just cause of war. For because reprisals and androlepsy, which is a certain kind of reprisal, are legal, the one who resorts to reprisals or androlepsy uses his own right, consequently he does no injury at all to another against whom he uses this violent remedy. Therefore, since there is no just cause of war, unless an injury has been done or is to be done, reprisals and androlepsy do not give the other party a just cause of war.

§ 605. *Hostilities are unjust by which reprisals and androlepsy are avenged*

§ 604.
§ 1110, part 1, Jus Nat.
§ 1111, part 1, Jus Nat.

Since reprisals and androlepsy do not give to the other party a just cause of war, and since war is unjust for which there is no just cause, if any nation on account of reprisals or androlepsy made by another brings war against the other, the war is plainly unjust, consequently illegal.

For wars to be unjust which are begun against one who uses the right of reprisals or androlepsy, it is necessary that the latter should be used for a just cause, which certainly is here assumed. For otherwise they are illegal, and those who use them do an injury to the other party. Therefore, since an injury is a just cause of war, reprisals and androlepsy done without right give just cause of war to the opposite party, and, when it seems wise to resort to arms, the war is just.

§ 1109, part 1, Jus Nat.

§ 1110, part 1, Jus Nat.

§ 606. *When a cause of reprisals and androlepsy is a just cause of war*

If reprisals and androlepsy cannot be used, the things which make them legal are a just cause of war; but as long as through them an injury can be repaired, or satisfaction can be obtained for irreparable injury, it is not allowable by the law of nature to declare war against the opposite party. For reprisals, of which androlepsy is a certain sort, are made with no other purpose than that you may acquire the right which the opposite party is unwilling to give you, consequently a violation of your right, and therefore an injury, is a reason for them. Therefore, since an injury is a just cause of war, and since reprisals and androlepsy cannot be used as a less violent remedy, according to the hypothesis; if reprisals and androlepsy cannot be used, the things which make them legal are undoubtedly a just cause of war. Which was the first point.

§ 592.

§ 586.
§ 859, part 1, Jus Nat.
§ 1109, part 1, Jus Nat.

But since one must not use harsher remedies as long as milder ones are sufficient for defence, and since reprisals and androlepsy are certainly a milder remedy than bringing war against an entire people, as long as an injury can be repaired by reprisals, or satisfaction can be obtained for an irreparable injury, it is not allowable by the law of nature to declare war against the opposite party. Which was the second point.

§ 982, part 1, Jus Nat.

§ 981, part 1, Jus Nat., and §§ 586, 592 h.

There are two ways by which it happens that one cannot acquire his right by reprisals and androlepsy, either because the opportunity is lacking to take the property or persons of another nation, or because that which is sought, or which is due, is much more valuable than are the things for the seizing of which a suitable opportunity can be found. Here further can be included the case of the opposite party opposing reprisals to just reprisals, and since this ought not to be done a new injury is committed, a just cause of war. Of course one must resort to arms when through continuous reprisals on either side the matter can have no end, since old injuries are ever increased by new.

§ 596.

§ 859, part 1, Jus Nat.

§ 1109, part 1, Jus Nat.

❧ CHAPTER VI ❧

Of the Law of War of Nations

§ 607. *What public war is*

That is called a public war which is waged between nations, or by those leaders who have the supreme sovereignty. Since nations are a number of people united into a state, in a public war a nation, by the united force of many, attacks the nation against which it brings war.

§ 5, part 8, Jus Nat.

> Hence it is that a public war in its external aspect is far different from that which occurs between individuals in a state of nature, and after states come into being the latter is usually called in common speech a fight or a duel or a violent contest. But it is a public war just the same—to apply the word rather to the status than to the action, although war seems to describe an action more than a status—if one enters into violent contest with another or even if a few battle with a few.

§§ 1088, 1090, part 5, Jus Nat.

Note, § 1102, part 1, Jus Nat.

§ 608. *What private war is*

That is called a private war which a private individual carries on with a private individual by his own authority, or which is carried on by several private individuals with several private individuals on their own authority.

> We have already proved elsewhere that private war is to be tolerated in a state only when no judicial decision can be obtained. But although public war differs very much from private in its external aspect, their laws, nevertheless, considered in themselves are the same in either form, and the nature of public war is to be determined from that of private war, as will become evident from what follows. Therefore, in

§§ 560, 562, part 8, Jus Nat.

Note, § 607.

the law of nature and nations war is to be defined in such a way that
the definition may be equally applicable to public and private war, and
from this is to be derived the law of war and the law in war. For just as
the necessary or natural law of nations consists only in the application
to nations of the natural law of individuals, so also the law of public

§ 4.

war and the law in public war consists simply in the application to
nations of the law of private war and the law in private war, which by
nature belongs to every man. And for that reason also we have spoken
of the law of war and of the law in war in "The Law of Nature," where
we have pointed out the rights belonging by nature to individual men,
in order that we might have definite principles from which the law
of public war and the law in public war could be proved. For unless
this should be observed, not only is it to be feared that errors may be
admitted instead of the truth, but also the law of public war and the
law in public war cannot be deeply investigated, and what is true cannot be unhesitatingly grasped.

§ 609. *What a mixed war is*

A mixed war is one which is public as to one party, private as to the other.

We have an example of mixed war if the ruler of a state wages war
with his rebellious subjects. For on the side of the ruler of the state the

§ 607.
§ 608.

war is public, on the side of the rebellious subjects it is private. From
a mixed war it is apparent that a private no less than a public war can
differ utterly in its external aspect from the war which individuals
wage with individuals in a natural state. And hence it is plainer why
in defining war no consideration is to be paid to the external aspect
which public war bears.

§ 610. *What soldiers are*

Those persons are called soldiers through whom the leader of the war
inflicts violence upon the other party with whom he is waging war.

Soldiers are the instrumental cause of the war, just as the leader is

§ 890, Ontol.

the principal cause. Of course the concept of the efficient principal
cause and the instrumental cause, which we have explained elsewhere,
is to be so modified as the difference between physical and moral cause

demands. Of course a moral cause is understood to be devoid of force if one's freedom of action be wanting; but when one acts by the right of another, he is thought of as under coercion coming from outside, and then he puts himself in the place of an instrument. Hence Grotius speaks of soldiers as instruments of war, and in general he classes men as instruments who so exercise their own volition that their will is dependent on that of another, and he likewise calls subjects the instruments of rulers.

§ 891, Ontol.

De Jure Belli ac Pacis, lib. 1, c. 5, § 3.

§ 611. *What comes under the name of arms*

Arms are defined as all things which we use for inflicting violence on another or for turning it away from ourselves, or for protecting ourselves against it.

Gaius[1] says the term signifies not only shields and swords and helmets, but clubs and stones. To-day therefore, after the method of warfare has assumed quite a different form because of the invention of gunpowder, under the term arms, not only swords and hand culverins, but also engines of war, balls of lead, iron, and stone, bombs, gunpowder itself, ladders for scaling walls, and all instruments the use of which is indispensable in the siege of cities, are properly included. But those things are not included in this category which are required as essential for preserving life, such as grain, clothing for soldiers, tents, and things akin to these. Moreover, the significance of a word is to be determined from the understanding of those skilled in an art, rather than by the observation of the inconsequential speech which prevails particularly among the unskilled.

See Dig. 50, 16, 41.

§ 612. *Of military officers and commanders*

Those persons are called military officers to whom a certain control over soldiers has been assigned by the sovereign power and to whom certain duties in war are entrusted. Those are properly called commanders to whom control over the whole army is assigned and to whom supreme command in war is entrusted. Therefore, officers are minor powers, some

§ 368.

1. Gaius was a famous Roman jurist in the second century A.D.

of whom are subject to others and farther removed from the sovereign power, others, however, are nearer to it according to the extent of power which they exercise: but those properly called commanders are nearest to the sovereign power.

It is not our purpose to explain all their differences and to describe the functions of each. For when we are simply demonstrating rights, generalities are sufficient. Moreover, their rights will depend upon the will of the sovereign power, which uses them in war as instrumental causes.

§ 613. *Whether the right of war belongs to nations*

§ 1104, part 1, Jus Nat.

§ 973, part 8, Jus Nat.

§ 1061, part 1, Jus Nat.

§ 1114, part 1, Jus Nat.

§§ 2, 3.

The right of war belongs to nations. For by nature the right of war belongs to every man against one who does not wish to allow him his perfect right, the right of self-defence also belongs to him, and the right of punishing the one who injures him, each of which is a right of war. Therefore, since nations in their relations to each other are regarded as individual free persons living in a state of nature, and since in their relation to each other they use nothing except natural law, or that belonging by nature to every man, the right of war belongs to nations.

§ 4, part 8, Jus Nat.

§ 26, part 8, Jus Nat.

§ 13, part 8, Jus Nat.

When men come together in a state, since they agree with each other that they will jointly provide that each may enjoy his right in peace and that each may in safety obtain that from the other, and that they will jointly defend themselves and theirs against any external force, they do not lose their rights nor renounce them, but determine to exercise them jointly, consequently the rights belonging to the individuals by nature coalesce in a common right. And since states have been established in harmony with natural law, their combined rights, such as belong by nature to individuals as regards their property and persons with respect to other persons, belong to the nation also as a nation as regards those things which belong to the nation, and as regards the entire nation with respect to outside nations. And therefore, the right of war belongs none the less to nations also in every case in which the right of war belongs by nature to individuals. And hence it is that what is to be determined concerning public war is derived from private war. The law of war is also in perfect accord with the purpose of the state, a certain part of which is security, that is, freedom from fear, especially of external force. But from this purpose is to be determined also the right of nation against nation, since states have been established in harmony with the law of nature. These things are carefully to be noted, since they help to a closer inspection not only of the right of war of nations but also of the other rights belonging to a nation against a nation, so that their truth is brought out into a perfectly clear light.

§ 12, part 8, Jus Nat.

§ 156, part 1, Phil. Pract. Univ.

§ 26, part 8, Jus Nat.

§ 614. *To what extent the right of war belongs to rulers of states*

Since the right of war belongs to nations, and that is included among sovereign rights, consequently it is included under the civil sovereignty, and since the civil sovereignty has been transferred to the ruler of the state, that he may exercise it, the right of war belongs to the ruler of the state also. And since it depends upon the will of the people whether it wishes to transfer sovereignty undivided or to retain some separate part for itself, or to transfer it on a definite condition to another or others, and since the right of the ruler of a state is to be determined from the desire which the people had, when they made the transfer; how far the right of war belongs to the ruler of the state and in what way he ought to exercise it are to be determined from the will of the people transferring the sovereignty, consequently from the fundamental laws, if there are any concerning the right of war.

§ 613.

§ 943, part 8, Jus Nat.

§ 810, part 8, Jus Nat.

§ 42, part 8, Jus Nat.

§ 64, part 8, Jus Nat.

§ 43, part 8, Jus Nat.

In a monarchy and in an aristocracy the right of war depends altogether upon the decision of the rulers of the state, but in mixed states the same can depend either upon the decision of the ruler of the state, or on the will of the people or of the nobles, or for beginning or ending a war the ruler of the state is bound at least to seek the consent either of the people or of the nobles. But in a democracy or a popular state since the sovereignty rests with the entire people, the right of war also rests with the people.

§ 133, part 8, Jus Nat.

§ 135, part 8, Jus Nat.

§ 131, part 8, Jus Nat.

§ 615. *The difference between a defensive and an offensive war*

A defensive war is defined as one in which any one defends himself against another who brings war against him. But that is called an offensive war which is brought against another who was not thinking of bringing a war, or when any one assails another with armed force.

§§ 607, 608.

Defensive war and offensive war occur no less between individuals than between nations, so that this distinction is common to both public and private war. Thus a defensive war arises if one defends himself against an aggressor or his property against robbery or his possessions against an invader; but an offensive war arises if one attempts by force to compel another either to restore what is his own or to perform what is due to him, or attempts to force him to a settlement of a controverted matter.

§ 616. *What a punitive war is*

§ 615.

A punitive war is defined as one in which a penalty is exacted from another. A punitive war, therefore, is a form of offensive war.

Thus he begins a punitive war who punishes by arms an injury to legates. That must also be classed as a punitive war which is brought against some nation on account of its idolatry, for in such a war we do not seek what is our own or what is due to us, we simply demand that the nation should give up idolatry, or that it should be utterly destroyed if it is unwilling to do so.

§ 617. *What is a just cause of war between nations*

§ 1109, part 1, Jus Nat.

§ 3.

A just cause of war between nations arises only when a wrong has been done or is about to be done. For by natural law a just cause of war arises only when a wrong has been done or is about to be done. Therefore, since no other law than natural law originally exists between nations, there can be no other just cause of war between them than a wrong done or about to be done.

§ 607.

§ 1109, part 1, Jus Nat.

This could likewise be shown in this way. The war which is waged between nations is a public war. But no war has a just cause except for a wrong done or about to be done. Therefore, also, there can be no just cause for a public war save a wrong done or about to be done, consequently there can be no other just cause of war between nations than a wrong done or about to be done.

Hence it is plain whence the justice of war is to be determined. Of course if any one brings war against another, there must be an inquiry as to the wrong the one has done to the other; now if there has been no wrong the war is not just, but if there should be a wrong the war then is just. From this, further, it is plain that the justice of a war between nations cannot be determined unless it should appear what indeed are the perfect rights of nations and how they can be violated. Therefore, an accurate decision cannot be reached concerning the justice of the war in any given case unless one is especially skilled in the law of nations and in general public law and consequently in the whole of natural law, and has been informed in adequate detail as to the nature of the facts to which the law is to be applied. The knowledge of the facts is to be sought from history, either written or unwritten. Of course by unwritten history we mean a recital of the facts given by those who have a knowledge of them. As long as the facts are not yet definitely determined a decision as to the justice of the war will be suspended, even if the theory of the law has been perfectly worked out. Just as on the other hand a decision fails if the theory is erroneous, even if, indeed, absolutely nothing should be lacking in certainty as to the facts. But do not persuade yourself that more may be allowed to rulers of a state than to private individuals, because they being put in a higher position rise superior to other human beings or private individuals; for they do not surpass private individuals except in so far as they represent the entire nation, and consequently have the right of the nation. But the right of a nation is only the right of private individuals taken collectively, when we are talking of a right existing by nature. Of course such a right belongs to a nation only because nature has given such a right to the individuals who constitute the nation. Therefore, after states have been introduced no other rights belong to rulers of the state, even such as have the most extensive power, than such as belong to individuals living in a state of nature. Every right is derived from these rights, even the right of war against rulers.

§ 859, part 1, Jus Nat.

§ 39.

§ 618. *When war is brought without just cause*

Since there is no just cause of war save a wrong done or likely to be done, the war that is brought without precedent or threatened wrong is not a § 617.

just war, consequently it is unjust, nor has any one a right of war except the one to whom either a wrong has been done or is offered or threatened.

§ 617.

Hence the right of war is easily distinguishable from a licence to war, with which it is frequently confused by those who simply assume that the right of war belongs to nations, and thence infer that it depends on their will whether and when they may desire to exercise it; for the right of war exists only when there is a just cause of war, which is the case only when an injury has either been done or is about to be done.

§ 619. *At what every war ought to aim*

§ 617.

In like manner because there is no just cause of war save a wrong done or about to be done, every war ought either to aim at repairing the wrong, if it can be repaired, or at satisfying the injured party for the wrong done, if it cannot be repaired, or at preventing the doing of wrong.

§ 615.
§ 616.

Therefore, war has a threefold purpose, namely, (1) to attain that which is our own or which is due to us, (2) to provide for security for the future by punishing the wrongdoer, (3) to prevent wrong to ourselves by defending ourselves through resistance to illegal force. The first two purposes are aimed at in an offensive war, the third in a defensive war, and the second of them in a punitive war.

§ 620. *How a vindicative war is defined*

A vindicative war can be defined as one in which we strive to gain that which is our own or which is due to us.

§ 615.
§ 616.

Since there are only three just causes of war, namely, (1) reparable wrong, (2) irreparable wrong, and (3) threatened wrong, which produce the three purposes which are permitted in a war, namely, (1) the attainment of one's own or that which ought to be one's own, (2) the establishing of security, (3) the preventing of threatened danger or the warding off of injury; undoubtedly there are three kinds of just war, which are distinguished by their different purposes. Therefore, since that is a defensive war in which the third is aimed at, a punitive war in which the second is aimed at, it remains for us to give a name to the war also in which the first purpose is aimed at, and this war it has seemed best to call a vindicative war in imitation of the vindication of one's property.

§ 543, part 2, Jus Nat.

§ 621. *Of the differences between justifying and persuasive reasons*

The reasons for a war are said to be justifying which are derived from a right of war belonging to us in a given case, or by which it is proved that a right of war belongs to us in a given case. But those reasons are persuasive which are derived from utility, or by which it is proved that it is to our advantage that war should be undertaken.

In an investigation concerning war the examination has a double aspect, namely, (1) whether there is a just cause of war, without which there is no right to wage war, and as being unjust, the war is also illegal, (2) if there should be a right of war, whether it is also to the advantage of the state to exercise its right. Therefore both the justifying and the persuasive reasons are to be considered, before war should be declared. The former reasons belong to the law of nature and nations, the latter are matters of statecraft or politics; the former make you act justly, but the latter make you act wisely. Those who distinguish reasons and causes call those justifying and persuasive causes which we have called reasons.

§ 618.

§ 1110, part 1, Jus Nat.

§ 1111, part 1, Jus Nat.

§ 622. *Of a war undertaken for persuasive reasons alone*

If one who undertakes war has none other than persuasive reasons the war is unjust. For if there are none other than persuasive reasons for undertaking war, since these are derived from utility, the sole cause of the war is utility, and not any wrong done or about to be done. But a war which is brought without precedent wrong is not a just war, consequently it is unjust. Therefore, if one who undertakes war has none other than persuasive reasons the war is unjust.

§ 621.

§ 618.

This is so evident that those are accustomed to invent justifying reasons who are driven to undertake war only by persuasive reasons. For no one wishes to seem unjust, although he may be so, unless he has put aside all sense of shame, or unless vainglory takes possession

of his blinded mind and leaves no place for sense of shame. If justifying reasons exist, persuasive ones ought to have this use, that one may
understand whether it is wiser to use his right than not to use it, lest
you may undertake a war of which you may afterwards repent when
the result does not correspond to your hopes. For although the result
can scarcely ever be certain, nevertheless it ought to have such a degree
of probability that you may be able to excuse your blunder. But of
these things one must speak in moral and political philosophy.

§ 623. Of the war which is waged for persuasive reasons, even though justifying ones be not lacking

If, indeed, justifying reasons are not lacking, but war is nevertheless undertaken rather for persuasive than for justifying reasons, such a war is not,
indeed, unjust as such, nevertheless the one who wages the war is a transgressor. For since justifying reasons are derived from a right of war belonging to
us in a given case, if justifying reasons are not lacking, we have a just cause of
war, consequently it is not unjust as such. Which was the first point.

But if, indeed, he who wages a war undertakes it rather for persuasive
than for justifying reasons, he would have no scruple in undertaking the
war, even if other than persuasive reasons did not exist, consequently he has
the intention of undertaking the war for persuasive reasons alone. Therefore, since a war is unjust which is undertaken for persuasive reasons alone,
even if justifying reasons are not lacking, but war is nevertheless undertaken
rather for persuasive than for justifying reasons, he who does this has the
intention of waging an unjust war; and since this is contrary to the law of
nature, he certainly is a transgressor. Which was the second point.

War is to be waged not only legally, but also with righteous motive,
a thing which is especially conducive to righteousness in action, to
which the law of nature binds us. If any one undertakes war for persuasive reasons, even though justifying ones are not lacking, he uses the
justifying reasons only as a pretext, because he does not wish to seem
unjust, even if he should have no scruple about being unjust. Therefore, if you should look at the spirit, there is no difference between
him and the one who, under the pretext of a just cause of war, engages
in war for persuasive reasons alone. And hence one may easily foresee
with what sort of scruple he is going to wage war, as of course he will

§ 621.

§ 1110, part 1,
Jus Nat.

§ 622.

§ 1111, part 1,
Jus Nat.

§ 440, part 1,
Jus Nat.

§ 139, part 1,
Phil. Pract.
Univ.

do nothing other than what he shall determine is to his interest. The vice with which war is begun persists in its conduct. For what justice is to be hoped from one who, although he makes a pretence indeed of justice, in very truth despises it?

§ 624. *What reasons are quasi-justifying*

Those reasons are said to be quasi-justifying which if properly reasoned out are recognized as contrary to law.

Namely that which is blazoned as a just cause of war but is not just but rather unjust. Therefore, when it is understood what indeed is a just cause of war between nations, it is not hard to see how quasi-justifying reasons are to be weighed, lest their appearance should impose on the unwary.   § 617.

§ 625. *What is the use of quasi-justifying reasons, and why war is undertaken on account of them*

Since quasi-justifying reasons are altogether excluded from the law of   § 624. war, he who alleges such has in fact no justifying reasons, and consequently quasi-justifying reasons are just pretexts, and since, therefore, war is undertaken simply for persuasive reasons, the war which is brought for quasi-justifying reasons is unjust, nay more, although quasi-justifying reasons may be mistakenly assumed for justifying ones, nevertheless since a just cause of war is lacking the war will still be unjust.

Not rarely, indeed, justifying reasons are brought forward by the warring parties, nevertheless that is usually done for no other purpose than that they may seem to take up arms rightly, although they do not care for the right. Therefore Plutarch says that kings very frequently use the two words war and peace as tokens, not for that which is just, but for that which is expedient.[2] Those who use the quasi-justifying

---

2. "Pyrrhus," chap. xii, in Plutarch, *Plutarch's Lives*, trans. Bernadotte Perrin, 11 vols. (London: William Heinemann; New York: G. P. Putnam's Sons, 1914–26), vol. 9, p. 381. The same reference to Plutarch is made by Grotius in his *The Rights of War and Peace*; see Grotius, *The Rights of War and Peace*, ed. Richard Tuck, 3 vols. (Indianapolis: Liberty Fund, 2005), vol. 2, bk. II, chap. xxii, 4, p. 1102. Wolff may have relied on Grotius rather than consulting Plutarch's text.

reasons evidently do not in fact care for justifying ones, but they are accustomed to disguise persuasive reasons, by which alone they are driven to undertake the war, by at least quasi-justifying ones. At the height of their prosperity they consider that the more just which is the more effective, agreeing with Spinoza that the law of nations is none other than the might of nature, so that as much is permitted as is within one's power.[3]

§ 626. *Of those who are brought into war neither by justifying nor by persuasive reasons*

The war of those who, influenced neither by justifying nor by persuasive reasons, are carried into wars, is not only unjust but also transgresses the law of humanity. For, since justifying reasons are derived from a right of war, if they are lacking, there is no just cause of war which would make the war allowable, so that it could be rightly waged. Therefore, since a war is unjust for which there is no just cause, the war of those who, influenced by no justifying reasons, are carried into war, is unjust. Which was the first point.

But if, indeed, no persuasive reasons exist, a war is brought on in which it does not seem expedient that arms should be taken up. Nevertheless, since we must represent to ourselves as a benefit that which we desire, those who, influenced neither by justifying nor by persuasive reasons, are carried into war, must represent to themselves war as such as a benefit; consequently, filled with a mistaken notion of good, they must gain pleasure from it, and consequently the slaughter and mangling of human beings and the destruction of property belonging to innocent people delights them. Therefore, since nothing is more opposed to the universal love between humans, which the law of nature teaches, than pleasure of this sort, and since charity, whose source is love, includes all the duties of man towards others, and that pleasure leaves no place for any duty to humankind, certainly the war of those who, influenced neither by justifying nor by persuasive reasons, that is, those who, eager

§ 621.

§§ 1110, 1111, part 1, Jus Nat.

§ 170, part 1, Phil. Pract. Univ.

§ 1110, part 1, Jus Nat.

§ 621.

§§ 892, 893, Psych. Emp.

§ 561, Psych. Emp.

§ 633, Psych. Emp.

§ 619, part 1, Jus Nat.

§§ 617, 620, part 1, Jus Nat.

---

3. See Benedict de Spinoza, *Theological-Political Treatise*, ed. J. Israel and trans. Michael Silverthorne and Jonathan Israel (Cambridge: Cambridge University Press, 2007), chap. 16, §3, pp. 196–97.

for war as such are carried into wars, transgresses the law of humanity. Which was the second point.

§ 654, part 1, Jus Nat.

To injure another for the sake of one's own advantage is contrary to the nature of man. Therefore, to injure many innocent people without deriving any advantage from it, because injury of itself gives pleasure, undoubtedly is so atrocious as to combat any idea of humanity. Certainly he renounces his human nature who is bad because he wants to be bad, nor can any greater wickedness be conceived of in a robber than that he takes pleasure in cruelty towards innocent persons from which he can hope for no gain.

§ 627. Of the right of war against those who from no justifying or persuasive reasons are carried into war

Since the war of those who, influenced neither by justifying nor persuasive reasons, are carried into wars, transgresses the law of humanity, it follows that belligerents of that sort, whom war as such delights, do not hesitate to injure any nations simply for self-gratification, evidently despising the natural obligation by which they are bound to other nations; and since the right belongs to nations as a whole to coerce the individual nations, if they are unwilling to satisfy their obligation, a right of war belongs to all nations in general against those who, in their eagerness for wars as such, are carried into wars for reasons neither justifying nor persuasive.

§ 626.

§ 173.

§ 13.

§ 159, part 1, Phil. Pract. Univ., and § 1103, part 1, Jus Nat.

Nature herself has united all nations into a supreme state for no other purpose than that for which individual states have been established. Therefore, a certain purpose of this supreme state also is the security of nations as a whole. Those who are eager for war as such destroy this security, and since it is to the advantage of all nations, and allowable for all to protect this, armed force therefore is just, which is resorted to by any nations against that sort of a monster of humankind. Since war properly speaking may not be engaged in except by those who by force seek their right against another, those who seek for war as an end in itself cannot be said to wage war, but they practise brigandage, and are to be compared to robbers whose malice is of the highest degree. Therefore, the right to punish them belongs to

§§ 8, 9.

§ 8.

§ 12, part 8, Jus Nat.

§ 273.

§ 1102, part 1, Jus Nat.

all nations, and by this right they can remove from their midst those fierce monsters of humankind, consequently they have the right to punitive war. Nothing is said by us which has not been recognized and expressed in the most ancient times by others. But we do not wish to repeat what can be read in Grotius and the commentaries on his work. And certainly it seems that nothing too harsh to be true can be said against those who plainly show that they are enemies of the whole human race.

§ 616.

De Jure Belli ac Pacis, lib. 3 [2], c. 22, § 2, and fol.

§ 628. *Of persuasive reasons just and unjust*

Those persuasive reasons for war are just, which are derived from the purpose of the state or from the common good of citizens, if they are accompanied by justifying ones; but those are unjust which are sought from some other source. For nations ought to perfect themselves and their condition, that is, ought to do their best to attain the purpose of the state. Nevertheless, since one must not use illegal means to attain a legal end, but when justifying reasons exist, the war is legal, that is, war is a legal means of attaining that which persuasive reasons suggest; if the persuasive reasons, which are accompanied by justifying ones, are derived from the purpose of the state or from the common good of citizens, they are just. Which was the first point.

§ 35.

§ 29.

§ 154, part 7, Jus Nat.

§ 621.

But if in truth persuasive reasons have no bearing on the purpose of the state, by which every right of a nation and consequently of the ruler of a state is to be measured, as when they arise from the display of force, in order to acquire riches or extend the limits of power, from vengeance, and many more things of this kind, which are not in accord with the duties prescribed by natural law, it is not to be doubted that these are vicious. Which was the second point.

§§ 9, 13, part 1, Jus Nat.

§ 240, part 1, Phil. Pract. Univ.

§ 30, part 8, Jus Nat.

§ 322, part 1, Phil. Pract. Univ.

Here it is assumed that war is undertaken for justifying and persuasive reasons jointly, so that it is undertaken for neither alone. Persuasive reasons must be introduced to find out whether it may be to the advantage of the state to undertake war, and therefore they are to be judged according to reason of state, but those are not to be considered which unbridled impulses suggest. For if the will should be affected by these, an act just in itself is vitiated by a certain defect, and the

§ 621.

justice of the war does not correct the defect, which is inherent in vicious impulses as such. We have already suggested above that it is by no means sufficient that war should be waged according to justice, but it must also be waged with righteous motive. Therefore one must also be on one's guard lest in the consideration of persuasive reasons something vicious may be admitted. It belongs to prudence to consider persuasive reasons, but whatever is vicious ought to be kept afar from it. No one could censure an excessive scrupulosity as not suitable for rulers of a state, for we have already before observed that without that purity of mind, righteousness in action cannot be conceived of, to which rulers of states are bound just as much as private individuals.

Note, § 623.

§ 257, part 1, Jus Nat.

Note, § 623.

§ 629. *When a defensive war is just, when unjust*

A defensive war is just in which one defends oneself against another who brings an unjust war; but a defensive war is unjust if the offensive war is just. For he who brings an unjust war has no just cause of war, consequently, since by war violence is done to another, he assails another by unjust force and attacks his property, consequently he attempts to harm him, and therefore to do him an injury. Therefore, since a wrong likely to be done gives a just cause for war, and since a war is a defensive one in which any one defends himself against one who makes war upon him, a defensive war is just in which one defends himself against another, who brings an unjust war. Which was the first point.

§ 1110, part 1, Jus Nat.
§ 1102, part 1, Jus Nat.
§ 669, part 1, Jus Nat.
§§ 859, 919, part 1, Jus Nat.
§ 617.
§ 615.

But the one who brings a just war wishes to compel another to repair an injustice done to himself, or to return what is his own or what is due him, or to give satisfaction for an irreparable injury, consequently to render his right to him, or to pay a penalty. Therefore, since he against whom the war is brought ought to render his right to the other, and is bound to suffer the punishment, no injury is done him. Therefore, since a war is not just which has no wrong as its cause, even a defensive war is not just if the offensive war is just. Which was the second point.

§ 619.
§ 921, part 1, Jus Nat.
§ 264.
§ 1071, part 1, Jus Nat.
§ 859, part 1, Jus Nat.

It is not in fact defence for one to set himself in opposition to force justly exercised, since he who uses force justly does not injure another. Therefore, the war of one who puts himself in opposition to a just war, is not in fact a defensive war. He is exercising his own right who takes

§ 617.
§ 972, part 1, Jus Nat.

§ 975, part 1,
Jus Nat.

up arms justly, nor does he injure another; but, on the other hand, he who takes up arms against him does this contrary to the right of the other, and consequently does him a wrong, so that the war, which at the beginning was offensive, ends in fact in a defensive war. No one will call that defence, if one puts himself in opposition to the execu-

§ 615.

tion of the decision of a judge whose power is just, nor when one uses force to avoid a penalty. No more then can that be called defence when any one resists one who is waging a just war. Since, nevertheless, in the concept of war morality is frequently not included, nor are the masses always agreed about it, therefore that is generally described as a defensive war in which any one opposes the one who brings war against him, whether he does it rightly or wrongly, and for this reason

§ 615.

he also is said to defend himself who opposes the one waging a just war against him. Of course he who does another a wrong ought to repair it or to give satisfaction for an irreparable wrong done, in order that the other may not need to regain his right by force. But when one has given cause for war, before they come to open hostilities, he ought to offer fair terms on which peace may be preserved. No one who has investigated the law of nature will call in question that we say nothing opposed to truth, consequently he will not be able to deny that nations and the rulers of states who have their power are bound by those principles; but it is quite another question whether you have persuaded them of this, and have rooted out the prejudices from their minds, blinded by which, they decide about their rights as they should not. Nevertheless it is certain that the human race will only then be happy if rulers of a state should examine more closely those principles by which they are bound, and should satisfy their obligation perfectly, and should not decide erroneously in regard to their right.

§ 630. *When an offensive war is allowable in a plain case*

An offensive war is allowable if your right is certain and you cannot obtain it otherwise than by force of arms, or if the other party should be unwilling to give satisfaction for a manifestly irreparable injury and you cannot obtain satisfaction otherwise than by force of arms. For every nation has the right to pursue its right against another nation by force,

§ 271.

if the other is unwilling to allow it, and the right to punish another

nation which has injured it. Nevertheless, since you must refrain from
arms, if by another course you can persuade the other to give your right
to you, and since then only is there a just cause for war, if there should
be no place for reprisals and androlepsy; or if it should not be possible
to make an agreement concerning the paying of penalty or to take it
in another way, you may not use that right until you cannot otherwise
than by force of arms bring it about that your right may be given you or
satisfaction rendered for irreparable injury. But since that is an offensive
war, which is brought upon another not contemplating it, or in which
any one assails another by force of arms; an offensive war is allowable, if
your right is certain and you cannot acquire it otherwise than by force of
arms, or if the other party should be unwilling to give satisfaction for a
manifest irreparable injury and you cannot obtain satisfaction otherwise
than by force of arms.

§ 272.
§ 1117, part 1, Jus Nat.
§ 606.
§ 582.
§ 615.

There are two things which are required to justify an offensive war,
namely, that you should have a right to something which ought to be
performed by another, and that you are not able to obtain it otherwise than by force of arms. The first brings into being the right of
war, but the other makes it allowable for you to use your full right.
Those, indeed, who rush to arms before milder remedies are tried are
urged by persuasive reasons to undertake war rather than by a desire
to acquire their right, and they merely invent justifying reasons, but in
this respect we have already proved above that they are transgressors.
Those who are driven by persuasive reasons to undertake war, eagerly
seize the opportunity by which they can bring war upon another in
their own right, although if one is to speak the exact truth you have
the right of making war only when you cannot otherwise acquire that
for which the law of nature gives the right of war. Since nothing is
more dreadful for the human race than war, we must not think that in
bestowing the right of war nature was prodigal. Only extreme necessity makes a place for this violent remedy. Those who believe otherwise turn the right into a license, as if it were allowable to determine at
will concerning the use of coercive means, and that the law of nature
should not regulate this also, just as it does the other actions of men.
The law of nature has given the right of war for a wrong done, but on
condition that you may use it only when the wrong cannot be repaired

§ 623.

otherwise or satisfaction cannot be given for irreparable injury in any other way. And finally it is logical that, while it prescribes duties both to individual men and to nations in general, it should not allow those things which can in no way be consistent with those duties. In the law of nature perfect harmony exists, and those things cannot conform to it which are mutually contradictory. The law of nature aims at happiness, both for individual men and also for nations. Therefore, it cannot allow anything altogether opposed to the happiness of the human race, and therefore it then finally allows war only when men render themselves unhappy by their own fault. Therefore, it has established very strict limits for war.

§ 396, part 1,
Phil. Pract.
Univ.

§§ 4, 5, part 8,
Jus Nat.

§ 631. *When in a doubtful case*

Offensive war is allowable if in a doubtful case one nation cannot be brought to a compromise otherwise than by force of arms. For if in a doubtful case one nation should be unwilling to accept a conference for an amicable agreement or compromise or for submission to arbiters, consequently also if it should refuse to accept fair conditions offered to it, the right of war against the one unwilling to accept belongs to the other, that thus the former may be driven to a compromise by force of arms. Therefore, since war is then rightly brought, and is offensive, an offensive war is allowable if in a doubtful case one nation cannot be brought to a compromise otherwise than by force of arms.

§ 572.

§ 615.

§§ 572 and fol.

§ 574.

Note, § 623.

Here we must reconsider those things which we proved above, and also our notes in the same place; but chiefly to be carefully considered is what we said concerning the voluntary law of nations and how far it is permitted among nations, so that we may depart from a rigorous interpretation of the law of nature only a little, lest those who usually rush to a decision without adequate consideration of a matter may imagine a contradiction where none exists. Indeed, it can happen and perchance frequently does happen, that neither party would desire to compromise in a doubtful case; nevertheless on this account he who has the right does not act properly, since at least that purity of motive is lacking with which even war ought to be waged.

§ 632. Whether it is allowable to decide a disputed case by force of arms

It is not allowable by the law of nature to desire to decide a disputed case by force of arms, or that war is by nature illegal which is undertaken for the purpose of deciding a disputed right. For since nations are to be regarded as individual persons, and if two persons agree with each other that a disputed question should be decided by a victory, this would be a duel; if nations wish to settle a disputed case by force of arms, or undertake a war for the purpose of deciding a disputed right, the war is the same as a duel. Therefore, since a duel is by nature illegal, the war also is by nature illegal, which is undertaken for the purpose of deciding a disputed right, and therefore, to desire to decide a disputed case by force of arms is by nature illegal.

§ 2.

§ 1090, part 5, Jus Nat.

§ 1091, part 5, Jus Nat.

We have already shown above, that from the law of private war we must determine the law of public war. A duel is undoubtedly war, that is, private war. Therefore, in whatever case a duel is illegal, in that case also public war is illegal. Just as the duel is not a proper method for deciding a controversy between private individuals; so war is not a proper method for deciding a controversy between nations. Since no one can easily call in question the former point to-day, it might seem remarkable that war is considered by many a method of deciding controversies between nations, although, nevertheless, the right of war as such belongs to no one in a doubtful case, and it is illegal to harass another in war, so that you may by force of arms extort what you claim. From the fact that nations have no judge, it by no means follows that it is only decided by the final victory who is in the wrong. For from the fact that nations have no judge it only follows that we must allow that any one should be judge in his own case. Each of the belligerents, therefore, assumes that the right belongs to him, but is denied by the other. Therefore, when they come to blows, each of the belligerents strives to compel the other party by force to allow him his right, or if he cannot obtain that, to consent at least to conditions to which he would in no way consent, unless he were reduced to extremities. And for this reason the final victory, by which the war is ended, is not considered

Note, § 608.
Note, § 1090, part 5, Jus Nat.
§ 608.

§ 1092, part 5, Jus Nat.

Note, § cited.

§ 1100, part 5, Jus Nat.

§ 1101, part 5, Jus Nat.

a decision of the controversy which caused the war, but the controversy is ended by compromise when peace is declared. Therefore, it will scarcely ever happen, that a war of nations would be equivalent to a duel, which is undertaken by agreement for the purpose of deciding a disputed right. Even if all nations should cherish this mistaken opinion, that their controversies should be decided by force of arms, this right would not be a natural right which nations ought to use one with the other, but would be a voluntary right, such as Grotius assumes was introduced by a certain tacit consent of nations, and should be referred rather to customary law. Then, indeed, the thing in controversy would belong to the victor, nor would there then be an agreement as to terms of peace. Since the contrary is the case, it is perfectly plain that war is not considered as a means of deciding a controversy, but of ending it, nor does the victor acquire a right by force of arms to that concerning which there is an agreement, but by virtue of the treaty of peace. It is a dangerous and deadly idea for a nation that, because they have no common judge, the right belongs to them to decide a controversy by force of arms. This gives licence to war, and turns the minds of all rulers of a state from that which the immutable law of nature prescribes in its care for the welfare of nations, as is plain from what has preceded. But it seems that the error arises from the fact that tribunals are deemed prior to war, and hence the conclusion is then drawn that when tribunals are lacking, there is a place for war, and therefore victory is improperly put on an equality with the decision of a judge, as if the natural state is not prior to the civil state, and in the natural state methods other than war did not exist for settling controversies, which the law of nature also prescribes for nations, so that war is at least a means of compelling a refractory party to consent to one of those methods, particularly to a compromise, as is sufficiently evident from those things which have been proved by us above. But since we may easily fall into errors of that sort, unless we have grasped the idea of the law of nature reduced to a system worthy of the name, therefore the necessity of doing that is clear, and for that reason we are compelled to establish a system of that sort. Nor do any of us doubt that those aided by these investigations will look deeply into the truth.

§ 1090, part 5, Jus Nat.

§ 24.

§ 4.

§ 633. *Whether a war can be just on each side*

War cannot be just on each side. For there is no just cause of war save a wrong done or likely to be done. Therefore, he alone has a just cause of war to whom a wrong has been done by the other party, or to whom the other party intends to do a wrong. Therefore, since a war is not just unless it has a just cause, a war is not just except on the part of the one to whom the other has either done a wrong or is attempting to do it, consequently it cannot be just on each side.

§ 617.

§ 1109, part 1, Jus Nat.

> Just as in the case of those who argue as to the truth of a proposition, the truth can be only with one party, since it cannot possibly happen that contrary or contradictory opinions can be at the same time true and false; so also it cannot happen that, if two are contending concerning right or wrong, the opinion of each is correct, when one asserts what the other denies. Justice in war is, therefore, only on the side of the one who has the correct opinion.

§ 634. *That on one side it is always unjust*

Since war cannot be just on each side, for whatsoever reason war may be waged, the cause of only one party is just, and that of the other is unjust, even if it should happen that each of the belligerents thinks that he is favouring a just cause.

§ 633.

> Although each of the belligerents may think that he is favouring a just cause, nevertheless the judgement of each is not on this account correct; but only one is right, and therefore the other is necessarily wrong. When that happens, each acts in good faith indeed; nevertheless not justly, since he alone can act justly who acts rightly. And therefore, in a doubtful case we have shown that a right to bring war does not arise from an injury on the part of another, since this is not manifest, but from a rejection of the means which the law of nature prescribes for settling controversies nor then is a right of war allowed for obtaining that concerning which there is a controversy, but a compromise is to be made by which the controversy may be settled. We have already suggested before that a victory is not properly put on an equality with the decision of a judge who declares the vanquished guilty. For we

§ 572.

Note, § 632.

have already shown elsewhere that they are mistaken who think that the vanquished is condemned by judgement of God through the final victory. If then a method of proof cannot be discovered on which side a war is just, either because of ignorance of the law of nature, or defect of accurate reasoning, or insufficient knowledge of facts, or false interpretation; judgement as to the justice of the war remains in suspense, even after the final victory, nor does the result of the war have any other effect than that by compromise through the treaty of peace an end is put to an undecided controversy, from which a right is acquired to that concerning which the agreement was made, however little right to it belonged to the victor before. Grotius, before defining this question, whether a war could be just on each side, distinguishes various meanings of the word just; but those distinctions have no bearing upon the law of nature and nations, since in it the meanings for terms are to be retained unchanged, which we have justified in the same definitions, and judgements are to be pronounced according to them.

Note, § 1091, part 5, Jus Nat.

De Jure Belli ac Pacis, lib. 2, c. 22, § 13.

§ 635. *Whether ignorance or irrefutable error concerning the justice of a war can be imputed*

The injustice of a war cannot be imputed to one who, because of ignorance or irrefutable error, thinks that he has a just cause of war when he has not. This is directly evident from the fact that in general ignorance and irrefutable error cannot be imputed.

§ 550, part 1, Phil. Pract. Univ.

§ 552, part 1, Phil. Pract. Univ.

§ 636. *When a punitive war is legal*

Punitive war is not legal except for one who has received irreparable injury, and when he cannot obtain satisfaction for it in any other way. For no one has a right of war except one to whom a wrong has been done. Therefore, since a penalty is exacted from another in a punitive war, and since we have a right to exact a penalty, that we may compel the offender not to injure us again in the future, and that we may be on guard, lest we following his example, or he himself may dare to injure others; a punitive war can be legal only in the case of one who has received irreparable injury. But a punitive war is an offensive war. Therefore, since an offensive war is legal on the occasion of an irreparable injury only if satisfaction cannot be obtained for it otherwise than by force of arms, a punitive

§ 617.

§ 616.

§§ 1058, 1062, part 1, Jus Nat.

§ 616.

war is not legal except for one who has received irreparable injury, and § 630.
when he cannot obtain satisfaction for it otherwise.

For a punitive war to be legal it is necessary that a wrong should
have been done to you by the one against whom the war is brought.
For by it provision is made for the security of the future, so that you
may be free from wrong by others; a thing which is entirely in harmony with the purpose of the state, so that it cannot be doubted that
a nation also has the right to punish a nation, that provision may be
made for its own security and the common security of nations. To no   §§ 12, 13, part 8,
purpose would the law of nature prohibit injury to nations if nation   Jus Nat.
were permitted to injure nation without punishment. Therefore, from   § 173.
the obligation of a nation not to injure arises the right of the injured
nation to punish. The satisfaction for irreparable wrong is punishment, and satisfaction has been given you in such a case if sufficient
provision has been made for security for the future. Therefore, since a
heavier punishment is illegal, when a lighter one is adequate, a public
war is legal only when satisfaction for an irreparable wrong cannot   § 1065, part 1,
be obtained otherwise. For the purpose of a punitive war is twofold,   Jus Nat.
one in relation to the punisher, the other in relation to other nations.
For it is not solely intended that the one who is punished should not
in the future do you a wrong again, but that he should also not dare
to do wrong to others. For from the punishment which he suffers he
ought to learn that he who does a wrong to another plans badly for
himself. Nothing is here said of nations which is not true of individuals in a state of nature, and of tribunals in a state, as is plain to those
who have mentally grasped all of the science of the law of nature in
proper sequence as we have laid it down in our system. If, then, any
one should still hesitate in regard to these matters, he should re-read
those things especially which we have proved concerning the right of
punishment in the first part of "The Law of Nature" and what we have
deduced therefrom in the eighth part concerning the right of punishment in a state.[4] So he will surely see with perfect clearness that one

4. See Christian Wolff, *Jus Naturae*, vol. 1 (1740; ed. Marcel Thomann,
Hildesheim: Georg Olms, 1972), chap. 3, §1061 ff., and Wolff, *Jus Naturae*, vol. 8
(1748; ed. Marcel Thomann, Hildesheim: Georg Olms, 1968), esp. pt. VII, chap. 3,
§832, pp. 632–34.

Note, § 632.

must not determine the natural state from the civil but vice versa the civil from the natural, and consequently the right of war of nations is to be discussed independently of the civil state, as we have already explained before.

§ 637. *Whether one nation can be punished by another nation for crimes and an offence towards God*

§ 636.

Since a punitive war is not legal except for one who has received irreparable injury from another, a punitive war is not allowed against a nation for the reason that it is very wicked, or violates dreadfully the law of nature, or offends against God.

De Jure Belli ac Pacis, lib. 2, c. 20, §§ 40 and fol.

Loc. cit., § 3.

Grotius defends the opposing doctrine. But his error arises from this, that he persuades himself that the evil in itself is such that it certainly can be punished, and that the right to punish belongs to him who is not equally guilty. But since he himself can find no natural reason for this right which is satisfactory, he is compelled to confess that it has not been determined by nature to whom this right is due, except that nature makes plain enough that it is most suitable that it should be done by the one who is superior, nevertheless not so as plainly to prove that this is necessary, except that the word superior is taken in this sense, that he who does ill, by that fact itself may be considered to have made himself inferior to every other. Who, pray, does not see that the mistake concerning evil punishable in itself has reduced Grotius to such straits that he cannot find a way by which he may extricate himself? Although the right to punish may belong to the superior in the state, nevertheless it does not take its source from the superior; but it belongs to him for no other reason than because the right to punish private citizens has been transferred to him and legislative power can have no effect without the right to

§ 40, no. 2.

punish, since civil obligation is introduced by fear of penalties. Grotius declares there is a just cause of war against those who are without reverence for parents, who eat human flesh, who practice piracy. But he confuses those things which are united with wrong to others with those by which no wrong is done to others. Our discussion here has to do with the latter, not with the former; for we shall see hereafter how much one nation may be allowed to punish another for wrong done to a third, when it itself has not been injured. But when we reject the erroneous opinion that a punitive war is legal against a wicked nation and one without reverence for God, we have no need for those qualifications which Grotius was compelled to give, in order that he might avoid absurd conclusions and might not convert a punitive law into a licence for war. Indeed it cannot be denied that in ancient history there are examples of punitive war against nations which had not injured other nations, but were either violating a law of nature as such, or were following customs not approved of by other nations, such as eating dog's flesh and burning, not burying, the dead, such as Grotius and his commentators mention, that need not be repeated by us;[5] nevertheless we are not to draw conclusions from the acts of nations concerning the law, but are rather to judge their acts by the law. It is not unknown that among the most ancient nations, although they were not devoid of culture, many errors were prevalent as to the law of nature, among which also is to be included this one as to the law of punishment. Furthermore, there is hardly a reason to doubt that those who had no just cause for war, have drawn a pretext from the law of punishment. But so far as concerns offences committed against God, no natural reason exists, through which it is evident that a right belongs to a nation to punish a wrong against God committed by a nation. And if such a right should be admitted, no result would follow therefrom other than reciprocal licence for war. God himself is capable of punishing a wrong done to himself, nor for that does he need human aid. Here are to be compared those things which we have proved and described above concerning the law of nations in regard to religion. But since nations have no right to punish an offence against God, there is no need for us, along with Grotius, to inquire in detail as to what are errors concerning God and what deeds of men are to be considered as wrongs against God.[6]

§§ 41 ff.

§ 259 ff.

Loc. cit., § 45.

5. See Hugo Grotius, *The Rights of War and Peace*, ed. Richard Tuck, 3 vols. (Indianapolis: Liberty Fund, 2005), vol. 2, bk. II, chap. xx, "Of Punishments," xli–xliii, pp. 1025–27.

6. See Grotius, *The Rights of War and Peace*, vol. 2, bk. II, chap. xx, "Of Punishments," xlvi–li, pp. 1035–52.

§ 638. *Whether atheism, deism, and idolatry are a just cause for a punitive war*

§ 636.

In like manner, since a punitive war is legal only for one who has received irreparable injury, punitive war is legal for no nation against another because it professes atheism, or deism, or is idolatrous.

§ 645, part 8, Jus Nat.

§ 644, part 8, Jus Nat.

§ 259.

Note, § 261.

§ 30, part 8, Jus Nat.

§§ 34, 42, part 8, Jus Nat.

No one can be punished in a state for atheism or deism. Therefore even if you should admit to the fullest extent that a nation has the right to punish another for deeds from which no wrong comes to itself, atheism and deism would not be a just cause for a punitive war. And since idolatrous worship arises from mistakes which are made concerning God, but no one can be punished for mistakes, the same thing must certainly be held concerning idolatry. Punishment of a nation hostile to the true religion can be intended for no purpose other than that the nation inflicting the punishment should introduce its religion into the state. But we have already proved above that it is illegal for one nation to compel another by force to introduce its religion into its state. Note what we have said above. No right belongs to nations other than that which has been granted to individuals by nature or that under the civil power, which takes its rise in association and, being determined by the purpose of the state, represents a potential part of it. And since rulers of a state have only the right which originally belonged to the people, no other right besides can belong to rulers of a state. But from neither right can one derive the right to punish a nation on account of atheism, deism, or idolatry.

§ 639. *When a war is at the same time vindicative and punitive*

§§ 505, 506, part 2, Jus Nat.

§ 542, part 2, Jus Nat.

§ 551, part 1, Jus Nat.

If any one seeks by force of arms that which has been taken from him unjustly by force, his offensive war is at the same time vindicative and punitive. The same is to be said of a war which is brought in order that a loss caused by a wrong should be repaired. For if what is his own has been taken away from any one unjustly by force, he who does the wrong is a robber. But an owner not only has the right to compel a robber by force to restore the property taken from him, but he has also the right to punish him. Therefore, if he makes war upon him to recover his property

by force of arms, since that is a vindicative war in which we strive to gain | § 620.
what is our own, but a punitive war is one in which a penalty is exacted | § 616.
from one against whom the war is brought; the war, which is obviously | § 615.
an offensive war, is at the same time both a vindicative and a punitive
war. Which was the first point.

But if war should be made with the purpose that a loss caused should
be repaired, the one making it does so that he may acquire what is due to | §§ 572, 580,
him. Therefore, since that is a vindicative war by which we strive to gain | part 2, Jus Nat.
that which is due to us, an offensive war is in this respect vindicative. But | § 620.
since, indeed, the loss is caused by a wrong, and by hypothesis the right
belongs by nature to a man, consequently also to a nation, to punish one | § 3.
who has done him wrong, and a punitive war is one by which a penalty | § 549, part 2,
is exacted from another; in that respect, a war which is made with the | Jus Nat.
purpose that a loss caused by a wrong should be repaired is a punitive | § 616.
war. Therefore it is plain that if the war is made with the purpose that a
loss caused by a wrong should be repaired, that war is at the same time
both vindicative and punitive. Which was the second point.

> Just as by one act property has been taken from its owner and also
> irreparable injury done him, in so far as the deed cannot be undone; so
> also, by one act of war, his property is regained and also he who did the
> injury is punished. But it is of importance that an offensive war, in which
> there are at the same time vindicative and punitive elements, should be
> distinguished from that which belongs to only one category. For more is
> allowable in the former than in the latter, as will be plain from what fol-
> lows. The same is true in the other case in which loss is caused by wrong.

§ 640. *Whether fear of a neighbouring power is a just cause of war*

The increasing power of a neighbouring nation and fear of the neigh-
bour's power is not a just cause of war. For nations ought to strive ear- | § 70.
nestly to become powerful, provided they do not use improper means. | § 72.
Therefore, if they increase their power by proper means, since they are | § 159, part 1,
exercising their own right, they do you no wrong. Therefore, since there | Phil. Pract. Univ.
is no just cause of war save a wrong done, the increasing power of a | § 975, part 1,
neighbouring nation is not a just cause of war. Which was the first point. | Jus Nat.
| § 617.

To be sure he who is powerful can cause loss or can injure in some manner, and it can happen that, relying on his power, he may wish at some time to cause loss or to injure in some way: nevertheless as long as he causes no loss in fact, nor injures in another way, and does not declare by any overt act an intention of doing anything else, no wrong has been done nor is it likely to be done. Therefore, since there is no just cause of war, unless a wrong has been done or is likely to be done, fear alone of a neighbour's power is not a just cause for war. Which was the second point.

§ 532, part 2, and §§ 859, 919, part 1, Jus Nat.
§ 617.

There are those who argue that fear of a neighbour's power is a just cause of war, for the reason that the right belongs to every nation to take those steps by which it can avoid danger of destruction, and escape those things which can bring it to ruin, or make it and its condition less perfect. But to attain this legal end it may not use illegal means; moreover, that war is not just, consequently is illegal, for which there is a cause other than wrong done, or likely to be done. There is no reason why you should object, that if war should be brought on account of fear of a neighbour's power, this is a case of wrong likely to be done, because the powerful can do a wrong. For a wrong cannot be considered as likely to be done because it is not impossible, or because another does not lack the power to do wrong; from this alone certainly it does not yet follow that he is about to do you a wrong, nay more, the intrinsic possibility[7] alone begets no probability, although it may be a sufficient reason that you should use all circumspection, lest something may be done by you which might develop into an extrinsic possibility, as the logic of probabilities suggests. Could any one in a state of nature justly declare that if one should far surpass others in strength, they should either expel him from their midst, or break his legs and arms? Fear is especially uncertain, so that it is to be considered as naught by one who deals with intrinsic possibility alone. But since a doubtful issue is to be wholly entrusted to divine providence, protection against uncertain fears must be sought from that source alone.

§ 34.
§ 37.
§ 71.
§ 1111, part 1, Jus Nat.

§ 1110, part 1, Jus Nat., and § 617 h.

§ 1192, part 1, Jus Nat.

7. An intrinsic possibility is determined by the inner essence of something. Extrinsic possibility depends on external circumstances. For example, it is intrinsically possible for a human being to be rational, but it is extrinsically possible for this person to achieve a certain social status.

§ 641. *Whether it is a just cause of war, if fortifications are built and there is planning for war in time of peace*

Since fear of a neighbour's power is not a just cause of war, there is no just cause of war if a neighbour unrestrained by any treaty should build a fortification on his own territory, which might cause loss some time, or if he should plan for war in time of peace, by enlisting soldiers, collecting a fleet, providing equipment for war. These things are in harmony with the purpose of the state, which is furthered by security, consequently a nation does all these things in accordance with its own right, nor in doing them does it do wrong to another nation, which can afford it a just cause of war.

§ 640.

§§ 12, 13, part 8, Jus Nat.

§ 30, part 8, Jus Nat.

§ 975, part 1, Jus Nat.

§ 617.

It is not unjust to look out for one's security; for men have united into a state especially for this purpose, that by their united strength they might furnish security for each other. Therefore the necessary means for attaining this end are legal. If you avail yourself of them in good time, a neighbouring nation has no just cause of complaint against you, for it has not been forbidden to do similar things. If it cannot do so, the weakness of another is not to be charged up to you, nor ought you, for the sake of another, to be negligent in those matters which are necessary for perfecting the condition of your nation. No one is so stupid as to persuade himself that another ought not to perfect his condition, because he himself cannot accomplish the same things as the other. But what is considered stupid in individual men ought to be considered no less stupid in nations. But those measures, taken in fear of a neighbour's power, are legal, by which provision is made for security in the future, if indeed it is to be feared that a neighbour relying on his power may persuade himself to do you a wrong. I say these means are legal, nevertheless they are not the only ones, since there are more to be enumerated in the Politics.

§§ 4, 12, part 8, Jus Nat.

§ 2.

§ 642. *What equilibrium among nations is*

Equilibrium among nations is defined as such a condition of several nations so related to each other in power that the combined power of the others is equal to the power of the strongest or to the joint power of certain ones. In our native vernacular it is called *das Gleichgewichte der Völcker* [the equilibrium of peoples].

The term is derived from the balance, in which an equal weight makes an equilibrium on either side. If then there is to be an equilibrium among nations, it is necessary that equal power of the others can always be opposed to the power of the one or the joint power of certain ones, in so far, to be sure, as those by entering into treaties are able to combine their power.

§ 643. *The effect and purpose of equilibrium*

§ 642.

Since equilibrium among nations consists in a condition such that the combined power of the others is equal to the power of the strongest or to the joint power of certain ones, if equilibrium among nations exists, it may happen that on the occurrence of war like force may be opposed to the one assailing by force, consequently it would not be necessary that one nation should succumb to the arms of the other,

§ 12, part 8, Jus Nat.

and so provision is made by that means for the common security of nations.

If nations were to live by such a standard of ethics, that they would perform for each other duties which by nature they owe, and if some would not injure others for their own advantage, equilibrium among nations would be of no use, as there would be no wars to be feared. Since the contrary is the case, equilibrium is especially useful to protect the common security. When this equilibrium is disturbed, it easily happens that a nation which persuades itself that it can injure other nations with impunity, is not afraid to injure them, especially when it promises no slight advantage to itself. If it should happen that a war arises, this nation, since it is much superior in strength, if it should not completely subjugate the opposing party, will compel it nevertheless to accept disadvantageous terms of peace. This, and no other, is the reason why equilibrium among nations began to be thought of. Certainly among us Europeans you may always hear a discussion of equilibrium, especially when there is talk of allies for war and a treaty of peace.

§ 644. *Of the disturbance of equilibrium among nations*

Since equilibrium among nations exists when their condition is such
that the power of the strongest or the joint power of several is equal to § 643.
the combined power of the others, it is disturbed if the power of the
strongest or the joint power of certain ones should surpass the joint
power of the others, consequently when the equilibrium among nations
is disturbed, it cannot happen that on the occurrence of war like force
may be opposed to the unjust force, and therefore one nation easily suc-
cumbs to the arms of another.

> Equilibrium among nations is especially conducive to their liberty
> and disturbance of the equilibrium is very dangerous to liberty. Nor is
> there any reason why European nations should struggle so fiercely for
> the preservation of equilibrium, save of course that the liberty of those
> which are less powerful may not be endangered.

§ 645. *Whether utility is a just cause of war*

Utility alone is not a just cause of war. For the reasons for war which are
derived from utility alone are only persuasive. But his war is unjust who § 621.
has no other than persuasive reasons. Therefore, his war is also unjust § 622.
who undertakes the war for no other reason than that he hopes for utility from it. Therefore, since the cause of an unjust war is not just, utility
alone cannot be a just cause of war. § 1110, part 1,
Jus Nat.

> It could be proved in the same way as we have shown above, that
> war undertaken for persuasive reasons is unjust, the proof being drawn
> of course from the lack of wrong, without which a just war cannot be § 622.
> conceived of. But it must be noted that utility here, just as also above § 618.
> when we were speaking of persuasive reasons, is taken with the broad-
> est meaning which we have assigned to the word. Hence under utility § 621.
> are included not only increase in power, but also desire for fame, pas- § 622, part 1,
> sion for vengeance, display of strength and things kindred thereto; for Phil. Pract. Univ.
> on account of the diversity of natural inclinations and of the desires
> and vices dependent thereon, the judgements of men as to what is of
> utility to themselves are varied indeed. Therefore, the present propo-
> sition extends much farther than it might seem, especially to those

who possess a mind affected by the concepts of civil law; for there are very many concepts which the reasoning of this law makes more restricted than they are and ought to be. We have another example of this in the concept of wrong, which in the law of nature extends much farther than it does within the narrow limits of the civil law. Therefore, although we have taught more than once that the terms used in the civil law are to be retained in the law of nature, and that their meaning is not to be changed rashly, nevertheless that is not to be extended to the prejudice of truth. The praetor does not care for trifles, nevertheless the law of nature does care, and those things which are tolerated and must be tolerated in the state, so that they are done without punishment, are not allowed by the law of nature, so as to become legal. The law of nature does not allow any departure from rectitude, although it imputes to the doer only that for which he is responsible, and it rejects all abuse or non-use of powers. And also it does not distinguish the things which are identical, and therefore for the purpose of extending concepts it admits something fictitious also, although that is not quite in harmony with the reasoning of the civil law, for which the purpose of the state sets up limits. If those points should be observed, then finally one can see into the likeness and unlikeness of the law of nature and civil law, as they really exist, nor is that which is simply civil confused with that which is natural, not without loss to the truth. The law of nature is not to be put on an equality with civil law for the sake of those who strive for this end. For if indeed they would be real priests of justice, it is necessary that they should correctly understand what belongs to the law of nature, and should recognize how the civil law has been made by adding to or subtracting from that according to the natural theory of civil laws, which we have given as proved in the eighth part.

§§ 669 and fol., part 1, Jus Nat.

§ 646. *Whether the preservation of equilibrium among nations is a just cause of war*

The preservation of equilibrium among nations is not a just cause of war. For equilibrium among nations is preserved for no other reason than that on the occasion of a war an equal force can be opposed to an unjust force, and that provision may be made for the common security

§ 643.

of nations, consequently for the utility of nations. If then war should be brought for the purpose of preserving equilibrium among nations, the cause would be none other than fear of a neighbour's power and personal utility to be hoped for from diminution of it or prevention of its increase. Therefore, since neither fear of a neighbour's power nor utility alone is a just cause of war, the preservation of equilibrium among nations cannot be a just cause of war.

§ 262, part 1, Jus Nat.

§ 640.

§ 645.

> Utility too much obsesses the mind of those who manage public affairs, so that, if they do not actually despise justice, they at least turn their minds away from it, or measure it by the utility in it. But the preservation of equilibrium, which does so much to establish the security of nations and protect their liberty, frequently obscures justice, so that scarcely anyone is considered just when arms have been employed for the preservation of equilibrium among nations, because it is not considered that to attain a legal end it is not allowable to use illegal means, consequently it is not seen that as far as the justice of the war is concerned the preservation of equilibrium is only a persuasive reason.

§ 643.

§ 71.

Note, § 621.

§ 647. Whether for the sake of equilibrium the right of any one can be taken away

Since the preservation of equilibrium among nations is not a just cause of war, no one is to be prevented by force of arms from obtaining that which is due to him, nor is he to be called to account so as to be compelled to leave to another what is his own or ought to be his, even if the equilibrium among nations is destroyed.

§ 646.

> Justice orders that we give every one his right, and this obligation binds nations also. Just as utility makes no exception in the case of private individuals, so also it makes none in the case of nations. Those who favour the opposite view are persuaded of this opinion by fear of a neighbour's power, a thing which ought to be guarded against in time, lest the growing power may at some time be harmful to them; but we have proved above that such fear is not a just cause of war. The violation of another's right is plainly a wrong. If then war should be brought for no other reason than lest another should be able to get his right, war is brought to do a wrong, and therefore the war is altogether

§ 926, part 1, Jus Nat.

§§ 264, 265.

§ 640.

§ 859, part 1, Jus Nat.

unjust. If it should be assumed, a thing which cannot be assumed without manifest injustice, that it is legal by any means to prevent another from acquiring his right, and to exert all of one's strength to the end that the right be allotted to another, because it is to your interest that he should not acquire it, the doors are opened wide for injustice and farewell is said to all reverence for law.

§ 648. *The same is explained in greater detail*

Since no one is to be prevented by force of arms from attaining that which is due to him, nor to be called to account so as to be compelled to leave to another what is his own or ought to be his, even if the equilibrium among nations is destroyed; the right to succeed to some kingdom can be taken away from no one, nor can any one be prevented from increasing his own territories in any legitimate way by new additions of land, nor from increasing his power in any other way, merely for the reason that equilibrium among nations may thus be disturbed.

Thus, for example, it is not legal to prevent some powerful king from succeeding to a kingdom in which the succession, established in that place by the law of inheritance, has devolved upon him, or if he is chosen by another nation which is free to transfer its sovereignty to any one it pleases. Likewise if through commerce a certain nation should become very powerful, you have no right to disturb its commerce, or by force to compel the nation with which it is trading to deal no longer with it. So you cannot interpret it as a wrong, if very powerful nations by their union disturb the equilibrium which existed, provided only that it is not done for the purpose of injuring you, since any nation by any legitimate means can provide for its security and take measures to increase its power. Self-preservation and self-perfection belong to the duties of a nation to itself. Therefore the law of nature also gives the right to them to use those means, without which they cannot preserve and perfect themselves, provided only they are not illegal or accompanied by some violation of your right. When therefore a nation uses its right, it does you no wrong. As long therefore as any nation does only that which it can do in its own right, it is not bound to consider whether that is advantageous to another or not.

§ 647.

§§ 31, 35.
§ 159, part 1, Phil. Pract. Univ.
§ 71.
§ 910, part 1, Jus Nat.
§ 975, part 1, Jus Nat.

§ 649. *Of the right of nations to preserve equilibrium*

Nations are not bound to preserve an equilibrium among themselves; nevertheless they have the right to preserve it, so far as that may be done without violation of the right of any nation. For nations ought to strive earnestly to be powerful, consequently to make themselves able to resist the unjust power of other nations, as far as possible, that therefore they may have no need of another's aid, to which only their own weakness gives them a right, the refusal of which must be endured. Therefore, the weakness of one nation can set no limits to the power of another, beyond which the other ought not to increase its power. Therefore, since a nation could not satisfy its own obligation, and the right of other nations would be extended in opposition to it, if they were bound to preserve the equilibrium, which requires that the joint power of the others can be exactly matched against the power of one or the joint power of certain ones; nations are not bound to preserve an equilibrium among themselves. Which was the first point.

§ 70.

§ 69.

§ 156.

§ 157.

§ 642.

But indeed equilibrium among nations is the means by which provision is made for their common security. Therefore, since one nation ought to contribute what it can to the preservation and perfection of another in what the other nation is not self-sufficient, and since nations are understood to have united into a supreme state, they are jointly bound also to look out for the common security; the law of nature therefore gives them the right to preserve an equilibrium among themselves. Which was the second point.

§ 643 h, and
§ 937, Ontol.

§ 166.

§§ 9, 10.

§ 13, part 8,
Jus Nat.

§ 12 h.

§ 159, part 1,
Phil. Pract. Univ.

Nevertheless, since no one ought to do anything contrary to the right of another or violate it, nations have a right to preserve equilibrium, so far as that can be done without violation of the right of any one. Which was the third point.

§ 910, part 1,
Jus Nat.

There are many prejudices which so fascinate the minds of many, that they cannot see the truth. Hence has arisen the idea that nations are bound to preserve an equilibrium among themselves. There are also flatterers who assume that nations are bound to preserve equilibrium among themselves, in order that they may please those whose interest it is that equilibrium be preserved, or who use it as a pretext for jealousy of a foreign power, and afterwards they only eagerly seek for reasons by which they may fashion their doubtful assumption into a likeness of the truth. This assumed obligation to maintain the equilibrium gains its most plausible pretext from the fact that in this way provision may be made for the common security of nations. But the law of nature provides for this by the duties towards each other which it prescribes to nations. And if they should strive with all their hearts to perform them, nothing would have to be feared by the weaker from the stronger. Moreover this immutable law does not admit of measures contrary to these, although it allows harsher measures for protecting security against plain violators of it. Natural obligation does not flow from depravity of morals, to which unbridled passions allure the unbalanced. But a right is merely allowed to protect one's self against the wrongs of others, without violating one's duties, so that no one may feel a loss except by his own fault. Purity of mind, which consists in a use in harmony with our duties of all our powers of mind, is to be sacredly guarded, and so finally in this most perfect law there is no contradiction at all, of which it is scarcely possible that human laws may be freed. Indeed, it cannot be denied that in the law of nature also there is some consideration for human weakness, with regard to which positive laws are passed, but only with the understanding that the obligation should not be extended to that which is impossible, and in estimating the seriousness of the offence, inasmuch as one sins with more excuse than another on account of the fact that non-use or abuse of one faculty or another is not to be imputed to him. But the law itself which compels one to act or not to act, demands the greatest effort which comes from the combined use of all the powers, when it insists upon righteousness in every act. Rulers of a state, who represent the people, as they are exalted above all, so also they ought to surpass all in every kind of intellectual and moral virtue, that all virtues may appear to be concentrated in them. And in that consists their glory, which makes them revered by all nations. But do not persuade yourself that more licence is allowed to those who are placed in a more exalted position than to private individuals, and that they deserve praise for the things which are censured in private individuals. Just as the obligation of preserving an equilibrium of powers among private individuals dwelling together in one place in a state of nature would not be assumed without absurdity, so that obligation is no less absurd, which some feign, of preserving the equilibrium among neighbouring nations.

§ 650. *From what source the right arises to overthrow a growing power*

If any nation should manifestly be considering plans for subjecting other nations to itself, these ought to provide for their common security by alliances, and the slightest wrong gives them the right to overthrow the growing power by armed force. For if any nation should manifestly be considering plans for subjecting other nations to itself, since every nation ought to preserve itself, and strive earnestly to become powerful, consequently to have strength to resist foreign attack, it is not to be doubted that nations which peril seems to threaten, ought to unite their forces and so ought to provide for their common security by alliances. Which was the first point.   § 31. § 70. § 69.

And since a wrong, both such as has been done or such as is likely to be done, is a just cause of war, and since even the slightest wrong, when done, is a wrong, as is self-evident, and since nations are not allowed simply for the purpose of increasing their own power to subject other nations to their power by force of arms, if a nation should manifestly be considering plans for subjecting other nations to itself, the fear that some injury is likely to be done is not a vain one, especially on the part of a nation to whom some injury, though a very slight one, has been done; if any nation should manifestly be considering plans for subjecting other nations to itself, the slightest wrong gives them the right to overthrow the growing power by armed force. Which was the other point.   § 617. § 72. § 859, part 1, Jus Nat.

> Therefore, we see that no danger threatens nations from those who misuse their power if they themselves, in the rigorous observance of the duties which are to be performed for others, allow nothing at all to be desired in their diligence, and guard with all care against doing injury to others, thinking of war and promoting their own interests with a pure mind. It is hardly wise to take up arms on account of a trivial wrong, because war draws a great mass of evils after it; but when there is fear, not without ground, of serious, nay of most serious, wrong, such as unwilling subjugation, not differing greatly from

destruction, which every nation is bound to avert from itself, there exists a perfect right of war, both to get satisfaction for it if committed and also to avert it if threatened. Therefore, in this case growing power not only has a place among persuasive reasons, but passes over into justifying ones also, in so far as the abuse of power is no longer doubtful.

§ 33.
§ 34.

§ 651. *When it is allowable to maintain equilibrium among nations by force*

Since nations ought to provide for their common security by alliances, if any nation should manifestly be considering plans for subjecting other nations to itself, and since the slightest wrong gives them the right to overthrow the growing power by armed force, and since nations ought to promote the common good by their combined powers, and consequently also ought in every legal way to provide for the common security; if any nation should manifestly be considering plans for subjecting other nations to itself and should inflict the slightest wrong on any one of them, the other nations have the right, for the purpose of preserving the equilibrium, to overthrow the growing power by armed force.

§ 650.

§ 12.
§ 71.

When, indeed, one who manifests the intention of doing wrong to others, does not hesitate to do a very trivial wrong, he is properly assumed to be likely to do a greater one. Wrong likely to be done cannot be avoided otherwise than by destroying the power of doing harm; for if indeed this should not be done, you can never be sure that the wrong is not going to be done. Danger that is still uncertain is rightly provided against by alliances; but if indeed it should already have progressed somewhat, so that one may foresee that it is likely to arise, who, pray, will say that one must wait until the kindling fire bursts into open flame, to be extinguished only with the greatest difficulty? The law of nature also suggests prudence, but to anticipate a crime is the part of prudence, lest delay may be fatal. And from those things which we have already proved, it is perfectly plain what ought to be determined concerning the preservation of equilibrium among nations.

§ 256, part 1,
Jus Nat.

§ 652. *Of the disturber of public security*

If any one relying on his power does not hesitate to disturb the common security of nations by arms unjustly assumed, other nations in general have a right to deprive him of power. For since nations are understood to §9. have united into a supreme state, they are bound to protect the common §§ 4, 13, part 8, security by their combined powers. Therefore, since the right belongs to Jus Nat. nations as a whole in the supreme state to coerce individual nations, if they are unwilling to satisfy their obligation, if any one relying on his §13. power does not hesitate to disturb the common security of nations by arms unjustly assumed, other nations in general have a right to deprive him of power.

> The disturber of the common security of nations in the supreme state does more harm than he who disturbs public tranquillity in a state. Therefore, just as in a state the right to punish one who disturbs the tranquillity of the state belongs to the people, consequently to the ruler of the state, who has the right of the people; so also in the supreme state the right to punish a disturber of the common security of nations belongs to all nations. But since it is not necessary that all nations should unite for a punitive war, which cannot indeed be done, this right can be exercised in general by those who have the most interest in diminishing the excessive power of the disturber, nay more, it is especially fitting that it should be so exercised. He declares himself an enemy of all nations who dares wrongfully to harass any other nation at will, and to inflict losses by force unjustly. Therefore, all nations have the right to repel unjust force by force, that the common security may be defended and preserved.

§ 653. *What aids or auxiliaries are*

Aids, or also auxiliary troops, or simply auxiliaries are defined as troops, both foot and horse, which one nation, not engaged in the war, sends to another nation carrying on war. In our native vernacular they are called *Hülfs-Völcker* [helpers].

> The term is properly a military one, which has later been transferred to signify the help which is brought to another in any case.

§ 654. *What subsidies are*

Subsidies to-day are defined as moneys, which are paid to a nation carrying on war by another nation, not engaged in the war, so that the nation can pay the expense of military service. In our native vernacular they are called *Subsidien-Gelder* [subsidy-moneys] likewise simply *Subsidien* [subsidies]. Nevertheless, also we have among us moneys with this name which are paid by a nation waging war to another for auxiliaries. You might call these also subsidy moneys.

Among the Romans, soldiers of the third rank were called *subsidia*, who were placed in the line of battle in the third rank, so that, if perchance the first rank were beaten, victory might be hoped for from them, when the contest was renewed afresh as it were. Consequently it was also said that a subsidy was sent, if auxiliaries were dispatched to a desperate case. To-day we are accustomed to call them *Succurs* [rescuers].

§ 655. *What treaties of war are*

Those are called treaties of war which are entered into for the purpose of war, as for auxiliaries, subsidies, and anything else which has to do with war. Since it depends upon the will of nations on what condition they may desire to enter into any treaty, treaties of war relate either to every war, both offensive and defensive, or to defensive only, nay more, auxiliaries and subsidies are promised either generally against all, or only against certain nations, or certain nations are excepted. Hence treaties of war are divided into offensive and defensive, and certain ones are offensive and defensive at the same time.

§ 382, part 3, Jus Nat.

It is not necessary to explain every difference in treaties, as regards the matter agreed upon, since concerning these any agreement you may please can be made, as shall of course have seemed best to the contracting parties, and one must abide by what has been agreed upon.

§§ 546, 547.

§ 656. *Of auxiliaries, subsidies, and assistance in war*

To a nation carrying on a just war it is allowable to send auxiliaries and subsidies and to aid it in war in any manner, nay more, by nature nation is bound to nation as to those things, if that is possible: but for an unjust war none of those things may be done. For by nature it is allowable to bring aid to one carrying on a just war, nay more, he who can, is bound to bring aid to one needing it: but anything that another does for the one who is carrying on an unjust war, is not legal. Therefore, since nations use no other law with each other than natural law, which individuals use with each other in a state of nature, it is allowable to send auxiliaries and subsidies to a nation carrying on a just war and to aid it in war in any other manner, if it can be done: but for an unjust war none of those things may be done.

§ 1116, part 1, Jus Nat.

§ 1115, part 1, Jus Nat.

§ 3.

It is plainly evident that such a natural obligation looks only to the duties which nations owe nations, since it exists only when it is in the power of the nation, whose aid is asked, to assume it, and as to that judgement should be with the nation itself.

§ 657. Of the wrong done by those acts to one carrying on a just war

Since it is not allowable to send auxiliaries and subsidies to one carrying on an unjust war, nor to do anything which can be of aid to him in any way, he who does any of these things, violates the right of the one whose arms are justly assumed; consequently if auxiliaries or subsidies should be sent to one carrying on an unjust war, or he should be aided in war in any way, he who does any of these things does a wrong to the other party, on whose side there is justice in war.

§ 656.

§ 859, part 1, Jus Nat.

Therefore there is the greatest difference between the one who helps the progress of arms justly assumed, and the one who involves himself in an unjust war; but since this distinction is plain, one need not speak at length concerning it.

§ 658. When treaties of war are allowable

It is not allowable to contract treaties of war with those who are carrying on an unjust war; but it is allowable to do this with those whose war is just. For it is not allowable to send auxiliaries, nor give subsidies, nor aid in any other way one who is carrying on an unjust war. For he who contracts a treaty of war with another agrees with him to send auxiliaries,

§ 656.

§ 655.

§ 377.

§ 170, part 1,
Phil. Pract.
Univ.

or to give subsidies, or concerning some other assistance in the war with him; consequently he binds himself to perform those things concerning which the agreement has been made. Therefore, since no one can bind himself to another to that which is illegal, it is not allowable to contract treaties of war also with those whose war is unjust. Which was the first point.

But on the other hand it is allowable to send auxiliaries and give subsidies and to be of aid in war in any other manner to one carrying on a just war, nay more, if any one can furnish these things, he is bound to do so.

§ 656.

§ 655.

§ 377.

Therefore, since in a treaty of war there is an agreement concerning these things, and he who promises binds himself to perform, it is allowable to contract treaties of war with those who carry on a just war. Which was the second point.

§ 621.

§ 30, part 8, Jus
Nat.

§ 610, part 1,
Jus Nat.

§ 160.

Since nothing is more deadly for nations than war, it is an especially hard thing to involve oneself in a foreign war. Therefore, in contracting treaties of war persuasive reasons especially are to be considered, namely, whether or not it may be to the advantage of the state that war be undertaken, a thing which is true even if a treaty is to be made with one whose arms are justly assumed. For since it is not allowable to do that which is opposed to the purpose of the state, he who cannot involve himself in a war without detriment to his subjects, does not have it in his power to take up arms in behalf of another, consequently he is not bound to do so. If then he should be unwilling to enter into a treaty, he does nothing which is opposed to his duties towards other nations.

§ 659. Of the tacit provision which exists in every treaty of war as such

§ 658.

Since it is allowable to contract treaties of war only with those who carry on a just war, if a treaty of war is entered into in time of peace, when there is as yet no thought of any particular war, that is understood to have been done with the tacit provision that the war shall be just.

This tacit provision belongs by nature to every treaty of war as such, since a treaty entered into for the purpose of an unjust war is by nature invalid, and its natural baseness will appear more clearly from those things which we are to prove later concerning law in war. By nature it is not allowable to enter into a treaty in time of peace, when there is as yet no thought of any particular war, except under this provision. Therefore, although it should not be expressly added, and there should be no need for its addition because of those things which we have mentioned, nevertheless it is always understood to have been added, or ought to be so understood. This is in harmony with justice, which nations in their relations with each other ought to cherish with the greatest care. For who, pray, would dare to approve an agreement whose purport is none other than this: "I will aid you in doing wrong, that you may aid me in doing the same"?

§ 926, part 1, Jus Nat. § 265.

§ 660. *When things promised in a treaty are not to be performed*

Since a treaty of war in time of peace, when there is as yet no thought of any particular war, is entered into with the tacit provision that the war shall be just, he who does not perform the promises made in the treaty for one carrying on an unjust war, does nothing which is contrary to the treaty.

§ 659.

For observing a treaty nothing else is required than that an ally should perform for his allies those promises to which he is bound. Therefore, since in a treaty of war no one can bind himself to aid an ally in an unjust war, to fulfil a treaty of war it is not in any way required, that one should further the success of an ally in arms unjustly taken up. Indeed, this is in no way included within the treaty, consequently if it should be denied, nothing is done contrary to the treaty.

§ 430, part 3, Jus Nat. § 658.

§ 661. *What the case of a treaty is*

The case of a treaty is defined as the combination of circumstances for which a treaty is made, whether they shall have been expressly stated or tacitly assumed.

A case in moral affairs is defined as the combination of all the circumstances concerning a certain action, and therefore it is determined by the circumstances. If, therefore, in the making of a treaty certain circumstances should be expressly stated, or even should be

§ 180, part 8, Phil. Pract. Univ.

understood as tacitly assumed from its nature, the case of the treaty is determined by those things, and consequently the treaty is understood to have been made only for this case.

§ 662. *When the case of a treaty exists*

§ 661.

§ 659.

Since the case of a treaty is determined by the circumstances under which the treaty is made, whether they shall have been expressly stated or tacitly assumed, the case exists if the circumstances exist which have been either expressly stated or tacitly assumed. Therefore, since in every treaty the tacit provision is assumed that the war is just, the case of a treaty does not exist if it is plain that the arms of the ally have been unjustly assumed.

Hence it is plain how a controversy is to be determined, if one should arise, concerning the case of a treaty, such as every one knows arises continually in regard to treaties of war. Of course inquiry is to be made not only in regard to the circumstances concerning which there is an express statement, but also in regard to those which are properly understood to have been tacitly assumed. And as regards these one must refer to the interpretation of treaties, and here those things are of use which we have proved in regard to interpretation in the entire third chapter of the sixth part of "The Law of Nature."[8] Since it is not only an exceeding hard thing to involve one's self in a foreign war, but also since cases may arise in which no sane man would have entered into a treaty, if he could have foreseen them, the case of a treaty is nowhere to be more carefully considered than in treaties of war. Therefore, although this has a place no less in other treaties than in these, nevertheless you would scarcely hear of a dispute concerning the case of a treaty, unless the fulfilment of a treaty of war is urged by an ally.

§ 663. *Of the right when the case of a treaty exists*

§ 662.

When the case of a treaty exists, the promises which have been made in a treaty are to be performed; when it does not exist, they do not have to be performed. For if the case of a treaty exists, the circumstances exist

8. See Christian Wolff, *Jus Naturae*, vol. 6 (1746; ed. Marcel Thomann, Hildesheim: Georg Olms, 1968), chap. 3, §§459–560, pp. 318–413.

for which the treaty was made, that is, under which one ally has bound himself to another to perform those things concerning which there has been an agreement in the treaty. Therefore, since nations ought to perform for each other those things concerning which there has been an agreement, when the case of a treaty exists, the promises which have been made in a treaty are to be performed. Which was the first point. § 377. § 380.

But if indeed the case of a treaty does not exist, the circumstances do not exist for which a treaty is made, that is, those under which an ally has bound himself to perform for another those things concerning which an agreement has been made in the treaty. Therefore, since no one can bind himself to another beyond his desire, one ally is not bound to another to perform those things concerning which there has been an agreement in a treaty, when the case of a treaty does not exist, consequently when this does not exist those things do not have to be performed which have been promised in a treaty. Which was the second point. § 662. § 377. § 382, part 3, Jus Nat.

We have an example by which the present proposition can be illustrated in that which has just been said concerning the tacit provision in every treaty of war, which is non-existent as such. But even without my suggestion it is plain that to the circumstances through which the case of a treaty is determined are to be referred also the conditions under which a treaty is contracted, so that then the case of a treaty does not exist when the condition fails. § 659.

§ 664. *Of the method of performing a treaty of war when the case of a treaty exists*

Since, if the case of a treaty exists, one ally is bound to perform for another the things which have been promised in a treaty, and since in a treaty of war there are promised aids, subsidies, and other things which are of assistance in war, such as arms, ships, provisions, horses; when the case of a treaty exists, the promised aids are to be sent, subsidy money is to be paid, arms, ships, supplies, horses, &c., are to be furnished. § 663. § 655.

Of course a treaty is fulfilled if those things are performed concerning which there has been an agreement in it, and therefore, when the case of a treaty exists, those things are to be performed concerning which there has been an express provision in the treaty, and the things

§ 428, part 3,
Jus Nat.

§ 466, part 6,
Jus Nat.

§ cited.

Note, § 466.

which a proper interpretation suggests are to be considered altogether
equivalent to express provisions. Whereas, both as regards those things
which are to be performed, when the case of a treaty exists, and as
regards determining the circumstances, on whose existence the case of
the treaty depends, a correct interpretation is to be allowed; therefore,
no less concerning the existence of the case of a treaty than concerning those things which are to be performed by virtue of the treaty,
controversies commonly arise, which it is plain, indeed, are likely to
be avoided if all terms should be expressly stated and without any
ambiguity; nevertheless it is not so easy to avoid them, as is more than
plain enough from those things which have been proved at length
concerning interpretation. Very great knowledge, wisdom, and foresight would be demanded in one who was to be capable of fashioning
a treaty, which should contain words not likely ever to be subject to
any doubt and only those plainly expressed; and certainly greater good
faith than can often be hoped for. Would that it were enough always
simply to say this: men fashion treaties from which the human ele-
ment is not lacking.

§ 665. *Of an ally involved in war*

If an ally, when he himself is involved in war, needs those things which
were to be performed for his ally by force of the treaty, he is not bound
to perform them: but if in spite of his own war he can perform, he is still
bound to do so, and in regard to that his judgement is to be accepted.
For if a treaty of war is made, since there is an agreement in it concerning
aids, subsidies, and other things which can be of use in war, one ally binds
himself absolutely to the other to those things which by nature he already
owed him. Therefore, since no nation is bound to do for another what it
does not have in its power to do, and since it does not have in its power
what it can do for another only by neglect of its duty to itself, if a treaty
of war is contracted, it is understood to have been made with this tacit
exception, unless he who promises what is promised should himself need
it at the time when it is to be performed. Therefore, since no one can bind
another to himself beyond his desire, if an ally, when he himself is involved
in war, needs those things which were to be performed to his ally by force
of the treaty, he is not bound to perform them. Which was the first point.

§ 655.

§ 377.

§ 656.

§ 160.

§ 610, part 1,
Jus Nat.

§ 382, part 3,
Jus Nat.

But if, indeed, in spite of his own war he can do those things to which he has agreed in the treaty, the reason fails by which he himself when involved in war is not bound to perform what he has promised to an ally, by virtue of the first point proved. Therefore, when a just excuse is lacking, as the obligations incurred by the treaty still continue, although one is involved in a war, he is nevertheless still bound to perform what was promised in the treaty. Which was the second point. §377.

§170, Ontol.

But since he who carries on a war and administers the state knows best of all how much his shoulders should bear and what they refuse to bear, therefore, whether or not in spite of his own war he can perform for his ally what he has promised in his treaty, is to be left to his judgement, especially since the other one, who needs his aid, may not readily be presumed likely to pass judgement against himself, although he ought to do so. Therefore, in that matter we must accept the judgement of the one from whom a performance of the treaty is sought. Which was the third point.

> The fortune of war is excessively uncertain and the outcome quite doubtful, nor can the dangers likely to arise therefrom be foreseen with certainty, nay more, they frequently arise contrary to all expectation. Therefore, it is the part of wisdom not to trust too much to one's strength, but rather to hope for less from it than it warrants. Therefore, since judgement is very difficult as to what can be done for an ally in spite of one's own war, certainly it is much better that a decision in regard to it should be left to him who ought to perform, lest he might have just reasons for complaint against the other party, if, while he is aiding another, it should happen that he himself should be in need of aid.

§ 666. *Of supplies promised in a treaty of war*

If supplies have been promised in a treaty of war but the promisor is suffering from want thereof, supplies need not be furnished to the ally. For he who is suffering from want has scarcely enough for his own needs. Therefore, since it is impossible that he who has scarcely as much as he himself needs should furnish supplies to another, and since there is no obligation to do that which is impossible, if supplies have been promised §209, part I, Phil. Pract. Univ.

in a treaty of war but the promisor is suffering from want thereof, supplies need not be furnished to the ally.

Every one sees that there is in a treaty this tacit exception, unless want should stand in the way; a thing which is quite in harmony with a just interpretation. If this occurs the agreement is invalid. In morals of course that is considered impossible which cannot be performed without violation of a necessary duty toward oneself, such as self-preservation. But we have made express mention of the present case for this reason, that it may appear that, even if you yourself are not involved in war, nevertheless other cases can still arise in which what has been promised in a treaty of war is rightfully refused to an ally. Those cases are easily distinguished provided you know what sort of an exception there is to every treaty through just interpretation.

§§ 537, 538, part 6, Jus Nat.

§ 633, part 3, Jus Nat.

§§ 536 and fol., part 6, Jus Nat.

§ 667. *Of two allies carrying on war*

If two allies should be carrying on war and the promises made to each in a treaty can be performed, they are to be performed; but if not, the ally is to be preferred with whom the earlier treaty exists. For treaties are to be considered sacred by nations, consequently that they may be secure from every violation, they are to be exactly fulfilled. If then two allies should be involved in different wars, and the promises made to each in a treaty can be performed, since nothing prevents you from fulfilling the treaty made with each, they undoubtedly are to be performed. Which was the first point.

But if indeed a case should arise, in which it is not possible to perform for each of the allies at the same time what has been promised, the earlier ally is preferred to the later. If then two allies should be carrying on war and the promises made to each in a treaty cannot be performed, he certainly is to be preferred with whom the earlier treaty exists. Which was the second point.

See what we have noted above in regard to that matter. But since it does not depend upon your will which of the allies you may desire to prefer, persuasive reasons are of no value here. For example, let us suppose that in an earlier treaty aids have been promised for nothing, but in a later one for a certain sum of money. Although the earlier

§ 547.

§ 546.

§ 386.

Note, § 386.

treaty may be burdensome to you, but the later one more favourable, nevertheless it is not allowable on that account to prefer the later to the earlier ally. Here also other reasons fail on account of which one is to be preferred to another, where you are still free to do as you please. But since in an unjust war those things are not to be performed which have been promised in a treaty of war, it would be superfluous to add that a later ally is to be preferred to an earlier one, if the earlier one should be waging an unjust war, but the arms of the later should be justly assumed; for since in this case no treaty would be understood to exist with the earlier ally, it cannot really be said that the later is being preferred to the earlier, but rather that what was promised is performed for the later, because a treaty must be observed, but is not performed for the other because nothing is due. Therefore no conflict of treaties occurs here to make an exception necessary. Indeed, if each ally should wage an unjust war, to neither would be due what was promised in the treaty, but it would have to be denied to each alike.

§§ 659, 660.

§ 659.

§ 668. *Of allies matched against each other*

If an ally should carry on war against an ally, the promises made in a treaty of war are to be performed for the earlier ally as against the later, unless the earlier agreement should have expressly specified otherwise, or unless the war of the earlier ally should be manifestly unjust, in which case the later is to be preferred to the earlier. For if in the earlier treaty it has simply been agreed that one should perform for the other this or that thing in the war; then it is plain that it must be performed against all men, consequently through the fact that a treaty is afterwards entered into with some one the right acquired in the former treaty cannot be diminished and taken away, so far as regards the new ally. Therefore, when there is no reason why an exception should be made for the later ally, and it is self-evident that the promises made in the treaty cannot be performed for each ally, the earlier ally certainly is to be preferred, consequently if an ally should carry on war against an ally, the promises made in a treaty of war are to be performed for the earlier as against the later. Which was the first point.

§ 667.

But if indeed it should have been expressly stated in the earlier treaty that those things concerning which an agreement has been made are not

§ 382, part 3,
Jus Nat.
to be performed, as against the one with whom a treaty is afterwards made, since no one is bound beyond that to which he has agreed, the promises made in a treaty are not to be performed for the one with whom there is an earlier treaty against the one with whom there is a later. Which was the second point.

§ 659.
And finally, if arms have been assumed by the earlier ally with manifest injustice, since an obligation arising from a treaty cannot be extended to unjust arms, nothing is due to the earlier ally. Therefore, when nothing prevents the performance for the later ally of the promises made in the treaty concluded with him, they will have to be performed as against the earlier ally. Which was the third point.

There are those who argue that the earlier ally is always to be preferred to the later, without any consideration of the justice of the war, for the reason that the decision as to the justice of the war is with the promisee not with the promisor. But this is the same as arguing that in contracting a treaty of war there is to be no consideration of the justice of the war; and it is not apparent how this can be admitted. For since it must be admitted that an unjust war is not to be waged, it cannot be admitted that aids, subsidies, and other helps are to be promised for an unjust war. But if, indeed, you ought not to promise to give aid in unjust war, you ought to have the decision also as to the justice of the war in which you are bound to aid another, and you cannot give to another the right to dispose of your conscience; a thing which would be more than servile, since not even a slave ought to do injustice on the order of his master, as no one denies. Let us suppose that I have promised you that I am willing to lend money to you whenever you need it, but that you should ask money of me for the purpose of whoring; will any one say that I am not to have the decision as to how you shall use the money, and therefore it must be given to you even if I know that you are going to spend it on prostitutes? But for nations and their rulers there is no other law than that which private individuals use in their

§ 3.
relations with each other in a state of nature. Since a promise for an illegal object is void, treaties of war are not to be extended to objects which are illegal. He who engages in an unjust war is to be warned to lay down his arms which he has unjustly assumed, rather than that

we should endeavour to further his cause. See what we have already suggested above.

Note §§ 659, 660.

§ 669. If allies of the same treaty should be matched against each other

If those who have been joined as allies in the same treaty are matched against each other, promises made in the treaty are to be performed for neither. If they have been joined as allies in the same treaty, aids cannot be furnished to each against each without manifest absurdity. Therefore, since agreements are to be so interpreted as to avoid absurdity, it is undoubtedly plain that the promised assistance cannot be rendered except against a stranger. If then allies are matched against each other, the promises made in the treaty are to be performed for neither.

§ 529, part 6, Jus Nat.

Of course in the present case you are bound to neither of the allies by the treaty, and no right is acquired by either from it. Here, therefore, there is no question as to which is to be preferred to the other.

§ 382, part 3, Jus Nat.

§ 670. Of allies excepted in a treaty of war

If a treaty of war shall have been entered into against all with the exception of allies, those alone are understood to be allies who now are such, but not those who are to be, unless it should be expressly stated, "both those who now are and who are to be." For interpretation of agreements must be made in accordance with what was probably the intent. But if allies should be mentioned in a treaty of war, the thought in the mind of the contracting parties is of those who now are allies, but they do not seem to think of those who are afterwards to be such, since otherwise they would not have said simply "allies," but would have expressly distinguished present and future allies. Therefore, if a treaty of war shall have been entered into against all, with the exception of allies, those alone are understood to be allies whom, at the present time, one or another of the contracting parties has as allies, but not those who perchance are to be. Which was the first point.

§ 512, part 6, Jus Nat.

But if indeed those who now are and those who are to be allies should be expressly excepted, since no one can be bound to another beyond his

§ 382, part 3,
Jus Nat.
desire, there is no doubt that one ally is not bound, when asked by his ally, to give aid to him against those whom he himself is to have as allies. Which was the second point.

§ 149, part 5,
Jus Nat.

§§ 546, 547.
It would be in fraud of a former treaty to make a treaty with one of its parties so that he would be involved in war with his former ally. Therefore, since all fraud ought to be far from every agreement, a treaty of that sort is diametrically opposed to the sanctity of treaties.

§ 671. *Of a treaty of war not observed without just cause of excuse*

If any one should not perform for his ally, who is carrying on war, the promises made in a treaty, when he has no just cause of excuse, he does him a wrong, and he is bound by nature to repair the loss which his ally suffers thereby. For if any one should have a just cause of excuse, because of which he cannot perform the promises made in the treaty, he is not bound to perform. Which was the first point.

§§ 665 and fol.

§ 547.

§ 546.
But since treaties are to be kept sacred by nations and therefore are to be strictly fulfilled, if there should be no just cause of excuse, as shown in point 1, the treaty certainly is violated, if those things are not performed, which were to be performed by force of the treaty. Therefore, since the ally has acquired a perfect right from the treaty to those things concerning which there was an agreement in it, and since wrong consists in the violation of a perfect right; if any one should not perform for his ally, who is carrying on war, the promises made in a treaty, when he has no just cause of excuse, he does him a wrong. Which was the second point.

§ 377.

§ 859, part 1,
Jus Nat.

§ 580, part 2,
Jus Nat.
Therefore, since the loss which the ally suffers when the assistance is denied him, which was to be given by virtue of the treaty, is caused by the wrong of the one denying, as proved in point 2, consequently is his fault; and since he is bound to repair all loss who has caused the same by his fault or fraud, if any one should not perform for his ally, who is carrying on war, the promises made in a treaty, when he has no just cause of excuse, he is bound by nature to repair the loss which his ally suffers thereby. Which was the third point.

There is no reason why you should say that, if one ally does not observe a treaty, the other is no longer bound to give assistance if it should happen that he himself is involved in war; this is not sufficient in the present case, because the one who relies on a treaty incurs the loss on account of the violation of the treaty, as is here assumed, a thing which it is plain enough does not always necessarily occur. A wrong is done in every case when a treaty is violated, but it is not always accompanied by a loss, either because fortune favours one's arms, or because the lack of the promised aid is supplied from elsewhere, just as it may often occur that there would be the same loss whether the promised aid should be sent or not.

§ 430.

§ 672. *What middle parties in war are*

In war those are called middle parties who are attached to neither belligerent party, consequently do not involve themselves in the war. They are commonly called neutrals because, for the purpose of the war, they favour neither party, and the condition of the nations which follow neither of the belligerent parties in war is called neutrality, and their lands are called neutral lands.

Neutrality concerns especially nations that are neighbours to the belligerents, or those whose lands are in the neighbourhood of the lands in which war is carried on, although it may also be extended to those which, since they are not too far away, can give aid in war to one party.

§ 673. *What a treaty of neutrality is*

A treaty of neutrality is defined as one made with some nation, with the purpose that it may be neutral.

Any nation, indeed, without a treaty itself being made, can be a neutral, in so far as it furnishes to neither of the belligerent parties the things which can be useful to it in war, which are usually furnished by allies, or furnishes to each party those things which nation owes to nation by nature independently of war; nevertheless, since it is frequently to the advantage of one of the belligerent parties, that one may not perchance enter into a treaty of war with the opposite party,

§ 672.

§ 377.

§ 859, part 1,
Jus Nat.

or even in the absence of a treaty give aid to it in case of necessity, and consequently no longer remain neutral, a treaty of neutrality is usually made, in contravention of which nothing can be done without wrong.

§ 674. *Whether neutrality is allowable by nature*

§ 30, part 8,
Jus Nat.

§ 610, part 1,
Jus Nat.

§ 160.

§ 656.

§ 672.

§ 417, part 2,
Theol. Nat.

§ 656.

§ 448, part 1,
Phil. Pract.
Univ.

§ 672.

It is allowable by nature for any nation to be neutral in war, if it should be to the interest of the state rather to abstain from war than to involve itself in it, or should the reason for the war be doubtful. For since every right of a people by nature should be determined by the purpose of the state, if it shall be to the interest of the state rather to abstain from war than to involve itself in it, it is plainly not in its power to give aid even to one carrying on a just war, consequently it is not bound by nature to give assistance. Therefore, since by nature it is certainly illegal to give aid to one carrying on an unjust war, by nature it is assuredly allowable for a nation to be neutral in war, if it shall be to the interest of the state rather to abstain from war than to involve itself in it. Which was the first point.

And if the reason for the war be doubtful, since it is not plain with which party justice lies in the war, and since it is not allowable to give aid to one fighting in an unjust war, and since he sins who acts without a clear conscience, one must join neither of the belligerent parties. Therefore, since a nation is neutral which is attached to neither of the belligerent parties, it is evident that it is allowable to be a neutral in a doubtful case. Which was the second point.

> The necessary law of nations which Grotius calls the internal law, and which must be considered not only in the court of conscience but also in rightly determining the glory of a nation, certainly demands that the question of justice should be considered in determining whether you ought to involve yourself in the war of another or whether you ought to refrain therefrom, nor is it sufficient that you should consider only what is in harmony with the welfare of the state. Therefore, there is no need that neutral nations should suspend their judgement concerning the justice of the war, although it may be wiser that they should not express it openly, nay rather, the welfare of the state demands silence sometimes, if not frequently. But although it is not necessary that they should express their judgement

to the belligerents, this nevertheless does not prevent them from taking account of the justice of the war in deciding what they are going to do in case of the present war, as they ought to do, unless they wish to break the law of nature.

§ 675. *Of neutrality that must be allowed*

Any nation must be allowed by either of the belligerent parties to be neutral, unless it has been bound by treaty to the other nation. For every nation must be allowed to abide by its own decision as to whether it can do anything for another without neglect of its duty towards itself, and if it should deny what is asked, that must be endured, consequently also it § 157. must be allowed to attach itself to neither, if it should not consider it to be in its interest to give assistance to either of the belligerent parties, and by virtue of the natural liberty belonging to it, what it may wish to do § 55, part 8, must be left to its own conscience, nor is it bound to give a reason to any Jus Nat. one why it may prefer to do one thing rather than another. Therefore, § 157, part 1, Jus since a nation is neutral which is attached to neither of the belligerent Nat., and § 3 h. parties, any nation must be allowed by either of the belligerent parties to § 158, part 1, Jus be neutral. Which was the first point. Nat., and § 3 h.

But if indeed a nation has been bound by treaty to either of the bellig- § 672. erent parties, since allied nations ought readily to perform for each other those things concerning which there has been an agreement in a treaty, § 380. and since their treaties ought to be sacred, that is, immune from every violation, a nation ought to do for its ally in war those things concerning § 547. which there has been an agreement in a treaty of war. Therefore, since § 546. a nation is not neutral which brings assistance to one of the belligerent parties in a war, and therefore becomes attached to the same, a nation § 672. which has been bound by treaty to one of the belligerent parties cannot be a neutral. Which was the second point.

Since by entering into a treaty to give assistance in war one nation binds itself absolutely to another, by that very act also it declares that § 377. it does not wish to be a neutral, and binds itself so that it may not be neutral, and in this way its neutrality is made illegal by the treaty. But it is self-evident, if the case arises in which the obligation contracted by §§ 660, 665, the treaty should fail, a thing which can happen as is plain from what and fol.

precedes, then that neutrality no longer is illegal, and consequently is legal. And therefore we have said specifically, unless the nation has been bound to the other, not of course if there was a treaty with the other belligerent party before the war, as is understood of itself; for here the question is not whether a treaty has been entered into, but whether the obligation incurred by the treaty exists in the case arising.

§ 676. Of the right to contract treaties of neutrality

A treaty of neutrality is allowable by nature, if by nature it is allowable for the nation with which it is contracted to be a neutral, and it must be allowed to contract a treaty of neutrality with one of the belligerent parties, unless it has been bound to the other nation by a treaty of war. For by nature it is allowable for any nation to be a neutral in war, if it shall be to the interest of the state to refrain from war, rather than to involve itself therein, or even if the justification for the war should be questionable. Therefore, since you are not forbidden to do those things which are allowable, it depends upon the will of every nation whether or not it may desire to bind itself to another to be neutral. Therefore, since by contracting a treaty it binds itself absolutely to another, and since that is a treaty of neutrality by which it binds itself to be neutral, it is plain that a treaty of neutrality is allowable, if it is allowable for the nation, with which it is contracted, to be neutral. Which was the first point.

And every nation must be allowed by either of the belligerent parties to be neutral, unless it has been bound by a treaty to one or the other. Therefore also it must be allowed by one of the belligerent parties to contract a treaty of neutrality with the other party, if it is bound by no treaty of war to the former. Which was the second point.

> By this treaty of neutrality that which was allowable by nature becomes a binding debt; which has no injustice in it of which the other belligerent party can complain, since it cannot compel the other to enter into a treaty of war with it.

§ 677. Of the obligation from a treaty of neutrality

He who enters into a treaty of neutrality, binds himself to the one with whom it is contracted, that he will not aid the opposite party in war,

§ 674.

§ 170, part 1,
Phil. Pract.
Univ.

§ 673.

§ 675.

nor in any way interfere with the movements of the former. For since a perfect obligation arises from a treaty, he who enters into a treaty of §377. neutrality with another binds himself to him in regard to those things concerning which there was an agreement in the treaty. Therefore, since it was agreed in it that he who is to be a neutral, or an adherent of neither party, should involve himself in the war in no way, the one who is to be a neutral is bound to involve himself in the war in no way. §672. Therefore, since he involves himself in the war to the prejudice of the one who contracts the treaty for the sake of his security if in any measure he should give aid in war to the opposite party, or should interfere with the movements of the former, he who contracts the treaty of neutrality binds himself to the one with whom the treaty is made, that he will not aid the opposite party in war, nor in any way interfere with the movements of the former.

He who contracts a treaty of neutrality with a belligerent, does that either for his own advantage or for the sake of the belligerent. In the former case he seeks the consent of the belligerent, that he may be the adherent of neither party; in the latter the belligerent desires that he should be the adherent of neither party. In the former case the security of the one who belongs to neither party is primarily considered, lest he may suffer some loss through war; in the latter case the security of the belligerent, lest his movements may be interfered with in some way, or lest the power of the opposite party may be strengthened. In the former case neutrality is granted to the one who wishes to be the adherent of neither party; in the latter it is sought by a belligerent. Therefore, although a treaty of neutrality ought to be respected by each of the contracting parties, nevertheless in the former case the one who wishes to be the adherent of neither party, in §547. the latter case the belligerent, ought to guard against doing anything contrary to the treaty.

§ 678. *The special obligation with respect to the party opposed to him with whom the treaty was made*

Since he who enters into a treaty of neutrality binds himself to a belligerent, that he will not aid the party opposed to him, he ought not to send §677. aids to the other belligerent party, nor furnish him with subsidies, nor provisions, nor arms, nor other things, such at least, as have a use in war, nor supply him with what can be of advantage in any way.

§ 677.

He who wishes to be the adherent of neither party, ought so to abstain from the war as to do absolutely nothing for the sake of the belligerents which can help one of the parties. And he has bound himself to this to the one with whom he made the treaty, with regard to the party opposed to him. So if provisions or war equipment should fail, he cannot supply them to the one in need, nor can he permit the party opposed to his ally to enrol soldiers in his territory, since this would be just the same as sending him aids. Likewise he cannot allow his subjects to lend him money, since this would seem to be just the same as giving subsidies.

§ 679. *The obligation directly affecting an ally*

§ 677.

Since he who enters into a treaty of neutrality binds himself to a belligerent that he will not interfere in any way with his movements; therefore he ought not to do anything which in any way can injure his ally, even although he does not directly aid his ally's opponent, who may be ignorant of what he is doing and for whom he is not performing any positive service, as when he delays auxiliaries coming to give assistance, while they are passing through his territories, with the purpose that they may not come in time, or if he should buy up produce from those of whom his ally is seeking it, with the purpose that the ally may not have an adequate supply. The same is understood in regard to any equipment for war.

§ 678.

The case is similar if a peaceful people should be persuaded not to allow soldiers to be enrolled in their territory, which before they did allow, or not to sell what would be useful for war. Of course the acts by which any one involves himself in war are of two sorts, some of which directly affect one of the belligerent parties, by which aid is furnished to it, but others only indirectly affect it, by which injury is done to it. The present proposition refers to the latter; the preceding proposition to the former.

§ 680. *Of the obligation of belligerents arising from a treaty of neutrality*

Belligerents entering into a treaty of neutrality bind themselves to the one who is the adherent of neither party, that they will not bring hostile force against him and his property. For since in a treaty of neutrality there is an agreement that the one who wishes to be neutral should be attached to neither of the belligerent parties; since one wishes to be the adherent of neither party with the idea of being exempt from the evils which war carries in its train, the belligerents certainly bind themselves to secure that exemption, and consequently they ought to refrain from all hostile violence against him. Therefore it is plain that they are absolutely bound by force of the treaty not to seek to bring any hostile force on him and his property.

§ 672.

§ 377.

Against those who are neutrals in war the belligerents have no right of war, since they are doing them no injury, which alone gives a right of war. Nay more, since they are allowed by nature, even without a treaty, to be the adherents of neither party, and are therefore exercising their own right when they wish to be neutrals; when they are such, they are doing no wrong to the belligerents. What, therefore, is allowable against an enemy is not allowable against those who are neutrals in war. And the belligerents, when they contract a treaty of neutrality, bind themselves by force of the treaty to that which is already due by nature. When, therefore, they agree to neutrality, they agree to the exemption from evils which war carries in its train, and so they bind themselves to secure that, consequently to abstain from all hostile violence against them. It would be absurd for belligerents to be free to cause losses to those who are neutrals in war, when these are bound to be on their guard against injuring in any way the other belligerent party.

§ 617.

§ 675.

§ 975, part 1, Jus Nat.

§ 681. *What sort of a treaty the treaty of neutrality contains*

Since belligerents entering into a treaty of neutrality bind themselves to the one who is the adherent of neither party, that they will not bring hostile force against him and his property, just as he also binds himself to them, that he will do nothing in favour of one which may injure the other, or by which his movements may be interfered with; a treaty of neutrality includes within itself, if not an agreement not to injure, at least an agreement not wilfully to harm, and it is a certain sort of treaty of friendship.

§ 680.

§ 677.

§ 394.

Above we have said that it was not necessary to enter into a treaty not to injure, because forsooth there is already by nature an absolute right not to have an injury done to one, nor is there then any need of acquiring it by an agreement. But just as at that time we made an exception in case any nation was of the opinion that it was allowable to injure foreign nations at will; so in the present case it is not superfluous to contract a treaty in regard to not injuring or at least in regard to not doing anything from which harm can result. For if arms are justly assumed by the one to whom any one allies himself, the harm which he does to the other is not strictly an injury; it becomes so because of an inaccuracy of speech such as frequently occurs. But there is no one who does not know that belligerents, although they ought not to do so, nevertheless in spite of natural obligation do commit many things by which wrong is done to neighbouring nations. Therefore, it is not superfluous that treaties of neutrality should be contracted, since a sense of shame is usually more efficacious than natural obligation; hence those are said to have put aside all sense of shame who have no scruple in violating the sacred faith of treaties. And in very fact there is a greater disgrace in such violation than in an act contrary to a prohibitive law in the present instance, and a sense of shame overcomes other depraved impulses, by which belligerents are stimulated to injure neighbouring nations which refrain from war without a treaty. But this is not the place to speak of these at greater length. It is sufficient to have aroused the attention of those who have enough acuteness to investigate such things more deeply. But a fuller treatment of them belongs to ethics or to the moral philosophy of nations.

§ 682. *When a treaty of neutrality is to be contracted with each of the belligerent parties*

Treaties of neutrality are to be contracted with each of the belligerent parties by that nation whose territory is near to the lands in which the war is carried on. For if the territory of any nation is near to the lands in which the war is carried on, it easily happens that losses may be caused and injuries inflicted on it, as well by one, as by the other of the belligerent parties. Therefore, since by a treaty of neutrality that is provided against by that nation whose territory is near to the lands in which the war is carried on, treaties of neutrality are to be contracted with each of the belligerent parties.

If the territory of a nation is far removed from the lands in which war is carried on, it is certainly to the advantage of one of the belligerent parties that the nation should not give aid to the other belligerent, as by furnishing auxiliaries or furnishing subsidies. And then by a treaty of neutrality provision can at least be made that this should not be done. But generally it happens that nations near to the theatre of war are accustomed to be neutral in it, and then a treaty must be contracted with each of the belligerent parties, provided each party   § 675. desires to agree to neutrality. For although each ought to consent, nevertheless nations and their rulers do not always do what they are bound to do by the law of nature. Indeed, if they would obey this law in the present case, there would certainly be no need of a treaty   § cited. of neutrality.

§ 683. Of those things which are to be done by neutral nations towards each of the belligerent parties

Those who are adherents of neither party ought to do for each of the belligerent parties what they are bound to do by the law of nations independently of the war, unless there has been an express agreement otherwise concerning certain things which may have a bearing on the war. For in a treaty of neutrality it is merely agreed that the nation which wishes to be neutral should not give aid to either of the belligerent parties, or interfere in the movements of the war in behalf of one party, consequently that   §§ 677, 639. it should conduct itself just as if there were no war. Therefore, it is plain that by that treaty it is in no way restrained from doing those things which are due by the law of nations independently of the war. Therefore, since one that is the adherent of neither party ought not to favour one party more than the other, it ought to do for each of the belligerent parties the things which are due by the law of nations independently of the war. Which was the first point.

But if, indeed, there shall have been an agreement otherwise, concerning certain things which have some bearing on the war, since treaties are   §§ 380, 547.

to be faithfully observed it is self-evident that it must abide by that which has been agreed upon. Which was the second point.

The war does not exist as regards those who are adherents of neither party, but they themselves are friends to both belligerents. Therefore those things are to be done for each of the belligerent parties which, independently of war, or in times of peace, are done by a nation for nations. What is done for one must also be done for the other, if it needs it. But it can be agreed that certain things also may be done which have some bearing on the war, or that those should not be done which in themselves have nothing to do with the war, but under existing circumstances can have some effect upon it, and then the former are to be done for each party, the latter to be denied each. Treaties of neutrality are not always devoid of all wrong, but as the less evil should be preferred to the greater, those things which cannot be changed must be endured.

§ 684. *What must be done by neutral nations for each of the belligerent parties*

Since one that is an adherent of neither party ought to do for each of the belligerent parties what one is bound to do by the law of nations, independently of the war; and since foreign nations must be allowed to come into our territory and procure goods for themselves at a fair price, and live there for proper purposes, and pass through our lands, and be received into our houses for proper rest, where, with their property, they can pass the night comfortably and safely, and enjoy healthful food and drink, and have feed supplied for their horses, and the services which they need furnished at a fair price; nay more, since toward foreigners living among us or passing through we ought to be courteous, unless entrance into our lands shall have been denied to foreigners for special reasons;—those who are adherents of neither party are bound to grant and allow to soldiers and subjects of each of the belligerent parties entrance to their territory and safe passage through their lands, that they may live there for a proper purpose, and procure for themselves the goods which they need at a fair price, and they ought to show themselves equally courteous to each party.

§ 683.

§ 58 h and
§ 594, part 6,
Jus Nat.

§ 692, part 6,
Jus Nat.

§ 689, part 6,
Jus Nat.

§ 350.

§ 351.

§ 295.

Of course the things which are done by a neutral nation for foreigners, if there is no war, are likewise to be done in time of war for each of the belligerent parties. And therefore there can be no difficulty in determining what can properly be done or ought not to be done by a neutral nation in any given case. For, as we have said, those things ought to be done which are to be done if there is no war; only, care is to be taken that nothing should be done which shows greater favour towards one party than another, lest just cause of complaint may be given to one party that neutrality has not been perfectly observed, a thing to be the more avoided as it is more easily a stimulus to troubles.

§ 685. *Examples of those things which by virtue of the treaty are to be performed and denied by a neutral nation*

Because those things concerning which there has been a special agreement are to be performed for neither of the belligerent parties or for both alike, if there shall have been an agreement that a neutral nation should not grant entrance into its territory, nor allow passage through, or that one may procure there provisions for oneself, entrance to their lands is not to be granted to the soldiers of either of the belligerent parties, nor is a passage through them to be allowed in the former case, but in the latter each party is to be allowed to seek provisions from the neutral lands. § 683.

It is my desire to bring forward these particular cases as by way of example, that it may appear how the general proposition is to be applied to particular cases, and lest there may remain any obscurity to prevent a perfect understanding.

§ 686. *Of the right of harmless passage of troops through foreign territory*

One nation ought to allow a harmless passage to the military forces of another nation. For a passage for just causes through a territory subject to our control can be denied to no one, unless there should be a well-founded fear of loss, that is, it must be allowed if it is harmless. Therefore, since nations use the same law with each other, and since the § 689, part 6, Jus Nat. § 3. § 613.

§ 156, part 1,
and § 55, part
8, Jus Nat.
right of war belongs to them, the decision as to how they may use their
right does not belong to another nation, whether properly or improperly; consequently, the passage of military forces for the sake of war is
to be considered a passage for a just cause, which must be allowed if it
is harmless.

De Jure Belli ac
Pacis, lib. 2, c.
2, § 13, n. 4.

§ 497.
    Grotius has already properly suggested that the objection cannot
be made that he who will allow the passage may fear the great number of those going across, for since there is no lack of methods for
taking precautions, which he also reviews, namely, that the troops
be taken across in separate divisions or unarmed, or that hostages be
demanded, the fear is not well grounded; and we have already indi-
Note, § 640.
cated above in a like case that an ungrounded fear does not take away
the right of another. Ideas which can give us some light are suggested
§§ 646 and fol.
also here and there among those passages which we have proved and
discussed above concerning the equilibrium of nations.

§ 687. *What is to be observed by those passing across*

§ 648.
Since by the law of nations passage is not to be allowed to military forces
unless it is harmless, military forces passing through a foreign territory
ought to go by the king's highway, nor turn into private property; if they
need anything, they ought to pay a proper price for it, and ought not to
seize the property of others, and they ought to refrain from every sort of
injury or wrong.

    For the right of harmless passage, which exists by nature and there-
§ 64, part 1,
Jus Nat.
fore cannot be taken from any one without wrong, is not to be turned
to licence, so as to be extended beyond the limits within which it
is restrained, and therefore the use of it cannot be accompanied by
the least loss to the one allowing it or to his subjects. But a certain
thing as yet doubtful is to be explained, which might occur to one or
another. We have said above that they have an erroneous idea who
Note, § 668.
argue that the decision as to the justice of a war is not with the one
who interferes in a war, but with those who wage it, nor can a treaty
of war be contracted with one who carries on an unjust war, but just
§ 658.
now we claimed that treaties of neutrality are to be contracted with
each of the belligerent parties, although nevertheless war cannot be

just on both sides. Likewise in the preceding proposition we assert that the passage of troops through its territory is to be allowed without exception by one nation to another, consequently with no consideration being given to the justice of the war; a thing which seems to be just the same as to argue, or at least to assume, that no nation can pass judgement for itself as to the right by which some other nation carries on war. But when a treaty is contracted with belligerents, that is done in order that the belligerents may bind themselves to allow that we, who seek a neutral part in the war, should not involve ourselves in it; a point which is in no way opposed to those things which we have proved before. For since a war is always unjust on the part of one of the belligerents, he who is attached to neither party does not involve himself in an unjust war, because that is illegal, nor in a just one, because he decides this is not in his power, consequently he is not bound to do this. And since the right of war belongs by nature to every nation, he abuses his right who wages an unjust war. Therefore, since by nature every one must be allowed to abuse his right, and every nation ought to avoid and ward off for itself danger of destruction, and those things which interfere with its perfection in any way, or render its condition less perfect, it can allow the harmless passage of troops through its territories even for an unjust war, if it cannot forbid it. Of course it is one thing not to prevent another from sinning when you are not bound to prevent it, but another to assist another to sin. However emphatically you may say that losses and dangers are to be warded off from another nation no less than from yourself, nevertheless that is to be understood only in the case in which it can be done without neglect of duty toward one's self, and in case of conflict duty towards one's self conquers duty toward others. Therefore there is no difficulty in what we have elsewhere suggested, that in allowing passage through your territory you must consider whether it is asked for just causes, in order that the act of another may not be imputed to you, because, although you were able to interfere, you were unwilling to do so; for in the present case it is assumed that you are not able to prevent the passage, unless you should desire to fail in your duty toward yourself; in morals, moreover, a moral impossibility is equal to a physical impossibility. And who does not know that war often occurs when one refuses passage,

§ 682.
§ 633.
§ 686.

§§ 672, 673.
§ 634.

§ 656.

§ 160.

§ 613.
§§ 156, 157, part 1, Jus Nat.

§ 36.
§ 33.

§ 156.
§ cited.
§ 229, part 1, Phil. Pract. Univ.

Note, § 689, part 6, Jus Nat.

or that what cannot be obtained by prayers is even sought by arms, and consequently the harmless passage becomes a harmful one?

§ 688. *Of asking for passage*

He who wishes to march with an army through the territory of another nation ought to ask for passage. For the passage ought to be harmless. Therefore, since by virtue of the natural liberty belonging to every nation, judgement rests with it as to whether or not the passage is harmless, and that it may be harmless, it is often necessary to agree as to one thing or another, nay more, frequently certain arrangements must be made that those making the passage without harm to those through whose boundaries they pass can have what they need; he who wishes to march with an army through the territory of another nation ought to ask for passage.

There is no reason why you should object, that passage through occupied territory is a right of harmless utility, which is a survival from the primitive common holding, and that a right which you have by nature is not to be obtained from another by entreaty. For that would only apply, if there were no just causes for denying passage, which prevent it from being considered the harmless use of the property of another. Although indeed by nature we ought to allow another the harmless use of our property, and hence comes the contract of loan, by which you grant to another the gratuitous use of your property; nevertheless it is not possible for this reason to claim for one's self the use of the property of another without the owner's consent, and therefore one is held only to acquire that by the contract. Therefore the same thing also is to be observed in the harmless use of those things which are in the ownership of nations, and he who is willing to consider carefully the details which have been proved of a loan, and who has an intellect trained to keen discrimination, will find among them more than one thing which can throw light upon the argument concerning the passage through occupied territory, and will advantageously apply it, particularly to the present case of marching with an army through the territory of another nation. In the present case there is the additional point, that the one through whose territory he wishes to march with an army ought to know with what purpose he is coming.

§§ 686, 687.
§ 55, part 8,
Jus Nat.

§ 156, part 1,
Jus Nat.

§ 687, part 6,
Jus Nat.

§ 418, part 4,
Jus Nat.

§ 3.

§ 689. *Whether by allowing passage wrong is done to the one against whom it is allowed*

He who allows passage with an army through his territory to one seeking it, does no wrong to him against whom there was need of it. For a harmless passage through its territory must be allowed by nation to nation. Therefore, since no one has the right to prevent another from doing what he is bound to do, if passage with an army through one's territory is allowed to one seeking it, nothing is done which is contrary to the right of the one against whom there was need of it. Therefore, since no wrong is done, if nothing should be done which is contrary to the right of another, he who allows passage with an army through his territory to one seeking it, does no wrong to him against whom there was need of it.

§ 686.

§ 170, part 1, Jus Nat.

§ 859, part 1, Jus Nat.

The disadvantage which the other belligerent party may feel from the passage gives one no right to take away the right of passage, nor a right not to submit to the passage. For his disadvantage is an advantage to the one crossing. Therefore, it would be a contradiction for any one to wish to measure his right by his advantage; of course there would be no reason why a right might not arise from the advantage of one just as much as from that of the other, unless indeed you are willing to admit that right belongs to the stronger, just as the bigger fish swallows the smaller. And then, for the purpose of maintaining equilibrium among nations, it might be allowable to diminish the power of the very strong by an armed force, even if no other cause of war should arise; a thing which we have shown above is contrary to the law of nature. We do not deny that those are governed by that perverse idea who, because they are very powerful, rely upon their power; but here it is not a question of fact but of law.

§ 646.

§ 690. *Whether he against whom passage is allowed can prohibit it*

Since allowing passage with an army through one's territory to one seeking it does no wrong to him against whom the army is advancing, if any one allows passage to the troops of another through his territory this is

§ 689.

to be endured by the one against whom it is allowed, nor has he the right to prohibit it.

§§ 343, 686.

Note, § 689.

§ 101, part 1, Jus Nat.

§ 18.

He who seeks passage and he who grants it are exercising their rights. And, as is self-evident, no one can have the right to prohibit any one from using his own right. See what we have just now remarked. As long as no wrong is done you, you must endure what another does. In truth the absurdity of refusing permission to cross is plain even from the fact that if you had need of the same you would bear it ill that another should wish to forbid that it be allowed you. But what you do not wish to be done to you, because of an innate right or one belonging to you by nature, that you may not do to another. What is allowed by nature to one nation, that is also allowed to another, and what is not allowed to one, the same is not allowed to another; natural equality is not in the least affected because one nation is more powerful than another, since the rights of nations are not derived from power.

§ 691. *If the one who seeks that passage may not be allowed should add threats*

§ 686.

§ 23, part 1, Jus Nat.
§ 690.
§ 689.

If any one seeks that passage may not be allowed to military forces against himself, that which is sought is rightly refused; but if, nevertheless, there is a well-grounded fear that he may bring war upon the one allowing passage, or may harm him in another way, passage can be denied. For one nation ought to allow harmless passage to the military forces of another nation. Therefore, since from this obligation the right arises of not yielding to the requests of one who seeks that passage may not be allowed, and since the seeker has no right to prevent that which can be done without injury to himself, if any one seeks that passage may not be allowed to military forces against himself, that which is sought is rightly refused. Which was the first point.

But if, indeed, there is a well-grounded fear that he against whom passage is allowed may bring war upon the one allowing it, or may harm him in another way, because the passage would not be harmless, whether loss should be caused by the passage itself, or should result therefrom, or it should give cause for loss, the passage would be no longer harmless. Therefore, since nation is bound to nation not to allow a passage harmful to itself, but one that is harmless; if there should be a well-grounded

fear that he against whom passage is allowed may bring war upon the   § 686.
one allowing it, or may harm him in another way, passage can be refused.
Which was the second point.

The fear is well grounded if one has just cause, or, if you prefer, sufficient reasons. For let us suppose that the one forbidding the granting
of passage threatens to declare war; when he is powerful enough to be   § 822, Psych.
able to add deeds to words, one has sufficient reason for fear, nor is   Emp.
the fear ill founded, since you are bound to avert all risk from yourself,
and therefore you gain a right to those things without which that can-   § 33.
not be averted. But although it is not allowable to use illegal means   §§ 34, 37.
to attain a legal end, this nevertheless does not prevent you from not   § 71.
suffering yourself to be dissuaded by well-grounded fear from allowing the passage, since the denial of passage cannot be said to be illegal,
as in case of conflict your duty toward yourself outweighs your duty
to another, and the loss arising from the denial of passage to the one   § 206.
asking it, or to a third party, for the sake of whom he wishes to cross,   § 630, part 2,
must be considered as fortuitous. And although it cannot be denied   Jus Nat.
that the one forbidding that passage be allowed is acting without right,
nay rather is violating your right, consequently is doing you an injury   § 690.
while attempting to interfere with you in the exercise of your right,   § 159, part 1,
this does not prevent you from not suffering yourself to be dissuaded   Phil. Pract. Univ.
from allowing the passage. For you have the right to those things   § 859, part 1,
without which loss cannot be averted. And in this way the denial of   Jus Nat.
passage puts on the character of defence against wrong, and therefore   § 686 h and
by your own right you may refuse passage as likely to be harmful   § 158, part 1,
Phil. Pract. Univ.
to you through the injury of a third party. You see how perfectly all   § 493, part 2,
things in the law of nature and nations harmonize with each other,   Jus Nat., and
provided only you have carefully examined the entire interrelation   § 159, part 1,
Phil. Pract. Univ.
of obligations and of rights derived therefrom; a thing which can be   § 972, part 1,
accomplished in no other way than by the aid of a system worthy of   Jus Nat.
the name, such as it has been our desire to establish.   § 973, part 1,
Jus Nat.

§ 692. *Of the one who wishes to cross without your consent*

Since passage may rightly be denied the one seeking it, if there should be
a well-grounded fear that he against whom it is allowed may bring war   § 691.

upon you, or may harm you in another way, you may resist by force one who is about to cross without your consent.

§ 686.
§ 688.
§ 859, part I,
Jus Nat.
§ 691.
§ 859, part I,
Jus Nat.
§ 973, part I,
Jus Nat.

Of course no right belongs to another to a passage harmful to you, and therefore he is bound to ask for the same, that you of course may decide whether or not it will be harmful to you. Therefore, since you do no wrong to him by denying passage, but in your own right you may prohibit it, he who prepares to cross without your consent does you a wrong; consequently since you have the right of self-defence, you may resist the same by force.

§ 693. *Of a harmless passage to be allowed for nothing*

§ 972, part I,
Jus Nat.

A harmless passage is to be allowed for nothing. For he who is willing to permit a passage, but not for nothing, has no just cause for preventing it. If, indeed, he should be afraid lest those crossing should cause a loss, consequently that it would not be harmless, the one intending to cross is merely bound to give adequate security, as by giving hostages, for a harmless passage, so that if loss should be caused contrary to expectation, it would be repaired. Therefore, since the one intending to cross has the right to cross, and since no one is bound to purchase from another the right which belongs to him by nature, a harmless passage is to be allowed for nothing.

§ 686.

There are indeed examples occurring in the history of the ancients of those who had to secure passage for a price, such as are cited in the commentators upon Grotius; but that purchase is a matter of fact, not of law, nor can any reason which has a pretence of right be assumed for it, as is indeed understood from the proof. Undoubtedly it is opposed to justice to be unwilling to give to another his right except for a definite price. Nevertheless, it is a matter of prudence, when the circumstances arise, to prefer to give money to one unjustly receiving it, than to defend one's right by force.

§ 926, part I,
Jus Nat.

§ 694. *Of the furnishing of necessaries for a passage*

If a passage is allowed, those things are not to be refused without which it cannot be accomplished; but for those things which one needs who is intending to cross, he is bound to pay a fair price. For let us suppose that you allow passage to another, but refuse those things which he needs for the passage. Since without them it is not possible for him to cross, this is undoubtedly just as if passage should be denied. Therefore, since it would be absurd to allow passage directly, but indirectly to refuse it; if passage is allowed, those things are not to be refused without which it cannot be accomplished. Which was the first point.

But since it is self-evident that the passage would not be harmless if those things were to be given for nothing which the one intending to cross needs, and since one nation is not bound to allow passage to another harmful to itself but one that is harmless, certainly one intending to cross is bound to pay a fair price for those things which he needs on the passage. Which was the second point.

§ 686.

The latter we have already intimated above, nevertheless it was not unwise that the same be insisted upon a second time, when we speak of the obligation to furnish necessaries to those intending to cross, since we shall at least have made plain at the same time that those crossing have no right to the things belonging to subjects of the country where they are marching, but that such things are to be procured at a fair price. In the same place we have shown that a fair price is to be paid by those crossing; but here we make especially plain that an unfair price is not to be exacted from them. And a fair or proper price is understood to be such as at the time is paid by natives for things of that sort or, if provisions grow dearer because of the passage, as much as afterwards has to be paid. Therefore it is plain that this is not a bare repetition of things already proved beforehand, which could rightly be called superfluous. It is easily understood that the obligation of furnishing necessaries for the passage is a part of the concession of the right of passage. For men need food and drink, horses need fodder and straw, and when it is necessary for those passing to stop at some place, it is necessary that they should be received into the houses by the inhabitants of the district. And hence also the need of seeking passage is plain, that an adequate supply can be procured everywhere and furnished without burden and loss to the inhabitants. For unless there should be such provision for those crossing, the passage would be harmful because of the fault of the one allowing it.

§ 687.

§ 695. *Of fear lest, if passage is allowed, the seat of war may be fixed in a peaceful land*

If it is to be feared that, if passage were allowed to one of the belligerent parties, the other party would ask for the same, and so the seat of war would be fixed in a peaceful country, the one whose permission is asked is not bound to allow passage. For since there is no one that does not see that, on the hypothesis of the present proposition, the passage would not be harmless, and since nation is bound to allow to nation only a harmless passage, on the hypothesis of the present proposition, he whose permission is asked is not bound to allow passage.

§ 686.

§ 696. *But if passage should be prepared for, without permission of the owner of a territory*

Since, if it is to be feared that, if passage were allowed to one of the belligerent parties, the other party also would ask for the same, and so the seat of war would be fixed in a peaceful country, the one whose permission is asked is not bound to allow passage; if one should wish to cross without the consent of the ruler of the territory, the ruler may resist by force, and, if there should seem to be need, he may take the side of the more powerful, that he may guard against the seat of war becoming fixed in his own district.

§ 695.

On the hypothesis of the preceding proposition it is readily understood that the fear is not groundless that the seat of war may be fixed in the territory of one from whom each of the belligerents seeks a passage, because those passing across can meet each other within the territory. Now there is no one who does not know what great losses may occur if the theatre of war shall have been in any territory, unless he is ignorant of the mass of evils which war draws after it. And we have already quite often said and proved, that a nation has a right to avoid losses. But if you wish to avoid losses as far as possible, it is undoubtedly necessary that you should take the side of the more powerful[9] and hasten his passage. But whether this may always be done is possibly doubtful, because it can happen that the war of the more powerful may be unjust,

9. Reading "potentioris" for "posterioris."

and it is not allowable to give aid to one carrying on an unjust war. But you are planning a just defence and are using the aid of the other for that purpose; a thing which it is understood is allowable. And you do not in any way give assistance to one carrying on an unjust war. Therefore, although the war may be unjust, in so far as he wages war for his purpose, nevertheless his arms are not unjustly assumed, in so far as your just cause is defended by them. Moreover, it is no contradiction that his arms are justly assumed in one respect but unjustly in another.

§ 656.

§ 990, part 1, Jus Nat.

§ 697. *Of loss caused by those passing through*

If those passing through shall have caused losses to the inhabitants, the one to whom passage was allowed is bound to repair them, and the ruler of the state ought to see to it that restoration is made to those to whom the losses were caused. For since the passage which is to be allowed ought to be harmless, those passing through ought to be on their guard that they do not cause even the least loss to the inhabitants of the district through which they pass. Therefore, since all loss caused by fault or fraud is to be repaired, if those passing through shall have caused losses to the inhabitants, the one to whom passage was allowed is bound to repair them. Which was the first point.

§ 686.

§ 580, part 2, Jus Nat.

And since a loss must be restored to those who suffer it, since, moreover, it is self-evident that unless that is done as soon as it has been suffered, it cannot possibly be done by the one to whom passage was allowed; therefore an estimate of the loss must be presented by the ruler of the state, who represents the people, consequently pleads the cause of the people, and he then ought to see to it that the loss should be restored to those who have suffered it. Which was the second point.

§ 93.

Rulers of states rightly demand from one whose forces have passed through their territory that they should repair all the loss which they have caused. For he ought sternly to forbid his men to cause any loss, and command the leaders of the soldiers that they should not allow them to dare to do anything which is not legal. If he does not do this, the loss has plainly been caused by his fault, consequently he himself is bound for his own fault. For however much either the soldiers or their leaders themselves have acted contrary to his desire, nevertheless he is still bound by their acts, because when he asked for passage, either expressly or at least tacitly he promised that it would be harmless, consequently he bound himself to restore the loss, so that to the extent of his promise he is bound to recognize their act as his act. But if, indeed, the loss shall not have been caused to the one allowing passage, but to his subjects, there is nothing indeed which is to be restored to him, but what is restored ought all to be restored to his subjects. Therefore, by no right indeed can he claim that for himself, since here eminent domain fails. His right is the right to protect his subjects, and therefore, in the present case, to see to it that the loss caused to them should also be restored to them, but the loss of his subjects ought not to be a profit to him.

§ 363, part 3,
Jus Nat.

§ III, part 8,
Jus Nat.

§ 698. *Of security that the passage will be harmless*

§ 697.

Since the loss caused by those passing through is to be restored, he who allows the passage has the right to demand adequate security from him to whom the same is allowed, and when the other is unwilling to furnish this, he has the right to refuse passage, when there is a well-grounded fear that the passage will not be harmless, or that the payment of the amount of the loss, if any should occur, would be obtained with difficulty.

§ 37.

Of course, we have already shown elsewhere that nations have the right to use those means by which they provide that their condition may not be less perfect. Therefore, from the obligation of the one passing through, that loss may not be caused, there arises not only the right of demanding reparation for loss caused, but also the right that loss be guarded against. And certainly it is better to guard against loss than to seek reparation. Moreover, cases undoubtedly occur in which the good faith of the one promising harmless passage is not sufficiently assured, e.g. if those passing through at another place have caused losses, if the one promising has not been sufficiently zealous in keeping faith, or if what he ought to give or restore can only with difficulty be obtained from him. The right to refuse passage, in regard to which there is not a little suspicion that it will not be altogether harmless, also arises from the fact that the loss is to be restored, if any is caused, a suspicion which is undoubtedly increased, if he who seeks passage should refuse to offer security.

§ 699. *Whether passage can be refused on account of a difference in religion*

Passage cannot be refused on account of a difference in religion. For that a harmless passage must be granted by nation to nation arises from that primitive common right, or community of property belonging by nature to the whole human race, by force of which any one can pass through any place as he may need or as it may seem best to him, but it does not arise from a mode of worshipping God, consequently not from religion. Therefore, since this right has no connexion with the religion to which a nation is devoted, which, intending to use a passage, asks for it, passage cannot be refused on account of a difference in religion.

§ 686.

§ 687, part 6,
Jus Nat.

§ 9, part 2,
Jus Nat.

§ 66, part 2,
Jus Nat.

§ 512, part 2,
Theol. Nat.

Here are to be reviewed those things which we have suggested above, when we were speaking of contracting treaties with a nation devoted to another religion. Whether a nation shall have been of one, or of another, or of no religion, is of no importance in allowing passage; nor is anything to be considered other than that the passage shall be harmless. Moreover, there is no just fear that a harmless passage is not to be expected from a nation devoted to another religion. For the dissent of all in religion does not produce hatred of the dissentients, and lead to the view that they can be injured at pleasure. But if a nation seeking passage is burning with hatred of that sort toward another through whose territory it wishes to go, then passage is not refused on account of diversity of religion, but because the passage is not harmless.

Note, § 429.

§ 700. *Or because the one asking passage can cross through another territory*

Passage through one's territory cannot be refused because one can pass through another territory. For if any one considers it necessary to cross with an army through another's territory, and there are two or more territories through which it can cross, individual nations are bound in the same way to allow a harmless crossing, nor does any natural reason exist, since the obligations of all are the same, why one rather than another should be bound to allow it. Therefore, the one having the need to cross has an equal right to cross through any territory, consequently by virtue

§ 686.

§ 17.

§ 55, part 8,
Jus Nat.

§ 156, part 1,
Jus Nat.

of natural liberty belonging to it, it has the choice of crossing wherever it may prefer. Therefore, passage through one's territories cannot be refused, because one can pass through another territory.

§ 18.

§ 686.

Indirectly those prove the same thing who give this reason, that others through whose territory it might be possible to pass can say in like manner that it is possible to pass through another's territory. For let us suppose that it is sufficient reason for denying passage, that he who seeks it can pass through another's territory. Since what is allowable for one nation is allowable for another, if it should be a just cause for denying passage to one, because he who seeks it can pass through another's territory, there will be the same just cause for the several individuals through whose territory it is possible to pass. Therefore, since all can at the same time rightly deny passage, there will be no right of passage; a thing which is certainly absurd. Of course it would be just the same as declaring that no right of passage through foreign territory belongs by nature to nations, but that it can be acquired only by agreements. Indeed those are not wanting who declare this; nevertheless we have proved above that this idea is not in accord with the truth.

§ 701. *Of a just cause for refusing passage*

§ 686.

§ 722, part 1,
Jus Nat.

There is no just cause for refusing passage other than that it would not be harmless. For one nation ought to allow harmless passage to another nation, consequently when the passage is harmless, it cannot justly be refused. Therefore, there can be no just cause for refusing passage other than that it would not be harmless.

§ 699.

§ 700.

Therefore, what we have just proved could be derived by way of corollary, namely, that on account of difference in religion, and because he who seeks passage could pass through another's territory, passage cannot be denied, because neither difference of religion, nor the possibility of passing through another's territory, make the passage through your territory harmful. By force of this general principle it is easily shown in each particular case whether or not passage may be rightfully refused, provided that in deciding what is harmful to you, you stray not from the truth, nor give way to unfounded fear. It is not enough that it perchance can happen that it may be harmful, but it is to be proved, or at least there ought to be a very great probability that it will be harmful. So it is not sufficient for refusing passage that it is the usual custom of almost all armies in passing to act harshly toward inhabitants, since that can be guarded against in part by one's own care, if by agents provision should be made that the passage may be comfortable and safe for those making it, and not too troublesome and harmful to the inhabitants, in part by adequate guarantee from the one seeking passage, that the officers of the soldiers will not be careless in the observation of rigour in military discipline, nor leave unpunished acts of the soldiers contrary to their prohibition.

§ 702. *When refusal of passage is a just cause of war*

Since there is no just cause for refusing passage other than that it would not be harmless, if it should be plain enough that it will be harmless, or that the one intending to cross would take sufficient precautions to secure that, a refusal is contrary to his right, and on this account is a wrong, consequently is a just cause of war.

§ 701.

§ 686.

§ 859, part 1,
Jus Nat.

Examples are not lacking of those who, because they were refused passage, have brought war upon those refusing, such as can be read in Grotius and his commentators. He cites the example of Moses, who, when he had to pass through foreign countries, at first to the Edomite and then to the Amorite offered these terms, that he would go along the king's highway nor turn aside on to private property, that if he had need of any of their property, he would pay them a proper price; and since these conditions assured a harmless passage, but were refused, he brought war for that reason upon the Amorite, and Augustine rightly declares that just wars were waged by the children of Israel against the Amorites.[10] No nation is bound to allow some other nation to take

§ 617.

De Jure Belli ac
Pacis, lib. 2, c. 2,
§ 13, n. 2.
Num. xx, xxi.

§ 687.

10. See St Augustine, *Sancti Aurelii Augustini quaestionum in Heptateuchum libri VII adnotationum in Iob liber unus*, ed. Iosephus Zycha (Prague: F. Tempsky; Leipzig: G. Freytag, 1895), p. 353: "notandum est sane quemadmodum iusta bella gerebantur. Innoxius enim transitus negebatur, qui iure humanae societatis aequissimo patere debebat." ("It must of course be noted how just wars are waged. For harmless passage was denied, which must be granted according to the most equitable law of human society" [my translation]).

from it any one of its rights, but if the other does not wish to allow it, the nation may acquire it by force.

§ 703. *Of passage allowed to property*

If passage is allowed an army, the same must also be allowed for all things which are needed in war. Passage is allowed an army for the purpose of carrying on war, as is self-evident. If then passage should be given to persons alone, but not at the same time to all things which are needed in war, this would undoubtedly be just the same as if passage should be absolutely refused. Therefore, it is plain that it is necessary that passage should also be allowed for all things of which those crossing have need in war.

The passage of war equipment and things necessary in any way for war is in itself included in the passage of the army, or is so clearly connected with it that neither can exist without the other. Therefore, if passage is allowed to the army, it is understood that it is at the same time allowed for things necessary for war and in war, so that the latter need not be demanded specially. Nevertheless it can happen that the passage of only certain things necessary for war may be demanded and allowed, because there is no need for passage of troops; since this passage can be less harmful, if in granting it no weighty reason comes from the other belligerent party, it alone is more readily allowed than passage with an army. But passage is properly denied to property for the same reason that it is rightly denied to troops. Therefore, it is not necessary that we should spend more time discussing these points. But we note by the way that the right of passage through foreign territories is in general less correctly proved solely through the right of commerce which belongs to nations; for it does not follow, if passage is to be allowed for the purpose of commerce, that the same is to be allowed for the purpose of war also; but it must undoubtedly be proved in general, that a harmless passage is to be allowed, and that this right belongs by nature to nations, not to be taken from them without wrong, as has been proved by us. And so finally, from what has been proved in general, it can be inferred, that for the purpose of war also harmless passage is to be allowed, nor can there be a just cause for refusing it, other than that it is not harmless to us.

§ 704. *Of safe passage of an army*

The passage is to be made safe for those who cross. For since no nation ought to injure another, neither ought he who allows the passage to injure those who cross, nor ought he to permit them to be injured by his subjects. Therefore, since those who cross ought to be free from all fear of injury, they are to be given safe passage.

§ 173.

That the passage may be safe is not then a matter to be requested, since the law of nature forbidding all injury without any exception is certainly immutable. Therefore, it is necessary that he who allows passage, since he cannot lawfully refuse, should neglect none of those things which are necessary to provide that those crossing may not be injured by his subjects. For otherwise the injury is his fault, and is imputable to him.

§ 695, part 1, Jus Nat.

§ 142, part 1, Phil. Pract. Univ.

§ 705. *What a declaration is*

A declaration is defined as a public announcement of war made against a nation or its ruler by another nation or its ruler. In our native vernacular we call it *den Krieg ankündigen* [a proclamation of war].

§§ 750, 758, part 1, Phil. Pract. Univ.

§ 700, part 1, Phil. Pract. Univ.

It is a military word, used formerly by the Romans, who declared war with certain solemnities.

§ 706. *The subject-matter of a declaration*

Since a declaration is a public announcement of war made by one nation against another, and since in war we seek by force our right against one who does not wish to give it to us, when there is a declaration or when war is declared, announcement is made to the opposing party what right of ours we wish to claim against it, consequently the declaration contains both an announcement of our desire to wage war and an indication of the reason why we have decided to wage war.

§ 705.

§§ 1102, 1103, part 1, Jus Nat.

Of course by this declaration or announcement of war nothing else is intended than that the other may understand that we have decided to bring war against him and for what reason we have decided it. But if already beforehand there shall have been some friendly discussion concerning the repair of a wrong done us, or concerning a right to be allowed us, or that satisfaction be given us for an irreparable injury, without success, war is declared, if we announce that we are going to seek by force of arms what we cannot acquire without them. For then the cause of the war is already known to the other party.

§ 707. *Of the method of declaring war*

Since a declaration or announcement of war is made with the purpose that the other party may understand that we have determined on war against him and for what reason that has been done, consequently nothing else is required than that this should come to the notice of the other; the method of announcing the war will naturally depend upon the will of the one announcing it, nor does it require special solemnities; consequently if a certain method of announcing a war has been introduced among certain nations, that belongs to the customary law of nations, and if any nation has accepted for itself a certain definite method of announcing a war, that is merely arbitrary, or a matter of civil law, and does not make law between nations.

Naturally it makes no difference how your decision to bring war may become known to another, provided it does become known. But there is no reason for doubting that certain nations can agree with each other concerning a method of declaring war, or can even introduce a definite method into their customs. Therefore, since stipulations are to be observed, especially among nations, and since customs have the force of tacit stipulations, as long as they are contradicted by no nation, if either of these exist, war certainly ought to be announced in that way. And because in a democratic state, such as Rome was under the consuls, the right of war rests with the people, in a mixed state it can depend upon the consent of the people or of the nobles or of certain ones chosen from the people; therefore, in forms of states of that sort laws can be passed concerning a declaration of war, which nevertheless it is self-evident do not bind other nations. But here it is to be observed that with some a declaration is to be distinguished from an announcement of war. For, according to them, among the Romans a declaration properly speaking was a solemn and public recital, made with a clear voice, of facts or of some right, which, on

§ 706.

§ 24.

§ 789, part 3,
Jus Nat.

§ 547.

the authority of Pliny, was followed by the announcement of war, if the other party refused satisfaction, so that the final announcement of war was involved in the declaration, and a precedent condition of declaration was involved in the announcement. But among the Romans there were different formulae and ceremonies for each, as one may see in Alexander ab Alexandro,[11] in Livy,[12] and in Cicero.[13] But since among us, indeed, those ceremonies and solemn formulae are not in use nor do they belong to natural law, therefore we have no need of distinguishing a declaration from an announcement. Nay more, since in the law of nations it would be sufficient, if it should be said that war is announced or proclaimed against another; we can do without the word declaration altogether, unless it were best that mention be made of it, because it occurs in other authors. But when we do not distinguish a declaration from an announcement of war, we follow Stephanus in the Thesaurus Linguae Latinae, where he expressly says that to declare is the same as to proclaim war and the declaration itself is a proclamation of war according to the authority of Servius.[14] But no one desires to dispute about a word.

Hist. XXVII. ii.

V.iii.
I.xxxii.
De Offic. I. xi.

§ 708. Of a conditional and absolute declaration of war

The declaration, or announcement, of war is conditional, if it is said that war will be waged, unless property should be returned or satisfaction given for a wrong, consequently it can be combined with an immediate recall of the property, or with a demand for satisfaction for irreparable wrong done. A declaration is absolute, if it is said without qualification that war will be waged to acquire that which is due or ought to be

---

11. Alexander ab Alexandro, *Genialium dierum libri sex* (Frankfurt, 1604), bk. V, chap. iii, esp. pp. 624–25. Alexander ab Alexandro (1461–1523) was a Neapolitan humanist.

12. See Livy, *From the Founding of the City*, trans. B. O. Foster, 14 vols. (London: Heinemann; Cambridge, Mass.: Harvard University Press, 1919–59), vol. 1, bk. I, chap. xxxii, 6, pp. 115–19.

13. See Cicero, *On Duties*, ed. M. T. Griffin and E. M. Atkins (Cambridge: Cambridge University Press, 1991), bk. I. 79, pp. 31–32.

14. Robertus Stephanus [Robert Estienne, 1503?–59], *Thesaurus linguae Latinae* (Basel, 1740), vol. 1, s.v. "clarigo," p. 537.

restored, consequently there is a place for it, if one is unwilling to give our right to us, or it is understood that he will not give it.

Note, § 707.

§ 3.

In the law of nature and nations we properly distinguish an absolute from a conditional announcement, although the distinction between a declaration and the announcement itself is not to be considered. The things which come from the fetial law of Rome, which was laid down in regard to the formalities of war, are not to be confused with the law of nature, which nations by nature use in dealing with each other.

§ 709. *Whether an absolute declaration ought to follow a conditional one*

§ 708.

Since a conditional announcement of war says that war will be waged unless property should be returned or satisfaction given for a wrong, if the other party is unwilling to return or restore, by that he agrees that we may strive to acquire by force of arms that which is refused; consequently if war should have been conditionally declared, and the other party should not wish to give us our right, there is then no need of an absolute declaration of war.

§ 427, part 3, Jus Nat.

Of course if the other party refuses to give us our right, it is then self-evident that we have no other means left by which we can acquire it, except by arms. Therefore, since we have already made it sufficiently plain to him that we will use this violent means, there is no need for us then to declare to him that we have not changed our mind. For that must be considered as true which any one says when he is bound to speak the truth, consequently the other party ought to blame himself for thinking that empty threats were added to a pretended intention. For it would scarcely be prudent to add empty threats, when you demand that the other party restore your right to you; there is no need to put it more expressly.

§ 710. *Whether in an offensive war there is always need of an announcement*

§ 615.

In an offensive war there is always need of an announcement. For an offensive war is brought against another who was not thinking of bringing war against us, if, of course, we can acquire our right, or satisfaction for §630. irreparable injury, only by force of arms, or if in a doubtful case we cannot otherwise prevail on the other party to perform. Therefore, since we must not resort to this remedy, which is especially to be avoided, because §631. it draws after it a great mass of evils for each of the belligerent parties, as long as there is even the least hope that without it we can acquire what we are striving to acquire by force of arms; it is therefore necessary that we should indicate that we are going to bring war upon another, in order that, before there may be a resort to arms, he can offer fair conditions for peace, and thus war may be avoided. Therefore, it is plain that in an offensive war there is always need of an announcement.

> It is the custom of brigands and robbers to make an unexpected attack by force on the body or property of another, since they have in fact no right to the property of another and to them nothing is due from another. But he who is bound to do anything for another, must be first dunned, so that it may be distinctly understood that he is unwilling to perform the same of his own accord, before you may use force to acquire your property or what is owed to you. Much more is that to be observed before there is resort to arms, because wars cannot be waged without slaughter and loss of many innocent people.

§ 711. *Of fair conditions offered to one declaring war*

If fair conditions of peace should be offered to one declaring war, he must refrain from war. For since in war we seek by force our right, which the other party does not wish to give to us, war is to be waged for no §1103, part 1, purpose other than that fair conditions of peace may be offered. If then Jus Nat. fair conditions of peace are offered to the one declaring war, there is no longer a reason for waging war; consequently the terms must be accepted and war refrained from.

> And hence the necessity of announcing an offensive war is plain, lest one may rush to arms without necessity; which is apparent only when, the peril being already present and threatening, the opposing party stubbornly persists in his design of not allowing you your right. The idea itself of a right of war suggests that a war is to be announced before it is brought, since in it we seek our right against him who is

unwilling to give it to us. Therefore, it is necessary that we should understand that he is unwilling to give it, and that he persists in this design. Therefore, the distinctions which Grotius suggests, to determine when in an offensive war an announcement is required by the law of nature and when not, are useless. For the reason why war is to be announced is universal and is extended to every right which is to be allowed you by another, from whatever source it may come. And what fair conditions of peace may be, is plain both from the cause of the war, and also from the expenses which the one announcing it has been compelled to incur, for the reason that the other party is unwilling to give his right to him; for the loss caused by his fault is to be repaired. But of that we shall have to speak more fully below.

§ 1103, part 1, Jus Nat.

§ 580, part 2, Jus Nat.

§ 712. *Of fair conditions not accepted*

Since war is to be refrained from, if fair conditions of peace be offered to one announcing it, if the terms should not be accepted a just offensive war becomes an unjust one.

§ 711.

For a just cause of war exists only until fair conditions of peace are offered. Therefore, since a just cause of war alone makes the war just, the war ceases to be just. Certainly, he who refuses to accept fair conditions of peace, cannot wage a war with the purpose of acquiring his right which is denied him, and for this reason he is driven to wage it either because of a passion for vengeance, because his right has not been given to him immediately, or in deciding upon the war persuasive reasons are considered, rather than justifiable ones, consequently he resorts to arms with the intention of injuring; a thing which is altogether illegal.

§ 1110, part 1, Jus Nat.

§ 173.

§ 713. *Whether a defensive war is to be announced*

A defensive war is naturally not to be announced. For an offensive war, which is announced, is either just or it is unjust. But if it is just, since then the defensive war is unjust, he against whom the war is announced ought to refrain from it, by offering fair conditions of peace. Therefore, the announcement of the war has no place. If, indeed, the one announcing the war should be unwilling to accept fair conditions of peace offered

§ 629.

§ 1111, part 1, Jus Nat., and § 711 h.

him, it is self-evident that it is necessary that the opposing party should defend himself; consequently it is not then required that he should indicate that he wishes to defend himself. Therefore, in case of the announcement of a just war a defensive war is not to be announced. Which was the first point.

But if, indeed, the offensive war which is announced shall have been unjust, the defensive war is just. Therefore, since it is self-evident that nothing else is left to him against whom the war is announced, except to resist one threatening injury, consequently to use his right of self-defence; if the offensive war shall have been unjust, the defensive war is naturally not to be announced. Which was the second point.

§ 629.

§§ 972, IIII, part 1, Jus Nat.

The reason which makes an announcement necessary in an offensive war does not apply in a defensive war, as is plain from the consideration of both proofs. If then an announcement should be made by each party, it is superfluous for the party waging the defensive war, a thing which is particularly plain if, after an invasion has been made by the other party, an announcement ought then to be made, or were to be made; for then defence does not admit of delay, but a present force which is to be resisted at once imposes the necessity of self-defence. But no one is assumed to be so foolish as not to wish to resist present force without delay, and to have to declare to the other his intention of defending himself. The supreme power owes defence to its citizens, who have united into a state for the purpose of defending themselves against the force of outsiders, and nothing is more natural than such defence, since even dumb animals themselves by a certain natural instinct are led to it, so that defence seems to be a sort of right common to men and beasts. Therefore, since the supreme power necessarily wages defensive war as part of its duty, it certainly seems incongruous to announce to another that we intend to do what we cannot omit without neglect of duty, nor without injury to our citizens. An offensive war depends on the will of the one waging it; for although he may have a just cause of war, namely, to acquire his right which is denied him, nevertheless it is frequently wiser to give up his right, which is undoubtedly allowable, rather than become involved in a deadly war, the result of which is doubtful, or else to leave the prosecution of his right in suspense, since what is put off is

§ 710, and preceding.

§ 4, part 8, Jus Nat.

§§ 630, 631.

§ 117, part 3, Jus Nat.

not taken away. Therefore, it is necessary that he should declare his will to another, if he has determined to bring war, as is plain from the above proof. But defence is both a physical and moral necessity

§ 710.

through what we have already said, nor is it a matter of whim whether or not you will defend yourself. But the consensus of nations, to which frequent appeal is made, neither admits the necessity in offensive war, nor allows its omission in defensive war, unless it is a customary right,

§ 24.

which, as we have already said, is effective as long as it shall be contradicted by no nation.

§ 714. *When it is allowable to omit an announcement of offensive war*

If he against whom war is to be announced does not admit envoys and there is no opportunity to send a letter, and the announcement cannot be made through a third party, the announcement of an offensive war is to be omitted. For if he against whom war is announced does not admit envoys, and there is no opportunity to send a letter, and the announcement cannot be made through a third party, there is no one who does not see that it is not in the power of the one who has determined upon war to announce it. Although, then, an offensive war must always be

§ 710.

announced, since nevertheless an obligation is not to be extended beyond

§ 109, part 1, Phil. Pract. Univ.

that which can be done, and the announcement is made impossible by the fault of the one to whom it was due, and consequently its omission is to be imputed to him; if he against whom war is announced does not

§ 700, part 1, Phil. Pract. Univ.

admit envoys, and there is no opportunity to send a letter to him, and the announcement cannot be made through a third party, the announcement of an offensive war is to be omitted.

The rule that the offensive war is always to be announced admits of no exception, but the impossibility of doing what it enjoins provides a legitimate excuse, nor has he a just cause for complaint that the announcement has been omitted, who has made it impossible by his own fault. For he shows by his very act that he does not wish that war should be declared before it is brought, and therefore no wrong is done him by omitting the declaration. Nay more, it is rightly inferred from this tacit consent, that he has concurred in the decision of the one bringing the war, whether he should wish it or not, so that then it is just the same as if the declaration had been by his own act, the purpose certainly failing for which otherwise there was need of the declaration, by virtue of the proof given above. But undoubtedly the case is very rare, that a third party would take upon himself an unpleasant task of that sort, so that it scarcely deserves consideration, and is merely one which is not always to be presumed impossible. Nevertheless, we have desired to mention it, lest we may seem to have omitted anything which may make an announcement impossible.

§ 710.

§ 715. *Whether retaliation is a just cause for omitting an announcement of war*

Retaliation is not a just cause for omitting an announcement of an offensive war, that is, it is not allowable to omit an announcement for the reason that the other party at another time has brought war upon us without an announcement. For the obligation to announce an offensive war is a natural one, from which no one can free himself. But if another does not fulfil a natural obligation, you are not therefore allowed not to fulfil it. Therefore, if the other party at another time has brought war upon you without an announcement, it is not on that account allowable for you to bring war against him also without announcement, and therefore retaliation is not a just cause for omitting an announcement of war.

§ 710.
§ 674, part 3, Jus Nat.
§ 631, part 1, Jus Nat.
§ 639, part 8, Jus Nat.

All retaliation is prohibited by natural law, nor is it allowable between nations, and on this account it has no place in an announcement of war. We have already shown elsewhere at some length that there is no right of retaliation. Since the law of nature prescribes a declaration, it also prohibits an omission of it. The unlawful act of another cannot render an act lawful for you which is unlawful by nature. This conflicts with the immutability of the law of nature and with that of the natural obligation derived therefrom. Every one will praise him who, although he might use what is wrongly called the right of vengeance, in announcing a war, refrains from it, for the manifest reason that retaliation is opposed to those vague notions of men concerning moral matters which nature herself implants in them, and which produce the moral sense, and that it is put forward only as an excuse. Nor do I hesitate to assert that those who use it as an excuse

§ 640, part 8, Jus Nat.
§ 577.
Note, § 640, part 8, Jus Nat.
§ 710.

§ 722, part 1, Jus Nat.

§ 142, part 1, Jus Nat.

are induced to omit the announcement not so much because of the idea of vengeance as for other persuasive reasons.

§ 716. *Of the time when an announcement of war can be made*

§ 710.

An announcement of war can be made by one who has already advanced with his army to the boundaries of the territory of the opposing party. For a war is to be announced with no other purpose than that the opposing party can avoid it by the offer of fair conditions of peace, as shown by virtue of the proof given above. But since delay ought not to be injurious to the one announcing it, since every one ought to avoid loss to himself, as far as possible, and since through fear of war one is induced the more readily to offer conditions by which it may be avoided the more imminent the danger is, it is not to be doubted that an announcement of war can be made by one who has already advanced with his army to the boundaries of the territory of the opposing party.

§ 493, part 2, Jus Nat.

Note, § 632.

War is not announced for the purpose that you may not assail another who is unprepared to resist, as is the practice of one who challenges another to a duel, to which war between nations is wrongly compared. Therefore one ready to make war is not bound to allow delay to the other, that he may enter the contest prepared. This is altogether at variance with the purpose for which war is announced, which is none other than that the opposing party, being apprised of our definite purpose of pursuing our right by force, may offer the conditions by which war may be avoided. Only a just war is allowable by the law of nature; but if an offensive war is just, the defensive war is unjust, and consequently delay need not be allowed one against whom war is declared, that he may become capable of defence.

§ 711.

§ 1111, part 1, Jus Nat.

§ 629.

§ 717. *Of entrance into the territory of another before an announcement of war*

§ 716.

§ 682, part 6, Jus Nat.

Since an announcement can be made, even if any one has already approached with an army to the boundaries of the territory of the opposing party, and since entrance into foreign territory without hostile intent is a matter of harmless utility, and consequently to be referred to the right surviving from the common holding, reserved by nature when other forms of ownership were introduced, it is the same whether you approach with an army to the boundaries of the territory of the opposing party, or enter into the territory itself before announcing war; war can be announced by one who has already entered with an army but without hostile intent.

§ 687, part 6, Jus Nat.

§ 561, part 6, Jus Nat.

Entrance with an army into the territory of another, which is made in a friendly spirit and for the purpose of avoiding war, is not an invasion; but it then begins to be such when done by force. The entrance is not illegal in itself, since the right arises from the obligation of averting loss from the subjects of another, for which purpose of course the declaration is made. In an individual case particular reasons frequently justify this entrance, arising especially from the stubbornness of the one refusing to allow you your right. Nevertheless here, as elsewhere, care must be taken lest, when there is a question simply of right, only persuasive reasons should be considered, for which there is a place allowed only in the execution of a right.

§ 495, part 2, Jus Nat., and
§ 159, part 1, Phil. Pract. Univ.

Note, § 706.

§ 621.

§ 718. *Of the duties of the inhabitants in that case and of the right of one advancing against those who fail therein*

If he who advances into the territory of another with an army before announcing war declares to the inhabitants that he is not coming with hostile intent, nor to inflict violence upon them, but to announce to the ruler of the state the reason for his coming, the inhabitants ought not to set themselves in forceful opposition to him, in fact those may be punished who should dare to do this. For since entrance without hostile intent into the territory of the opposing party, before war is declared, is allowable, no injury is done to the inhabitants. Therefore, there is no reason why it should be allowable to resist him; nay, since no one ought to interfere in any way with another in the exercise of his right, the inhabitants ought not to set themselves in opposition to him. Which was the first point.

§ 717.

§ 975, part 1, Jus Nat.

§ 655, part 2, Jus Nat.

But since ignorance does not excuse those who have been warned, a thing which is self-evident, since the act itself of abstaining from the use of violence removes distrust, as those who wish to oppose by force

§ 717.

§ 859, part 1,
Jus Nat.

§ 1061, part 1,
Jus Nat.

§ 549, part 2,
Jus Nat.

one who is entering violate his right, consequently do him injury, and as every one has the right by nature to punish the one who has harmed him, or done him an injury, it is allowable to punish the one who, according to the hypothesis of the present proposition, dares to inflict violence on him. Which was the second point.

> There is no reason why the opposing party should complain of the entrance into a territory devoid of a guard, when no hostile force is used, before it is understood that the opposing party does not wish to offer fair conditions of peace to the one announcing war, but according to hypothesis wishes to repel force by force. Since, nevertheless, he does not abstain from hostile violence, that it may be possible to repel force by force, but that fair conditions of peace may be offered, it is self-evident that a delay dangerous to himself is not to be allowed by one announcing war.

§ 719. *Of the beginning of warlike operations*

§ 493, part 2,
Jus Nat.

When war is announced and fair conditions of peace are not offered at once, it is allowable to begin warlike operations. For let us suppose that warlike operations are not to begin immediately. Since delay is allowed him against whom the war is brought, he may enter the war better equipped. Therefore, delay is dangerous to the one declaring war. Therefore, since we ought to ward off all loss from ourselves, it is absurd not to begin warlike operations immediately, when, on the announcement of war, fair conditions of peace are not immediately offered.

> Since one must not resort to arms, unless gentler means are tried, it is assumed that the cause for announcing the war is adequately recognized and understood by the one against whom it is announced, so that there is no need of deliberation. For the purpose is simply that he may declare his intention, whether he prefers to allow the right which he has hitherto denied, or to suffer the other party to acquire it by force. But if he should prefer the former, there is no reason why he should not immediately declare the same to the other party, since both the justifying and persuasive reasons are plain to him, or at least are unknown only by his own fault, which he ought to impute to himself, because he has not earlier investigated and considered them,

when he was not ignorant that for that reason it was possible to come to blows. Therefore, if he wishes to devise delays, it is rightly assumed that he intends nothing else than that he may become better equipped to repel force by force, a thing which he has a right to prevent who brings a just war, as will appear more clearly hereafter.

§ 720. *In case of a conditional announcement*

If the war has been conditionally announced, it is allowable to begin war-like operations immediately, when the condition arises. For if a war has been conditionally announced, there is no need of an absolute announce- §709. ment when the condition arises. Therefore, nothing stands in the way of an immediate resort to arms. Therefore, it is allowable to begin warlike operations immediately, when the condition arises.

It is especially advantageous in a war to anticipate rather than be anticipated, and it is of the greatest importance that you should keep the war from your boundaries, and that it should rather be waged in the enemy's territory. It is not to be thought that the law of nature binds us to those things which are opposed to prudence, since it really binds us to observe prudence. §258, part 1, Jus Nat.

§ 721. *How an announcement of war is to be understood*

If the ruler of one state declares war against the ruler of another state, it is understood that a public war has been declared by one entire nation against another. For war is waged between nations, who have the right of war. Therefore, since rulers of a state represent their nation when they §607. have dealings with other nations, and since they have the right which §613. belongs to the people, if the ruler of one state declares war against the ruler of another state, it is just the same as if one nation should announce §39. war against another, and the announcement is made by the right of the people, consequently the war which the ruler of one state declares against the ruler of another state is understood to have been declared by the entire nation against an entire nation.

There is no one who does not voluntarily admit this; for we are all unanimously accustomed to say that war is announced by a nation against a nation, as that the Turks declare war against the Persians, that war exists between the British and the Spaniards, and in the same way the name of the country is taken as the name of the nation and it is said that France is waging war with England, especially do we say in the German idiom, *Franckreich habe Krieg mit Engelland* [France has a war with England]. But here it had to be proved by us that the act of the ruler of the state was to be considered as the act of the whole state, lest it should be thought that what is considered as a right consists in a wrong, as those frequently think who have not been trained in general public law and in the law of nations.

§ 722. *Who enemies are*

Those are called enemies who are at war with each other; in our native vernacular they are called *Feinde* [foes].

§ 626, part 1, Jus Nat.

§ 662, Psych. Emp.

§ 144, Disc. Praelim.

Enemies are different from private foes. For a private foe pursues another with hatred, consequently his mind is inclined to take pleasure from the unhappiness of another. But a just war is not waged in hatred towards the opposing party, but from a sense of right, and one whose war is unjust at least thinks that he has the right, or wishes to seem to others to think so. Nevertheless, by an inaccuracy of speech which the scientific method does not tolerate, it happens that those who are enemies are likewise said to be foes. And in our vernacular the word enemy is confused with the word foe, possibly because our ancestors saw that it could scarcely happen that he who is an enemy should not be likewise a foe, if attention is turned to the licence with which wars are usually carried on even among Christians themselves.

§ 723. *That individual subjects of one belligerent are enemies of the subjects of another*

§ 722.

§ 721.

Since those are enemies who are at war with each other, and since when war is declared by the ruler of one state against the ruler of another, war is understood to have been declared against the entire nation by an entire nation, when war is announced, all the subjects of the one against which it is announced are declared to be enemies of the subjects of the one announcing war, and when there is a resort to arms on either side, the subjects of each are enemies of the subjects of the other.

So if war is made by the Germans with the French, all the Germans are enemies of the French and all the French are enemies of the Germans, even those who are not hostile to each other, but united by the closest bonds of friendship. But these points will appear more clearly below, where we are going to speak of the method of carrying on a war.

Note, § 722.

§ 724. *Enemies of each other remain such wherever they may live*

Since the subjects of each of the belligerents are enemies of the subjects of the other, since moreover they remain such, even if they live or stay in a foreign territory, and therefore much more if they live in an uninhabited place, since they do not become temporary citizens in another place, as they do in a foreign territory; those who are enemies of each other remain such, in whatever part of the world they live.

§ 723.
§ 324.
§ 303.

Not from the place in which any one has a domicile, but from the association by which he is made a member of a state and is one of a nation, does it come about that he becomes an enemy. Therefore, as long as he remains a member of the state, he is also to be considered an enemy. Nor is this prevented because one who lives in a foreign territory, or stays there, takes on the character of a temporary citizen. For he is regarded as a temporary citizen in so far as he is subject to the laws of the place, as long as he lives or stays there, although he retains the rights which belong to him in his own nation, nor through the fact that he becomes subject temporarily to the laws of the place in which he is, is the obligation terminated by which he is bound to his own nation.

§ 303.
§ 300.

Note, § 324.

§ 725. *Whether women and children are in the number of enemies*

Likewise because subjects of one of the belligerents are enemies of the subjects of another, it is self-evident also that in the number of subjects women and children are also included, nay even infants; therefore women also, and children, nay even infants, are in the number of enemies.

§ 715.

Now the question is not whether the same right exists against all who are in the number of enemies; but only what persons are considered among enemies. For in regard to the former, we shall speak in the following chapters, where we are going to discuss law in war.

§ 726. *Of the property of enemies*

§ 723.
§ 725.

Since subjects of one of the belligerents are enemies of the subjects of another and women also and children, nay even infants are in the number of enemies, all of the property which belongs to any subject of one of the belligerent parties with respect to that of the other party is property of an enemy, even that which belongs to women, children, and infants.

§ 607.
§ 722.

§ 289.

War is waged between nations, and therefore one nation is the enemy of another nation. Therefore, since the goods of individuals of one nation taken together with respect to those of another nation are regarded as the goods of that nation, all the property which belongs to the subjects of one of the belligerent parties is considered by the other party as enemy property, that is, as property of an enemy.

§ 727. *When property of the enemy is to be considered as such*

§ 726.

§ 724.

Since all the property of those who are enemies is enemy property with regard to those to whom the people are enemies, since moreover they remain enemies of each other in whatever part of the world they live, the property of enemies remains the property of enemies in whatever place it may be.

§ 722.

Of course it is property of the enemy because it belongs to the enemy. But it continues to belong to the enemy, into whatsoever place it may be transferred, consequently it is the property of an enemy in any place. But because enemies are only enemies to each other who are at war with each other, therefore also their property is property of an enemy only with reference to them. Therefore, if the property of my enemy should be transferred to a peaceful territory, with respect to the inhabitants it is not the property of an enemy, nevertheless it remains such with respect to my enemy.

§ 728. *Of property not belonging to an enemy captured in an enemy's territory*

On the other hand, because the property of my enemy so far as I am concerned is the property of an enemy and remains such wherever it may be, the property of one who is not my enemy so far as I am concerned is not the property of an enemy, even if it should be found in the territory of an enemy. Nevertheless, since it ought to be certain that the property which is in the territory of an enemy does not belong to my enemy, but to another who is not my enemy, and consequently that ought to be proved, property captured within the territory of an enemy is presumed to belong to the enemy, until the contrary shall be proved. The same is understood of merchandise, nay even of persons, who are in an enemy's ship, provided it is navigating the sea.

§ 726.

§ 727.

> Of course, whatever belongs to an enemy is the enemy's, and therefore, what is an enemy's depends upon the person to whom in fact all rights real and personal belong. If then the person shall not be my enemy, neither the corporeal nor the incorporeal property can be enemy property to me, nor can it become enemy property for the reason that it is in an enemy's territory, for the place where things are has no effect on the ownership, nor does it change anything therein. But why property found in the territory of an enemy is to be assumed to belong to an enemy is evident also from this, because otherwise my enemy could present any property at his pleasure as property of some other person, who is not my enemy, if credence had to be given to his bare assertion. Therefore, it is necessary that it be proved, that the truth may prevail over a presumption.

§ 729. *Of those things which are due to my enemy*

The property of my enemy so far as I am concerned is the property of an enemy and remains such wherever it may be, even in friendly territory. This includes incorporeal things and therefore personal rights, which my enemy has. Therefore, those things which are due to my enemy, even if the debtor is not an enemy, are included in the category of enemy's property.

§ 726.

§ 727.

§ 408, part 1, Jus Nat.

For example, let us suppose that Titius, who is not an enemy, owes my enemy three thousand dollars; the right to this debt so far as I am concerned is included in the category of enemy property. Those things which are due to my enemy certainly belong to him, and on this account are properly reckoned among the property of an enemy.

Note, § 728.

§ 730. *Of those who are allied to an enemy*

§§ 106, 150, 151, part 2, Phil. Pract. Univ.

§ 722.

He who allies himself with my enemy, as by sending him troops or subsidies, or by assisting him in war in any manner, is my enemy. For he who allies himself to my enemy, as by sending him troops or subsidies, or by assisting him in any manner, engages in war against me, and therefore becomes a participant in the war. Therefore, since one is an enemy when a war exists between him and me, he who allies himself with my enemy, as by sending troops or subsidies, or by assisting him in war in any manner, is my enemy.

§§ 106 and fol., part 2, Phil. Pract. Univ.

§§ 671 and fol., part 1, Phil. Pract. Univ.

§ 180, part 2, Phil. Pract. Univ.

The things which we have said at length elsewhere of joining in the acts of another are easily applicable to war. Likewise the points which we have proved elsewhere of the imputation of the act of another, which depends upon such joint action, are applicable without difficulty to joint action in war. Nevertheless, since all joint action is not equally harmful, therefore not every one can be judged by the same law. But since it would be too tedious to inquire into every difference which the diversity of cases according to the variety of circumstances increases, it is not allowable for us in the present instance to go into such complications.

§ 731. *Of the property of those who ally themselves with an enemy*

§ 730.

§ 726.

Since he who allies himself with my enemy, as by sending troops or subsidies, or by assisting him in any way, is my enemy, since moreover the property of my enemy so far as I am concerned is the property of an enemy, the property of the one who allies himself with my enemy, as by sending troops or subsidies, or by assisting him in war in any way, so far as I am concerned is the property of an enemy.

There seems to be no need then of showing that under enemy's property are here included all goods generally of the subjects of one who involves himself in war, since that is plain enough by force of previous proofs.

§ 732. Of the right against the persons and property of those who ally themselves with an enemy

Likewise, since he who allies himself with my enemy, as by sending troops or subsidies, or by assisting him in war in any way, is my enemy, § 730. and all his property, so far as I am concerned, is the property of an enemy, whatever is allowable against an enemy or the property of an § 731. enemy, the same is also allowable against them and their property who ally themselves to my enemy in war, as by sending troops or subsidies or by assisting him in any way.

What sort of right this is we shall show below. But here we are assuming the existence of the difference which distinguishes a just from an unjust war. For it is on the basis of this [difference] that we must §§ 617 and fol. decide whether or not a given person may rightly be considered an enemy, or, in case we wish to avoid the question of morality as involved in the concept of enemy, whether or not a given person rightly shows himself hostile to another; since, aside from that question of morality, it matters not which of these two view points you may choose.[15]

§ 733. Of the right of war against one who allies himself to my enemy

Since the same thing is allowable against one who allies himself to my enemy and against his property, as against an enemy and the property of § 732. an enemy, it is allowable to enter his territory with an armed force, and to conduct hostile operations there, or bring war upon him.

This may not be done under the right of retaliation, which we have already proved elsewhere does not exist, a statement which we have Note, § 715.

15. [The last two sentences of this paragraph are involved and obscure in the Latin. A somewhat arbitrary translation has been necessary in order to make the passage intelligible.—Tr.]

§ 974, part 1,
Jus Nat.

Note, § 732.

§ 1116, part 1,
Jus Nat.

§ 1115, part 1,
Jus Nat.

§ 987, part 1,
Jus Nat.

again emphasized above, but by the right of defence against an aggressor. Here also must be understood what we have just now noted; for it is allowable to give aid to one carrying on a just war, but he who does anything for the sake of one who is carrying on an unjust war does a wrong to him on whose side the war is just, and in this respect he is then on an equality with an aggressor.

§ 734. *Whether it is allowable to bring war without announcement against one who allies himself with my enemy*

If war is brought against one who allies himself to my enemy, as by sending troops or subsidies, or assisting him in any other way, there is no need of an announcement. For he who allies himself to my enemy, as by sending troops or subsidies, or by assisting him in any other way, declares by that very fact that he wishes to be a participant in the war carried on against me. If then I bring war against him, it is equivalent to a defensive war. Therefore, since by nature a defensive war is not to be announced, if I bring war upon one who allies himself to my enemy, there is no need of an announcement.

§ 615.

§ 713.

Therefore, much less is there need of an announcement of war, if any one not even when warned is willing to refrain from giving aid to my enemy in war, since it is plain enough that the same act is allowable for me against him which is allowable against an enemy and his property, and that I am allowed to enter his territory with an armed force and conduct hostile operations there, in order to repel force by force.

§ 732.

§ 733.

§ 735. *Of the extension of the announcement of war*

Since war can be brought against one who allies himself with my enemy, as by sending troops or subsidies, or by assisting him in any other way, without an announcement, when war is declared against any one, it is understood to have been declared against all those who ally themselves with him, or who are going to ally themselves with him during the continuance of the war; consequently, since the one announcing a war declares that all the subjects of the one against whom the announcement

§ 734.

is directed are considered as his enemies and enemies of his subjects, §723. when war is declared against any one, they and all their subjects who ally themselves to the enemy of the one announcing, or they who are going to ally themselves during the continuance of the war, are declared to be enemies of the one announcing the war and of his subjects.

He has no just cause of complaint who involves himself in another's war, if war is brought against him by the one against whom he gives aid to another, without a declaration, since he himself is already acting as his enemy, and he knows that he is included in the number of his §730. enemies. Therefore, his territory and all the goods of his subjects are in fact property of an enemy, nor is there need that by an announcement of war they should be so declared. If he has not shrunk from the risk of bringing aid to another in war, he should charge it to himself that he has not thought of that which he knows, or at least could not but know, would possibly result.

§ 736. *If any one should furnish an ally the troops, or subsidies, or other things which he has promised*

If a treaty of war against everybody has already been made, before the present war was thought of, he who sends the promised troops, or subsidies, or assists his ally in any other manner in war, as the treaty demands, is an enemy of the one against whom war is carried on by his ally. For when a treaty of war is made against everybody, since it is made for §655. the purpose of war, the parties mutually promise, or one promises the other, that he will give aid as to whatever has been agreed upon, in a war undertaken against any one. Therefore, since he is my enemy who contrary to my interests sends troops or subsidies to my enemy, or assists him in war in any way, when one makes a treaty of war against everybody §730. with someone, when he is not as yet thinking of a definite war, by that very fact he declares that he will be an enemy of the one who is going to become an enemy to his ally. If then by force of a treaty against everybody already entered into, before there was a thought of the present war, he sends troops, or subsidies, or assists his ally in any other manner in war, he becomes an enemy of the one against whom war is carried on by his ally.

§ 672.

§§ 380, 547.

Undoubtedly he implies that he wishes to be neutral in war, and to give aid to one of the belligerent parties therein; yet he who wishes to be a neutral in war ought not to attach himself to either party, nor to involve himself in the war in any way. But it is no excuse that, since treaties are to be sacredly observed, any one may wish to perform those things at least for his ally, to which he has been bound before there was any thought of the present war, but in other respects be unwilling to involve himself in the war, and prefer to cultivate friendship with the one against whom war is being carried on. For he who makes a treaty of war with another against everybody declares that he wishes to attach himself to his side in every war, consequently also in the present war. Therefore, he cannot be a neutral if he should perform the things promised in the treaty. Of course no one can attach himself to one of the belligerent parties except by bringing aid to him in war in every way. Therefore, one contracting a treaty of war declares by that very act that, if it should happen that his ally becomes involved in war, he

§ 672.

does not wish to be a neutral. If he should wish to be a neutral, an exception would have to be added to the stipulation, that he may be allowed not to give the promised aid, if it should happen not to be to his advantage to involve himself in the war. But no one will contract in this way, since the obligation might be suspended at the will of the one promising, nor would there be any certainty of the performance for the sake of which we bind another to us.

§ 737. *The definition and purpose of the publication of a war*

He is said to publish the war who makes it plain to other sovereign powers and to his subjects that war has been undertaken by him. Therefore, the publication of a war is the indication of it, made by the one who has undertaken the war, to other sovereign powers and to his own subjects. Therefore, it is plain that the publication is made with the purpose that it may be understood both by the rulers of other nations and by the subjects of the one carrying on the war, that he has undertaken a war with this or that nation.

Publication differs from an announcement. For a war is announced to the one against whom we have determined to bring war, that he may understand that we are going to pursue our right against him by force; but war is published for the nations which it does not affect, and for the subjects of the one by whom the war is carried on, in order that they may not be ignorant that we are at war with this or that nation. Therefore, they are different both as regards the subjects to whom the indication is made, and as regards the purpose with which it is made. Therefore, the two acts are quite different, and one of them can occur without the other.

§ 706.

§ 738. *When there is a place for the same*

Since a war is published with the purpose that it may be understood, both by the rulers of other nations and by the subjects of the one carrying on war, that he has undertaken a war with this or that nation, the publication of war has a place both in defensive and in offensive war, and whether it shall have been announced or not.

§ 737.

> Publication of war is not made carelessly; therefore, it ought to be a matter of concern to those to whom the publication is made, that they should learn that he, by whose authority the war is published, has undertaken a war with this or that nation. And hence it is evident what ought to be plainly shown in the publication according to the variety of circumstances.

§ 739. *Of the method of publishing a war*

Since the one publishing a war indicates to those to whom it is published that war has been undertaken by him against this or that nation; since, moreover, we can proclaim anything to another by words expressed orally or in writing; war can be published to rulers of other nations either through ministers, whom any one may have at their court, or by letters sent to them, and to subjects either by criers or by rescripts, nay more, to either by writing expressed in print.

§ 737.

> Since the invention of the art of printing, publication of everything is best made by writing expressed in print, copies of which can be distributed at the courts of princes, and can be procured at a small price and read by subjects and any one else. But publication is usually made

in the royal city by criers. In our native vernacular criers are called *Herolde* [heralds], and are persons who by order of the supreme power orally announce anything in public in solemn form.

§ 740. *Of a manifesto and counter-manifesto in war*

The writing expressed in print by which an offensive war is published is to-day called a manifesto; and that which is opposed to it by the other belligerent party in a defensive war is called the counter-manifesto. We call the former *ein Manifest* [a manifesto] and the latter *ein Gegen-Manifest* [a counter-manifesto]. Each is usually called by the common name of a declaration of war, *eine Kriegs-Declaration*. Since an unjust war is illegal, and whatever is done in it is equally illegal, and since no one wishes to seem to wage war unjustly, that is, without just cause, in manifestos not only is there indicated the fact that war has been undertaken with this or that nation, but also for what reason it has been undertaken, that is, the justifying reasons for war are set forth. But since he on whose side the war is defensive does not wish to seem to wage an unjust war, in the counter-manifesto the justifying reasons set forth in the manifesto are refuted, and if there are any justifying reasons besides, which the defendant can allege in his behalf, they are explained. And since, moreover, through manifestos and counter-manifestos war is published to subjects also of each of the belligerent parties, in them is laid down not only that the subjects of one of the belligerent parties are to consider the subjects of the other as enemies, but also what they ought to do or not to do while the war continues.

§ 1111, part 1, Jus Nat.

§ 1112, part 1, Jus Nat.

§ 1110, part 1, Jus Nat.

§ 621.

§ 738.

We have already said that in the manifestos and counter-manifestos, or declarations of war, justifying reasons for war are to be laid down; the persuasive reasons indeed are to be concealed, since through them one may know whether or not it is to one's advantage to undertake war, and are not to be published, as they are state secrets, and the desire to make them public is opposed to that prudence to which the law of nature binds us. Since war cannot be just on both sides, it is easily evident that cogent justifying reasons cannot be presented to a neutral by each of the belligerent parties. But if indeed the cause of war be doubtful, each party has probable reasons

§ 258, part 1, Jus Nat.

§ 633.

which have the appearance of truth; otherwise the other party puts forward only quasi-justifying reasons. Now justifying reasons are set forth in declarations of war particularly for the sake of foreigners, that they may be able to decide as to the justice of the war; and they are explained for the sake of subjects, that their complaints concerning the undertaking the war may be cut off or at least mollified. But it is self-evident that only for the sake of the latter are the commands and prohibitions inserted, as to what ought to be done, or not done, by them while the war continues.

§§ 624, 625.

§ 741. *Whether declarations of war are laws as regards subjects*

Declarations of war are laws as regards subjects, in so far as definite things are commanded or forbidden in them. For legislative power belongs to the superior, and only members of the state or subjects are bound by laws promulgated by it. Therefore, since a rule, in accordance with which we are bound to direct our actions, is a law, and that is imperative which binds one to do, and prohibitive which binds one not to do, declarations of war are laws as regards subjects, in so far as definite things are commanded or forbidden in them.

§ 813, part 8, Jus Nat.

§§ 965, 967, part 8, Jus Nat.

§ 141, part 8, Jus Nat.

§ 131, part 1, Phil. Pract. Univ.

Since those are enemies who are at war with each other, if war is published to subjects, from that very fact it is then understood that they are enemies of the subjects of the opposing party and the enemy's subjects are also enemies to them, and therefore, in so far as they ought to be enemies the declaration of war has already of itself the force of law as regards subjects; nevertheless, since the ruler is accustomed expressly to enjoin upon his subjects that they are to consider the subjects of the other party as enemies, and that they themselves are enemies to them, and besides he forbids and commands some things in particular, therefore we say that the declaration of war is a law, in so far as definite things are commanded or forbidden in it. Indeed, a declaration of war regarded as such can be said to be a law as regards subjects only in so far as there is contained in it tacit direction that the subjects of the other, with whom there is war, are to be considered as enemies.

§ 163, part 1, Phil. Pract. Univ.

§ 722.

§ 742. *Of those things which are to be avoided in declarations of war*

In declarations of war one must refrain from words and expressions which breathe forth hatred and a desire for vengeance, nor must one use an argument prompted by ill will. For war ought to be carried on without hatred of the opposing party, and therefore of the enemy, and since the mind ought to be a stranger to all desire for vengeance, the desire for vengeance ought to be afar from every war also. Therefore, since belligerents ought not to indulge in hatred and desire for vengeance, it is not allowable in declarations of war to use words and expressions which breathe forth hatred and desire for vengeance. Which was the first point.

Since an argument prompted by ill will cannot be used in a declaration of war, except with the intention of turning the hatred of other nations upon the enemy, but this intention betrays a desire for vengeance, to which the mind of the belligerent ought to be a stranger; in declarations of war one must not use an argument prompted by ill will. Which was the second point.

It is unseemly that learned men, if they do not know how to restrain the tongue, should contend not so much with arguments as with insults, the base offspring of a feeble mind, and that they should give rein to depraved impulses. Therefore, it is much more unseemly for rulers of states, who ought to refer to the glory of their nation the royal acts, in the number of which is also the declaration of war, to imitate the perverse customs of the learned, which they ought not to tolerate in those matters. In declarations of war the facts are to be reviewed and to them are to be applied the principles of the law of nature and nations; a thing which can be done without any harshness of words and without argument prompted by ill will. If any one has not observed the treaty or does things contrary to it, review what has been promised in the treaty, and what the ally has not done, or what he has done to the contrary, refer to that when you appeal to the sanctity of treaties between nations; but far be it from you to call your enemy a breaker of treaties and a traitor, for whom there is nothing so sacred that he does not desecrate it. There is no reason why you should object, that if the facts should be examined closely and the law

§ 1119, part 1, Jus Nat.

§ 722.

§ 948, part 1, Jus Nat., and § 3 h.

§ 1049, Log.

§ 947, part 1, Jus Nat.

§ 948, part 1, Jus Nat., and § 3 h.

§ 51.

§ 284, part 8, Jus Nat., and § 740 h.

§ 650, part 8, Jus Nat.

§ 740.

applied to them, then it is a proper inference on the part of others that he is a breaker of treaties and a traitor, that he has no regard for his word, and that for him there is nothing so sacred that he does not desecrate it. And you cannot argue that it is just the same whether you give reasons to your reader by which your point is proved or call by its right name the defect existing in the enemy, nor is a wrong done him by speaking the truth, because otherwise you would have to refrain from the enumeration of his acts. You are, indeed, very greatly mistaken if those things seem to you to be the same. For by a declaration of war nothing is aimed at other than that it may be made plain to others for what reason war has been undertaken by you. But for this it is sufficient that the acts and the principles of the law of nature and nations applicable to them are understood by others, and it is not required that you should set forth your opinion of the vices of your enemy. If then you do this, it is not done with the intention of instructing others, but of harming your enemy, or detracting from his reputation, and can proceed from nothing else than from hatred towards the enemy and from desire for vengeance and other perverse impulses akin thereto. For that which is attributable to impulse and a feeling of aversion, upon which the passions rest, has not the least connexion with reason. The things which we have already said are readily applicable also to an argument prompted by ill will, inasmuch as it is diametrically opposed to the purpose with which a declaration of war ought to be made. But if you urge further, that it can happen that one may characterize by its own proper name that which he recognizes is in accord with the truth, or at least seems to himself to so recognize, even if it is inspired by no hatred of the enemy, and no desire for vengeance, and is not prompted by other depraved passions, the answer is easy indeed. Let us for the moment concede that these things are so, which, nevertheless, from what has just been said, it is plain enough cannot be conceded; still no one will be able to deny, with any appearance of truth, that rulers of states ought to act the part of a good man, since this obligation binds all in general; but it is the duty of a good man to avoid even those things which he might legally do, if it is to be feared that he may suggest to anybody a suspicion hostile to his good name. Therefore, those care little for the reputation of the ruler of a state, who have the task of drawing up

§§ 737, 740.

§ 967, part 5, Jus Nat.

§ 968, part 5, Jus Nat.

a declaration of war, if they are still so far devoid of self-restraint that they do not know how to moderate their language.

§ 743. *Of love and affection for enemies*

§ 617, part 1,
Jus Nat.
§ 618, part 1,
Jus Nat.
§ 722.
§ 1119, part 1,
Jus Nat.
We ought to love and cherish an enemy as ourselves. For every man is bound to love and cherish every other man as himself. Therefore, since he is your enemy who is at war with you, and since war can be waged without hatred toward him, consequently this does not stand in the way of love; we ought to love and cherish an enemy as ourselves.

§ 623, part 1,
Jus Nat.

§§ 618, 619,
part 1, Jus Nat.

§ 142, part 1,
Phil. Pract.
Univ.

§ 632, part 1,
Jus Nat.
If war were to interfere with love and affection to enemies, which is enjoined upon us without any restriction, since a natural obligation is absolutely unchangeable, war would never be allowable. A law of nature cannot make laws for that without which you cannot satisfy an obligation of nature. But if love and affection toward an enemy seems a hard doctrine to some, they confound a public enemy with a private foe, and consequently they think that love for private enemies is wrong, as they think those deserve hatred. But how far they are from the truth is evident from what we have proved elsewhere.

§ 744. *Of a friendly feeling toward an enemy*

§ 743.

§ 625, part 1,
Jus Nat.

§ 633, part 1,
Jus Nat.
Since we ought to love and cherish enemies as ourselves, and since we are also friendly toward the one whom we love, we ought also to be friends of our enemies; and since we ought also to be friendly to those who are private foes, it is not allowable to have hostile feeling toward a public enemy, however much he be a foe to us.

Note, § 722.
We have already suggested above that a public enemy differs from a private foe, nor is it necessary that he who is a public enemy should likewise be a private foe. But here it had to be shown that the decision is not with us, as to whether we should wish to be friendly or hostile to public enemies. I am not indeed ignorant that very many will be opposed to this, especially in this profane age, in which religion and honesty are brought into contempt, nay are considered a mockery, and these are likely to ridicule the love of public enemies and a friendly feeling toward them. But we are not affected by the ridicule of

those who are of evil disposition, for whom the approach to the secrets of truth is closed up, mindful of that statement of Epictetus, that if any one has determined to be a philosopher, he must understand that he will be mocked by the multitude. We proclaim the truth, we do not write to please those who have a mind alien to the truth. But would that love of enemies might drive its roots deep into the hearts of all belligerents. For then only might it be hoped that wars would be waged with the religious scruples with which they ought to be waged, by those means which we shall point out in the following chapter, nor would the law of war, of itself deadly enough to nations, be turned to hostile licence, nor would the perils of war become limitless.

§ 745. *Of the right of conscription of soldiers*

Those who have the right of war have also the right of conscription of soldiers. It is evident that a public war cannot be carried on without soldiers. Therefore, if any one has the right of war, he also has the right of conscription of soldiers. $ 610.

> The right of conscription of soldiers is so closely connected with the right of war that the latter could not exist without the former. But since every right is open to abuse, so also the right of conscription of soldiers can become an abuse. Therefore, since the right of war has already been made plain by us, it is not alien to our purpose to explain also the right of conscription of soldiers.

§ 746. *To whom it belongs*

Since those who have the right of war have also the right of conscription of soldiers, since moreover nations have the right of war, nations therefore have the right of conscription of soldiers; consequently if a nation transfers the right of war to the ruler of the state, it transfers to him also the right of conscription of soldiers, and therefore he has the right of conscription of soldiers. But since a people, when it transfers the power, can restrain the exercise thereof according to certain fundamental laws, since, moreover, the ruler of a state has no greater right than the people wished to transfer to him; if the right of conscription of soldiers shall have been restricted by the fundamental laws, he can exercise the

§ 745.

§ 613.

§§ 36, 77, part 8, Jus Nat.

§ 43, part 8, Jus Nat.

right in no other way than in accordance with them, consequently in the conscription of soldiers he can do nothing which is opposed to the fundamental laws.

If there are no fundamental laws concerning the conscription of soldiers, the law of nature alone rules this act; for this reason we must prove here what is in harmony with it and what is not in harmony with it.

§ 747. *Whether this is a sovereign right*

§ 745.

§ 943, part 8, Jus Nat.

Since he who has the right of war has also the right of conscription of soldiers, consequently since the right of conscription of soldiers is most closely connected with the right of war, and since the right of war belongs among sovereign rights, the right of conscription of soldiers belongs among sovereign rights.

§ 207, part 8, Jus Nat.

§ 60, part 8, Jus Nat.

§ 9, part 8, Jus Nat.

§ 207, part 8, Jus Nat.

The idea itself of sovereign rights suggests the same thing. For since civil sovereignty consists in the right to determine those things which are required to promote the public good, and since for this it is further required that citizens should be safe from injury by others and from the external violence of enemies, and that the state itself should be sufficiently powerful to resist this, but since it is self-evident that this cannot possibly be accomplished without soldiers, it is manifest that the right of conscription of soldiers belongs to the exercise of civil sovereignty, and therefore to sovereign rights.

§ 748. *How the ruler of the state ought to exercise the right of conscription of soldiers*

§ 77, part 8, Jus Nat.

If the right of conscription of soldiers shall have been determined by no fundamental law, the ruler of the state can exercise it as it seems best, nevertheless he ought so to exercise it that the public good may not be interfered with, or that it may receive no harm therefrom. For if the right of conscription of soldiers shall have been determined by no fundamental law of the state, since nothing has been enjoined upon the ruler of the state which he is bound to observe in the conscription of soldiers, it has been left to his judgement as to how the same is to be exercised, consequently he can exercise it as it seems best to him. Which was the first point.

But since the civil sovereignty, consequently also the right of conscription of soldiers, ought to be so exercised that the public good may be promoted, as far as that is possible, and since every ruler of a state, on whatever condition the sovereignty has been transferred to him, is bound to do those things which are required to promote the public good, and not to do those things which are opposed to it, if the right of conscription of soldiers shall have been determined by no fundamental law, he ought so to exercise it that the public good may not be interfered with or that it may receive no harm therefrom. Which was the second point.

§ 747 h, and
§ 207, part 8,
Jus Nat.

§ 809, part 8,
Jus Nat.

§ 84, part 8,
Jus Nat.

> The liberty to exercise the civil sovereignty is not to be confused with licence in exercising the same. For since the civil sovereignty is to be determined from the purpose of the state, nor is it understood to have been transferred to the ruler of the state, on whatever condition it may have been transferred, for any other purpose than that it should be exercised for the benefit of the state, the liberty to exercise the sovereignty of the state by no means terminates the obligation of the ruler of the state arising therefrom, and on this account it is proper at least for him to decide what may be for the advantage of the state, from the purpose of which a reason is to be sought for that which is decreed.

§§ 30, 31, part 8,
Jus Nat.

§ 88, part 8,
Jus Nat.

§ 749. *What soldiers are to be enrolled*

In case of extreme necessity all subjects who are able to serve are bound to perform military services; aside from this case those are not to be enrolled as soldiers who are able to perform other useful and necessary services to the state and to contribute to the expenses of war. For in a state individuals are bound to contribute to the whole those things which they can contribute to the common good of the state, consequently even their services for defending the state against the violence of enemies. If, therefore, necessity should demand that every one of the subjects in general should come under arms; in this case of extreme necessity all who can are bound to perform military services. Which was the first point.

But since the common good of the state, to which individuals ought to contribute what they can, consists not only in this, that the state should

§ 28, part 8,
Jus Nat.

§ 9, part 8,
Jus Nat.

§ 209, part 1,
Phil. Pract. Univ.

§ 19, part 8,
Jus Nat.

be defended against the external force of enemies, but it is also required for it, that the state should abound in those things which contribute to the necessity of life, its advantage and pleasure, and that provision should be made for the happiness of individuals and that every one should be safe from the injury of others, and on this account not all can perform the same service for the state, but one ought to do one thing, another do another; so all in general are not bound to perform military services, unless there shall have been extreme need, as proved above. Therefore, those who can perform useful and necessary services to the state other than military services, and, since the war imposes no slight expenses, to be paid by the state as a whole, those who are able to contribute thereto are not to be enrolled as soldiers. Which was the second point.

§ 9, part 8, Jus Nat.

§ 775, part 8, Jus Nat.

That the state may be safe and prosperous, not only has it need of soldiers, but also of very many others, who follow different kinds of lives, as is not only plainly taught by experience but as is abundantly evident *a priori* from those things which we have proved at length in the eighth part of "The Law of Nature" concerning the constitution of the state. Just as in the human body all the members have not the same function, but each one contributes to the preservation of the body that for which it is best adapted; so also in a state, which is comparable to the human body, there are diverse functions, necessary to its preservation and safety, which the members of the state are bound to share with each other. Since it is for a ruler to take care that those may not be wanting who are needed for attaining this or that particular purpose, he ought undoubtedly to see to it that those are not compelled to bear arms who can perform another necessary and useful service for the state, especially if they excel in that walk in life which they follow, but that, if no special necessity presses, those should be set aside for soldiers who, either because of want, or carelessness, or lack of skill, do not make themselves useful to the state in that walk in life which they follow. If these things should be considered, it will not be difficult to determine how the ruler may properly exercise the right of conscription of soldiers, and when he abuses it; of course persuasive reasons alone do not make legal a method of conscription of soldiers, which does not observe the law. Skill devoid of the protection of law is not skill, but is to be considered as abuse.

§ 399, part 8, Jus Nat.

§ 750. *Whether soldiers are to be enrolled without their consent*

No one is to be enrolled as a soldier without his consent, unless necessity demands it. For all are not bound generally to perform military services for the state except in case of extreme necessity, and, aside from this, one is not to be enrolled as a soldier who is willing and able to perform other useful and necessary services to the state, and is able to contribute to the expenses of war. If then necessity should not demand that the ruler using his supreme power should compel the unwilling to follow a military career, no one is to be enrolled as a soldier without his consent.

§ 749.

§ 114, part 2, Jus Nat.

§ 116, part 8, Jus Nat.

The enrolling of soldiers unwilling to serve certainly belongs to the eminent power of the ruler of the state, since the liberty of individuals in a state, as regards those actions which tend to promote the public good, should not be restricted beyond that which the purpose of the state demands. If then those should not be lacking who voluntarily prefer to follow a military career rather than perform other services for the state, there is no reason why the unwilling should be compelled to bear arms. But since it is the duty of the ruler to determine the number of those in every walk of life who are to be allowed to follow that career, and to see to it that men who are fitted for the same may not be lacking, it is undoubtedly necessary that those who for any reason are found to be unsuited to the pursuit in life which they ought to follow should be set aside for a military career rather than others. If then these should be unwilling to be enrolled as soldiers, necessity undoubtedly demands that they should be enrolled, though unwilling. And so it comes about that those may make themselves useful to the state who otherwise were not likely to become useful to it. This is in harmony with the right of the whole over individuals, consequently the right belongs to the civil sovereignty to use coercion on those who are unwilling to perform their duty, or who show themselves negligent in performance, that they may perform, that is, that they may make themselves useful to the state. But do not persuade yourself, since licence is distinguishable from liberty in the exercise of the right of conscription of soldiers, that by that fact the right of the ruler is diminished. Sovereignty embraces many and varied rights. Therefore, one right ought not to be so exercised that it may infringe

§§ 33, 47, part 8, Jus Nat.

§ 401, part 8, Jus Nat.

§ 399, part 8, Jus Nat.

§ 32, part 8, Jus Nat.

§ 29, part 8, Jus Nat.

§ 28, part 8, Jus Nat.

upon another right. This is guarded against only by the proper use of a right, not by its abuse. For it is certain that all sorts of confusion arise, as soon as you depart from a right use of law, which the purpose of the state determines, and the public safety, the supreme law of the state, demands. All things in a state are connected one with the other, and the purpose of the state, for the sake of which men entered into the state, makes this connexion. Whatever therefore is in it, it is not to be considered in itself, but in its relation to other things which tend to accomplish the purpose of the state. The state cannot be perfect in its details, nor do just complaints of citizens cease, unless that should be observed in the government of the state. Therefore, it is of the greatest importance that nothing be done without the full purpose in view; they will understand this well enough who are endowed with the keenness of intellect which is needed for managing the state rightly and properly.

§ 30, part 8, Jus Nat.

§ 86, part 8, Jus Nat.

§ 88, part 8, Jus Nat.

§ 4, part 8, Jus Nat.

§ 751. *Who are not bound to service in wars*

He who is not suited for service in wars, is not bound thereto. For it is impossible for one to enter into service in wars, who is not suited thereto, as is self-evident. Therefore, since no one is bound to do that which is impossible, he who is not suited for service in wars, is not bound thereto.

§ 209, part 1, Phil. Pract. Univ.

Every obligation, which is a form of moral necessity, assumes a physical possibility of performance. If then any one is not able to bear arms, nature bars him from service in wars, and therefore he cannot bind himself thereto, nor can he be bound by the law of nature.

§ 752. *Who those persons are*

Because those are not bound to service in wars who are not suited thereto, infants, children, old men, and other feeble persons are not bound thereto, likewise those very cowardly in military matters, and those who have any other defects of spirit which interfere with the use of arms.

§ 751.

Nature does not keep women from service in wars, and they, as experience proves, are not incapacitated for it because of their sex; for instances are not lacking of women who have even openly fought in war, or concealing their sex have associated themselves with companies of men. Likewise it is a rule of civil law, if slaves are kept out of war, as was formerly the case at Rome; for it did not always seem wise for that treacherous body of men to be trained to arms. There is also no natural reason why clergymen should be restrained from service in war.

§ 753. *Of enrolling soldiers in foreign territory*

No one is allowed to enrol soldiers in a foreign territory without the consent of the ruler, and if indeed it should be allowed by him, only those who are willing may be enrolled. For in a foreign territory no one can claim any right for himself, nor is the ruler of the state bound to allow § 293. subjects to depart, whose aid he needs for defending the state. Therefore, no one is allowed to enrol soldiers in a foreign territory without the con- § 406, part 8, sent of the ruler. Which was the first point. Jus Nat.

But since any one can depart from the state with the consent of the § 407, part 8, ruler, nevertheless since by virtue of the obligation by which the whole § 28, part 8, is bound to individuals, one cannot be driven from the state except for Jus Nat. the commission of a crime; the ruler can indeed allow foreigners to enrol §§ 589, 595, soldiers in their territory, but only under this condition, that they may part 8, Jus Nat. enrol only those who are willing. Which was the second point.

The stipulation between the individuals and the whole, by which the state has been established and to which assent also as many as § 4, part 8, afterwards associate themselves with the state, carries with it a mutual Jus Nat. obligation, namely, the obligation on the part of the individuals not to depart from the state, without the express or tacit consent of the corporate body, consequently of the one who has the right of the corporate body, and the obligation on the part of the corporate body that no citizen is to be driven from the state without his consent. This stipulation ought to be observed by the ruler of the state, to whom, along with the right of the corporate body or people, its obligation also has passed over. Neither party can free itself from its obligation, § 674, part 3, consequently can do nothing which is opposed to it, although either Jus Nat. party can give up its right corresponding to the obligation of the other § 117, part 8, party, by which act that obligation is extinguished. Therefore, when Jus Nat. a ruler allows a foreigner to enrol soldiers in his territory, this permis- § 97, part 3, sion includes a conditional surrender of the right of the corporate Jus Nat. body over the individuals, namely, that they should be free to depart from the state either permanently or temporarily, as may seem best to them, if they should so desire. For liberty to depart does not include the obligation of not returning, as in case of banishment.

§ 754. *Whether one enlisting soldiers in a foreign territory without the consent of the ruler does a wrong*

§ 753.

§ 859, part 1,
Jus Nat.

§ 581, part 8,
Jus Nat.
§ 7, part 8,
Jus Nat.

§ 301.

Since no one is allowed to enrol soldiers in a foreign territory without the consent of the ruler, if any one dares to enlist soldiers, he violates the law of that nation, and therefore he does a wrong to the other; and since this wrong is a crime committed by a foreigner, since, moreover, foreigners committing an offence in alien territory are to be punished in accordance with the laws of the place, if a foreigner dares to enlist soldiers in a foreign territory without the consent of the ruler, he can be arrested and punished.

He who enlists soldiers in foreign territory without the consent of the ruler or without obtaining his permission, does it either without the knowledge of his own ruler or with his order or tacit approval. In the former case an offence is committed by the one who enlists the soldier, but there is no wrong on the part of the one whose subject he is; but in the latter case, since he whose subject enlists the soldier concurs in his offence, the law of nations is violated by him, and the wrong done by him is to be distinguished from the offence which the one enlisting the soldier commits. Frequently persuasive reasons suggest that the wrong be concealed, and the offence of the one enlisting the soldier be punished so much more severely, that others may learn

wisdom from his misfortune; for the right of punishment is limitless, the limits to it being determined only from existing circumstances, by which one must determine how much punishment may be sufficient

to avert the danger of injury in the future. Therefore, since even capital punishment may be allowed, if crimes cannot be checked without it, it is not to be doubted that those can be punished by a capital

penalty who enlist soldiers in foreign territory without obtaining the permission of the ruler. It is altogether opposed to public security that

a foreigner should enter alien territory and enrol soldiers there as he pleases, or should carry off citizens either directly by secret violence or by false inducements. Therefore, it would seem neither unjust nor harsh, if this crime should be prevented by hanging, as has frequently been known to happen.

§ 603, part 8, Jus Nat.

§ 755. *What kidnapping is*

Kidnapping is defined as the abduction of a person who is subject to the power of some other person. Therefore, since he abducts a person who fraudulently takes him from the control of the one to whom he is subject and asserts that he has some right over him, and since the taking away of the property of another, that is of property subject to the ownership of another, done without the knowledge and consent of the owner, in order to make it one's own, is theft; the act by which kidnapping is accomplished is equivalent to the act of theft, and therefore is rightly considered the theft of persons.

§ 146, part 2, Jus Nat.

§ 498, part 2, Jus Nat.

Kidnapping and theft certainly are of the same genus and differ only in species, a difference which depends upon the object on which the offence is committed. In kidnapping the right, which another has over a man, is taken from him, but in theft, the right which he has in a thing. In the former case the offender asserts a right over a person which does not belong to him, but in the latter a right in a thing. Therefore, by the authors who treat of crimes, the theft of a person, which is called kidnapping, is properly included among the species of theft. Nothing is thereby asserted which is not in harmony with the concepts of genera and species, and in harmony with the method by which the concept of genus is formed, if the concepts of species are given, and on the other hand, that by which the concepts of species are formed, if the concept of genus is given. Nor would it be difficult to apply the definition of kidnapping, which we have given, to examples of the texts of the Civil Law, except that such prolixity would not be in accord with our present plan, and that, from what follows, it would be plain enough that these examples are not out of harmony with that definition.

§§ 236 and fol., Ontol.

§§ 711, 712, Ontol.

§ 756. *Against what persons kidnapping is committed*

Since kidnapping is committed, if any one abducts a person subject to the power of some other person, and so treacherously takes him from

§ 755.
§ 1081, part 7,
Jus Nat.
§ 661, part 7,
Jus Nat.
§§ 306, 428,
part 7, Jus Nat.
§ 141, part 8,
Jus Nat.
§ 114, part 8,
Jus Nat.

his power, and asserts that he has some right over him, and since slaves are subject to the power of the master, children to the power of their parents, a wife to the power of her husband, and subjects in a state to the power of the ruler, including his eminent power; he is guilty of kidnapping who sells the stolen slave of another, or even knowingly buys him, or persuades him to escape from his master and conceals him; he who steals another's children and holds them in slavery as his own, or to be purchased at a set price by the parents, or for any other dishonourable purpose; he who steals another's wife, for a dishonourable purpose; he who steals another's subjects, in order to reduce them to slavery, or to compel them to serve in wars.

§ Criminal.
pt. 2, qu. 83,
no. 91, f. 363.

It has pleased us to cite these examples of kidnapping, that a decision may be the easier in other cases where kidnapping has occurred. The example cited by Carpzov[16] proves that a case is possible in which children are stolen for the purpose of getting a ransom. So undoubtedly it is kidnapping, if any one steals a wife from a husband that he himself may marry her, or where pandering is allowed, as it is understood is the case among some nations, for example, the Chinese, that he may make money from the use of her body, or be paid by another who wishes to take her away and enter into a marriage contract with her. How else than kidnapping may you classify a seizure by one carrying away by force a chaste woman for immoral purposes or even for the purposes of marriage, or carrying away a daughter without the consent of her parents, because they are unwilling to approve of her marriage.

§ 757. *Of those who force stolen subjects of others to perform services in wars*

Those who force the subjects of others, who have been carried away by treachery, to perform services in wars, infringe upon the eminent power of the one whose subjects they are. For eminent power belongs to the ruler in a state, by virtue of which in case of necessity he can dispose of

§ 114, part 8,
Jus Nat.

16. Benedict Carpzov, *Practica nova rerum criminalium imperialis Saxonica* (Leipzig, 1723), pt. II, quaestio 83, no. 91. The case described by Carpzov is on p. 240 in that edition.

the person of a citizen for the public good, consequently he can enrol him as a soldier even though he is unwilling. If then any one treacherously captures foreign subjects, over whom it is self-evident that he has no right, and forces them to perform services in the wars, consequently enrols them as soldiers without their consent, he assumes for himself the eminent power of the one whose subjects they are, and takes it from him. Therefore, since he violates the right of another who takes it from him and claims it himself, he who treacherously captures foreign subjects and forces them to perform services in the wars, infringes upon the eminent power of the one whose subjects they are.

§ 750.

§ 610.

§ 239, part 1, Phil. Pract. Univ.

Since the right belongs to every nation not to allow any other one to take from it any right, and to punish another nation which injures it, it cannot seem harsh that a foreigner should be punished by hanging, who enrols soldiers in an alien territory without its consent, especially, if a foreigner as a private individual, which is presumed in a doubtful case, should have done that of his own accord, since he does not hesitate to deprive the ruler of the state of what is easily his most important sovereign right, especially when milder measures for avoiding the risk are not sufficient.

§ 267.

§ 272.

Note, § 754.

§ 747 h, and § 114, part 8, Jus Nat.

§ 1065, part 1, Jus Nat.

§ 758. *Whether a wrong is done to the nation*

Since those who compel the subjects of others, who have been carried away by treachery, to perform services in war infringe upon the eminent power of the one whose subjects they are, and since a wrong consists in the violation of the right of another, those who compel the subjects of others, who have been carried away by treachery, to perform services in war do a wrong to him whose subjects they are, consequently since the right which is violated is a right of the people transferred to the ruler of the state, they do this to the nation itself, and therefore if they do it by the order or permission of their ruler, he himself does the wrong, but the wrong is understood to have been done by a nation to a nation.

§ 757.

§ 859, part 1, Jus Nat.

§ 42, part 8, Jus Nat., and § 39 h.

§§ 654, 675, part 1, Phil. Pract. Univ.

They do not realize the extent of the wrong, who do not grasp the concept of sovereign rights and especially that of eminent power, or at least they do not realize it with sufficient distinctness, nor do they consider how serious the violation of a sovereign right by a foreigner may be. For although the ruler of a state has no right against a foreigner, nevertheless on that account the foreigner may not violate, at pleasure, the right belonging to the ruler of the state as such; otherwise, of course, it would have to be granted that any one who is not subject to the right of another can do what he pleases contrary to the right of the other. But every one sees how absurd this would be, inasmuch as it is diametrically opposed to the law of nature, unless one is labouring under dense ignorance of the whole law of nature, and has given up the common understanding of that which one is unwilling to have done to him by another. And for this reason it is not presumed of the ruler of the state that the carrying away of the subjects of another for services in war is done with his consent, unless his desire should be so plain that the truth overcomes the presumption. But although the kidnapping should be committed with his consent by those to whom it was entrusted to enlist soldiers; nevertheless punishment is justly imposed upon them, since one is not bound to obey a ruler who commands what is contrary to the law of nature, nor does an evil deed cease to be such for the reason that it is done by the order of a ruler, nor does illegal obedience take from another a right gained because of the wrongful act.

§ 910, part 1, Jus Nat.

§ 1044, part 8, Jus Nat.

§ 759. *When kidnapping for services in war is a justifying reason for war*

Since the ruler of a state does a wrong to another nation, if by his order or permission kidnapping is committed for the purpose of services in war, and since a wrong done is a just cause of war, and since those are justifying reasons for a war which are derived from a right of war, kidnapping for the purpose of services in war, committed by the order or permission of the ruler of the state, is to be counted among the justifying reasons for war.

§ 758.
§ 617.
§ 621.

Although, indeed, it may not be wise to rush to arms immediately, on account of kidnapping for the purpose of services in war, committed by the order or permission of the supreme power, nevertheless in declarations of war it can be included among the justifying reasons. Nor does it make any difference, however severe a punishment has been inflicted on the kidnappers; for they have paid the proper penalty for a wrong done by themselves, but satisfaction has not yet been given for the wrong to the supreme power.

§ 760. *What a stipend is*

A stipend is defined as the money which is paid to soldiers and their officers for their support, or the wages which are paid for military labour, or services in wars. Nevertheless this does not constitute the entire stipend, since to it may also be charged clothing and personal entertainment, and immunities from all the personal burdens to which subjects are bound to contribute.

§ 761. *Of the payment of the stipend*

Since stipends are paid to soldiers and their officers for their support, moreover since it is evident that he who devotes himself to military service can gain nothing in any other way, stipends are to be exactly paid to soldiers. §760.

> Nothing ought to be of more importance to sovereign powers than that stipends should be exactly paid, lest by their fault soldiers may cause losses to others, and by necessity be led to thefts, robberies and cheating; for begging is not becoming to a soldier, whom the supreme power is bound to support, nor ought he to waste away his body with hunger, whom strength of body ought to grace. Therefore it is to the reproach of the supreme power if the stipends are not carefully paid.

§ 762. *Of the personal lodging of soldiers*

Lodging is due to soldiers, and individual possessors of houses are bound to provide lodging for them according to the measure of their abilities. It is self-evident that soldiers as well as other men need a suitable dwelling, wherever they are. Therefore, since it is not enough to provide for their apparel by furnishing clothes and for their food by paying their wages, §760. they must then also be received into the houses of others and the necessities for their dwelling must be furnished them, and therefore lodging is due to them. Which was the first point.

But indeed to provide lodging for soldiers, that they may either spend the night there in transit or dwell in them, when they live in any place, and may have the use of things necessary for their dwelling, is undoubtedly a burden to the possessors of the houses, who are bound to furnish these things for nothing, as proved above. Therefore, since the burdens of state are to be borne by all, since, moreover, individuals ought to contribute to those things according to the measure of their abilities, individual possessors of houses are bound to receive soldiers in military hospitality. Which was the second point.

§ 755, part 8, Jus Nat.

§ 777, part 8, Jus Nat.

It is known more than well enough to-day that these lodgings for soldiers, which are included in public duties and are equivalent to a tax, are quite a heavy burden, especially if the soldier has stayed permanently or passed through often. Those feel this particularly, who before were free from it. And since burdens diminish the values of immovable property, it is not remarkable that, when these lodgings are permanent, the value of buildings is greatly diminished, not without much loss to those who bought them, when that burden was not imposed upon them. And for this reason in many places in which soldiers are permanently quartered, small buildings are erected at public expense, as dwellings for the soldiers; a thing which undoubtedly ought to be done, if possible.

§ 930, part 8, Jus Nat.

§ 931, part 8, Jus Nat.

§ 932, part 8, Jus Nat.

§ 763. The duty of a ruler in regard to the lodging of soldiers

§762.

Since individual possessors of houses are bound to provide lodging for soldiers, and as those lodgings are quite a heavy burden as such, careful provision must be made, that they may not become too burdensome because of the misconduct of the soldiers, nor more expensive than necessary.

It is fitting that this be a matter of special care on the part of the ruler, which he is bound to exercise in imposing taxes and public burdens, among which lodgings for soldiers belong. We have already suggested before, that in administering the state no definite course is to be established in regard to any one class of public affairs, except in relation to everything else, since all things ought to be directed to the same end, for which states have been established, just as God

§ 932, part 8, Jus Nat.

§ 930, part 8, Jus Nat.

decides none of those things which occur in the world without regard to anything else, but in relation to the whole universe. A state is ruled with very little wisdom, if in every class of affairs and in each class every particular affair is considered absolutely without any regard at all being given to other things.

Note, § 750.

§ 4, part 8, Jus Nat.

§ 510, part 1, Theol. Nat.

§ 678, Psych. Rat.

§ 764. To whom immunity from lodgings for soldiers is to be allowed

Immunity from lodgings for soldiers can be allowed to persons to whom that can be counted as a part of their salary, or as a reward for services to the state. Immunity from having to provide hospitality to soldiers is a privilege. Therefore, since privileges ought not to be given except for the sake of the public good, consequently since care should be taken that they should not tend to the prejudice of others, immunities from hospitalities to soldiers are not to be allowed in such a way that the other possessors of houses will be burdened too much. It is therefore necessary that there should be a reason, determined from the proper administration of the state, why that should be allowed to certain persons. Therefore, since salaries are to be so arranged that they can support those who perform public duties, and, if in course of time prices of goods should be greatly increased, they are to be increased in proportion to the increase in prices, and since furthermore the ruler of the state can charge the gain or advantage from privileges granted in consideration of office as a part of salary, immunity from having to provide lodgings to soldiers can be granted to persons for whom that can be considered as a part of their salary. Which was the first point.

§ 762 h, and § 853, part 8, Jus Nat.

§ 872, part 8, Jus Nat.

§ 907, part 8, Jus Nat.

§ 908, part 8, Jus Nat.

§ 906, part 8, Jus Nat.

A ruler ought to confer a privilege on parents for noteworthy services to the state, likewise on children or kinsmen, and therefore much more on those deserving well in themselves, consequently since this is done with no other purpose than that others also may be induced to deserve well, those privileges have the character of rewards, by which citizens are persuaded to deserve well of the state. Therefore, since immunity from providing lodgings to soldiers, to which otherwise every possessor of a house is bound, is a special privilege, it is not to be doubted that it can be counted as a reward for services to the state, and consequently, by force

§ 659, part 8, Jus Nat.

§§ 295, 296, part 1, Phil. Pract. Univ.

of those things which have been proved, it can be granted to the persons
for whom it can be considered a reward for services to the state. Which
was the second point.

It depends indeed upon the will of the ruler, to whom he may
wish to give a privilege; since nevertheless he cannot wish without a
motive, and since privileges ought not to be given, except for some
public good, it is not a matter of indifference what motive one uses.
It must be derived from the public good; a thing which it is quite
plain is done, if the advantage derived from the privilege is counted
either as a part of a salary or as a reward for services to the state.
We have shown elsewhere, that no one can be bound by civil law
to perform noble deeds in behalf of the state, except by conferring
civil dignities, which ought to be rewards for striking merits, to be
conferred therefore only on the well deserving, in order of course that
they themselves may be further stimulated to deserving well and that
others may be stimulated by their example. But since immunity from
providing lodgings for soldiers is to be granted to persons for whom
this can be counted as a reward for services to the state, and since this
seems no less to serve, in order to bind those who can deserve well
of the state, to deserve well thereof, civil dignities do not seem to be
the only means of binding one to a performance of noble deeds for
the state. But we have indeed already answered this doubt, since the
general statements there may easily be applied to the present case.
But it must be understood besides that although civil obligation may
be created by rewards, nevertheless those are not always given with
the purpose that those receiving them may be bound to act, but also
with the intention of rewarding them. And therefore also immunity
from providing lodgings for soldiers is given by way of reward, since
it is given as a reward for services to the state, and since it must not be
readily granted, lest others may be too heavily burdened, this concession is not properly fitted to binding citizens to serve the state well
and nobly, especially because anything noble is hardly to be expected
from those who are influenced by hope of gain, not by desire for glory.
Gifts by way of recompense are meant rather for past service than to
stimulate service in the future, especially for service of the sort which
is continuous. If you should properly consider all these things, I do
not doubt that you will recognize that there exists no other way in

§ 762.

§ 21, part 4,
Jus Nat.

§856, part 8,
Jus Nat.

§ 889, Psych.
Emp.

§ 872, part 8,
Jus Nat.

§ 771, part 8,
Jus Nat.

§ 768, part 8,
Jus Nat.

§ 766, part 8,
Jus Nat.

§ 298, part 1,
Phil. Pract.
Univ.

Note, § 771,
part 8, Jus Nat.

§ 298, part 1,
Phil. Pract.
Univ.

§ 771, Psych.
Emp.

general to induce subjects to serve the state nobly, except the conferring of civil dignities. But as in every other matter, so also as regards immunities from hospitalities to soldiers, justifying reasons are to be distinguished from persuasive ones; for there is a place for the latter particularly when there is an opportunity to decide to whom immunity is to be more wisely granted, if it is to be counted as a part of the salary. Finally, we remark in passing that what has been proved concerning the immunity from providing lodgings to soldiers (which are equivalent to a tax), as being counted as part of salary, is similarly understood of immunity from any personal burdens. Immunity from tax includes immunity from providing lodgings to soldiers as the genus includes its species, and therefore in the interpretation of privileges the argument from the former is properly applied to the latter, unless the words of the privilege suggest an exception.

§ 930, part 8, Jus Nat.

§ 906, part 8, Jus Nat.

§ 765. Of mercenaries

Mercenary soldiers are foreigners, who voluntarily enlist for military service. Therefore, their obligation to services in war comes from the stipulation by which they bind themselves thereto, either for services in a certain war or for a certain time, for provisions and a certain sum of money contracted for in advance, consequently, since stipulations are to be observed, the promises made to mercenary soldiers must be observed. That stipulation is usually called a capitulation.

§ 789, part 3, Jus Nat.

It is a sort of mixed contract of hiring and sale. For in so far as there is an agreement for performing military services for provisions, that is, for pay and clothing, it is a contract of hiring, but in so far as he who enrols his name for military service sells his liberty for a certain sum of money, it is a sale. It is of course just as if one sells himself into slavery. But one cannot be a mercenary soldier unless he is a foreigner; for a ruler has a right to enrol his subjects as soldiers, although they may voluntarily give in their names for military service, and they are likewise bound by nature to perform military service, but the ruler exercises that right either according to fundamental laws, or when such laws do not exist, as it shall seem best to him. Therefore, there is no need of a stipulation to create an obligation, which in fact already

§ 1194, part 4, Jus Nat.

§ 937, part 4, Jus Nat.

§§ 1080, 1091, part 7, Jus Nat.

§ 746.

§ 749.

§ 746.

§ 748.

§ 114, part 8,
Jus Nat.

exists by nature. Nor is there place for a capitulation, as it is opposed to the eminent power belonging to the ruler. But we must not confuse with mercenary soldiers the auxiliaries which a sovereign power sends, allowing their use to a belligerent for a certain sum of money, which goes by the name of subsidy. For here no stipulation exists between the sovereign power which wages the war, and the individual soldiers whom he uses as instruments in war; but the treaty is entered into

§ 369.

with another sovereign power which has no connexion with the war.

§ 766. *No fraud is to be committed in the hiring of soldiers*

§ 765.

§ 149, part 5,
Jus Nat.

Since mercenary soldiers are soldiers by stipulation, since, moreover, every stipulation ought to be devoid of all fraud, in hiring soldiers all fraud is illegal.

Hirers of soldiers act under the mandate of the sovereign power either express or tacit, in so far as the hiring is not prohibited, but is at least tacitly ratified in so far as the sovereign power receives into his army the foreigners who have enrolled in his service. And the sovereign power is never presumed to have permitted the hirers to commit fraud, since nothing is to be presumed which is not becoming to his sovereignty.

§ 767. *Of the promise under oath of soldiers*

§§ 646 and fol.,
h, and § 1043,
part 8, Jus Nat.

§ 665.

§ 301, part 1,
Phil. Pract.
Univ.

§ 393, part 3,
Jus Nat.

§ 916, part 3,
Jus Nat.

All soldiers are bound to promise under oath that they will not desert the military service undertaken by them. Indeed, subjects enrolled as soldiers are already bound by nature to service in wars, consequently not to become deserters, and mercenary soldiers are bound by their stipulation to the same thing; since, however, this obligation, which common men esteem lightly, is not sufficiently strong to prevent desertion, it is necessary that a positive obligation should be introduced, which does not exceed their comprehension, and whose meaning they can grasp. Therefore, since that can be introduced only by a penal sanction, certain penalties are decreed against deserters, and that soldiers may know that those have been rightly decreed, they bind themselves by promising not to desert the service in war, and since the good faith of those enlisting for military service is very doubtful, and consequently not sufficiently assured, they are bound to promise that under oath.

No more effective means for preventing desertion can be devised than the giving of a promise strengthened by an oath with the added fear of a penalty for desertion, and therefore this is the method best fitted to prevent soldiers from becoming deserters. Nay more, when this promise is sworn to, it can even happen that soldiers who fear God may serve with a sense of duty. But of these things I need not speak more fully at present, as they belong to civil prudence or politics. It is advantageous that penalties be added to stipulations also, since it depends on the will of the contracting parties how they may wish to agree with each other. Therefore hired soldiers agree to a penalty for desertion, although their entire obligation arises from their stipulation, and is merely strengthened by a promise under oath, which creates no new obligation. He who enlists for military service, by that very act subjects himself to military laws, so far as he transfers the control of his actions to the one to whom he owes military service, and he makes his actions dependent upon the other's will.

§ 118, part 1, Phil. Pract. Univ.

§ 11, part 3, Jus Nat.

§ 765.

§ 768. Of the natural disgrace of desertion

Since soldiers promise under oath that they will not desert the military service undertaken by them, and since he is a traitor who does not keep his promises, and he is a perjurer who does not observe his oath, deserters are traitors and perjurers, and their treachery is the greatest of all.

§ 767.
§ 768, part 3, Jus Nat.
§ 932, part 3, Jus Nat.
§ 935, part 3, Jus Nat.

It is scarcely to be hoped that you may persuade rude men of that sort, often strangers to uprightness of character, who voluntarily enlist for military service, or even those who are chosen as soldiers from subjects lacking a sense of duty, that this is disgraceful. Therefore the fear of punishment, human as well as divine, ought to effect that which reason cannot effect. And therefore, it is evident, how important it is that soldiers should not become impious and that even that abject fear of God should not be extinguished in them.

§ 769. Of kidnapping committed on desertion

Since soldiers promise under oath that they will not desert the service in wars; consequently, since a right against them established by every possible means belongs to the sovereign power, and since he is guilty of kidnapping who steals one who is subject to the control of some other

§ 767.

§ 755.

person; he who secretly takes away soldiers who are deserters, or conceals them, is guilty of kidnapping, consequently he who assists in any way in the desertion becomes a participant in the kidnapping.

Therefore, it can seem harsh to no one if he should be severely punished for this offence.

§ 770. *What military law is*

Military law is defined as the body of laws, in which provision is made for those things which ought or ought not to be done by soldiers and their officers, or for the things which are allowed them. Therefore, in military law we treat of the duties of soldiers and their officers, of the punishments of those who fail in their duty, and of the right of officers of soldiers, also that of their chief commanders.

§ 149, part I, Phil. Pract. Univ.

Military law is a positive law, and to it also can be applied what has been proved concerning the theory of the civil laws in the eighth part of "The Law of Nature," provided only that the attention be directed at the same time to warlike acts. There exist military laws of many nations which are easily recalled for examination by one who has closely examined the law of nature and of nations and especially the law of war and in war, so that it does not now seem to be our business to distinguish what is natural in them from that which is merely positive, or to establish any natural theory of military law. Sheer dread of prolixity, which is at variance with our present purpose, forbids us to enter upon such digressions.

§ 771. *Of the right of minor authorities in war*

The right of minor authorities in war is to be determined either by the will of the sovereign power as expressly declared in its mandate or its military law, or from the nature of the function entrusted, or of the duty laid down in the law. For minor authorities in war, such as commanders, act under no other right than that which has been granted them by the sovereign power. Therefore, the will of the sovereign power is known, if it has been expressly declared in the military law, as is self-evident, and since it is plain from a mandate what the sovereign may have desired to

§ 368.

be done or not to be done by the minor authority, and since it is understood that only so much right is bestowed on the minor authority as is required to enable it to perform its function and do its duty, to which it is bound by military law; the right of minor authorities in war is to be determined either by the will of the sovereign power, as expressly declared in its mandate or its military law, or from the nature of the function entrusted or of the duty laid down in the law.

§ 640, part 8, Jus Nat.

We speak here of the entire right which belongs in war to the minor authorities, both over the soldiers or officers of the soldiers subject to them, both as regards all warlike acts, and as regards all matters which arise on the occurrence of war. Therefore, here the question is not merely how far the sovereign power is bound through them, but this especially is aimed at, that we may have a general principle, from which a definite judgement can be reached concerning that which minor authorities do or do not do lawfully, and whether they claim a greater right than in truth belongs to them, or whether they do not use their right when they could and ought to use it. If the right is to be determined from the nature of the function entrusted, customs also have great weight, so that that is rightly assumed to come within the limits of the function of minor authorities, which it is known has always been and is to-day performed by them. There is no need now of adding more particular details; it is sufficient for us to have found out how we ought to know the will of the sovereign power, on which depends all the right of the minor powers.

§ 772. *How a minor authority binds a sovereign power in war*

What a minor authority in war promises within the limits of its mandate, or of the function entrusted to it, either by virtue of its duty prescribed by law, or of the right granted to it thereby, to that it binds the sovereign power. For since the right of the minor authority in war is to be determined, either by the will of the sovereign power as expressly declared in its mandate or its military law, or from the nature of the function entrusted to it or of the duty laid down by the law; whatever a minor authority in war promises either within the limits of its mandate, or of

§ 771.

the function entrusted to it, either by virtue of its duty prescribed by law, or of the right granted to it thereby, it promises that by the right of the sovereign power vested in it, consequently it is an agent in giving the promise. Therefore, since an agent in giving the promise does not bind himself, but the one who is using him as agent, what a minor authority in war promises within the limits of its mandate, or of the function entrusted to it, either by virtue of its duty prescribed by law, or of the right granted to it thereby, to that it binds the sovereign power.

§ 721, part 3, Jus Nat.

§ 722, part 3, Jus Nat.

§§ 722 and fol., part 3, Jus Nat.
§ 788, part 3, Jus Nat.

§ 246, part 5, Jus Nat.

§§ 640 and fol., part 4, and §§ 213 and fol., again 258 and fol., part 5, Jus Nat.

§ 640, part 8, Jus Nat.

§ 213, part 5, Jus Nat.
§ 253, part 5, Jus Nat.
Dig. 1. 3. 12.
§ 472, Psych. Emp.

Note, § cited.

Since we have spoken elsewhere of a promise made through an agent, the things which we have proved concerning it are easily applicable to the promises, consequently to the stipulations, of minor authorities in war. Here also those things are useful which have been proved concerning the mandate and the factor's contract, which is similar to the mandate, and the ship captain's contract. For since the principal entrusts to another as his agent something to be done, which the agent takes upon himself, and the factor is put in charge by another of some business of his own, just as a captain is put in charge of a ship by its owner; a minor authority in war, if the sovereign power expressly enjoins something upon it, or gives it full power under military law, is like an agent; in so far as a certain function is entrusted to it, or some duty is imposed upon it under military law, by which it is bound to do or not to do certain things, it is like a factor or ship captain. These things are to be properly understood by those who administer justice, that they may know, when in a certain case the meaning of the laws is plain, how they ought to proceed in like cases, because it is impossible to provide expressly in the laws for all particular cases. Upon this basis rests also that great heuristic principle which we have called the principle of reduction, and it is of the very greatest value not only in the art of investigation, but also in proof. I should wish then that to those points which we here suggest those might turn their attention who may be inclined to work out the general truths, which are involved in particulars.

§ 773. *When their promises are sponsions*

A minor authority in war is understood to have given by sponsion that which it promises outside of the limit of its mandate or of its function, or duty prescribed by law, or without any right granted to it by law.

For since it would be the same whether something should be promised within the limits of its mandate or within the limits of the function entrusted to it, or of its duty prescribed by law, or of the right granted by law, because the promise would always be made by right of the supreme power vested in the minor authority; if it promises anything outside of the limits of its function or duty prescribed by law, or without any right granted to it by law, it must be considered to have promised that outside the limits of its mandate. Therefore, since promises of minor authorities made without the mandate of the supreme power are sponsions, if minor authorities in war promise anything, the promise without a mandate, or outside the limits of its mandate and function entrusted to it, or of its duty prescribed by law, or made without any right granted to it by law, is a sponsion.

§ 771.

§ 465.

Since we have proved above what things are to be understood in regard to sponsions, those things are to be applied to promises of authorities in war under the circumstances of the present proposition. Therefore, there is no need of repeating here the things that are plainly understood from the foregoing discussion. But just as we have suggested as to the previous proposition, that those things can be applied to minor authorities which have been proved elsewhere of a mandate, of a factor's contract, and of a ship captain's contract; so also the same thing is here understood in particular of those things which the agent does outside the limits of his mandate, the factor or ship captain outside the limits of his office or outside the law thereof. The reason is plain from those things which we have just noted. It still needs to be said, that those things which are here proved concerning minor authorities in war, are likewise to be understood concerning any other minor authorities whatsoever, since in the proof minor authorities are assumed to act by virtue of a right conferred on them by the supreme power, either expressly or from the nature of the function or duty specifically prescribed; a thing which is common to all minor authorities.

§§ 465 and fol.

Note, § 773.

§ 774. Of a minor authority which pretends to a greater right than it has

If a minor authority in war pretends to a greater power than it has, it is bound to the one with whom it has dealt, both for the loss and for a penalty. For if a minor authority in war pretends to a greater right than it has, since it does this knowingly and willingly, it acts fraudulently.

§ 701, part 1, Phil. Pract. Univ.

Therefore, since a stipulation entered into by it without right is a sponsion, consequently the sovereign power is not bound by that, if it should

§ 773.

be unwilling to ratify it; if, because no ratification has followed, the other

§ 468.

party, with whom the contract is made, should incur loss, that is caused by the fraud of the minor authority. Therefore, since he who has caused a loss produced by fraud ought to repair it, if a minor authority in war

§ 580, part 2, Jus Nat.

pretends to a greater right than it has, it is bound to the one with whom it has dealt, for the loss. Which was the first point.

If a minor authority in war pretends to a greater right than it has, and therefore persuades another to enter into a stipulation, which, if it should not be observed, results in loss to the other, it is guilty of fraud. But since

§ 147, part 5, Jus Nat.

every stipulation ought to be free from fraud, either of the contracting

§ 149, part 5, Jus Nat.

parties has the right to demand from the other party that he shall not be guilty of fraud, consequently if the minor authority in war pretends to a greater right than it has, in order to persuade the other party to enter into the stipulation, it does him a wrong. Therefore, since every one has

§ 859, part 1, Jus Nat.

the right by nature to punish the one who does him a wrong, if a minor

§ 549, part 2, Jus Nat.

authority in war pretends to a greater right than it has, it is bound to the one with whom it has dealt, not only for the loss as proved above, but

Point 1.

also for the penalty. Which was the second point.

Point 2.

Each is likewise proved in this way. It is plain, as proved above, that the minor authority, according to the hypothesis of the present propo-

§ 683, part 2, Jus Nat.

sition, is a defrauder. But he who defrauds another is bound to him

§ 684, part 2, Jus Nat.

not only for the loss, but also for a penalty. Therefore also, if a minor authority in war pretends to a greater right than it has, it is bound to the one against whom the right has been claimed, both for the loss and for a penalty.

Even if he with whom a contract is fraudulently made is not defrauded, nevertheless the sovereign power, which ought not to allow fraud by the minor authorities, can punish the one who has committed the fraud by pretending to more than he had. The sacredness of good faith, which is especially befitting sovereign powers, is hostile to

Note, § 550.

every sort of fraud. Therefore, it ought not to allow minor authorities to act fraudulently, when they desire to seem to promise in its name. Therefore, it is proper to punish the bad faith of the minor authority. Nay more, when a minor authority pretends to a right which it has not, but which belongs to the sovereign power, and which therefore it cannot exercise without its consent, it does in fact wrong it, and injures it. Therefore, not only by the law of nature has the sovereign the right to punish it, but also by virtue of its sovereign power.

§ 859, part 1, Jus Nat.

§ 920, part 1, Jus Nat.

§ 1061, part 1, Jus Nat.

§§ 579, 832, part 8, Jus Nat.

§ 775. *How far minor authorities bind subordinates*

Minor authorities bind subordinates within the limits of those acts which they are accustomed to command. For those acts which minor authorities are accustomed to command to subordinates are a part of the function entrusted to them, consequently they command those acts by virtue of the right granted them by the sovereign power. Therefore, since this is the same as if the sovereign power, whom its subjects are bound to obey, were to command those things, minor authorities bind subordinates within the limits of those acts which they are accustomed to command, consequently also, if they make promises, within the limits of those acts which they are accustomed to command, they bind their subordinates.

§ 771.

§ 1043, part 4, Jus Nat.

So an officer binds his soldiers, a magistrate his citizens. But what these things are which a minor authority can command is understood from the function entrusted to it. What things are to be referred to this power is plain not only from the fact that it cannot properly perform its duty without them, but also from the fact that they are accustomed to be performed by a minor authority, since custom is the best interpreter.

§ 776. *How far minor authorities cannot bind subordinates*

Minor authorities cannot bind subordinates without their consent outside the limits of those acts which they are able to command. For if minor authorities cannot command certain acts, they have no right over them. Therefore, they cannot determine concerning those things at their

§ 156, part 1, Phil. Pract. Univ.

pleasure without the consent of the subordinates, consequently they cannot bind them, without their consent, outside of those acts which they can command.

§ 368.

§ 771.

Minor authorities derive all their right from the sovereign power, and therefore they cannot claim a greater right for themselves against subordinates and their property than has been granted them; how great this was we have proved before. Therefore, they cannot bind their subordinates without their consent to those things which they cannot command by virtue of the right belonging to them. For this reason their consent must be asked. But it must be observed that subordinates also are here understood to be minor authorities, which are subject to the right of other minor authorities of a higher order, for it is understood that one is subordinated to the other, and it is to the interest of the state that this should be done. We do not descend to the details which are explained in what follows. It was in order to prove those [details] that these matters have been discussed first. See what we have said of magistrates and of public duties. For every right of magistrates and of those who perform a public function rests upon the same general principle of exercising one's right through another, and all kinds of minor authorities are in truth simply magistrates.

§§ 162, 163, part 8, Jus Nat.

§§ 884 and fol., part 8, Jus Nat.

§ 162, part 8, Jus Nat., and § 368 h.

❁ CHAPTER VII ❁

Of the Law of Nations in War

§ 777. *Whether any right in war belongs to one waging an unjust war*

He who wages an unjust war has no right in war. For whatever is done in an unjust war is illegal. Therefore, since no one can have a right to that which is illegal, there can be no right to those things which are done in an unjust war. Therefore, he who wages an unjust war has no right in war.

§ 1112, part 1, Jus Nat.

§§ 156, 170, Phil. Pract. Univ.

It is also proved in this way. Since he who carries on an unjust war has no just cause of war, he has no right to wage the war; consequently no right in war can belong to him.

§ 1110, part 1, Jus Nat.

> We might assume the present proposition as an axiom, without any proof. For he who wages war, necessarily has or ought to have some purpose; since in an unjust war this purpose cannot be legal, neither can the means be legal which are used for obtaining this purpose, and acts done in war are such means; consequently no right in war can belong to one waging an unjust war.

§ 778. *The effect of an unjust war*

Since he who wages an unjust war has no right in war, all force in an unjust war is illegal, and those whom an unjust belligerent kills, he kills without right, the things which he takes from the enemy, he takes with unrighteous force, and whatever loss he causes him, he causes wrongfully; consequently, since those are robbers who seize property by force without the consent of the owners, with the intention of keeping it for themselves, since those are invaders, who without any right drive others

§ 777.

§ 170, part 1, Phil. Pract. Univ.

§§ 505, 506, part 2, Jus Nat.

by force out of possession of their immovable property, and since it is understood to be characteristic of bandits to kill the innocent and lay waste their property, he who wages an unjust war is a robber, an invader, and a bandit.

In every period the more civilized nations have recognized that unjust belligerents are to be classed with robbers, invaders, and bandits, and that those things which are done by them in a war waged without any right are to be considered robbery and brigandage. An act does not change its nature, whether it is done by one person or another; but rather the person committing the act gets his name therefrom. A bandit is one who engages in brigandage; a robber one who engages in robbery; nor indeed does brigandage cease to be such, or robbery cease to be such, because it is done by one person rather than by another. But there is no need that we should be too tedious in enumerating things which thus far have never been called in question by any one of those who have commented on law in war. This at least we note, that from this it is clearer than daylight that unjust war is not only opposed to the personal glory of the ruler of a state, but also to the glory of his nation, for which he ought to care.

§ 47.

§ 51.

§ 779. *Of the right of those who ally themselves with one waging an unjust war*

He who allies himself with one waging an unjust war has no right in war, or whatever he does, he does without right. For he who allies himself with one carrying on an unjust war, does whatever he does in it for the sake of the one who is waging the unjust war, a thing which is self-evident. Therefore, since whatever he does is illegal, in the same way as before it is plain that he who allies himself with one carrying on an unjust war can have no right in war, or that he does without right, whatever he does.

§ 1115, part 1,
Jus Nat.

§ 777.

He who allies himself with one waging war takes his side in the war, as is evident. He does nothing therefore in his own right, but in the right of the one whose fortunes in war he follows. If then the latter has no right in war, as he cannot have in an unjust war, no right can belong to the former.

§ cited.

§ 780. *The effect of this alliance*

Since he who allies himself with any one waging an unjust war has no right in war, therefore, it is plain, as before, that whatever he does is to be considered as robbery, invasion, and brigandage.

§ 779.

§ 778.

Just as he who allies himself with robbers, invaders, and brigands, is himself a robber, invader, and brigand, a thing which no one calls in question, therefore also the one allying himself with one waging an unjust war, who is to be considered as a public robber, invader, and brigand, acts the part of a public robber, invader, and brigand. There is the same wickedness in the act of those who involve themselves in an unjust war, as in that of those who undertake an unjust war, since they have a common cause. But so much the wickeder is it to ally yourself with the one who is waging an unjust war if, without this alliance, the war could not be waged, since he encourages robbery, invasion, and brigandage, who ought to prevent it as far as he can. For since every one is bound to ward off loss from another as far as possible, he is also bound to ward off, as far as possible, the dangers and losses which are caused him in war. Neglect of this duty is wicked by nature; if then it should be added to the wickedness of his deeds in an unjust war, it certainly increases the same.

§ 495, part 2, Jus Nat.

§ 781. *Of the right in a just war*

That is allowable in war, for one who is waging a just war, without which he cannot acquire his right from the other party; that is not allowable which does not help to attain this purpose. For by the law of nature a right in war exists only to that without which one cannot attain the right, for the sake of which the war is waged. Therefore, since nations and their rulers use natural law in their relations with each other, that is allowable in war, for one who is waging a just war, without which he cannot acquire his right from the other party, but that is not allowable, which does not help to attain this purpose.

§ 1113, part 1, Jus Nat.

§ 4.

War is waged for no other purpose than to acquire our right, which another does not wish to allow us. That we may attain this end, adequate means must be employed. The right of war belongs to

§ 1102, part 1, Jus Nat.

§ 613.

nations. Therefore, the right must also belong to them to those things which are necessary for exercising this right, that is, to those measures without which the purpose cannot be accomplished. The right would have been given to no purpose, unless those things also were allowed without which there would be no use of the right. But it is to be noted, since the outcome of war is doubtful, in determining that which is necessary for the purpose aimed at in a war, that certainty is not required, but probability is sufficient; for certainty of knowledge is far beyond human wisdom, however great it be.

§ 782. *Of force allowable in war*

§ 781.

§ 1102, part 1, Jus Nat.

Since that is allowable in a just war, without which one's right cannot be acquired from the other party, and since in war we pursue our right by force, that force is allowable in war without which we cannot acquire our right, consequently one must abstain from force in acquiring those things which can be acquired without force, as, for example, by starvation.

§ 1117, part 1, Jus Nat.

The right to war does not indeed exist, unless you cannot persuade the other party in any way to grant your right to you; a thing which is especially clear from those things which we have proved of the method of settling controversies between nations. Therefore, there is no right in war to the force which is proper to war if you can acquire in some milder way what is obtained by force. For no greater force can be used against an enemy than necessity demands, which alone excuses one using force and transfers all the blame to the one against whom it is used.

§ 783. *With whom the decision rests as to the need for those things which ought to be done in war*

§ 55, part 8, Jus Nat.

§ 39.

§§ 613, 614.

§ 156, part 1, Jus Nat.

§ 781.

The decision as to the need for those things without which he who is waging war cannot obtain his right, is to be left to him. For nations by nature are free, consequently also rulers of a state who represent them and who wage war by their right. Therefore, since by force of natural liberty it must be allowed that each one in determining his actions should follow his own judgement, as long as he does nothing contrary to your right, a thing which in the present case does not occur when he is exercising his own right; the decision as to the need for those things, without which he who is waging war cannot obtain his right, is to be left to him.

No nation which the war does not concern can claim for itself the decision as to the need of those things without which the purpose of the war cannot be obtained; for that is not only contrary to the natural liberty of nations, and no state can claim sovereignty over another without impairing this, but it is also impossible in itself, since when the case arises counsel must be taken in the arena as the proverb says. But much less can this decision be given to the opposing party, since it would be absurd for an enemy to be appointed judge in his own case, who, since he would not confess that his cause of war is unjust, would declare all force used against him illegal. The question as to the abuse of law in war would always be in dispute between belligerents; therefore the decision cannot be entrusted to that one of the contesting parties who complains of the abuse. This would be the same as if any one should wish to claim for the plaintiff the decision of a case in court, a thing which any one recognizes is absurd. There is, therefore, no way left except to leave to the conscience of the belligerent to decide what may seem necessary for accomplishing the purpose of the war.

§ 784. *In what warlike force consists*

Warlike force consists only in the use of arms. In war we pursue our right by force. Therefore, since nations cannot pursue their right against others by force, otherwise than by force of arms, as is self-evident, warlike force consists only in the use of arms.

§ 1102, part 1, Jus Nat.

Indeed, even in a state of nature, when you cannot defend your rights against another with your hand, the law of nature itself makes the use of arms allowable, permitting only so much for the defender as is sufficient to ward off injury, and when any one has been injured, as much as is sufficient to ward off danger of future injury. If then your hand is not of sufficient strength, the insufficient strength given by nature is to be supplemented by the use of tools, that is, by the use of arms. Nature has given hands to men that they may use them in defence of themselves and their right; but she has also given them powers of the mind, by the use of which it is possible to invent and

§ 980, part 1, Jus Nat.

§ 1059, part 1, Jus Nat.
§ 981, Ontol.
§ 611.

use tools, by which the insufficient strength, which she has denied the hands, is supplemented. Therefore, the use of arms is not less natural than that of the hands, each of which nature is rightly said to have combined with the other. Men differ from brutes in this respect, that they are aided in their actions by tools, with the use of which brutes are unacquainted. But all warlike operations are not restricted to war-like force, for force is not used against the enemy in all cases, much less do all acts which become a cause of war come from that same source, as will be made plainer from what follows.

§ 785. *Warlike acts, warlike operations, hostilities*

Whatever an enemy does in any way whatsoever for the purpose of war, is a warlike act. A warlike operation however is defined as a warlike act, by which force is used against an enemy, or a way is prepared to use force against him or to withstand force on his part. Warlike operations, by which actual force is used against an enemy or property, are called hostilities.

Thus it is a warlike act to pitch tents; for they are pitched not with the purpose that force can be used against an enemy, but that soldiers may defend themselves from the inclemency of the weather. In like manner the bringing of gunpowder into camp is a warlike act, since it is done indeed for the purpose of war, but at the same time neverthe-less actual force is not used against an enemy or his property, nor is a way prepared to use force against him. It is a warlike operation to build up a platform for engines of war and to surround yourself with a wall; for the former is done that you may be able to use force, and the latter that you may be safe from the incursions of the enemies, and may be able more easily to resist their onslaughts. The following, however, are hostilities: to lay waste the property of the enemy, to kill the enemy, to capture the property of the enemy or the enemies themselves. Warlike acts might be more minutely classified and sub-classified as a genus into its species, nor would that be difficult for one who, when he has carefully examined them all, using those controlling concepts of genera and species of things which we have given in the Philosophia Prima, turns his attention to the method by which gen-era are determined from species, and on the other hand, species from

§§ 236 and fol., Ontol.

genera; but there is no need of such over-nicety at present, although that would at least tend to establish an accurate theory of the method of waging war and of the duties of the several officers of soldiers. The method of carrying on war can be learned from Julius Caesar and Polybius, a thing which the most highly accomplished leaders do not deny. For although on the invention of gunpowder warlike operations seem to have put on another form, nevertheless the method of conducting a war is still the same, since the use of instruments varies only the effect of warlike operations, according to their diversity. But it is sufficient for us to turn our attention to the difference which we have explained in our definitions. For in warlike acts in general, both the obligation is considered, by which minor powers are bound to the sovereign, and the right belonging to them against subordinates within the limits of their function; but in hostilities the right belonging to the sovereign power in war is considered, as it is by his right that the war is waged when force is used against an enemy or his property, and the other warlike operations are governed by the common law relating to warlike acts.

§ 710 and fol., Log.

§ 786. Of expenses incurred for war

Expenses incurred for war are also due by nature to him who wages a just war. For he who wages a just war pursues his right by force against an enemy, which he cannot acquire otherwise than by force of arms, consequently the other party, whose war is unjust, is in the situation that he may be compelled to pay the expenses for the war. If then he who has incurred them were not to receive payment, loss would be caused to him by fault of his enemy. Therefore, since no one ought to cause loss to another, and that caused by one's fault ought to be repaired, expenses incurred in war are due by nature to him who wages a just war.

§§ 629, 630.

§ 488, part 2, Jus Nat.

§ 495, part 2, Jus Nat.

§ 580, part 2, Jus Nat.

It can undoubtedly happen that expenses incurred in war may exceed the debt which is sought in the war; but since that occurs by the fault of the one who does not wish to give his right to another, he may charge it to himself, if he should pay the penalty of his imprudence. Nor is there any reason why any difficulty should be caused by a war waged in a doubtful case in which it is merely sought that the enemy should be brought to a compromise by force of arms, or in a

§ 572.

defensive war, by which it is sought that he should refrain from unjust force. For in either case he who wages war pursues his right, and he who does not wish to allow the same is in such a situation that he must pay the expenses of the war. Therefore, although there is no certain debt which is sought, nevertheless the expenses incurred for a just war are to be paid by the other party.

§ 787. *What beyond the limit of the debt it is allowable to take from the enemy*

He who is waging a just war may occupy, even beyond the limits of his debt, territory and places of the enemy and may seize any other property, with the purpose of persuading the enemy to end the war, but with the intention of restoring it when the war is ended. It is self-evident that the consent of each of the belligerents is needed to end the war. Therefore, if he with whom you have a war is unwilling to consent to end it, when you have acquired what is due to you, the war is certainly to be continued until he does consent. But since there is need of a motive, if he is to desist from the war, and since the motive consists in a representation of evil, you can persuade the enemy to desist from war in no other way than by occupying his territory and places situated therein. Therefore, he who is waging a just war may occupy, even beyond the limits of his debt, territory and places of the enemy, and any other property, with the purpose of persuading the enemy to end the war. Which was the first point.

§ 889, Psych. Emp.
§ 890, Psych. Emp.

But since, indeed, those things which are seized or occupied beyond the limit of the debt may be seized or occupied only with the purpose that the enemy may be persuaded to end the war, and since this purpose will have been attained if at length he consents to it, when the war is ended, the things which have been occupied or seized are in your hands without any reason. Therefore, since there is no reason why you should retain them after the war is ended, and since no one ought to be made richer at another's expense, those things which have been occupied or seized with the purpose that the enemy may be persuaded to end the war must be restored when the war is ended; consequently it is not allowable to occupy or seize them without the intention of restoring them. Which was the second point.

§§ 583, 585, part 2, Jus Nat.

There is no reason why you should argue, that if the enemy should have known that those things are to be restored to him, which have been occupied or seized, this motive would have little effect. For since the expenses incurred for the war are owed to the one occupying or seizing, it is allowable to charge up no less the fruits derived from them in the meantime, than the things themselves, under the given circumstances, both for the expenses and for the losses produced by the existing causes, or the irreparable injuries caused thereby, for which satisfaction must be given. Therefore, restitution does not diminish the efficacy of the motive, even if you suppose the war is waged with the greatest conscientiousness; although this may be rarely assumed, nevertheless it is to be assumed in the natural law of nations, as there it is to be proved how war is to be waged with the greatest conscientiousness, nor is any indulgence to be given to the customs of nations at variance with the rigour of that law. It is undoubtedly hard and attainable with difficulty, as we do not in the least deny, but voluntarily concede, to wage war with that conscientiousness which the natural law of nations demands, nor is it less difficult to impose that upon sovereign powers; but we are not concerned with this now, as we are teaching what the law of nature to which all actions are subject, even those of sovereign powers, enjoins, what it forbids, what it allows, and not inquiring how sovereign powers are to be induced to perform their duty, and not to abuse their right, and whether it is possible to persuade them thereto.

§ 786.

§ 788. Of property taken away and losses caused by unjust force

He who wages an unjust war is bound to restore property taken by force from another whose war is just, and to repair losses caused in any way. For he who wages an unjust war is a robber. But a robber is bound to restore stolen property to the owner. Therefore, he also who wages an unjust war is bound to restore property taken by force from another whose war is just. Which was the first point.

§ 780.

§ 524, part 2, Jus Nat.

Furthermore, whatever he does in war, who is waging an unjust war, he does without right and losses are caused without right to the other party, whose war is just; consequently with fraud, or, if he should think

§ 778.

§§ 701, 717, part 1, Phil. Pract. Univ.

that his war is just, with fault. Therefore, since loss caused by fraud or fault must be repaired, he who wages an unjust war is bound to repair losses caused in any way. Which was the second point.

§ 580, part 2,
Jus Nat.

He undoubtedly contracts very great debts who wages an unjust war, if he had to abide by the law of nature, since he is bound not only for the expenses incurred for the war, but, by force of the present proposition, he is bound to restore things seized by unjust force, and to repair any losses caused. There is the added consideration that he is also bound to the other party for a penalty. If these things were properly considered and respect paid to conscience, he would not, relying on his power, rush with such headlong haste to arms who is not yet convinced or completely persuaded as to the justice of his cause of war, since in morals persuasion on account of the most valid reasons is equivalent to conviction.

§ 786.

§ 789.

§ 789. Of the obligation to pay a penalty for unjust hostilities

He who wages an unjust war is bound to pay a penalty to the other for the hostilities which he commits. For he who wages an unjust war does wrongfully those things which cause losses to the other. Therefore, since hostilities are all those warlike operations by which force is used against an enemy and his property, and therefore losses are caused to an enemy through hostilities, he who wages an unjust war does a wrong to his enemy by all hostilities. Therefore, since the one to whom a wrong is done has the right to punish the offender, he who wages an unjust war is bound to pay a penalty to the other for the hostilities which he commits.

§ 778.

§ 785.

§ 488, part 2,
Jus Nat.

§ 549, part 2,
Jus Nat.

This is also shown in this way. He who wages an unjust war is a robber. But by the law of nature we have the right to punish a robber. Therefore, the injured party has a right to punish the one who wages an unjust war; consequently the one is bound to the other for a penalty.

§ 778.

§ 551, part 2,
Jus Nat.

Of course nation is bound to nation for the penalty for a wrong, in so far as satisfaction is to be given for the wrong. For it is self-evident that there is no place here for penalties, either capital, or those affecting the person, or those which consist in infamy, such as are inflicted in a state by the sovereign upon those committing crime, but only for those which consist in payment and therefore have the character of a fine. Therefore, infamy does not attach to these penalties as to civil penalties. Just as there is no derogation from the dignity of the ruler of a state, if a penalty is added to a stipulation, so there is no derogation therefrom, if he should pay something by way of penalty to one whom he has injured by unjust force.

§ 790. *Of the right against persons in a just war*

A right against persons arises in a just war from defence of oneself and one's property. For since in hostilities force is used against both persons and things, he who wages an unjust war, either in fact assails with illegal force, or at least attempts to assail our body or our property. Therefore, because by nature every one has the right to defend both himself and his property, consequently to ward off force by force, a right against persons arises in a just war from defence of oneself and his property.

§ 785.

§ 778.

§ 973, part 1, Jus Nat.
§ 691, part 2, Jus Nat.
§ 972, part 1, Jus Nat.

In so far as he who wages an unjust war assails our body by force, he is an aggressor; but in so far as he assails our property by force, he is a robber. Therefore, we defend both ourselves or our body, and our property by force against persons. Therefore, since in a just war we have no dealing with the person of the enemy, except in so far as we attempt to ward off any unjust force from ourselves, or from our property, all acts in a just war, which are aimed at the person of enemies, belong to defence, and therefore, a right against persons in a just war cannot arise other than from defence of oneself and one's property. Those who do not regard this, tacitly assume that anything you please is allowable in war, and therefore turn the right into licence, which is an imaginary right and cannot belong to any man.

§ 150, part 1, Jus Nat.

§ 791. *How that is to be determined*

Since a right against persons arises in a just war from defence of oneself and one's property, and since he defends himself who resists one intending or attempting to injure him, in order that the other may not injure him, or that he may avoid injury as far as possible, the right against persons in a just war is to be determined from that which is necessary to resist the violence which an enemy is attempting or intending to use

§ 790.

§ 972, part 1, Jus Nat.

against us or our property, or to repel him from us and from our property, consequently so much is allowable in a just war against the person
of an enemy as is sufficient to ward from us and our property the force
used by him.

§ 785.

§ 427, part 3,
Jus Nat.

Either the peril is present, when the body is in fact assailed, or our
property is assailed, or it is threatened, inasmuch as it is certain that
the enemy has the intention of doing this, and consequently a just
fear of danger is never absent, as long as the war continues. Therefore,
we need not wait until the enemy actually uses force on us or our
property, but the crime is to be anticipated. He who manifests the
intention of injuring, is the same as one actually attempting to injure.
But as soon as the enemy takes up arms, he manifests the intention to
begin hostilities. What, therefore, is plainly indicated, is considered as
true against him; consequently the opportunity for anticipating the
crime must not be neglected.

§ 792. Of the right against the person of the subjects of belligerents

§ 790.

§ 791.

§ 723.

§ 982, part 1,
Jus Nat.

Because a right against persons arises in a just war from defence of oneself
and one's property, and therefore is to be determined from that which is
necessary to resist an enemy by force or to repel him from us and from
our property; the subjects of the one who is engaging in unjust war,
although they are considered enemies, as long as they refrain from all
violence, and do not show an intention to use force, may not be killed
nor may violence be inflicted in any way upon their persons, nor may
they be treated badly; consequently it is never allowable to kill children,
boys, girls, those weakened by age, the sick, those who are weak, bodily
or mentally, and those who have already surrendered themselves, or wish
to do so. And since harsher measures are not allowable in defence, when
milder ones, nay, the mildest, are adequate; if their intention or good
faith is suspected, the arms which they have in their houses are to be
taken away, in order that they may not be able to commit any hostile act.

There is no reason why you should object, that subjects of a belligerent by their resources resist the restoration of our right, consequently concur in unjust hostilities, and make themselves participants

in the crime which is committed by the enemy against our citizens, because they approve of the act of their state, or at least ought to approve. For the right of defence does not extend to killing, except when that is a necessary means of preserving your own life, or avoiding bodily injury. If this danger does not exist, one loses his right to kill an aggressor and a robber, consequently also an enemy. For the right to punish is not extended beyond the need of avoiding danger of threatened injury, much less does it make vengeance, which is illegal in itself, legal in those who, more by their own misfortune than their fault, incur the misfortunes of war. Furthermore it is to be noted, since one may go to the aid of another in very different ways, not all who aid another can be punished in the same way, and charity, which cannot be separated from the use of a right in war, demands that a thing, which is attributable to misfortune, should not be considered a fault and certainly not made equivalent to fraud. Charity so moderates the use of the right to punish an enemy, that nothing may be done which seems contrary to it, except in case of conflict between love for one's self and for one's enemy. The law of nature is everywhere consistent with itself, nor does it allow anything contrary to what it enjoins or forbids, so that the former should not be done rightly, but the latter should. A right granted by virtue of that most sacred law is never to be exercised except with a sense of duty. Those who think otherwise turn right into licence, which can belong to no man. What men must be permitted to do without punishment, they are not understood to be allowed by the law of nature to do rightly. The right against persons in war is not the right of the promiscuous slaughter of those who are in the category of enemies, so that the cruellest customs of robbers would become law, and war would be waged without any religious scruple; if you should grant that, the cruelty of an enemy will be an empty word, which nevertheless is disapproved by the common sense of mankind, it being plainly proved that nature herself is opposed to the right of absolutely limitless slaughter of enemies.

§ 1013, part 1,
Jus Nat.

§ 778.

§ 1059, part 1,
Jus Nat.
§ 640, part 8,
Jus Nat.

§ 743 h, and
§ 620, part 1,
Jus Nat.

§ 229, part 1,
Jus Nat.

§ 150, part 1,
Jus Nat.

§ 793. *Of unjust customary law concerning persons in war*

Since the subjects of the one who is waging an unjust war may not be killed, nor may violence be inflicted in any other way upon their persons, as long as they refrain from all violence, and do not show an intention of

using force, or if in a doubtful case provision may be made by a milder
measure that they may not do anything hostile; since, moreover, their
children must always be spared, the boys, the girls, those weakened by
age, the sick, those who are weak, bodily or mentally, and those who
have already surrendered themselves, or wish to do so; if a general licence
to inflict violence upon the persons of enemies has been introduced by
the customs of certain nations, that is to be considered as a part of the
customary law of nations, but one that is especially unjust, by which
immunity simply is allowed to the one exercising it, but a true right is
not conferred upon him.

Grotius indeed refers that licence to the voluntary law of nations;
nevertheless he is wrong in this: since the voluntary law of nations
belongs to all nations, it ought not to be common only to some of
them. For although we may admit a certain voluntary law of nations,
nevertheless we distinguish it from the customary law, from which it
differs just as do civil laws, which seem to have some injustice in them,
from those which have manifest injustice, and as just laws differ from
the perverse customs of certain nations. That customary law, by which
licence is allowed an enemy to inflict violence on the persons of enemies, is more suitable for barbarous nations than for the more civilized,
among whom it is especially to be censured. But how far they get away
from the truth, who set that forth as a law of nature, is evident from
those notes which we have made on the previous proposition.

§ 794. *Whether it is allowable to kill those captured in war*

Likewise, because it is not allowable to kill the subjects of a belligerent,
as long as they refrain from all violence and do not show an intention to
use force, or as long as you can provide in another way that this may not
happen, it is not allowable to kill those captured in war, not even immediately, much less at any other time, unless some especial offence shall
have been committed because of which they are liable to punishment.

In former times, indeed, even among nations not barbarous it
was considered right to kill those captured in war at any time, since
it is just the same whether you exercise your right immediately or
after an interval, for the reason that the right that is postponed is

---

§ 792.

§ 24.
§ 418, part 3,
Jus Nat.

De Jure Belli
ac Pacis, lib. 3,
c. 4.

§ 22.
§ cited.

Note, § 792.

§ 793.

not lost; from this nevertheless it cannot be proved that it belonged to the voluntary law of nations, as it seemed to Grotius. For since the voluntary law of nations is to be derived from natural law in the same way as the civil law is derived from natural law, but when civil laws are derived from natural laws, especial care must be taken, lest certain common errors may be assumed to be a law of nature; the voluntary law of nations cannot rest on the errors which are considered a law of nature. Moreover, it is well understood that certain gross errors were at one time prevalent as to the law of nature even among learned and cultivated peoples. But if captives commit an offence, a right to punish arises from their own offence, not from the fact that they are in the category of enemies. Therefore, the right arising from the wrong of one who is in the category of enemies is not to be confused with the right against an enemy as such. In the law of nature all things are to be properly distinguished which are different, lest their confusion should lead us into error, from which then more errors follow.

§ 22.

§ 992, part 8, Jus Nat.

§ 631, Log.
§ 627, Log.

§ 795. *When one ceases to be an enemy*

As soon as an enemy is in my power, he ceases to be an enemy. For those are enemies who are at war with each other. But since he who is in my power can no longer in any way resist me in the prosecution of my right, as soon as he is in my power I can have no further war with him; consequently he ceases to be an enemy.

§ 722.

§ 461, part 2, Jus Nat.

He who comes into my power is vanquished and the war with him ceases which existed before, consequently it is not possible any longer for him to inflict violence on my person. Therefore, there is no longer any reason why he ought still to be called an enemy. But if, while he is in your power, he does a malicious wrong of some sort, he is punished on account of the wrong, not because he is an enemy. But it is to be noted that power here simply denotes physical capacity to dispose of something according to one's liking, without consideration of what can be done rightly. Therefore, since a person may be said to be in our power in the same sense as a thing is said to be, on this account, for the sake of brevity, we have appealed to the same definition as is readily applicable to persons.

§ 1089, part 5, Jus Nat.

§ 461, part 2, Jus Nat.

§ 796. *Whether captives are enemies*

§ 795.

§ 461, part 2,
Jus Nat.

Since one ceases to be an enemy as soon as he is in my power, and since one who has been captured is in my power, those who are captured in war, or captives, cease to be enemies, consequently all hostilities cease against captives.

From this it is also plain that by the law of war captives cannot be killed. Nor is there reason why you should object that an excessive number of captives might be a burden and a peril. For from that it can in no way be conceived how the right to kill them should arise. For unless you can correct the difficulty in another way, or avoid the peril, they are rather to be sent away than killed, an agreement being made with them, or, if their good faith is doubted, with the sovereign power, that they should not perform military service while the war lasts, or within a certain number of years, as is even to-day usually done among Christian nations. For those are not strangers to cruelty who kill captives. And Diodorus Siculus properly calls the sparing of captives a common right and says that those sin beyond a doubt, who do not shrink from this crime.[1] But if you insist that the killing of captives can be a motive for ending the war, especially if all in general are killed, the answer is easy; one must not use illegal means for the sake of a legal end. Nor has it always been proved that the killing of all captives in general is a motive for ending the war; for it can just as well happen that by this deed the mind of the enemies may be exasperated; and such exasperation does not counsel moderation. There have been also in every time those to whom that cruelty is hateful. See examples thereof among the commentators on Grotius, which we think it is superfluous to repeat here.

§ 71.

De Jure Belli
ac Pacis, lib. 3,
c. 11, § 13.

§ 797. *Whether it is allowable to kill those who have been surrendered unconditionally*

§ 795.
§ 461, part 2,
Jus Nat.
§ 792.

Since one ceases to be an enemy as soon as he is in my power, and since one surrendered unconditionally is in my power, it is not allowable to kill those who have been surrendered unconditionally.

1. See Diodorus of Sicily, *The Library of History,* ed. and trans. C. H. Oldfather, 12 vols. (London: William Heinemann, 1933–67), vol. 5, bk. XIII, chap. xxvi, p. 193.

There is no reason why you should object that he who has surrendered unconditionally transfers all right in himself to me; for he cannot transfer a greater right than he himself has in himself. But no one has a right over his own life. Therefore he cannot transfer that to me. If he has committed a capital offence, he is not punished as one who has surrendered, but for the crime, so that not even in this case is the killing legal, unless that crime should deserve capital punishment. Moreover, those things are to be reread which we have noted above, that you may not make those who have surrendered, or all captives generally, defendants on a capital charge. It also must be understood that although subjects are bound to patient obedience, however badly the superior rules, that is, abuses the right which he has over the people, nevertheless on this account those are not to be subjected to punishment for his act, since no one can be punished for the act of another. For although the act of the ruler of a state is to be considered the act of the nation, nevertheless one must not argue without circumspection from the entire nation to individuals. For there is no one to whom it does not seem absurd, that a whole nation is to be given over to slaughter, or even that it has deserved that penalty, for unjust hostilities; indeed, there is no reason why a few should expiate the crime of an entire state, for which their lives cannot be put in pledge. For although not only the property of subjects, but also their persons may be bound for the debts of a state, nevertheless the pledging cannot go beyond their natural liberty, as we have proved above concerning hostages.

§ 351, part 1, Jus Nat.

Note, § 792.

§ 1043, part 8, Jus Nat.

§ 39.

§ 1084, part 8, Jus Nat.

§ 39.

§ 351, part 1, Jus Nat.

§ 495.

§ 507.

§ 501.

§ 798. *Whether the stipulation of those bargaining that their lives are to be saved can be repudiated*

Since it is not allowable to kill those who have surrendered unconditionally, the stipulation of those bargaining, either in a battle or in a siege, that their lives shall be saved, is not to be repudiated, consequently neither is that of those who lay down their arms in battle.

§ 797.

Not only those who offer to lay aside their arms if the pledge should be given that their lives are to be saved, but also those who in fact throw aside their arms in battle, bargain that their lives are to be saved. For the will can be expressed both by words and by act. But if you should object that this depends on the will of the enemy, to that objection a full answer has been repeatedly given in what precedes, so that it would be superfluous to serve the cabbage so frequently warmed over.

§ 799. *Whether promises to an enemy, a robber, and a brigand are to be observed*

The things which are promised to an enemy as enemy, nay, even to a robber and a brigand as robber and brigand, must be observed. For if you promise something to an enemy as an enemy, since you know that he is an enemy, nor could you make the promise, with a reservation of the right belonging to you against an enemy, you give up your right against him, consequently it is extinguished. Therefore, since it is now just as if he were not your enemy, and since promises are by nature to be observed, there is surely no reason why promises to an enemy as an enemy are not to be observed, consequently they must be observed. Which was the first point.

In exactly the same way it is shown that promises to a robber as a robber, and to a brigand as a brigand, must be observed. Which was the second point.

§ 95, part 3, Jus Nat.

§ 97, part 3, Jus Nat.

§ 431, part 3, Jus Nat.

Of course when you have dealing with an enemy as an enemy, it is tacitly assumed that your right against an enemy ought not to be considered, in so far as it is lessened by what is agreed upon, and as you consent to abide by what has been agreed upon, but not by what might rightly be done otherwise, unless the contrary had been agreed. If, therefore, promises were not to be observed, the agreement would be void. But it is absurd to assume that enemies when agreeing together have intended to accomplish nothing. And, if you should wish to assume that only he, to whose advantage it is that the promises be observed, intended the agreement to be effective, that would be just as if the promise depended upon the will of the promisor, which must be considered no less absurd.

§ 800. *Of good faith promised an enemy, a robber, and a brigand*

§ 799.

Since the things which are promised to an enemy as an enemy, nay, even to a robber and a brigand as robber and brigand, are to be performed, and since he who keeps his promises keeps faith, good faith is to be observed with an enemy, nay, even with a robber and a brigand.

§ 759, part 3, Jus Nat.

Whereas if it is allowable to break a pledge given to an enemy, promises made to an enemy are turned into mere illusions; and it is to the interest of each of the belligerent parties that this should not happen. For the outcome of those things which are done in war is doubtful.

§ 801. *When it is not allowable by the customary law of nations to kill enemies*

Because promises to an enemy as an enemy are to be observed, if a promise has been made to enemies that their lives will be saved, it is not allowable to kill them, although the custom has been introduced that otherwise it may be allowable to kill them.

§ 799.

If all nations were to recognize what sort of a right against the persons of enemies exists by nature, the stipulation that their lives should be safe would be altogether superfluous; for that savagery by which violence is inflicted on the persons of enemies who have come under the power of their enemy would never have to be feared, and by the consent of all, the use of such savagery would be considered contrary to the law of nations. Therefore, we have restricted that stipulation to the case in which the perverse customs of offenders allow for cruelty, which is abhorred by that perfectly righteous law which has been established by nature herself.

§§ 790 and fol.

§ 802. *Whether killing is allowable, if it is necessary to inspire terror*

If it should be necessary to inspire terror, it is not allowable on this account to kill captives, those who have surrendered or wish to surrender themselves, or to maltreat their persons. For although terror is a motive for ending war, consequently for either offering or accepting fair terms of peace, or that others learning from the misfortune of another what is to be avoided by themselves may cease to resist, since the war is waged that this may be brought about; nevertheless, since it is not allowable to use

§ 890, Psych. Emp.

§§ 630 and fol.

illegal means to acquire a legal end, since, moreover, it is not allowable to
kill those who have been captured in war, those who have surrendered or
who wish to surrender themselves—and as soon as they have come under
our power, they are no longer to be considered as enemies—if it should
be necessary to inspire terror, it is not allowable on this account to kill
captives, those who have surrendered or wish to surrender themselves, or
to maltreat their persons.

It is not sufficient that we do this or that thing by way of redress
of our right. For since everything which is done with that purpose
is to be considered as a means, one must examine further to find
out whether or not such a means is also allowable. Otherwise a right
in war would be turned to mere licence, as is the case in that which
Grotius called the voluntary law of nations, which he teaches is to be
tempered with innate justice, and which can belong to no man, and
war would be waged without religious scruples. Therefore, Grotius
properly observes that the advantage which is hoped for in the future
from terror, can be included in the causes on account of which the
right to punish is not given up, if that right exists, because a captive,
or one who has surrendered or wishes to surrender, has committed an
act worthy of punishment.

§ 803. *Who are deserters*

They are called deserters who flee from our side to enemies and who support their cause in war against us. Soldiers are frequently such deserters. It is
readily evident, whether the deserters are soldiers or our citizens, that those
who betray to the enemy the plans which are being considered by us, or in
what condition our affairs are, or plan hostilities against us in any other way,
are guilty of a dreadful crime, which may be punished as a capital offence.

The right to kill deserters belongs to the ruler of the state, not so
much as a right in war as a sovereign right to punish. If then they are
punished, they are punished not as enemies, but as subjects who have
committed a crime against the state. Therefore, those things which
have been stipulated and agreed upon with an enemy, are not to be
applied to deserters, except in so far as express mention has been made
of them, so that it may be understood that the penalty is remitted.

Marginal notes:

§ 794.
§ 797.
§ 798.

§ 795.

§ 937, Ontol.

§ 150, part 1,
Jus Nat.
De Jure Belli
ac Pacis, lib.
3, c. 11, § 16,
no. 3.

§ 581, part 8,
Jus Nat.

§ 628, part 8,
Jus Nat.

§ 832, part 8,
Jus Nat.

§ 804. *Whether a too obstinate resistance gives the right to kill an enemy*

The right to kill an enemy does not arise because he has resisted too stubbornly. For he who resists warlike force, by which he himself or his property is assailed, either has a just cause for carrying on war or he has not. I say that in either case no right arises to kill the enemy because of a too stubborn resistance.

He who has a just cause for carrying on war is allowed to use only so much force against the person of the enemy as is sufficient to ward off the violence of the enemy from his own person or property; consequently he may resist him as long as he can. If then he resists him too stubbornly, he is exercising his own right; consequently he does no injury to his enemy for which he is to be punished. Therefore, the right to kill him does not arise because he has resisted too stubbornly. § 791.

§ 170, part 1, Phil. Pract. Univ.
§ 975, part 1, Jus Nat.

All force is illegal on the part of one who has no just cause for carrying on war; consequently if he resists the just force by which he himself or his property is assailed, he is equivalent to an aggressor and a robber, and the one who assails his person or property with just force is equivalent to a defender. Therefore, since the right of defence against an aggressor or robber is not extended so far as to kill him, except when peril of life or mutilation of limbs cannot otherwise be avoided, or when his property cannot be protected otherwise, and since this peril ceases as soon as he is no longer resisting a just force; the right also to kill one resisting a just force ceases, consequently, for the reason that he has resisted bravely, no right can arise to kill an enemy, which arises only by way of self-defence and defence of one's property.

§ 549, part 1, Jus Nat.
§ 778.
§ 979, part 1, Jus Nat.
§ 778.
§ 972, part 1, Jus Nat.
§ 1013, part 1, Jus Nat.
§ 699, part 2, Jus Nat.

§ 790.

There is no reason why you should object in the case of one resisting legal force that the enemy deserves punishment for the killing of our citizens and the destruction of our property. As for the fact that one who kills another, or who is a robber, is punished in a state by capital punishment, that is a civil punishment, to be determined from the purpose of the state according to existing circumstances, nor can civil laws be applied to the right of defence and to the right in war, which is to be derived from the principles of the law of nature. Those who think that the one who resists a just force can be killed in accordance with the right of vengeance,

§ 636, part 8, Jus Nat.

§ 640, part 8, Jus Nat.

which is forbidden by the law of nature, wander far from the truth and make an improper application of the very right of vengeance which they invoke, as is perfectly plain from those things which we have already noted in various places. Who will say that an aggressor may rightfully be killed when he desists from violence and there is no further need of defence? But nations use no other natural law than that which belongs to individual men in a state of nature. Much less is the right to kill an enemy on account of too stubborn resistance to be allowed him who merely thinks that he has a just cause of war, and his enemy an unjust cause. For mistake gives no right, nor in a doubtful case is a controverted right to be decided by arms, but he has a just cause of war who cannot persuade the other party to make a compromise, consequently his purpose is that he may compel his opponent to do so by force of arms.

§ 4.

§ 632.

§ 805. *Whether it can be extended to those who have not resisted*

§ 804.

Since the right to kill an enemy does not arise because he has resisted too stubbornly, much less on account of too stubborn resistance is it allowable to kill others who are in the category of enemies, but have not resisted the force brought upon them, such as the inhabitants of a besieged city, and those who were not in it, but were captured elsewhere, especially after they have abandoned a hostile intent.

Resistance may be made either in a siege or in a battle, or in individual combats. What is allowable in those acts is to be determined by the law of defence, and is not to be extended beyond them. Not all who are in the category of enemies are to be judged by the same law, so that any acts of a stranger could be charged to them as responsible principal persons. We have already more than once suggested that in the law of nature details must be carefully differentiated, since frequently the law may vary because of the most trivial circumstances.

§ 806. *Whether resentment because of disaster suffered may give a right to kill an enemy*

§ 804.

In like manner because the right to kill an enemy does not arise because he has resisted too stubbornly, neither does resentment because of disaster suffered give a right to kill an enemy.

An enemy is not to be killed except from necessity, because he resists legal force, and therefore the right to kill terminates as soon as the necessity ceases. He who on account of resentment because of disaster suffered kills an enemy who has come into his power either in battle or afterwards, does this only from desire for vengeance, which has no place by the law of nature even in defence, much less outside of it. In fact, in true defence a man is not killed by intent, but his death is rather to be attributed to accident, to which the fraud or fault of the aggressor has contributed. And for the reason that one who resists legal force may be bound to another to pay a penalty on account of hostilities which he commits, one may not infer that he can be killed, since there are other kinds of punishment, by which violence is not inflicted on the persons of enemies, which the natural law of nations makes legal, as is plain from the following proposition.

§ 790.

§ 999, part 1, Jus Nat.

§ 948, part 1, Jus Nat.

Note, § 992, part 1, Jus Nat.

§ 789.

§ 807. *Of the punishment of those who resist a just force too stubbornly*

If there is too stubborn resistance to a just force, not only is there a right to exercise a greater force, but also a right to other things which can have the effect of punishment, as in a siege, that they should be compelled to surrender themselves, either unconditionally or on harsh terms, that they should pay a certain sum of money, that they should give over their cities and homes to plunder, and in a battle there is a right to more than compensation for the loss. For he who wages an unjust war and consequently stubbornly resists a just force is bound to the other for a penalty. Nevertheless, since it is not allowable to kill an enemy on account of that resistance when he comes into our power, the penalty cannot be killing, but ought to be something else. Therefore, since any property corporeal or incorporeal can be taken away as a punishment, in a siege it has the effect of a punishment, that the besieged should be compelled to surrender themselves either unconditionally or on harsh terms, that they pay a certain sum of money, that their cities and homes be given over to plunder, and in a battle the right to more than compensation for the loss has the effect of a punishment. Which was the first point.

§ 789.
§ 804.

§ 589, part 8, Jus Nat.

§ 788.

But since one resisting a just force assumes the character of an aggressor, as we have proved above, and since only so much is allowable against an aggressor as is sufficient to ward off an injury, consequently as much

§ 804.
§ 980, part 1, Jus Nat.

as is necessary for repelling force by force, and since, furthermore, the force is allowable in war without which we cannot attain our right; if there is too stubborn a resistance to a just force, a right arises because of the resistance to exercise a greater force. Which was the second point.

Those who extend the right of punishing an enemy too far, and turn it into a general licence to inflict violence upon the persons of enemies, have no love for the human race, under which even enemies are included as to the love due them, nor do they shrink from cruelty. The law of nature, which has in view the happiness of all human beings, does not tolerate anything opposed to it except in case of conflict of one's happiness with that of another, and in case of losses on both sides it orders the one, who is at fault, to bear the loss. The more civilized nations to-day see to it that they agree to better terms, unless in the siege of cities matters have gone to extremities, but the besieged may be compelled to accept harsher terms, when they resist too stubbornly, although even in determining these terms a right is not to be turned into licence; nevertheless that is a thing which must be left to the judgement of the one deciding on the terms.

§ 743.

§§ 280, 614, 698, part 1, Jus Nat.

§ 229, part 1, Phil. Pract. Univ., and § 206 h.

§ 629, part 2, Jus Nat.

§ 783.

§ 808. *Of individual combats*

Individual combats, which do nothing towards acquiring one's right or towards ending the war, are illegal. For whatever is done in war to acquire one's right, consequently to end the war, is legal, since on account of its doubtful outcome no one can be certain of that which he has attained in war, and since it is to the advantage of the belligerents that war be at length ended; but what does not conduce to the end in view is illegal. If then individual contests do nothing towards acquiring one's right, or towards ending the war, they are illegal.

§ 781.

Hostilities are a means of attaining the end for which the war is waged. If you have a right to the end, you will also have a right to the means without which the end cannot be obtained. Therefore, necessity makes hostilities legal, which otherwise it would not be allowable to engage in, not the necessity of itself, but so far as it arises from the end to which you have a right. For necessity of itself is not capable of begetting a right, except in so far as the precedent right, from which it springs as from its source, makes a place for it. And therefore, the law of nature prescribes the narrowest limits for this necessity, beyond which it forbids it to wander. Therefore, from the purpose of the war all right in war is to be determined. Now we pursue our right by war, and in a doubtful case we have the right to compel the opposing party to a compromise. Therefore, he who has a just cause of war desires especially, nay rather he ought to desire, that the war may be ended as quickly as possible, and therefore it is rightly considered the purpose of the war, that it should be ended, or that there should be peace. Hence it is commonly said that war is waged for the sake of peace. Therefore, in determining the right to hostilities, one must consider no less carefully whether the hostilities contribute anything towards ending the war, than whether they tend to the attainment of one's right. But in so far as he who wages a just war has also the right to compel an enemy to desist from war and accept fair terms of peace, he attains his right therefore when he compels the other party to desist from war and make peace. And therefore, we have above included this right itself under the right for obtaining which war is waged. The same is seen most clearly in a defensive war, in which we defend our right against him who tries to take it from us by force. For a defensive war is undertaken for no other purpose than that the enemy may be compelled to desist from war, and we may be able quietly to enjoy our rights.

§ 1102, part 1, Jus Nat.

§ 572.

§ 781.

§ 809. *Of the right over captives taken by the one whose war is unjust*

He who wages an unjust war has no right over captives, but is bound by nature to restore them. He who wages an unjust war has no right in war, and all his force is illegal. If then he captures certain ones in war, he takes them without right, consequently he can acquire no right over those captured by his unjust act. Therefore, he has no right over those captured. Which was the first point.

§ 777.

§ 778.

Since he who wages an unjust war carries off the subjects of another without right when he captures them, he is guilty of kidnapping or theft of people, as was proved above, and he is a robber. Therefore, since a thief and a robber are bound to restore property stolen and carried away, consequently also a person who has been carried off, he who wages an

Note 1.
§ 141, part 8, Jus Nat., and § 775 h.

§ 778.
§ 524, part 2,
Jus Nat.

§ 755.

unjust war is bound by nature to restore those captured. Which was the second point.

Since kidnapping is the theft of people, a thief and a kidnapper are judged by the same law. But just as an unjust belligerent is a robber when he takes the property of enemies, so is he a kidnapper if he takes persons who are the subjects of an enemy whether they are soldiers or civilians. Therefore, as a kidnapper is bound to restore people who have been abducted, so also an unjust belligerent is bound to restore those who have been captured.

§ 810. *Of diminishing the strength of one waging an unjust war*

§ 781.
§ 1102, part 1,
Jus Nat.

Whatever he does who has a just cause for waging war to diminish the strength of one waging an unjust war, is allowable. For that is allowable for one who is waging a just war, without which he cannot acquire his right. Therefore, since he pursues by force his right against the one whose arms are unjustly taken up, consequently he cannot attain the same unless he should repel his force by force, and diminish the strength of the other, so that he may be finally compelled to desist from war; whatever he does who has a just cause for waging war, to diminish the strength of one waging an unjust war, is allowable.

§ 972, part 1,
Jus Nat.

One who defends himself against unjust force resists the same in order that he may avert the threatened injury, consequently his object in war is to compel the opposing party to desist from war. No one wages war without confidence in his resources, on the failure and exhaustion of which he cannot continue it. Nor does any one readily enter into a contest with one whom he recognizes as his superior in strength, unless he should wish to incur the stigma of rashness and pay the penalty for it. Therefore, he whose intention is to compel the enemy to desist from war is bound to reduce his forces and take them away from him. Therefore, if any one has the right to compel another to desist from war, he also has the right to diminish his forces, as a means without which the end for which he ought to strive cannot be obtained. Nevertheless this right ought not to be extended beyond that which is necessary to diminish his forces, lest you should seek to acquire a legal end by means which are illegal and for which, therefore, there is no necessity.

§ 71.

§ 811. *Of the right to capture enemies*

He who wages a just war is allowed to capture any enemies, both in so far as they resist in any way the restoration of his right, or prevent the end of the war, and by way of androlepsy. For that is allowable in war for the one who wages a just war, without which he cannot acquire his right from the opposing party. Therefore, since that cannot be done, if there is resistance to the restoration of his right, he may capture the enemies resisting him, in order that they may not be able to resist him longer. Which was the first point.

§ 781.

Likewise, since the forces of one waging an unjust war are diminished if those are captured who are preventing the end of the war, and since what one does who has a just cause for waging war to diminish the strength of one waging an unjust war, he is allowed to do; he who wages a just war is allowed to capture enemies who prevent the end of the war. Which was the second point.

§ 810.

Finally, since androlepsy is committed that he who does not wish to do so may be compelled to return a right to us or to our citizens, and since we pursue our right by force in war, and those things are allowed us without which it is not possible to attain it, if the enemy can be persuaded by the capture of certain persons to desist from the war, and return our right for which the war is waged, it is allowable to seize those persons by way of androlepsy. Which was the third point.

§ 593.

§ 781.

Before the question may be asked, what sort of a right against captives belongs to an enemy, it undoubtedly has to be shown that a right to capture enemies belongs to a belligerent. For if it should not be allowable to capture enemies, there can be no right then against those captured. And when it is understood for what reason they may be captured, then it can further be inferred what sort of persons may legally be captured, lest this right should be extended beyond the limits which it ought to have.

§ 812. *Of the right to capture soldiers and their officers*

§ 811.
§ 610.

Since it is allowable to capture enemies who resist the restoration of a right, and soldiers, through whom force is brought against the opposing party with whom war is waged, and their officers, to whom a certain control over the soldiers has been assigned by the sovereign power, and

§ 612.

to whom certain military duties are entrusted, are the principal persons who resist the restoration of a right, it is allowable to capture soldiers and their officers whenever the opportunity is offered to capture them.

§ 810.

If many soldiers are captured, that also tends to diminish the strength of the enemy, which diminution makes their capture legal. And it frequently contributes much, both towards ending the war, and also towards interfering with its success, if the chief leaders should be captured, whose skill has great effect in war.

§ 813. *Of those who are captured by way of androlepsy*

§ 811.

Because it is also allowable to capture enemies by way of androlepsy, and androlepsy is committed with the purpose that he may be compelled to restore your right who does not wish to restore it, it is allowable to cap-

§ 593.

ture noble women also and maidens, men conspicuous for their dignity and having leisure for the administration of the state, nay even boys, girls, and infants, children of the sovereign powers, and the sovereign powers themselves; consequently, if those besieged surrender themselves unconditionally, by the law of androlepsy it is allowable to carry away any persons, nay, if it shall so seem best, surrender is not to be allowed, except under this condition, that certain persons shall become captives.

So it can be agreed that all garrison soldiers with their officers should be made captives on account of a too stubborn resistance. Otherwise persons are not to be led away into captivity whose loss or prolonged captivity the sovereign power does not bear easily.

§ 814. *Of the right over captives*

Captives do not become slaves by the law of nature; nevertheless it is not contrary to natural law that they should be reduced to slavery for an offence that deserves that penalty. He who wages a just war may capture any enemies, both in so far as they resist in any way the restoration of his right and prevent the end of the war, and by way of androlepsy; consequently in order that the enemy may be compelled to desist from war and return his right. Therefore, since a right cannot be extended beyond the purpose for which it was given, and since it is not necessary for that purpose that captives should become slaves, but it is sufficient that they be detained until they should be freed by their friends, captives do not become slaves by the law of nature. Which was the first point.

§ 811.

§ 593.

But, indeed, if captives should have committed an offence for which they can be punished, since even liberty can be taken away as a punishment, and since this is taken away if they should be reduced to slavery, when the offence of captives deserves that punishment, they may be reduced to slavery. Which was the second point.

§ 589, part 8, Jus Nat.

§ 1117, part 7, Jus Nat.

When that cruel licence to commit violence on the persons of enemies was considered a right, captives were killed at pleasure, but when the atrocity of that was recognized they were reduced to slavery. From this the Emperor says that they are called *servi* because generals order their captives to be sold, and thus *preserve* them and do not put them to death. But since slavery was extended beyond the limits prescribed by the law of nature, as is usually done to-day by the nations among which slavery has been received, it can still be doubted whether slavery of that sort is to be preferred to death, or whether one would not prefer death rather than endure it, especially since the right of killing a slave is not thereby taken away, but always remains undiminished in the master's hands. But even though the right to kill a slave is taken away, slavery is not in harmony with the law of nature, unless an offence has been committed by the captive which deserves such a punishment. Those things which are done in war by unjust force are imputed to the nation as a whole, and not to the individuals as individuals. Therefore, although we assume that the act of the corporate body deserves punishment, nevertheless, since no one can be punished for the act of another, and since any one of those who share the punishment with each other is punished for his own act, by which he concurs in the act of another, individuals cannot submit to that punishment which the corporate body deserves. Moreover, in a state it is not inconsistent that individuals regarded as such and the corporate

Institutes, I. iii, § 3.

§§ 1080 and fol., part 7, Jus Nat.

§ 1084, part 1, Jus Nat.

§ 1083, part 1, Jus Nat.

§ 142, part 8, Jus Nat.

§ 778.

§ 39.

§ 4.
body should be opposed to each other as distinct persons, a thing which is perfectly clear in a democratic state, where the entire people is sovereign but the individuals are subjects. Therefore, although an unjust belligerent may be a robber and a brigand, and robbery and brigandage may be chargeable to the nation which the ruler of the state represents, nevertheless on this account it is not to be said that any one of the individual persons is guilty of robbery and brigandage. And since the punishments which are decreed against robbers and brigands in a state are civil punishments, and nations are subject to natural law in their relations with each other, nations cannot be punished for using unjust force in war in the way in which it is customary for robbers and brigands to be punished or as has been introduced by
§ 1059, part 1, Jus Nat.

§§ 1063, 977, part 1, Jus Nat.
a positive law. By the right to punish provision is made for security in the future, and from this purpose in the existing circumstances is to be determined how much is allowable to attain that purpose. Therefore, those are too hasty in their judgement who confuse the individuals of the corporate body with the corporate body, the penalties allowed by the law of nature of nations with the penalties decreed by positive law against robbers and brigands, and who make the different methods of concurring in the act of another identical with the act itself. Grotius with his keenness seems to have sufficiently distinguished them, although he has not fully explained all the details.[2]

§ 815. *Of the right over captives*

§ 814.

§ 794.

§ 811.

§ 593.
Since captives do not become slaves by the law of nature, nor is it allowable to kill them, soldiers and the officers of soldiers are to be detained until the war is ended, in order that they may not be able to injure us further or resist the restoration of our right, but those who have been captured by way of androlepsy are to be detained until the right has been restored.

§ 777.

§ 790.
 A right over persons in a just war, for in an unjust war there is no such right, arises from a defence of oneself and one's property; consequently soldiers and their officers are captured in order that they cannot longer resist the restoration of a right, but those who are captured by way of androlepsy are captured for no other purpose than that the

---

2. See Grotius, *The Rights of War and Peace,* ed. Richard Tuck, 3 vols. (Indianapolis: Liberty Fund, 2005), vol. 3, bk. III, chap. 3, I–II, pp. 1246–51.

enemy may be forced to desist from war, or by way of security for the restoration of our right by the enemy, in which case they put on the character of hostages, and therefore they are judged in accordance with the law of hostages. From the purpose therefore, on account of which the right to capture enemies has been granted by nature, is it to be determined what is allowable against captives.

§ 497.

§ 816. *Of the restitution of expenses incurred for captives*

If captives are to be released, the expenses incurred for their support or for other things are to be refunded by their nation. For they are captured on account of the act of their nation, for which certainly the war is waged. Therefore, the debt which has been contracted for expenses incurred for their support, or for other things, is understood to have been contracted by their own nation; consequently their own nation is bound to refund these expenses, if they are to be released.

§ 607.

Here we are speaking of that which by nature ought to be done, but not of that concerning which nations agree with each other during the continuance of the war, or when a treaty of peace is made. For it is more than well known that those things which are allowable by nature, such as the right of demanding expenses incurred for captives, can be changed by agreement.

§ 170, part 1,
Phil. Pract. Univ.

§ 817. *Of stipulations made for captives*

If stipulations concerning captives have been made between belligerents, as that they may be ransomed at a certain price, and are to be returned if the price is paid, the agreements must be observed. Since the things which are promised to an enemy as an enemy are to be observed, stipulations concerning captives made between belligerents are to be observed. Therefore, since the things promised in stipulations would be observed if those things should be performed concerning which there had been an agreement, if stipulations concerning captives have been made between belligerents, the agreements must be observed.

§ 799.

§ 788, part 3,
Jus Nat.

§ 430, part 3,
Jus Nat.

Thus if there has been an agreement concerning the price of ransom, the nation, which is bound by nature to free its subjects, is bound to pay the price agreed upon for redemption, and he who holds

§ 816.

them captive is bound to return them on payment of the price. But to release and to return are not the same thing. For those who are released are restored to their own control, so that they have the liberty either to return to their friends or to depart as they may wish; but those who are returned are restored to their own nation. It is quite important that this distinction be considered in the case of soldiers captured and ransomed during the continuance of the war. For an intention of returning to the army is scarcely to be presumed of a soldier given his liberty. But if, indeed, he should not return, he is equivalent to a deserter, and he incurs the penalty of desertion, a thing which those who have contracted for the redemption of captives during the continuance of the war must be believed to have wished to avoid. But it is self-evident that the justice of the war is not to be considered in these stipulations.

§ 818. *Of the release of captives*

He who holds captives can release them under any condition he pleases, and what they promise when they are released they are bound to observe, nor can they be prevented from observing it, either by their own nation, or by the one who has control over the nation. For he who holds captives has the right to retain them until the war is finished, if they are soldiers or their officers, or until the right is restored on account of which they have been captured by way of androlepsy, or until they are to be restored according to agreement. But since any one can give up his right, as far as he pleases, as long as he does nothing contrary to the right of a third person, he who holds captives can release them under any condition he pleases. Which was the first point.

But since, indeed, those who are released agree to the terms under which they are released, consequently promise that they will do nothing contrary thereto, and since even those things are to be observed which are promised to an enemy as an enemy, captives are bound to observe what they promise when they are released. Which was the second point.

Finally, since he who holds captives has the right to detain them until they are to be restored, if he should release them before he is bound to do it, his enemy, to whose power they are subject, is presumed to assent to the condition of their release, and consequently he also is bound through their promises not to demand anything from them contrary to

§ 815.

§ 817.

§ 117, part 3, Jus Nat.

§ 361, part 3, Jus Nat.

§ 799.

the promises. Therefore, they cannot be prevented by their own nation, or by the one who has control over the nation, from abiding by their promises. Which was the third point.

It makes no difference whether the release be made on the motion of the one who is holding the captives, or be secured by the entreaties of the captives.

§ 819. *Of release granted on promise of return and of the condition of not serving as a soldier*

Since he who holds captives can release them under any condition he pleases, and since what they promise when they are released they are bound to observe, if they are released for a certain period, on condition that they return to captivity, they are bound to return when the period has elapsed, and since he cannot be said to have returned into captivity who secretly enters the territory of an enemy, intending to escape again afterwards, he is bound to make a public return to captivity. In like manner those who are released on the condition that they may not serve as soldiers while the war continues, or for a certain time, cannot serve as soldiers during the continuance of the war, nor before the agreed time has elapsed. The same is understood in regard to any other conditions agreed upon.

§ 818.

A release is usually allowed to commanders and other officers of soldiers on promise of return, for the purpose of caring for their private business. Captives are released on condition of not serving as soldiers, if officers are released with the soldiers whom they command, as happens in the case of conditional surrender. But it is self-evident that the conditions under which a dismissal or release is granted cannot be such as are opposed to the right of the one to whose power the captives are subject. So the condition would be illegal, that never afterwards should the one released serve as a soldier, when the sovereign power whose subject he is has a war with any nation whatever, or even only with the one releasing him, since this nation has the right to detain the captive only during the continuance of the war. The same thing is understood if the condition affixed to the release should be contrary to agreements made concerning captives.

§ 117, part 3, Jus Nat.

§ 815.

§ 820. *Of destroying property in an unjust war*

§ 177.

In an unjust war all destruction of the property of an enemy is illegal. For he who wages an unjust war has no right in war. Therefore, since by nature no one ought to destroy the property of another or damage it, and since he does that who destroys the property of an enemy, as is self-evident, he who wages an unjust war ought not to destroy any property of the enemy, consequently in an unjust war all destruction of the property of an enemy is illegal.

§ 647, part 2,
Jus Nat.
§ 170, part 1,
Phil. Pract.
Univ.

§ 821. *Of the restoration of the loss caused by destruction*

§ 820.

§ 488, part 2,
Jus Nat.

§ 580, part 2,
Jus Nat.

Since in an unjust war all destruction of the property of an enemy is illegal, and since loss is caused thereby to an enemy who has justice on his side in the war, and since loss caused by fraud or fault is to be restored, he who in an unjust war destroys the property of an enemy is bound to restore the loss caused by the destruction.

This is a part of the debt arising from the war, which it is none the less allowable to seek by force than the original claim, for which the war was undertaken.

§ 822. *Whether a ravager in an unjust war is liable to a penalty*

§ 820.

§ 239, part 1,
Phil. Pract.
Univ.

§ 859, part 1,
Jus Nat.

§ 549, part 2,
Jus Nat.

Since in an unjust war all destruction of the property of an enemy is illegal, if he who wages an unjust war destroys the property of an enemy, he acts contrary to the right of the other with whom he is at war; consequently he does him a wrong, and therefore, since every one has the right by nature to punish the one who does him an injury, he who in an unjust war destroys the property of an enemy is bound to the other, with whom he is at war, for a penalty.

§ 636.

§ 789.

Since even in a just war we may seek a penalty, by the unjust destruction of property the right of the one who has taken up arms justly is increased. But because the unjust ravager is bound for a penalty to the other, with whom he is at war, from this also it might be inferred that he may be bound for a penalty, on account of the hostilities which

he commits; for ravaging is included in the category of hostilities. In
like manner the preceding corollary might be inferred from this, that   § 785.
losses caused in any way to one waging a just war are to be repaired.   § 788.
Since in an unjust war all destruction of the property of an enemy is   § 820.
illegal, all questions cease which are debated as to non-destruction,
in as much as they are pertinent only in case of a just war, in which
the right to destroy is to be restrained within its own limits, that its
exercise may not be accompanied by wrong.

§ 823. *Of the right to destroy the property of an enemy in a just war*

In a just war the destruction of the property of an enemy is legal, if without it we should not be able to pursue our right by force, if the strength
of the enemy thereby be diminished, and our own increased, if finally
the destruction be caused as a just penalty. For that is legal in a just war
without which we cannot attain our right from the enemy. Therefore,
since we pursue our right by force, if it should happen that it is inter-   § 781.
fered with, unless the property of the enemy should be destroyed, such   § 1102, part 1,
destruction is legal. Which was the first point.   Jus Nat.

Whatever serves to diminish the strength of one waging an unjust
war, and consequently to increase our strength, is legal in a just war. If   § 810.
then by the destruction of the property of an enemy the strength of an
enemy be diminished, our own increased, the destruction thereof in a
just war is legal. Which was the second point.

Finally, since any corporeal property can be taken away as a pun-   § 589, part 8,
ishment, for no other purpose indeed than that the one who is to be   Jus Nat.
punished should lose it, and consequently incur loss, and so far as con-   § 588, part 8,
                                                                                Jus Nat.
cerns the one to be punished it is the same whether his property should   § 486, part 2,
be taken from him, or destroyed, or spoiled; in a just war it is legal to   Jus Nat.
destroy the property of an enemy. Which was the third point.

But since, indeed, a heavier penalty is illegal, when a lighter one is   § 1065, part 1,
adequate, and since in so far as the punisher exceeds the limit, he injures   Jus Nat.
the one who is to be punished; if destruction of the property of an enemy   § 1067, part 1,
is done by way of penalty, the penalty ought to be just, that is, such as the Jus Nat.
offence of the enemy deserves. Which was the fourth point.

Loss is caused the enemy by destruction, but no gain accrues to us thereby, as if the ships of the enemy should be burned, if their engines for use in war should be made useless, if their buildings should be set on fire, if the trees in the orchards and the vines in the vineyards should be cut down, if crops and grain should be trampled down in the fields, if movable property either useful or ornamental or even necessary should be destroyed, and other things akin to these. Since hostilities in war are due to the force by which we pursue our right in war, which consists either in collecting a debt or imposing a penalty, and therefore all our right in war is to be determined thereby, the right to destroy the property of an enemy is not to be determined otherwise, unless you should wish to assume a thing which can be assumed only in contravention of the law of nature, that there is absolutely no place left in war for justice, which orders us to give each one his right, and that right in war becomes mere licence, to which none can be entitled. If you should object that when an enemy wrongfully seizes and destroys our property and kills our citizens, we likewise can, by the right of vengeance, seize and destroy his property and kill his citizens, you assume more than one thing which cannot be granted. For we have already proved elsewhere, and have several times before insisted, that the right of vengeance does not exist, but has been invented contrary to the law of nature. But this especially is to be noted, that this is not a question of what is allowable by virtue of reasons arising during the war, but what right by virtue of war belongs to a just belligerent; consequently what he may be allowed to do, no act of the enemy being assumed. For if he should commit a wrong with unjust force, since he deserves punishment, destruction even of his property has a place as a just penalty, as the present proposition plainly declares. It is plain, of course, from the above proofs that in our method of treatment there must be consideration of wrongs committed in war also. Furthermore it is to be noted that the question now is not whether any one may think that he has a just cause of war, but what is fitting for one who in fact does have a just cause. For right does not arise from your opinion but from the truth. Therefore we are not to discuss at present what weight is to be given to opinion, for that we shall investigate more closely hereafter, nor can that be done, unless it is understood beforehand what is in harmony with the truth. Other things might still be

§ 781.

§ 927, part 1, Jus Nat., and § 265 h.

§ 926, part 1, Jus Nat.

§ 150, part 1, Jus Nat.

§ 640, part 8, Jus Nat.

§ 549, part 2, Jus Nat.

§ 782.

suggested, except that they have already been made plain in previous discussions or might be more properly inculcated in what follows. This at least may be added, that the belief that one's cause is just does not make it right, but he who cherishes such a belief simply persuades himself that he has a right arising from a just cause, so that then in proving the right to destroy the property of an enemy the opinion of a belligerent deserves no attention.

§ 824. *Of allowable destruction of the fruits of the field, crops, houses, orchards, and vineyards in warlike operations*

Since in a just war the destruction of the property of an enemy is legal, if without it we cannot attain our right, since moreover in war camps §823. must be established and then must be surrounded with a rampart and a ditch, when that cannot be done unless fruits or crops are trodden down, fields spoiled, sometimes even buildings torn down, orchards and vineyards uprooted, and the same is true in the siege of cities and in battles; it is allowable to spoil the fields of the enemy, trample down the fruits and crops in them, tear down the buildings, uproot the orchards and vineyards, if the laying out of camps, the siege of cities, and battles demand it.

Here no distinction is made between different things, whatever sort they may be, nor are their qualities considered; for the right over things arises not from their qualities but from the need of destroying them, which the right to war renders legal. Indeed, the ruler of our state himself destroys the property of citizens by the power of eminent domain, if defence against hostile force demands the destruction. The law of nature, which gives us a right to war, gives also a right against §§ 110, 111, the property of enemies, as far as that is necessary in waging war; for part 8, Jus Nat. otherwise the former right would be useless, if it were not allowable to claim the latter. § 613.

§ 825. *Of the destruction of cities, villages, and towns*

In like manner, because the destruction of cities, towns, villages after they have come into our power accomplishes nothing toward attaining our right, nor is the strength of the enemy thereby diminished nor ours increased, as is self-evident, it is not legal to tear down or destroy cities, towns, and villages after they have come into our power. Nevertheless, since destruction is legal as a just punishment, the destruction of cities, towns, and villages is legal, if some special offence has before occurred which deserves such a punishment.

§ 823.

§ cited.

I say some special offence ought to occur beforehand, not only on the part of those who inhabit the cities, towns, and villages, but likewise of the sovereign power with whom there is war, because all the property of subjects alike with public property is looked at as property of the nation, and the act of the sovereign power is imputed to the entire nation. But the justice of the punishment is to be determined from its purpose, to decide of course how much is to be inflicted for the terrorizing of the enemy, that provision may be made for security in the future.

§ 289.

§ 39.

§ 826. *Of the demolition of fortifications*

Since the power of resistance is diminished if fortifications should be demolished, when it seems best to abandon them after they have been captured, as is indeed self-evident, their demolition is legal.

§ 823.

The building of fortifications requires very great expenditures. Therefore, by their demolition a very great loss is inflicted on the enemy. But since in an unjust war the other party, whose cause is unjust, is the cause of the loss, the unjust belligerent, who has imposed the necessity upon the just belligerent of using the means from which the loss results to him, should blame himself for the loss, however much it may be. Of course, the act of the just belligerent ought to be viewed from two standpoints, from his own and from that of the unjust belligerent. From the former standpoint, it is the means without which the end which the just belligerent seeks and ought to seek cannot be attained; but from the latter, it is the act from which loss arises for the unjust belligerent. The just belligerent seeks his end, not the loss, and he acts on account of that end, not for the sake of the loss, since he prefers, if it can be done, that his act should not be accompanied by loss. Therefore, the real cause of the loss is not the one from whose deed that results, but the one who induced the necessity of the action. And therefore, the loss is not imputed to the just belligerent,

§ 527, part 1, Phil. Pract. Univ.

but to the unjust. See what we have proved elsewhere already and have discussed, when we were speaking of self-defence, and of one who punishes another. And so then it is plain how war can be waged with the greatest religious scruple, without affecting the love which we owe even to an enemy, and without any desire for vengeance, from which every one ought to keep his mind free. See what we have proved and discussed elsewhere concerning defence, and concerning punishment. But do not persuade yourself that those things which belong to virtue are confused by us with those things which belong to law. For in the law of nature, when we speak of that which it is allowable to do, nothing can be admitted as allowable which is opposed to duty; for the law of nature which confers a right for the sake of performing our duties, just as it controls all other acts of men, likewise controls also those which pertain to the exercise of a right. And therefore, the abuse of a right, not its use, consists in those things which are opposed to duty, and the abuse is to be endured by those who can claim for themselves no right over the actions of another by virtue of natural liberty, as we likewise have proved clearly in regard to ownership. Justice, which is itself a virtue, and the other virtues are bound to each other by a sisterly bond, and they are not to be considered as enemies, between whom there is continual war. When, therefore, the question concerns the law of nature, the following argument has no force: When property comes into the power of an enemy it is his; consequently as owner he can destroy it at will. For let us assume for the time that by the law of nature itself the property of an enemy belongs to the party into whose power it comes; to destroy it without just cause is an abuse of ownership forbidden by the law of nature. But what must be endured unpunished between nations is another question, of which we shall speak later. Those who do not distinguish in the civil law what things are to be endured, so that human affairs can be settled, and because by force of natural liberty each one must be allowed to do as he pleases, as long as he does not do what is contrary to your right, and what things the law of nature urges; really admit the voluntary law of nations in that sense which we have explained, while they seek to oppose it, confusing it with natural law, and opposing law to virtue as though contrary to it, just as if what is to be considered as law among men were really law. Those trained in the concepts of the civil law, which

§ 993, part 1, Jus Nat.

§ 1075, part 1, Jus Nat.

§ 743.

§ 948, part 1, Jus Nat.

§§ 998, 999, part 1, Jus Nat.

§§ 1077, 1078, part 1, Jus Nat.

§ 159, part 1, Phil. Pract. Univ.

§§ 167 and fol., part 2, Jus Nat.

§§ 926, 927, part 1, Jus Nat.

§ 170, part 2, Jus Nat.

§§ 157, 158, part 1, Jus Nat.

§ 22.

[On the Laws, I.
xv. 42, xxii. 58.]

are not sufficiently developed, have corrupted the pure doctrine of the law of nature; so much the more indeed as they have been strangers to all philosophy, from the depths of which Cicero has long taught that all knowledge of law is to be drawn, not from the pandects, or decrees of the praetors, nor from the opinion of the learned, as is the custom of those of our time who are skilled in the law. Finally, we suggest what we have already insisted upon more than once, but can never be insisted upon enough, in the law of nature there ought to be one harmony, one concord, which we trust will shine out clearly from our system.

§ 827. *Of the destruction of tombs and monuments and of violence to the bodies of the buried*

§ 700, part 6,
Jus Nat.
§ 823.

Since the destruction of tombs and monuments erected to the memory of the dead and violence to the bodies of the buried accomplish nothing toward diminishing the resistance of the enemy nor toward increasing our strength, and since the dead are not in the category of enemies, destruction of tombs and burial monuments of the dead and violence to the bodies of the buried are illegal.

§ 802.

There is no reason why you should object that such things can be done to terrorize the enemy and induce him to end the war and accept fair conditions of peace, a thing which is rightly intended by one who is waging a just war. For no terrorizing is allowable in war, however it may be inspired in the enemy, as is plain from the above proof concerning the killing of captives for the purpose of inspiring fear, and from our annotations. Those measures are never to be approved which indicate a desire simply to injure the enemy, when they do not have even the least influence upon the war. Incidentally we mention that the things of which we have spoken in the present proposition are called things religious in the terminology of the Roman law, for by that law any place is said to become religious through burial of the dead.

§ 828. *Of the destruction of sacred things*

For the same reason the destruction of sacred things is illegal, such as temples, and the altars in them, images and other decorations, and since in matters which arise between nation and nation, no difference in religions is to be considered, you gain no right to destroy sacred things because an enemy favours a religion which is different from your own, and which in your judgement is false.

§§ 259 and fol.

This destruction is much more disgraceful, if the enemy professes the same religion as your own, since a form of divine worship is interfered with, which in accordance with your judgement is to be favoured in every way, however superstitious the worship may be; for he indeed sins who acts according to a mistaken conscience, and therefore, in judging the act of another a mistaken conscience is also to be taken into account. Since every war ought to aim either at repairing a wrong, if it can be repaired, or at satisfying the one injured for the wrong done, if it cannot be repaired, or at avoiding the doing of a wrong, and since the religion of an enemy in no way affects this end, as is self-evident; it gives you no right to a thing to which you have no right otherwise. Here the question could be raised whether it would be allowable to take from an enemy sacred things which are movable, so that you yourself may make the same use of them as he does; but that we shall examine later. For here we are speaking simply of destruction, by which indeed loss is caused to the enemy; but it is attended with no advantage to you, as we have before mentioned. But of that destruction, which we have said was much more disgraceful, we have an example in the catholic who destroys a sacred image for the purpose of injuring and wronging an enemy.

§ 441, part 1, Phil. Pract. Univ.

§ 619.

Note, § 823.

§ 829. *Of the destruction of things which bear fruit*

Hence, furthermore, it is plainly illegal to destroy a thing bearing fruit, which we ourselves hold, in order that it cannot produce fruit for the enemy during the continuance of the war, since this contributes nothing of importance toward making or conducting war, consequently the destruction of fruit-bearing trees which do not interfere with warlike operations is illegal.

§ 823.

It is readily evident that such things are not done, except for the sole purpose of doing injury, although nevertheless an injury ought not to be done for its own sake.

Note, § 827.

§ 830. *Of destruction of hay, straw, food, and drink of enemies, nay even our own*

§ 823.

Since the strength of the enemy is increased, if he has an abundance of the things which he needs to carry on war in any way, and is diminished, if he is deprived of them, it is allowable to destroy not only hay and straw which the enemy has collected for use in war, and to set fire to gunpowder, but also to destroy flour and food and drink, nay more, not only must this be done, in order that our property of this sort may not come into the power of the enemy, but also our other property which is useful in war may be destroyed, in order that it cannot be used against us.

§ 170, part 2, Jus Nat.

§ 169, part 2, Jus Nat.

Note, § 825.

Perchance some will wonder that we give a reason why it is allowable for us to destroy our property so that it may not be useful to the enemy in war, since by virtue of ownership we can dispose of our property as it seems best to us. But those who thus think do not consider that there is also an abuse of ownership, prohibited by natural law, although it cannot be checked by a third party who has no right over our actions. See what we have noted a little while ago.

§ 831. *Of taking from an enemy things which are sacred*

§ 1102, part 3, Jus Nat.

§ 786.

§§ 512 and fol., part 8, Jus Nat.

§ 787.

If you can make use in war of certain sacred things, you may take them from the enemy within the limit of what is due as a debt or penalty. The same is understood of those things of which you can make the same use in divine service, if they are seized for such use. For he who wages a just war, since he wages it with the purpose of attaining his right, certainly must take care to increase his powers in every way; and since the other party, whose war is unjust, is bound to pay the expenses, he may increase his strength from the resources of the enemy. If then you can make use in war of certain sacred things, since it is not altogether repugnant to the nature of sacred things that they become profane, it is allowable to take them from the enemy. Since, nevertheless, it is not allowable to take away more than the amount of the debt, under which is likewise included what is due as a penalty, except with the intention of restoring it, if you can make use in war of certain sacred things, you can take them from the enemy within the limit of what is due as a debt or penalty. Which was the first point.

But if the sacred things have no use at all in war, nevertheless you should wish to make use of them as the enemy does, and take property from the enemy within the limit of your debt, under which is likewise included what is due as a penalty, you are not bound to restore it at the end of the war; if you take away for your own use sacred things having no use in war and charge the things taken as a debt or penalty, it is allowable to take them away. Which was the second point.

§ 787.

Sacred things are silver vessels and silver images and statues. It is allowable to sell them, if temporary misfortune and other necessities force this sale, in order to aid the wretched. Therefore, since money can be coined from the silver, since too the silver can be sold, if you should need money for paying the expense of war, which the enemy owes, and for which all his goods are pledged, it is not to be doubted that within the limit of your debt you may take from the enemy sacred silver vessels and silver images and statues, especially if your citizens cannot contribute what they ought to contribute. But except from necessity one must not go to these extremities, lest we may seem to wish to disturb the sacred things of the enemy, for war is not waged with the church but with the state, not for religion, but to acquire our right. Therefore, it is not proper to exercise a right to sacred things other than such as the church has by nature, since nations in their relations with each other use only natural law. But if the belligerents are devoted to the same religion, if through it the natural law of the church is interpreted more strictly, from this it must be decided what may be done rightly, in order that they may not sin against their conscience. For although you may assume that conscience may be mistaken, nevertheless it is understood that nothing ought to be done contrary to a mistaken conscience. You have here an illustration of the first point of the present proposition; an illustration of the second would be the following. If a catholic wages war with a catholic, no one doubts that one of them can transfer a miraculous image from an enemy church to one of his own. The same thing is true in regard to other precious images and utensils which he transfers from an enemy church to one of his own, for the same use in divine service which they had before; but that this may be done rightly, it must be within the limit of the debt and the penalty. We have already described the persuasive reasons which prevent the exercise of a perfect right, and

§ 514, part 8, Jus Nat.

§ 786.

§ 495.

§ 4.

§ 441, part 1, Phil. Pract. Univ.

§§ 743, 744.

here we speak simply of the right, not of its exercise, which the precepts of religion control no less than do those of the law of nature. The most perfect law prescribes this, that we should show ourselves fair to all, even to enemies themselves. Therefore, no one should think that we defend superstition and idolatry. For such it would be to devote any sacred things to superstition and idolatry; nevertheless, war is not waged for the purpose of uprooting superstition and idolatry, nor do enemies cease to be superstitious and idolatrous if those things should be taken from them; a thing which in the other case, in which the same use is made of them, could certainly not occur. Arms are not a suitable instrument for destroying superstition and idolatry. For others are to be persuaded to the true worship of God, and when that cannot be done, we must allow every nation to indulge its own impulse.

§ 261.

§ 832. *Of the right of a ruler of a state to sell the sacred things of the church on account of war*

If the burdens of war should fall too heavily upon subjects, the ruler of the state can apply the sacred things, especially the superfluous, useless, and valuable ones, to the expenses of the war. Nay, this right belongs to the church also, if what is demanded by an enemy cannot be contributed from another source. In imposing burdens the ruler of a state ought to take care that his subjects should not be reduced to poverty. Therefore, since the sacred things, especially the superfluous, useless, and valuable ones, can be sold to aid the wretched in times of misfortune, and since the ruler of the state by force of eminent domain can dispose of the property of citizens in case of necessity for the benefit of the state; if the burdens of war should fall too heavily upon subjects, the ruler can apply the sacred things, especially the superfluous, useless, and valuable ones, to the expense of war. Which was the first point.

§ 777, part 8, Jus Nat.
§ 512, part 8, Jus Nat.
§ 513, part 8, Jus Nat.
§ 523, part 8, Jus Nat.
§ 514, part 8, Jus Nat.
§§ 110, 111, part 8, Jus Nat.

But since the ruler of the state, when he does this, in fact disposes of the right over sacred things belonging to the church, as proved above, therefore, from this it is now apparent that the church also can apply the sacred things, especially the superfluous, useless, and valuable ones, to the contribution which is demanded by the enemy, if that cannot be made up from another source. Which was the second point.

Here we speak only of that which is allowable by nature. If religion puts an obstacle in the way of alienation of some things, that is not the present question. But in the latter case it must be kept in mind that a right belongs to the enemy, to whom contribution must be made, to take away the sacred things, which right could not belong to him if they were in themselves inalienable. But when the church does not wish to use its right, the enemy either will exercise his right or will reduce the wretched to poverty by plundering or other harsher measures; a thing which the church ought certainly to provide against by the exercise of its right.

§ 831.

§ 514, part 8, Jus Nat.

§ 833. *Whether it is allowable to capture enemies or the property of enemies in peaceful territory*

It is not allowable to capture enemies or the property of enemies in peaceful territory. For belligerents have no right against one who does not involve himself in the war; consequently in a peaceful territory he can claim no right of war for himself. Therefore, since aside from the right of war, belligerents can claim no right for themselves in the territory of another, neither is it allowed them to enter a peaceful territory with an armed force and to capture in it enemies and the property of enemies.

§ 293.

§ 166, part 8, Jus Nat.

Civil sovereignty in his own territory belongs to the ruler of the state, and foreigners residing in it and their property are subject to his right, as if they were temporary citizens. If then a belligerent in a peaceful territory should claim some right for himself over enemies and the property of enemies, that would be done contrary to the right of the owner of the territory; consequently he would do him a wrong, a thing which is not allowable. Therefore through the right of the owner of the territory the right of a belligerent in a peaceful territory over the enemy and the property of the enemy is suspended, but is not taken away, because it cannot be exercised without wrong, for which he is bound to pay a penalty to the owner of the territory. But it is another question if the owner of the territory should permit it, a thing which he certainly can do, unless he should be a neutral in the war.

§ 167, part 8, Jus Nat.
§ 303.
§ 239, part 1, Phil. Pract. Univ.

§ 859, part 1, Jus Nat.
§ 911, part 1, Jus Nat.

§§ 724, 727.
§ 549, part 2, Jus Nat.
§ 117, part 3, Jus Nat.
§ 672.

§ 834. *Whether it is allowable to take a captive or captured property through peaceful territory*

It is not allowable to take captives or captured property through peaceful territory. To take captives and captured property to places of safety is an act of war, by which hope of recovery is taken from the enemy. Therefore, he who allows captives and captured property to be taken through his territory aids the other belligerent party in the war, consequently involves himself in it. Since, therefore, the owner of a peaceful territory does not wish to involve himself in the war, the passage of a belligerent with captives and captured property is not without harm, consequently the right of passage through foreign territory ceases, which otherwise is included in just claims. Therefore, since the owner of a territory can prohibit belligerents with captives and captured property from crossing his territory—and in the present case it may be presumed from what has been proved above that he does not wish to allow it—and no foreigner contrary to the prohibition of the owner of a territory is allowed to enter it, it is not allowable to take captives and captured property through peaceful territory.

He who takes captives and captured property through peaceful territory claims for himself a right in the territory of another which does not belong to him. Therefore, since no one can do this, if he should dare to do it he violates the right of the owner of the territory, and consequently, as is before evident, he is responsible to him for the wrong done. But it is another question if the owner of the territory on request should allow that, for it is wholly up to him to determine whether or not he wishes to involve himself in the war in this way. Nor should you object that one nation ought to allow harmless passage to the military forces of another nation, consequently passage with captives and captured property ought much more to be allowed; for it is plain from the proof, that to take captives and captured property through peaceful territory is not to be classed as a harmless passage. And besides it is understood that the passage with an army through foreign territory ought not to be made unless it is allowed by the owner of the territory on request. Therefore, although passage with captives and captured property through peaceful territory might be harmless, nevertheless

§ 689, part 6, Jus Nat.

§ 295.

§ 293.

§ 239, part 1, Phil. Pract. Univ.

Note, § 833.

§ 686.

§ 688.

the right of the owner of the territory is violated, in so far as it is done without formal request being made to the one with whom rests the decision as to the crossing and the reason, if there should be any, for forbidding it. He intrudes upon the control of the state, who wishes to assume for himself the decision as to what is to the advantage of the state itself: a thing which is illegal. Nor, furthermore, is it the same thing to pass with military force through foreign territory and to take captives and captured property through it. For the first of these acts is allowed, because you have no right to interfere with the war; but the second act cannot be allowed, unless by the means which we have already mentioned you wish to aid one of the belligerents in warlike acts or, if you prefer, to assist in a warlike act, consequently desire to involve yourself in the war. If you should desire to interfere with the war, or even to interfere with aid for the war, then you would involve yourself in the war by taking the part of one of the belligerents: a thing which does not happen if you do not claim for yourself a right to interfere in that in which you have no right to interfere. This first act is not to be taken amiss by the other belligerent party, but the latter is not to be borne. It has seemed best to explain these things a little more fully, lest one should imagine a contradiction where there is none.

§ 257.

§ 690.

§ 835. *Of allowing safe departure to the citizens of an enemy when war is declared*

When war is declared, a safe departure within a definite time is to be allowed foreigners who are citizens of the enemy, or of that nation against which war is declared. Since foreigners, as long as they live in alien territory, are considered as temporary citizens, when they are allowed to live or stay there they are understood to have been received into the number of temporary citizens. But when the war is announced, all the subjects of the one against which it is announced are declared to be enemies of the subjects of the one announcing war, and remain such in whatever part of the world they live. Therefore, since it is inconsistent for one to be an enemy, against whom we seek our right by force, and a temporary citizen, whose actions are subject to the laws of the place, when war is announced, by that very fact it is declared that the subjects of the nation against which war is threatened are no longer to be considered as

§ 303.

§ 723.

§ 724.

§§ 722 h, and 1102, part 1, Jus Nat.

§ 299.

temporary citizens in the other's territory, and by the publication that fact itself is made plain to foreigners who are residing in the territory of the nation announcing war. Therefore, since no foreigner may enter a territory contrary to the prohibition of its ruler, and consequently may not remain there, when publication is made to those who are subjects of one against whom war is declared, they must depart. Which was the first point.

§ 737.

§ 295.

But as long as they are in the territory of the one announcing the war, since they are bound to conform their actions to the laws of the place, and consequently ought not to entertain a hostile intent, they cannot be considered as enemies. Therefore, no hostile act against them is allowed, as long as they are not in the other's territory contrary to the prohibition of its ruler. Nevertheless, since they are bound to depart, as proved above, a safe departure within a definite time is to be allowed, within which they can get outside the boundaries of the territory. Which was the second point.

§ 300.

Point 1.

Since the ruler of a territory is not understood to allow foreigners to live in his territory or reside there, except on the condition that they should conform their actions to the laws of the place, and that those entering the territory should tacitly bind themselves to this, between the ruler of the territory and the foreigner living in it there exists a tacit stipulation, by which the latter promises temporary obedience, the former, protection, under which is also included a safe departure. Therefore, since stipulations are to be observed, even those that are tacitly agreed upon, from the tacit stipulation a safe departure is to be allowed, if a reason arises because of which the ruler of a territory can no longer allow the foreigner, who was before admitted, to remain in his territory, and the foreigner is bound to obedience, so that he must depart within the time set for him. This is in conformity with the rule that the sanctity of a tacit pledge is to be observed no less than that of an express one.

§ 299.

§ 300.

§ 555.

§ 789, part 3, Jus Nat.

§ 556.

§ 556.

§ 836. *How the same are to be declared enemies*

Since, when war is declared, a safe departure within a definite time is to be allowed foreigners who are citizens of the enemy, or of that nation

§ 835.

against which war is declared, in the declaration of the war they must be ordered to depart within a definite time, and when this has elapsed they are to be considered as enemies.

Of course the subjects of one against whom war is declared immediately become enemies when the announcement is made, since nothing prevents them from being considered as such; but if they are residing in the territory of the one announcing the war, the right derived from the tacit stipulation under which they were admitted to the territory prevents them from being considered enemies immediately on the announcement, since, as we said before, that includes a free and safe departure, which cannot be made without delay. It is understood that safe entrance is not allowed without a safe departure, whether this be permitted expressly or tacitly. Therefore, in the present case also the law of nations guarantees a safe departure, when it commands that the good faith of nations be kept sacred. But it is the duty of the ruler of the territory, who must assure a safe departure, to fix the time within which the foreigner must depart from his country after the expiry of which they are no longer to be considered as temporary citizens but as enemies.

Note, § 835.

§ 837. *Of those who stay beyond the allotted time in the territory of the enemy*

Since the citizens of the one against whom war has been declared, if they should not depart from the territory of the one announcing the war within the time fixed in the declaration of war, are to be considered as enemies, since, moreover, it is allowable to capture any who are enemies, those who stay beyond the time allotted them in the declaration of war in the territory of the enemy, into which they have come before the war, can be detained as captives, nevertheless they cannot be killed.

§ 836.

§ 811.

§ 794.

They of course are ranked in the same condition as citizens of the enemy. For although otherwise the ruler of a territory can under definite penalty prohibit a foreigner from entering his territory, because of the loss to the state which is to be feared from the entrance of foreigners, and although it is known that the Chinese formerly forbade the entrance of foreigners under pain of death, nevertheless there is a difference in the present instance, in which on account of war it is not

§ 269 h, and § 625, part 8, Jus Nat.

Note, § 296.

allowable to remain in the territory of an enemy for a purpose which does not bear on the war and which is not of itself injurious to the state. It is one thing to live in the territory of an enemy for a matter of this sort, and another to come into it with the intention of planning some hostile design; and this very difference is considered in the case of an enemy, whenever he comes into our power.

§ 838. *Of one who cannot depart because he is prevented by superior force*

Since the citizens of an enemy who have come into our territory before the war are bound to depart within a definite time after a declaration of war has been made, and since no one is bound beyond that which is possible, if any one cannot depart within the prescribed time because he is prevented by a superior force, such, that is, as he cannot resist, delay must be allowed him.

§ 836.

§ 209, part 1, Phil. Pract. Univ.

Here especially belongs the case of one who overtaken by illness is compelled to keep to his bed. For then a delay must be allowed until he recovers. Here we speak of delay which ought to be allowed, but not of that which is obtained by way of a favour for the purpose of expediting one's business affairs. For the latter is a matter of mere indulgence.

§ 27, part 4, Jus Nat.

§ 839. *Of the confiscation of property of an enemy in the territory of one who is waging a just war*

Movable property of an enemy in one's own territory can be confiscated, within the limit of his debt and the penalty, by one who is waging a just war. For since it is allowable to do that to an enemy without which one cannot acquire one's right, and since all the property of hostile subjects may be held in pledge for the debt of their nation, since moreover the property of an enemy remains such, wherever it may be, it is evident that the movable property of an enemy in one's own territory can be confiscated by a just belligerent. Nevertheless, since, beyond the limit of the debt, within which is also included what is due as a penalty, captured property is to be restored at the end of the war, movable property of an

§ 781.

§ 495.

§ 727.

§ 787.

enemy in one's own territory can be confiscated within the limit of his debt and penalty by a just belligerent.

Here is understood not only the primary debt for which the war was undertaken, but also that arising in the war itself, both from injury done in it, and from expenses incurred in it, inasmuch as the unjust belligerent ought to pay them. Here, likewise, is included money, in as much as it is usually included in movable things. Such confiscation is in accord with the law of nature, which commands us to abstain from force when we can acquire without it what otherwise it is not possible to acquire except by force. § 786.

§ 782.

§ 840. *Of not paying a debt to an enemy*

Since he who is waging a just war can confiscate movable property of an enemy in his own territory, within the limit of his debt and the penalty, nay even beyond that limit with the intention of restoring it when the war is ended, he can also prohibit the debtors of the enemy, his own citizens, from paying the debt to their creditors during the continuance of the war; nay more, he can command that they pay the debt to him, when the day of payment comes. § 839.

§ 787.

This prohibition is already included under the general prohibition which is usually made in the declaration of war, namely, that there shall be no dealing with the enemy during the continuance of the war. It falls heavily indeed upon those whose property is confiscated; but this is a necessary evil which war brings with it, and is a misfortune which it is not possible to avoid. Nevertheless, it is not to be considered harder than if the enemy invades the country in which we dwell and carries away from us our property, or exacts a contribution. And when we speak of a right in war, that is not to be determined from the loss which is caused to the subjects of the enemy, nor from the sorrow by which their souls are tortured, but from the purpose of the war, from which that right springs, as from its source, as is quite plain from what has been proved heretofore. War is nothing but the mother of disasters, which, therefore, a ruler of a state strives to avoid, as far as possible, if he has at heart consideration for the happiness of his subjects.

§ 841. *Of immovable property possessed by your citizen in the territory of an enemy*

If a citizen of one of the belligerents possesses immovable property in the territory of another, it is the property of an enemy as regards the former but not as regards the latter. For those who possess immovable property in foreign territory, as far as it is concerned are subject to the law of the people, or of the one who has the right of the people, although they themselves may remain foreigners, consequently as possessors of it they are regarded as his subjects. Therefore, since all property which belongs to any subject of one of the belligerent parties is the property of an enemy as regards the other party, if a citizen of one of the belligerents possesses immovable property in the territory of the other, it is the property of an enemy as regards the former, but not as regards the latter.

§ 167, part 8,
Jus Nat.
§ 141, part 8,
Jus Nat.

§ 726.

Just as there is no contradiction in the fact that he who is your citizen or subject may as a possessor be the subject of one in whose territory he possesses immovable property, so there is no contradiction in the fact that the property of the one who is not your enemy is the property of an enemy as regards you, and that as possessor of that property he may be considered an enemy. A possessor is a moral person, not to be extended beyond the possession, which it is possible to separate from the physical individual without affecting its other moral characteristics.

§ 70, part 1,
Jus Nat.

§ 842. *And in general of whatever is possessed by any foreigners*

Nay more, in general immovable property possessed by a foreigner in the territory of an enemy is the property of an enemy. This is shown in the same way as in the preceding proposition.

It is, of course, just the same whether he who possesses immovable property in the territory of one of the belligerents is a citizen of the other belligerent, or of another who has no connexion with the war. For that property is the property of an enemy does not depend upon the person, but upon the things themselves which are possessed, in so far, of course, as they are subject to the jurisdiction of the one to whom the territory belongs.

§ 331.

§ 843. *What military contributions are*

Military contributions are defined as a collection of money and other fungible things for supporting an army, exacted from the subjects of the enemy.

> When an enemy enters into the territory of one with whom he is at war, or even when entrance is open to him, and exacts from his subjects money, grain, food for his horses, and anything else of which he has need for the support of his army, all such things are included in military contributions, because individuals are bound to contribute proportionately.

§ 844. *Of the right to demand contributions*

Since military contributions are demanded and exacted for the purpose of supporting the army, and since the expenses incurred for a war are due to the one who is waging a just war, consequently those things which are necessary to support an army are due to him, he therefore has the right to demand and to exact military contributions. Nevertheless, since no one can be bound beyond that which is possible, and since also we ought to love the enemy as ourselves, nor cherish hostile feeling towards him, contributions ought to be exacted according to the extent of the capacities of those who are bound to give them.

§ 843.
§ 786.

§ 209, part 1,
Phil. Pract. Univ.

§ 743.
§ 744.

> Since nothing is done rightly in an unjust war, there is no right to demand contributions in it. Moreover, no one should be surprised that we require that in determining the amount of just contributions there should be consideration of the love of enemies, on the ground that we are confusing that which is a matter of right with that which is a matter of virtue; for the determination of the amount has nothing to do with the right, which in itself is unlimited, but with the exercise of the right, which never can be separated from virtue, unless you should wish to consider an abuse of the right and a proper use thereof to be one and the same thing. See what we have said above in regard to that point.

§ 777.

§ 826.

§ 845. *What pillaging is*

Pillaging is a forceful taking away by soldiers of movable things from the houses of enemies or from other places where they are kept or hidden away. In our native vernacular it is called *die Plünderung* [plundering].

Thus soldiers are said to pillage a city if they are allowed, or if they are ordered, to rush into any houses and carry away from them whatever movables they choose: a thing which frequently occurs in the storming of cities. The houses also are said to be pillaged.

§ 846. *When it is allowable*

§ 844.

§ 1112, part 5, Jus Nat.

§ 845.

Pillaging is allowable if just contributions should not be paid, or even if it should be done within the limits of the penalty. For just contributions are a debt, which the belligerent collects by right of war. Therefore, since by nature every one is allowed to take in place of that which is due to him, when he cannot collect that from the debtor, any other property which is worth as much; and since in pillaging of houses any movable property found in them, or even hidden away, is taken away from them, if just contributions should not be paid, pillaging is allowable. Which was the first point.

§ 589, part 8, Jus Nat.

§ 845.

§ 1065, part 1, Jus Nat.

Furthermore, since any corporeal property can be taken away by way of penalty, which is in the ownership of the one from whom the penalty is exacted, and when houses are pillaged any movable property is forcibly taken from them by soldiers, pillaging therefore can be done by way of penalty; consequently, since a heavier penalty is illegal when a light one is sufficient, pillaging is allowable if it should be done within the limits of the penalty. Which was the second point.

Note, § 844.

In pillaging of cities and houses excesses are avoided with difficulty, because soldiers claim an unbridled licence as a right. Therefore, it should hardly be resorted to unless the greatest necessity should demand it. And lest the right may be abused, those things are to be considered which we have just now noted concerning the amount of contributions, especially when pillaging takes the place of contribution.

§ 847. *Whether property is to be destroyed in pillaging*

If cities and houses are pillaged, the property which is exposed to pillage is not to be destroyed, except in so far as the pillaging is done by way of just punishment. For cities and houses are pillaged, if just contributions should not be paid, or within the limits of the penalty, consequently that we may obtain those things which are rightly demanded from the enemy for supporting the army or for military supplies, or what is due by way of penalty. Therefore, since in plundering property is destroyed that the enemy may feel the loss, and we gain no advantage, if cities and houses are pillaged, the property which is exposed to pillage is not to be destroyed. Which was the first point. § 846.

§§ 843, 844.

Nevertheless, since the property of an enemy can be destroyed by way of a just penalty, if the penalty can be extended beyond pillaging it is allowable to combine it with destruction, in order, of course, that those things may be destroyed which cannot be taken away for one's use. Which was the second point. § 823.

> Pillage and destruction are certainly to be distinguished as two separate acts. In pillage property is carried away for the profit of the one taking it; in destruction it is spoiled, simply to cause loss to the owner. Therefore, not all property which is in a house can be pillaged, but all property can be destroyed. To destroy things which cannot be carried away, especially necessary things, when pillaging only is allowable, is certainly to be classed as a wrong, not as a lack of charity. For although charity is a reason for refraining from destruction in pillaging, nevertheless the right does not cease to exist because one refrains from exercising it, when charity merely refrains from the wrong.

§ 848. *What booty is*

Booty is defined as movable property of the enemy captured in war by soldiers. The Romans distinguished booty [*praeda*] from spoils [*manubiae*], which they defined as money taken in by the quaestor from the sale of booty.

> According to Gellius, respectable writers either thoughtlessly or carelessly have classed booty as spoils, and spoils as booty.[3] Thus if an

---

3. See Aulus Gellius, *The Attic Nights,* ed. and trans. John C. Rolfe, 3 vols. (London: William Heinemann, 1927–28), vol. 2, bk. XIII, chap. xxv, 31, pp. 499–501.

enemy conquered in battle is compelled to retreat, those things which he leaves in his flight are called booty; with which also are classed the things which are thrown away by him when the victor pursues him as a fugitive. In like manner, those things are classed as booty which are intercepted on their way to the enemy, or are taken from him on any other occasion.

§ 849. *Whether plundering [taking of booty] is allowed*

§ 781.

§ 786.

§ 810.

§ 848.

§ 239, part 1, Phil. Pract. Univ.

Since in a just war it is allowable to take any movable property of an enemy, both to collect a debt, under which a penalty also is included, and expenses incurred for the war, and also to diminish his power of action, and since booty consists of the movable property of an enemy captured in war, consequently when the booty, however great it may be, does not satisfy those purposes; plundering of the enemy is allowable in a just war whenever an occasion is presented for plundering, consequently it is not unjust to have plunderers in war.

In our native vernacular plunderers are called *Partheygänger* [adventurers], and are employed for no other purpose in war than to seek eagerly for booty, a thing which is not necessarily done with the intent of injuring, so that injury of itself is aimed at, but for purposes which are legitimately sought, that is, in accordance with the law of war.

§ 850. *Whether things carried away in pillaging are included in booty*

§ 845.

§ 848.

Since in pillaging movable property belonging to the enemy is carried away, and since booty consists of movable property of the enemy, the things which are carried away in pillaging are included in booty.

Plundering and pillaging differ. For plundering can occur without pillaging, as when things on the way to the camp of the enemy are captured by the hands of the soldiers; but it is always included in pillaging. And hence a camp abandoned by the enemy is said to be pillaged. In defining booty consideration is given not so much to the act by which property is taken, as to the quality of the property, namely,

§ 848.

that it is property of the enemy and likewise movable.

§ 851. *Of property which does not belong to the enemy found in their hands*

Property which does not belong to the enemy, although it may be found in their hands, since it is not the property of the enemy, does not form part of the booty, consequently in case of plundering it remains the property of those to whom it belongs, and, therefore, must be restored to them.

§ 728.

§ 467, part 2, Jus Nat.

> The right to plunder arises from war, which cannot be extended beyond the property of enemies.

§ 722.

§ 852. *To whom the booty belongs*

All booty belongs to the sovereign powers which are at war. For war is waged by those agents who have the supreme sovereignty, consequently by sovereign powers. Therefore, since the war is theirs, all right in war is also theirs. Therefore, since plundering is done by virtue of the right which is given in war to one waging a just war, the booty also belongs to the sovereign powers which are at war.

§ 607.

§ 368.

§§ 849, 777.

> Although plundering may be done by soldiers, nevertheless it is not done by the right of soldiers, but by the right of the sovereign power, which uses the soldiers as instruments in warlike acts, or in execution of its own right in war.

§ 853. *Whether any of the booty belongs to the soldiers capturing it, or to their officers*

Since all booty belongs to the sovereign powers which are at war, neither the individual soldiers who capture the property of the enemy with their own hands, nor their officers, have any right to the booty; consequently if any one of them appropriates any of the booty he commits a theft, and is like one who steals public money.

§ 852.

§ 498, part 2, Jus Nat.

> A theft by which public money is taken is called a peculation, hence the retention of booty is equivalent to the crime of peculation, whether the taking has occurred on the orders of leaders within the limits of their powers or by the command of the sovereign power,

or on private initiative, without their knowledge. Both soldiers and
officers serve for pay, with which they ought to be content. Rewards
of bravery are to be expected from the sovereign power, and no one
can give rewards to himself from the property of another. Therefore
the peculation committed on the booty is not excused because the one
committing it has shown himself a brave man and has done his work
well, and consequently has deserved a reward.

§ 854. *Whether any of the booty of the auxiliaries belongs to the one sending them*

Since all booty belongs to the sovereign powers which are at war, and
§ 852.   since the war is not that of the auxiliary troops, but they simply aid the
§ 653.   others in war, consequently do nothing in their own right, but in the
right of the one whom they aid; when plundering is done by the auxiliaries the booty does not belong to them, nor to the one sending them.

There is no difficulty in all these matters, so that there should be
no dispute, although Grotius calls it quite a serious one, as to who
De Jure Belli   acquires the booty, for the reason that the more recent interpreters of
ac Pacis, lib. 3, the law vary widely; but this is a thing at which you should not won-
c. 6, § 8.   der, since they do not usually determine questions from the underlying concepts of things, but rather defend their preconceived opinions
by extrinsic reasons.

§ 855. *How the sovereign power can dispose of it*

Because the booty belongs to the sovereign powers which are at war,
§ 852.   and since any one can dispose of his property as shall seem best to him;
§ 118, part 2,   sovereign powers therefore can dispose of the booty as they please, con-
Jus Nat.   sequently can make rules concerning it by military law, or signify their
desire in any other way in particular cases; then too they can make agreements concerning it in stipulations with the auxiliaries.

From this it undoubtedly arises, that in former times the Romans
De Jure Belli   did not dispose of booty in the same way, as Grotius relates. But for
ac Pacis, lib. 3, the purpose of avoiding prolixity we do not wish to repeat those things
c. 6, § 16.   here, although those arguments have their use in politics which have
none in law.

§ 856. *Of giving booty to plunderers*

Finally, since it is allowable to have plunderers in war, and since the sov- ereign power which they serve can dispose of the booty as shall seem to its advantage; if no other pay has been set aside for the plunderers, it is possible to give to plunderers the booty gained by them.

§ 849.

§ 855.

There is nothing in this which can be called unjust in itself. Never-theless it will be difficult to avoid the abuse of a right granted to plunder-ers, who are stimulated by the desire for gain, for which they are eager. But it must be observed that the booty is said to be divided, when either the collected booty itself or the money derived therefrom is distributed by way of pay or reward among the individual soldiers and their officers; but it is said to be seized, if what each has captured with his own hand is left to him. But concerning those things which the sovereign power has deter-mined, a decision is to be made in accordance with political principles.

§ 857. *Whether deceit is allowable in war*

Deceit is allowable in war, whether it consists in pretence, or falsehood without the plighted word, or in concealment. For if those things to which the belligerent has a right can be obtained in war without force, he must refrain from force in obtaining them. If then certain things can be obtained by deceit, that is by pretence or falsehood without the plighted word, since in the case of a promise we are bound to speak the truth even to an enemy, or if certain things can be obtained by concealment, for securing which there would otherwise be need of force, one must use deceit rather than force, consequently deceit is allowable in war.

§782.

§§ 790, 800.

§ 170, part 1, Phil. Pract. Univ.

Deceit in itself, whether it consists in an affirmative act, as pre-tence and falsehood, which can be considered as a species of pretence, or in a negative act, as by concealment, is in no way dishonourable, but according to existing circumstances is now licit, again illicit. And because of this the Roman jurists divide deceit into good and bad. It might seem strange that those writers strive to make difficulties who assume that all force is allowable in war, when nevertheless deceit causes less harm than force, if their perverse method of dealing with questions were not known, nor are those who have treated the law of

§§ 338 and fol., part 3, Jus Nat.

Note, § 854.

nature without an understanding of the true system accustomed to
derive results from causes by a consecutive course of reasoning.

§ 858. *What stratagems are and when they are allowable*

Stratagems are unexpected acts of war dependent upon cunning. Therefore, when acts of war are allowable, stratagems also are allowable, and

§ 782.   since acts of war may consist both in force and in deceit, stratagems can

§ 852.   consist both in force and in deceit.

> Hence Cicero refers stratagems to the counsel of the commander,
> by which of course acts of war are determined. And military prec-
> edents or counsels are usually cited by which those who come later
> are led to do similar things. Examples of stratagems may be found
> in the historians, who have described wars, especially the method of
> conducting them, and also in the authors who have written on mili-
> tary science.

§ 859. *Of the acquisition of the ownership of property captured in war*

The ownership of movable property captured in war is acquired by the
sovereign power, for the expenses incurred in the war are due to it. There-

§ 786.   fore, since it is understood that they are huge, so that the value of the
movable property captured does not equal them, consequently it can
always be charged against them, and hardly ever or indeed never has
the penalty to be considered to which the unjust belligerent is rightfully

§ 789.   bound for his several hostile acts, since, moreover, by the maturing of the
right, ownership of the property taken is acquired in place of the debt

§ 1119, part 5, owed; ownership of movable property captured in war is acquired by the
Jus Nat.   sovereign power of the nation by which it is captured, and to which the
expenses are due, and to which the unjust belligerent is bound to pay a
penalty for his several hostile acts.

> It has seemed best to add the present proposition, lest any one may
> claim that we are wrong in tacitly assuming that the sovereign power
> which is at war acquires the ownership of property captured in war,
> while before we claimed the booty for the sovereign power, although

the same thing might already have been plain enough from the right
to capture.

§ 852.

§ 860. *When ownership begins*

Since movable property is understood not to have been captured in war
until it is held in such a way that we can freely dispose of it, and since ownership thereof is acquired by the sovereign power; the movable property
of an enemy does not become subject to the ownership of the sovereign
power until it is held in such a way that it can dispose of it as it pleases.

§ 859.

> You cannot be said to have captured a thing, when the enemy can
> still take it from you, as when he pursues you as you flee with the
> property that has been seized or carried away by force. For the act of
> capture is perfected only when the enemy can no longer resist and has
> given up the intention of recapture. Therefore, when the enemy can
> no longer pursue you, when you have come with the captured prop-
> erty within fortifications, or into a place which he does not dare to
> enter, then it is plain in that case that you have captured the property
> and consequently the sovereign power has the ownership of it.

§ 861. *Captured property cannot be vindicated*

Property captured in war cannot be vindicated by those who owned
it before from any possessor. For the ownership of movable property
captured in war is acquired by the sovereign power which is at war, consequently those who had owned it before cease to be owners. Therefore,
since the right of vindicating one's property from any possessor belongs
to the owner, the property captured cannot be vindicated from any possessor by those who owned it before.

§ 859.

§ 544, part 2,
Jus Nat.

> He who loses ownership loses also all right derived from ownership,
> consequently also the right to vindicate the property; for that belongs
> to the owner, as owner, consequently it can belong to none but the
> owner. The owner excludes all others from any of his rights over the
> property, and therefore also from the right to vindicate. Therefore let
> us suppose that the property captured is sold to some one in a peace-
> ful territory and by him is sold again to some other one of the nation

§ 120, part 2,
Jus Nat.

with whom the captor is at war; he who had owned it before cannot vindicate it from him.

§ 862. *What occupation in war is*

All property of an enemy, but especially immovable property, including cities and territories, is said to be occupied, when it is brought by the enemy under his power. Hence, occupation in war is an act by which the property of an enemy is brought by force of arms under one's power.

§ 461, part 1, Jus Nat.

At what time property becomes subject to our power we have explained elsewhere, namely, when it is physically possible that we may dispose of it as we please. Thus, for example, a city is occupied when we have compelled it by force of arms to surrender, or when it is reduced to such a state that the soldiers of the garrison and the inhabitants can no longer resist us.

§ 863. *Of the occupation of sovereignty*

§ 862.

§ 498, part 1, Jus Nat.

§ 230, part 8, Jus Nat.

Since the property of an enemy is occupied when it is brought by an enemy under its power, and since the civil sovereignty is an incorporeal thing, the civil sovereignty can be occupied and has been occupied, either wholly or as to some part of the subjects, if either the entire nation or some part of it can no longer resist the exercise of sovereignty, but is bound to subject itself thereto; consequently if cities and territories are occupied, the sovereignty is occupied at the same time.

Cities and territories and the sovereignty in them or over the persons who live in those places are occupied by one and the same act. Thus a city has not been occupied until no one in it resists longer by force of arms and then too those who are in it are understood to submit to the victor. But it is just the same, whether they should surrender themselves or should be compelled to cease resistance because of failing strength, and thus as conquered should come into the power of the victor.

§ 1089, part 5, Jus Nat.

§ 864. *When the sovereignty has been occupied those become subjects who were enemies*

Since on the occupation of the civil sovereignty the right over individuals belonging to all the people in the state, consequently to the ruler of the

state, has been occupied, and since those are subjects over whom we have
sovereignty, when the civil sovereignty has been occupied, either wholly or
as to some part of the subjects, either the people as a whole, or a certain
part of the people, become subjects, and since they no longer resist the
force of the one occupying, as the fighting ceases, they cease to be enemies,
consequently, when cities and territories are occupied, since the civil sovereignty is occupied at the same time, if cities and territories are occupied,
those who live in them become subjects and cease to be enemies.

§ 42, part 8,
Jus Nat.
§ 32, part 8,
Jus Nat.
§§ 60, 141,
part 8, Jus Nat.
§ 863.
§ 1088, part 5,
Jus Nat.
§ 722.

§ 863.

Since in war we pursue our right, our object is merely to reduce the
enemy to such a condition that he can no longer resist the restoration
of our right. Therefore there is no war with one who no longer resists
this, consequently he is not an enemy.

§ 1102, part 1,
Jus Nat.

§ 722.

§ 865. Of the right against those who had been enemies after the sovereignty has been occupied

Since if the sovereignty is occupied, those who had been enemies become
subjects, and cease to be enemies, consequently with them there is now
no war, the right of war against them is also extinguished, consequently
none of those things are allowable against them which were allowable
against an enemy, but only those things are allowable which by right of
sovereignty are allowable against subjects.

§ 864.

§ 722.

Hence, from the things which have been proved in the eighth part
of "The Law of Nature" we easily determine what sort of a right exists
over the vanquished in each case, when the sovereignty has been occupied. Therefore, those are greatly deceived who persuade themselves
that they still have the same right against the vanquished which they
have against enemies, not directing their attention to the source of this
right, and those deviate even further from the truth who think that
more is allowable against the vanquished than against enemies, being
altogether ignorant of the source of the right.

§ 790.

§ 866. Of the occupation of eminent domain and of the ownership of a nation

Eminent domain and power, and also ownership over a nation are occupied at the same time as sovereignty. For sovereignty includes eminent

domain over the property of citizens and eminent power over their persons as its potential parts, consequently he who holds sovereignty, has eminent domain and eminent power. Therefore, eminent domain and eminent power are held at the same time as sovereignty. Which was the first point.

§§ 111, 114, part 8, Jus Nat.

In like manner, since the ownership of a nation is bound up with its sovereignty, ownership of a nation is held at the same time as sovereignty. Which was the second point.

§ 305.

It is understood from what precedes that the ownership of a nation is not to be confused with the ownership of lands which are subject to private control. Therefore, if the cities and territories of an enemy are occupied, the ownership of the lands which are subject to private control is not occupied, but they remain the property of those to whom they belong, except in so far as they are subject to eminent domain, and the ownership of the nation is understood to have been occupied along with the sovereignty merely over the things which have not been brought into the ownership of private individuals, since they are in the ownership of the nation. But just as the occupation of sovereignty does not take away the right of punishing one for an act which he committed when he was an enemy, if that act should deserve the penalty of confiscation, there is still a place for that after the sovereignty is occupied. For what is taken away as a penalty is not occupied by right of war, consequently has no connexion with occupation in war.

§ 862.

§ 867. *Of the right arising from impossibility of defence*

A nation loses its sovereignty over its subjects whom it cannot defend against the force of an enemy, and the obligation by which they are bound to it comes to an end. For men unite into a state, that by their united strength they may defend themselves against external force. Therefore, if a nation cannot defend some part of itself against the force of an enemy, it cannot keep the stipulation by which the state was established, consequently that part is no longer bound to it by the stipulation. Therefore, the right which the entire nation has acquired over the part, namely, the right of sovereignty, it loses, and the obligation by which the part was bound to the nation is extinguished.

§ 4, part 8, Jus Nat.

§ cited.

§ 827, part 3, and § 534, part 6, Jus Nat.

§ 32, part 8, Jus Nat.

Withdrawal from a state is allowable, if it is unwilling or unable to satisfy its obligation; it is, of course, just the same if the stipulation by which society was formed should not be fulfilled either voluntarily or by compulsion; and it is understood that this stipulation has been made on no other terms than with the tacit provision that each party can satisfy the obligation by which it is bound to the other, consequently that things should remain in the state in which they now are. When, therefore, the purpose fails for which a society was formed, the society also ceases to exist, consequently the rights and obligations which arise therefrom are extinguished.

§ 868. *When it is allowable to surrender to an enemy*

Since those whom its own nation cannot defend against the force of an enemy are no longer bound to it, and its sovereignty over them is extinguished, they can rightly surrender to the sovereignty of an enemy and become his citizens; consequently when a part of a nation is conquered and can no longer be defended by its nation, the vanquished rightly surrenders to the sovereignty of the victor, whether this be done by stipulation or by the act itself, in so far as it does not resist him, whether it gives up the intention of resisting or is compelled to give it up.

§ 867.

§ 1089, part 5, Jus Nat.

Here an unwilling act is equivalent to a voluntary one, since necessity must be obeyed.

§ 869. *What sort of sovereignty is acquired by the victor over the vanquished*

When cities and territories are conquered, such sovereignty is acquired over the vanquished as exists in the people, unless it shall have been agreed otherwise by stipulation. For when cities and territories are occupied, sovereignty over the vanquished is also occupied, and since the vanquished cannot be defended longer by their sovereign, they rightfully surrender to the sovereignty of the victor. If then they surrender without any stipulation, the sovereignty which the enemy acquires over them can be none other than that which exists as such, consequently such as is originally in the people. Which was the first point.

§ 863.

§ 868.

§ 33, part 8, Jus Nat.

§ 789, part 3,
Jus Nat.

§ 430, part 3,
Jus Nat.

But since stipulations must be observed, if surrender has been made by a stipulation, since one must abide by what has been agreed upon in it, the sovereignty which the victor acquires over the vanquished will be such as has been agreed upon. Which was the second point.

§ 867.

§ 790.

§ 156, part 1,
Jus Nat., and
§ 783 h.

§ 56, Ontol.

It cannot be said that such a sovereignty is acquired as the ruler of the state had, for his right is extinguished as soon as he can no longer defend his subjects. But much less can it be said that such a sovereignty is acquired over the vanquished as the victor has over his own subjects, for the right which he acquires must attach to the persons who are subjected to him, and it passes over to him by force of the subjection. And although his right over the persons arises in a just war from the defence of himself and his property, that nevertheless does not belong to sovereignty, and however much it should be assumed to belong to it, a thing which cannot be assumed without manifest absurdity, nevertheless there would be no reason why it ought to be such as the victor has over his own subjects. If you should assume that the sovereignty is taken away as a penalty on the vanquished, since the determination of the penalty would then depend upon the will of the victor, no reason would exist why such sovereignty should be taken away as he has over his own subjects. Therefore, nothing is left except that he acquires such sovereignty as exists in the people, unless some change should have been made in the stipulation of subjection.

§ 870. *The same is explained more specifically*

§ 869.
§ 34, part 8,
Jus Nat.
§ 57, part 8,
Jus Nat.
§ 62, part 8,
Jus Nat.

Since the same sovereignty is acquired over the vanquished in conquered cities and territories as exists in the people, unless there has been an agreement to the contrary, and since sovereignty is originally the peculiar property of a people and is likewise supreme and complete, the victor acquires over the vanquished in conquered cities and territories a complete and supreme sovereignty as his own peculiar property, unless there shall have been an agreement to the contrary.

This is understood both of the sovereignty over a whole nation and over a part that has been conquered.

§ 871. *Of the origin of patrimonial kingdoms*

Since the victor acquires over the vanquished complete and supreme sovereignty as regards ownership, he holds the same in his patrimony, consequently since a kingdom is a patrimonial one, if the sovereignty is in the patrimony of the king, patrimonial kingdoms arise by right of war.

§ 870.

§ 40, part 8, Jus Nat.

§ 155, part 8, Jus Nat.

There are those who think that the origin of patrimonial kingdoms is due solely to the right of war; but we have elsewhere shown that there is no objection to saying that they may arise also by the will of the people, although that may not easily happen, and, therefore, in a doubtful case it may not be assumed that the kingdom is patrimonial.

§ 40, part 8, Jus Nat.

§ 248, part 2, Jus Nat.

§ 872. *Of the right of the victor to make changes in the conquered state*

If a victor has acquired sovereignty over the vanquished without any stipulation, he can change as he pleases the form which the state had before. For if a victor has acquired sovereignty over the vanquished without any stipulation, he holds the sovereignty in his patrimony, and it is a patrimonial kingdom, which arises through occupation by war. But if the kingdom is a patrimonial one, the king can change the form of the state. If then the victor has acquired sovereignty over the vanquished without any stipulation, he can change as he pleases the form which the state had before.

§ 871.

§ 291, part 8, Jus Nat.

There is no reason why you should object that a kingdom does not come into existence if sovereignty is acquired over a certain part of the people. For a kingdom is not determined by the number of its subjects and the size of its territory, but by the form of the state, which can be the same in a large and a small territory. Therefore, whatever part of the enemy's territory may have been occupied, since it is different from the territory which the victor had held before, and does not of itself belong thereto, it will exist as a kind of kingdom.

§ 139, part 8, Jus Nat.

§ 873. *Of the change in form of a conquered state*

Since a victor who has acquired sovereignty over the vanquished without any stipulation can change as he pleases the form which the state

§ 872.

had before, the decision lies with the victor as to whether he may wish to combine the sovereignty with his own, or to keep it separate, and whether in this second case he may wish it to be the same as it had been in the king from whom it was taken, or whether he may wish to fashion certain fundamental laws as regards the management of the state, or the succession in it, as may seem best.

§ 870.   Of course a victor who has acquired full sovereignty has the right to determine as he pleases, both concerning the method of holding the sovereignty and of exercising it; how extensive this right may be is understood from those things which have been proved concerning general public law in the eighth part of "The Law of Nature."

§ 874. *When sovereignty of a slave-owner is acquired*

A slave-kingdom is not acquired by occupation in war except within the limits of a just penalty. For in a slave-kingdom all the subjects are
§ 270, part 8, Jus Nat.   reduced to personal servitude. Therefore, since captives, to whom those are compared who are subject to the sovereignty of an enemy after their cities and territories have been occupied, do not become slaves by nature, since nevertheless it is not contrary to natural law that they should be reduced to slavery for an offence worthy of that penalty, a slave-kingdom
§ 814.   is not acquired by occupation in war except within the limits of a just penalty.

Absolute sovereignty is confused with the sovereignty of a slave-owner by many who are ignorant of the law of nature, when they ought not to be, as they are lacking in accurate concepts of those characteristics which belong to sovereignty. And therefore it happens that subjects are considered as slaves, and eminent power and eminent domain are confused with the power of a master. Undoubtedly the sovereignty of a slave-owner is the most severe penalty which is inflicted on any nation, if you relinquish the right to kill, so that the case is very rare in which the sovereignty of a slave-owner is acquired over a nation. But there exists also a mixed sovereignty, made up of civil power and that of a slave-owner; a thing which can be modified in various ways, since sovereignty may contain very many potential parts.

§ 875. *When power over the person does not belong to an enemy*

An enemy has no power over one who does not oppose him by force. For an enemy does not need any defence against one who does not oppose him by force. Therefore, since a right against the person does not arise in a just war except for defence of oneself and one's property, an enemy has no power over one who does not oppose him by force.

§ 972, part 1,
Jus Nat.

§ 790.

Force is allowable against an enemy, in so far as without it one cannot acquire one's right. If then any one does not oppose an enemy, there is surely no reason why he should assail him with force. Examples are not lacking in the history of the ancients of those who knew how to use their power in war properly. An example is the case of those who allowed the farmers near their camp to till their fields.

§ 876. *Of rapes committed in war*

Since an enemy has no power over one who does not oppose him by force, since, moreover, women and maidens do not resist an enemy by force, especially when they have come into the power of the enemy, soldiers ought not to be allowed by their officers to commit rape on women and maidens, nor, since it is illegal in itself, does the right of war excuse it, much less justify it.

§ 875.

§ 461, part 2,
Jus Nat.

§ 335, part 7,
Jus Nat.

The same thing is true whether the captive women are taken into camp to be prostituted to the soldiers, or whether they are raped after cities and territories are captured, or the soldiers rush into places not surrounded by a wall or entrenchment. It undoubtedly is a foul crime, to be abhorred by all who have not thrown aside all sense of honour, and is absolutely alien to the warlike force by virtue of which we secure our right. Compare what we have said above. Nor is there reason why you should object that rape is not allowed except when there is need of terrorizing. For here the same reason exists for not allowing it, by which we proved above that, for the purpose of terrorizing, the persons of captives or of those who have surrendered or who wish to surrender themselves are not to be harshly treated.

Note, § 808.

§ 802.

§ 877. *Whether by nature it is allowable to destroy the enemy by poison*

§ 722.
§ 791.

By nature it is allowable to destroy the enemy by poison. For as long as he is an enemy, he resists the restoration of our right, consequently so much force is allowable against his person as is sufficient to repel his force from us or our property. Therefore, if you are able to remove him from our midst, that is not illegal. But since it is just the same whether you kill him with a sword or with poison, as is self-evident, since forsooth in either case he is removed from our midst that he may not longer resist and injure us, by nature it is allowable to destroy an enemy by poison.

There is no reason why you should object that an enemy is killed secretly by poison, so that he cannot protect himself from that so easily as from open violence; for he is not always killed by open violence who is killed by a sword or the use of other arms. For let us suppose that you secretly enter a place where the leader of the hostile army is asleep, and kill him with a sword. No one surely will deny that this is allowable by the law of war and is just the same as if he should be pierced by a bullet when unexpectedly seen from a distance. Therefore, from the fact that by poison a secret attempt is made against the life of an enemy, the right to remove him from our midst, if a favourable opportunity occurs, is not changed. It must be attributed to the generous spirit of those who have been unwilling to use this means when they might have done so, being influenced by the glory associated with carnage, which they were unwilling to besmirch with something generally considered a stain. Therefore, if you judge the deed in accordance with natural law, it is not a crime, a name by which the Roman writers called it. Besides it is to be considered that war is not waged as an end in itself, but for the sake of peace, and therefore, also, those means are not illegal which can contribute anything toward end-

§ 71.

ing the war, provided they are not illegal in themselves, as the removal of an enemy is not. Moreover, it often contributes not a little to the purpose of the war if the enemy should be killed, and whether the result which is aimed at is to be hoped for from his killing is included

§ 621.

among the persuasive reasons for choosing this means; for those things which we have said as to persuasive reasons for undertaking war are to be understood also as to any other matter to which we have a right.

§ 878. *Whether it is allowable to use poisoned bullets or arrows*

Since by nature it is allowable to destroy the enemy by poison, it is not   § 877. by nature illegal to use poisoned bullets or arrows.

> An enemy is killed in order to diminish his strength, and diminu-
> tion of his strength is sought, not his death. If then you use poisoned
> bullets or arrows, so that, if the enemy should not die from the wound,
> he nevertheless would die from the poison, consequently his destruc-
> tion would become so much the more certain; that which makes the
> killing of the enemy allowable, also makes the use of poison allowable.
> Of course it is just the same whether you get rid of the enemy by a
> single or by a double mortal wound.

§ 879. *Whether it is allowable to poison springs*

By nature it is not allowable to poison springs. For the use of water is
general, as is self-evident; consequently it happens that those are killed
by drinking it who oppose an enemy by force none the less than are those
who do not oppose him. Therefore, since no force is allowable against
one who does not oppose you by hostile force, consequently the use of
poison is not allowable, which takes the place of force; by nature it is not   § 875. allowable to poison springs.

> Those whom it is not allowable to kill with the sword, it is not
> allowable to destroy by poison. But those who do not oppose our
> force may not be killed. Therefore, it is not allowable to destroy them
> by poison. The right in war is not to be extended beyond its limits.
> But if you should object that by this reasoning it would be illegal to   § 792.
> throw bombs into a besieged city, it must be understood that these
> cases which are considered equivalent are in fact not at all comparable.
> For a besieged city is resisting with hostile force, and by the throwing
> of the bombs, by which the destruction of buildings particularly is
> aimed at, we use as it were a means of compelling the enemy to sur-
> render the city. But if the springs should be poisoned, the destruction
> of the enemy cannot be brought about in such a way that it would
> not threaten the lives of those also who certainly may not be killed
> by right of war. Nay more, since it may not be possible to counteract

§ 877.

the effect for a long time, it can happen that injury may be done, not to one whom it is allowable to kill with poison, but to others, against whom we had not the same right.

§ 880. *Of the polluting of waters without poison so that they cannot be drunk*

§ 782.

It is allowable by nature to pollute waters without the use of poison, so that they cannot be drunk. For if waters are polluted in this way, the enemy cannot quench thirst by use of them, and therefore is compelled by thirst not to resist our force longer. Therefore, since one must abstain from the use of force, if without it that which is sought can be acquired, as in the present instance, by the effect of thirst, it is allowable by nature to pollute waters without the use of poison, so that they cannot be drunk.

De Jure Belli
ac Pacis, lib. 3,
c. 4, § 17.

This was done both in former times and in a more recent period; for example, see Grotius and commentators who refer to this passage. Moreover, water has been polluted either with hellebore or cinders and other mineral refuse, or with corpses, naphtha, and lime. The bad taste shows that the water is spoiled even if it is not evident to the sight, so that one must refrain from drinking it, and consequently he is compelled to suffer from thirst, who cannot procure pure water elsewhere. Starvation and thirst go along together. Therefore, as it is not censurable to coerce an enemy by starvation to surrender, for example, or desist from war and make peace, so neither can one be censured if he compels an enemy to do the same thing because of thirst. Therefore, it cannot be considered one and the same thing to poison waters and to pollute them without the use of poison, so that they cannot be drunk.

§ 881. *What an assassin is*

An assassin is defined as one who, hired for a price, kills an enemy through treachery and deceit. In a way he is equivalent to a hired murderer who for money kills a person on the order of another.

The difference between an assassin and a hired murderer lies in the fact that an assassin takes his order from one who can kill another by right of war, but a hired murderer takes his order from one who is forbidden to kill another, so that his act is treacherous homicide or a capital crime.

§ 882. *Whether it is allowable to kill an enemy by sending an assassin*

Since deceit is allowable in war, consequently, since it is allowable to   § 857.
kill an enemy even by treachery and deceit, and since it is just the same
whether this is done by one or more, since, moreover, an assassin kills an   § 881.
enemy by treachery and deceit, it is not illegal by nature to kill an enemy
by sending an assassin.

It matters little that an assassin does this for a stipulated price, for
the money is given that the assassin may risk his life. But if some one
should voluntarily offer himself, and should wish to play the part of
an assassin without pay, he would not change the character of the act
thereby. So likewise it is just the same whether there shall have been
several assassins or only one.

§ 883. *Who are spies*

Those are called spies who seek to find out in what condition the affairs
of an enemy are and what he is planning against us. In the German
vernacular they are called *Spionen* [spies]. Therefore, it is plain that spies
perform a useful service for those who send them, but that they injure
the enemy against whom they are sent.

There is no more common practice in war than hiring spies, since it
is of the greatest importance that we should find out what the enemy
is planning.

§ 884. *Whether it is allowable to send spies*

Since it is important for one who sends spies to find out in what condition the affairs of an enemy are, and what they are planning against him,
that he may wisely plan the acts of war that serve to secure his right, and
since he may do what is necessary to attain this end, it is allowable for   § 781.
him who is waging a just war to send spies.

Spies not infrequently cause more damage than do assassins, and   § 883.
satisfy more easily the expectation of the one who sends them. Nevertheless, the function of the spy is considered less odious than that of
the assassin. Therefore, also, the punishment of spies is less severe

than that of assassins, if they should be caught. But no one doubts that it is allowable to use the aid of spies; whether the same thing applies to assassins might seem doubtful from the fact that necessity gives a right to kill an enemy, if it should not be possible to defeat his attack otherwise, consequently it seems an enemy can be killed only in battle. But although indeed this doubt may seem plausible, nevertheless the plausibility is easily removed from it. As long as the war lasts, the enemy plans to use force or to oppose himself to just force, merely awaiting the opportunity for attaining his purpose. Therefore, he is constantly on the footing of one who is using force or opposing a force justly exerted, as long as the war continues; consequently the right which belongs to one waging a just war against him continues, as much as is necessary to reduce him to the condition in which he can no longer oppose himself to just force. If then necessity makes a place for murder, it is allowable if any opportunity is presented. And it is understood that the necessity exists if he cannot be captured.

§ 791.

§ 885. *Of the right to punish spies and assassins*

By the law of nature, the one whose cause is just has the right to punish spies and assassins sent by his enemy, nay more, the one sending the assassins is especially liable to him for their wrongs. For whatever an unjust belligerent does to the prejudice of one whose arms are justly taken up, is done by no right, but rests on wrong; consequently the acts of those whose aid he uses are mere wrong. Therefore, since by nature every one has the right to punish the one who does him a wrong, by the law of nature the one whose cause is just has the right to punish spies and assassins sent by his enemy, and the one sending the assassins is himself especially liable to him whose cause is just.

§ 777.
§ 778.

§ 549, part 2,
Jus Nat.

Since by nature the unjust belligerent has no right in war, consequently has not the right to oppose the warlike acts of a just belligerent, the right to punish spies or assassins sent by a just belligerent cannot be defended by the law of nature, except in so far as these go to excess in the exercise of their right, as by killing one whom they were able to capture. For he who goes beyond the limit in defence to which all acts of just warfare are comparable, injures another; consequently the injured party has the right to punish him. Nowhere do we

§ 777.

§ 1002, part 1,
Jus Nat.

depart farther from the law of nature than in war; why this cannot be otherwise we shall show later. It seems harsh indeed that the lives of the very greatest leaders are exposed to the treachery and violence of assassins, but since the fault rests in themselves, not in the one sending them, they ought to impute it to themselves, that they have preferred to expose themselves to treachery and violence, rather than to avoid all risk of loss by yielding to a righteous cause.

§ 1061, part 1, Jus Nat.

§ 886. Of the end of difficulties and war between nations

All difficulties and also even war itself between nations ought to have an end, and an effort ought to be made that they can do so. For every difficulty which is begun ought to have an end, and an effort ought to be made that it can do so. Therefore, all difficulties, even war itself between nations, ought to have an end, and an effort ought to be made that they can do so.

§ 70, part 7, Jus Nat.

We have shown the same thing concerning the difficulties of private individuals in the state and concerning their suits in court. Therefore, since nations are understood to have united into a state whose individual members are individual states, to them also that might be applied which has been proved concerning the affairs and lawsuits of private individuals in a state of which they themselves are members.

§ 983, part 8, Jus Nat.

§ 9.

§ 887. How for that reason a voluntary law of nations is developed

Since all difficulties and even war itself between nations ought to have an end, and an effort ought to be made that they can do so, if it be impossible that the difficulties of nations and even war itself can have an end, if we keep to the rigour of the law of nature, we must depart from it, and consequently the conclusions of the law of nature must be changed as much as is necessary to attain that end, and to this all nations are bound to agree. Therefore, since the voluntary law of nations is developed from the necessary or natural law in the same way as the civil law is developed from natural law, since, moreover, in the civil law the conclusions which are drawn from the law of nature are changed for the purpose of ending difficulties and terminating suits, so far as is sufficient to attain that

§ 886.

§ 22.

§ 986, part 8,
Jus Nat.
end; if the conclusions of the law of nature are changed for the purpose of ending difficulties between nations and terminating suits, so far as is necessary to attain that end, a voluntary law of nations is developed out of the necessary law of nations.

If in this way a voluntary law of nations should be proved, it cannot be said to be a fiction invented gratuitously, just as it cannot be said that civil laws, in so far as it is necessary that they depart from the rigour of natural law, are to be considered as fictions. Likewise, it is not to be feared that the voluntary law of nations may be extended beyond its limits, and turned to unbridled licence, just as the civil laws themselves are in this way kept within just limits, that the will of the legislator may not get off the track, by virtue of those things which we have proved concerning the natural theory of civil laws in the eighth part of "The Law of Nature." The agreement also of nations which the law of nature demands, cannot be considered as a fiction,

Note, § 9.
in as much as the law of nature supplies it, however much should be lacking, by caring for the happiness of nations as far as is possible in their weakness, or obstinacy and wickedness, that are to be endured like tares incapable of being uprooted. But if on account of the tacit agreement which the law of nature demands and, if it is lacking, supplies, as we have said, you should wish to say that this belongs to the law of nature, which we say is a part of the voluntary law of nations although we yield in names, provided we are agreed in the fact itself,

§ 145, Disc.
Praelim.

§ 631, Log.
nevertheless the demonstrative method does not allow things which are different to be indicated by the same name, especially where it is to be feared that this may be done to the detriment of the truth, and that if one error is admitted, more will follow.

§ 888. *What war is to be considered just by the voluntary law of nations*

By the voluntary law of nations, so far as regards results, war is to be

§ 558, part 1,
Jus Nat.

§ 153, part 1,
Jus Nat.

§ 156, part 1,
Jus Nat.

§ 158, part 1,
Jus Nat.
considered as just on either side. For all nations are free by nature, consequently by nature no nation has any control over the actions of another, and by virtue of liberty each must be allowed to follow its own judgement in determining its actions, as long as it does nothing contrary to the right of another, nor has any nation the right to demand that another should give to it a reason for its actions. Therefore, since no nation can

assume for itself the functions of a judge, and consequently cannot pronounce upon the justice of the war, although by natural law a war cannot be just on both sides, since nevertheless each of the belligerents claims that it has just cause of war, each must be allowed to follow its own opinion; consequently by the voluntary law of nations the war must be considered as just on either side, not indeed in itself, which forsooth it implies, but as regards the results of the war.

§ 580, part 8, Jus Nat.

§ 540, part 8, Jus Nat.

§ 633.

§ 634.

§ 887.

Therefore, it cannot be said that the question as to the justice of the cause is in suspense, until by the final victory the decision of God, arbiter of wars, determines who had the just cause, so that the vanquished is to be considered an unjust belligerent, doomed to pay the penalty rightfully both to God and to the victor. War is not a suitable method for deciding the controversies of nations. And just as the opinion of those is wrong who think that God so directs the brave as to indicate his own will, so the opinion of those is not without error who think that God so directs arms that he who has the unjust cause is conquered, and the final victory which puts an end to the war, the enemy being reduced to such a condition that he can no longer resist the force of the other, is always with the just belligerent. It frequently happens that the victory is due to the strength of the more powerful enemy, or even to the skill and caution of the contestant. But who, pray, will say that his cause is just who prevails in arms because of skill, or his who has used the greater caution? But much less is it right to decide that God for reasons of that sort vindicates the justice of his cause who has it not, and declares the other worthy of punishment, and gives to his enemy a right under which all things are allowed against an enemy.

Note, § 632.

Note, §§ 295, 296, part 5, Jus Nat.

§ 889. *What is allowable in war under the voluntary law of nations*

Since by the voluntary law of nations, as regards results, war is to be considered as just on either side, what is rightly allowable for one belligerent in war is also allowable for the other.

§ 888.

By the voluntary law of nations each one of the belligerents is considered equally right. And therefore, you may not listen to one of the belligerent parties accusing the other of violation of the law of nations, as long as the other does nothing which is considered illegal in war. The voluntary law of nations does not make warlike acts legal which are not so by natural law, but simply common to both belligerents, although by the law of nature they belong only to the one waging a just war.

§ 890. *Of the limits of the voluntary law of nations in war*

Because that which is allowable by the law in war for one of the belligerents is also allowable for the other by the voluntary law of nations, without any consideration of the justice of the war, since, moreover, by nature the unjust belligerent has no right, but the right of a just belligerent is to be determined by that which is necessary, according to one's own judgement, to acquire one's right from the opposing party, and is not extended beyond this limit; the voluntary law of nations allows nothing except that which is allowable by the law of nature to a just belligerent, or which must be allowed him; consequently if an extension is made by the customs of nations beyond the limits within which the law of nature restrains the right of war of a just belligerent, it is to be referred to customary law.

§ 889.
§ 888.
§ 777.
§ 783.
§ 781.

§ 24.

Therefore, that excessive licence which Grotius admits in the voluntary law of nations, and which some put forward as the law of nature itself, and which we have repeatedly commented on in preceding notes, is to be referred to the perverse customs of nations. Here belongs, for example, the right to kill indiscriminately women, children, infants, old men, and other persons who do not oppose a hostile force, and the right to plunder cities and houses and to destroy any property of the enemy, this right being extended so far that one may do as he pleases.

§ 891. *Of what character is the voluntary law of nations in war*

The voluntary law of nations does not give to one waging an unjust war a true right to warlike acts, but simply immunity from punishment for the action. For one waging an unjust war has no right to warlike acts, but he is only by the voluntary law of nations to be permitted to do that which

§ 777.
§ 889.

is allowable for a just belligerent, although by the law of nature he ought to abstain from it. Therefore, since he merely acts without punishment who is allowed by others to act, although he is bound by nature to the opposite course, the voluntary law of nations does not give to one waging an unjust war a true right to warlike acts, but merely immunity from punishment for the action.

§ 788.

§ 418, part 3, Jus Nat.

Therefore, the voluntary law of nations, which puts an unjust belligerent on an equality with a just one, is from his standpoint wrongly called law. Nor does the opinion that an unjust belligerent entertains as to the justice of his cause, transform his immunity from punishment for the action into a right, since that arises not from his opinion, but from the truth, although some consideration must necessarily be given to opinion in the voluntary law of nations, in order that a war can have an end, consequently when it is ended, that the seeds of a new war may not remain. He who acts under a mistaken belief nevertheless sins, since his mistake does not bring it about that an action contrary to the law of nature is not such, but is in conformity with that law, except in so far as an unavoidable mistake cannot be charged to him, so that he may deserve to be excused. But those assuredly are not to be excused who knowingly defend the unjust cause of their ruler, and confirm his mind in error.

Note, § 419, part 3, Jus Nat.

Note, § 823.
Note, § 887.

§ 441, part 1, Phil. Pract. Univ.

§ 552, part 1, Phil. Pract. Univ.

§ 892. *The method of acquiring in war*

By the voluntary law of nations warlike occupation is the ordinary method of acquiring ownership and sovereignty over belligerents. For the ownership of movable property captured in war and sovereignty over the vanquished in the captured cities and territories are acquired by the sovereign power which is at war, together with the dominion of the nation, and likewise control over the captives. But since all the property of the enemy, consequently also incorporeal property such as are rights against persons, are understood not to have been acquired until they have been brought under the control of the one acquiring them, consequently have been occupied by warlike force, and since by the voluntary law of nations as regards results war is to be considered as just on either side; by the voluntary law of nations warlike occupation is the ordinary method of acquiring ownership and sovereignty over belligerents.

§ 869.

§ 859.

§ 868.

§§ 814 and fol.
§ 497, part 1, Jus Nat.

§ 498, part 1, Jus Nat.

§ 461, part 2, Jus Nat.

§ 862.

§ 888.

Dig. 50, 17.

Warlike occupation, therefore, is included in the Roman law among the methods of acquisition which belong to the law of nations, although the law of nations which we call voluntary is referred to the same category with the law of nature peculiar to men, undoubtedly for the reason that even that may be considered a part of natural law which by virtue of natural liberty must be allowed by others, although in itself it was not allowable by the law of nature, such as is the abuse of ownership and of natural liberty, or the right over one's own actions, so far as it does not incline towards wrong to another. Indeed, from these acts, although they are illegal in themselves as regards the one acting, nevertheless a true right arises for another whose act is devoid of fault. For example, although it may not be allowable in itself to sell books which you need very much, in order to waste the money on extravagance and dissipation, nevertheless by the purchase title passes, if there be no defect in the transaction as such. Likewise in a just war the abuse of right in war is distinguished from its use by those characteristics which we have proved on several occasions in the discussion of the limits of that right; but the decision in regard to it rests with the belligerent, and others must abide by it. But the abuse of it

§ 783.

Note, § cited.

§ 1004, part 1,
Jus Nat.

§§ 1067, 972,
973, part 1,
Jus Nat.

§ 1088, part 1,
Jus Nat.

§ 55, part 8,
Jus Nat.

§ 209, part 1,
Phil. Pract.
Univ.

Note, § 826.

gives a right also to him whose cause is otherwise unjust, to certain warlike acts, such as excess in defence against an assailant, and excess in punishment of one who is punished, whose resistance is otherwise illegal. Therefore, the rights of belligerents are so involved with their underlying causes, that they cannot be untangled by any one, even if an arbiter should especially be appointed, much less without a judge or arbiter, such as nations free by nature are not bound to recognize. Since a natural obligation cannot be extended beyond what is possible, necessity itself demands that as regards the results arising from warlike acts the war should be considered as just on the part of each belligerent, as in the transfer of ownership or of any particular right, a flaw existing in the intention of either party, which accompanies the act necessary for a transfer, does not affect the act itself. But law and morality are not on this account opposed as enemies, as we have already noted beforehand. Virtue can never be far separated from the operation of law, unless you may wish to err, nevertheless a flaw existing in the intention of one party cannot vitiate the effect of law for others who have no part in it. If in war it were necessary that the intrinsic justice of individual acts be determined, innumerable controversies would arise therefrom and quarrels which would have no end. But just as no state is ruled without great wrong, so also a war cannot be waged without wrong. The law of nature itself commands that such things be endured that justice may be preserved in general, just as nature and the creator thereof allow imperfection in a part, that perfection may be preserved or even a higher perfection attained in the whole. For there is nothing more natural than that in case of conflict the whole should be preferred to the part. But nations in general are regarded as constituting a supreme state, as a whole and as to the several parts; consequently the individuals who make up a certain nation are as it were parts of a part. But that we may not be more prolix than might seem necessary, we leave to the personal meditation of our readers what might further be said. §§ 9, 10.

§ 893. Of the right to punish spies and assassins by the common law of belligerents

By the voluntary law of nations spies and assassins are punished by either belligerent; nay more, the law of nature does not seem to prevent one whose cause is unjust from punishing the former as doing him a wrong, the latter as murderers. The just belligerent can punish those sent by his enemy as spies and assassins by virtue of the right in war which he has §885. by nature. But by the voluntary law of nations what is allowable for one §889. party is also allowable for another. Therefore, by the voluntary law of nations spies and assassins are punished by either belligerent. Which was the first point.

But since, indeed, assassins are hired for a price to kill an enemy through treachery and deceit, and spies are not compelled by the power §881. of the sovereignty to which they are subject to injure the enemy by §883. betraying his plans and finding out in what condition his affairs are, their act can be looked at from two points of view, both in so far as it is their own and the act of a perfectly free will which no law restrains, and in so far as it depends upon the will of the one acting or agreeing thereto. With regard to the former, the act of spies is considered as an act by which a wrong is done to him to whose prejudice it results, and the act §530, part 2, of assassins is regarded as murder. Therefore, since both a wrong which Jus Nat.

§ 549, part 2,
Jus Nat.
§ 881 h, and
§ 1061, part 1,
Jus Nat.

Note, § 885.

§ 777.
has been done and murder can be punished, the law of nature does not seem to prevent one whose cause is just from punishing spies as doing him a wrong, and assassins as murderers.

Although an unjust belligerent cannot punish spies and assassins by right of war, which he does not have by nature; since, nevertheless, on this account the right otherwise belonging to him by nature may not be taken away, it seems nothing can prevent him from using it. For although he may not rightly oppose a just force, nevertheless the act of spies and assassins is not equivalent to this, in whatever way a just belligerent may legally use their assistance at their own risk. Therefore, there is this difference between a just and an unjust belligerent in punishing a spy or assassin, that the former has a double right to a penalty, but the latter only a single right. Since one would be sufficient, there is no need that he should seek protection from the voluntary law of nations.

§ 894. *Of captured property and persons returning to their own nation*

If captured property and persons are returned to their own nation, both by nature and by the voluntary law of nations they are restored to their original status, that is, the property must be returned to those who had owned it before, and all rights must be restored to the persons which they had before, even all rights over themselves. He who wages an unjust war

§ 788.

§ 809.

§ 4, part 8,
Jus Nat.
is bound by nature to return both captured property and persons, and since the sovereign power is bound to defend its subjects and their rights against external force of enemies, it is bound by nature to claim for its subjects property captured by the enemy with unjust force and to free captives. If then captured property or persons return to their own nation, since this is just as if they had been restored by the enemy or recovered from him; undoubtedly property ought to be returned to its owners from whom it had been taken by unjust force, and persons restored to their own control, and consequently all rights restored to them which they had before, even all rights over themselves. Which was the first point.

§ 1119, part 5,
Jus Nat., and
§ 781 h.
But although, indeed, a just belligerent acquires ownership in property captured by just force, at least conditionally, which later, indeed, cannot be limited because of a debt arising in the war; nevertheless, when

the same property is returned to its nation, so that the hope of recovery §787.
becomes nothing, or at least doubtful, it becomes equivalent to property
which has been wrongfully taken from one nation by another and for
which the common property of subjects of the former has been pledged
to the latter, consequently a new debt is contracted, for which satisfac- §495.
tion is due to the latter. But when property is returned to its own nation, §586.
from which it had been taken by an enemy as compensation for a debt,
for which just as much property of other subjects had been bound, and §§781, 586.
even now remains bound, as proved above, there is indeed no reason why §495.
the sovereign power ought to acquire that property, especially since in
the present case he has no further right in war. Therefore, the property §56, Ontol.
must be restored to those who had owned it before, like property which §777.
had never been captured from them by the enemy. And the same thing in
like manner is understood of captives, over whom a belligerent has a certain right, and therefore they are to be restored to their own control, all
their own rights and the rights of others over them having been restored §§814 and fol.
to them. Which was the second point.

Finally, by the voluntary law of nations as regards results, the war
is considered as just on either side; consequently it is the same as if an §888.
unjust belligerent should act lawfully in war. But if the war were indeed
just, by the law of nature property and persons when they are returned to
their own nation are restored to their original conditions, as proved
above. Therefore, by the voluntary law of nations captured property and Point 1.
persons when they return to their own nation are restored without distinction to their original condition. Which was the third point.

By nature owners retain title in property carried off by unjust force,
in as much as it cannot be taken away without their consent. Therefore, when it comes back in any way to its own people, it must be §336, part 2,
restored to its owners by those into whose power it comes. Therefore, Jus Nat.
it can grant no other right over captured property returning to the §467, part 2,
nation, from which it had been taken, to an unjust belligerent, than Jus Nat.
that which belongs to a just belligerent, especially since by his own §889.
decision the property is considered as wrongfully taken by the enemy.
Therefore, by the voluntary law of nations captured property returning to its own nation is restored to its former owners without making any distinction between a just and an unjust war. And the same

thing is understood of captives returning to their people. Those who contend by virtue of the decision of their state, that the restitution to their original condition of captured property and persons, when they are returned to their people, is derived from the law of nature, and not from the voluntary law of nations, differ not in fact, but only in words. See what we noted a little while ago.

Note, § 887.

§ 895. *How those things are to be regarded*

§ 894.

Since captured property and persons are restored to their original condition when they are returned to their own nation, they can be regarded as if they never had been in the power of the enemy.

§ 894.

For no change is made in the rights over property and persons because they have been in the power of the enemy. Therefore, because the same condition would have existed if they had never been in the power of the enemy, when they return to their nation they are to be considered in the same situation as the others which have never come into the power of the enemy.

§ 896. *Of postliminium and to what law it belongs*

The restoration to their original condition of property and persons captured by the enemy and their return into the power of their nation is called postliminium. And therefore, it is plain that postliminium belongs no less to the law of nature than to the voluntary law of nations.

§ 894.

The law of nature supports postliminium, in so far as there are reasons for it derived from the principles of the law of nature, for those things which belong to the law of nature ought to have natural reasons, derived from the very concepts of the things; but the voluntary law of nations, in so far as the law of nature does not oppose it, must be allowed to depart from the rigour of the law of nature in practice. Since, then, there are some things which are in perfect accord with the law of nature, and others which are to be endured, if the law of nature is not opposed, because they cannot be changed, or so that a greater wrong may be avoided; it has seemed to us more fitting that they be distinguished from each other by name also, and not called by a common name, lest some one may think that virtue can ever be

§ 189, part 1,
Phil. Pract.
Univ.

separated from the exercise of right, if you should wish to act rightly, as you are bound to do by nature, and should confuse with a true right immunity from punishment in action between nations, which is only incorrectly said to be a right. Since the law of nature, whose obligation is certainly unchanging, insists that war must be waged with the highest sense of right, it is not allowable to sin for the reason that your sin has to be endured by others.

§ 891.

§ 142, part 1, Phil. Pract. Univ.

§ 897. *What things return by postliminium, and what are received*

Persons are said to return by postliminium who, after capture in war by the enemy, come again under the power of their own nation. And property is said to be received by postliminium which, after capture in war by an enemy, comes again under the power of its own nation. Without any distinction nevertheless both property and persons are said to return and be received by postliminium.

Pomponius distinguishes two kinds of postliminium, namely, that either we return or we receive something. Nevertheless Paulus, who was later than Pomponius, says that people also are received by postliminium. That distinction is not made in the law of nature, so that it is just the same whether things and persons together or separately should be said to be received and to return. But when Grotius says that postliminium is the right which arises on the return to the threshold, that is, to the boundaries of the state, that indeed does not play the part of a definition, for the reason that not all of the elements are present by which this right is established in its essentials, so that therefrom the other things may be proved which depend on that right; if, nevertheless, return is explained thus, that return is the same thing as to come into the power of their own nation from the control of the enemy, under which they had been, since to capture and to bring under one's power mean the same thing, and power should be accepted in the physical sense, it is not far from the truth to say that it is the right by which property is restored to owners, persons to their own control, that is, postliminium arises on return, in so far, of course, as it depends upon the fact of return, that you may become a sharer in it. For it is plain from a previous proposition that there is another source of this

Dig. 49. 15. 14.

Dig. 49. 15. 18 [49. 15. 19.]

De Jure Belli ac Pacis, lib. 3, c. 9, § 2.

§ 461, part 2, Jus Nat.

§ 851, Ontol.

§ 894.

right, whether it is considered a law of nature or a voluntary law of
nations to which that law is not opposed. But it is plain enough that
in more than one way property and persons captured by the enemy
can return to the control of their nation; nevertheless that variation is
not to be considered in postliminium, since this right has been proved

§ cited.

without reference thereto.

§ 898. *Whether there is postliminium with allied nations*

There is postliminium with an allied nation. Since he who allies himself
in war with another who is at war is to be considered as one person with

§ 161, part 7,
Jus Nat.

him, consequently an allied nation, so far as regards war, is the same as
the other nation with which it is allied; it is just the same whether property and persons captured in war should return to their own nation or
to an allied nation. Therefore, when postliminium exists with one's own

§§ 894, 896.

nation, it will also exist with an allied nation.

> The proof which we have given of postliminium, both as regards
> the law of nature and as regards the voluntary law of nations, can be
> applied to an allied nation also; but there is no need of repetition,
> since an allied nation makes the cause of the other nation its own,
> consequently, the right which on account of the war belongs to the
> other nation ought also to belong to it, and since it follows the deci-
> sion of the other nation, which the other nation considers right, it also
> ought to consider it right. Of course the decision is the same as to the
> cause of the war and as to acts of war not illegal in themselves arising
> therefrom in any way, and by virtue of natural liberty this must be left
> to either nation by other nations.

§ 899. *Whether there is postliminium with neutral nations*

With neutral and peaceful nations there is no postliminium. For neutral
nations attach themselves to neither of the belligerent parties, and peace-

§ 672.

ful nations, which do not involve themselves in the war, are similar to
them, although they have not declared to the belligerents that they do
not wish to attach themselves to either party. Therefore, since the war
is to be considered as just on either side by nations not involved in the

§ 888.

war, warlike acts committed by either party are considered legal, and consequently, since by the voluntary law of nations warlike occupation is the ordinary method of acquiring ownership and sovereignty over belligerents, things which have been captured by one party or by the other in war are understood to have been acquired by the captors. If, then, property and persons captured in war come to those nations, they are not on this account restored to that condition in which they had been before they were captured, so that the property is to be restored to its owners and persons to their own control, and consequently there is no postliminium with neutral and peaceful nations. § 892.

§ 896.

So if captured property should be sold in a neutral and peaceful nation, he who had been its owner cannot claim it. Between neutral and peaceful nations there is no intrinsic difference. For neither nation involves itself in the war and by force of natural liberty both permit every one to follow his own judgement as to warlike acts and as to the cause of the war, consequently each is necessarily bound to recognize as lawful the act of either party, for otherwise it would be necessary to accuse each party of injustice, which would be absurd, or at least one or the other, and so, if either followed the judgement of one party in war, it would attach itself to that side, and therefore would not be neutral or peaceful. Therefore, the difference between a neutral and a peaceful nation is simply that the former declares either to each of the belligerent parties or to one of them that it does not wish to involve itself in the war, or it even enters into a treaty of neutrality; but the latter by act alone refrains from war. Therefore, since as regards neutral and peaceful nations there is no war, neither are the rights arising from war, which affect belligerents as such, to be extended to them. There are those, indeed, who extend postliminium to neutral and peaceful nations also, but how much they are in error is plain enough from what has been just said. § 634.

§ 672.

§ 673.

§ 900. *Whether those who have surrendered have postliminium*

They do not have postliminium who, defeated by armed force, have surrendered themselves to enemies. For those who, defeated by armed force, surrender themselves to enemies declare by that very fact that they wish to remain with the captor, consequently they pledge good faith. §§ 758, 427, part 3, Jus Nat.

Therefore, since good faith pledged to an enemy is to be observed, since they who have surrendered themselves to enemies cannot be restored to their original condition without violating good faith, they do not have postliminium.

§ 800.
§ 896.

Of course, one who has surrendered cannot by his own act withdraw from the power of the enemy and return to his people. It is of course just the same as though he should flee from his own people to the enemy and espouse their cause, and for this reason he is rightly considered a deserter. For good faith among nations pledged in whatsoever way ought to be held sacred, nor can postliminium avail against it, nor is the one to whose power the surrendered have submitted, bound to recognize postliminium.

§ 803.

§§ 550, 556.

§ 901. *Whether surrendered cities and provinces can release themselves from the enemy*

Since they do not have postliminium who, captured by arms, have surrendered themselves, neither cities nor provinces which have surrendered themselves to the enemy can use postliminium, and thus release themselves from the enemy.

§ 900.

§ 896.

Corporate bodies have no other rights than have individuals, since the right passes over from individuals to the corporate body, so that the right of corporate bodies is made up of the rights of all the individuals taken together. And any corporate body, such as a city and a province, ought to preserve pledged faith no less than should individuals.

§ 902. *Of postliminium in things retaken by force of arms*

Those things which are recovered by force of arms from an enemy have postliminium. For when they are retaken, they are returned to their own nation, as is self-evident. Therefore, since things captured in war which are returned to their own nation have postliminium, those things also must have postliminium which are recovered by force of arms from an enemy.

§§ 894, 896.

Every nation is bound to defend the rights of its subjects against external force, and therefore ought to use every effort to recover from the enemy what has been captured, if that is possible. Therefore there is no reason why one ought to acquire for himself things recovered in war from the enemy, but he acquires the things for those who had owned them before, and therefore he restores them to the original status which they had before.

§§ 4, 28, part 8, Jus Nat.

§ 903. Of surrendered persons dismissed by the enemy, or of things deserted, or recovered by us through agreements

Surrendered persons dismissed by the enemy, and surrendered property or cities deserted by the enemy, or recovered by us through agreements, have postliminium. For if persons surrendered to the enemy are dismissed by him, and surrendered property and cities are deserted by him, he gives up his right over them. Therefore they acquire the right they had before; consequently they are restored by the act itself to that condition in which they had been before. Therefore, since this restitution is postliminium, if surrendered persons should be dismissed by the enemy, and surrendered property and cities should be deserted by him, they have postliminium. Which was the first point.

§ 95, part 3, Jus Nat.

§ 894.

§ 896.

Furthermore, since every nation ought to defend the rights of its subjects, consequently ought to use every effort to recover those things which it was obliged to surrender to the enemy, if that can be done, and restore them to their original condition, it is not to be doubted that surrendered property recovered through agreements should have postliminium. Which was the second point.

§§ 4, 28, part 8, Jus Nat.

In the hypothesis of the present proposition the reason why postliminium is lacking in the case of those surrendered does not apply, namely, breach of faith. Therefore, although those who have surrendered themselves and their property cannot release themselves from the enemy's right, so that on that account there can be no place for postliminium, nevertheless that no longer stands in the way when the enemy gives up his right. When a surrender is rescinded, it is just as if it had never been made; consequently the rights also of the surrendered are restored, as there is no reason why they should be taken away from them by our act, but this is rather contrary to the obligation by which we are bound to our subjects, as is evident from the proof.

§ 900.

§ 97, part 3,
Jus Nat.
The right of one who gives up his right is lost. Therefore, it would be absurd to consider that it was transferred to the nation to which it had belonged before the property had been deserted or returned by the enemy.

§ 904. *Of slaves received under postliminium*

If slaves are received under postliminium, they are to be restored to their owners. For those things which are received under postliminium are
§ 896.
restored to their original condition. Therefore, the one who had been your slave, if received under postliminium, is your slave. Therefore, if slaves are received under the right of postliminium, they are to be restored to their masters.

Of course those who return or are received under postliminium, are regarded as though they never had been in the power of the enemy.
§ 895.
Since, therefore, they would have remained the property of their masters, they will also belong to them when they are received under postliminium. However fictitious it may be, that they have never been under the power of the enemy, nevertheless, nothing prevents us from using that fiction for purposes of proof. For although the Cornelian Law[4] assumes that those captured in war never were captured, nevertheless, the fiction is not due to the Roman law, but is in harmony with the
§ 895.
law of nature, and therefore also it can be used as a principle in proof of that. He who is skilled in the method of proof and the art of reasoning, well understands how much use is made of fictions of that sort in the investigation and proof of things which are in accord with the truth.

§ 905. *Whether captives lose their rights and whether rights over them are extinguished*

Those captured in war do not lose their rights, nor are the rights over them extinguished; both are simply in abeyance. For when those captured in war return to their people, all the rights which they had are restored to

---

4. This is the *Lex Cornelia de Captivis,* which was believed to provide for the civil succession to the estate of a person who had been taken captive by an enemy, and who then died in that state.

them and all rights over them must be restored. But since rights which $§ 894.$
were lost, and consequently were transferred to others, would be no longer under their control, and therefore the possessors would not be bound
to restore the same rights to them, as no reason for restitution existed, $§ 467$, part 2,
nor could extinct rights, which have become non-existent, be restored to Jus Nat.
them; those captured in war do not lose their rights, nor are the rights
over them extinguished. Which was the first point.

But since, indeed, their own rights cannot be restored to them, nor
can the rights of others over them be restored until they have returned
from captivity, since, moreover, no one can claim them for himself before
hope of a return has ceased, both the rights of captives and the rights $§ 336$, part 2,
over them remain in abeyance until they either return, or it has become Jus Nat.
certain that they never will return. Which was the second point.

> There is no reason arising out of the captivity why a captive ought
> to lose his rights, since by nature he is to be compared to one absent,
> who is prevented from returning, and concerning whom it cannot
> be definitely determined whether he is likely to return or not. Nor
> is there any reason why in that case one should depart from the law
> of nature, so as to come to the contrary decision by virtue of the vol-
> untary law of nations. Therefore there is nothing left, except that the
> rights should remain in abeyance.

§ 906. *Of a will made in captivity*

Since those captured in war do not lose their rights, as the free power of $§ 905.$
disposing of their property has not been taken away from them, although
while the war lasts none of their property may be sent to them while they $§§ 994, 999,$
are detained by the enemy, by nature a will made in captivity is valid. part 7, Jus Nat.

> Of course the rights of captives are in abeyance only as regards their
> exercise, not for a moral reason, since in fact there is none, but from
> a physical impossibility, and since this does not prevent the making
> of a will, there is indeed no reason why a will made in captivity ought
> not to be valid. By nature captives do not become slaves, although
> they can be reduced to slavery for an offence, nor is it contrary to $§ 814.$
> nature that slaves should hold their own property with full legal right, $§ 1108$, part 7,
> and since by nature the master has a right only to the services to be Jus Nat.

performed by the slave and over other actions in so far as they have some bearing on those services, by force of slavery to which any one is reduced the master does not acquire all rights which belonged to the slave prior to the servile status, consequently not his property, if he has any; and while he is in servitude, nothing belongs to the master except that which is acquired through his services. The things which are contrary to those principles have been introduced by the customs of barbarous nations and afterwards spread to more civilized states, or have been added or altered by them through their ignorance of the law of nature, since when one error is allowed more follow.

§ 1096, part 7, Jus Nat.

§ 1107, part 7, Jus Nat.

§ 907. *Of civil laws and customs and stipulations of nations in regard to postliminium*

Those things which are laid down in the civil law in regard to postliminium are valid only with one's own nation; but those which have been introduced among certain nations by custom, or have been determined by stipulations, are to be considered among those nations as customary or stipulative law. For civil laws bind only the members of that state by which they are enacted. If, then, certain laws concerning postliminium have been established in a certain state, they are valid only with their own nations. Which was the first point.

§ 967, part 8, Jus Nat.

Furthermore, since customary law is that which has been introduced by long usage and observed as law, and stipulative law is that which arises from agreements entered into between different nations, those things which have been introduced by custom among certain nations concerning postliminium, or have been determined by stipulations, are to be observed among those nations as customary law or as stipulative law. Which was the second point.

§ 24.

§ 23.

Therefore, nothing can be determined concerning postliminium from the Roman law, however closely it should agree with the law of nature. For nothing can be admitted concerning this agreement before it has been proved from another source that this belongs to the law of nature, or even to the voluntary law of nations accepted in that sense in which we accept it, and which, if the law of nature is not contrary to it, takes its place. But when the Roman law is in accord with the law of nature, or with the voluntary law of nations, it is not valid law

§ 887.

in regard to postliminium because it belongs to the Roman law, but because it belongs to the law of nature or the voluntary law of nations, and it would be equally valid if nothing had been said concerning it in the Roman law, or if the contrary had been said. The same thing is true in every other case. Nor is it sufficient that the agreement of the Roman law with the law of nature should be proved, if all that is expressed in it concerning postliminium can be derived from some general principle, unless it shall have been proved beforehand that that principle is a part of the law of nature, and that those things which are presumed in addition for the purpose of deriving other conclusions therefrom are a part of the same law. And if something is to be attributed to necessity not in opposition to the law of nature, it must be carefully scrutinized, lest that may be taken for the law of nature   Note, § 887. which ought to be referred to the voluntary law of nations. Those things which are to be understood in regard to postliminium in peace and during truces will be proved in their own place.

§ 908. *Of marriage*

Marriage is subject to postliminium. For since those captured in war   § 905. do not lose their rights, they do not lose their right to their spouse, consequently marriage is not dissolved by captivity. Since, therefore,   § 894. by postliminium all rights which one had before captivity are restored to him on his return, by virtue of postliminium a wife also is restored to one on his return.

And hence it is plain, as long as there is hope of return, the woman cannot marry another man.

§ 909. *Of the right of private individuals in war*

The subject of a belligerent without the mandate or permission of the sovereign power cannot use hostile force against enemies or the property of enemies. For a war is waged by those leaders who have supreme sovereignty,   § 607. consequently by those sovereign powers as leaders who have a right of war.   § 368. Therefore, since it belongs to the sovereign power to determine concerning   §§ 613, 614. warlike acts or hostilities by which force is used against enemies, no sub-   § 785. ject can claim for himself a right to engage in hostilities, and consequently without the mandate or permission of the sovereign power it is not possible to use hostile force against enemies or the property of enemies.

There is no one who doubts that the right of war is a potential part of civil sovereignty. Therefore, just as a subject has no right to any act which concerns the exercise of civil sovereignty, except by the consent of the sovereign power, so also a subject can have no right in war in himself, but if it should be necessary to allow a subject to begin hostilities, he can get the right from no other source than the sovereign power. Therefore, Grotius is mistaken in arguing that by the law of nature all hostilities are allowed to private individuals, and in thinking that the law of nature has been changed at all in that regard by the voluntary law of nations, since he extends the voluntary law of nations beyond the limits within which it is to be admitted, for the reason that he has sought to deduce it from the acts of nations, of which the records of the ancients have preserved knowledge, a very insecure foundation.[5]

§ 910. *Of arming ships against an enemy*

§ 909.

Since the subject of a belligerent without the command or permission of the sovereign power cannot use warlike force against enemies or the property of enemies, it is not allowable to arm ships against an enemy by private authority.

Those who command armed ships of that sort we usually call "Privateers," a word that is not of German origin. Therefore, those who ally themselves with them on their own responsibility are equivalent to pirates, because they act with no authority, and reasons of state stand in the way of allowing any chance individual to arm ships, on account of the abuse readily to be apprehended, since, influenced by the desire for gain, they may attack friends or those who are not enemies, no less than enemies, and it is always a dangerous thing for anything to be done in war under private auspices.

5. See Grotius, *The Rights of War and Peace,* ed. Richard Tuck, 3 vols. (Indianapolis: Liberty Fund, 2005), vol. 1, bk. I, chap. III, 2, pp. 241–42.

§ 911. *Of those concessions which are tacitly granted*

Because it is allowable to use force against enemies or the property of enemies by the private concession of the sovereign power, and since a tacit consent is true consent, since, moreover, it is not difficult to foresee that, if anything should be done on private initiative which has an especially important effect in war, because it seriously injures the enemy and helps us very much, the opportunity offered must be seized by the decision of the sovereign power; in such a case ratification by the sovereign power is rightly presumed, that is, the sovereign power is understood to have tacitly granted the right to such an act. And for the same reason an act is allowable for the private individual which is justified by the right of defence belonging by nature to every person, which cannot be taken from him.

§ 909.

§ 662, part 1, Phil. Pract. Univ.

§ 973, part 1, Jus Nat.

There is an example in point, if property useful in war is being carried to the enemy, or if some chief commander should be captured, and if, in the latter case, resistance should be offered to the capture.

§ 64, part 1, Jus Nat.

§ 912. *Of private hostilities of soldiers*

Soldiers cannot commit hostilities without the order or permission, express or implied, of their officers, and the officers can order these within the limits of their authority. For it is the duty of those who are in control of soldiers to decide when hostilities are necessary and to order them, inasmuch as they act within the limit of their authority by right of the supreme power, so that it would be just as if the sovereign had ordered hostilities. Therefore it is plain, as said before, that soldiers cannot commit hostilities without the order or express permission of their officers or at least with their tacit permission, or for the purpose of defence, just as we have shown in regard to other private individuals.

§ 771.

§ 900.

§ 911.

The examples of tacit permission which we have before given have a place here also. Although of course soldiers have been enrolled or hired for the purpose of hostilities, nevertheless in their service they do not depend on their own will, but on the will of those who are

Note, § 911.

their officers; if they do anything outside their line of duty, they do
not do that as soldiers, and therefore they are equivalent to private
subjects. Therefore, the things which have been proved concerning private individuals are readily understood concerning soldiers.
And in like manner the same thing is understood of officers who
are subordinate to others. All results in war are quite doubtful and
they bring after them other unexpected results, so that one should
not easily presume the consent which is necessary. Therefore, the
advantage ought to be evident and the loss to the enemy plain, that
the presumption may justify a private act. But it is self-evident that
if a soldier should have been forbidden by the military law to fight
without an order, there is no room for a presumption, and one fighting without an order is bound in any event to pay the penalty of a
transgressor of the law. For although it is a provision of the law of
nature that a soldier should not fight without an order, nevertheless,
since a law as a positive law ought to have some effect, if the order
has been given even without qualification, or with a threat added
that a soldier should not act without command, or if the prohibition
has been made when they went on service, it is therefore necessary
that the liberty to fight without an order should be kept within quite
narrow limits.

§ 913. *What a truce is*

§ 788, part 3,
Jus Nat.

A truce is defined as a suspension of acts of war by both belligerent parties for a stipulated time; consequently a truce is made by agreement.

Thus a truce is made to bury the dead, likewise to hold a conference that terms of peace may be considered.

§ 914. *Whether a war is ended by a truce*

§ 913.

Since in time of a truce warlike acts are simply suspended, war is not
ended by a truce, but continues even if the truce has been agreed upon
for a considerable time.

A truce is often made for a short time, according to the different
purposes for which it is agreed upon. If, indeed, it is agreed upon
for several years, either of the belligerent parties reserves for itself the

right which it claims to have, nor on that account is the war brought to an end. Of course in questions of morality a right is one thing, the exercise of the right another. The latter can be suspended without impairing the former. In Livy, we have examples of truces for a hundred years, in Justinus, one of fifty years.[6] So also kings can make a truce for the duration of their lives, reserving the controverted right for their successors.

[Livy, *Histories*,] Bk. 3, 1, 15, and 7, 20.

[Justinus, *Histories*,] Bk. 3 [chap. 7.]

§ 915. *What is not allowed in time of a truce*

Likewise, because a truce is made by agreement and in it a suspension of warlike acts is promised by both parties, and since stipulations even between enemies are to be observed, in time of a truce no hostile act is to be committed; consequently if any such act is committed by either party, the other party immediately has the right to resort to warlike acts without delay, unless there has been an agreement to the contrary.

§ 913.

§ 799.

§ 827, part 3, Jus Nat.

§ 916. *Whether when a truce is ended war must be declared anew*

Since a war is not ended by a truce, there is no need of a new declaration when the truce is ended.

§ 914.

By virtue of the agreement warlike acts are not suspended beyond the stipulated time, since no one can acquire a greater right from another than he wished to transfer to him. Therefore, when the time of the truce is ended, each party knows for himself that warlike acts are suspended no longer, but are allowable to him; for each party knows that the other party wishes to resume hostilities. Therefore, there would be no reason for a new declaration.

§ 382, part 3, Jus Nat.

6. See Livy, *From the Founding of the City,* trans. B. O. Foster, 14 vols. (London: Heinemann; Cambridge, Mass., Harvard University Press, 1919–59), vol. 1, bk. I, chap. xv, 5, p. 57, and vol. 3, bk. VII, chap. xx, 8, p. 425; Justinus, *Epitome of the Philippic History of Pompeius Trogus,* trans. J. C. Yardley, intro and notes R. Develin (Atlanta, Ga.: Scholars Press, 1994), bk. 3, chap. 7, p. 52.

§ 917. *Of the publication of a truce*

§ 913.

Since for the time of the truce warlike acts must be suspended, as soon as the agreement has been made in regard to it, publication should be made by each of the belligerent parties.

And therefore a day thereafter is usually set from which the truce is to begin.

§ 918. *The effect of a truce*

§ 914.
§ 913.

Since during the time of a truce the war is not ended, but warlike acts are simply suspended, all things ought to remain just as they are, nor should any changes be made in them which affect the enemy.

A truce ought not to be deleterious to either party. Therefore each ought to refrain from those things which are done with the intention of injuring the enemy.

§ 919. *When a truce begins to be binding*

§ 789, part 3,
Jus Nat., and
§ 799 h.

The parties to a truce are bound immediately on the completion of the contract, the subjects of each from the moment of publication. For the obligation of the contracting parties arises from the stipulation. Therefore, the parties are bound immediately on the completion of the contract. Which was the first point.

§ 1043, part 3,
Jus Nat.

§ 775.

Since the sovereign power may bind its subjects by its stipulations and the subjects are bound to obey the commands, since, moreover, minor powers may bind their subordinates within the limits of those acts which they are accustomed to command, since, moreover, no one can be bound to do that of which he is ignorant, as is self-evident, therefore the subjects of the contracting parties cannot be bound until after the truce has been

§ 851, Ontol.

published to them. Therefore, since their obligation depends upon publication, they are immediately bound from the moment of publication.

The obligation of the contracting parties comes from their own will, but that of their subjects from the will of superiors to whose right they are subject. Hence, the truce when published is said to receive the form of law as regards the subjects and the subjects are bound as by a law. It is easily seen that the contracting parties ought to publish a truce without delay, so as to satisfy their obligation.

§ 920. *Of the reckoning of the time of a truce*

If a truce has been stipulated for a definite time, as for a hundred days or for three years, the days or years are to be reckoned from the moment of completion of the contract: if it has been stipulated as up to a certain day, as to the first of March, the truce is ended at daybreak: if it has been said that it ought to begin from a certain day, the truce begins exactly at daybreak on that day. For a truce is valid for the time agreed upon and is binding immediately on the completion of the contract, unless there has been an express agreement otherwise, since then one must abide by the agreement. Therefore if, for example, the truce has been made for a hundred days, since it was then agreed that it ought to continue through a hundred days, one hundred days are to be reckoned from the moment of the completion of the contract, each of which, of course, consists of twenty-four hours, each hour of sixty minutes. Which was the first point. § 913. § 919. §§ 382, 789, part 3, Jus Nat.

But if it has been said that the truce is to continue up to the first of March, it is quite evident that the intention of the contracting parties was that it ought not to continue longer than till daybreak on the first of March: for if it had been meant to be still valid during that day, it should have been said that it was not to continue beyond the first of March. Since the latter expression manifestly includes the first of March, the former certainly excludes it. Therefore, the truce comes to an end at daybreak of the day up to which it was agreed upon. Which was the second point.

Finally, if it has been said that it is to begin from a certain day, as from the first of March, the words of the contracting parties show with sufficient clearness that they had in mind that the truce should begin on the first of March at daybreak. Which was the third point.

When the words of the contracting parties show plainly enough what their intention was, there is certainly no reason for determining on other principles whether the day added as a *terminus ad quem* ought to be excluded or included. Therefore, we pass by that dispute as being unnecessary. Nevertheless, the computation of the time of a truce cannot be considered superfluous. For let us suppose that while a city was besieged, a truce was made up to the first of August, and the siege, suspended on account of the truce, was resumed on the first day of August, and the city captured; the question is whether the city has been captured rightfully or wrongfully if on the second of August an army arrived which was sufficient to compel the enemy to desist from the siege.

§ 921. *Whether during the time of a truce the property and persons of the enemy can be captured*

The property or persons of the enemy cannot be captured during the time of a truce. For during the time of a truce all warlike acts ought to cease, of whatsoever character indeed they may be. Therefore, since the capture of the property or persons of enemies is certainly a warlike act, it is not allowable to capture either one or the other during the time of a truce.

§ 913.

§ 785.

> During the time of a truce an enemy is not to be considered as an enemy, nor is his property to be considered the property of an enemy, since the exercise of every right of war has now been suspended, and what was otherwise allowable in war has now become unallowable by virtue of the agreement.

§ 922. *Whether during a truce postliminium exists*

During the time of a truce there is no postliminium. For as long as the truce continues, all things ought to remain in the condition in which they are, nor ought there to be any change in them. Therefore, whatever things have been captured by the enemy before the truce ought to remain under his control, consequently, they cannot be restored to their original condition during the truce. Therefore, since property and persons are restored to their original condition by postliminium, during the time of a truce there can be no postliminium.

§ 918.

§§ 894, 896.

> And hence it is plain that even if captured property or persons should be by chance restored to us during a truce, they are to be returned to the enemy.

§ 923. Of subjects of the enemy wishing to desert and of unguarded places

During the time of a truce it is not allowable to receive subjects who wish to desert to the enemy, much less to bribe the enemy's garrisons and invade places held by them. For during the continuance of a truce, no change must be made in those things which affect the enemy, conse- § 918. quently, those who were subjects of the enemy before the truce ought to remain so during its continuance. Therefore, even if they should wish to desert, they are not to be received. Which was the first point.

In the same way it is plain that it is not allowable during a truce to persuade the garrisons to revolt by means of money or promises, conse- quently, by corrupting them to invade places of the enemy held by them. Which was the second point.

When subjects of the enemy who wish to desert are received, the sov- ereignty, which the enemy had over them, is undoubtedly taken away. Therefore, their reception is equivalent to the occupation of incorpo- real property of the enemy, and with respect to the one to whom the § 862. property belongs, it is understood that the occupation was by force, in so far as he would have resisted, if he had been consulted in the mat- ter, so that it could not have been occupied except by force of arms. Therefore, that reception is certainly to be considered as a warlike act § 913. which is suspended during a truce. In war all acts are rated as hostile by which we attain a thing which ordinarily it was not possible to acquire except by force of arms, for the reason that the particular circumstances remove the act from the category of force. An enemy always intends to use force in whatever he plans against the persons or property of enemies; but when no one opposes him, force is lacking as regards that act. But in the present instance there is no need of these niceties, since it is plain enough from the purpose of the truce, which the contracting parties intend and ought to intend, what their intention is, for from this it can be determined what is allowable and what not.

§ 924. Of places abandoned by the enemy and unguarded places

During a truce it is allowable to occupy places abandoned by an enemy, § 249, part 2, but not unguarded places. For the places which an enemy abandons, he Jus Nat.

no longer wishes to claim as his own. Since, therefore, places abandoned by the enemy do not affect him if they are occupied, nothing is changed in them which affects him, consequently nothing is done which is contrary to the truce. Therefore, during a truce it is allowable to occupy places abandoned by an enemy. Which was the first point.

§ 918.

But even if places are unguarded, nevertheless they are still the property of the enemy. Therefore, since the property of an enemy cannot be captured during a truce, it is not allowable to occupy unguarded places of the enemy. Which was the second point.

§ 921.

> The distinction is not to be considered whether the guard has been given up before the truce, or after it was made; for the absence of a guard is not sufficient evidence of abandonment, and much less is an inadequate guard to be considered as abandonment, if it appears otherwise that the enemy desires to claim such a place as his own.

§ 925. *Of a safe departure and return*

During a truce it is allowable for either party to go back and forth. For while the truce continues the property or persons of enemies cannot be captured, and all hostilities cease which can be committed in any way. Therefore, since a truce guarantees security for property and persons, during a truce it is allowable for either party to go back and forth.

§ 921.
§ 913.

> Nevertheless, the mind of the one who goes and returns ought to be free from all design of injuring the enemy. Therefore, if an enemy fears lest this going and returning may be injurious to him, it is agreed in the stipulation for a truce that it shall not be allowed.

§ 926. *What is allowable within one's own boundaries and outside of them during the continuance of the truce*

During the continuance of a truce any one can do whatever he pleases within territory indisputably his own; but within disputed territory he can do nothing which may be to the prejudice of the enemy. For since during a truce all things ought to remain in the condition in which they are, nor is anything to be changed in regard to them which affects the enemy, there is no one who does not see that within disputed territory

§ 918.

nothing can be done which may be to the prejudice of the enemy. Which was the one point.

But since that cannot be held as true against a promisor which he has not made sufficiently plain, the intention of the contracting parties is not extended to the point that neither party may do anything, within territory indisputably his own, by which he provides for his own security, since an enemy would not have been able to prevent that if the war had continued. Therefore, unless there has been some special agreement concerning these matters, during the continuance of a truce any one can do whatever he pleases within territory indisputably his own. Which was the other point. §§ 428, 382, part 3, Jus Nat.

> A truce is not made with the purpose of helping the enemy and injuring ourselves. But when we cannot provide for our security unless that is done to the prejudice of the enemy, so that his condition becomes more difficult if the war is continued, such action at least is to be avoided in places in dispute. For when the position under the truce ought to remain the same as it was before, the condition of neither ought to come out worse than it was before, so when the truce is ended the situation shall be just as if there had been no truce, and the war had not been interrupted thereby, but had continued uninterruptedly. Those things, therefore, which can be done for the sake of one's security within territory indisputably one's own, when there is no war, can also be done when war is suspended, consequently during a truce. § 913.

§ 927. *Special cases*

Since during the continuance of a truce any one can do whatever he pleases within territory indisputably his own, it is allowable to withdraw farther into one's territory with one's army, to rebuild walls and enrol soldiers; but since aside from those things nothing may be done by which the condition of the enemy is made worse, one must refrain from every act which aims at occupying a besieged city or, on the other side, defending the same. § 926.

§ cited.

> The latter is plain from the fact that warlike acts are suspended during a truce; for if these should be continued, the war is in fact continued, a thing which is altogether opposed to the stipulation of the truce. § 913.

§ 928. *Other cases*

§ 927.

Since nothing may be done during the continuance of a truce which aims at defending a city besieged before the truce, it is not allowable to rebuild a fortification broken down by the artillery of the enemy, nor to send auxiliaries or other necessities to the city in trouble.

A siege is not terminated by a truce, but is simply not continued, and all things on either side ought to remain in the same condition as they are at the very moment when the truce begins.

§ 929. *Of those who happen to be found within the territory of the enemy when the truce is ended*

He who is prevented by superior force, as by sickness, from withdrawing outside the territory of the enemy, and any other one caught therein, has no right to return when the truce is ended. For when the truce is ended, there is immediately an opportunity for warlike acts. Therefore, since it is allowable to capture an enemy in war, as soon as the truce is ended the enemy can exercise his right, and, consequently, can detain as captives any hostile persons caught within his territory, consequently these have no right to return.

§ 916.

§§ 811, 889.

It is no objection that, when war is declared, a foreigner who is a citizen of the enemy must be allowed a safe departure within a certain time, and that delay must be allowed those detained by superior force. For it is one thing, when war begins, and another when it is continued on the termination of a truce. Concerning the definite beginning of the former one could not determine, since a person might enter the territory of one with whom a war has afterwards arisen with his own nation, and a safe departure was at least tacitly promised him when he entered, without any limitation. But one entering the territory of an enemy or hostile localities during the time of a truce is not ignorant of the fact that when the truce comes to an end the war immediately goes on, so that there is no need of a new declaration; consequently he is not ignorant of the fact that he can be captured if caught by the enemy in hostile territory, nor that it is not impossible that he cannot return in good time if he is prevented by superior force. He goes at his own risk into hostile localities during the time of a truce, a thing

§ 835.

§ 838.

§ 836.

§ 916.

which cannot be said of one who comes into hostile territory before the war. There is the further fact that he also knows that a safe return has not been tacitly promised him by the truce, except for so long as the truce continues.

§ 930. *The classification of truces*

Truces are general, by which all warlike acts are suspended, and special, by which only certain stipulated acts are suspended. Since a truce is made by a stipulation which is to be observed, since, moreover, neither party can acquire a greater right from such a stipulation than has been expressly declared or necessarily implied from the truce, special truces are not to be extended beyond the hostilities concerning which there has been an express agreement, and the warlike acts necessarily connected therewith.

§ 913.

§ 799.

§§ 382, 427, part 3, Jus Nat.

So if during the siege of a city a truce is allowed for the purpose of burying the dead, only the warlike acts directed toward the continuance of the siege by the one party, and the defence of the city by the other party, ought to cease, but that is not to be extended to other acts with which the continuation of the siege and the defence of the city against it do not interfere. Nor during the continuance of the truce is it allowable for either side to go back and forth between city and camp, since such going and coming, during the continuance of the siege which is not ended by the truce, is not harmless.

§ 931. *Of the stipulative law of a truce*

If in the stipulation of a truce it has been expressly agreed that certain things can be done which are otherwise not allowable, or that certain things cannot be done which are otherwise allowable, the former will be allowable during the time of the truce, the latter will not be allowable. For no one can acquire a greater right from another than he wished to transfer to him, nor can one be bound to another beyond his desire. Therefore, if it has been expressly agreed that certain things can be done which are otherwise not allowable, those things will be allowable, and on the contrary if it has been expressly agreed that certain things cannot be done which are otherwise allowable, those things will not be allowable.

§ 382, part 3, Jus Nat.

The law between the contracting parties will be what they arrange as the law of the truce. Then, indeed, they must determine by the agreement what is allowable and what not, and not by the nature of a truce, whence one determines what by the law of nature is allowable by a truce or not, in so far as that law governs the truce, just as it does any other human acts. For example, it is allowable during a truce for

§ 925.

either party to go back and forth, but it will not be allowed if there has been an express agreement that it may not be done, and consequently if one acts contrary to the agreement he can be detained as a captive.

§ 932. *Who can make a truce*

General truces cannot be made except by sovereign powers; special ones can be made by commanders-in-chief within the scope of their authority, when existing circumstances make that necessary. For in a general truce all warlike acts are suspended for a certain time agreed upon. Therefore,

§§ 913, 930.
§ 607.
§ 368.
§§ 613, 614.

since a war is waged under the direction of those who have supreme sovereignty, consequently under the direction of the supreme powers, and since they have every right in war, it depends solely on their own will whether the war ought to be continued, or warlike acts suspended for some time. Therefore, general truces cannot be made except by sovereign powers. Which was the first point.

But certain duties in war are imposed on commanders-in-chief,

§ 771.

and they have the right which arises from the nature of the function entrusted to them, or is required for properly exercising it. Therefore,

§ 930.

since in special treaties only certain acts are suspended, when existing circumstances make it necessary, commanders-in-chief also can make treaties. Which was the second point.

Thus in the siege of a city commanders who direct the warlike acts on either side can agree upon a truce for the purpose of burying the dead, or that the consent of the sovereign power to the surrender of the city may be secured under strict conditions. The former case also occurs after a battle. But greater circumspection is necessary on the part of the giver than of the one asking; for necessity governs the latter, and it is to his advantage, as in the cases which we have just given. Nevertheless, there may be the same necessity on either side, and the same advantage for each, as if after a battle each party has to bury its dead. Also a commander-in-chief ought not to do what he does within the scope of his authority, if that would have a great effect on the war, unless the lesser powers are called into conference, lest some fault can be imputed to him, since those who are absent usually judge things which have been done in war according to their results. But this is a question of policy and is not to be confused with a matter of right.

§ 933. *On whose good faith a truce depends*

Since general treaties cannot be made except by sovereign powers, but special ones frequently also by commanders-in-chief, who do by the right of the sovereign power whatever they do within the scope of their authority, and therefore bind the sovereign power by their stipulation, treaties rest upon the good faith of the sovereign powers.

§ 932.

§ 368.

§ 772.

> The good faith of sovereign powers is sacred. Therefore, that sanctity attaches also to the good faith in a truce. And therefore, a private individual deserves no light punishment who dares to do anything contrary to a truce.

§ 758, part 3, Jus Nat., and § 915.

§§ 550, 369.

§ 934. *Of private acts which are contrary to a treaty*

If a private individual should do what is contrary to a truce, the good faith of the truce is not violated, unless the act was performed by the order of the sovereign power, or ratified by it: but the individual is to be punished and property captured by him is to be returned. For if a private individual should do what is contrary to a truce, without the consent of the sovereign power, consequently, if an order has not been given beforehand, and ratification has not followed, the act of the private individual, which depends in no way upon the will of the sovereign power, cannot be imputed to it. Therefore, since a truce rests upon the good faith of the sovereign powers, if a private individual does what is contrary to a truce, and the sovereign power has not ordered or ratified it, the good faith of the truce is not violated. Which was the first point.

§ 650, part 1, Phil. Pract. Univ.

§ 933.

But if the sovereign power has ordered it, the act of the private individual must be imputed to the sovereign, and since it would be just the

§ 654, part 1, Phil. Pract. Univ.

same whether he has ordered or ratified it, it must be imputed to him
also, when it has ratified. Therefore, since a truce rests on the good faith

§ 933.   of the sovereign powers, it certainly is violated if a private individual
should do anything by the order of the sovereign power, or if after he has
acted, the sovereign has ratified it. Which was the second point.

Finally, if a private individual who has done anything contrary to
a truce should not be punished by the sovereign power, and property

§ 921 h, and   wrongfully captured should not be restored, the sovereign power would
§ 859, part 1,   ratify this act, consequently it itself would violate the good faith upon
Jus Nat.
                 which a treaty rests; as proved above, such a private individual who has
Point 2.
                 done anything contrary to a treaty is to be punished, and captured prop-
erty is to be restored. Which was the third point.

A private act, therefore, gives no right to the other party to continue
warlike acts further, immediately upon the making of the truce, unless
the consent of the sovereign power is proved, which consent indeed
is evident from the fact that the sovereign is unwilling to punish the
offender and restore the captured property. Of course as long as the
consent is not proved, the presumption is in favour of the sovereign.

§ 859, part 1,   Therefore the injured party does wrong if on account of the private act
Jus Nat.   he withdraws immediately from the agreement for the truce, before
Note, § 933.   his right is denied him. He deserves no slight punishment who dares
§§ 581, 626,   to do anything contrary to a truce. Therefore the sovereign power
part 8, Jus Nat.
                 rightly punishes him as guilty of a crime, nor does the injured party
§ 549, part 2,
Jus Nat.   less rightfully demand a penalty for the wrong done him.

§ 935. Of the penalty added to a stipulation for a truce

If a penalty has been added to the stipulation for a truce, on the payment
of the penalty the truce continues. For if a penalty has been added to the
stipulation for a truce, the contracting parties undoubtedly understand
that the agreement is that on payment of the penalty the truce contin-

§ 915.   ues, since otherwise there would have been no need of adding a penalty.
Therefore, since stipulations must be observed, if he who has acted con-
§ 789, part 3,   trary to a truce has paid the penalty, the truce ought to continue.
Jus Nat.

If, then, on the violation of a truce the injured party uses violence,
he does wrong, since according to the agreement he ought simply

to demand from the offender the stipulated penalty. But when the offender is unwilling to pay the penalty at the time when the injured party withdraws from the agreement, the latter is no longer bound thereby, and so he has the right to resume warlike acts.

§ 382, part 3, Jus Nat.

§ 915.

§ 936. *If the agreement should be in the alternative, that either a penalty should be paid or there should be a resort to arms*

If the agreement is in the alternative, that either a penalty should be paid or there should be a resort to arms, the choice is with the injured party. For if there is an agreement in the alternative, that either a penalty should be paid or there should be a resort to arms, that is, of course, when the truce is violated by the other party, the choice cannot be that of the offender, since by refusing to pay the penalty he would withdraw from the agreement; consequently, the injured party would have the right to resume warlike acts, nor would there then be need of a contract in the alternative. Therefore it is necessary that the injured party should have the option.

§ 915.

Therefore it is up to the injured party whether he may wish to demand the penalty and leave the truce in force, or receive the penalty offered by the offender, or indeed whether he too may wish to withdraw from the agreement.

§ 937. *What safe passage is*

Safe passage is defined as the right to move freely hither and thither, granted either to persons or to property. Since this right does not belong to every one in general but is granted only to a certain person or to certain particular persons, with regard to the transportation either of themselves or of their property, since, moreover, a concession of that sort is a privilege, the concession of safe passage is a privilege.

§ 853, part 8, Jus Nat.

Since it is allowable in war to capture the persons and property of enemies, and since the decision as to those things which are to be done in war is to be left to those waging the war, safe passage in war can belong to no one except by special concession. And therefore it is a kind of privilege.

§§ 811, 889.

§ 783.
§ 853, part 8,
Jus Nat.

§ 938. *Whether he to whom safe passage has been granted can substitute another for himself*

§ 937.

§ 864, part 8,
Jus Nat.

Since the concession of safe passage is a privilege, and since a privilege given to a person is restricted to him so that it cannot pass from him to another, if safe passage has been granted to a person as a person, another person cannot use the same safe passage. But since it is just the same whether property is carried by one or by another, if safe passage is given to things, they can be transferred to the place to which they are to be carried by another than their owner.

Of course, one must see what is the matter at stake, a thing which is clear from the reason why security has been sought and granted. Thus if the security promised to goods has also been promised to the persons by whom they are to be carried, and when nothing has been expressly said concerning the persons by whom they are to be carried, the owner has been left free in transporting them to use the assistance of those whom he wishes.

§ 939. *Whether one who has been allowed to come can send another, and vice versa*

§ 938.

Since if safe passage is given to a person as a person, another person cannot use the privilege; if one is allowed to come, he cannot send another, nor vice versa.

§ 427, part 3,
Jus Nat.

Of course no one can claim a greater right for himself than has been granted to him. Moreover, more is not allowed than has been expressly stated.

§ 940. *How security is to be furnished*

§ 937.

Since safe passage is granted for the purpose of security, security is to be furnished even outside the territory of the one granting it, both for the persons and property for which it is given, until they shall have come to a place where they are safe.

Of course safe passage is allowed with the purpose that they are to fear nothing from a hostile force, until either persons or property have come to a place where they are safe.

§ 941. *How the right of safe passage is to be determined*

In like manner because safe passage depends wholly upon the will of the one granting it, the right of the one to whom safe passage is granted must be determined by the will of the grantor, and this is understood from the purpose for which it is given; consequently, he to whom the right is given to go out or to cross over has not the right to return, and he to whom security has been granted for some particular business is understood to have it granted until that business has been finished.

§ 937.

See what we noted a little while ago.

Note, § 939.

§ 942. *Whether, if a journey is allowed, the return is allowed*

If safe passage is allowed to make a journey, the return is also included in it. For since a journey is not ended until you have made a return, the return also is part of the journey. Thus if safe passage is allowed for making a journey, the return also is understood to be allowed.

§ 941.

Although it may be plain enough what has been intended when safe passage has been granted to one seeking it, nevertheless it is wiser that express mention be made of the return, lest one may be drawn into a controversy as to how great a right has been granted.

§ 943. *Whether under safe passage property and attendants are included*

If safe passage is granted to make a journey, under that are also included the things which are usually taken for a journey, and an attendant or two without whom it would be unbecoming to travel. It is self-evident that one making a journey cannot do without things which he needs on his journey, that is, either on the road or in the place to which he is going, nor indeed can a journey be made without attendants by one with whose dignity it accords that he should not travel without attendants, nor by one who has need of the services of attendants. Therefore, if safe passage is granted to make a journey, under it are also included things which one making a journey needs on his journey; consequently, those things which are usually taken for a journey, and an attendant or two for the care of his person, without whom it would be unbecoming to travel.

Note, § 942.   Nevertheless it is better, as said before, that express mention should
be made of the property, and the number and name of the persons
should be indicated.

§ 944. *Whether safe passage granted to a father includes his son and wife*

Safe passage granted to a father does not include his son and wife. For it
is self-evident that a son and wife do not usually accompany a father on
a journey, as if he could not make the journey without them. Therefore,
if a father alone seeks safe passage for himself, the one granting it could
not have thought of the son and wife. Therefore, since the right of the
§ 941. father is to be determined by the will of the one granting it, safe passage
cannot be extended to a son and wife; consequently, that given to the
father does not include the son and wife.

§ 937.   The concession of safe passage is a privilege which cannot be
extended beyond the person to whom it is given. The reasoning is
different in the case of attendants, as is plain from the proof of the preceding proposition, inasmuch as they are understood to be included
in the privilege.

§ 945. *Of safe passage granted for a definite time*

Safe passage granted for a definite time comes to an end when the time has
elapsed. If it has been granted at the will of the grantor, it remains effective
so long as the grantor does not declare a revocation, and it is annulled by
his death. For since the right of the one to whom safe passage has been
§ 941. granted is to be determined by the will of the grantor, if it has been granted
for a definite time it is evident that the grantor has not wished that it
should be good beyond that time. Therefore, when the time has elapsed
for which it has been given, it comes to an end. Which was the first point.

But if it has been given at the will of the grantor, it is no less evident
that the safe passage ought to remain effective, until the grantor declares
a contrary will. If, then, he should declare a revocation, the safe passage
is no longer effective. Which was the second point.

Finally, since the one who is dead ceases to have a will, his will continues no longer, consequently it is just as if the grantor had declared a

revocation, therefore the safe passage is extinguished by his death. Which was the third point.

If it has been given at the will of the grantor, the privilege is called a precarious one, revocable at pleasure at any time. Since, nevertheless, the safe passage is granted for the sake of security, that cannot be taken away by revocation before the one to whom the privilege has been granted is in a place of safety, consequently, it is wrong to revoke it in such a way that he may be captured, or his property be taken. But if safe passage has been granted for a definite time, it cannot be understood from that alone that one may come repeatedly, because the limit may also be fixed with the purpose that the going and return should not be prolonged indefinitely. Therefore, it is from the purpose that we must draw our judgement, that we may be agreed on the intention of the grantor.

§ 1124, part 5, Jus Nat.

§ 1125, part 5, Jus Nat.

§ 937.

§ 941.

§ 946. Whether safe passage comes to an end by the death of the grantor

Safe passage does not come to an end by the death of the grantor. For the safe passage was granted by virtue of the right of the grantor, a thing which no one calls in question. Therefore, from this grant a genuine right has been acquired by one to whom the safe passage has been given, which cannot be taken from him. Therefore, since it no longer depends upon the will of the grantor, as it would if it had been given at the will of the grantor, it cannot come to an end at the death of the grantor.

§ 937.
§ 336, part 2, Jus Nat.
§ 945.

The things which have been legally done by a living man do not become void at his death, but as having been legally done they continue in force. But safe passage is usually granted in writing, so that it can be proved what was given and in what way it was given.

§ 947. Whether safe passage includes the right to reside in security in any place

Safe passage does not include the right to reside in security in any place. For safe passage is the right to move safely hither and thither. Therefore,

§ 937.

since the right to move about is one thing, the right of residence another thing, it is not understood that the one to whom the former right has been granted has the latter at the same time granted to him. Therefore, safe passage does not include the right to reside in security in any place.

Let us suppose, for example, that a city in which he is staying who has safe passage is captured by an enemy; if he himself also should be captured in it, nothing is done which is opposed to his safe passage.

§ 948. *Whether the price of ransom of a captive can be transferred to another*

§ 12, part 3, Jus Nat.

§ 789, part 3, Jus Nat., and § 799 h.

The right to demand from a captive a stipulated price for ransom can be transferred by the captor to another. For any one can transfer his right to another at pleasure. Therefore, since one who holds a captive has the right to demand the price of ransom as soon as an agreement has been made in regard to it, the right to demand from a captive an agreed price for ransom can be transferred by the captor to another.

§ 814.

§ 794.

§ 859, part 1, Jus Nat.

Since by nature captives do not become slaves, nor may they be killed, their ransom is quite in accordance with the law of nature, unless an exchange of captives can be made. Therefore, since it is allowable to agree upon a price for ransom, an agreement made in regard to it is not illegal, and therefore there arises for one who holds a captive a genuine right to demand an agreed price, of which as of any other right one can dispose at pleasure without wrong to a captive.

§ 949. *Whether an agreement concerning the price can be rescinded on account of ignorance of the wealth of the captive*

§ 789, part 3, Jus Nat., and § 799 h.

An agreement concerning the price cannot be rescinded because it is found out that the captive is richer than he was believed to be. For the amount of the price has been determined by mutual consent of the contracting parties, and since stipulations must be observed, from the stipulation the right arises on the one side to demand the agreed price and the obligation arises on the other side to pay it. Therefore, he who holds the captive cannot exact a greater price than had been agreed upon, nor can the agreement concerning the price be rescinded because it is found out that the captive is richer than he was believed to be.

The stipulation gets its value from the will of the contracting parties, and not from the amount of the property of the captive of which the captor was ignorant when he made the agreement concerning the amount of the ransom. The reasoning is different if there has been fraud, in regard to which he is separately bound for the loss sustained.

§ 950. *Whether the price of the ransom is due if the captive dies before liberation*

If the captive should die with the price of the ransom unpaid, before an opportunity to depart has been allowed him, or if he was to be taken over to the enemy but died on the way; the agreed price is not due. For the price of ransom is due for the freedom which the captor is bound to give to the captive. But since in either case assumed in the present proposition he cannot give him freedom, as is self-evident, the price of ransom is not due to him.

The performances are mutual in a stipulation concerning the price of ransom. The captor is bound to restore liberty to the captive, and the captive is bound to pay the price. These performances are mutually interdependent, so that if one should fail, the other also would fail.

§ 951. *Whether it is due if one who has been ransomed dies in freedom*

If one who had been a captive should die in freedom when the price has not yet been paid, the price is due. For in that case the captor has fulfilled the agreement. Therefore, the captive also was bound to fulfil it at the very moment when he had gained his freedom. From the moment, therefore, of his liberation the price of ransom is no longer regarded as such, but as a debt due for just cause. Therefore, although he should die after being freed before he has paid the price, nevertheless the debt is not extinguished by his death.

§ 789, part 3, Jus Nat., and § 799 h.

A captive is understood to be at liberty as soon as opportunity has been granted him to depart. If he should delay his return and should die before he returns, the fault is his own.

§ 952. *If a captive should pledge himself for the price of ransom*

If there has been an agreement that the price of ransom should be due at once, and the one who had been a captive should be held simply as security for the debt, on his death, if the price is not yet paid, it is still due. For in that case, as the stipulation has been perfected by virtue of the agreement, the price of ransom is no longer regarded as such but as a debt due for just cause, for which he who before had been a captive has pledged himself or his liberty. Therefore, since by the death of the captive before the price is paid, the situation is such as it would be if the pledge had perished; on his death the debt still exists, consequently, if the price is not yet paid, it is still due.

§ 1142, part 5, Jus Nat.

§ 1188, part 5, Jus Nat.

> He who holds a captive, satisfies his obligations as soon as he frees him from captivity and grants him the opportunity to depart. Therefore, if he remains as a pledge, this is another cause upon which, not the debt, but the security for the debt rests.

§ 953. *Of a term fixed for payment*

If there has been an agreement that the price should be paid on a certain day, and if before that time the one should die who had been a captive, the price is due; but if it has been added that on the day of payment he should still be among the living, it is not due. For since one must abide by what has been agreed, each conclusion is evident from the method of agreement.

§§ 789, 430, part 3, Jus Nat.

> Of course in the first case the day was added as the date for payment, which does not suspend the right to collect the debt as by a condition, but defers the enforcement of it; but in the second case, the added condition that the released captive must still be among the living on the day of payment, suspends the right to demand the price, so that the same does not become definitely due unless the condition is fulfilled.

§ 954. *Of one who is released on stipulation that he would cause another to be released*

If one is released on stipulation that he will cause another to be released, he is bound to return to prison if the other should die before his release;

he is not bound if he should die after his release. For if any one should be released on stipulation that he will cause another to be released, the release of the other is considered as in the nature of a condition on which the promised release depends. Therefore, since a conditional promise has not been fulfilled until the condition occurs, and as long as this is not certain, the promisee cannot say that anything is due to him, such as, in the present instance, release; if any one is released on stipulation that he will cause another to be released, he is bound to return to prison, if the other dies before his release; he is not bound, if he should die after his release.

§ 468, part 3, Jus Nat.

§ 497, part 3, Jus Nat.

Suppose by way of example that one has been captured by the Spaniards, the other by the French, and the former should be released by the Spaniards, on stipulation that the other also should be released by the French. If there has been an agreement that each should be delivered to his people at a certain place and one should die before the delivery, what right then exists is to be determined in accordance with the present proposition. But it is easy to be seen that in the present case delay in delivery can be imputed, so that delivery may be assumed which cannot be accomplished on account of delay of the other, although the captive has died before delivery.

§ 955. Of one who is captured a second time, when the price of ransom is not yet paid

If one who has been released should be captured by another, when the price of ransom is not yet paid, the price is due to each. For when any one is released by the one who holds him captive, the captor is bound simply to give a safe return to his own people, and when this has been furnished, he has satisfied his obligation, for the captive has been released from the captivity in which he was held. Therefore, the price of ransom is now due for a just cause. Consequently, since in the stipulation for the price of ransom it was not agreed that if the war should continue afterwards he should be safe from all violence of the enemy, that does not prevent him from being captured by another, if the opportunity were presented. If, then, this should happen, he is bound to pay the price of the ransom for his release, just as if he had not been captured before. Therefore, if one

who has been released should be captured by another when the price of
ransom is not yet paid, the agreed price is due to each.

Unless that price has been definitely determined by agreement
between the belligerents, the same price is not to be paid to each, but
that is to be paid to either which has been agreed with him.

§ 217.

§ 956. *Whether what he has with him is captured with his person*

If an enemy does not despoil his captive, or the captive secretly keeps anything with him, it remains the property of the captive. For if the enemy
does not despoil the captive, or the captive secretly keeps anything with
him, that which he keeps with him the enemy does not bring under his
control, consequently he does not occupy. Therefore, since property of
an enemy not taken by his enemy remains the property of those to whom
it belonged, as is self-evident; if an enemy does not despoil his captive,
or the captive secretly keeps anything with him, it remains the property
of the captive.

§ 461, part 2,
Jus Nat.

§ 862.

Since by nature captives do not become slaves, and since it is not
in accordance with natural law that a slave should not be able to hold
property of his own, the present proposition is a part of the law of
nature, and does not apply to these nations alone by which slavery is
not received. If the rule has been introduced by the customs of certain
nations, that captives should become slaves and that all the property
which they have with them should be acquired along with their person, that must be referred to the customary law of nations, and is to
be considered unjust.

§ 814.

§ 24.
§ 239, part 1,
Phil. Pract.
Univ.

§ 957. *Whether that can be charged to the ransom*

Since that which he keeps with him belongs to a captive, if an enemy
does not despoil his captive, or if a captive should secretly keep anything
with him, that cannot be charged to the price of ransom.

§ 956.

For the one holding the captive it is just the same whether the price
paid should be paid from that which the captive has with him, or from
another source, since he pays out of his own resources. The price of

ransom by some is usually expressed by the Greek word *lytron,* in German, *Löse-Geld* [ransom].

§ 958. *Of a hostage given to redeem a captive*

If any one has been given as a hostage to redeem a captive, on the death of the captive the hostage is freed. For he who is given as a hostage to redeem a captive is put in pledge for his redemption. Therefore, when by his death the reason for the pledge ceases to exist, the pledge also comes to an end. If, therefore, any one is given as a hostage to redeem a captive, on the death of the captive the hostage is freed.

§ 497.

The hostage ought to be considered as a person substituted for the captive. The right, therefore, which belongs to the one who holds the captive, is the same over the hostage as it was over the captive. But if the captive dies, the right of the captor over him is extinguished. Therefore, on the death of the captive, his right over the hostage ought also to be extinguished.

CHAPTER VIII

Of Peace and the Treaty of Peace

§ 959. *What peace is*

§ 1102, part 1,
Jus Nat.

Peace is defined as that condition in which we are at war with no one. Therefore, since in war we pursue our right by force against another who is unwilling to concede it to us, in peace we need strive by force with none in order to pursue or protect our right, consequently we quietly enjoy our right.

§ 911, part 1,
Jus Nat.

§ 1109, part 1,
Jus Nat.

Peace is the opposite of war, so that when there is war peace does not exist, and therefore there is peace when there is no war. If, therefore, one should understand what the condition is in which war exists, one knows at the same time what the condition is when peace exists. Here the meaning is general, as is that also of war, so that it can be understood no less of individual men living in a state of nature than of nations. Since all wrong is forbidden by nature, and since there is no just cause of war unless a wrong has been done or is threatened, by nature peace is prior to war; but when on the termination of war a treaty of peace is made, peace is subsequent to war. For when one withdraws from war, he returns to peace. Frequently, indeed, the name "a peace" is applied by some to a compromise concerning the cause of the war and concerning those acts which have been committed in it; nevertheless this is not in harmony with the common usage of speech, by which we say that a nation is at peace which is not involved in war, and moreover while war continues we call those peaceful nations which do not involve themselves in the war and in no way make it their own. Nay, we say that even the belligerents themselves are at peace with these. Therefore, no reason persuades or compels us to introduce uncertainty in terminology, which we ought to avoid, especially in sciences such as the law of nature and nations ought to be.

§ 960. *Whether peace exists during a truce*

Since by a truce war is not ended, but continues, since, moreover, war does not exist in peace, during the time of a truce there is not peace. Nevertheless, since during a truce all warlike acts of either belligerent party cease, so that if the truce should be made for a long time, as for twenty, nay fifty, or a hundred years, it would be just the same as if there were no war, as is sufficiently plain; if a truce should be made for a long time, since during the time we must refrain from war, that truce is equivalent to peace.

§ 914.
§ 959.

> Nevertheless, a truce made for even the longest period is still different from peace. For when a truce is made the parties refrain from war merely for a certain time, and when the time has elapsed, a return to war lies open for the same cause; but when peace is made, an agreement is made in regard to the cause of the war, so that that war is ended, nor can it be undertaken a second time for the reason for which it had been waged. Therefore, in the case of a truce made for a long time a certain status exists intermediate between war and peace, which approaches more nearly to peace than to war, since it does not differ from peace except that it is combined with an expectation of war, which does not exist in peace.

§§ 890, 891, part 5, Jus Nat.

§ 961. *Of cultivating peace*

Nations are bound by nature to cultivate peace with each other. For every nation ought to grant to another its right, and in a doubtful case nations ought to settle controversies with each other either amicably or through compromise, or through mediation or through an arbiter, consequently each and every nation ought to be on its guard, lest it may be the cause which compels another nation to seek its right by force against it, and that therefore there may be an opportunity for war. Therefore, since those cultivate peace with each other between whom there is no war, nations are bound by nature to cultivate peace with each other.

§264.

§ 570.

§ 1102, part 1, Jus Nat., and § 572.

> The law of nature which strives for the happiness of the human race as a goal, looks no less to the security of individuals than to that of nations, which does not exist except in peace. Therefore, he who gives

§ 959.
§§ 396 and fol., part 1, Phil. Pract. Univ.

to another a just cause of war sins deeply against the law of nature. Nothing is more opposed to the nature of men than is war, for which the law of nature allows place only as a means of defence, as for an unavoidable evil. But war has its beginning in the injustice of those who are unwilling to allow to others their right or in their unfairness, in that they avoid the milder remedies by which in a doubtful case the controversy can be settled, or finally in their wickedness, in that they do not shrink from injuring others. If then injustice, unfairness and wickedness were hated words, all war would be banished from the earth, and all nations and all individual men would enjoy perpetual peace.

§ 962. *The obligation of the ruler of a state to preserve peace with regard to his subjects*

The ruler of a state owes it to his subjects to strive in every way to preserve the peace. For men have united into a state so that they may quietly enjoy their right and may acquire this safely from another, and the whole is bound to the individuals to contribute, as far as it can, to that purpose. Therefore, since it is quite plain from what precedes, and is known from the common experience of every one, how much war is opposed to that purpose, the whole is bound to the individuals to do its best that war may be avoided, consequently that peace may be preserved. Therefore, since sovereignty has been transferred to the ruler of the state, and therefore also together with it all obligation which is attached to it, the ruler of the state ought to take care that peace should be preserved; consequently he owes it to his subjects to strive in every way to preserve peace.

§ 4, part 8, Jus Nat.

§ 28, part 8, Jus Nat.

§ 959.

§ 42, part 8, Jus Nat.

This is a perfect obligation, since it comes from the stipulation which was made between king and subjects by virtue of the transfer of sovereignty made to him, and it depends upon the original compact by which the state was established. Since the welfare of the commonwealth is the supreme law of the state, the obligation of the ruler is to be determined thereby. But he who has learned what the public welfare is, and is not ignorant of how much evil war brings with it, will see readily that nothing is more opposed to the welfare of the state than war, and nothing more conducive to it than peace, so that

§ 403, part 3, Jus Nat.

§ 86, part 8, Jus Nat.

§ 17, part 8, Jus Nat.

there is no need of further discussion on that point. Hence further it follows, that if the ruler of the state should recklessly undertake a war which he could and ought to avoid, he violates the perfect right of his citizens, and does them an injury, although on account of the irresistible character of the sovereign power, they may be bound to endure it, being bound to obey with patience the one who commands wrongly, consequently one who acts contrary to the public good or the welfare of the state.

§ 859, part 1, Jus Nat.
§ 1041, part 8, Jus Nat.
§ 1043, part 8, Jus Nat.
§ 85, part 8, Jus Nat.

§ 963. *And with regard to other nations*

Every ruler of a state owes it to other nations to strive in every way to preserve the peace. For nations are bound by nature to cultivate peace with each other; consequently each one ought to take care that peace may be preserved for the sake of other nations also. Therefore, since the ruler has the right of his nation, consequently every obligation also is imposed on him which is attached thereto, so that the ruler of the state is bound to do that which one nation ought to do for another; every ruler of a state by nature owes it to other nations to strive in every way to preserve the peace.

§ 961.

§ 39.

The ruler of a state by nature owes it both to his subjects and to other nations by virtue of the present proposition to strive to preserve the peace, but not to both in the same way. For in regard to his subjects the obligation is a perfect one; in regard to other nations it is an imperfect one. In the former case the wrong is to be endured because of the duty of the subject; in the latter case his neglect of duty is to be endured by virtue of the natural liberty belonging even to nations, consequently to their rulers, the repudiation of an imperfect obligation not being a just cause of war.

§ 962.
Note, § 962.
§ 402, part 3, Jus Nat.
Note, § 962.
§ 55, part 8, Jus Nat.
§ 39.
§ 157, part 1, Jus Nat.
§ 409, part 3, Jus Nat.

§ 964. *In how many ways that may be done*

Since any ruler of a state by nature owes it to other nations to strive in every way to preserve the peace which all nations are bound to cultivate with each other, not only ought the ruler himself to avoid war as far as he can, but ought also to do his best to dissuade others from recklessly undertaking war.

§ 963.

§ 961.

Refraining from war has a double aspect. The ruler of a state ought not only to refrain from it himself, but he ought also to make every effort that others may refrain. By the former course he proves that he desires the happiness of his subjects, by the latter that he desires that of other nations. And in this way he satisfies no less his duty towards other nations than that towards his own nation. But if those things were observed which have been proved concerning the method of settling controversies between nations and concerning the law of war, and if rulers of states were to use that wisdom by which the state is to be directed, according to those principles which are to be proved in the Politics, the occasion for war would be rare, and nations would enjoy perpetual peace.

§ 162.

§ 1010, part 8,
Jus Nat.

§ 965. *What a disturber of the public peace is*

A disturber of the public peace is defined as one who harasses other nations in reckless and unjust war. In our native vernacular he is called *ein Friedens-Stöhrer* [a violator of the peace]. Since the evils which arise from war affect not only the belligerent nations, but also stealthily invade neighbouring nations, and even those far removed, a disturber of the public peace injures not only those which are at war but also neighbouring nations, and even those far removed.

The injuries vary in accordance with differences in the circumstances. By way of example, I wish to mention at least one. Let us suppose that peaceful nations are engaged in commerce with each other, or even with those which are at war, and their dealings are made more difficult by the war; now since the subjects of peaceful nations are compelled to purchase their goods at a higher price, they experience no little loss of money because of the war, so that it is just as if they were bound to contribute to the expenses of the war. And so no little loss is caused by belligerent nations even to those who are at peace, by the fault assuredly of the disturber of the public peace, who could or ought to have avoided the war.

§ 488, part 2,
Jus Nat.

§ 966. *Of restraining them*

Since disturbers of the public peace by reckless and unjust wars harass other nations, and injure not only these, but also other peaceful nations, since, nevertheless, they ought to strive in every way to preserve peace among nations, they do not satisfy the obligation by which nations as members of a supreme state are bound to each other to promote the common good, consequently every nation has the right to compel disturbers of the public peace to cease the disturbance.

§ 965.

§§ 963, 964.

§ 12.

§ 13.

The law of nature considers the common welfare of nations no less than that of individuals, and therefore it cannot allow any individual to disturb the public peace by reckless excess. And although the desire to preserve the peace is in itself an imperfect obligation, nevertheless it does not remain such in the case of the disturber of the public peace. For he acts wrongly either openly by force or recklessly. In the former case he is not without malice, in the latter he is not without fault. And since he harasses nations by wars simply for his own advantage, or influenced by vain glory, and consequently satisfies his avarice or ambition at the expense of the common safety of nations; he shows a hostile intention towards all, so that the fear of his inflicting injuries is not vain but well founded. Therefore, as he threatens danger to the nations in general he is rightfully checked by any combination of forces.

§ 963.

§ 705, part 1, Phil. Pract. Univ.

§ 777, part 1, Phil. Pract. Univ.

§ 967. *How this right is to be used*

Since every nation has the right to compel disturbers of the public peace to cease the disturbance, consequently that degree of force may be used against them without which they cannot be compelled to cease the disturbance; those who are harassed with arms by disturbers of the public peace may rightfully enlist any nations in arms against them, so that indeed their power may be diminished and that they can no longer cause a disturbance.

§ 966.

It is to the advantage of all nations, especially of neighbours, that there should be no disturbers of the peace who, relying on their power, manifestly misuse the right of war. Therefore, although a direct injury is not done to them, which is the sole just cause of war, nor is such an injury feared from a neighbouring power, however much you should lack a just cause for bringing war yourself, nevertheless there is no lack of a persuasive reason for bringing aid to those who are harassed with

§ 617.

§ 640.

§ 656.

§ 650.

§ 652.
Note, §§ 650
and fol.

arms, and for sending subsidies to them, or assisting them in war in any other way, a thing which is allowable in itself. There is the added consideration that the slightest injury may give a right to destroy by force of arms a growing power, if any nation has manifest designs of subjecting other nations to itself, and all nations in general have the right to diminish the power of one who, relying on arms taken up unjustly, does not hesitate to disturb the common security of nations. See what we have noted above.

§ 968. *Of treaties of war against disturbers of the public peace*

§ 967.

§ 655.

If nations are afraid of a disturber of the public peace, they ought to make treaties of war in proper season. For nations rightfully ally themselves against a disturber of the public peace with the one who is harassed by his attacks. Therefore, since treaties of war are entered into for the purpose of sending auxiliaries, subsidies, and anything else which has to do with war; since, moreover, it is self-evident that treaties of war can be made whenever it may seem best, even when there is as yet no thought of making war, and the combined force can deter one, who otherwise, relying on his power, would rush to arms, so that he may refrain therefrom; since, moreover, milder measures are always to be preferred to harsher ones and more certain ones to those that are doubtful; if nations are afraid of a disturber of the public peace, they ought to make treaties of war in proper season.

§ 967.

Of course in the present instance treaties have a double effect. For either the disturber of the public peace is deterred from his design of making war, or, if he rushes to arms, his force can be at once bravely resisted, so that the strength of the one attacked may not be wasted or diminished before he is rescued; experience tells us plainly enough how much weight this has in war, nor is it difficult of proof *a priori.* That the treaties of which we are here speaking are allowable, is evident from what has been proved before.

§ 969. *How long a just war may be continued*

§ 1102, part 1,
Jus Nat.

A just war may be continued until you have acquired your right, and the other party no longer opposes your righteous force. For war is waged in order to acquire a right, and therefore the purpose of war is to acquire that right. Therefore, since you continue to seek your right until you have acquired it, as is self-evident, a just war may be continued until you have acquired your right. Which was the first point.

But, indeed, although you may seem no longer to have a just cause to continue the war, as soon as you have acquired that for which the war was begun, nevertheless the end of the war does not depend upon your will, unless the enemy also agrees to lay down arms. If, then, he should continue the war with the intention of recovering those things which you have rightly taken from him, and should still oppose your righteous force, it is allowable to continue the war against an unjust force until the enemy no longer opposes your righteous force. Which was the second point.

It is understood from what precedes that we seek in war not only that which was due to us before the war, but also that which arises in the war itself, as the expenses, and whatever springs from the losses caused by the enemy during the war and from fresh injuries inflicted. Moreover, he who is unwilling to desist from fighting, even if the reason for the war has already ceased to exist, pays a just penalty for his obstinacy. War may begin by the will of one party, unless it is a defensive one which we do not have it in our power to avoid; but it can end only by the consent of both of the belligerent parties. If then one who ought to do so is unwilling to consent to the end of the war, he has himself to blame, if he experiences a greater loss than he would have suffered had he immediately granted his right to the other party. But it is plain without my saying it that this is said only of the right to continue the war; the question is not whether it is expedient to continue the war until you have completely acquired your right. Fortune does not always favour the just cause, so that therefore not rarely you may be compelled to give up part of your right, in order that you may not expose yourself and your friends to greater risks. And therefore it frequently happens that a just war is injurious to the one waging it, and advantageous to him whose cause was unjust.

§ 970. *How long in a doubtful case*

In a doubtful case it is allowable to continue the war until the other party either offers a compromise or accepts one offered. For in a doubtful case you wage war lawfully, in order that by force of arms you may drive another to a compromise which he does not wish to make. If then while the war is going on you again offer a compromise to him and he accepts it, or if he offers the same to you there is no longer any reason why war should be waged. Therefore, with the ceasing of the reason which makes the war allowable, the war also may no longer be continued. Therefore, in a doubtful case it is allowable to continue the war until the other party either offers a compromise or accepts one that is offered.

§ 631.

When it is said that a compromise is offered, it is not sufficient that the offerer declare that he is ready to make a compromise, but the conditions of peace must be set forth, or a conference must be arranged while the war is going on, in which a method of compromise may be considered. For otherwise there is a doubt that the compromise will be completed, and only when it is completed does the war come to an end. And since in war not only is deceit allowable, but the resort to it is also common, if the compromise should not be offered in express terms the suspicion of fraud is not absent, especially if other circumstances should increase the suspicion.

§ 857.

§ 971. *How long war may continue against a disturber of the public peace*

War against a disturber of the public peace may continue until sufficient provision has been made for security in the future. For since the right belongs to all nations in general to compel a disturber of the public peace to cease his disturbance; if any ally themselves to the nation which is harassed by his arms, it wages war for the sake of the common security. Therefore, war may continue against him until sufficient provision has been made for security in the future.

§ 966.
§ 967.

The determination of what is sufficient to provide for the common security of nations in the future depends upon the particular circumstances. For provision is made either that the disturber of the public peace shall change his desire to cause a disturbance, or that his power shall be taken away. There is greater trust in the latter method than in the former, not only because a change of mind is not easily presumed, but also because old habits are easily resumed. That determination is a matter of prudence, which controls all use of a right, and is not out of harmony with the law of nature, since by that also we are bound to prudence. Therefore, those things which it has seemed best to note here and there as to what is the part of prudence, are mentioned by us for no other purpose than that it may appear that for the proper conduct of affairs it is needful that the civil prudence which is discussed in political science, should be combined constantly with the law of nature. The law of nature itself urges this combination, not only in so far as it binds us to prudence, but also in so far as it compels us to right action.

§ 258, part 1, Jus Nat.

§ cited.

§ 189, part 1, Phil. Pract. Univ.

§ 972. *When war may be continued until the other party has been conquered*

Because one belligerent cannot be persuaded to offer or accept fair terms of peace, war may be continued until he has been completely conquered, in order indeed that he can no longer resist. For you may continue a just war until you have acquired your right, and the other party can no longer oppose your righteous force, and in a doubtful case, until the other party either offers a compromise or accepts one offered, consequently until the other party accepts or offers fair terms of peace. If, therefore, neither can be obtained from him, the cessation of war does not depend on your will. Therefore, the war is to be continued until with his failing strength he can no longer resist your force, but may be compelled to desist from war, consequently until he has been completely conquered.

§ 969.

§ 970.

§ 1089, part 5, Jus Nat.

It is one thing to be conquered in a battle, another to be conquered in war. The one conquered in a battle cannot continue it, or by flight or departing with his army he at least declares that he does not wish to continue it; but he alone can be said to be conquered in war who cannot continue the war, or who at least declares in words that he does not wish to continue it, and seeks peace. Victory in battles is always doubtful, and the same one is not always victorious. Therefore, it also happens that one may allow a victory to another, lest his strength may be used up which ought to be preserved for a better purpose, that is, to continue the war. For if one whose powers are so weakened that he can no longer resist, or at least so diminished that he may foresee that he will accomplish nothing against another superior to him in

§ 1089, part 1, Jus Nat.

strength, consequently in the former case, being reduced to extremities, is compelled to desist from war; in the latter case, fearing that he
may straightway be reduced to extremities, wishes to desist from war,
then only can he be said to be conquered in war, and it is called a final
victory in war by which war is at length ended and peace restored. For
since force of arms is not a suitable means for deciding the controversies of nations, as the final victory, if he whose cause is unjust should
gain it, manifestly does not make the unjust cause a just one, so also
in a disputed case it cannot decide that justice in the war is with the
one who has carried off the victory; consequently the final victory can
give no right to the victor which he did not have without it. And, if we
assume that this error is made by certain nations, so far is it from being
capable of being considered as law of nature, that it cannot even be
considered as voluntary law of nations, but as unjust customary law,
which is mistakenly considered as law, when it is not, and those who
reason more correctly are not bound to abide by it, and those who
are conscious of error in themselves cannot have a clear conscience
towards another.

Note, § 632.

§ 992, part 8, Jus
Nat., and § 22 h.

§ 24 h, and
§ 239, part 1,
Phil. Pract.
Univ.

§ 973. *Of the continuation of an unjust war*

§ 777.

He who wages an unjust war has no right to continue the war. For one
who wages an unjust war has no right in war. Therefore, he has no right
to continue the war.

§ 778.

> One waging an unjust war is a robber, an invader, and a bandit.
> Who then can inquire whether robbery, invasion, and brigandage may
> be continued?

§ 974. *When a just belligerent becomes an unjust one*

§ 969.

If he whose war was just should be unwilling to end it, even if he has
acquired his right, he becomes an unjust instead of a just belligerent.
The same thing is true, if in a doubtful case he should be unwilling to
accept fair terms of peace. For although a just belligerent may continue a
war until he has acquired his right, and the other party no longer wishes
to oppose his power, if one who has acquired his right is unwilling to
end the war, he has no right to continue it. If then he should continue

it he acts without right; consequently he becomes an unjust belligerent instead of a just one. Which was the first point.

In like manner, because in a doubtful case it is allowable to continue the war until the other party offers a compromise, it is evident that in the same way he becomes an unjust instead of a just belligerent if he should be unwilling to accept a compromise which has been offered. Which was the second point. §970.

> Undoubtedly arms are unjustly assumed which protect no right, and as soon as the cause of the war ceases to be just, the right to war also ceases. He who continues a war without just cause can have none other than persuasive reasons for continuing the war. But a war which has no other reasons than persuasive ones is an unjust war. Those err greatly from the truth who think that a war can lawfully be continued until the final victory puts an end to it, or that in a doubtful case a controverted right may be decided by such victory, especially if it should be assumed to be a part of the law of nature that either belligerent party may depend upon his own judgement as to the justice of his cause. As it is well known that in a defence one becomes an aggressor instead of a defender if he goes beyond the limit, so it is no less sure on the basis of the present proposition that one becomes an unjust instead of a just belligerent when in war he goes beyond the limit, inasmuch as he goes to excess in defending his right which is denied by the other party.
>
> §621.
> §622.
>
> §1003, part 1, Jus Nat.

§ 975. *When war is ended*

When peace is made, war is at an end. Since in peace there is no war, if there is an agreement for peace, a contract is made that there should be no war. Therefore, since when a treaty for peace is made, the belligerents are immediately bound to observe what has been promised on each side, when peace is made, war is at an end. §959.

§789, part 3, Jus Nat.

> War and peace are mutual contradictions, so that they cannot exist together. As long, therefore, as war continues, there can be no peace, and as soon as peace is declared, war cannot continue. When, therefore, there is an agreement of peace, by that very fact it is also agreed that the war ought to be ended.
>
> §959.

§ 976. *The effect of the making of peace*

§ 975.
§ 722.

§ 785.

Since when peace is made, war is at an end, but since those are enemies who are at war with each other, and since hostilities are warlike operations by which force is in fact used against an enemy or his property; when peace is made those who were enemies cease to be enemies and all hostilities cease on either side.

§ 960.

§§ 913, 914.

Since peace is not made during the time of a truce, those who were enemies before the truce continue also to be enemies during the truce. That they are protected from hostile acts, does not come from the fact that they are not enemies, and that their property is not the property of enemies, but from the fact that hostilities are in fact suspended until the time of the truce has elapsed, the right to hostilities being reserved. It is one thing not to have a right, another not to exercise it. Therefore, since he can have a right who does not exercise it, he who retains a right can bind himself to another not to exercise it during a certain time. But when peace is made, the right itself to hostile acts is extinguished, so that there is no place for them because of the lack of the right, not because the right to exercise it has been taken away.

§ 977. *Who can enter into a treaty of peace*

§ 607.

§ 975.

Only those who have the supreme sovereignty can enter into a treaty of peace. For a public war is waged by those leaders who have the supreme sovereignty; consequently it is for them to decide concerning war, as may seem best to them, therefore also to determine whether the war is to be ended or continued, just as it was for them to decide whether the war was to be undertaken or not. Therefore, since when peace is made, war is at an end, only those who have the supreme sovereignty can enter into treaties of peace.

§ 943, part 8, Jus Nat.

Just as the right of beginning a war and of determining hostile acts, either through one's self or through others, belongs undoubtedly to the right of war, so also does the right to end the war, consequently also the right to make peace. Therefore, just as the right of war belongs among the sovereign rights, so also the right to make peace belongs thereto.

§ 978. *The same is considered in greater detail*

Since only those who have the supreme sovereignty can enter into a treaty of peace, since, moreover, the supreme sovereignty in a democracy rests in the people, in a monarchy with a monarch, in an aristocracy with the nobles, and since in a kingdom it can be limited in a certain way, or diminished; in a democratic state treaties of peace can be entered into only by the people, in a monarchy by the monarch, in an aristocracy by the nobles, in a kingdom by the king either along with the people, or with the consent of certain others, or without it, as may have been determined by the fundamental laws.

§ 977.

§ 131, part 8, Jus Nat.

§ 133, part 8, Jus Nat.

§ 135, part 8, Jus Nat.

§ 139, part 9, Jus Nat.

> The forms of composite states are determined by their fundamental laws and, therefore, from these it is plain how much the right of the king has been limited, in order that in the administration of the state he cannot do what may seem best to him. The right to make peace is of the very greatest importance, not in that the war is ended, which is the desire of all the citizens, as long as the war continues, since there is no safety in war, and all demand peace; but in that there must be a settlement of those things which affect the state, and in the settlement many things can be done to the prejudice of the state. And, therefore, the making of peace is not entrusted to the judgement of others, without the express ratification of the sovereign power by virtue of a general enactment. That we shall show more clearly from what follows, where the method of making peace will be explained.

§ 979. *Who cannot make peace*

Since only those who have the supreme sovereignty can enter into a treaty of peace, consequently only sovereign powers, and since no minor power has supreme sovereignty, no minor power can enter into a treaty of peace, as a magistrate, or a leader in war, even though a commander-in-chief, or a governor appointed by a supreme sovereignty, nor any other private person, such as the most eminent individuals in a democratic state or in a monarchy.

§ 977.

§ 368.

§ cited.

> In our native vernacular we call governors *Stadthalter* [magistrates], but the most eminent individuals we call *die Stände* [the estates].

Moreover, it can be established by a fundamental law that peace cannot be made without the consent of the governor or of the most eminent individuals. But the situation is different if the king himself should be unwilling to make peace without the consent of the governor or the most eminent individuals. For then neither those whose consent he requires perform the function of counsellors alone, nor is he bound to ask their consent, nor does their dissent prevent him from doing what may seem best to him. See what we have proved and commented on elsewhere.

§§ 79, 80, part 8, Jus Nat.

§ 980. *Of a king who is an infant, a minor, or of unsound mind*

If the king is an infant, a minor, or of unsound mind, as insane or of weakened intellect, he cannot make peace. It is self-evident that the king as an infant or minor cannot exercise sovereignty because of immaturity of judgement, and if he is of unsound mind because of lack of judgement. Therefore, although he may have a right to make peace, nevertheless he cannot exercise it, and consequently cannot make peace.

§§ 767, 768, part 7, Jus Nat.

Who in fact are to be considered minors and adults by the law of nature, we have explained elsewhere. But just as by the civil law a certain age is fixed, that private individuals may be considered majors, or adults; so also in kingdoms a certain age is usually fixed by the fundamental laws, at which those are to be considered capable of administering the sovereign power whom immaturity of judgement keeps from the exercise of it. But when kings themselves cannot administer the sovereignty, tutors or curators are given to them who administer in their name.

§ 981. *Who then can make peace*

If the king is not capable of administering the sovereignty, the making of peace is in the hands of those to whom the administration of the sovereignty belongs. For if the king himself is incapable of administering the sovereignty, the administration of the sovereignty must be entrusted to others, whether this be done by the fundamental laws, or by the will of the people, or in the testament of his father, or in any other way.

Therefore, since those to whom the administration of the sovereignty belongs can do the same in fact as the king was able to do, if he were administering the sovereignty, the peace which the king could have made they also can make.

§ 978.

It is easy to see that the administrators of the sovereignty have no greater right than the king, in whose name they do whatever is done by them. Therefore, if by the fundamental laws the right to make peace has been restricted in any way, the administrators cannot exercise it any other way. It is also self-evident that if by a definite law any limitation has been made upon the making of peace during the time of the administration or the right to make peace, the administrators can do nothing contrary to that. So they themselves cannot make peace if it has been said that the nobles should do so, or certain persons who are named; and they can do so only with the consent of those whose consent the fundamental law requires.

§ 982. *When a captive king can make peace*

When the kingship is patrimonial, a captive king can make peace. For if the kingship is patrimonial, the king possesses the sovereignty by the right of ownership, and consequently he can dispose of it as a whole, and likewise of the several rights belonging to it, as may seem best to him. Therefore, since in a peace a disposition is made of rights included in the civil sovereignty, a thing which will show more clearly in what follows, a captive king, even though he is subject to the right of one who holds him captive, and therefore is not altogether free, since he does nothing contrary to the right of another, and therefore does no one an injury in whatever way he disposes of his right, can make peace.

§§ 40, 155, part 8, Jus Nat.

§ 118, part 2, Jus Nat.

§ 135, part 1, Jus Nat.
§ 859, part 1, Jus Nat.

There are not lacking those who claim that kingdoms cannot be held in absolute ownership by a king; nevertheless, since we have shown the contrary, those conclusions are not false which necessarily follow from the concept of a patrimonial kingship. The objections which are made to patrimonial kingship come from a confusion of sovereignty and the method of holding the sovereignty. In the ownership itself of things, the right of property and the right to enjoy and use are to be distinguished. Therefore, since property in sovereignty makes a

§ 39, part 8, Jus Nat., and § 871 h.

§ 39, part 8, Jus Nat.

kingship patrimonial, it has those characteristics certainly which necessarily flow from the right of property, namely, the right of disposing
of the substance itself of sovereignty. Since all sovereignty ought to be

§ 131, part 2,
Jus Nat.

exercised in such a way that the public good is promoted, as far as that
can be done, that applies no less in the case of patrimonial kingship
than in one held in usufruct, for the method of exercising sovereignty

§ 809, part 8,
Jus Nat.

does not in the least depend upon the method of holding sovereignty,
but is to be determined from the purpose for which sovereignties were
introduced or states established, which is not in the least altered by
the method of holding them. Indeed, even in the kingdom of a slave-
owner by the law of nature those things are not allowable which are
opposed to the happiness of subjects, so as to make it comparable with

§§ 275, 276,
part 8, Jus Nat.

a tyranny, yet it differs very greatly from a patrimonial kingship. Those
things which belong to the law of nature, so far as regards the exercise

§§ 155, 264,
part 8, Jus Nat.

of sovereignty or the method of exercising it, remain the same even in
a patrimonial kingship, just as on the other hand none of those things
which pertain to the method of holding sovereignty is to be included
under the exercise of sovereignty. The abuse of a right in the exercise of sovereignty can equally occur whatever the method of holding the sovereignty; and certainly those are mistaken who persuade
themselves that one is included in the other, if sovereignty should be
held by the right of ownership. The abuse of a right in a patrimonial
kingship cannot exist, except in so far as he does not dispose of those
things which concern the alienation of the kingdom and change in the
form of the state, as is in accordance with the duty of a ruler, unless
you should wish to confuse the sovereignty of a slave-owner with a
patrimonial sovereignty. Since reference is made only to the method
of holding the sovereignty, when it is called patrimonial, through the
fact that it is patrimonial there is no change made in the sovereignty
itself, consequently in no part of it. The sovereignty remains such as
it is by nature, as nothing corporeal or incorporeal is changed, for
the reason that it is held by exclusive right of ownership. Therefore,
indeed, all things go up in smoke which are urged against patrimonial kingship and which assume that sovereignty itself has therefore
become changed, so that it does not remain what it is by nature if it
should be held in full ownership, just as other things, both corporeal
and incorporeal, are held by their masters. And undoubtedly it is false

that an owner has a full right of abuse of a thing by virtue of the law
of nature, inasmuch as he is restrained by the law of nature, and others
who have no right over the actions of an owner must simply endure,
or, if you prefer, tolerate him. Nay, if you should wish to speak accurately, it is not so much an abuse of sovereignty as an unbridled desire
for a right which does not belong to a ruler. Therefore, when a ruler
does the things which cannot be done by right of sovereignty, the acts,
which by their nature do not fall under the exercise of sovereignty, are
not an abuse of sovereignty, but rather of the power which the right
assumes. Therefore, an owner is not said to abuse his ownership, or
the right which he has in the thing, but to abuse his own property,
and that such abuse of the thing must be allowed him by another does
not depend upon ownership but upon natural liberty. For although,
because of that liberty, the owner can dispose of his property as he
pleases, nevertheless that does not destroy the natural obligation of so
using his own property as to satisfy a certain natural obligation, and
therefore the abuse of the thing is prohibited by natural law, although
others have no right to interfere with the abuse. Therefore, the abuse
of one's property is in no way included in the right of ownership, so
that by virtue thereof this is allowable in an owner. The law of nature
would be self-contradictory if it were to give a right to do what it
forbids. And although sovereignty as well as corporeal things may be
said to be held in ownership, nevertheless, sovereignty and ownership
are not therefore to be confused, as a corporeal thing is not confused
with ownership because it is said to be subject to it. For property is
one thing, a method of holding property another. But we have already
shown elsewhere that it is not objectionable to say that an aristocracy
also may be patrimonial. Ownership simply counts as a method of
holding, so that a kingdom becomes patrimonial, consequently those
things which flow from a right of ownership, in so far as that is distinguished from the right to use and to enjoy, have a place only in it and
not in other types of kingdom.

§ 170, part 2,
Jus Nat.

§ 169, part 2,
Jus Nat.

§ 169, part 2,
Jus Nat.

§ 118, part 2,
Jus Nat.
§ 167, part 2,
and § 159, part 1,
Jus Nat.

§ 170, part 2,
Jus Nat.

§ 169, part 2,
Jus Nat.

§ 156, part 8,
Jus Nat.

§ 983. *Of a captive king whose kingdom is not patrimonial*

If the kingship is not patrimonial, a captive king can make peace by
promising his own private property, or public property, on condition of

ratification, or through those to whom he has entrusted the administration of the sovereignty; but if the king has made no disposition of it, he
can make peace who has the next hope of succession. For a captive king
disposes of his private property by his own personal right, not by right
of sovereignty. However, therefore, the free exercise of sovereignty may
be interfered with while he is in captivity, that nevertheless cannot in
any way prevent the captive as a private individual from disposing of his
property. In so far, therefore, as the one making peace promises his own
private property, he is able to make peace. Which was the first point.

Likewise, although through his captivity he may have been reduced
to such a condition that it is to be feared lest he may be compelled to
promise to the enemy, to the prejudice of his own nation, things which
he would not have promised when he was free; nevertheless, if he should
promise nothing except on condition of ratification, that is no longer to
be feared. Therefore, he can also make peace by promising public property on condition of ratification. Which was the second point.

By captivity the right is not taken from the king, but only the free
exercise of it is interfered with. Therefore, just as one who is absent can
entrust his affairs to another, so also can a captive. Therefore, if peace
should be made by those to whose care the administration of the sover-
§ 978.   eignty was entrusted by him, since the right of making peace also belongs
to the sovereignty, there is no doubt that he can make peace through
them. Which was the third point.

Finally, if the captive has made no arrangements concerning the administration, it is just the same as though he were dead, because the sovereignty cannot be exercised by him, since he is absent, and, while he
remains a captive, its free exercise is interfered with, nor can it be exercised
through others, since he has named no one who should act in his name.
But if indeed he were dead, the sovereignty, so far as regards its exercise,
§ 279, part 8,   since the kingship is not patrimonial, would according to the hypothesis
Jus Nat.   pass over to his successor. Therefore, it ought to pass over to him, so
long as the king is to be considered as dead, consequently, so long as he
is detained in captivity, and entrusts the administration to no one, and is
unable to do so. Therefore his successor also can make peace. Which was
the fourth point.

But if there has been a different provision introduced by the fundamental laws or by the customs of a certain nation, this will be the peculiar law of that nation, by which other nations are not held.

§ 984. *Of making peace with an invader or a usurper of the sovereignty*

It is allowable to make peace with an invader or a usurper of the sovereignty, if the subjects have pledged their faith to him. For, if subjects have pledged their faith to an invader or usurper, indisputably by paying homage, they have given their promise to him, and consequently have bound themselves to him, that they are willing to admit by their acts that the royal acts are lawful. Therefore, since nations are free by nature, and one nation must abide by the decision of any other nation in those matters which affect its own state, consequently when the subjects treat with the ruler of a state they are held to follow possession; and since the making of peace is a royal act, it is not to be doubted that it is allowable to make peace with an invader or a usurper of the sovereignty to whom the subjects have pledged their faith.

§ 363, part 3, Jus Nat.

§ 284, part 8, Jus Nat.

§ 55, part 8, Jus Nat.

§§ 157, 556, part 1, Jus Nat.

§ 150, part 2, Jus Nat.

§ 977 h and § 284, part 8, Jus Nat.

An invader of sovereignty is one who without a right occupies the sovereignty by force or fraud. But it can also happen that a people may wrongfully eject their king and offer the sovereignty to another. He cannot be called an invader with reference to the people, although with respect to the king, whose right cannot be taken away, he could be called an invader. But with respect to either of them he is called a usurper, since, indeed, he, as the possessor of the right of another, is exercising a right that does not belong to him. The sovereignty of a people is its own special property. Therefore, other nations have no right to interfere with it, however wrongfully they dispose of it; a thing which nevertheless does not always happen as regards an invader. But since one who has a true right does not lose his right because he has lost possession, what we have said to the effect that nations should follow possession does not prevent them from giving their assistance in the recovery of possession to one who has a true right.

§ 1073, part 8, Jus Nat.

§ 336, part 2, Jus Nat.

§ 34, part 8, Jus Nat.

§ 169, part 2, Jus Nat.

§ 1077, part 8, Jus Nat.

§ 357, part 2, Jus Nat.

§§ 617, 656.

§ 985. *Of making peace by the people or by the nobles.*

In a democratic state the majority of the people, in an aristocracy the majority of the nobles, can make peace, although the minority should dissent. For in a democratic state the people have a right to make peace, in an aristocracy the nobles have the right. But in a democratic state that which seems best to the majority is considered as the will of the whole people, and in an aristocracy that which seems best to a majority of the nobles is to be considered as the will of all. Therefore, in a democratic state the majority of the people, in an aristocracy a majority of the nobles, can make peace, although the minority should dissent.

§ 978.

§ 157, part 8,
Jus Nat.

§ 79, part 7,
Jus Nat.

There is no one who does not recognize that it is according to nature that a majority or plurality vote should be decisive. But although that can be changed by agreement, nevertheless in a treaty of peace that can scarcely ever, or even never, be brought about, since the treaty must reach a conclusion. But, how a people may wish to exercise its right, when the individual citizens cannot conveniently be called to a common assembly, must be entrusted to custom.

§§ 127 and fol.,
part 7, Jus Nat.

§ 986. *How peace can be made*

Peace cannot be made in such a way that the one to whom a right is due acquires it completely. Only a compromise is possible. For let us suppose that peace ought to be made as the rigor of justice demands, so that a right is allotted to the one who claims it; he whose cause was just, not only ought to acquire his original right, for which the war has been waged, but likewise all the expenses incurred for the war; property seized by unjust force during the war would have to be restored to him, and losses caused in any way would have to be repaired. Nay more, for injuries done during the war the opposing party would be bound to him for a penalty, for which satisfaction would have to be made, and security given for the future. But, on the other hand, a just belligerent is bound to restore the things which he has occupied beyond the limit of his debt. And because the deeds even of a just belligerent are illegal, if without them he could have attained his purpose, he also is bound to restore to the other party the losses caused him and to pay the penalty for the wrong done, since

§ 926, part 1,
Jus Nat.

§ 786.

§ 788.

§ 789.

§ 787.

now he is equivalent to an unjust belligerent. It is readily evident, if it were necessary for a treaty of peace to be made in this manner, that it would be impossible for one to be concluded; but a war then could not be ended except by the destruction of one or both of the belligerent nations. Peace, then, cannot be made in such a way that the one to whom a right is due can acquire it completely. Which was the first point.

But since, indeed, it cannot happen, when a treaty of peace is made, that by a careful examination of all the details it may be determined how much is to be assigned to one party or restored to the other, as proved above; therefore, it is necessary that, putting aside the question of right, the parties should agree as to who ought to have the property in dispute and what one party ought to restore to the other, what to retain, or what one party ought to be bound to perform for the other. Therefore, since a treaty of that sort is a compromise, peace can be made only through a compromise. Which was the second point.

§§ 879, 882, part 5, Jus Nat.

Experience fully confirms that peace is made only by compromise. And therefore also an agreement made concerning peace gets the name of a compromise, so that a conclusion is usually reached between belligerents through a compromise. If the cause of the war shall have been in dispute, there is no just cause of the war, and it is only a matter of driving the opposing party by force of arms to a compromise. The only issue therefore is to bring about a compromise between the belligerents. And what mode is allowable for defending oneself, for recovering one's property, and for demanding penalties even in a just war, cannot be determined from external evidences. And we have already proved above that the decision in regard to the necessity of those things without which he who wages a war cannot obtain his right is to be left to the individual himself. If, then, belligerents complain to each other of wrongs done in war, the cause in dispute between them can be settled in no other way than by compromise. For otherwise on account of those wrongs the war would have to be continued until they were finally compelled to compromise.

§ 631.

§ 783.

§ 987. *The effect of a treaty of peace*

Since a treaty of peace is a compromise, and since a contest is ended by a compromise, when a treaty of peace is concluded the war is ended,

§ 986.
§ 880, part 5, Jus Nat.

consequently no further right to hostilities belongs to either of the belligerents; and since, when a compromise is effected, the claim is extinguished, nor may it be renewed, nor may there be a return to the matter in dispute, even if afterwards you may be able to prove that it is yours or is owed to you; when peace has been made, war cannot be renewed as regards that cause for which the war was waged.

§ 890, part 5, Jus Nat.

§ 891, part 5, Jus Nat.

Therefore, it is said that perpetual or everlasting peace is concluded, not because neither of the belligerent parties wishes to bring war against the other in the future, but because either is unwilling to engage in war for the same reason for which war is waged at present. If, indeed, the compromise is only a special one, there is no general renunciation of the claim to the thing in regard to which the compromise was made, which may be had on other grounds than those which were in mind at the time; nevertheless this does not stand in the way of a perpetual peace, provided you use the precaution of renouncing all claims which can be made in any way to the same thing. For thus a general compromise will be made, by which all right to that thing for which the war was waged is extinguished, and everything which can be referred thereto.

§ 889, part 5, Jus Nat.

§ 888, part 5, Jus Nat.

§ 988. *What sort of reasons are to be considered in a treaty of peace*

Likewise, since peace cannot be made in such a way that the one to whom a right is due acquires it completely, but only a compromise is possible, in a treaty the cause of the war is not determined, nor are the controversies which may have been stirred up by the acts of the war, consequently neither party convicts the other of injustice and wrong, therefore, in a treaty of peace justifying reasons are not considered, but each of the contracting parties is bound to direct his attention to persuasive reasons.

§ 986.

§ 884, part 5, Jus Nat.

§ 621.

When conditions are to be offered, or when offered are to be accepted, there ought not to be an absolute neglect of justifying reasons in the deliberations of one who has desired to consider conscience no less than his own advantage; nevertheless such reasons have no place in the common deliberations of the contracting parties. In a compromise, each one gives up something of his own right which he claims to have, and it is the task of prudence to consider how much may wisely be given up; and prudence advises that, depending on circumstances, not a little is to be yielded even to the power of the opposite party. One must yield to necessity, which is an irresistible weapon.

§ 883, part 5, Jus Nat.

§ 989. *What an amnesty is*

Amnesty is defined as complete and lasting forgetfulness of wrongs and offences previously committed. Therefore, when an amnesty is given, since all deeds are consigned to perpetual oblivion and everlasting silence, no one can be accused or punished for acts before committed.

The term amnesty had its rise among the Athenians, who, on the proposal of Thrasybulus, after the thirty tyrants were driven out, passed a law that no one should be accused or punished after oblivion had been decreed of wrongs and offences committed on either side, and this law Cicero says was called by them the law of forgetfulness.[1] The term is retained by us in the German language to-day, and we usually call such oblivion *eine Amnestie* [an amnesty], since there is no other word, and we have not chosen to invent a new one. But from the definition it is more than plain that the effect of decreeing amnesty is that acts wrongfully done are to be considered as though they had not been done; from which immunity for them naturally arises.

1. Wolff appears to be relying on Grotius, *The Rights of War and Peace*, bk. II, chap. IV.viii.3, where Grotius refers to a passage in Cicero's *On Duties* on Aratus of Sicyon (Cicero, *On Duties,* ed. M. T. Griffin and E. M. Atkins [Cambridge: Cambridge University Press, 1991], bk. II.82, pp. 96–97). That passage, however, is not on the law of forgetfulness in ancient Athens. Wolff seems to be confusing Grotius's comments on Thrasybulos with Cicero's on Aratus of Sicyon. Moreover, Grotius's observations on Thrasybulos appear to be based on an error. For as Barbeyrac comments, "I know not where our Author [Grotius] found what he says of Thrasybulos." He then proceeds to reconstruct the likely origin of Grotius's erroneous opinion in a misreading of another work; see Grotius, *The Rights of War and Peace,* ed. Richard Tuck, 3 vols. (Indianapolis: Liberty Fund, 2005), vol. 2, bk. II, chap. IV.viii.3, p. 495, n. 7.

§ 990.

§ 988.
§ 987.

Since in a treaty of peace neither party convicts the other of wrong, and since when peace has been made as regards that cause for which the war was waged, war cannot again be renewed, consequently the war and whatever was done in it is consigned to perpetual oblivion and everlast-

§ 989.

ing silence, and since an amnesty is complete and lasting forgetfulness of wrongs and offences previously committed; in a treaty first of all there must be an agreement for an amnesty, and this is contained in every treaty of peace as such, even if there should be no agreement for it.

This is to-day observed, so that when parties contract for peace they agree in the first place to an amnesty, and, therefore, the first article is devoted to the amnesty. But although express mention of amnesty should not be made, nevertheless it is understood that those who deliberate concerning peace tacitly agree to it. For since they do not do that in order that the cause of the war and the controversies which

§ 988.
§ 987.

might have been stirred up by the acts of the war should be decided, but that the war may be ended by a compromise, and peace may thus be restored between the belligerents; it is undoubtedly necessary that

§ 959.

they should wish that there should be everlasting oblivion of the war and of the acts which were committed in the war, and that one should not be called to account by the other for the things done. Indeed, unless this may be considered as certain, the war cannot be said to be ended when peace is concluded, since from it enmities survive liable to

§§ 962, 963.
§ 11.
§ 86, part 8,
Jus Nat.

renew the war, which the common safety of nations demands should be completely ended, and the common safety is certainly the highest law in the supreme state, just as it is in each individual state.

§ 991. *How peace can be agreed upon*

In a treaty of peace an agreement must be made, either that all things should be restored to the place in which they were before the war, or that they should remain in the place in which they are, or that certain things captured in war should be restored and other things retained, and that certain other things besides should be performed. For since in the treaty of peace neither party convicts the other of injustice and wrong, con-

§ 988.

sequently the things captured in war may not be declared to have been

wrongfully seized, but a compromise must be made on the terms which
can be agreed upon; that which has been agreed upon is to be considered $ 986.
as law. Therefore, since one can agree only to that which can in some
way be done; since, moreover, it is necessary either that all things should
be restored to the place in which they were before the war, or that they
should remain as they then are, that is, at the time in which peace is
concluded, or that only certain things captured in war should be restored
and other things retained; since, moreover, there are other performances
also to which nations can mutually bind themselves, a thing which is
here assumed to be sufficiently well known of itself; in a treaty of peace
an agreement must be made either that all things should be restored to
the place in which they were before the war, or that they should remain
as they then are, or that certain things captured in war should be restored
and other things retained, and that certain other things should be performed in every case of that sort.

A negotiation for peace can have no other outcome than that the
peace should be concluded in the way in which the belligerents can
agree with each other. Each says that he has a just cause of war and that
he has done no wrong in the war. Nothing, therefore, is left except to
agree as to how it can be brought about that the right which springs
from the agreement may be guaranteed by the sanctity of treaties. If
you should say that a compromise of that sort ought to be made before
the disputants go to war, it will not be difficult to show that this can
scarcely be done. For if, indeed, any one driven by no necessity should §§ 546, 547.
show himself too indulgent, especially to one seeking unjust terms or
those that are at least too harsh, one would undoubtedly have to fear
that others would abuse his kindness, and thus he would not provide
for his own security. Therefore, a case of this sort gives a reason for pre-
ferring war rather than offering a ready ear to one seeking terms that
are unjust or unfair, although it may be that one may be compelled to
agree to them, if the fortune of war is less favourable.

§ 992. *Of the things concerning which nothing has been said in a treaty of peace*

Those things concerning which nothing has been said in a treaty of
peace remain as they are. For, since neither of the contracting parties is

§ 988.   convicted of injustice or wrong, the property which has been occupied in
           war is generally considered as occupied as if by right, and in like manner
           the things which have been done on either side are understood to have
           been done as if without wrong, and to this result especially contributes
§ 989.   the fact that there is an amnesty in every treaty of peace as such. There-
§ 990.   fore property captured in war belongs to the one who occupied it, and
           as he who has allowed them to occur ought to bear losses, he who has
           spent money cannot recover it. Therefore those things concerning which
           nothing has been said in a treaty of peace remain as they are.

           By the treaty of peace no change is made in those things which were
           done in the war, except in so far as some definite agreement has been
§ 22.   made in regard to them. For otherwise wars would spring out of wars,
§ 984, part 8,   a thing which is to be guarded against between nations, just as in a
Jus Nat.   state care must be taken that lawsuits may not arise out of lawsuits.
           But if there is an express agreement for an amnesty, which is a wise
           thing to make, since a stipulative right is less apt to be called in ques-
           tion than the voluntary and natural, or necessary, law of nations, there
           is in truth an agreement also to this effect, that those things concern-
           ing which nothing has been said should remain as they are.

                      ## § 993. *Of losses caused in war*

§ 992.   Since those things concerning which nothing has been said in a treaty
           of peace remain as they are, there is no action for the recovery of losses
           which have been caused in war, unless there has been an agreement
           otherwise.

           But if there has been an agreement otherwise, the losses are to be
           restored according to the agreement, but not as for a debt contracted
           under the law of war. The same thing must be held as to those things
           which remain as they are. They are retained in accordance with the
           agreement, by virtue of the clause of amnesty either expressly added
           or existing in the treaty as such. And, therefore, doubt is removed as
§ 777.   to unjust acquisition on the part of him whose war is unjust, inas-
           much as he occupies nothing legally, unless perchance from accidental
§ 787.   causes, and also on the part of the one whose war is just, if he has
           taken anything beyond the limit of his debt. Furthermore, it is plain

that by the law of nature on account of the uncertainty of that which may be rightly done in war, only when peace is made is it clear what things have been really acquired by each one of the belligerent parties, so it happens that among peaceful nations while the war continues the things acquired are to be considered the property of him who has occupied them in war, and should be considered as such within the limits of his state. The doubtful right becomes certain and fixed by the treaty of peace. § 892.

§ 994. *Of debts contracted or wrongs done before the war or outside the field of war during its continuance*

Debts which were contracted before the war, likewise wrongs done before it, but for which the war was not waged, or even debts contracted elsewhere while the war was going on or wrongs done outside the field of war, are not understood to be released by the treaty of peace, unless there has been an express statement concerning them. For the clause of amnesty, whether there has been an express agreement in regard to it or whether it exists simply in the treaty of peace as such, cannot be extended beyond the war and those things which have been done in the war, since it is not certain that the contracting parties have thought of any but these things. Therefore, by the treaty of peace, only those things are understood to have been released which have to do with the present war and which have been done in it. Therefore the debts which were contracted before the war, likewise wrongs done before it, on account of which nevertheless the war was not waged, or even debts contracted elsewhere while the war was going on or wrongs done outside the field of war, cannot be understood to have been remitted by the treaty of peace. Which was the first point. § 990.

But if there has been an express statement concerning those things in the treaty of peace, the clause of amnesty is extended to them because then there is no reason for doubt that they have been remitted along with other things. Which was the second point.

Although in the treaty of peace care must be taken that war should not arise from war, yet the amnesty as such is not for this reason extended to those things which have been done before or outside the Note, § 992.

war. For suppose that there had to be a second resort to arms on account of a debt or wrong of that sort; nevertheless it cannot be said that a new war arises from the preceding one which had been ended by the peace. Nevertheless, this can find a place among persuasive reasons that an amnesty should be so expressly extended that no cause may exist for any new war.

§ 995. *Of private debts of that sort*

Those debts which arise from private contracts, or from a private wrong in time of war, are not considered as released by the peace. For this debt does not arise from the fact that it was made in the war, but from a stipulation, and since this is to be observed even with an enemy, the war § 799. does not prevent the debt from being contracted, although it prevents it from being collected. Therefore, it is plain that these debts of private § 994. individuals incurred beforehand are not considered as released by the treaty of peace.

> For example, let us suppose that my debtor along with his own country comes under the control of the enemy. It is self-evident that the interest when it falls due cannot then be collected by me. Indeed, if I were to seek to bring an action, the enemy could adjudge that to himself by way of spoil. For since my right arises from the contract, it has no relation to the war, nor can those arguments be extended to it which are given in regard to the remission of debts in a treaty of peace. Therefore, when the bar is removed, after peace has been made, I can demand the interest. But the argument is different if an enemy in war has adjudged to himself a debt in the name of booty. For then it is included among those things which are retained by warlike force. The same is understood of penalties.

§ 996. *Whether movable property is included under things to be restored*

If there has been an agreement in a treaty of peace that all things are to be restored to the position in which they were before the war, movable property is not included under things to be restored. For since care must § 886. be taken that troubles should have an end, the agreement in a treaty of peace is therefore to be made for no other reason than that restitution can be effected. But if movable property had to be restored, since he to whom it is to be restored would be bound to prove his ownership against the possessor, and if it had perished would have to prove its value, that the loss might be restored, consequently not only would it have to be proved besides who held the captured property, but also that it had been taken from him by warlike force, and it is, therefore, readily evident to how many and how great difficulties the restitution of movable property captured in war would be subject, so that it could not be effected among the parties contracting for peace. Therefore if nothing has been expressly determined concerning the restitution of certain movable property, the contracting parties are understood not to have thought of it. If, then, there has been an agreement in a treaty of peace that all things are to be restored to the position in which they were before the war; movable property is not included under things to be restored.

§ 545, part 2, Jus Nat.

§ 572, part 2, Jus Nat.

Therefore, in this case also amnesty is to be extended to movable property, whether this has been expressly agreed or is simply contained in the treaty of peace as such. But it is self-evident that if there has been a statement concerning the restoration of certain things, these are to be restored; for here the question is simply what is the law in a case where there has been a general agreement that all things should be restored, no express mention being made of movable things. But on account of those difficulties which we have mentioned and others which might have been added concerning the restitution of movable things, except perchance of certain things whose restitution is not difficult, it is customary not to make agreements in treaties of peace but simply to stipulate a definite sum by way of recompense.

§ 990.

§ 997. *When peace begins to be binding*

As soon as a treaty of peace has been perfected the belligerents are immediately bound, but the soldiers and subjects of each are bound from the moment of publication. This is shown in the same manner as that by which we have proved the same above concerning a truce.

§ 919.

It is self-evident that an agreement can be made otherwise, as that peace should begin on a certain day. And then one must abide by the agreement.

§§ 376, 547.

§ 998. *Of the restoration of things captured after treaties of peace have been made*

§ 997.

Since a treaty binds belligerents immediately, as soon as it has been perfected, but not soldiers and subjects before publication; what soldiers do during their service in war, they do with impunity, nevertheless things captured after treaties of peace have been made and losses inflicted on either side are to be restored.

§§ 785, 987.

Of course a war is finished at once, consequently the things which are done after treaties of peace have been made are wrongfully done; therefore, he who does a wrong is bound to restitution. But since their inevitable ignorance may excuse soldiers, they are not liable to a penalty.

§ 999. *Of contributions exacted after a treaty of peace has been made*

§ 998.

Since a treaty of peace binds belligerents immediately, as soon as it is made, neither belligerent has a further right to any act of war, and since the exaction of a contribution is certainly an act of war, no contributions may be exacted after a treaty of peace has been made, unless they were due before, but not yet paid.

§§ 785, 987.

Nevertheless it is wiser, especially when there is an agreement in regard to restitution, that it should be expressly agreed that there should be no further exactions of contributions, when also the exaction of those already proclaimed, but not yet paid, can be forbidden.

§ 1000. *Of the fruits of things to be restored by virtue of peace*

If property is to be restored by virtue of the peace, the fruits also are to be restored from the day of the granting of peace, but not those gathered or due before the peace. For as soon as property is to be restored he who is bound to restore it has no right in it, a point which is self-evident. Therefore the right to take the fruit in the meantime cannot belong to him. But since at the very moment at which he who holds the thing is bound to restore it, the right of the other begins to whom the thing is to be restored, the right to take the fruit begins to be in him at the same §23, part 1, moment. Therefore, if a thing is to be restored by virtue of the peace, Jus Nat. the fruits also are to be restored which have been gathered from the day of the granting of peace. Which was the first point.

But since, indeed, through the amnesty, which is contained in every treaty of peace, the deeds which were committed in the war are forgiven, §990. the fruits gathered before the peace are not to be restored, consequently §989. not those which were due before the peace, which he who holds the property can demand as his own. Which was the second point.

> Of course in the treaty of peace there is no consideration as to whether the fruits have been gathered rightly or wrongly; but even if it is assumed that they have been gathered altogether wrongly, nevertheless the wrong having been forgiven through the amnesty the restitution of the fruits also is given up.

§ 1001. *Of the rights connected with the property restored*

If property is to be restored by virtue of the treaty of peace, the rights connected with the property are to be restored. For property is to be restored as it was captured in war; for that is understood to have been the intention when the agreement was made for its restitution. Therefore, since the property was captured together with the rights connected with §512, part 6, it, they also are to be restored with the property. Jus Nat.

§ 1002. *Of the restoration of fortified places*

If fortified places are to be restored, the fortifications which existed when the places were occupied may not be destroyed before the restitution. It is plain from the proof of the present proposition, that property is to be restored such as it came into the power of the enemy. Therefore, it §1001. is also plain that if fortified places are to be restored, the fortifications which existed when the places were occupied by the enemy may not be destroyed before the restitution.

> This would be just the same as if one who was to restore a city should set fire to the houses before the restitution, or should lay waste the country that was to be restored. But the conclusion is different

if the enemy himself has built fortifications while he held the place; for then he can decide in regard to these as it may seem best to him, unless there has been an agreement that the fortified place should be restored in the condition in which it now is. Likewise it is plain that it is understood that through the amnesty there is a release of liability, if the fortifications have been destroyed during the continuance of the war, while they were held by the enemy.

§ 1003. *Of the names of districts left to another by the treaty of peace*

The names of the districts left to another by the treaty of peace are to be determined by the usage of experts of the present time. For in the interpretation of treaties one must not depart from the common usage in speech, unless there are urgent reasons to the contrary, and indeed the usage of that time must be observed, in which the treaty was made, as it exists among experts. Therefore, the names of the districts left to another by the treaty of peace are to be determined by the usage of experts of the present time.

§ 470, part 6,
Jus Nat.

§ 471, part 6,
Jus Nat.

§ 478, part 6,
Jus Nat.

Words are symbols of things. Therefore, in a treaty of peace one cannot think of other meanings for things than those which they have at the time when the treaty is made, among experts, such as those are who make agreements for peace.

§ 1004. *Of things that are to be restored to their original state*

If by virtue of the treaty of peace certain things are to be restored to the condition in which they were before the war, the final condition is understood which existed when the war began, unless there should be a reference to a definite year. For a treaty of peace admits of no other interpretation than that which was intended. Therefore, when the contracting parties agree with each other that certain things should be restored to the condition in which they were before the war, since they could not have thought of a condition different from that in which things were when the war began, unless they should have referred to a definite year; the final condition is certainly understood which existed when the war began. Which was the first point.

§ 512, part 6,
Jus Nat.

But if then they should refer to a definite year, then such a condition must be understood as having existed in that year. Which was the second point. § 427, part 3, Jus Nat.

The contracting parties do not desire their agreement to be meaningless when they arrange for the restoration of things to the original condition. Therefore, if they are to understand each other, the reference can be only to the condition which existed when the war began. Hence that which was captured by the enemy and recovered by us during the war remains ours, and is not to be restored to him, because it was ours when the war began.

§ 1005. *Of those who voluntarily have lawfully subjected themselves to one of the belligerents*

If an independent people, or even those whom their own nation could not or would not defend during the continuance of the war, has voluntarily subjected itself to one of the belligerents, the restitution agreed upon in the treaty of peace does not apply to them. For if an independent people and those who are equivalent to such, namely, such as their own nation cannot or will not defend, has voluntarily subjected § 867. itself to one of the belligerents, that has no direct connexion with the war, although it may happen on the occasion of the war, since the belligerent has not subjected them to himself by an act of war, but they themselves have subjected themselves to his control, consequently the belligerent has acquired his right from the agreement. Therefore, since in a treaty of peace there is a settlement of those things which have been done by an act of war, and therefore the stipulated restitution cannot § 986. extend beyond them, this cannot apply to an independent people, or even to those whom their own nation could not or would not defend, when during the continuance of the war they have voluntarily subjected themselves to one of the belligerent parties.

But if a surrender has been made by a dependent or inferior people, the enemy can indeed acquire no right, consequently the surrendered people whom he wrongfully holds subject to himself, he is bound to restore, even if there should have been no agreement concerning restitution. But it is self-evident that there can also be an agreement

that those should be restored to their original condition who have
voluntarily or in accordance with their own right surrendered themselves. For in a treaty of peace an agreement can be made by way of
settlement in regard to matters which have no relation to the war
which has been waged or to those things which have been done in the
war, provided only express mention should be made of them, just as in
§ 991.   every settlement concerning definite points an agreement can be made
                          as to matters which have no bearing on the question in dispute. Peace
                          is made for the purpose of ending the war. Therefore, in the minds of
§ 881, part 5,   the contracting parties only those things are considered which have
Jus Nat.   been done by warlike force, and, therefore, when there is a question of
§ 959.   restitution, they think only of restoring those things which have been
§ 857.   carried away by hostile force, or by fraud.

§ 1006. *Of reference to other preceding treaties*

If in a treaty of peace reference should be made to other preceding treaties,
those things will be effective in regard to the stipulated matter which have
been more fully stated in them. For there is no one that does not see that
only for the sake of brevity is a reference made to other preceding treaties,
in order that the same statements should not have to be repeated there
a second time. Therefore, it is evident that the contracting parties agree
in regard to those things which have been more fully stated in preceding
treaties in regard to the matter agreed upon. Therefore, since a treaty is
made by mutual consent, if in a treaty of peace reference should be made
§ 819, part 3,   to other preceding treaties, those things will be effective in regard to the
Jus Nat.   stipulated matter which have been more fully stated in them.

It is clearly understood that what is said here concerning treaties of
peace is likewise true concerning any other treaties and stipulations.
Moreover, this reference to preceding stipulations is very common,
and can also be done in such a way that the whole of some preceding treaty may be renewed, and what is now made may be simply a
renewal of some former treaty, or the present treaty may include a
confirmation of former treaties, either without any change or with
some variations. Of course such provisions will depend upon the will
of the contracting parties.

§ 1007. *Of the alienation of sovereignty by a treaty of peace and of things in the ownership of the people*

If by the treaty of peace either the entire sovereignty or a part of it is to be alienated, and if the kingship is patrimonial, the king can make the alienation without the consent of the people; but if, indeed, it is held in usufruct, for an alienation there is required in the former case the consent of the people, in the latter case both that of the people and that of the part in regard to which the alienation is made, declared either by words or acts, when namely a king being in a very great crisis cannot obtain peace otherwise, or a ratification follows, when the people without protest do homage to the one newly acquiring them. The same thing is understood of property, which is in the ownership of the people or of some corporation. For if the kingship is patrimonial, the king, as may seem best to him, can transfer the sovereignty to any outside person, and unless special reasons prevent, he likewise can also divide it into its particular parts. Therefore, nothing prevents him from alienating by a treaty of peace either the entire sovereignty, or a part of it, without the consent of the people, a thing which is in harmony with the nature of a patrimonial kingship. Which was the first point.

§ 283, part 8, Jus Nat.

§§ 294 and fol., part 8, Jus Nat.

§ 115, part 8, and § 131, part 2, Jus Nat.

But if the kingdom shall be held in usufruct, he cannot alienate the sovereignty, but his act is *ipso jure* void, and if he should seek to transfer it, the people can resist. If, then, the kingship is to be alienated by the treaty, the consent of the people in whom the title to the sovereignty rests is required for this act. Which was the second point.

§ 1058, part 8, Jus Nat.

§ 34, part 8, Jus Nat.

But since the entire people is bound to individuals and consequently to any part of itself to promote the welfare of that part, since it cannot free itself from this obligation, the sovereignty over that part cannot be alienated without its consent. Which was the third point.

§§ 17, 28, part 8, Jus Nat.

§ 674, part 3, Jus Nat.

Since consent can be expressed both by words and acts, and for the alienation of sovereignty through a treaty of peace made by a king holding this sovereignty in usufruct both the consent of the people is required, as proved above, and of that part in regard to which the alienation is made, as proved above, if the sovereignty is to be alienated through a treaty of peace by a king holding this sovereignty in usufruct either over the whole people or over a part of it, it is just the same

§ 660, part 1, Phil. Pract. Univ.

Point 2.

Point 3.

whether the consent is declared expressly by words, or tacitly by deed. Which was the fourth point.

§ 133, 139, part 8, Jus Nat.

If the right of making peace belongs to the king (for otherwise the present question has no pertinence), because it has been transferred to him by the will of the people, to that also the people has declared by its very act that it will consent, because it was necessary to obtain peace. If, then, the king being in an extreme crisis should be compelled to alienate either the entire sovereignty or some part of it in order to obtain peace, he is not then bound to require express consent. Which was the fifth point.

Finally, if the king by a treaty of peace has alienated the sovereignty, either as a whole or in part, and the people has ratified this in some way, for example, if it should not countermand it and should voluntarily do homage to the one newly acquiring it; since this would be just as if it had consented before the treaty of peace was completed, the alienation is valid. Which was the sixth point.

When property which is in the ownership of the people is alienated by a treaty of peace, there is a disposal of the right of the people, just as when the sovereignty is alienated. Therefore it is quite plain that the things which have been proved concerning the alienation of sovereignty are in the same way understood of the alienation of property which is in the ownership of the people, so that there is no need of separate proof.

The decision in regard to that which is necessary for obtaining peace certainly lies with the king, as in general the decision concerning the things which are necessary for preserving and perfecting the state lies with him, unless a special method of action has been laid down by the fundamental laws. And so much the more readily in the present instance do we abide by the decision of a king, because no king will give up to another the sovereignty over a certain part of his people, much less over the whole people, unless driven by the direst necessity, so that he cannot secure peace any other way. Therefore, never, or scarcely ever, can a case be conceived of in which there is not the tacit consent of the people and of that part in regard to which an alienation is made, to the order for alienation either of the sovereignty as a whole or of a particular part. It is further to be suggested as regards the part that, just as a part of the people has a right to submit to the sovereignty of the enemy, if its own nation cannot defend it against a hostile force, so on the other hand, the people ought no less to have the right to separate a certain part from itself, if it cannot preserve itself otherwise, especially since it is not destroyed but becomes a member of another state. But what applies in the case of a people, or a part of some people, is much more easily applicable in regard to public property and the property of a corporation, especially since the ownership of a nation is connected with its sovereignty and passes over to the ruler of a state in the same way in which the sovereignty is transferred to him. Here we must especially note that what things are proved concerning the alienation of sovereignty, must not be understood of things surrendered in war or occupied by force; for when there is a settlement in war concerning the latter, how far they are to be restored, there is no question in the treaty of peace as to whether or not they are to be given up. If peace can be obtained in no other way than that all things should remain as they are, or that not everything should be restored, the need of the consent of the people ceases of itself. And as regards public property and property of a corporation, it must be considered besides that the ruler of a state has eminent domain over them also, by virtue of which in case of necessity he can dispose of them as public safety demands.

§ 868.

§ 164, part 7, and § 4, part 8, Jus Nat.

§ 88.

§ 305.

§ 306.

§§ 92, 102.

§§ 93, 103.

§ 1008. *Of private property and persons*

In a treaty of peace the ruler of a state can dispose of private property of subjects by virtue of eminent domain, nay more, of the persons of individuals by virtue of his eminent power. For by virtue of eminent domain the ruler of a state can dispose of the private property of subjects and by virtue of the eminent power he can dispose of their persons also in case of necessity, for the sake of the public safety. The ruler of a state owes this to his subjects, that he should preserve the peace in every way, consequently also that he should restore peace when it is disturbed and that he should avoid war, as far as he can, consequently also that he should strive to end a war, if he should become involved in it, and since in a treaty of peace the cause of the war is not determined, nor are the controversies determined, which may have been stirred up by the acts of the war, but in the settlement peace must be made under those conditions which can be obtained; he who makes the treaty of peace cannot dispose according to his liking concerning those things which are granted to the other party in the treaty

§§ 110, 111, part 8, Jus Nat.

§§ 113, 114, part 8, Jus Nat.

§ 962.

§ 964.

§ 988.

§ 986.

§ 991.

of peace. Therefore it is evident that, since in a treaty of peace there must be a disposition of the private property of subjects or even of their persons themselves, this is done in case of necessity for the sake of the advantage of the public. By virtue, therefore, of eminent domain, the ruler of a state in a treaty of peace can dispose of the private property of subjects, and by virtue of his eminent power can also even dispose of their persons.

To what, then, the state is bound to those whose property or persons have been disposed of does not belong to the treaty of peace, and it has been proved elsewhere.

§ 119, part 8, Jus Nat.

§ 1009. *Of allies in war*

Allies also are included in a treaty of peace. If, nevertheless, there has been a separate war with them, peace is to be expressly concluded with them also. For those who associate themselves in war with another belligerent party, by sending troops or subsidies, or assisting in any other manner, do whatsoever they do in war, not in their own name, but in the name of the one with whom they are allied and whose cause they defend. Whatever, therefore, they do in war, has reference to the war which is waged by the one with whom they are associated. Therefore, since through the amnesty which exists in every treaty of peace as such, although it has not been expressly agreed upon, all deeds committed in war are consigned to perpetual oblivion and everlasting silence, so that no one can be accused or punished for things done in the war; the amnesty is extended to the allies also. Therefore in a treaty of peace the allies also are included. Which was the first point.

§ 990.

§ 989.

But if, indeed, a separate war has been waged with them, the things which have been done in it have nothing at all to do with the war of the one with whom they are allied, although the former war has arisen because of the latter. Therefore, the treaty which has been made for ending the former, cannot be extended to the latter also. Therefore, it is necessary that peace should be expressly concluded with the allies also. Which was the second point.

It happens in more than one way that a separate war arises with the allies. One who is united by treaty to a belligerent can, in his own name, declare war in favour of such belligerent against another belligerent, and can wage war against such other in another place, with his own army, either openly defending the cause of his ally, or making pretext of another cause. Likewise, on the other hand, by the one against whom troops or subsidies are sent or other assistance is furnished, war can be declared on the one sending or furnishing aid, and against him hostile acts may be committed or even without a declaration of war arms may be used against him, so that by that very fact there is a separate war with him. Therefore, there is no one that does not see that in these cases it is necessary for a separate treaty of peace to be made by the allies. Therefore, it is also evident that allies can make a separate treaty of peace, so that the war in which they themselves are engaged may be ended, unless the treaty contained the provision that one of the allies may not make peace without the other.

§ 1010. *What rebellion is*

Rebels are defined as subjects who without just cause take up arms against the ruler of the state. And that condition is not called war but rebellion, in our native vernacular *ein Aufruhr* [a tumult]. Moreover, in a rebellion the attempt is made either to deprive the ruler of the state of his sovereignty or to compel him to accept certain limitations on it.

When it is unlawful and impious for subjects to take up arms against the ruler of the state is to be determined from the principle of general public law as proved in the eighth part of "The Law of Nature." Frequently desperation makes subjects rebel, if the ruler of the state for his own advantage burdens them too heavily, or deprives them of the rights and privileges which they enjoyed, or if there is anything else that makes his rule intolerable. For although they are bound to obedience with patience, nevertheless patience, if imposed on too much, finally turns into fury, so that they attempt to shake off the yoke that seems to be unbearable. § 1043, part 8, Jus Nat.

§ 1011. *What civil war is*

But civil war is defined as one in which subjects take up arms for a just cause against the ruler of a state. Therefore, since rebellion has an unjust § 1010.

cause, but civil war a just cause, a rebellion is not a civil war and civil war is not rebellion; consequently subjects who stir up a civil war are not rebels. In a doubtful case citizens who take up arms against the ruler of a state are called in our native vernacular *die Misvergnügten* [the disaffected], or by a term borrowed from the French and but slightly changed, *die Malcontanten* [the malcontents], as being discontented with the present régime.

§ 257.

Since the decision does not rest with foreign nations as to matters arising between subjects and ruler of any state, inasmuch as they ought not to intrude themselves in the affairs of others; they will not call it rebellion if subjects take up arms against a ruler, unless the wrong on the part of the subjects is perfectly plain; they will rather speak of *innerliche Unruhe* [internal unrest], in our native vernacular, and of malcontents using force against a ruler.

§ 1012. *Whether civil war is allowable*

Since that is a civil war in which subjects take up arms for a just cause against the ruler of a state, and since arms are not understood to be taken up for a just cause, except when it is allowable to resist the ruler of a state by force, a thing which we have proved elsewhere is allowable in certain cases; a civil war is allowable in every case in which it is allowable to resist the ruler of a state by force. Since it is allowable for subjects simply to petition, when the ruler commands what seems too harsh or unjust, and, if he cannot give a hearing to their petitions, they are bound to obey, nay more, not even magistrates have not the right to resist his wrongful acts. Therefore, if there should be resistance to the wrongs of a ruler of a state, this is not civil war, but rebellion.

§ 1054, part 8, Jus Nat.

§ 1051, part 8, Jus Nat.

§ 1052, part 2, Jus Nat.

§ 1053, part 8, Jus Nat.

§ 1011.

§ 1044, part 8, Jus Nat.

§ 1045, part 8, Jus Nat.

Of course a ruler is not to be obeyed when he commands what is opposed to the law of nature; if, nevertheless, he should dare to punish a justifiable disobedience, that is to be patiently endured. Nevertheless, that the innocent may escape from punishment, it is allowable for them to flee and become suppliants to another nation, which can urge extradition of the property which they left behind. But this is not the place to say more concerning these and other matters affecting the question.

§ 1013. *What riot is*

We define a riot as that situation in which a crowd congregates and uses force against magistrates or minor powers or their property, and also against private persons and their property, or at least threatens it. In our native vernacular we call it *ein Aufstand* [an uprising].

Riot undoubtedly differs from rebellion, since in the latter armed force is used against the sovereign power, but in the former only against minor powers or private individuals. Rebellion approaches more closely to civil war, from which it differs only in the justice of the cause, than does riot to rebellion. We have an example of riot in the case of peasants, who along with slaves, women, and maid-servants, armed with clubs, stones, mattocks, and other implements, resist magistrates and interfere with the administration.

§ 1014. *What sort of an offence it is*

Since riot disturbs the public peace it is a crime or a public wrong, and those arousing a riot or encouraging it or mingling in it are guilty of a crime; consequently according to the variation in circumstances they are to be punished by their ruler.

§ 11, part 8,
Jus Nat.
§ 581, part 8,
Jus Nat.
§ 626, part 8,
Jus Nat.

Of course both the authors of riot deserve punishment and those who unite in it and assist it in any way, although frequently it is necessary that the penalty be remitted through an amnesty.

§ 989.

§ 1015. *Of the things promised to rebels and rioters*

The promises which are made by the sovereign powers to rebels and rioters in order to quell the rebellion or riot are to be observed. This is shown in the same way as we have shown above that those promises are to be kept which are made to an enemy as an enemy, to a robber and brigand as a robber and brigand.

§ 799.

A treaty of peace is not indeed made with rebels and rioters, since only sovereign powers make peace with each other; nevertheless this does not

§ 977.

prevent an agreement being made for settling a rebellion, or riot if to settle it otherwise is impossible, or at least unwise. But these stipulations, even if they are bare promises on the part of the ruler, are no less to be observed than are treaties made with an enemy during a war.

§ 1016. *Of amnesty promised to rebels and rioters*

§ 1015.

Since the promises which are made by the sovereign power to rebels and rioters in order to quell a rebellion or riot are to be observed, if amnesty has been promised, no one can be accused or punished for those things which have been done in the rebellion or riot.

I choose to suggest an amnesty by way of example; but according to the diverse circumstances other examples also can be cited, as that certain burdens should be lifted, that privileges should be restored, and other things which have given a reason for rebellion and riot, the penalty against the instigators of the rebellion and riot being reserved.

§ 1017. *Whether a treaty of peace binds the people and their successors*

§ 959.

§ 424.

A treaty of peace also binds the nation, or people, and their successors. It is evident that a treaty of peace is made for the benefit of the rest of the state, and that it is a real treaty. But a real treaty made by the ruler of a state for the benefit of the state binds the nations also and their successors. Therefore, a treaty of peace also binds the nation, or people, and the successors of the ruler of the state.

To make peace pertains to the exercise of sovereignty, which is a function of the ruler of the state. Therefore, in regard to the acts affecting the sovereignty, which have been left and ought to have been left to the decision of the present ruler of the state, the successors have no right, so that the consent to the treaty of peace of those who hope to succeed them need not be asked. Therefore, the successors cannot object on the ground that the peace was made to their prejudice. It could not have been made, save on the conditions which could be obtained in the given circumstances.

§ 1018. *Of not allowing delay in the performance of agreements*

Those agreements which have been made in a treaty of peace, to give, to return, or to restore, must be performed without delay. For if no mention of time has been made, it is certainly understood that the agreement was that they should be performed immediately; but if some time has been mentioned, that performance should occur within the time agreed upon. If, then, it has not been left to the will of the one bound to perform, when he may wish to perform, since stipulations must be observed; those agreements which have been made in a treaty of peace, to give, to return, or to restore, must be performed without delay.

§ 789, part 3, Jus Nat.

See what we have proved elsewhere concerning the prompt payment of a debt, and likewise of delay illegal in itself, and of the satisfaction thereof.

§§ 665, 666, part 5, Jus Nat.
§ 652, part 3, Jus Nat.
§§ 653, 654, part 3, Jus Nat.

§ 1019. *Of the right of postliminium in those things which are restored by a treaty of peace*

Things which are restored by a treaty of peace have the right of postliminium. For every nation, and consequently the ruler of the state, is bound to defend the rights of his subjects against external force of enemies, consequently to do his best that things captured by the enemy should be recovered. Therefore, however they may be recovered, they are to be restored to their original condition, since no reason exists why any change should be made in that; for that the things have been captured by an enemy is no reason. Therefore, things which are restored by a treaty of peace have the right of postliminium.

§ 39.
§ 428, part 8, Jus Nat.

§ 56, Ontol.
§ 896.

Since by the law of nature captives do not become slaves, but when peace is made they are to be released, consequently are either to be exchanged or released for a certain price, in regard to which it is wise that an agreement be made, as is the custom among Christians; by the law of nature the question ceases to exist as to whether and when captives have the right of postliminium under a treaty of peace. The state owes it to them that it should free them from captivity and restore them to their original condition.

§ 814.
§§ 815 and fol.

§ 817.

§ 1020. *When peace is said to be broken*

Peace is said to be broken if the treaty of peace should not be observed, or if any one does anything which he could not or ought not to do by virtue of the treaty, or if he does not do what he ought to do by virtue of it. Therefore, both a positive act and a negative act contrary to the treaty of peace are described as a breach of peace, in our native vernacular *ein Friedensbruch* [a breach of the peace]. Moreover, any treaty in general is said to be broken in the same sense. And he who breaks the peace, or the treaty, is called a breaker of the peace, or of the treaty.

§ 759, part 3,
Jus Nat.

A breach of the peace is a most abominable wrong, since the offender breaks the good faith which ought to be sacred among nations, and incurs the stigma of treachery.

§ 550.

§ 766, part 3,
Jus Nat.

§ 1021. *Of the renewal of an old war*

Since, when peace has been made, as regards that cause for which the war was waged, war cannot be renewed, neither can it be renewed because of the amnesty which is contained in every treaty of peace, even if there has been no express agreement concerning it, for the things which have been done in that war, and since he breaks the peace who does what he ought not to do by virtue of the treaty of peace; he breaks the peace, who, for the same cause for which the war has been waged or for those things which were done in it, that is, without any new cause, uses warlike force.

§ 987.

§ 990.

§ 989.

§ 1020.

He who rushes to arms again without any new cause for it acts contrary to what is in every treaty of peace. Because in this case the breach of the peace is so evident, it means that no one will readily take up arms again after peace has been made, unless under pretext of a fresh cause. The name of disturber of the peace is too odious among nations for any one not to guard against it.

§ 1022. *What articles of peace are*

Articles of peace are defined as the several parts of the agreement, by which those things are distinguished concerning which any specific agreement has been made. Moreover, articles are connected, in which an agreement is made concerning things that belong to the same cause, and separate, in which an agreement is made regarding things that concern each a different cause. Therefore, since there are as many different stipulations as there are things concerning different causes, connected articles of peace concern the same peace, while separate articles make some separate peace.

This is not peculiar to instruments of peace, for it can also happen that other instruments may treat of different things at the same time; for example, if one sells his house and promises a hundred for another consideration. Here the contract of purchase and sale and the stipulation from which the hundred is due are different contracts.

§ 1023. *Of the breach of the peace in separate articles*

Since there are as many different treaties of peace as there are distinct articles and only connected articles concern the same peace, if the peace §1022. of separate articles is broken, it continues in the others.

In the same way, indeed, in the similar case which we have cited by way of illustration, he who hands over the house, but is unwilling to Note, §1022. pay the hundred, does not violate his contract of sale but only his stipulation. It is of very great importance to determine accurately whether or not the treaty of peace as a whole has been broken if a single article of the treaty has been violated. And, therefore, connected articles are to be distinguished accurately from those that are separate from each other, lest the diverse and separate obligations, one of which does not depend upon the other, should be confused in a common treaty. Of course, if a wrong should be committed in one article, a separate one, and on that account there should be a resort to arms, the war would have no bearing on those things concerning which there was an agreement in the other articles. In a treaty of peace nothing is properly considered except the cause of the war and those things which have been done in the war. But by stipulations other promises are added §991. which have no bearing on this.

§ 1024. *Whether peace is broken for a trivial offence*

The peace is broken even if provisions of slight importance should be violated. For the peace is broken when anything is done contrary to that §1020.

which has been said in the treaty of peace. Therefore, since this would occur if provisions even of slight importance are violated, the peace is broken even if provisions of slight importance should be violated.

§ 546.

§ 759, part 3,
Jus Nat.

Of course that good faith should be sacred, consequently that a promise is inviolable does not depend upon the fact that the thing promised is of great importance, but upon the fact that it has been promised. Good faith is violated if the promise of a thing, even of slight importance, should not be observed.

§ 1025. *Of war brought for a new cause*

§ 987.

§ 1020.

The peace is not broken if war is brought for a new cause. By the treaty of peace it has been agreed only that war would not be again undertaken for the cause on account of which war was waged. If, then, war should be brought for a new cause, that would not be contrary to the treaty of peace, consequently the peace is not broken.

§ 617.

Note, § 987.

It is just the same whether the wrong which gives a cause for war was committed before the previous war, or during its continuance, or afterwards. See also what we noted above, as to how the same cause can assume the form of a new cause.

§ 1026. *Of a treaty of war entered into against one with whom you have made peace*

§ 1025.

Since the peace is not broken if war should be brought for a new cause, and since it is just the same whether you bring war against another in your own name or ally yourself to a third party, since in either case you act in a hostile manner against him with whom you had made an agreement of peace; the peace is not broken, even if you afterwards ally yourself to a third party who is bringing war against him with whom you made peace.

Therefore, it is evident that it is not illegal to make a treaty of war against one with whom you had made peace, nor can he accuse you of treachery, unless peace has been made on the condition that you are not thereafter to ally yourself in war to any one against him. For then the obligation arises from a special agreement, by which the right otherwise belonging to you by nature has been taken away. Nevertheless, this treaty is a separate article, not connected with the rest, unless it should be added expressly that the peace is to be broken, if this should be done, so that the concession of the things, in regard to which an agreement has been made, would depend upon it as upon a protestative condition.

§ 1022.

§ 1027. Of allies and subjects acting contrary to the treaty of peace

If those who had been allies in war, or your subjects, without your consent or subsequent ratification, should do anything contrary to the treaty of peace, the peace is not broken. For as soon as a war is finished, and consequently a peace made, those who had been allies in the war cease to be such. Therefore, since their act no longer depends on your will, it cannot be imputed to you. Therefore, if they do what is contrary to the treaty of peace, the peace cannot be said to have been broken by you. Which was the first point.

§ 975.

§ 650, part 1, Phil. Pract. Univ.
§ 1020.

In like manner it is plain that if any one of your subjects without your consent or subsequent ratification should do what is contrary to the treaty of peace, that act is not dependent upon your will. Therefore, even as before it follows that the peace is not broken. Which was the second point.

Subjects are bound to him with whom peace has been made, to repair the loss, but to you for the penalty. And hence it is evident what ought to be done, that you may not by ratification make the deed of your subjects your own. Moreover, in order that ratification may be proved, as Grotius rightly says, three things are required, namely, knowledge, power to punish, and neglect to do so; a manifest act or one reported by him to whom the wrong is done assures the first; the second is presumed, unless there has been open insurrection of the subjects; finally the third is shown by such lapse of time as is usually taken for punishing crimes in any states.

§ 580, part 2, Jus Nat.

§ 647, part 8, Jus Nat.

De Jure Belli ac Pacis, lib. 3, c. 20, § 30.

§ 1028. Of subjects who serve as soldiers with others carrying on war

If your subjects serve as soldiers with others carrying on war, without your command, the peace is not broken. For if subjects in a state have not been prohibited from serving as soldiers with others, either as mercenaries or without pay, a thing which is otherwise permitted cannot be understood to have been forbidden by a treaty of peace, unless there has been an express agreement that afterwards they should not serve as soldiers against the other. Therefore, since nothing is done contrary to the treaty of peace, if they should serve as soldiers, peace cannot be said to be broken on this account.

§ 1020.

De Jure Belli
ac Pacis, lib. 3,
c. 20, § 31.

Grotius indeed does not think that is to be allowed, unless it should appear from plausible arguments that the contrary was intended. Yet he produces no reason for his belief. But, on the other hand, no reason appears why that ought not to be allowed by the treaty of peace, which had been allowable otherwise, when nothing has been agreed to the contrary concerning it in the treaty of peace. But the situation is different if they should serve as soldiers by decree of the state, for then you would aid the enemy of the one with whom you had made peace.

§ 1029. *If subjects are injured contrary to the articles of peace*

If your subjects are injured contrary to the articles of peace, the peace is broken. Of course peace is made, not only for the state as a whole, but also for the individual members of it, or the subjects whom the entire nation ought to protect against the injuries of strangers. If, then, your subjects are injured contrary to the articles of peace, that undoubtedly is contrary to the treaty of peace, consequently the peace is broken.

§ 28, part 8,
Jus Nat.
§ 1022.
§ 1020.

§ 723.

§ 1027.

Just as war affects individual subjects, so also peace. And just as a treaty of peace binds individual subjects, so also provision is made for the security of individuals by it. But here those things are to be kept in mind which were proved a little while ago concerning the deeds of the subjects of an offending state.

§ 1030. *Of allies included in a treaty of peace*

§ 1020.

If force of arms is used against allies included in a treaty of peace, the peace is broken. For it is self-evident that that is done contrary to the treaty of peace, consequently that the peace is broken.

This is true even if the contract has not been made with them. For by the stipulation we have the right to bring aid to the injured party against the assault and to compel the offender to fulfil his promise, although from it no right has been gained for the injured ally.

§ 1031. *Of allies waging war on their own account*

If your allies are waging war, not for your sake, but on their own account, peace made with you does not affect them, nor does that affect you which has been made with them. For then it is plain that your war and the war of your allies are separate wars. If, therefore, you make peace, a settlement is made only of the cause of your war and of the things done in it, but not of the cause of the war of the allies and of those things which were done in it. And the same is understood if your allies should make peace. Therefore, peace made by you does not affect your allies who have waged separate wars, nor does their peace affect you.

In this case peace cannot be made except by your consent and that of your allies, and although the articles of peace may be contained in the same instrument, those nevertheless which are referred to your cause are different from those which concern the cause of the allies. §1022. Nevertheless they can promise a guarantee to each other, and then the individuals are bound to bring aid against the one who breaks the §451. peace with either. §443.

§ 1032. *If it is not your fault that you do not fulfil the promise*

If it is not your fault that you do not fulfil what was promised in a treaty of peace, you do not break the peace. For since no one can be bound to another beyond that which is possible; if it is not your fault that you do §209, part 1, not fulfil what was promised in a treaty of peace, by that fact nothing Phil. Pract. Univ. is done contrary to the treaty of peace, consequently you do not break the peace. §1020.

It is not your act that you cannot fulfil; but it is an accident which you were not able to foresee when you made the treaty, nor avoid when the treaty had been made. But an accident which you could

§§ 638 and fol.,
part 1, Phil.
Pract. Univ.
not avoid cannot be imputed to you. To this applies the case, if you
yourself involved in war cannot send the promised troops or subsidies,
or if the thing has perished which you were bound to deliver, or if it
§ 665.
has been carried away by thieves or robbers or even by some enemy.

§ 1033. *Of peace broken by one party*

If the peace is broken by one party, the other party is not bound to
observe the treaty of peace; nevertheless he can do so if he should so
§§ 369, 962,
977.
desire. For an agreement of peace is a treaty. But if one party violates
a treaty, the other party also can withdraw from it. Therefore, even if
§ 430.
the peace should be broken by one, the other can withdraw from the
treaty of peace, consequently he is not bound to observe it. Which was
the first point.

But he who breaks a treaty of peace loses his right which he derived
from it, since you are no longer bound to observe it, as proved above;
since, nevertheless, he cannot by his act free himself from the obligation
§ 674, part 3,
Jus Nat.
§ 336, part 2,
Jus Nat.
by which he is bound to you, nor can he take from you the right gained
by the treaty of peace; if you should still wish to observe the treaty of
peace, you can do so. Which was the second point.

> Therefore, it is for you to determine what is the wiser course,
> whether the treaty of peace should be dissolved, or should stand, and
> that you should simply demand its fulfilment or reparation of the loss
> caused. And however much it has been added, that by such an act the
> peace would be considered broken, that does not affect the situation,
> since it would be absurd that an obligation should be made to depend
> on the whim of the contracting parties.

§ 1034. *Of a penalty added to a treaty of peace*

If a penalty is added to a treaty of peace, the option is with the one to
whom the wrong is done, whether he desires himself to withdraw from
it or to accept the penalty offered. When a penalty is added to a treaty of
peace, the contract is not put in the alternative, either that the penalty
should be paid or the treaty of peace dissolved; for this is not consistent
with a treaty of peace, by which it is intended that war should not be

again renewed for the same cause for which the war has been waged, nor should any one be accused or punished for the deeds committed in it. Therefore, since through the penalty added for him whose right gained from the treaty has been violated, that is, the one to whom the wrong has been done, his right to withdraw from the treaty of peace, which the other has broken, is not taken away, since, nevertheless, if he should not wish to do so, he is not compelled to withdraw from it; it is understood that by the addition of the penalty nothing else is intended except that he, to whom the wrong has been done, may choose whether he himself prefers to withdraw from the treaty of peace or to accept the penalty offered.

§ 987.

§§ 989, 990.

§ 859, part 1,
Jus Nat.

§ 1033.

> It would not further the security of the peace if any one might free himself by offering a penalty. But since it is not always wise to undertake a war, it is to the interest of the one to whom an injury has been done that he should avoid a war which he does not wish to undertake, yet that the other may not have violated the treaty with impunity. So of course the addition of a penalty does not diminish the obligation of keeping the peace and thus make the obligation subject to the whim of the contracting parties; but it merely makes better the condition of the one to whom the wrong was done, so that when the peace is broken his right gained from the treaty of peace is not taken from him, nor, if it is not wise to undertake the war, he is simply bound to endure the wrong done him without penalty and without any reparation.

§ 1035. *Whether the exception of duress by fear or force is good against a treaty of peace*

A treaty of peace is not invalid because it has been extorted by warlike force or by fear. For let us suppose that a treaty of peace ought not to be valid because it is said to have been extorted by warlike force or by fear. No peace will be valid unless it has been made by those who are equal in power; since this is a thing which is difficult to prove, especially among nations which have no judge, so that there is no opportunity of determining the question, there will be no peace which any one can be bound to observe, consequently it will always be possible to renew war for the same reason. Which certainly is absurd.

This is also shown directly in this way. By virtue of the amnesty which is contained in every treaty of peace as such and which is usually expressly agreed upon in the first place of all by both parties, all things done in the war are consigned to perpetual oblivion and everlasting silence, consequently by that very fact there is a tacit renunciation of the exception that a settlement has been extorted by warlike violence or fear. For that reason, force and fear cannot be alleged against the same. Therefore, a treaty of peace is not invalid because it has been extorted by warlike force or by fear.

§ 990.
§ 989.

Fear is undoubtedly just, which is due to arms taken up justly. But since in a treaty of peace the justice of the war is put on one side, and a settlement is made on the basis that nothing wrong has been done in the war by either of the belligerent parties, there is no consideration by the parties whether either party is moved by just or unjust fear to make peace under these conditions. Therefore, there is no need of saying that from the law of nations the rule has been introduced that all fear inspired in war should be considered as just.

§ 988.

§ 1036. *Of mediation*

If mediators should be employed to make peace, each of the belligerents ought to agree in regard to them. For a mediator pleads the cause of either party, and it depends upon the will of the parties whether or not they wish to accept the one who voluntarily offers his services, consequently also it depends upon the will of one party whether he wishes to accept the one offered by the other party. Therefore, it is necessary that each of the belligerent parties should agree to those who are to be employed as mediators to make peace.

§ 924, part 5, Jus Nat.

§ 926, part 5, Jus Nat.

§ 658, part 5, Phil. Pract. Univ.

We have already proved elsewhere what is to be held concerning a mediation, and anything besides that may arise for consideration is easily derived from those conclusions.

§§ 925 and fol., part 5, Jus Nat.

§ 1037. *Whether mediators are bound to give a guarantee*

A mediator is not bound to give a guarantee. For a mediator is bound only to give his assistance in settling the matter in controversy between the litigants, but he has no right to settle it himself, consequently if he is employed to make peace, he ought to endeavour simply by warning, persuasion, and exhortation to persuade those who are deliberating on the terms of peace to make a settlement. But since, when he does this, he does not promise aid against the one who has not observed the agreements, he does not bind himself to guarantee it. Therefore, he is not bound to give a guarantee.

§ 923, part 5, Jus Nat.

§ 929, part 5, Jus Nat.

§ 443 h and § 393, part 3, Jus Nat.

Nor does it make any difference if he has subscribed the treaty of peace. For he subscribes as a witness, not as a guarantor, or, as others prefer to say, a guaranty, unless he has expressly bound himself to guarantee, a thing which it is self-evident can be done.

§ 1038. *Whether a mediator has the right to interpret the treaty of peace*

A mediator has no right to interpret the treaty of peace. For a mediator is chosen simply in order that he may use his efforts to make peace. Therefore, since no right of interpreting the treaty of peace is conferred upon him, since, moreover, no one can acquire a greater right than the one who transfers it has wished to confer upon him, nor is anything to be effective as against the transferor, except that which he has clearly indicated, a mediator therefore can have no right to interpret the treaty of peace.

§ 923, part 5, Jus Nat.

§ 382, part 3, Jus Nat.

§ 427, part 3, Jus Nat.

If the right of interpreting the treaty of peace were to belong to the mediator, it would have to be transferred to him by the consent of those who make the peace. But express consent is lacking, because nothing is said concerning it in the treaty of peace; tacit consent is also lacking, because that is not included in the mediation. It is one thing to use your efforts that those wishing to make peace may agree to terms of peace, in order that the parties negotiating may not withdraw without accomplishing anything; and it is another thing to declare what is to be understood by ambiguous words in a treaty of peace, or to interpret it. The consent of the parties to the articles of a treaty of peace, by which consent the treaty has been made, does not depend upon the manner in which the mediator may have understood the words, whose meaning is called in question.

§ 459, part 6, Jus Nat.

§ 1039. *Of the publication of peace*

The publication of peace is the act by which it is announced, both to soldiers and subjects, that peace has been made, consequently that the war is ended. Since, therefore, when war is ended all warlike acts ought to cease, so that the things which have been captured by the soldiers in the prosecution of the war after peace was concluded are to be restored, and losses caused by them are to be repaired, and fresh contributions cannot be demanded or exacted, peace ought to be published to the soldiers without delay. But since the same necessity does not exist as regards subjects, peace can be published to subjects whenever it may seem best.

§ 975.
§ 785.

§ 998.
§ 999.

The news that peace has been made usually comes to subjects before it is published to them, especially when it has been published to the soldiers. Yet war is published to subjects by authority of the state, and so far as they are concerned the declaration of war has the force of a law, inasmuch as certain things are commanded or forbidden in it. Therefore it is necessary that peace also be published by authority of the state, since just as it pertains to the sovereign power to make laws, so also it has the right to annul or abrogate them. The method of publication is a matter of choice.

§ 737.
§ 741.
§ 813, part 8, Jus Nat.

§ 818, part 8, Jus Nat.

§ 1040. *Of the effect of the publication as regards subjects*

Since by the publication of peace it is announced to subjects that war is ended, those things which were illegal on account of the war are again legal from the day of publication, nor are the subjects of the one with whom the war had been waged to be any longer considered by them as enemies, and whatever rights were acquired by them through peace they can now use, and they are bound to observe as a law whatever has been especially agreed.

§ 1039.

Of course the publication of peace has a [legal] effect corresponding to that of the publication and declaration of war.

Of the Law of Embassies

§ 1041. *Who are called ambassadors*

Ambassadors are defined as persons who are sent by one nation or its ruler to another nation or its ruler for some affair of state. In our native vernacular they are called *Gesandten* [envoys].

> In the law of nature there is no distinction between ambassadors as regards their rank, but this distinction comes from the customs of nations, and therefore is not to be considered at present.

§ 1042. *What they are by the law of nature*

Since certain affairs of state are entrusted to ambassadors who are sent to another nation, by the law of nature ambassadors are mandataries of their nation or of the one who has the right of the nation, that is, of the ruler of the state. § 1041.

> Hence also, when sent, they are furnished with a mandate, and in this respect the same things are true of them which we have proved elsewhere of mandataries. §§ 649 and fol., part 4, Jus Nat.

§ 1043. *Who are agents*

Those persons are generally called agents who care for the private affairs of the ruler of a state or even of his subjects in his name in dealing with another nation. Since it depends upon the will of the one appointing them what he may wish to entrust to them, nothing prevents one from entrusting to agents any public business as well, especially that of less importance.

Of these we need say nothing at present. For if they are foreigners, they have no other right than that of foreigners living in alien territory; but if they are citizens, as they can be, they are subject to the same law as other citizens are. The term ambassador is a relative one, because it refers to the one to whom they are sent; but inasmuch as they are engaged in the service of the one who sends them, they are usually called the ministers of the sender, very often with an added phrase stating the court of the one to whom they have been sent. So an ambassador sent by the King of Sweden to the King of the French is called the minister of the Swedes at the court of the most Christian king. The ambassadors of the pope are called by the special name of papal or apostolic nuncii. But those things that are merely arbitrary are alien to our purpose, and therefore there is certainly no reason why we should say much concerning them.

§ 1044. *Of the right to send ambassadors*

§ 170.
§ 171.
§ 189.
§ 191.
§ 370.
§ 377.
§ 166.
§ 12.
§§ 9, 10.
§§ 173, 268.
§ 267.
§ 269.
§ 589.
§ 589.
§ 619.
§§ 586, 589, 630, and fol.
§ 961.

Nations have a perfect right to send ambassadors to other nations. Every nation has a perfect right to seek the duties of humanity from another nation, if it cannot itself do what it desires, nor can it be forbidden without wrong, nor can its request be harshly treated. It has a right, though an imperfect one, to engage in commerce with another nation, as to which it can bind that nation absolutely to itself by stipulations. In like manner they are able to make treaties for the sake of the public good, and in this way they can bind each other absolutely to certain performances and to allowing certain things, in accordance with that duty imposed by nature, by which one nation ought to contribute what it can to the preservation and perfection of another in that in which it is not self-sufficient, so that they may promote the common good as members of the supreme state. No nation is bound to allow itself to be injured by another, for example, by allowing the other to take away some right from it, or to intrude upon its administration, and many other things which have been repeatedly fully proved in previous discussions; nevertheless one must not proceed to violent remedies, as reprisals, androlepsia, and finally public war itself, unless one cannot otherwise obtain one's right or reparation for wrong done. Nay more, when war has broken out, since nations are bound to cultivate peace with each other, and it is not

allowable to continue a war indefinitely, in the midst of arms one must $\quad$ §§ 969 and fol.
think of peace, and one nation ought to offer to another conditions
under which it is to be made. Therefore, it is plain that there are very
many interests of state to be considered between nations, and care is to
be taken that they can be effected. But it is self-evident that these matters $\quad$ § 886.
cannot be understood except by mutual conferences and decisions. And
since nations themselves cannot come together, and since very many
obstacles, which change according to the diversity of circumstances, prevent rulers of states, who have their right, from doing that, it is neces- $\quad$ § 39.
sary that they should send to each other certain persons furnished with $\quad$ § 1041.
a mandate to transact public business, that is, ambassadors. Therefore, $\quad$ § 159, part 1,
Phil. Pract. Univ.
since by nature a man has a right to those acts without which he cannot
satisfy a natural obligation, and since that is a perfect right, nations have $\quad$ § 905, part 1,
Jus Nat.
a perfect right to send ambassadors to other nations.

Nation has no less need of nation than man of man. And however
much you assume that there is some nation which is self-sufficient,
nevertheless others exist which need its aid, not to be refused, except
in case of conflict of duties toward itself and other nations. Therefore,
the necessity of transacting affairs of state between nations cannot be $\quad$ § 206.
called in question, provided you turn your attention to those things
which have been proved heretofore, however much you desire to treat
as superfluous the obligation by which they are bound to each other
as members of a supreme state which nature herself has established $\quad$ § 12.
between them for the sake of mutual aid in perfecting themselves and
their condition and to promote the common good by their combined
strength. The necessity of dealings with each other carries with it a $\quad$ § 8.
necessity for embassies without which dealings are impossible. Each,
therefore, has a sufficient reason in the nature itself of nations, by
which the law of nations is unalterably established. He who understands these points clearly, as they are understood if the points proved
before should be carefully considered, can have no doubt of the right
to send ambassadors.

§ 1045. *Of admitting ambassadors*

Since nations have a perfect right to send ambassadors, and since it would $\quad$ § 1044.
be contrary to that right if the ambassadors should not be admitted,

§ 239, part 1,
Phil. Pract.
Univ.

§ 910, part 1,
Jus Nat.

§ 859, part 1,
Phil. Pract.
Univ.

ambassadors are to be admitted by the one to whom they are sent, consequently, since whatever is done contrary to the perfect right of another is a wrong, if they are not admitted a wrong is done to the sender, unless that occurs in case of a conflict of the duties of a nation towards itself and towards other nations.

§ 206.

De Jure Belli ac
Pacis, lib. 2,
c. 18, § 3.

Those who claim that it is merely a matter of choice whether or not anyone wishes to admit ambassadors, come to a rash decision, as is plainly evident from what we have just proved. But hasty decisions can scarcely be avoided, unless a system worthy of the name should be kept firmly fixed in mind, so that the truth fully understood in all its relations may, so to speak, ever float before our eyes. Grotius divides the reasons on account of which we are not bound to admit ambassadors into three classes, the first of which depends upon the one who sends the ambassador, the second on the one who is sent, the third, finally, on the purpose for which he is sent. Although, indeed, he is wrong in deriving the whole law of embassies from the acts of nations, as though none of it belonged to the necessary or natural law of nations, from this source he derives that threefold classification of just causes for which ambassadors can be rejected. It is quite plain that if you wish to decide whether the admittance of ambassadors conflicts with the duties of a nation towards itself, the special circumstances are to be considered, which are found in a given case, both in the one who sends the ambassador, and in the one who is sent and the purpose for which he is sent, together with your own present circumstances; but that the decision may be final, and not out of accord with truth, it is necessary that some duty towards yourself or your nation should be violated, if under such circumstances ambassadors were to be admitted. So it is quite evident that an ambassador is not to be admitted who is sent to disturb the peace of the state, nor if one should be sent who is guilty of the crime of treason, because this verges on contempt of the one to whom he is sent, nay more, on an offence against him, inasmuch as the right belonging to him to punish this atrocious crime is violated. In like manner, since reckless acts are not allowable according to the law of nature, ambassadors are properly rejected if it is already plain to us about what they are sent and we are unwilling to agree thereto. But we do not wish to tarry

§ 278, part 3,
Jus Nat.

on the details of these definitions. We merely give this warning that
when the need for admitting ambassadors is plain, if, for example,
they offer peace, no cause can be alleged why we should be unwilling
to admit them. But then also it is plain that the one to whom the
ambassador is sent has no duty towards himself or his nation with
which the admittance of the ambassador conflicts. Furthermore, this
also is to be considered, that it is one thing for an ambassador simply to be rejected, but another for the particular one to be rejected
who is sent, a situation which must be understood to exist when the
cause of rejection depends upon the character of the one who is sent.
And since, then, another person can be sent, the right of admitting
ambassadors is not yet violated if any one should desire that another
person should be sent, nor on this account can the one sending him
complain of a wrong done him. In the acts of nations, or of their rulers, not only are those things to be distinguished which must be done
by law from those which have been introduced only by custom, both
licit and illicit, but also from those which prudence suggests.

§ 1046. *Whether those allied by a treaty on unequal terms can send ambassadors*

Those allied by a treaty on unequal terms have the right to send ambassadors. For a nation which is allied to another by a treaty on unequal terms
is bound to perform more for the other than is performed by the other
for it. But in this there is no reason why rights ought to be taken from   § 398.
it which belong to other nations, and why the nation should not remain
free as it had been before. Therefore, since nations have the right to send
ambassadors to other nations, the same right also ought still to belong to   § 56, Ontol.
a nation which is allied to another by a treaty on unequal terms, to the   § 1044.
nation itself, that is, to which it is allied.

Of course, by a treaty on unequal terms the other nation gains a
right only to those things which have been promised in the treaty,
namely, that more should be performed for it than it is bound to
perform in return. Therefore, since it cannot claim for itself against
the nation which is allied to it by a treaty on unequal terms more than
it has gained by force of the treaty, by virtue of our previous proof

all reasons continue to exist for which nations have the right to send ambassadors. But all discussion in regard to the one who has the right to send legates has little weight in the law of nature, and owes its origin rather to the customary law of nations, by which many things have been introduced that do not belong to the law of nature, whether you consider the rights of ambassadors or their dignity and rank. The right to send ambassadors does not depend so much upon the personality of the sender as upon the business for which the ambassador is sent. For the need of the latter gives rise to the right to send ambassadors. But those things which are merely arbitrary are not found in the concepts themselves of things, nor are they a part of that right which has been established by nature.

§ 1047. *Of permanent ambassadors*

Permanent ambassadors are defined as those who reside for several years at foreign courts.

> Permanent embassies, such as are common to-day, have been intro-duced only in more recent times, previously they were unknown; and particularly in our extravagant period, especially since the splendour of royal luxury is assumed to be proper for ambassadors, they have to be supported at great expense.

§ 1048. *To what law they belong*

Since transactions between nations are not everyday affairs nor are they continuous, as is plain enough by virtue of our previous proof from the arguments which prove the need of embassies, and as the ancient custom to which permanent embassies were unknown abundantly proves, since, moreover, permanent ambassadors, as they reside at foreign courts, and observe what is done there and inquire into them and report them to him who sent them, are in the category of spies, consequently the reason fails on account of which nations have the right to send ambassadors; the right to have permanent ambassadors at foreign courts is not a natural right, nor does the voluntary law of nations, which is to be determined by the purpose of the supreme state, for mutual assistance, that is, in perfecting oneself and one's condition by promoting the common good

§ 1044.

Note, § 1048.

§ 883.
§ 1044.

§ 14.

by their combined powers, demand permanent embassies; consequently they do not belong to the customary law of nations. § 8.

The customary law of nations is not effective except among nations which approve of it by a certain tacit consent, consequently so long as it seems best to them, and since nations are free, and, therefore, no one in acting depends on the will of another, no nation for the sake of other nations is bound to approve of that which has been introduced by custom alone; consequently if any nation should be unwilling to abide longer by that, it must be allowed to stand by its decision.

§ 24.

§ 55, part 8,
Jus Nat.

§ 153, part 1,
Jus Nat.

§ 1049. *Whether permanent ambassadors must be admitted*

Since the right to permanent embassies at foreign courts is not a natural right, nor does the voluntary law of nations demand them, permanent embassies are rejected without violation of the necessary and voluntary law of nations, consequently, since no absolute right of the one wishing to send them is violated, no wrong is done to the one wishing to send them, if they are not admitted.

§ 1048.

§ 859, part 1,
Jus Nat.

It is evident from what we have just noted that custom does not stand in the way. For if any one should be unwilling to agree to that which prevails by custom alone, from this it simply follows that he himself cannot claim by virtue thereof some right that he does not allow to another; consequently in the present instance his permanent ambassadors are not to be admitted, if he himself should wish to send any. It cannot be said that this is done by the right of retaliation, as we have proved elsewhere that no such right exists; this arises from the right of natural liberty belonging to every nation, because of which he who now sends permanent ambassadors does not wish to admit those of another. Of course, when the customary right has been abrogated, which is considered a perfect right by virtue of a certain tacit consent, there is then no right to send permanent ambassadors, likewise no obligation to admit them. Therefore, there is no need of any special law by which it may be allowable not to admit them. Frequently the ruler of a state owes it to his nation both that he should not send permanent ambassadors and that he should not admit those sent by another, as is understood from those arguments by which we have

Note, § 1048.

§ 640, part 8,
Jus Nat.

§ 1048.

proved that permanent embassies do not belong to the law of nature nor to the voluntary law of nations.

§ 1050. *Who are to be sent as ambassadors*

§ 250.

§ 648, part 1, Jus Nat.

§ 538, part 1, Jus Nat.

§ 1041.

§ cited.

§ 332, part 1, Theol. Nat.

§ 194, part 1, Phil. Pract. Univ.

§ 204, part 1, Phil. Pract. Univ.

§ 203, part 1, Phil. Pract. Univ.

Those are to be sent as ambassadors who are eminent in rank in the state of the sender. For every ruler of a state ought to consider the ruler of another state as his equal. Therefore, since every one ought to show the respect to another which he deserves, consequently, the ruler of a state, when he has dealings with another, ought to show by his words and deeds that he considers him equal to himself, or as equally the ruler of a state; and since ambassadors are sent to the ruler of another state to transact some public business with him; by the very sending of ambassadors we ought to show that we recognize the one to whom they are sent as equally a ruler of a state, consequently as one who is eminent above other persons, both private and public. Therefore, since the sender as ruler of a state deals with a ruler of a state, it is especially fitting that those should be sent as ambassadors who are eminent in rank in the state of the sender; consequently this is in harmony with mutual propriety between nations. But there exists also a natural law of propriety, and this obliges us to prefer polite to impolite action. Therefore, those are to be sent who are eminent in rank in the state of the sender.

§ 250.

Therefore it is not a matter of mere custom that men of the first rank should be sent as ambassadors, but it is especially in harmony with the law of nature, which desires that attention should be given not only to the business for which ambassadors are sent but also to the persons who manage it. Business is conducted by an ambassador either with the king himself or with the most important ministers to whom the duty is entrusted. If, then, the sender ought to recognize the one to whom he sends an ambassador as his equal, in the management of the business, he ought to employ those who, if not equal in rank, are, nevertheless, not too much below him, therefore, men of the first rank in his own state. Questions of prudence belong to politics. But it is in harmony therewith that frequently some attention should be paid to opinion as well as to the customs also which depend upon opinion, as far as this can be done without contravention of duty.

§ 1051. *How ambassadors are to be received and treated*

Ambassadors are to be received and treated with respect. This is shown in the same way in which we have proved the preceding proposition.

Not only does the natural equality of rulers of a state demand this, but those things also are to be considered here which arise accidentally, especially things that are permanent, as they pass over to successors.

§ 250.
Note, §§ 249, 250.

§ 1052. *If they come from an enemy*

Since ambassadors are to be received and treated with respect, and since this obligation, being derived from the laws of nature, is natural and therefore unchangeable, consequently is not changed by the fact that the sender and the one to whom the ambassador is sent are enemies, ambassadors even when sent by an enemy are to be received and treated with respect.

§ 1051.

§ 186.

The respect which rulers of states owe to each other is not incompatible with war. Both parties, the sender as well as the one to whom the ambassador is sent, continue to be rulers each of his own state, even if there is war between them, since they are waging it as rulers, consequently even if they are enemies. In war we seek our right by force from another, but this pursuit of our right by force does not demand that we should refuse another the respect which is his due. For this denial accomplishes nothing in the attainment of our right. As we ought to love and cherish our enemy as ourselves, but certainly not to hate him, and as hostilities do not put an end to the duties which we owe others, consequently, not to the respect due to them; so much less does war, which can and ought to be waged without hatred of the participants, prevent an enemy from showing the respect to an enemy which is due. It is a vulgar error, and from it vulgar customs arise, that he is unworthy of respect with whom we have a quarrel. But the customs of those whom fortune has lifted above the lot of other men to the Gods above ought to be removed by all the greater interval from this vulgar error.

§ 614.
§ 722.
§ 1002, part 1, Jus Nat.

§ 632, part 1, Jus Nat.

§§ 620, 624, part 1, Jus Nat.
§ 648, part 1, Jus Nat.
§ 1119, part 1, Jus Nat.
Note, § 722.

§ 1053. *Whether it is allowable to insult or despise them*

Since ambassadors sent by the enemy are to be received and treated with respect, and since insults are the opposite of respect, insults are not to be

§ 1052.
§§ 538, 811, 812, part 1, Jus Nat.

§ 722, part 1,
Jus Nat.

§ 860, part 1,
Jus Nat.
offered to ambassadors sent by the enemy, consequently he who insults them does a wrong to the sender. In the same way the same thing is understood of contempt for ambassadors sent by the enemy.

§§ 787, 860,
part 1, Jus Nat.

§ 790, part 1,
Jus Nat.

§ 852, part 1,
Jus Nat.

§ 810, part 1,
Jus Nat.
Since nations employ the law of nature in their relations with each other, those points which we have proved elsewhere in regard to not despising others, or loading them with insults can, nay ought to, be applied to them. It is scarcely necessary for me to suggest that it is no excuse that like is returned for like, were it not that there are some who excuse wrong under the specious plea of the right of retaliation.

§ 1054. *How the law of nature provides for the dignity of the one who sends and the one who receives ambassadors*

§ 1050.

§ 1051.

§ 1053.
Since it is in accordance with the law of nature, not only that those persons should be sent as ambassadors who are eminent in rank in the state, but also that those sent should be received and treated with respect, even if they should be sent by an enemy; the law of nature provides for the dignity of the sender and of the one to whom an ambassador is sent.

§ 135, part 1,
Phil. Pract.
Univ.
The law of nature flows from the essence and nature of men as from its source, as is perceived very clearly from a system worthy of its name, such as we have established. Therefore, those whom it makes equals it also provides for equally.

§ 1055. *Of the representative character of the ambassador*

§ 1042.

§ 661, part 4,
Jus Nat.
The representative character of an ambassador is defined as the token of the representation of the sender before the one to whom he is sent. Since by the law of nature ambassadors are mandataries of the ruler of the state from whom they are sent, consequently they represent the person of the sender as regards the business committed to them by him, so far as they act in the name and by the right of the sender, as if it were done by him himself present in person; by the law of nature representative character consists in the power to do in the name and by the right of the sovereign power any public business with another sovereign power. Therefore, it does not belong to this right to extend the representation to the dignity itself of the sender, or his majesty, consequently by the law of nature an

ambassador is not the same moral person as the sender, so that it would §206, part 8, be just as if the sender himself were present and the other, to whom he is Jus Nat. sent, ought to consider him as equal to himself or equally the ruler of the §250. state. Therefore, a special representative character, which is defined as the power of bearing the personality of the sender, is not a part of the law of nature, and since there is no need of it either from the business to be done or from the dignity of the sender, which can be assured without it, it does not belong to the voluntary law of nations; but if introduced by customs §1052. it is a part of the customary law, and if introduced by agreement, it is a §22. part of the stipulative law. Although that fictitious and assumed character, §24. which inheres in an ambassador by the nature of things, is called special §23. in distinction from natural, it is here called common, because it belongs to every ambassador as such, and cannot be separated from him.

The law which has been established by nature itself disregards those things which have been invented in regard to property and persons by the fancy of men either by mistake or by the impulse of an erratic mind. For that law never turns away from the necessary relation of all things, so that the righteousness which it demands in the case of individuals is observed in the whole structure of all human actions, and this righteousness cannot be perfect, unless it should be referred §189, part 1, to other actions related to the one given. Therefore, it does not allow, Phil. Pract. Univ. without reason, a departure from its strict rule in the positive or civil law, and just as it prescribes from what source reasons are to be taken in the civil law for permitting a departure from that rule, so it commands that the same rule be observed in the voluntary law of nations, §991, part 8, nor does it approve generally of the stipulative and customary law, Jus Nat. since it is never at variance with itself. But it is not now our purpose to weigh special representative character on the scales of reason. This §22. belongs to civil policy, which is controlled by universal public law. §§23, 24.

§ 1056. Of those things which flow from special representative character, or are superadded to it

Since special representative character is not a part of the law of nature, nor of the voluntary law of nations, those things concerning ambas- §1055. sadors which are derived as a necessary consequence from their special

representative character are not a part of the law of nature nor of the
voluntary law of nations, and much less are those things which are added
gratuitously to expand it.

Just as those who reason badly claim many things on account of
extrinsic reasons, when intrinsic reasons derived from the very concepts of things are lacking, so the same thing happens in regard to the
special representative character of ambassadors. Since that depends
altogether on freedom of invention, whatever may seem best may be
added to it, and among men of contradictory character the things
which involve a contradiction can be excused, provided only they are
not physically impossible.

§ 1057. *Whether nations are bound to recognize it*

§ 1056.

In like manner, since special representative character is not a part of the
natural law of nations, either necessary or voluntary; no nation is bound
to recognize it unless by agreement.

§ 382, part 3,
Jus Nat.

§ 23, part 1,
Jus Nat.

§ 859, part 1,
Jus Nat.

§ 1051.

§ 1053.

It does not depend solely upon the will of the sender what character
he may wish to impress upon his ambassador; for no one can bind
another beyond his will and acquire against him any right which cannot be gained without his consent. If, then, any one does not wish to
recognize that right, nor to do the things which proceed from it or
are annexed to it, he does no wrong to the sender, provided only he
does not refuse to give due respect to the ambassador, nor hold him in
contempt or heap insults upon him.

§ 1058. *How ambassadors are regarded in respect to their*
private acts

§ 1055.

By the natural law of nations ambassadors are regarded in respect to
their private acts as foreigners living in alien territory. For by the natural
law of nations ambassadors represent the person of the sender as regards
the business for which they are sent; consequently as regards those acts
which are required to conduct that business they differ from other foreigners, who are living as private individuals in alien territory for business of their own, but as regards their own private acts, which have no

bearing upon that business, they do not differ from other foreigners. Therefore, in respect to those acts they cannot be regarded otherwise than as foreigners living in alien territory.

An ambassador as an ambassador is not admitted except for the public business which has been entrusted to him. Therefore, he can be regarded as ambassador only in respect to the acts necessary for transacting that business; in respect to other matters, therefore, not affecting this, or in respect to private matters, since he cannot be regarded as an ambassador, there is nothing left except to look on him as a foreigner who is living in alien territory, nor does his admittance as ambassador make any change as regards his private acts. His admittance involves nothing except that he, to whom he is sent, is willing to do those things which the matter entrusted to him demands, observing due respect to him as ambassador. If prudence suggests anything besides, that is not a matter of law.

§ 1041.

§ 1051.

§ 1059. *Of the extraterritoriality of an ambassador*

Since by the natural law of nations ambassadors are regarded in respect to their private acts as foreigners living in alien territory, extraterritoriality, by which ambassadors with their retinue and their baggage or property are assumed to live outside the territory, and the houses in which they reside are assumed to be outside the territory, is not a provision of the natural law of nations, and since without it the business entrusted to an ambassador could be transacted, there is indeed no extrinsic reason why there should be a departure from the law of nature in this respect; and, therefore, this extraterritoriality is not a part of the voluntary law of nations, consequently it cannot be acquired except by stipulation, either express or tacit, subject to the exception in the case of conflict with the duty of the one to whom he has been sent toward his own nation.

§ 1058.

§ 22 h and § 991, part 8, Jus Nat.

§ 206.

Those who derive the extraterritoriality of an ambassador from their so-called representative or special character are greatly mistaken, since it does not follow from this. Indeed, the king himself is not a king except in his own territory, but in alien territory he is regarded as a private individual, except in so far as such respect is shown to him as is properly due to the ruler of a state. For just as in his own territory

§ 250.

§ 285, part 8,
Jus Nat.

the king is looked on as a private person in respect to his private acts, so much the more ought he to be looked on as a private person in alien territory in which he has no right to any royal act, a fact which is self-evident. Assume, therefore, that an ambassador represents the person of the sender so far as regards rank, nevertheless, you may not fashion extraterritoriality out of that. This must be referred to those things which are fashioned out of the so-called representative character. But it is another question whether or not it is wise to determine by agreements some of the things which are improperly derived from extraterritoriality. But that is foreign to our present design.

§ 1060. *Of the jurisdiction over the person, the retinue, and the baggage of an ambassador*

§ 1058.

§ 300.

§ 302.

§ 1059.

Since by the natural law of nations ambassadors are regarded in respect to their private acts as foreigners living in alien territory, and since the acts of foreigners are subject to the laws of the place, and the effect of the laws as regards them is the same as in the case of citizens, if foreigners commit an offence, they are to be punished according to the laws of the place and their controversies concerning their right are to be decided by the judge of the place in accordance with the same laws; ambassadors, therefore, in respect to their private acts, together with their retinue and their baggage or property, by the natural law of nations are subject to the jurisdiction of the place both civil and criminal, and as is before evident, no change has been made by the voluntary law of nations in regard to these matters. From this, then, it is clear that their baggage can even be put in pledge for debts contracted.

In the retinue are included wife, children, servants, officials: such as a minister of religion, physician, and secretary of legation; in the baggage anything serving the necessity, comfort, and pleasure of life.

§ 1061. *Of the independence of an ambassador of the sovereignty of the one to whom he is sent*

§ 1060.

Since in respect to their private acts ambassadors together with their retinue and baggage are subject to the jurisdiction of the one to whom they are sent, the independence of the ambassador of the sovereignty of the one to whom he is sent, as long as he lives in his territory, is not a part of the natural and voluntary law of nations; consequently it is not a part of that law, that he should have jurisdiction over his retinue, much less does the right of asylum in the house where the ambassador resides belong to him.

The independence of the sovereignty of the one to whom an ambassador is sent and the right of extraterritoriality are the reciprocals of each other. Therefore, what has been said of the one must also be understood of the other.   § 1059.

§ 1062. *Of the assumed sanctity of an ambassador*

Because the independence of an ambassador of the sovereignty of one to whom he is sent is not a part of the natural or voluntary law of nations, § 1061. therefore, the inviolability or the sanctity of the independence of an ambassador of the sovereignty of the one to whom he is sent is not a part of the common law of all nations.

Those who claim that the sanctity of an ambassador is a part of the common law of all nations imagine a right which does not exist. If anything of that sort belongs to an ambassador, it all arises from the concession of the one to whom he is sent, and since it cannot have its source in anything other than an agreement, either express or tacit, if anything is done contrary to that sanctity, the wrong consists in the violation of the agreement. If, then, anything is done in violation of it, it cannot be said that the law of nations has been violated, but the act is contrary to an express pledge of faith or is contrary to an accepted custom, as the independence has either been agreed upon by a stipulation, or is observed by custom.

§ 1063. *Of the assurance of security to foreigners*
in one's territory

Foreigners, as long as they live in alien territory, ought to be safe from every injury, and the ruler of the state is bound to defend them against it, that is, security is to be assured to foreigners living in alien territory. For as long as foreigners live in alien territory they are temporary citizens. § 303.

§ 532, part 8,
Jus Nat.
Therefore, since the ruler of a state ought to see to it that every one is safe from injury by others, foreigners also, as long as they live in alien territory, ought to be safe from every injury. Which was the first point.

§ 535, part 8,
Jus Nat.
§ 573, part 8,
Jus Nat.
§ 303.
For in a state also care must be taken that each one should be given his own right, and if the wrong cannot be repaired, he who did it is to be punished. Therefore, since the ruler of a state ought to defend his citizens against the wrongs of others, he is bound to defend foreigners also against any wrongs as long as they live in his territory. Which was the second point.

Each of these points is also shown in this way. The ruler of a state
§ 317.
ought not to allow any one of his subjects to cause a loss or do a wrong to
§ 318.
the citizen of another nation, and if this has been done, he ought to compel him to repair the loss caused and to punish him; unless he does this,
§ 316.
since he tacitly approves of the act, the nation itself must be assumed to have done the wrong or inflicted the injury. Therefore, since foreigners living in alien territory remain citizens of their own nation, notwith-
§ 324.
Note, § cited.
standing that in respect to certain acts they are regarded as temporary citizens in that territory, foreigners, as long as they live in alien territory, ought to be safe from every injury and the ruler of the state is bound to defend them from injuries.

Finally, that security is to be assured to foreigners living in alien territory is proved in general in this way. Since the ruler of a territory is not supposed to allow foreigners to live in his territory, except on the condition that their actions should be subject to the laws of the place, and
§ 299.
since they tacitly bind themselves to this on entering it, between the ruler
§ 300.
of the territory and the foreigner living in it there exists a tacit agreement, by which the latter promises temporary obedience, the former protec-
§ 555.
tion. Therefore, since tacit agreements of that sort are to be observed,
§ 556.
the ruler of the territory is bound to protect foreigners, consequently not to allow them to be injured contrary to the right common to all
§ 695, part 1,
Jus Nat.
men by nature. But if he does not allow foreigners living in his territory to be injured by others, he assures security to them. Therefore, the ruler
§ 917, part 1,
Jus Nat.
of a state is bound to assure security to foreigners living in his territory. Which was the third point.

By the law of nature foreigners in alien territory are safe from injury, in so far as the right of security belongs to every man by nature, and

the ruler of the territory takes upon himself the protection of the for- §918, part 1, Jus Nat.
eigner by allowing him the right to enter it and live in it, and the protection, therefore, rests upon tacit good faith, which is sacred among
nations, consequently it certainly ought to be free from every viola- §456.
tion. Since by the very fact that the ruler of the state admits foreigners §556.
into his territory and permits them to live there, he receives them into
the number of citizens for the time during which indeed they live
there, he owes the same protection to them as to his own citizens. And §303.
since by nature foreigners have the right for just reasons to live for a
time in alien territory, a right which cannot be denied except in case §692, part 6, Jus Nat.
of conflict of duties toward one's own nation and other nations; by the
law of nature itself he is therefore bound to give security to foreigners,
to whom he has granted the right to exercise their privilege of living in §206 h and §64, part 1, Jus Nat.
his territory, when he has no just reason for forbidding it. Therefore,
by the law of nature sufficient provision is made for the security of
foreigners living in alien territory for a lawful purpose.

§ 1064. *Of the security of ambassadors*

Ambassadors are entitled to security not only by the law of general
application to foreigners but also by the law peculiar to ambassadors,
even if they come from the enemy. Ambassadors have a dual personality,
namely, that of a private person as regards their private acts, but that of
a public person as ambassadors, as having been sent by their own nation
to another nation on some affair of state. §1041.

Since by the natural law of nations ambassadors are regarded in
respect to their private acts as foreigners living in alien territory, since, §1058.
moreover, security is to be assured to foreigners living in alien territory,
the same must be assured to ambassadors also. Therefore, ambassadors §1063.
are entitled to security by the law of general application to foreigners in
alien territory. Which was the first point.

But since the law of nature provides for the dignity of the sender §1054.
also, and, therefore, ambassadors are to be received and treated with §1051.
respect, a wrong done to ambassadors ought to be considered more serious than one done to a foreigner who is a private individual, in so far as
the former is directed in a way at the sender, whose dignity ought to be
a special incentive not only to those who act, to be on their guard lest
they do wrong, but also to him, to whom the ambassador has been sent,

to object vigorously and effectively to the wrong and guard against it in every way. And when an ambassador is admitted, that is, he to whom he is sent agrees that he should come to him as ambassador, he also tacitly promises both the respect due to an ambassador, and also that special security. Therefore, since the obligation arises even from the tacit agreement no less than from the express one, and since when this obligation is added to the natural one it makes it stronger, a certain special security belongs to ambassadors because of the law peculiar to them. Which was the second point.

§ 658, part 1, Phil. Pract. Univ. § 560.

Finally, since by the above proof, by which we have shown the right to send ambassadors, it is apparent that there is no less need for sending ambassadors in time of war than in time of peace, and although they come from an enemy, they nevertheless do not come as enemies because they do not come with the intention of doing any hostile act, and, therefore, they are to be received and treated with respect just as if they came as ambassadors in time of peace; it is evident in the same way as before, that ambassadors, even if they should be sent by an enemy to an enemy, have the right to security not only by the law of general application to foreigners, but also by the law peculiar to ambassadors: a thing which is so much the plainer, if safe passage should be given by the one who admits them, since in this case the security of one living in hostile territory is assured him also because of the concession, even if otherwise it should not be contained in it. Which was the third point.

§ 1044.

§ 1052.

Points 1 and 2.

§ 937.

§ 947.

Not from any so-called representative character nor from any fictitious extraterritoriality is the security of ambassadors derived, either of the general or special type, but from the fundamental principles of the law of nature, a point which we trust has been established by us. But it is evident from those proofs which we have brought forward that there exists also a natural law of embassies, which nations are bound to use in their relations with each other, that does not in fact depend wholly upon their will. And hence, furthermore, is understood when ambassadors are injured contrary to the law of nations, which ought to be held sacred among nations, since it is in itself unchangeable, so that the most serious complaints concerning its violation are justifiable, nor may one offer an excuse for its violation, which customs seem to allow too readily.

§ 546.

§ 1065. *Of the sanctity of ambassadors*

Since ambassadors are entitled to security by the law peculiar to themselves, so that the public welfare of nations demands that it be immune   § 1064.
from every violation, as the necessity for embassies, which gives rise to
the right to send ambassadors in time of war and peace, abundantly
proves and previous demonstrations more fully confirm; since, more-   § 1044.
over, that is sacred which the public welfare of nations demands should   § 1064.
be immune from every violation; the security of ambassadors is sacred,   § 546.
and, therefore, their person also is to be considered sacred, and this sanctity is transferred from their person even to their equipment and retinue.

And this is that genuine sanctity, which the law of all nations protects, which is not fashioned by the will of men, but which has God
Himself as its source, He who is the author of the law of nature. But   § 273, part 1,
it in no way affects this sanctity, that ambassadors are not indepen-   Phil. Pract. Univ.
dent of the sovereignty of the one to whom they are sent, but rather
are subject to his jurisdiction as regards their private acts; for that
perfectly just law provides no less for the security of him to whom an   § 1061.
ambassador is sent and for his citizens, than for that of the ambassa-   § 1060.
dors, just as it also properly provides for both the dignity of the sender
and of him to whom the ambassador is sent. This law is also perfectly
plain, so that it needs no qualification such as the laws determined by   § 1053.
the will of men demand. And although the sanctity of ambassadors
which we have proved rests also upon the tacit good faith of the one
admitting them, nevertheless, since the law of nature demands this,
as is evident from previous proofs, it renders that good faith itself also
sacred. There is no need that an ambassador should be independent   § 556.
of the sovereignty of the one to whom he is sent, and not subject to
his jurisdiction; for he can show himself independent, if he refrains
from those acts which are subject to his jurisdiction, and unless he
does this, he does not consider his own dignity nor that of the one
sending him. It is not at all fitting that an ambassador inflict injury
on those among whom he lives, or fail to pay that which he owes on
a contract, so that there should be need that a suit be brought against
him or that his goods be put in pawn when he is ready to leave. But
it is much more unfitting for him to offend in such a way that there

should be need of public censure, or for him to commit crimes which are worthy of more serious penalty. He who wishes to be considered sacred ought to shrink from doing wrongs to others. And he who desires to be honoured for the sake of the one who sends him ought to strive with every effort to show himself worthy of the honour itself. But if in spite of these things the ambassador should be injured, the wrong done to him is made so much the more serious and will be so considered by the judgement of all right-thinking men.

§ 1066. *Of the stipulative and customary law of ambassadors*

If any nations have agreed with each other upon certain laws of embassies and upon the method of treating ambassadors with respect, or have introduced certain things by their customs, those provisions bind only the contracting parties and those nations by whose long usage these customs have been introduced, as long as they are willing. Since no one can bind others beyond their will or acquire any right against them, but since nations can bind themselves to each other absolutely by stipulations, if any nations have agreed with each other upon certain laws of embassies and upon the method of treating ambassadors with respect, or have introduced certain things by their customs which are equivalent to a tacit agreement, those provisions bind the contracting parties, but not other nations which have not entered into the stipulation, and those who have accepted those customs, but not other nations which have not tacitly agreed to them. Which was the first point.

§ 382, part 3, Jus Nat.

§§ 377 h, 393, 368, part 3, Jus Nat.

But since stipulations can be abrogated by the contracting parties, if they should be unwilling to abide by them, and since no reason compels nations to observe faithfully and continuously customs introduced by their predecessors, if any nations have agreed with each other upon certain laws of embassies and upon the method of treating ambassadors with respect, or have introduced certain things by their customs, those provisions are valid, as long as they are willing. Which was the second point.

§ 839, part 3, Jus Nat.

The law of embassies, such as is now in use, is almost wholly to be referred to customary and stipulative law, and is contained in the doctrine of representative character and extraterritoriality, which as sources of the law of embassies the natural law of nations and the general voluntary law of all ignore, as is evident from what precedes. It is not for us to write a history of the law of embassies, but to show what the immutable law of nature enjoins or forbids in regard to embassies, and to distinguish this from the stipulative and customary law.

§ 1067. *Of credentials*

Credentials are defined as those documents which the sender gives an ambassador, directed to the one to whom he is sent, and in which he declares that he is his ambassador. Since certain business is to be trans- §1041. acted with the ambassador, and, therefore, the one to whom the ambassador is sent ought to understand concerning the will of the sender, the ambassador must be instructed in his credentials, and since he is the man- §1042. datary of the sender the credentials contain the sender's express mandate. §652, part 4, Jus Nat.

Hence it is easily understood what things are to be introduced into the credentials.

§ 1068. *When an ambassador ceases to be such*

If an ambassador is recalled by the sender, or if the sender or the one to whom he is sent dies, the ambassador ceases to be an ambassador. For when he is recalled by the sender, the sender declares that he does not desire that the one who had been sent as an ambassador should any longer perform the function of an ambassador. Therefore, since the ambassador gets all his right from the sender and acts in dependence upon his will with the one to whom he has been sent in the name of the sender §1042. as his mandatary; if the sender recalls an ambassador he ceases to be an ambassador. Which was the first point.

In like manner, because the ambassador is a mandatary of the sender, §1042. and since a mandate is extinguished by the death of the principal, on the §754, part 4, death of the sender he who had been an ambassador ceases to be such. Jus Nat. Which was the second point.

Finally, since the ambassador has been given the right to act with the one to whom he is sent only in regard to the matter entrusted to him; and since as mandatary of the sender he can do nothing contrary to the §1041.

§ 1042.

§ 673, part 4,
Jus Nat.

scope of his mandate, and therefore, it is not plain whether the sender would wish to act with his successor concerning that matter, or through him whom he had sent; on the death of the one to whom an ambassador had been sent he ceases to be an ambassador. Which was the third point.

It is necessary to know how long the ambassador is to be considered as such, since nothing is validly done with him, except so long as he retains the character of ambassador. And, therefore, if an embassy is to be continued with the successor of the one to whom the ambassador had been sent, there is need of new credentials, which he also needs if the sender should have died. This is above all necessary in the permanent embassies which are in use to-day.

§ 1067.

THE END OF THE LAW OF NATIONS

BIBLIOGRAPHY

Primary Sources by Christian Wolff

Aërometriae elementa. Leipzig, 1709.

"Christiani Wolfii . . . Oratio de *Sinarum philosophia practica.*" In Christian Wolff, *Meletemata mathematico-philosophica quibus accedunt dissertationes,* "Sectio III. Scripturas Wolfianas varii argumenti continens velut programmata, orationes, epistolas, praefationes," pp. 22–126. Reprint of 1755 edition. Hildesheim: Georg Olms, 1974. Also reprinted as "Discourse on the Practical Philosophy of the Chinese (1721–26)." In *Moral Enlightenment: Leibniz and Wolff on China,* edited by Julia Ching and Willard G. Oxtoby, pp. 145–86. Monumenta Serica 26. Nettetal: Steyler Verlag, 1992.

Christian Wolffs eigene Lebensbeschreibung. Edited by Heinrich Wuttke. Leipzig: Weidmann, 1841.

Cosmologia generalis, methodo scientifica pertractata, qua ad solidam, inprimis Dei atque naturae cognitionem via sternitur. Frankfurt, 1731.

Jus naturae methodo scientifica pertractatum. 8 vols. Frankfurt and Leipzig/ Halle and Magdeburg, 1740–48.

Jus naturae methodo scientifica pertractatum. Reprint of 1740–48 edition, edited by Marcel Thomann. 8 vols. Hildesheim: Georg Olms, 1968.

Philosophia moralis sive ethica, methodo scientifica pertractata. 5 vols. Halle, 1750–53.

Philosophia practica universalis, mathematica methodo conscripta. Leipzig, 1703.

"Philosophia practica universalis, mathematica methodo conscripta." In Christian Wolff, *Meletemata mathematico-philosophica quibus accedunt dissertationes.* Reprint of 1755 edition. Hildesheim: Georg Olms, 1974.

Philosophia practica universalis, methodo scientifica pertractata. Frankfurt and Leipzig, 1738–39.

Philosophia prima sive ontologia methodo scientifica pertractata. Frankfurt and Leipzig, 1730.

Philosophia rationalis sive logica. Reprint of 1740 edition, edited by J. École. 3 vols. Hildesheim: Georg Olms, 1983.

Philosophia rationalis sive logica, methodo scientifica pertractata. Frankfurt and Leipzig, 1728.

Psychologia empirica, methodo scientifica pertractata. Frankfurt, 1732.

Psychologia rationalis, methodo scientifica pertractata. Frankfurt, 1734.

Theologia naturalis, methodo scientifica pertractata. Frankfurt, 1736–37.

Vernünftige Gedanken von dem gesellschaftlichen Leben der Menschen und insonderheit dem gemeinen Wesen zur Beförderung der Glückseligkeit des menschlichen Geschlechtes mitgeteilt. Halle, 1721.

Vernünftige Gedanken von der Menschen Thun und Lassen. Halle, 1720.

Vernünftige Gedanken von Gott, der Welt und der Seele des Menschen, auch allen Dingen überhaupt. Halle, 1720.

Primary Sources by Other Authors

Alexander ab Alexandro. *Genialium dierum libri sex.* Frankfurt, 1604.

Augustine, Saint Aurelius. *Sancti Aurelii Augustini quaestionum in Heptateuchum libri VII adnotationum in Iob liber unus.* Edited by Iosephus Zycha. Prague: F. Tempsky; Leipzig: G. Freytag, 1895.

Breuning, Christian Heinrich, ed. *Verordnungen, und Constitutiones, den rechtlichen Prozess und andere streitige Faelle betreffende. Wie auch des Durchlauchtigsten Hochgebohrnen Fuersten und Herrn, Herrn Johann Georgen des Andern, . . . Decisiones Electorales Saxonicae, oder Erledigung derer Zweifelhafften Rechts-Faelle.* Leipzig, 1746.

Campanella, Tommaso. *La città del sole: Dialogo poetico / The City of the Sun: A Poetical Dialogue.* Translated by Daniel J. Donno. Berkeley: University of California Press, 1981.

Carpzov, Benedict. *Jurisprudentia forensis Romano-Saxonica. Editio V.* Leipzig, 1668.

———. *Practica nova rerum criminalium imperialis Saxonica.* Leipzig, 1723.

———. *Processus juris in foro Saxonico.* Leipzig, 1708.

Cicero, Marcus Tullius. *On Duties.* Edited by M. T. Griffin and E. M. Atkins. Cambridge: Cambridge University Press, 1991.

————. *On the Republic. On the Laws.* Translated by Clinton W. Keyes. Cambridge, Mass.: Harvard University Press, 1928.

————. *Pro Archia. Post reditum in Senatu. Post reditum ad Quirites. De domo sua. De haruspicum responsis. Pro Plancio.* Translated by N. H. Watts. Cambridge, Mass.: Harvard University Press, 1923.

Conring, Hermann. *Opera.* 6 vols. Brunswick, 1730.

Descartes, René. *A Discourse on the Method.* Edited and translated by Ian Maclean. Oxford: Oxford University Press, 2006.

Diodorus of Sicily. *The Library of History.* Edited and translated by C. H. Oldfather. 12 vols. London: William Heinemann, 1933–67.

Flaccus, Verrius, and Sextus Pompeius Festus. *De verborum significatione libri XX ex editione Andreae Dacerii cum notis et interpretatione in usum delphini.* 2 vols. London: A. J. Valpy, 1826.

Gellius, Aulus. *The Attic Nights.* Edited and translated by John C. Rolfe. 3 vols. London: William Heinemann, 1927–28.

Grotius, Hugo. *De Jure Belli ac Pacis Libri Tres.* Edited by J. F. Gronovius. Amsterdam, 1712.

————. *The Rights of War and Peace.* Edited by Richard Tuck. 3 vols. Indianapolis: Liberty Fund, 2005.

Justinian. *Digest.* Edited by Alan Watson. Philadelphia: University of Pennsylvania Press, 1998.

————. *Institutes.* Translated and with an introduction by Peter Birks and Grant McLeod with Latin text by Paul Krueger. London: Duckworth, 1987.

Justinus. *Epitome of the Philippic History of Pompeius Trogus.* Translated by J. C. Yardley, introduction and notes by R. Develin. Atlanta, Ga.: Scholars Press, 1994.

Leibniz, G. W. *Opera philosophica quae exstant Latina Gallica Germanica omnia.* Edited by J. E. Erdmann. Berlin: G. Eichler, 1840.

Livy. *From the Founding of the City.* Translated by B. O. Foster. 14 vols. London: William Heinemann; Cambridge, Mass.: Harvard University Press, 1919–59.

Plutarch. *Plutarch's Lives.* Translated by Bernadotte Perrin. 11 vols. London: William Heinemann; New York: G. P. Putnam's Sons, 1914–26.

Pufendorf, Samuel. *Two Books of the Elements of Universal Jurisprudence.* Edited by Thomas Behme. Indianapolis: Liberty Fund, 2009.

Spinoza, Benedict de. *Theological-Political Treatise*. Edited by J. Israel and translated by Michael Silverthorne and Jonathan Israel. Cambridge: Cambridge University Press, 2007.

Stephanus, Robertus. *Thesaurus linguae Latinae*. Basel, 1740.

Strabo. *The Geography of Strabo*. Translated by Horace Leonard Jones and J. R. Sitlington Sterrett. 8 vols. London: William Heinemann; New York: G. P. Putnam's Sons, 1917–32.

Thomasius, Christian. *Essays on Church, State, and Politics*. Edited and translated by Ian Hunter, Thomas Ahnert, and Frank Grunert. Indianapolis: Liberty Fund, 2007.

———. *Institutes of Divine Jurisprudence, with Selections from the Foundations of the Law of Nature and Nations*. Edited and translated by Thomas Ahnert. Indianapolis: Liberty Fund, 2011.

Tschirnhaus, Ehrenfried Walther von. *Medicina mentis, sive tentamen genuinae logicae, in qua disseritur de methodo detegendi incognitas veritates*. Amsterdam, 1687.

Vattel, Emer de. *The Law of Nations*. Edited by Béla Kapossy and Richard Whatmore. Indianapolis: Liberty Fund, 2008.

Weigel, Erhard. *Philosophia mathematica, theologia naturalis solida*. Edited by Thomas Behme. Stuttgart–Bad Cannstatt: Frommann–Holzboog, 2013.

Secondary Sources

Ahnert, Thomas. *Religion and the Origins of the German Enlightenment: Faith and the Reform of Learning in the Thought of Christian Thomasius*. Rochester, N.Y.: Rochester University Press, 2006.

Arndt, Hans-Werner. *Methodo scientifica pertractatum: Mos geometricus und Kalkülbegriff in der philosophischen Theoriebildung des 17. und 18. Jahrhunderts*. Berlin: Walter de Gruyter, 1971.

Beck, Lewis White. *Early German Philosophy: Kant and His Predecessors*. Bristol: Thoemmes Press, 1996.

Bianco, Bruno. "Freiheit gegen Fatalismus: Zu Joachim Langes Kritik an Wolff." In *Aufklärung und Pietismus*, edited by Norbert Hinske, pp. 111–55. Heidelberg: Lambert Schneider, 1989.

Gaukroger, Stephen. "Picturability and Mathematical Ideals of Knowledge." In *The Oxford Handbook of Philosophy in Early Modern Europe*, edited by

Desmond Clarke and Catherine Wilson, pp. 338–60. Oxford: Oxford University Press, 2011.

Guicciardini, Niccolo. *Reading the Principia: The Debate on Newton's Mathematical Methods for Natural Philosophy from 1687 to 1736.* Cambridge: Cambridge University Press, 1999.

Haakonssen, Knud. "Christian Wolff (1679–1754)." In *The Oxford Handbook of the History of International Law,* edited by Bardo Fassbender, Anne Peters, Simone Peter, and Daniel Högger, pp. 1106–9. Oxford: Oxford University Press, 2012.

———. "German Natural Law." In *The Cambridge History of Eighteenth-Century Political Thought,* edited by Mark Goldie and Robert Wokler, pp. 251–90. Cambridge: Cambridge University Press, 2006.

———. "Samuel Pufendorf (1632–1694)." In *The Oxford Handbook of the History of International Law,* edited by Bardo Fassbender, Anne Peters, Simone Peter, and Daniel Högger, pp. 1102–5. Oxford: Oxford University Press, 2012.

Hellmuth, Eckhart. *Naturrechtsphilosophie und bürokratischer Wertehorizont: Studien zur preußischen Geistes- und Sozialgeschichte des 18. Jahrhunderts.* Göttingen: Vandenhoeck und Ruprecht, 1985.

Hinrichs, Carl. *Preußentum und Pietismus.* Göttingen: Vandenhoeck und Ruprecht, 1971.

Hochstrasser, Tim. *Natural Law Theories in the Early Enlightenment.* Cambridge: Cambridge University Press, 2000.

Hüning, Dieter. "Christian Wolffs Begriff der natürlichen Verbindlichkeit als Bindeglied zwischen Psychologie und Moralphilosophie." In *Die Psychologie Christian Wolffs: Systematische und historische Untersuchungen,* edited by Oliver-Pierre Rudolph and Jean-François Goubet, pp. 143–67. Tübingen: Max Niemeyer, 2004.

Hunter, Ian. *Rival Enlightenments: Civil and Metaphysical Philosophy in Early Modern Germany.* Cambridge: Cambridge University Press, 2001.

Israel, Jonathan. *Radical Enlightenment: Philosophy and the Making of Modernity.* Oxford: Oxford University Press, 2001.

Saine, Thomas P. "Who's afraid of Christian Wolff?" In *Anticipations of the Enlightenment in England, France and Germany,* edited by Alan Charles Kors and Paul J. Korshin, pp. 102–33. Philadelphia: University of Pennsylvania Press, 1987.

Thomann, Marcel. Introduction to *Jus Gentium* (1749) by Christian Wolff, edited by Marcel Thomann, pp. vii–li. Hildesheim: Georg Olms, 1972.

Tuck, Richard. *The Rights of War and Peace: Political Thought and the International Order from Grotius to Kant*. Oxford: Oxford University Press, 1999.

Wiesenfeldt, Gerhard. *Leerer Raum in Minervas Haus: Experimentelle Naturlehre an der Universität Leiden, 1675–1715*. Amsterdam: Koninklijke Nederlandse Akademie der Wetenschappen; Berlin: Verlag für Geschichte der Naturwissenschaften und Technik, 2002.

Wollgast, Siegfried. *Ehrenfried Walther von Tschirnhaus und die deutsche Frühaufklärung*. Berlin: Akademie-Verlag, 1988.

Wurtz, Jean-Paul. "Über einige offene oder strittige die Medicina Mentis von Tschirnhaus betreffende Fragen." *Studia Leibnitiana* 20, no. 2 (1988): 190–211.

INDEX

abandonment: of property in
war, 667–68; river channels,
abandoned, 91–92; truces,
abandoned territory during,
679–80

absolute declarations of war, 527–28

academies, admission of foreigners
to, 254

Acta Eruditorum (journal), xi

affirmations strengthening treaties
and other agreements, 401–3

agents, defined, 753–54

agreements. *See* treaties and other
agreements

aids or auxiliary troops, 485, 486–87,
545–46, 636

Alexander ab Alexandro, *Genialium
dierum libri sex,* 527

Alexander the Great, 408

alien territory, foreigners living
in: academies, admission of
foreigners to, 253–54; citizenship
of, 237–38; death in alien territory
and ownership of goods, 240–41;
disputes between, settling, 219;
enemies, citizens of enemies
in time of war regarded as,
626–27; exclusion from right
of succession (law of alienship),
240–41; health, for reasons of,
254–55; immovable property of,
244–48; law of alienship not in

harmony with law of nations, 244;
marriages, contracting, 248–50;
obligations and rights of, 238–39;
safe departure allowed to citizens
of enemies, in time of war, 625–26;
security of, 767–69; succession to
goods of deceased citizen, 242–44;
as temporary citizens, 219–20, 767;
war, citizens of enemies in, 625–28;
wills made by, 239–40. *See also*
ambassadors; exile and exiles

alien territory, passage through: for
going to an academy for purposes
of study, 256–57; lodging-houses
and inns, access to, 259–60;
navigation through occupied seas,
263–65; peaceful territory, enemies
or property of enemies taken in
or transported through, 624–25;
for trade and commerce, 255–56.
See also harmless passage of troops
through foreign territory

alienation and pledge: androlepsy or
viricaption (subjects of another
nation taken by pledge), 373, 435–
38, 444–46, 605, 606–7; citizen
property retained by pledge, 369;
head of state's consent to, 78–79;
king's private property retained
by pledge, 369; in natural law,
358, 362; peace treaties alienating
sovereignty or ownership by

This book is set in Adobe Garamond, a modern adaptation by Robert Slimbach of the typeface originally cut around 1540 by the French typographer and printer Claude Garamond. The Garamond face, with its small lowercase height and restrained contrast between thick and thin strokes, is a classic "old-style" face and has long been one of the most influential and widely used typefaces.

Printed on paper that is acid-free and meets the requirements of the American National Standard for Permanence of Paper for Printed Library Materials, Z39.48-1992. ♾

Book design by Louise OFarrell,
Gainesville, Florida
Typography by Apex CoVantage
Madison, Wisconsin
Printed and bound by Edwards Brothers Malloy
Ann Arbor, Michigan